TADATOSHI FUJIMAKI

When I was a kid, I was sure that by this age I would be a respectable and perfect adult. However, now that I am this age... Forget "perfect"—there's so much I still don't know or understand. Plus, there's nothing respectable about most of my thoughts and actions. Basically, I pretty much haven't changed since middle school.

Hopefully, I can grow up soon.

—2011

Tadatoshi Fujimaki was born on June 9, 1982, in Tokyo. He made his debut in 2007 in *Akamaru Jump* with *Kuroko's Basketball*, which was later serialized in *Weekly Shonen Jump*. *Kuroko's Basketball* quickly gained popularity and became an anime in Japan in 2012.

Kuroko's BASKETBALL

15 & 16

SHONEN JUMP Manga Edition
BY TADATOSHI FUJIMAKI

Translation/Caleb Cook
Touch-Up Art & Lettering/Snir Aharon
Design/Julian [JR] Robinson
Editor/John Bae

KUROKO NO BASUKE © 2008 by Tadatoshi Fujimaki
All rights reserved.
First published in Japan in 2008 by SHUEISHA Inc., Tokyo.
English translation rights arranged by SHUEISHA Inc.

The stories, characters and incidents mentioned in this
publication are entirely fictional.

Printed in the U.S.A.

Published by VIZ Media, LLC
P.O. Box 77010
San Francisco, CA 94107

10 9 8 7 6 5 4 3 2 1
First printing, October 2017

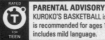

PARENTAL ADVISORY
KUROKO'S BASKETBALL is rated T for Teen and
is recommended for ages 13 and up. This volume
includes mild language.
ratings.viz.com

www.viz.com

www.shonenjump.com

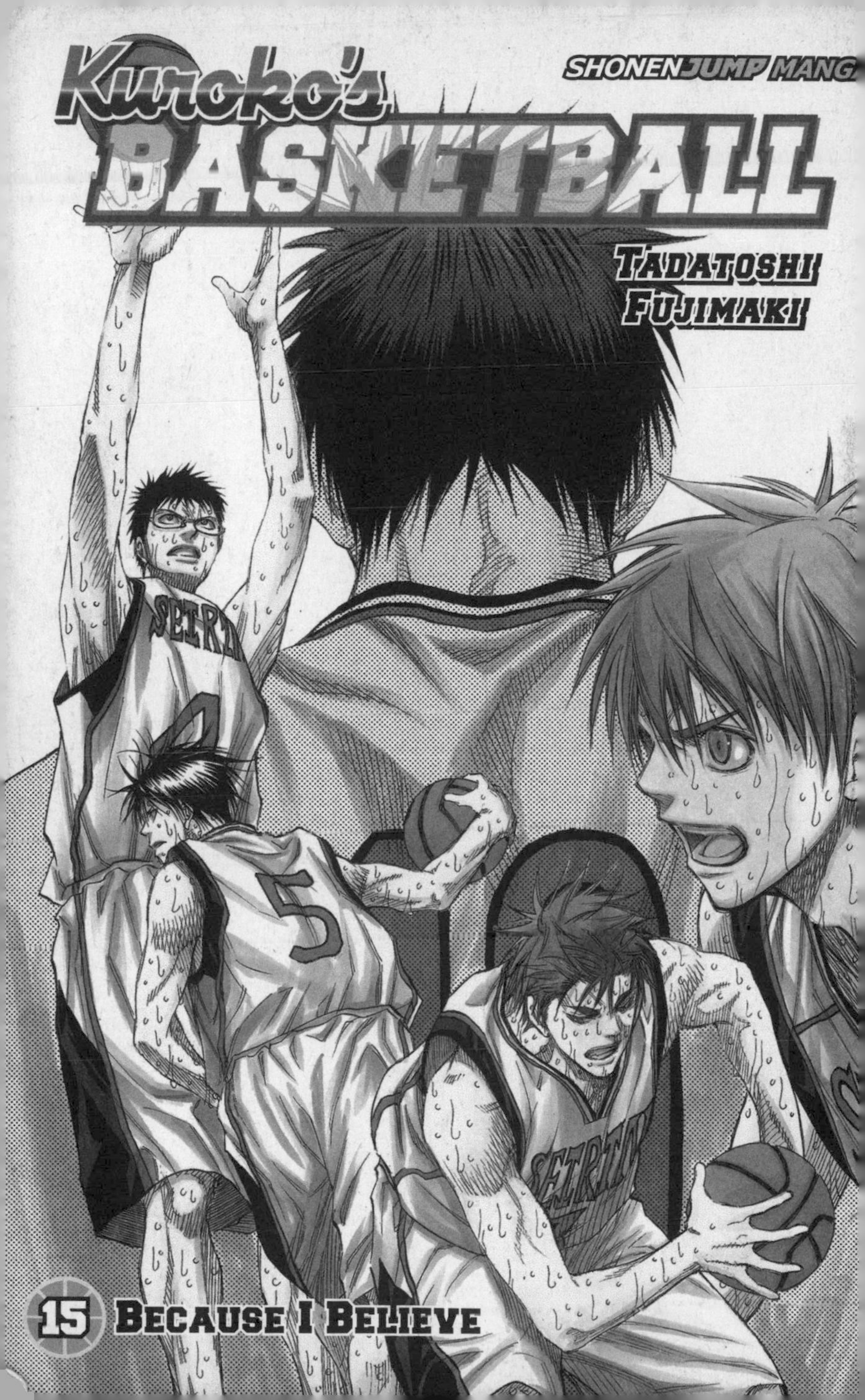
Kuroko's
BASKETBALL
SHONEN JUMP MANG
TADATOSHI
FUJIMAKI
15
BECAUSE I BELIEVE

Characters

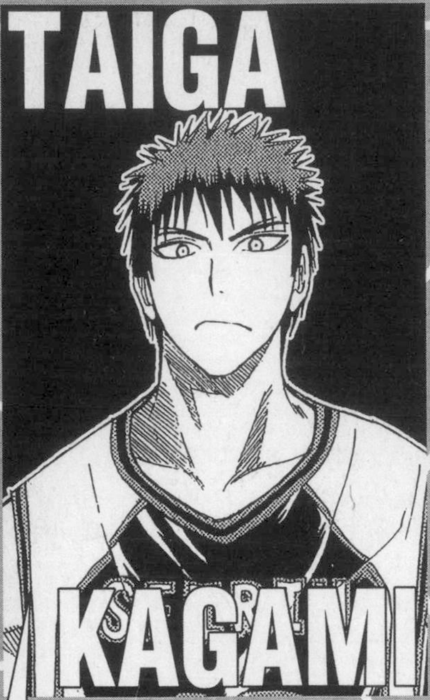
TAIGA
KAGAMI

A first-year on Seirin High's basketball team. Though he's rough around the edges, he's a gifted player with a lot of potential. His goal is to beat the Miracle Generation.

A first-year on Seirin High's basketball team. Gifted with a natural lack of presence, he utilizes misdirection on the court to make nearly invisible passes.

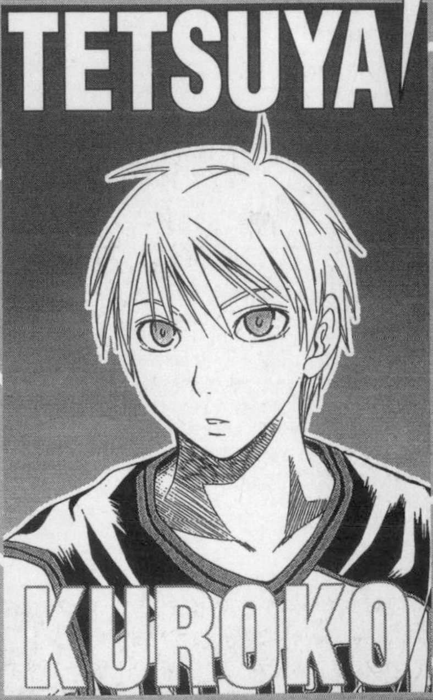
TETSUYA
KUROKO

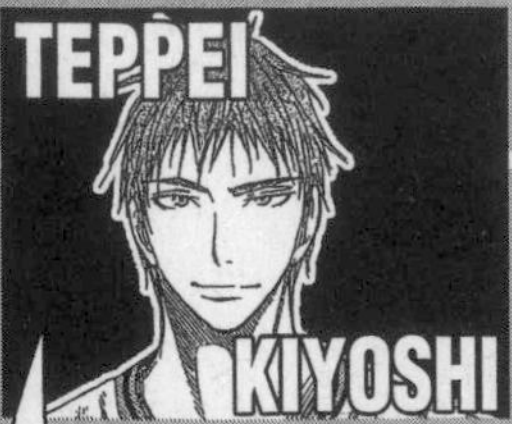
TEPPEI
KIYOSHI

A second-year on Seirin High's basketball team and the club's founder. He was hospitalized but returned shortly after Inter-High.

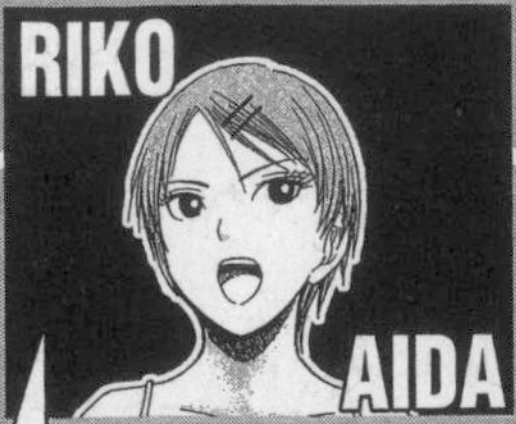
RIKO
AIDA

A second-year and coach of the Seirin High basketball team.

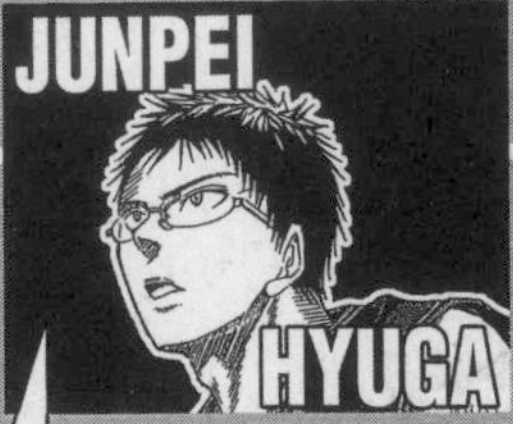
JUNPEI
HYUGA

A second-year on Seirin High's basketball team. As captain, he led his team to the Finals League last year despite only playing first-year players.

KUROKO'S BASKETBALL

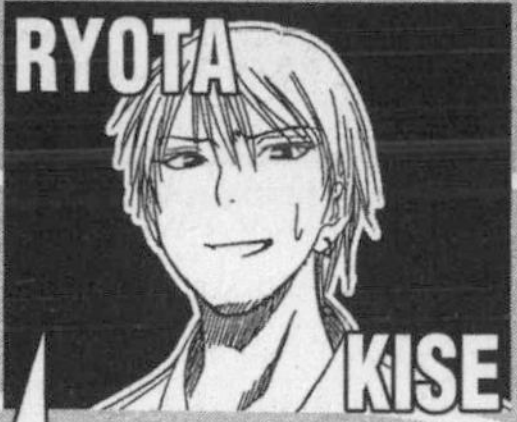
RYOTA
KISE

One of the Miracle Generation. Any basketball move he sees, he can mimic in an instant.

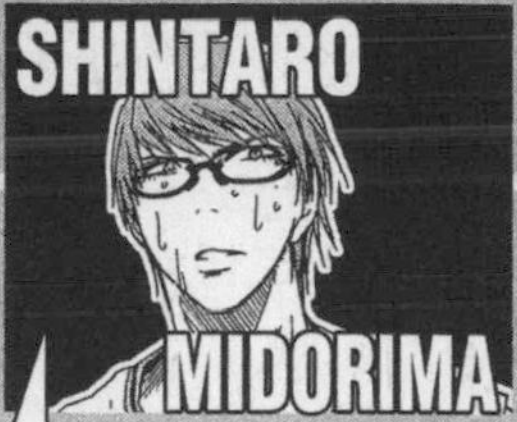
SHINTARO
MIDORIMA

A first-year at Shutoku High, he's the top shooter of the Miracle Generation.

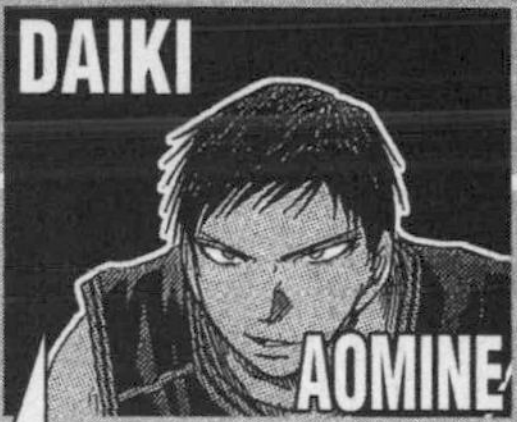
DAIKI
AOMINE

The ace of the Miracle Generation and Kuroko's former friend, he's now a first-year at To-oh Academy.

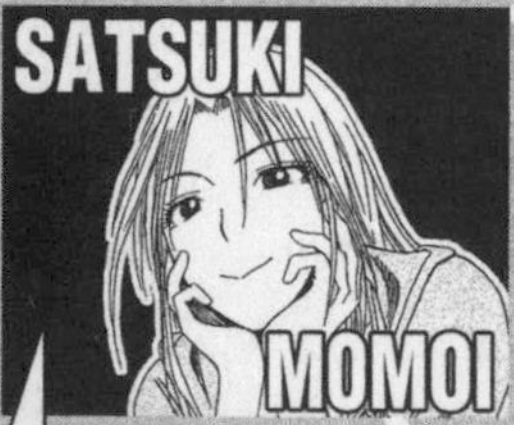
SATSUKI
MOMOI

A first-year member of To-oh Academy's basketball team, she was the team manager for the Miracle Generation. Is she really Kuroko's girlfriend?!

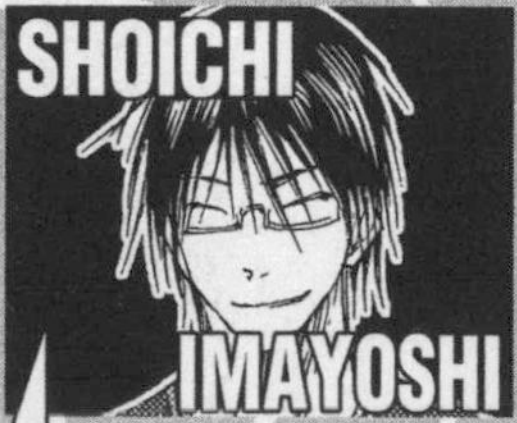
SHOICHI
IMAYOSHI

The third-year captain of To-oh Academy's basketball team, he's a cunning point guard.

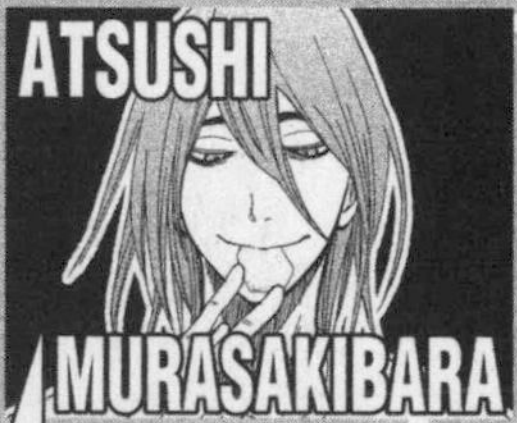
ATSUSHI
MURASAKIBARA

One of the Miracle Generation. A first-year on Yosen High's basketball team. He plays center, but he doesn't actually enjoy basketball all that much.

Teiko Middle School is an elite championship school whose basketball team once fielded five prodigies collectively known as "the Miracle Generation." But supporting those five was a phantom sixth man—Tetsuya Kuroko. Now Kuroko's a first-year high school student with zero presence who joins Seirin High's basketball club. Though his physical abilities and stats are well below average, Kuroko thrives on the court by making passes his opponents can't detect!

Seirin lost during the Finals League of Inter-High, but they can still win the next prize...the Winter Cup! Their first game of the tournament is against To-oh and Aomine, and the talent difference means an uphill battle for Seirin. Kuroko's moves are at the core of Seirin's offensive strategy, but none of them are working against To-oh's stingy defense. However, Kuroko's defeat has awakened Kagami, and Seirin is riding on his momentum...

STORY THUS FAR

TABLE OF CONTENTS

127TH QUARTER:
ALL OPTIONS EXHAUSTED

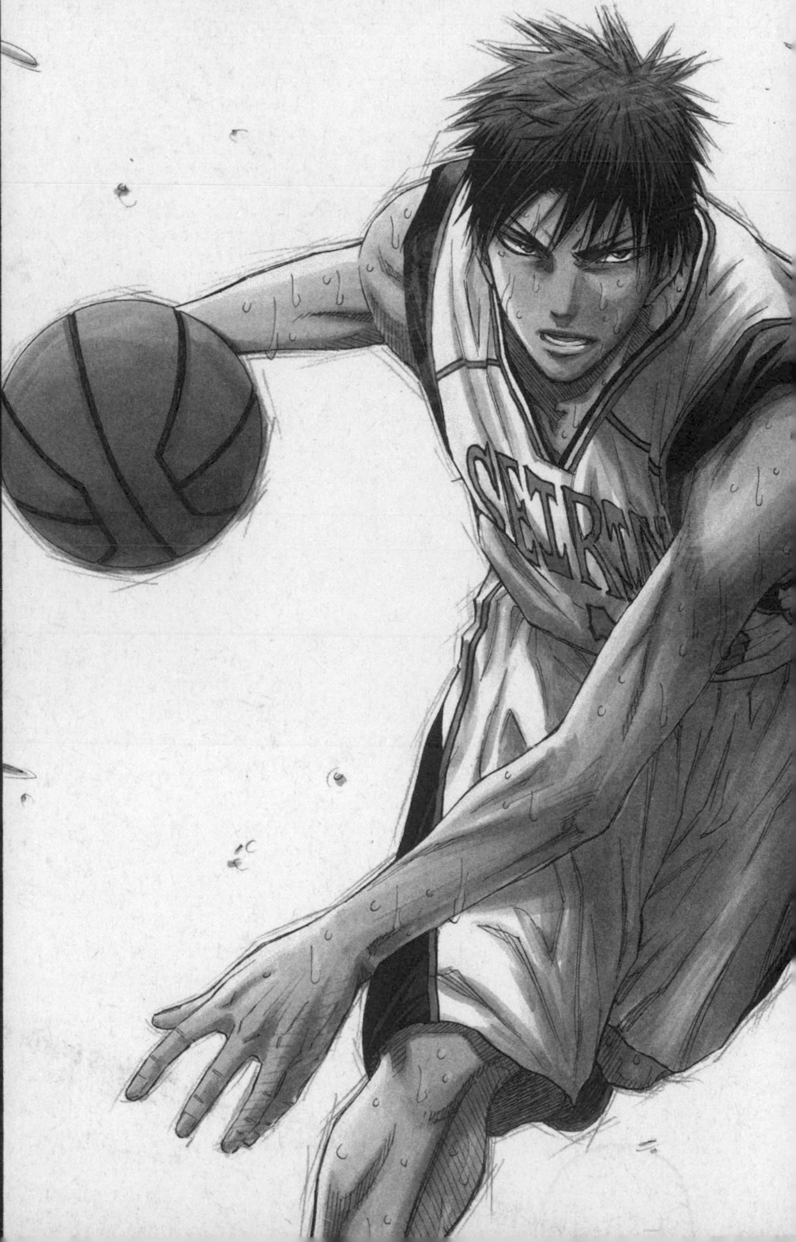

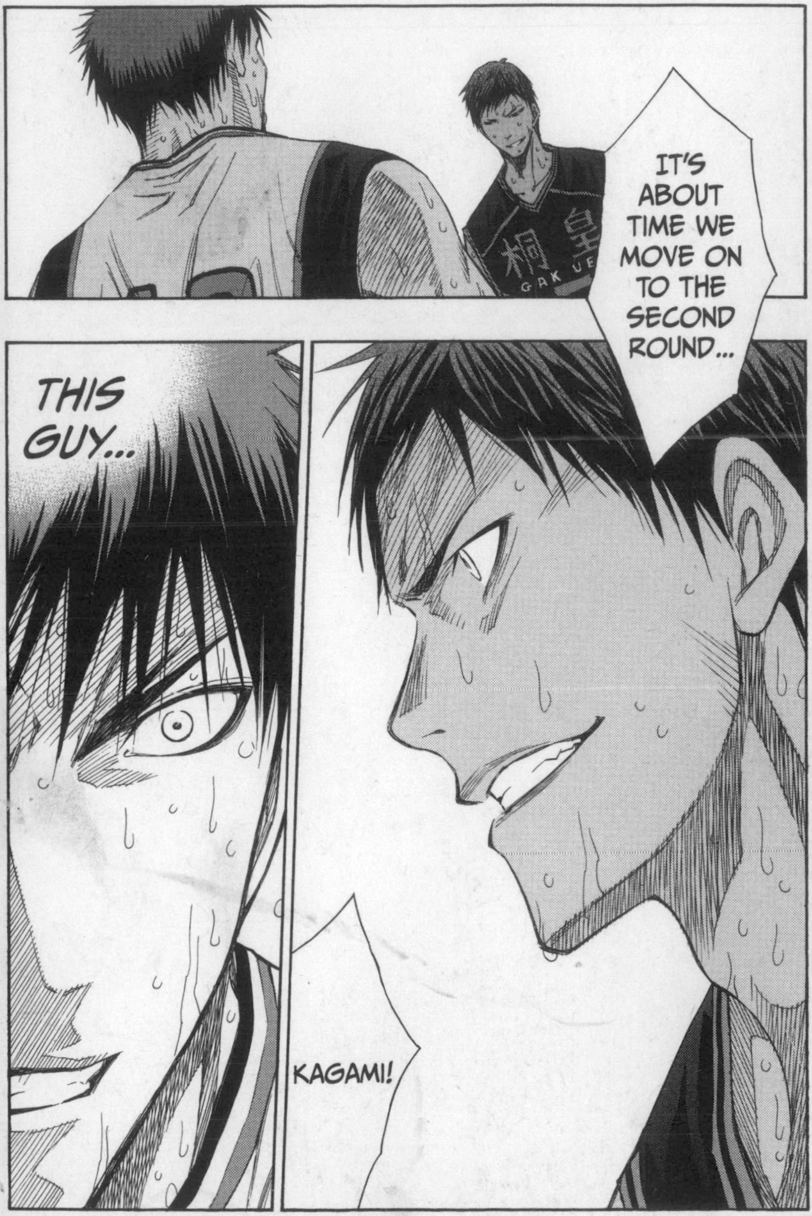
IT'S ABOUT TIME WE MOVE ON TO THE SECOND ROUND...
KAGAMI!
THIS GUY...

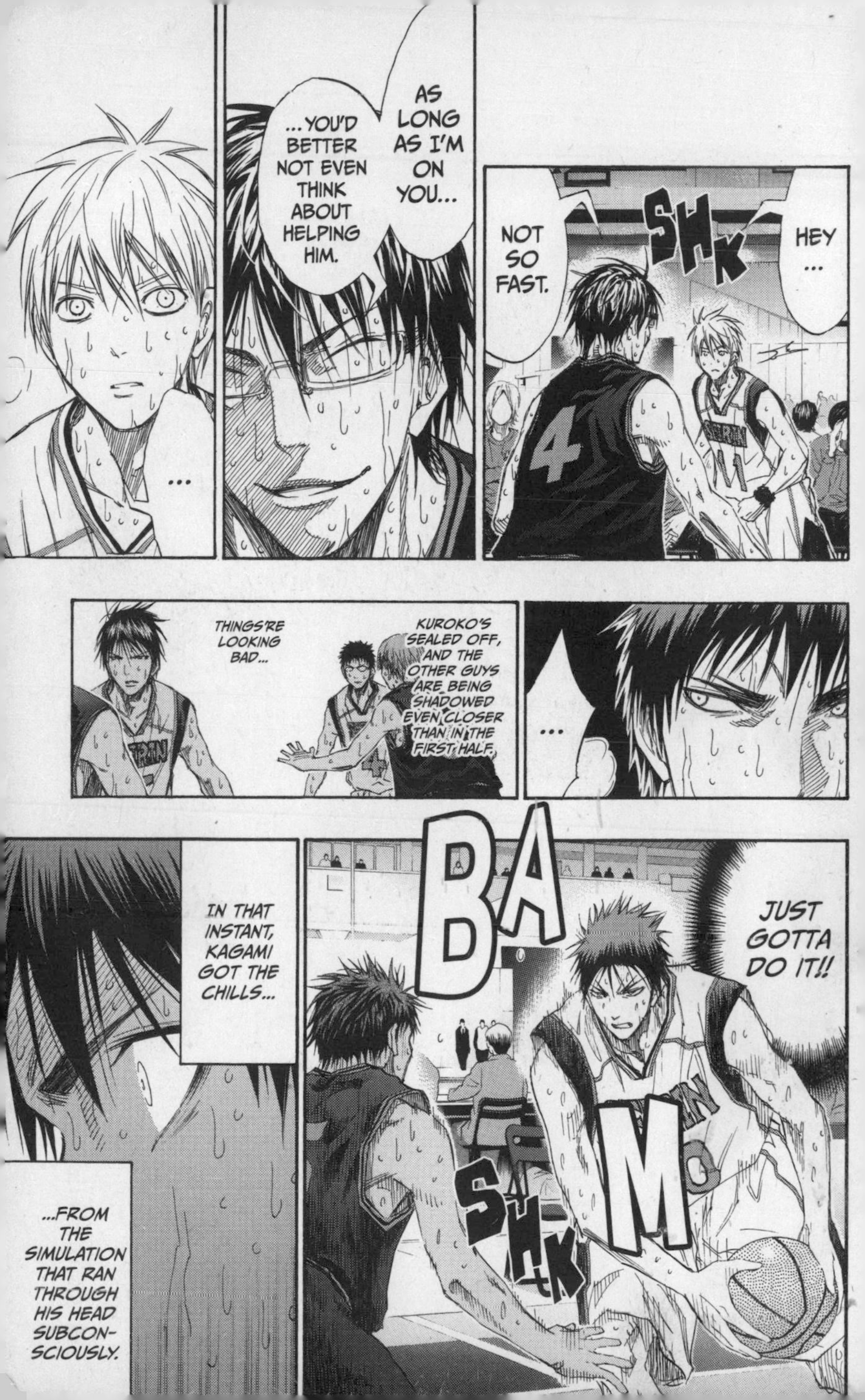
HEY ...
SHK
NOT SO FAST.
AS LONG AS I'M ON YOU...
...YOU'D BETTER NOT EVEN THINK ABOUT HELPING HIM.
...
...
KUROKO'S SEALED OFF, AND THE OTHER GUYS ARE BEING SHADOWED EVEN CLOSER THAN IN THE FIRST HALF.
THINGS'RE LOOKING BAD...
BA
JUST GOTTA DO IT!!
M
SHK
IN THAT INSTANT, KAGAMI GOT THE CHILLS...
...FROM THE SIMULATION THAT RAN THROUGH HIS HEAD SUBCONSCIOUSLY.

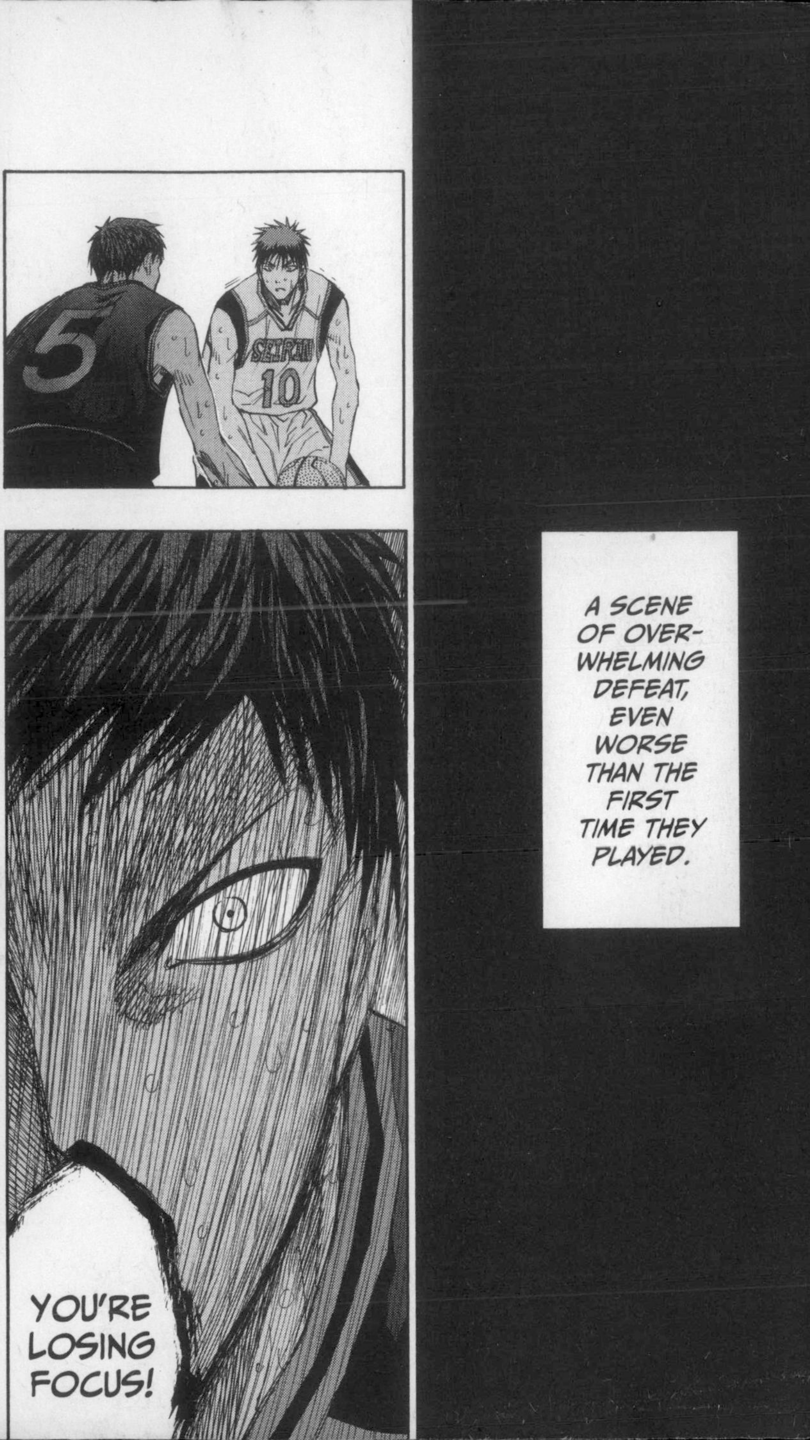
A SCENE OF OVER-WHELMING DEFEAT, EVEN WORSE THAN THE FIRST TIME THEY PLAYED.
SEIRIN
10
5
YOU'RE LOSING FOCUS!

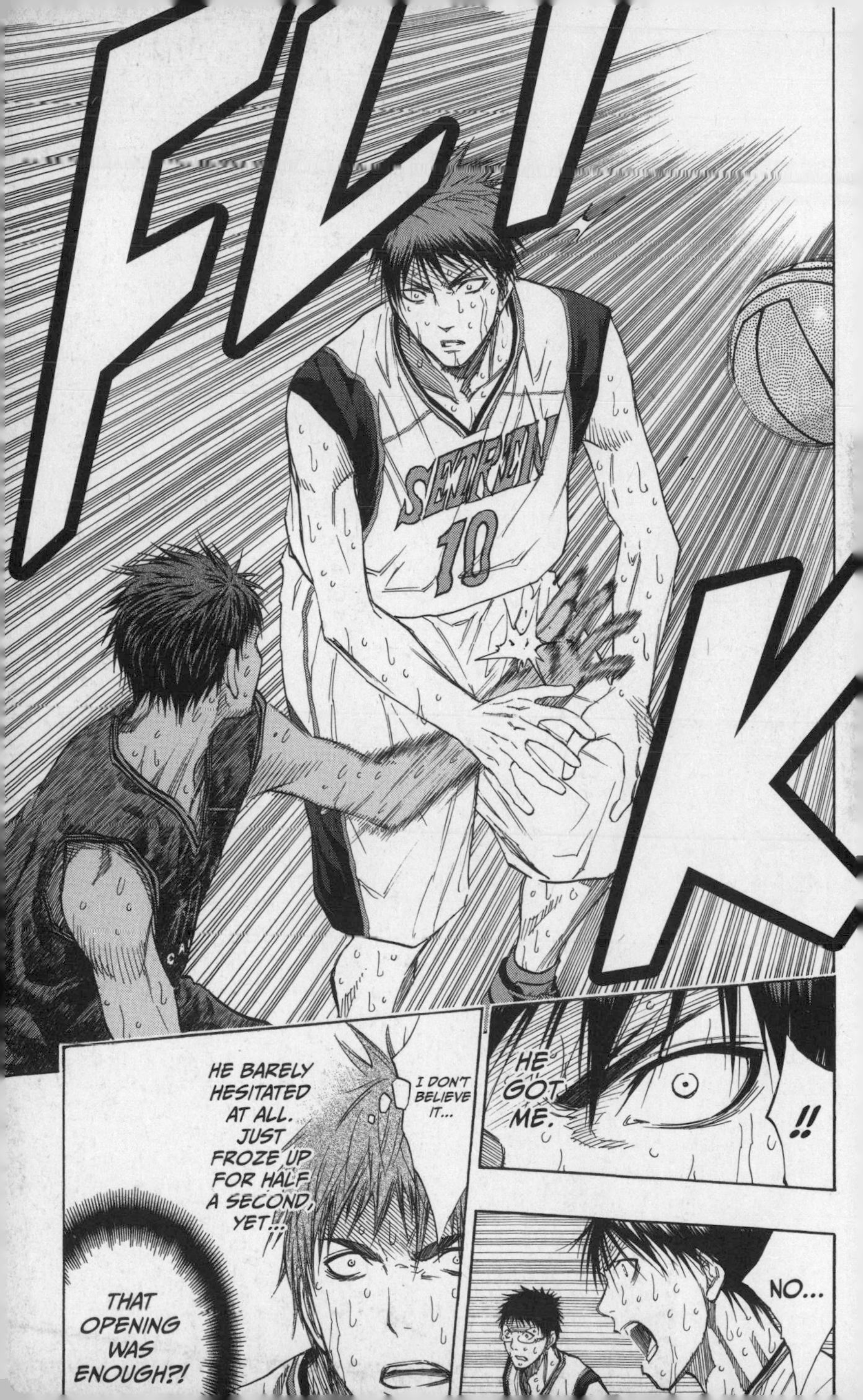
FLIK
SEIRIN
10
HE GOT ME.
!!
NO...
I DON'T BELIEVE IT...
HE BARELY HESITATED AT ALL. JUST FROZE UP FOR HALF A SECOND, YET...!!
THAT OPENING WAS ENOUGH?!

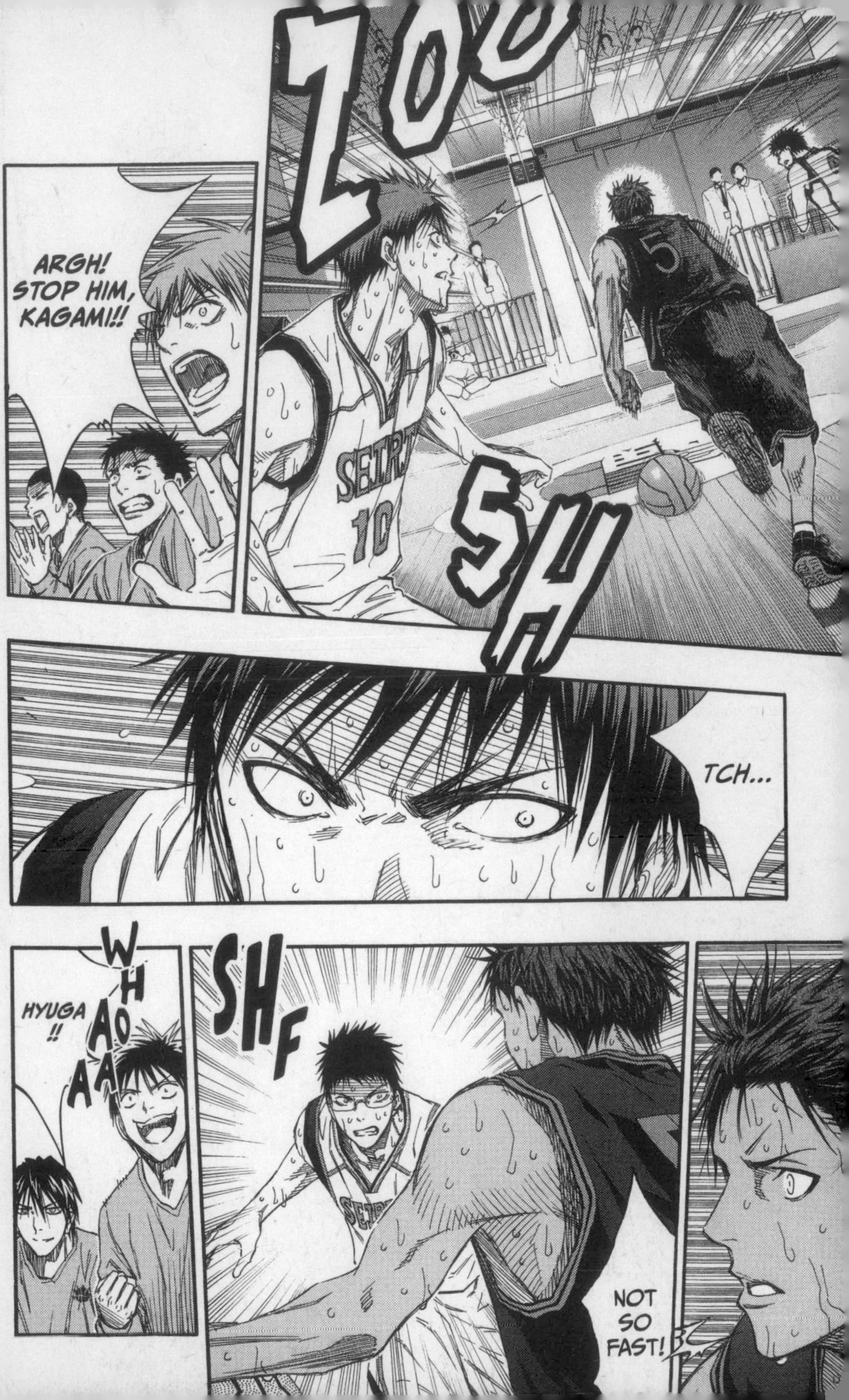
ZOO
SH
ARGH! STOP HIM, KAGAMI!!
TCH...
NOT SO FAST!
SHF
HYUGA !!
WHOAAA

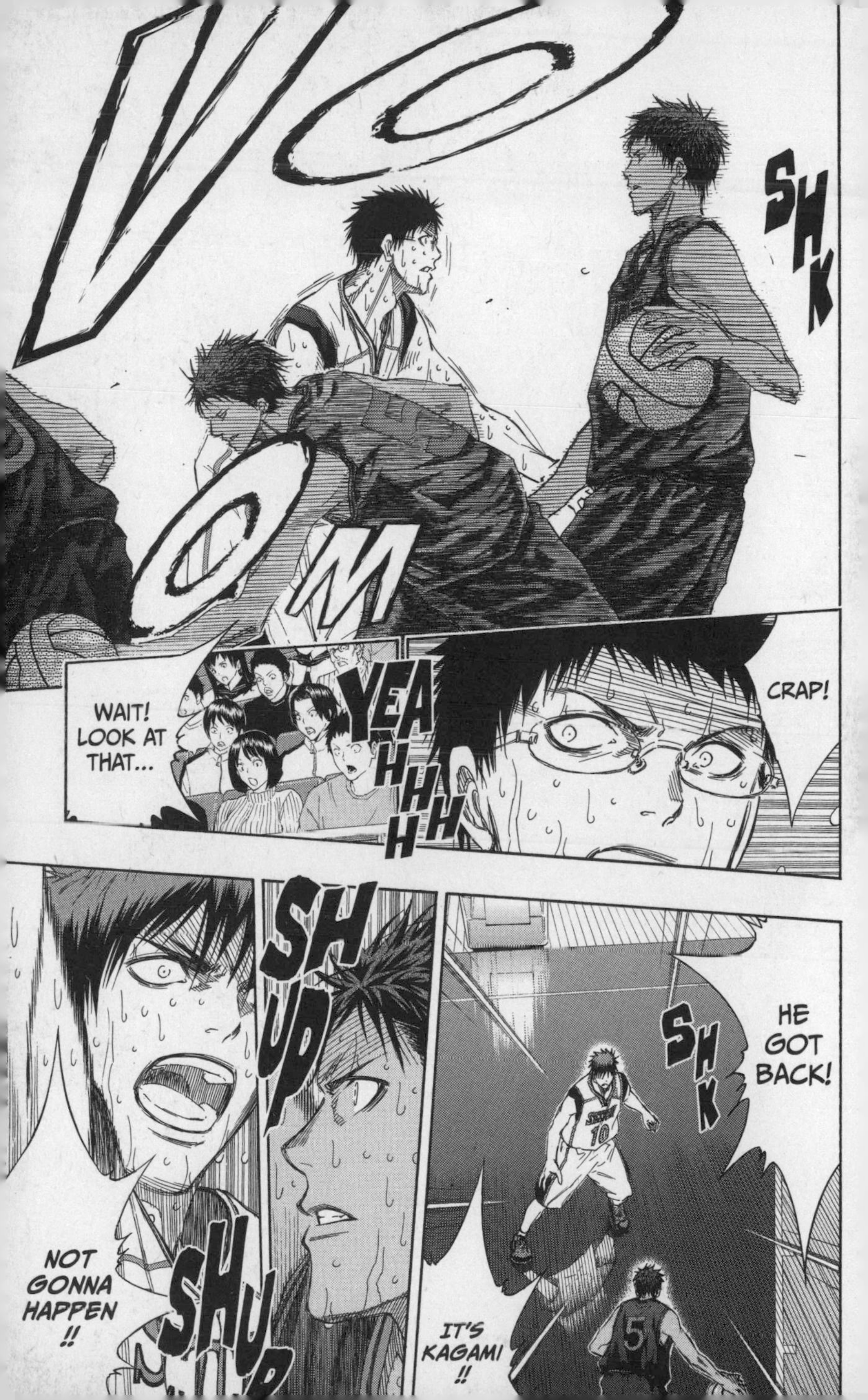
SHK
VOOM
CRAP!
YEAHHHHH
WAIT! LOOK AT THAT...
HE GOT BACK!
SHK
IT'S KAGAMI!!
SHUP
NOT GONNA HAPPEN!!
SHU

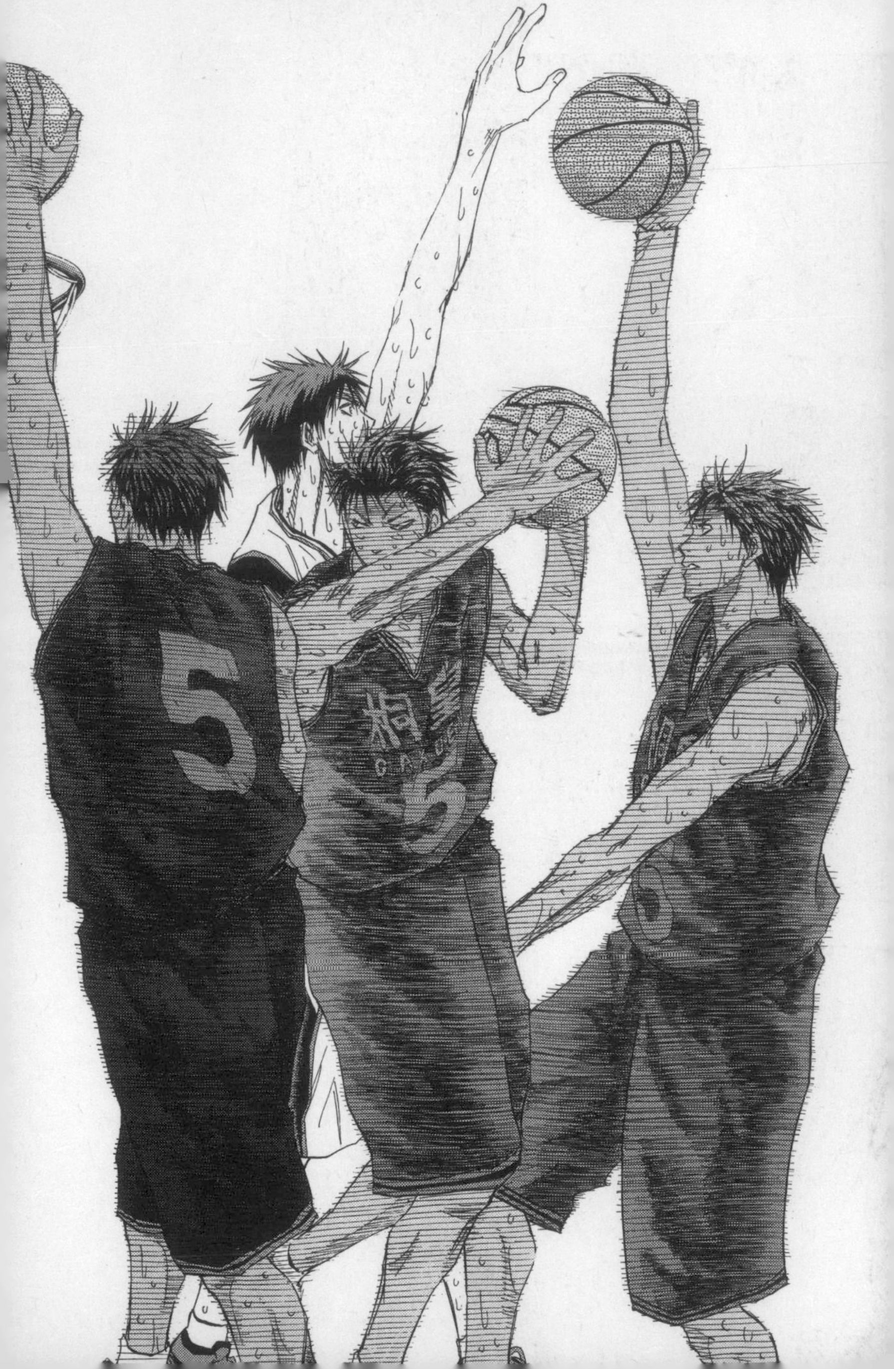

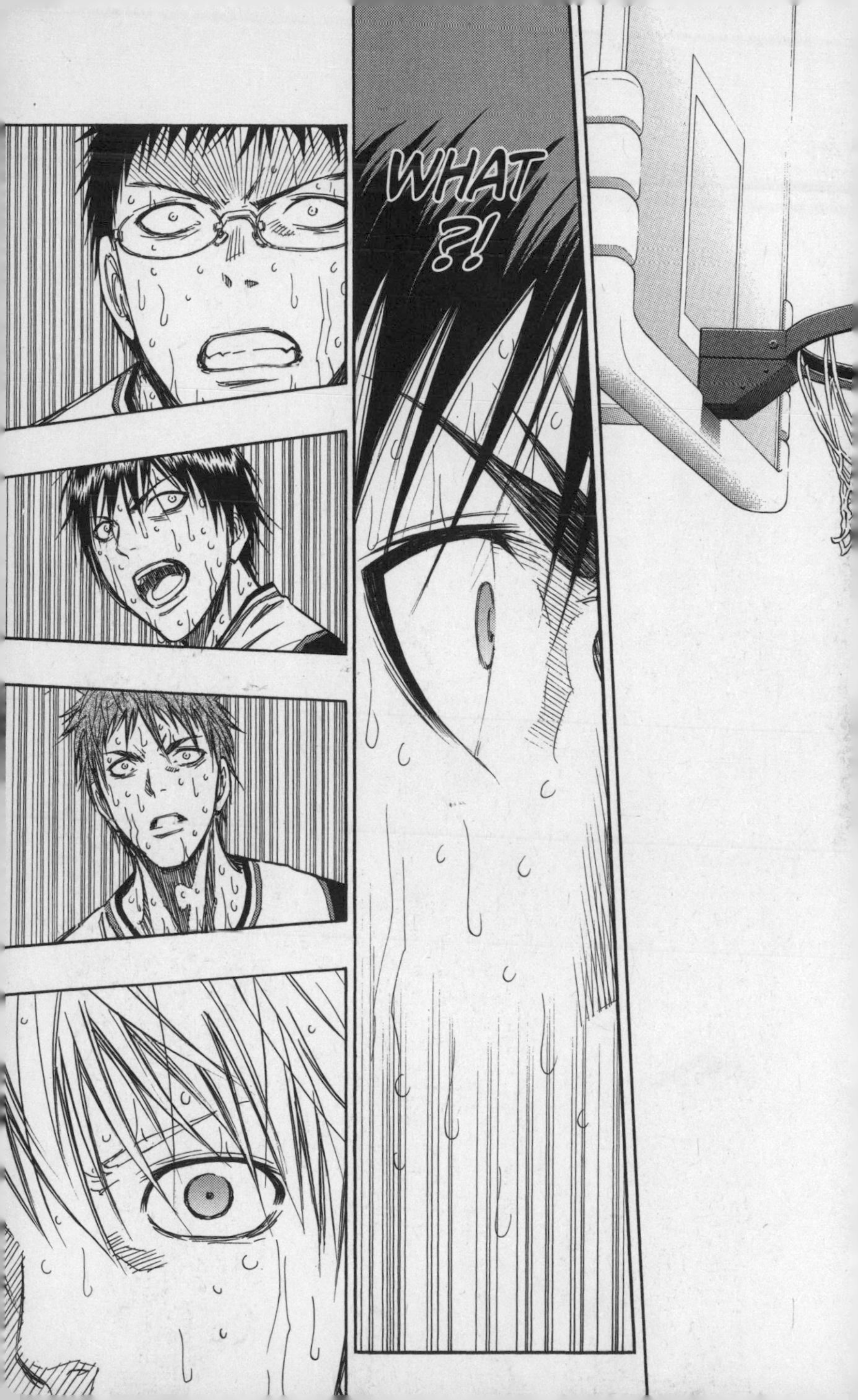
WHAT ?!

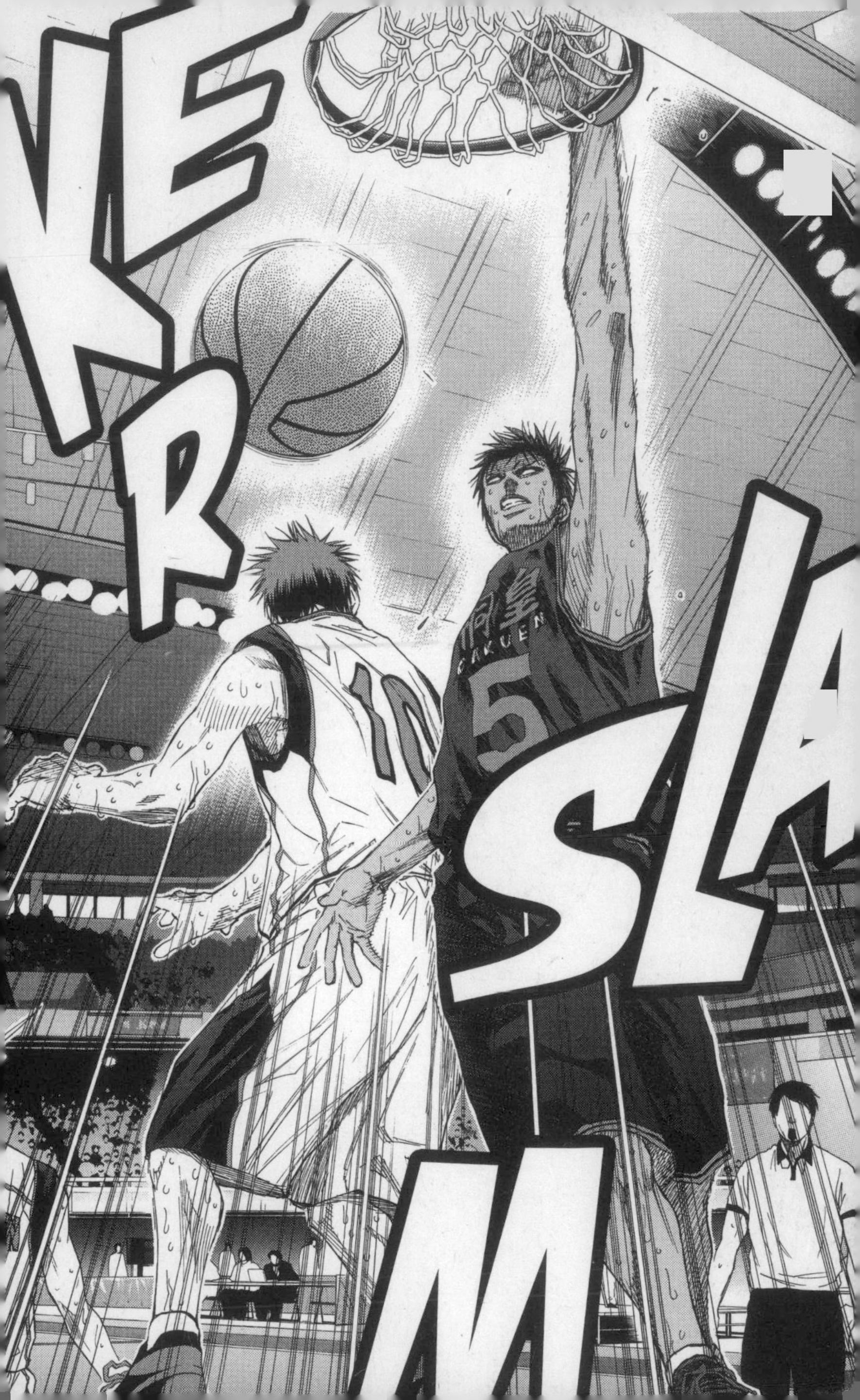
SLAM
GAKUEN

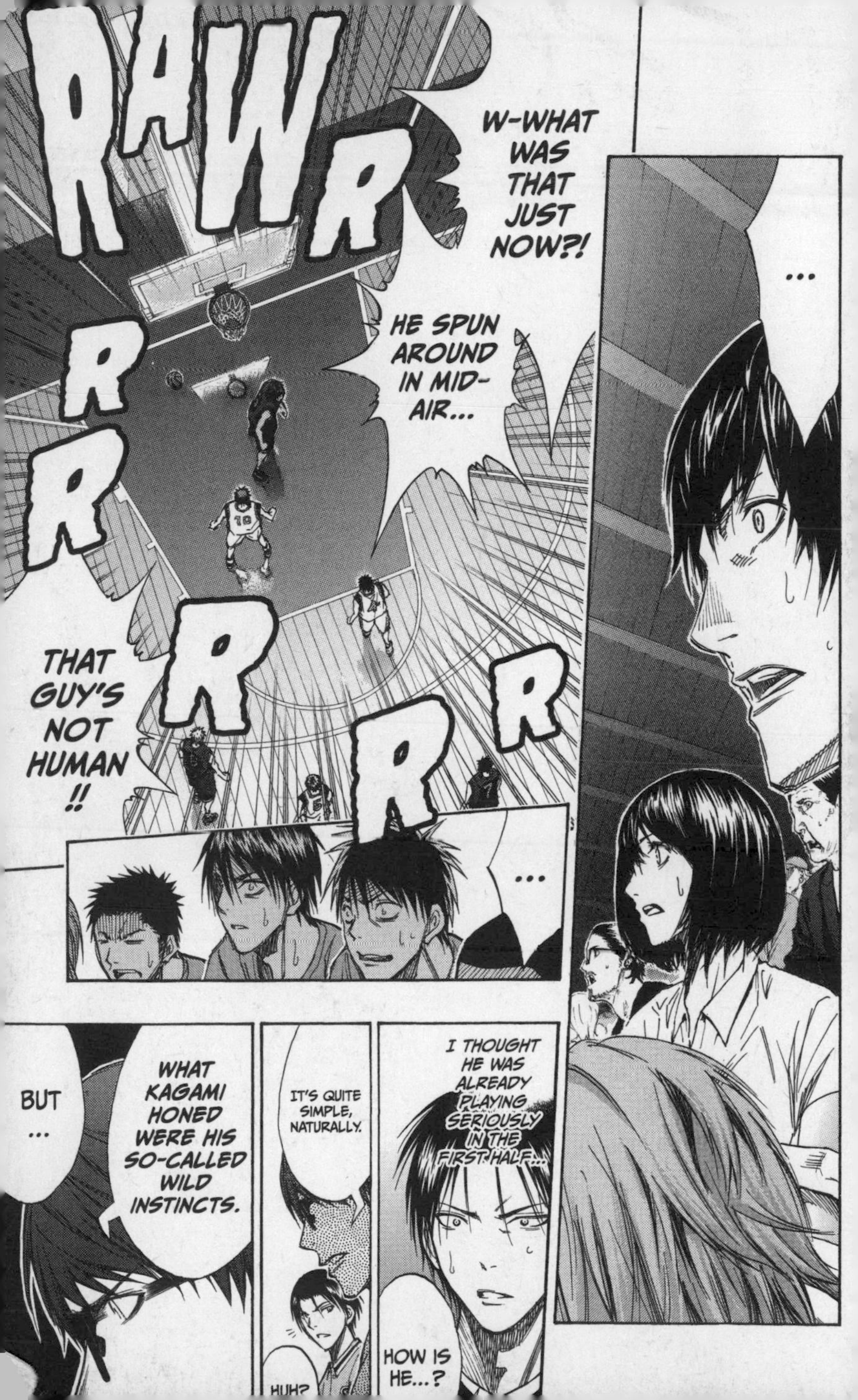
...
RAWR RRRRR
W-WHAT WAS THAT JUST NOW?!
HE SPUN AROUND IN MID-AIR...
THAT GUY'S NOT HUMAN!!
...
I THOUGHT HE WAS ALREADY PLAYING SERIOUSLY IN THE FIRST HALF...
HOW IS HE...?
IT'S QUITE SIMPLE, NATURALLY.
HUH?
WHAT KAGAMI HONED WERE HIS SO-CALLED WILD INSTINCTS.
BUT ...

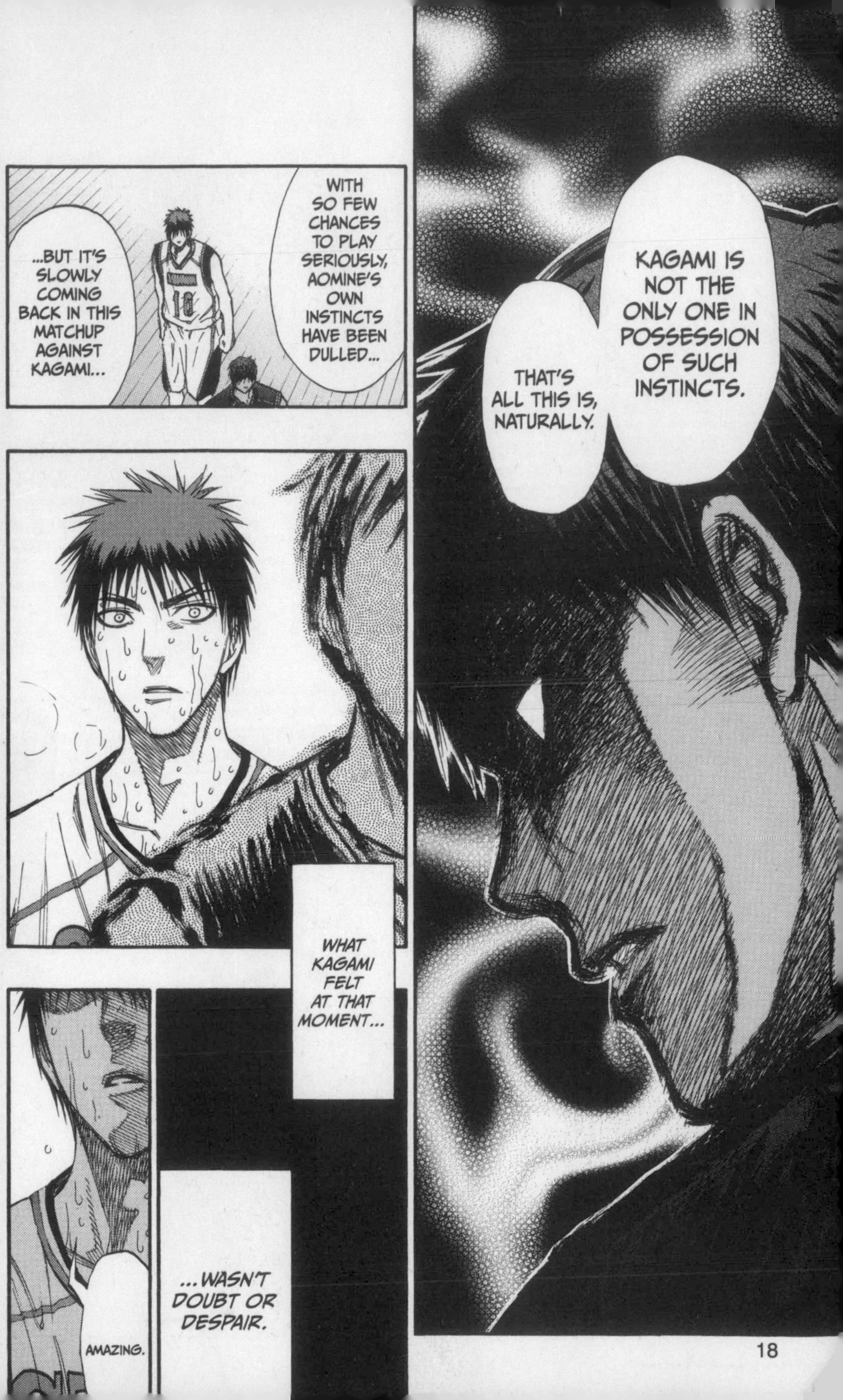
KAGAMI IS NOT THE ONLY ONE IN POSSESSION OF SUCH INSTINCTS.
THAT'S ALL THIS IS, NATURALLY.
WITH SO FEW CHANCES TO PLAY SERIOUSLY, AOMINE'S OWN INSTINCTS HAVE BEEN DULLED...
...BUT IT'S SLOWLY COMING BACK IN THIS MATCHUP AGAINST KAGAMI...
WHAT KAGAMI FELT AT THAT MOMENT...
...WASN'T DOUBT OR DESPAIR.
AMAZING.

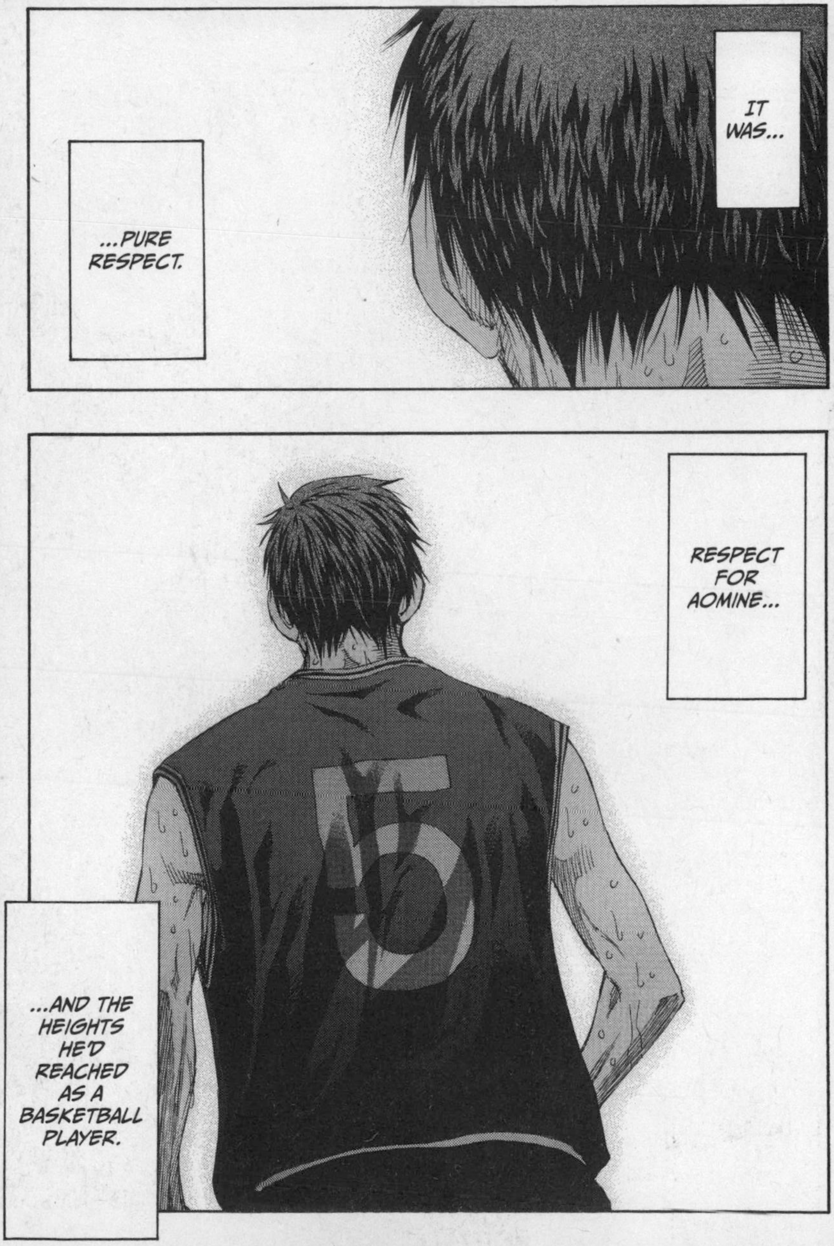
IT WAS...
...PURE RESPECT.
RESPECT FOR AOMINE...
...AND THE HEIGHTS HE'D REACHED AS A BASKETBALL PLAYER.

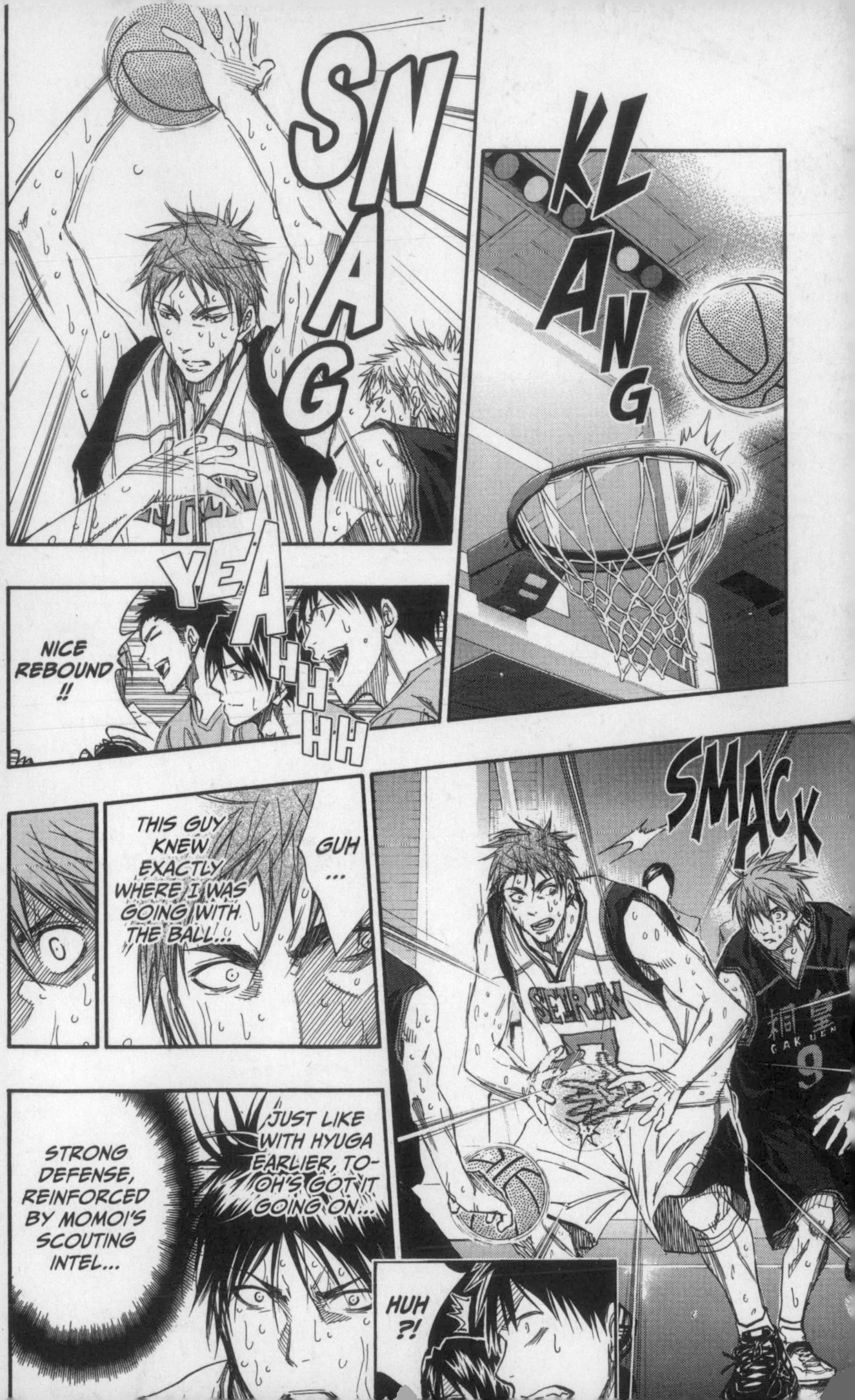
KLANG
SNAG
YEAAHHHHH
NICE REBOUND !!
SMACK
HUH ?!
GUH ...
THIS GUY KNEW EXACTLY WHERE I WAS GOING WITH THE BALL...
JUST LIKE WITH HYUGA EARLIER, TO-OH'S GOT IT GOING ON...
STRONG DEFENSE, REINFORCED BY MOMOI'S SCOUTING INTEL...

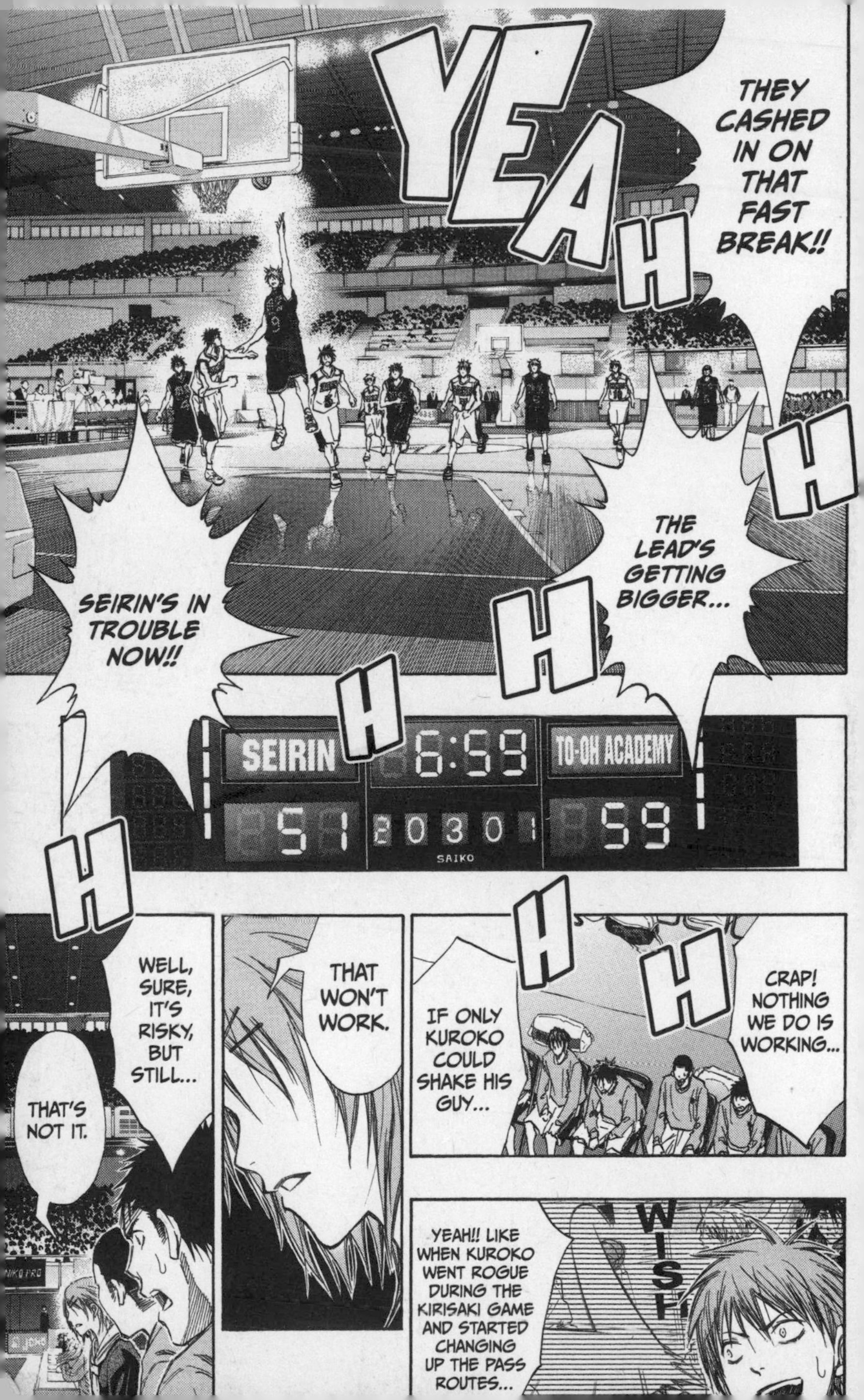
YEAHHHHHHH
THEY CASHED IN ON THAT FAST BREAK!!
THE LEAD'S GETTING BIGGER...
SEIRIN'S IN TROUBLE NOW!!
SEIRIN 6:59 TO-OH ACADEMY
51 2 0 3 0 1 59
SAIKO
CRAP! NOTHING WE DO IS WORKING...
IF ONLY KUROKO COULD SHAKE HIS GUY...
YEAH!! LIKE WHEN KUROKO WENT ROGUE DURING THE KIRISAKI GAME AND STARTED CHANGING UP THE PASS ROUTES...
WISH
THAT WON'T WORK.
WELL, SURE, IT'S RISKY, BUT STILL...
THAT'S NOT IT.

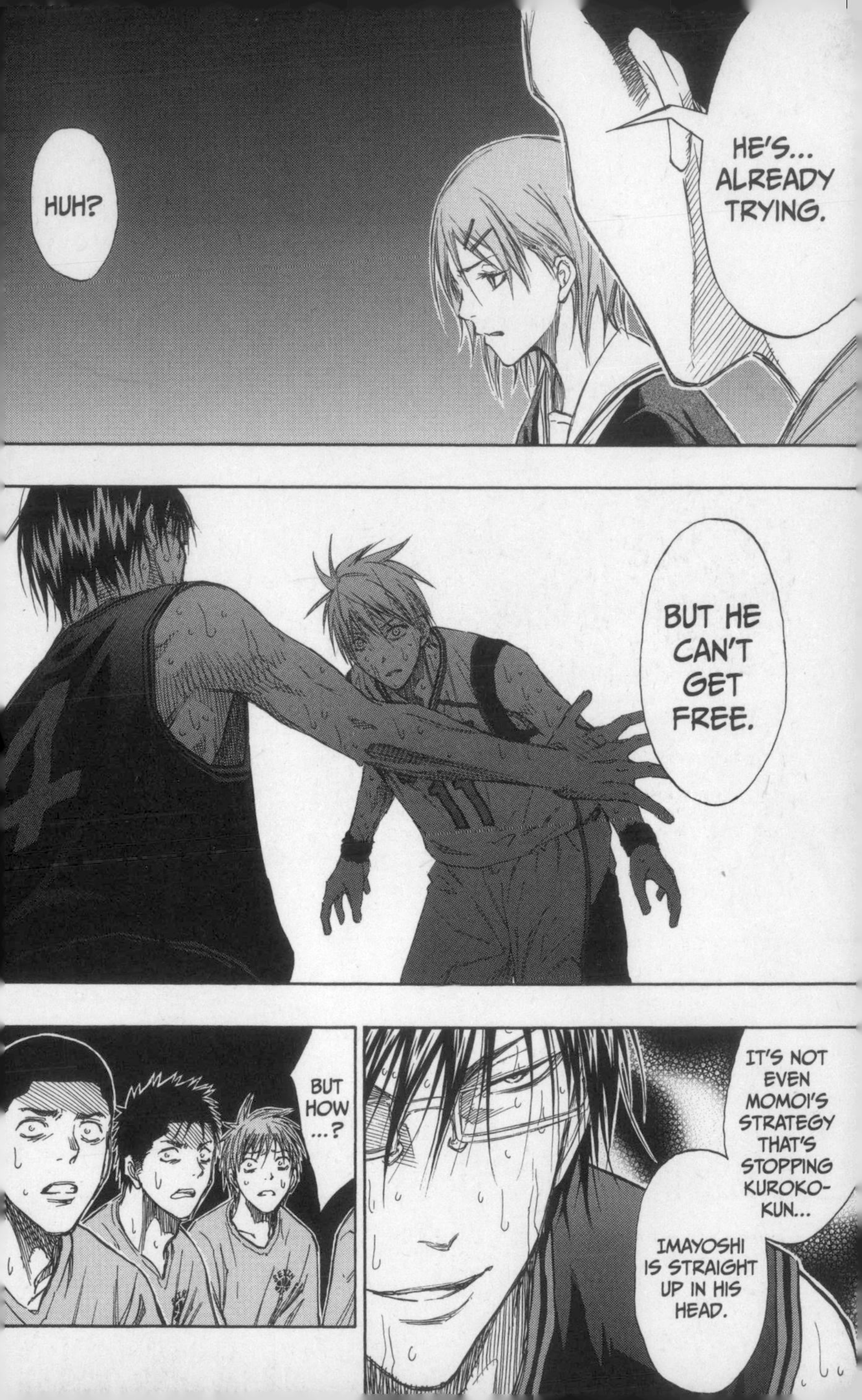
HE'S... ALREADY TRYING.
HUH?
BUT HE CAN'T GET FREE.
IT'S NOT EVEN MOMOI'S STRATEGY THAT'S STOPPING KUROKO-KUN...
IMAYOSHI IS STRAIGHT UP IN HIS HEAD.
BUT HOW ...?

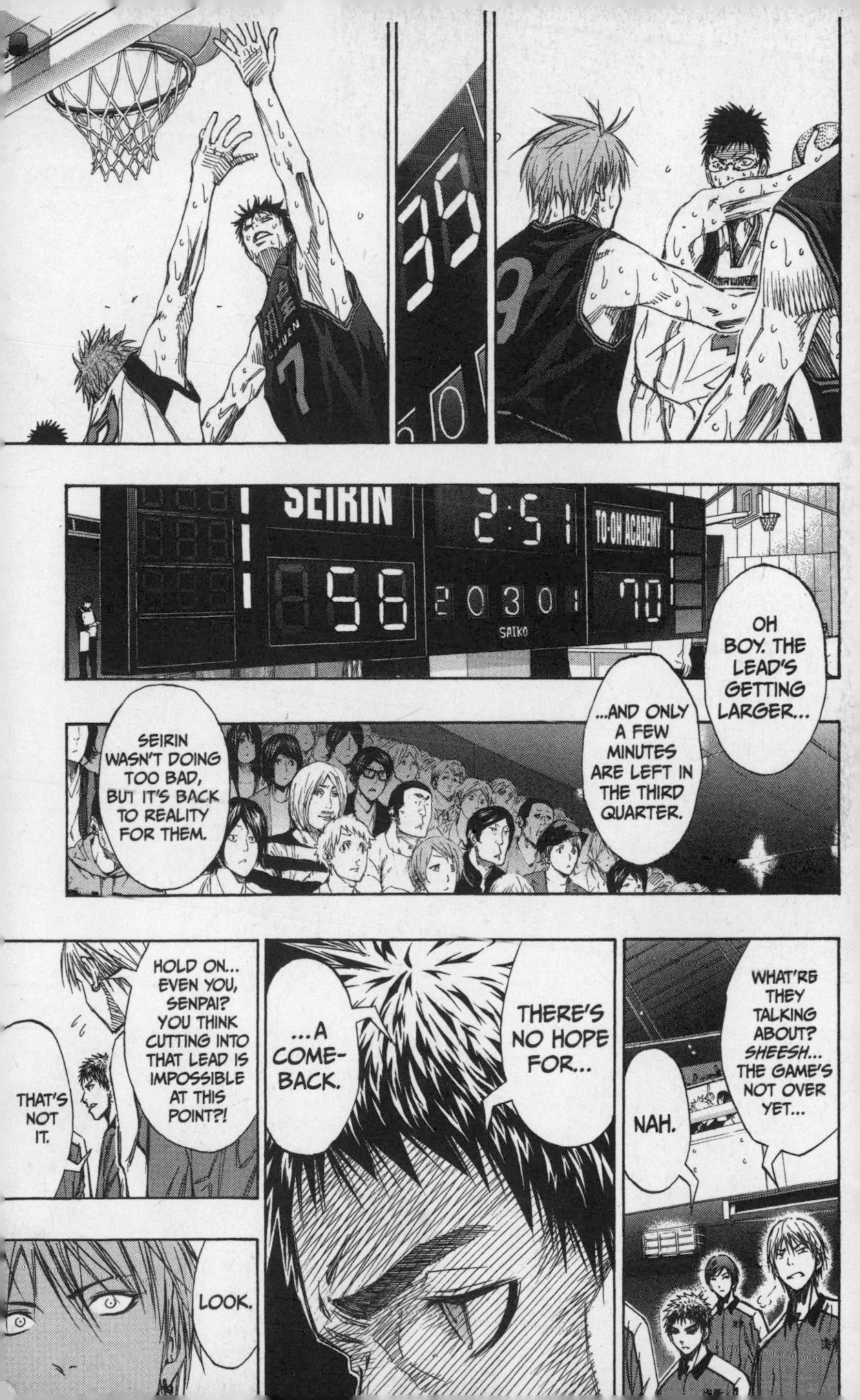
SEIRIN
2:51
TO-OH ACADEMY
56
70
SAIKO
OH BOY. THE LEAD'S GETTING LARGER...
...AND ONLY A FEW MINUTES ARE LEFT IN THE THIRD QUARTER.
SEIRIN WASN'T DOING TOO BAD, BUT IT'S BACK TO REALITY FOR THEM.
WHAT'RE THEY TALKING ABOUT? *SHEESH*... THE GAME'S NOT OVER YET...
NAH.
THERE'S NO HOPE FOR...
...A COMEBACK.
HOLD ON... EVEN YOU, SENPAI? YOU THINK CUTTING INTO THAT LEAD IS IMPOSSIBLE AT THIS POINT?!
THAT'S NOT IT.
LOOK.

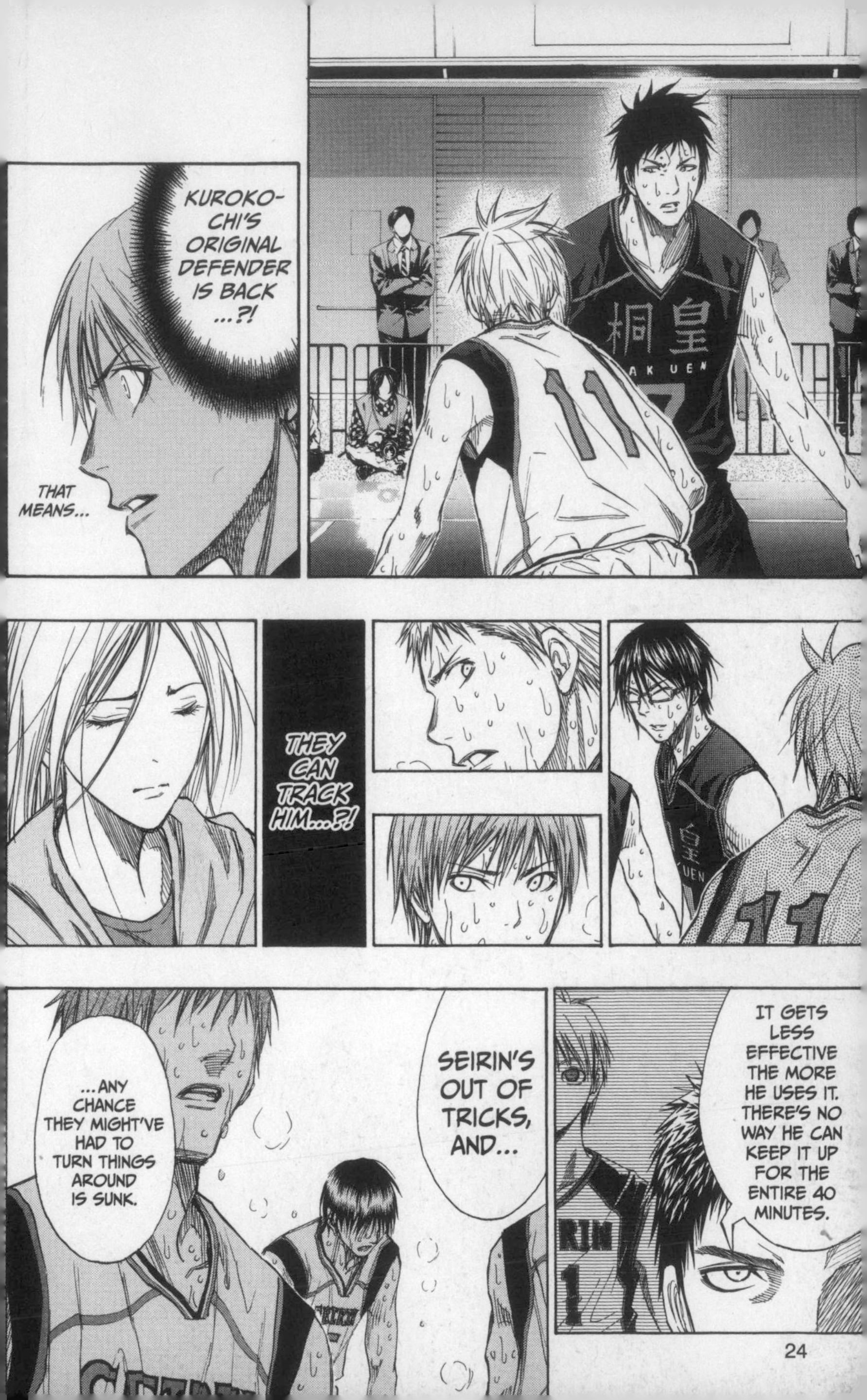
KUROKO-CHI'S ORIGINAL DEFENDER IS BACK ...?!
THAT MEANS...
THEY CAN TRACK HIM...?!
IT GETS LESS EFFECTIVE THE MORE HE USES IT. THERE'S NO WAY HE CAN KEEP IT UP FOR THE ENTIRE 40 MINUTES.
SEIRIN'S OUT OF TRICKS, AND...
...ANY CHANCE THEY MIGHT'VE HAD TO TURN THINGS AROUND IS SUNK.

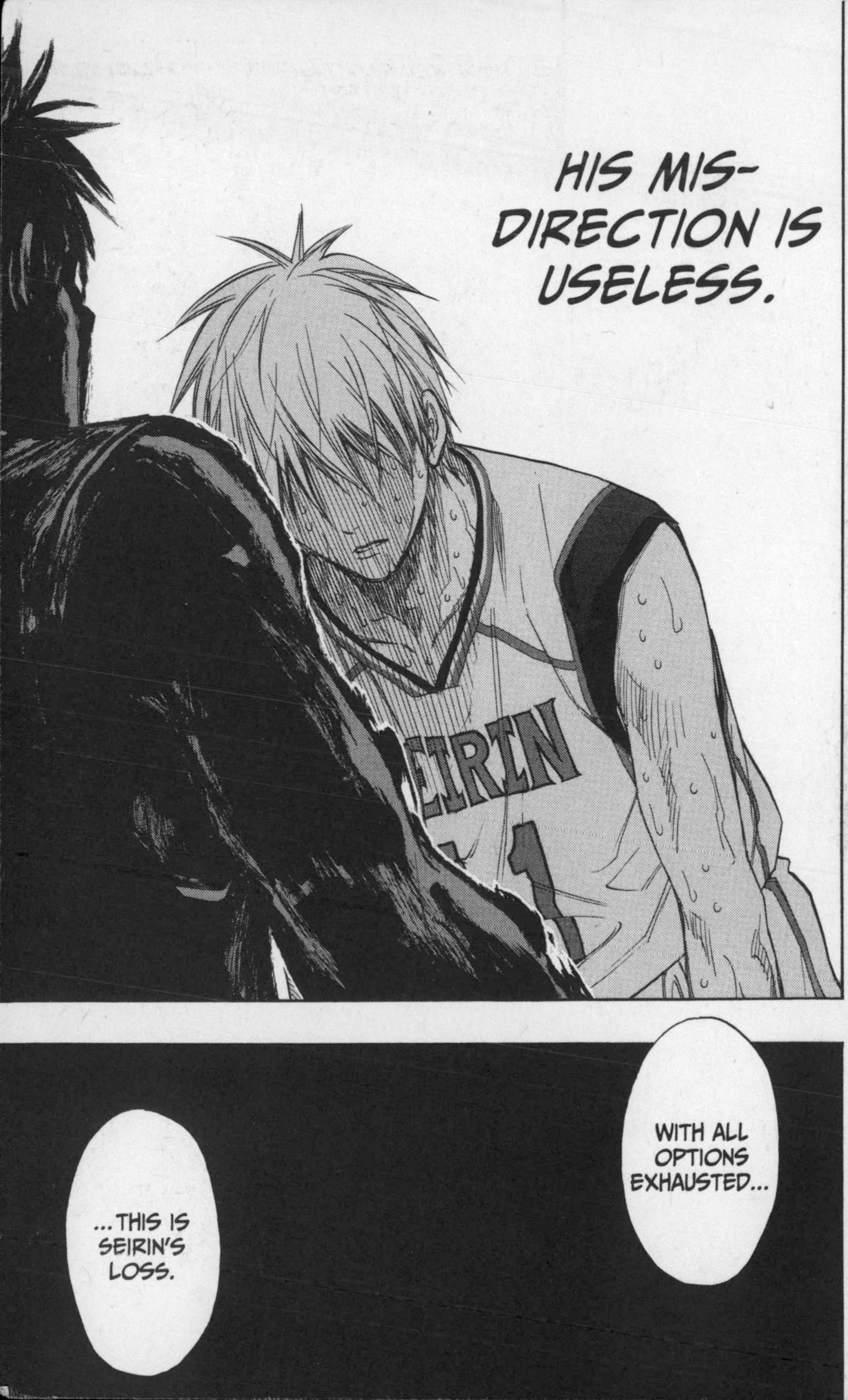
HIS MIS-DIRECTION IS USELESS.
WITH ALL OPTIONS EXHAUSTED...
...THIS IS SEIRIN'S LOSS.

KUROKO'S BASKETBALL BLOOPERS

TAKE 6

YOU IDIOT!!

SO DIZZY...

HURGH...

TMP

WHAT?!

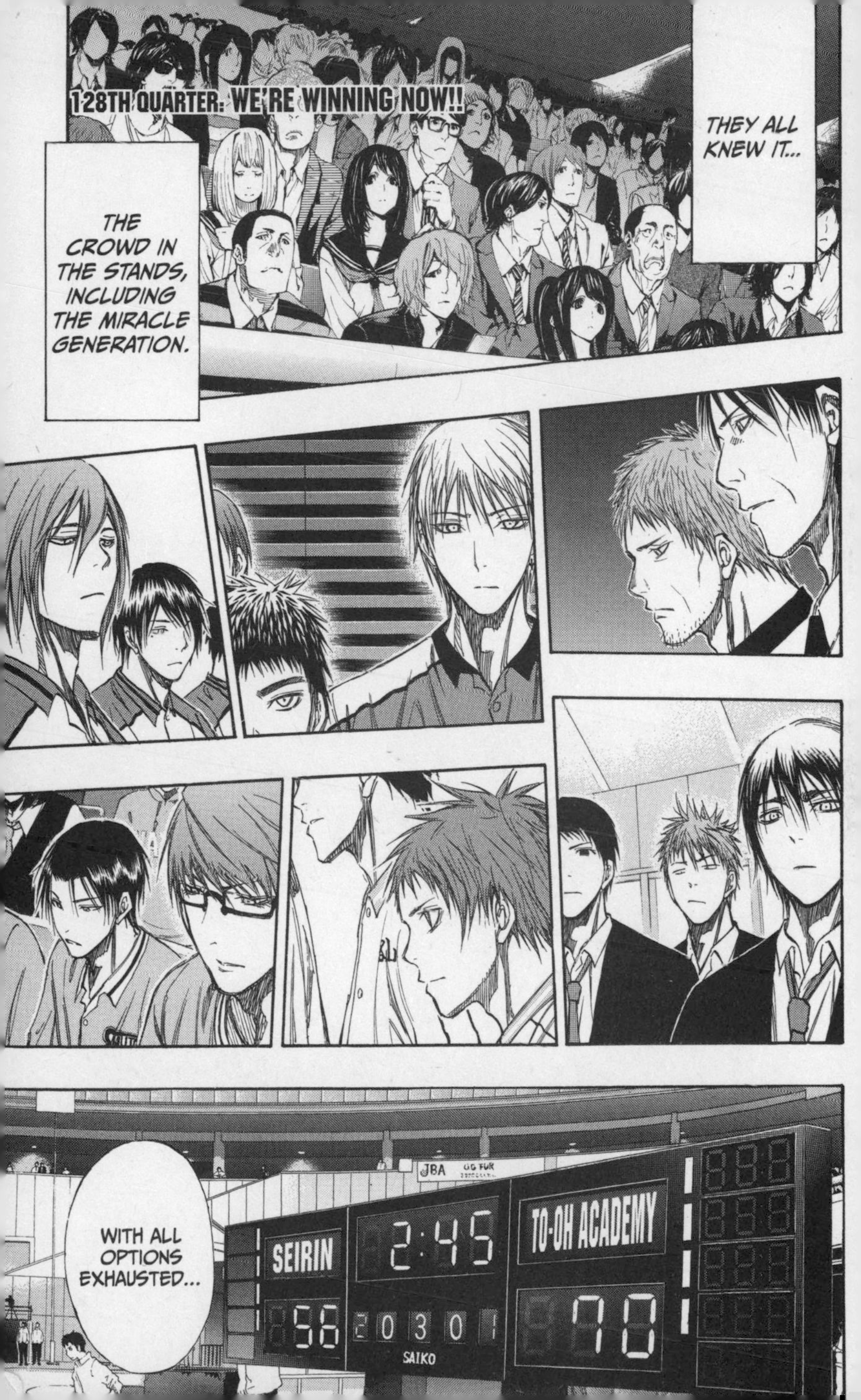
128TH QUARTER: WE'RE WINNING NOW!!
THEY ALL KNEW IT...
THE CROWD IN THE STANDS, INCLUDING THE MIRACLE GENERATION.
JBA
TO-OH ACADEMY
2:45
SEIRIN
70
56
SAIKO
WITH ALL OPTIONS EXHAUSTED...

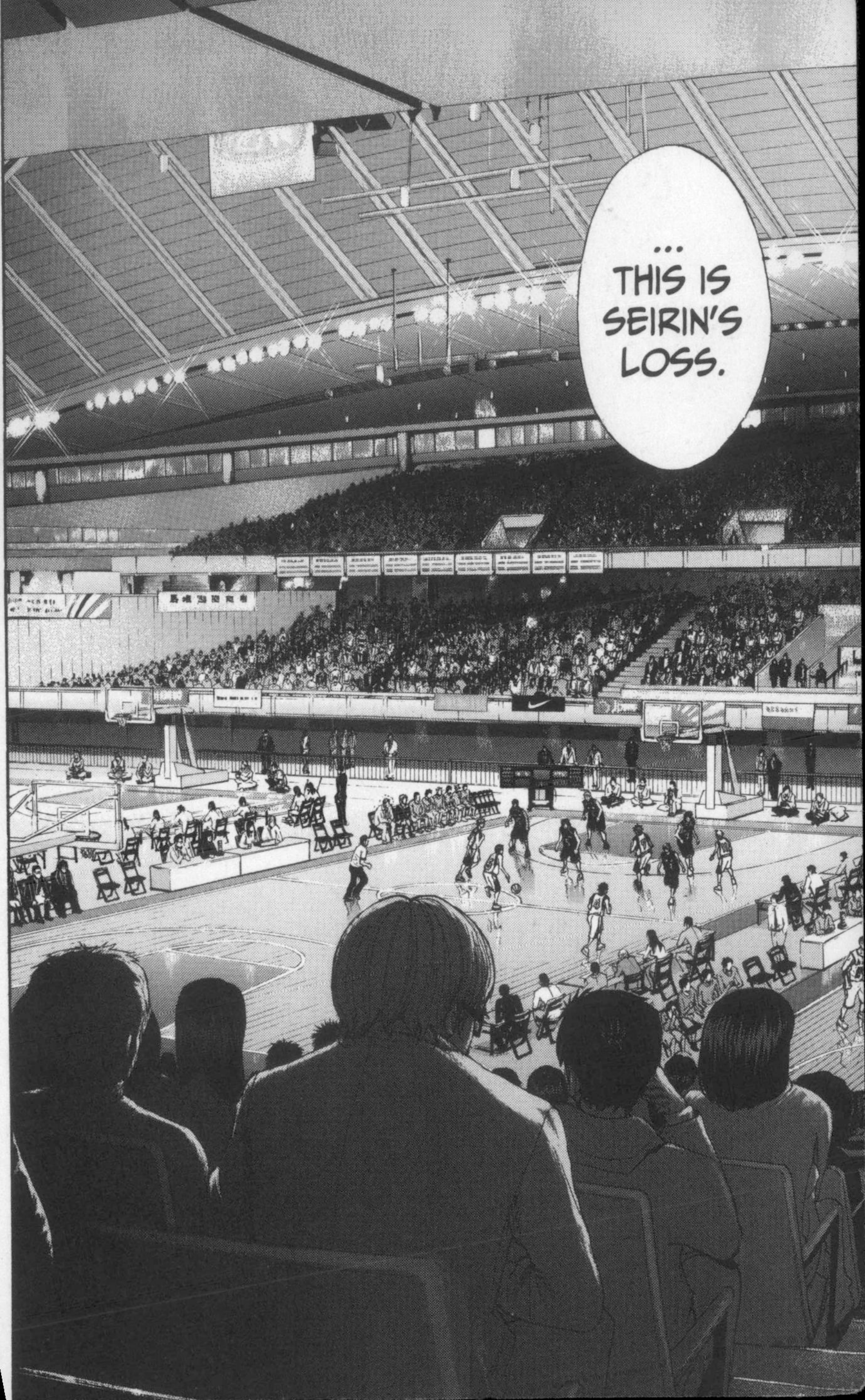
... THIS IS SEIRIN'S LOSS.

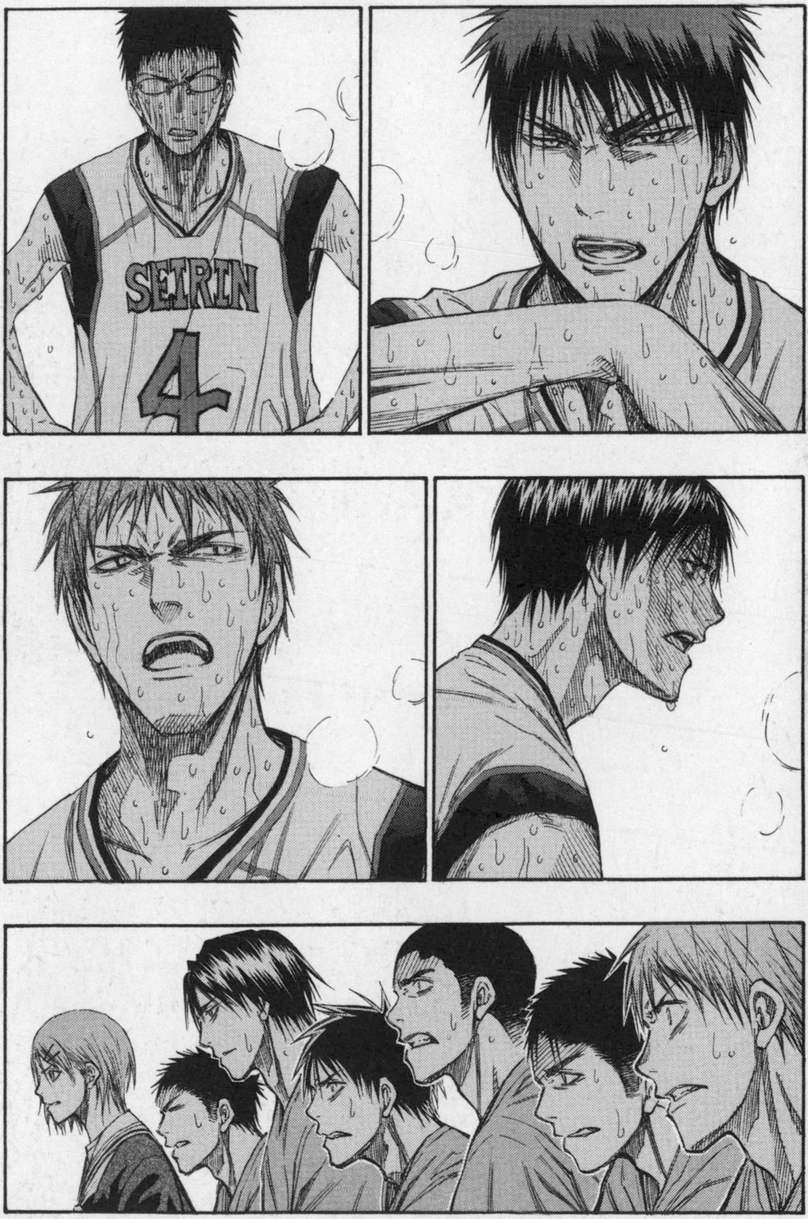
SEIRIN
4

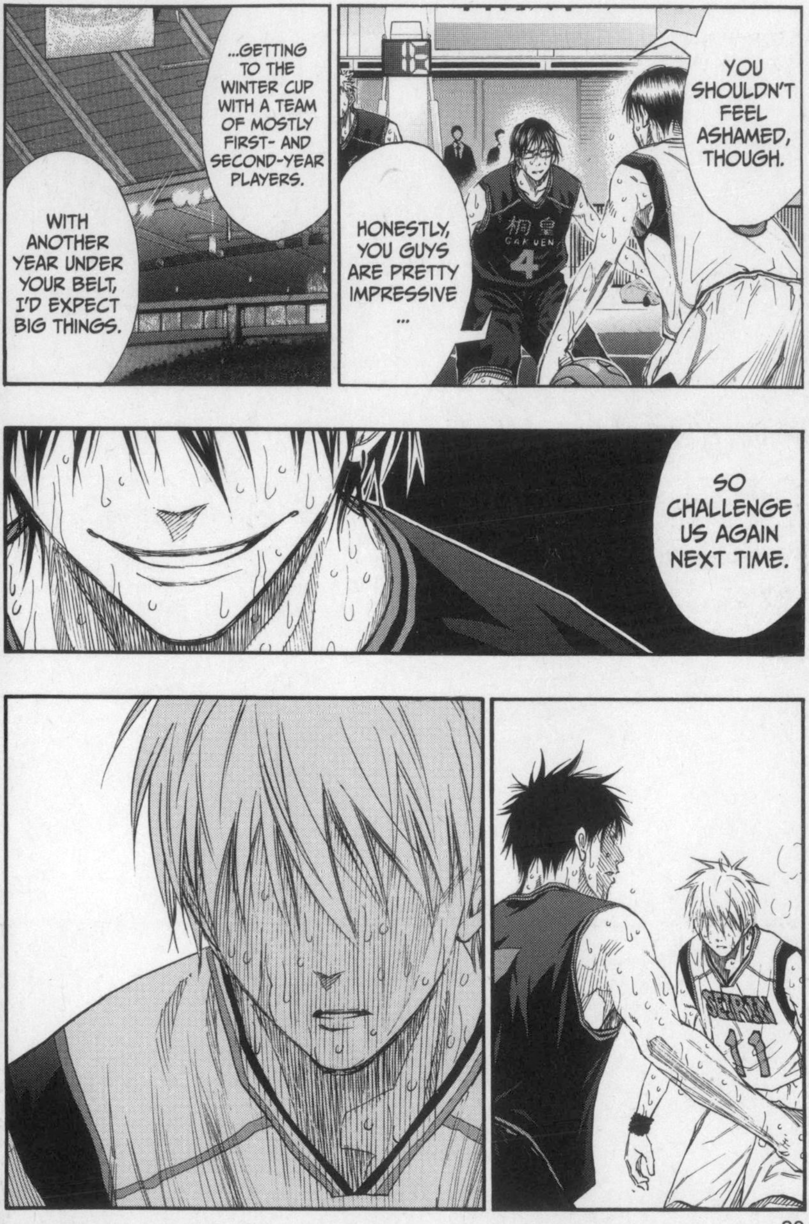
YOU SHOULDN'T FEEL ASHAMED, THOUGH.
HONESTLY, YOU GUYS ARE PRETTY IMPRESSIVE...
...GETTING TO THE WINTER CUP WITH A TEAM OF MOSTLY FIRST- AND SECOND-YEAR PLAYERS.
WITH ANOTHER YEAR UNDER YOUR BELT, I'D EXPECT BIG THINGS.
SO CHALLENGE US AGAIN NEXT TIME.

128TH QUARTER: WE'RE WINNING NOW!!

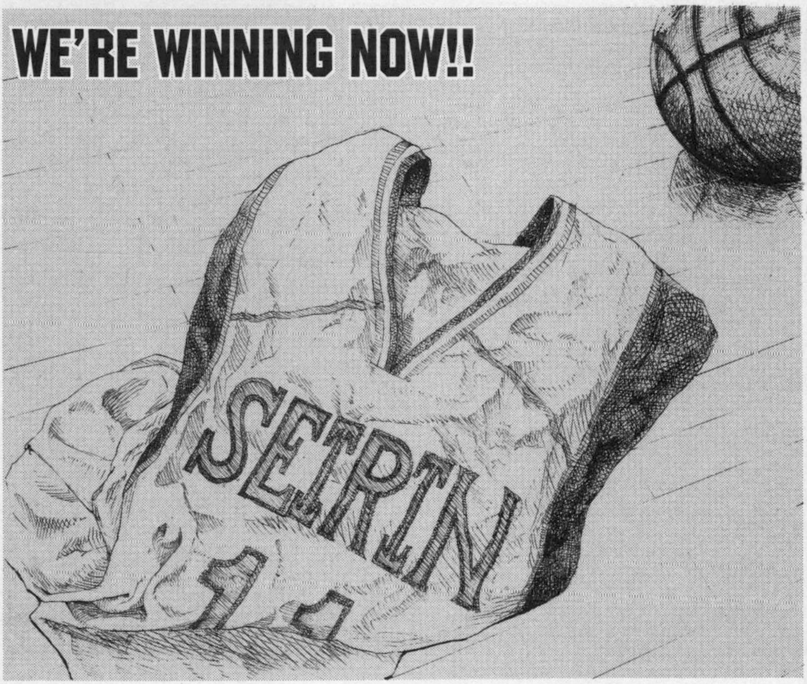

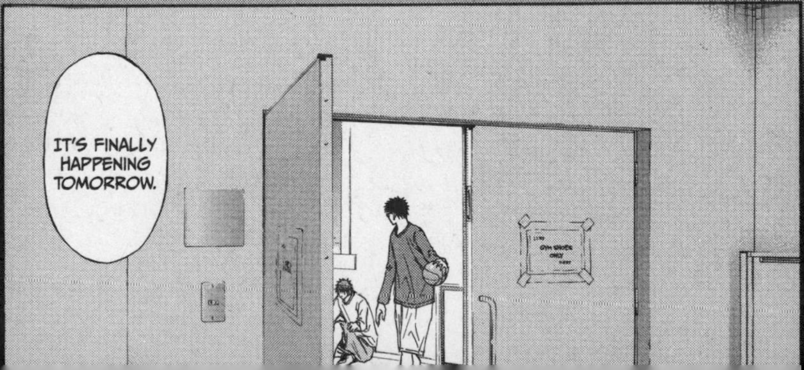
IT'S FINALLY HAPPENING TOMORROW.

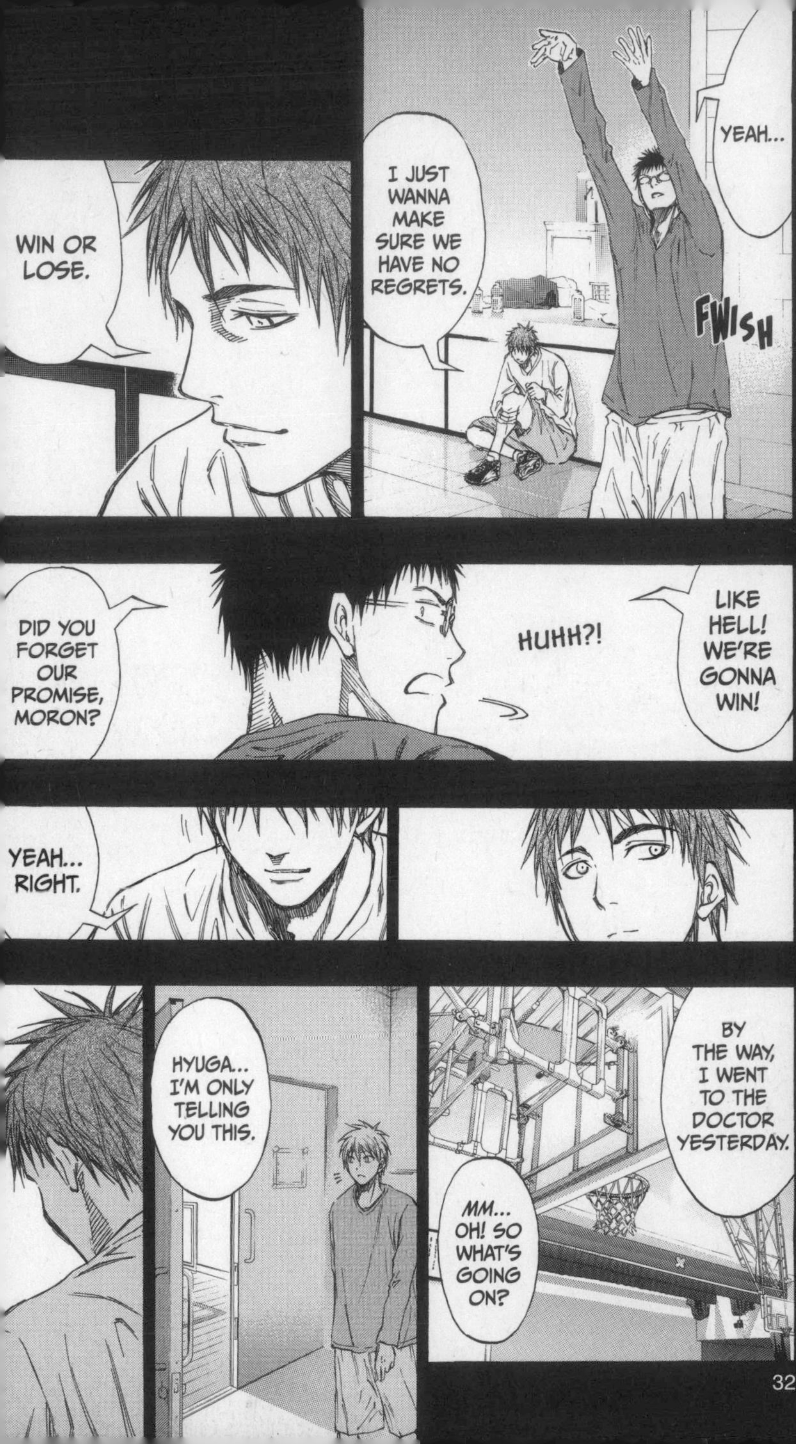
YEAH...
FWISH
I JUST WANNA MAKE SURE WE HAVE NO REGRETS.
WIN OR LOSE.
LIKE HELL! WE'RE GONNA WIN!
HUHH?!
DID YOU FORGET OUR PROMISE, MORON?
YEAH... RIGHT.
BY THE WAY, I WENT TO THE DOCTOR YESTERDAY.
MM... OH! SO WHAT'S GOING ON?
HYUGA... I'M ONLY TELLING YOU THIS.

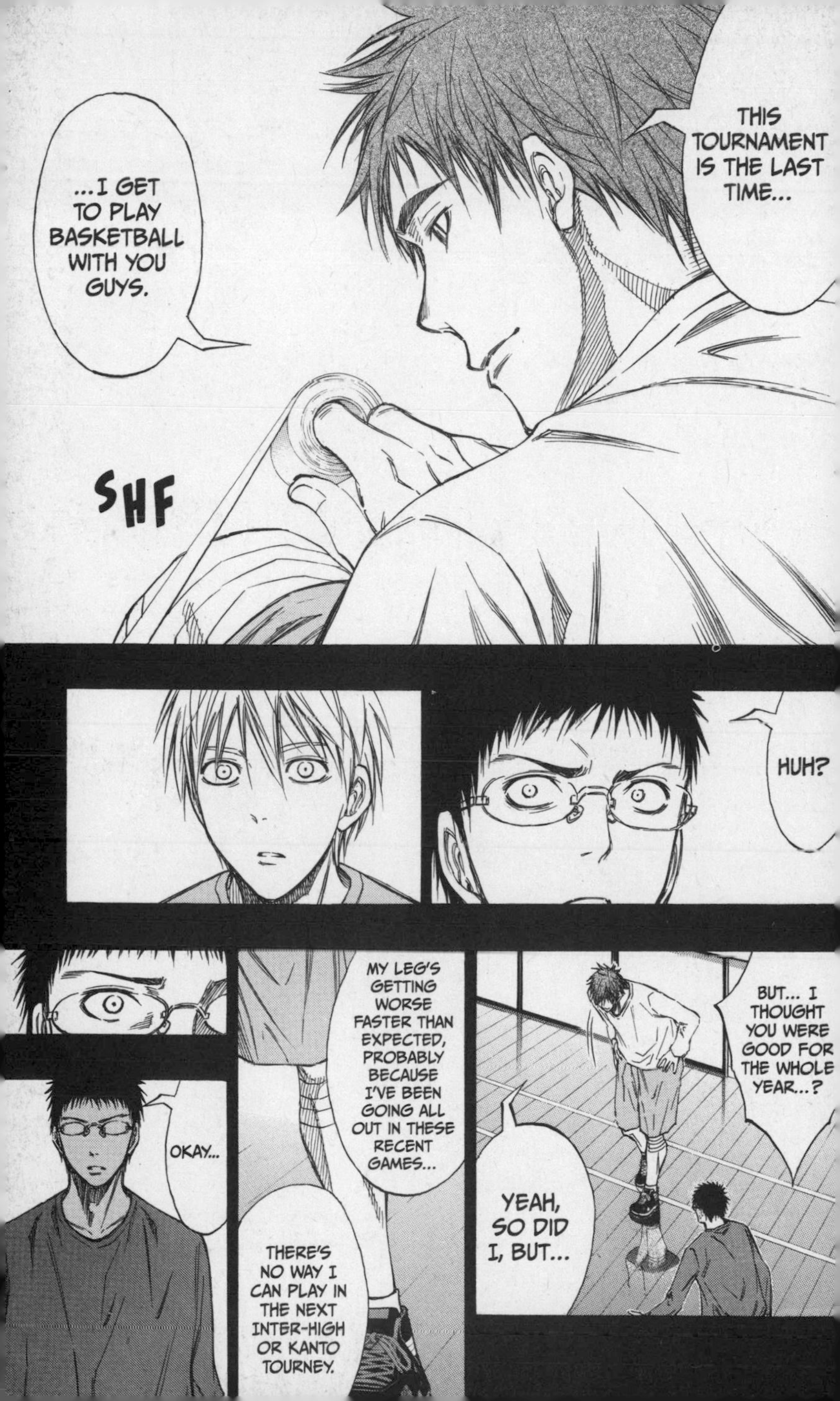
THIS TOURNAMENT IS THE LAST TIME...
...I GET TO PLAY BASKETBALL WITH YOU GUYS.
SHF
HUH?
BUT... I THOUGHT YOU WERE GOOD FOR THE WHOLE YEAR...?
YEAH, SO DID I, BUT...
MY LEG'S GETTING WORSE FASTER THAN EXPECTED, PROBABLY BECAUSE I'VE BEEN GOING ALL OUT IN THESE RECENT GAMES...
THERE'S NO WAY I CAN PLAY IN THE NEXT INTER-HIGH OR KANTO TOURNEY.
OKAY...

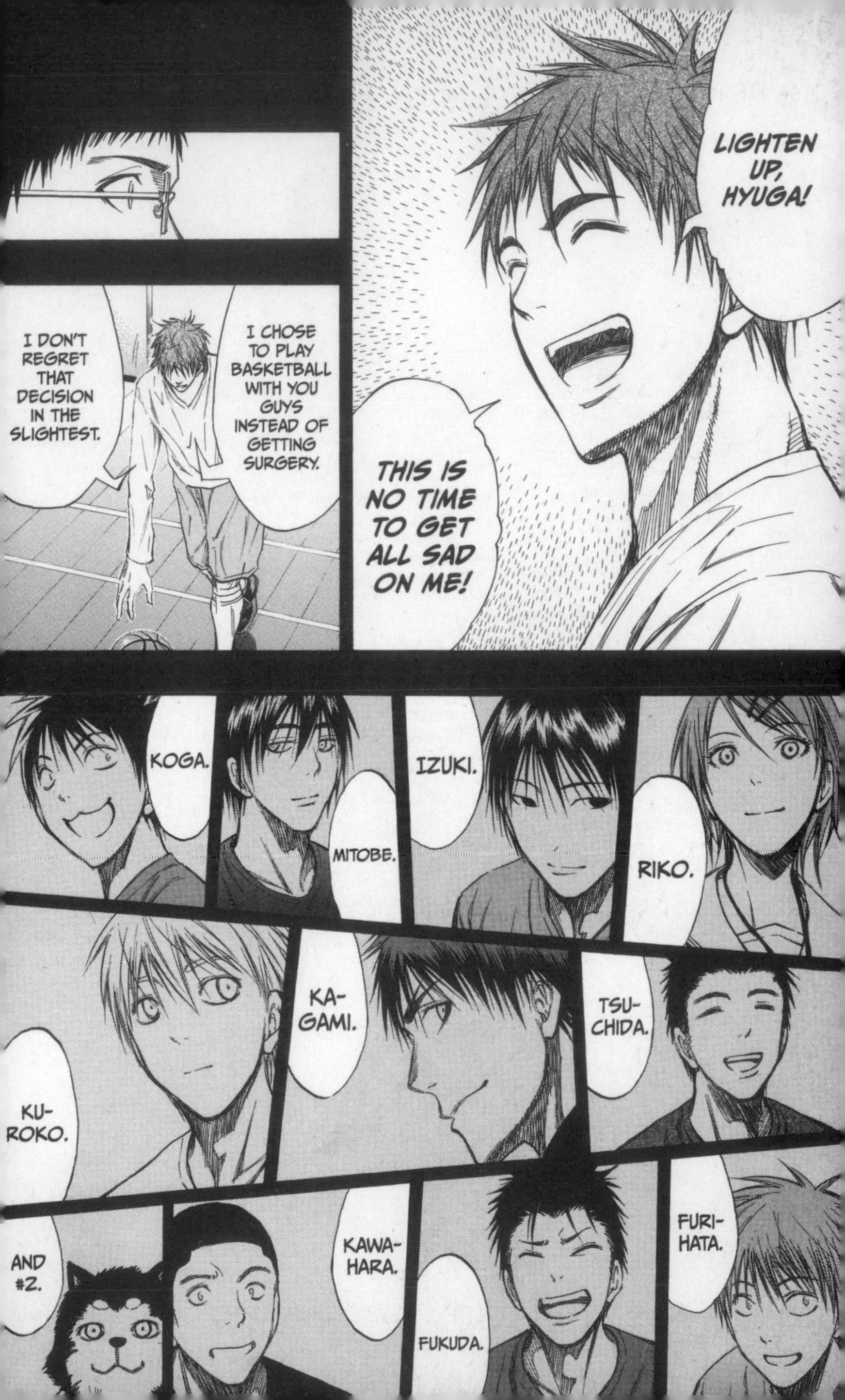
LIGHTEN UP, HYUGA!
THIS IS NO TIME TO GET ALL SAD ON ME!
I CHOSE TO PLAY BASKETBALL WITH YOU GUYS INSTEAD OF GETTING SURGERY.
I DON'T REGRET THAT DECISION IN THE SLIGHTEST.
RIKO.
IZUKI.
MITOBE.
KOGA.
TSU-CHIDA.
KA-GAMI.
KU-ROKO.
FURI-HATA.
FUKUDA.
KAWA-HARA.
AND #2.

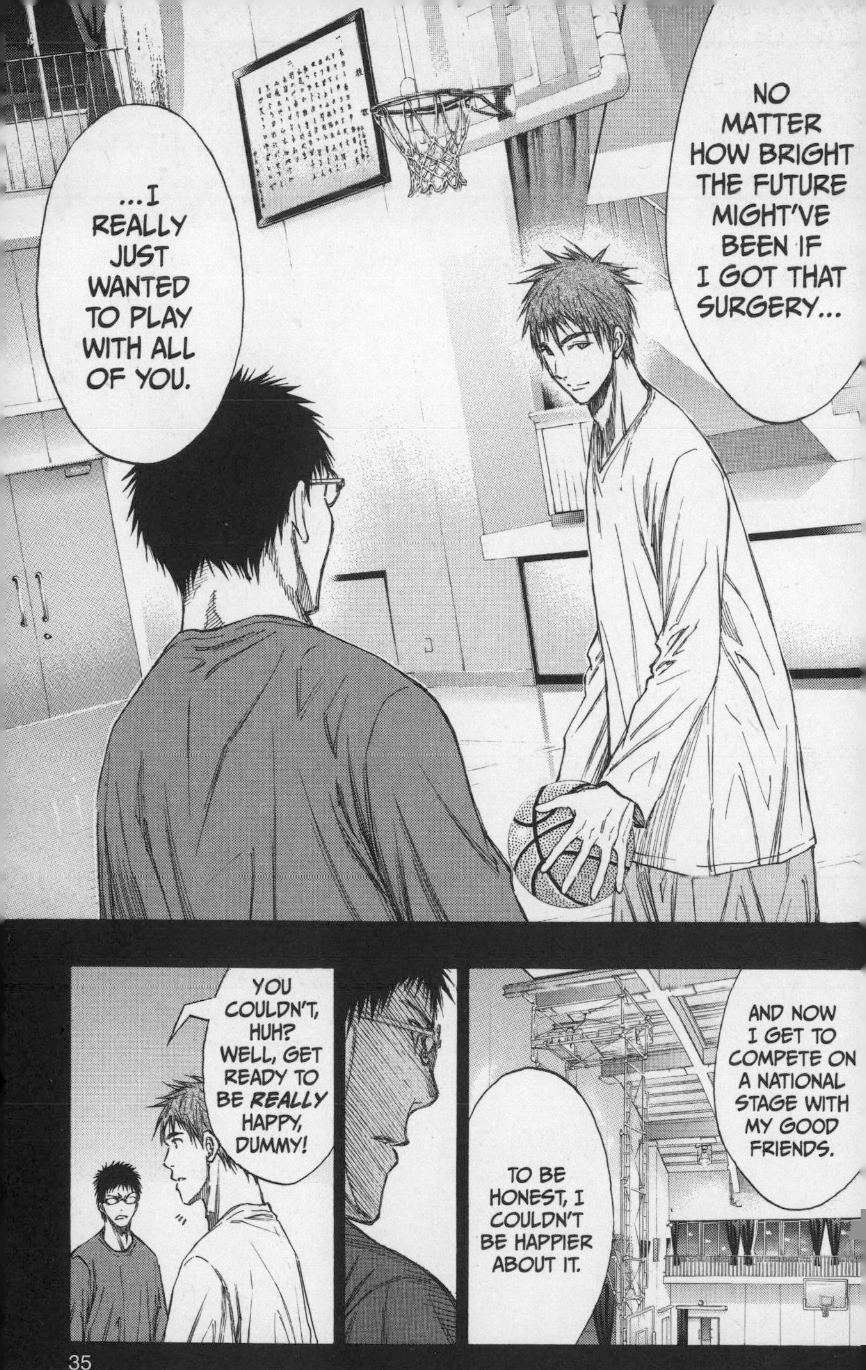
NO MATTER HOW BRIGHT THE FUTURE MIGHT'VE BEEN IF I GOT THAT SURGERY...
...I REALLY JUST WANTED TO PLAY WITH ALL OF YOU.
AND NOW I GET TO COMPETE ON A NATIONAL STAGE WITH MY GOOD FRIENDS.
TO BE HONEST, I COULDN'T BE HAPPIER ABOUT IT.
YOU COULDN'T, HUH? WELL, GET READY TO BE *REALLY* HAPPY, DUMMY!

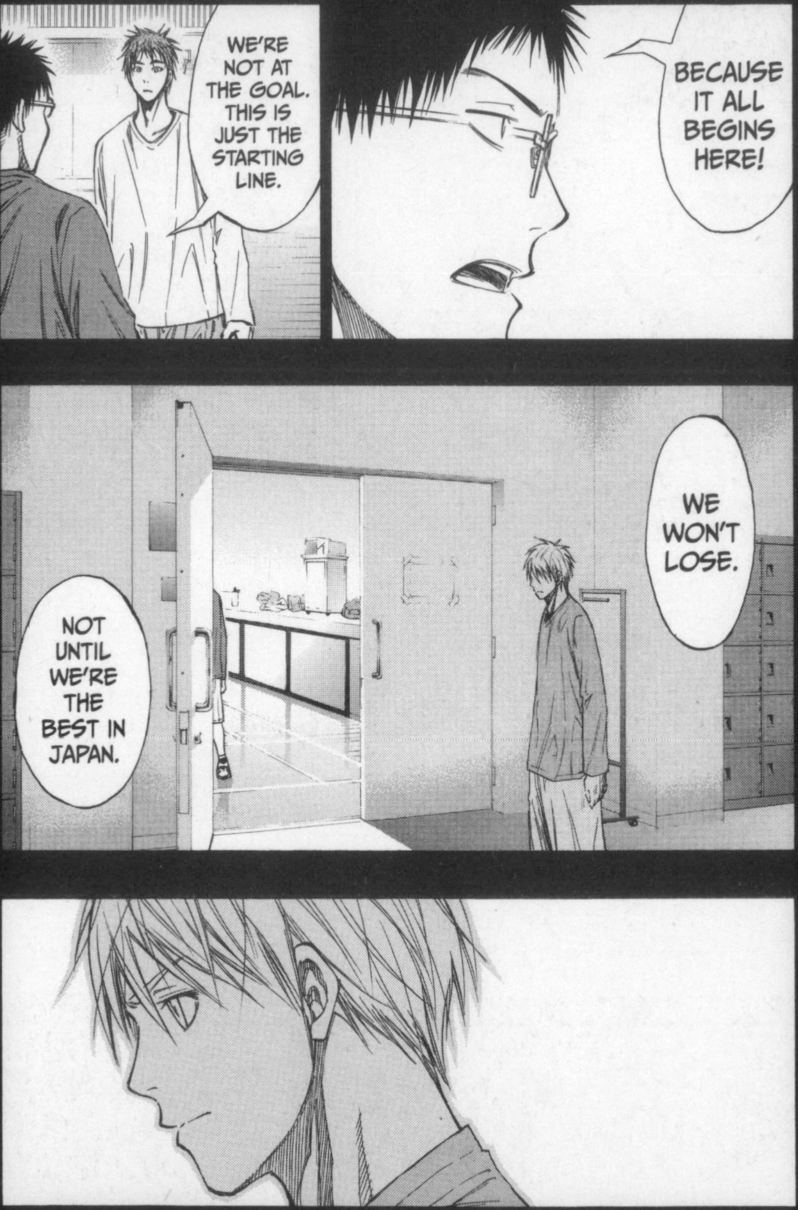
BECAUSE IT ALL BEGINS HERE!
WE'RE NOT AT THE GOAL. THIS IS JUST THE STARTING LINE.
WE WON'T LOSE.
NOT UNTIL WE'RE THE BEST IN JAPAN.

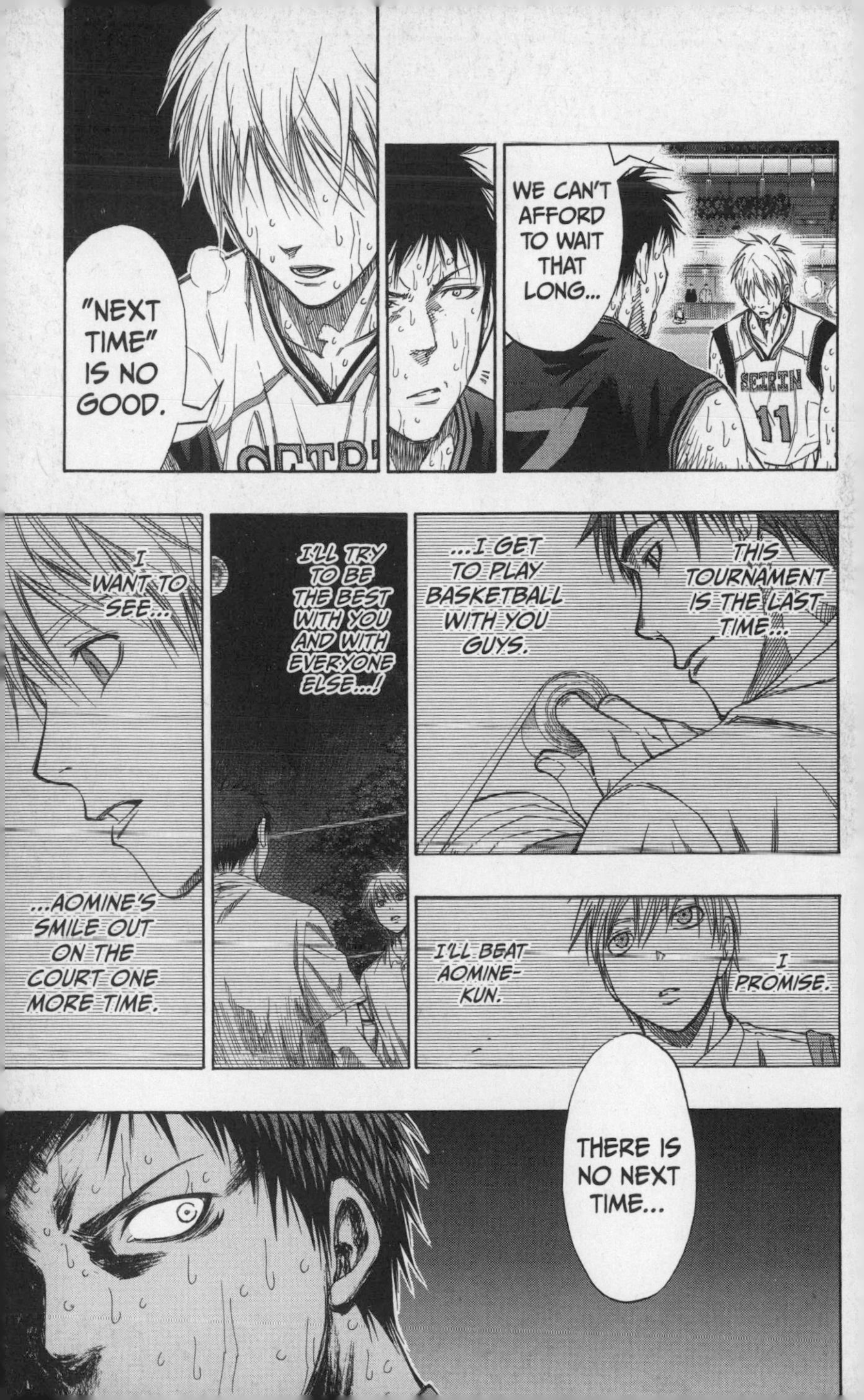
WE CAN'T AFFORD TO WAIT THAT LONG...
"NEXT TIME" IS NO GOOD.
THIS TOURNAMENT IS THE LAST TIME...
...I GET TO PLAY BASKETBALL WITH YOU GUYS.
I PROMISE.
I'LL BEAT AOMINE-KUN.
I'LL TRY TO BE THE BEST WITH YOU AND WITH EVERYONE ELSE...!
I WANT TO SEE...
...AOMINE'S SMILE OUT ON THE COURT ONE MORE TIME.
THERE IS NO NEXT TIME...

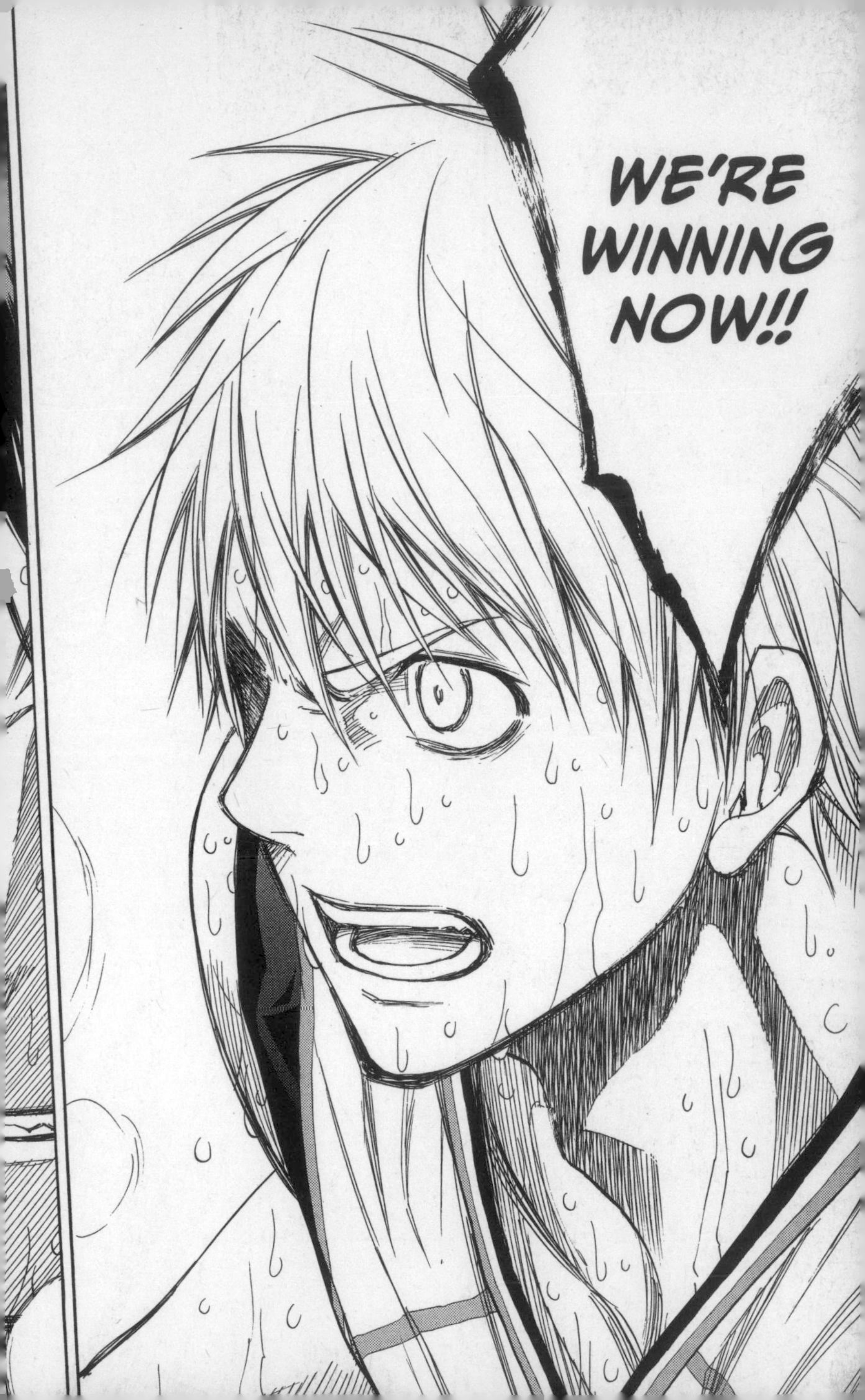
WE'RE WINNING NOW!!

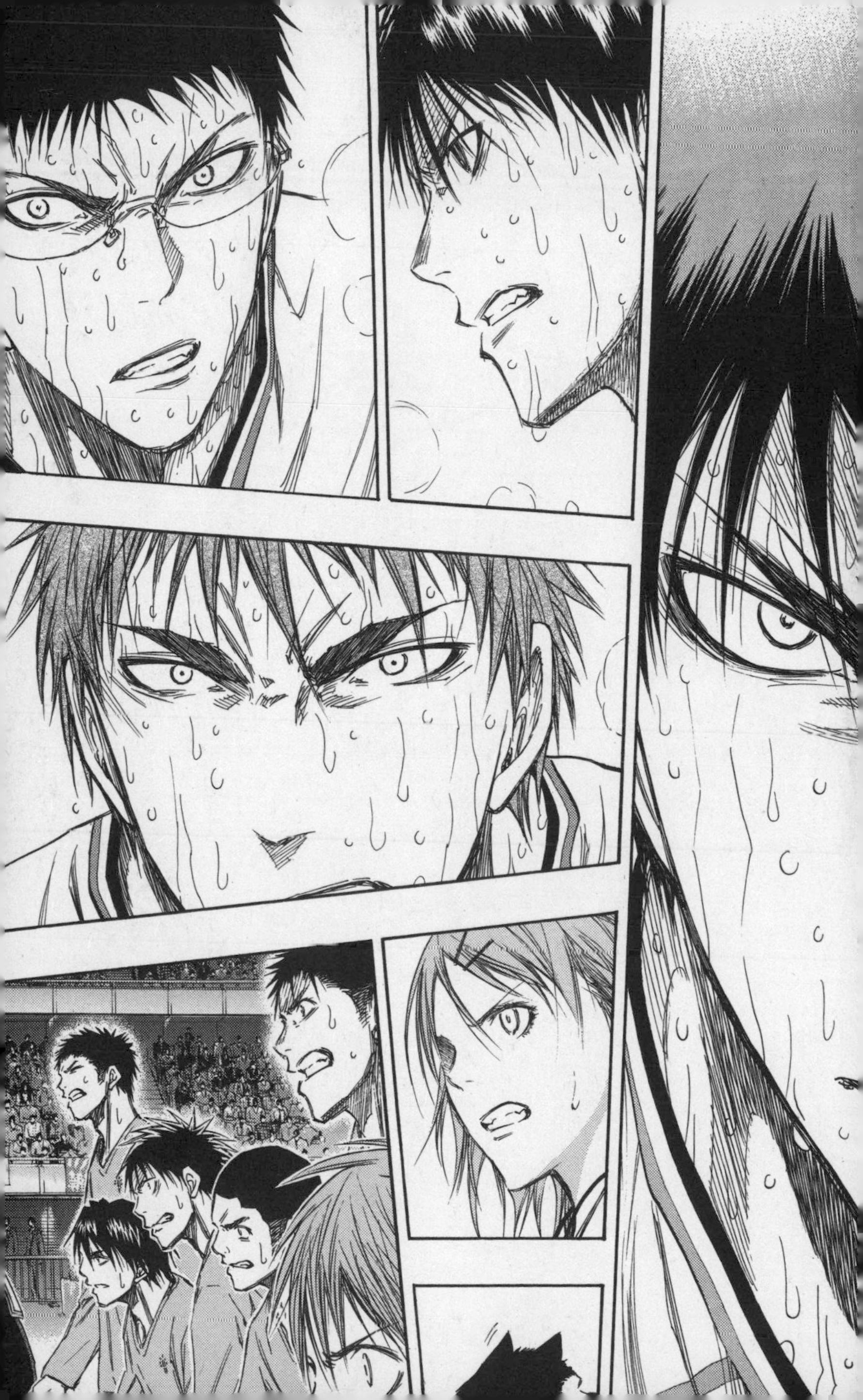

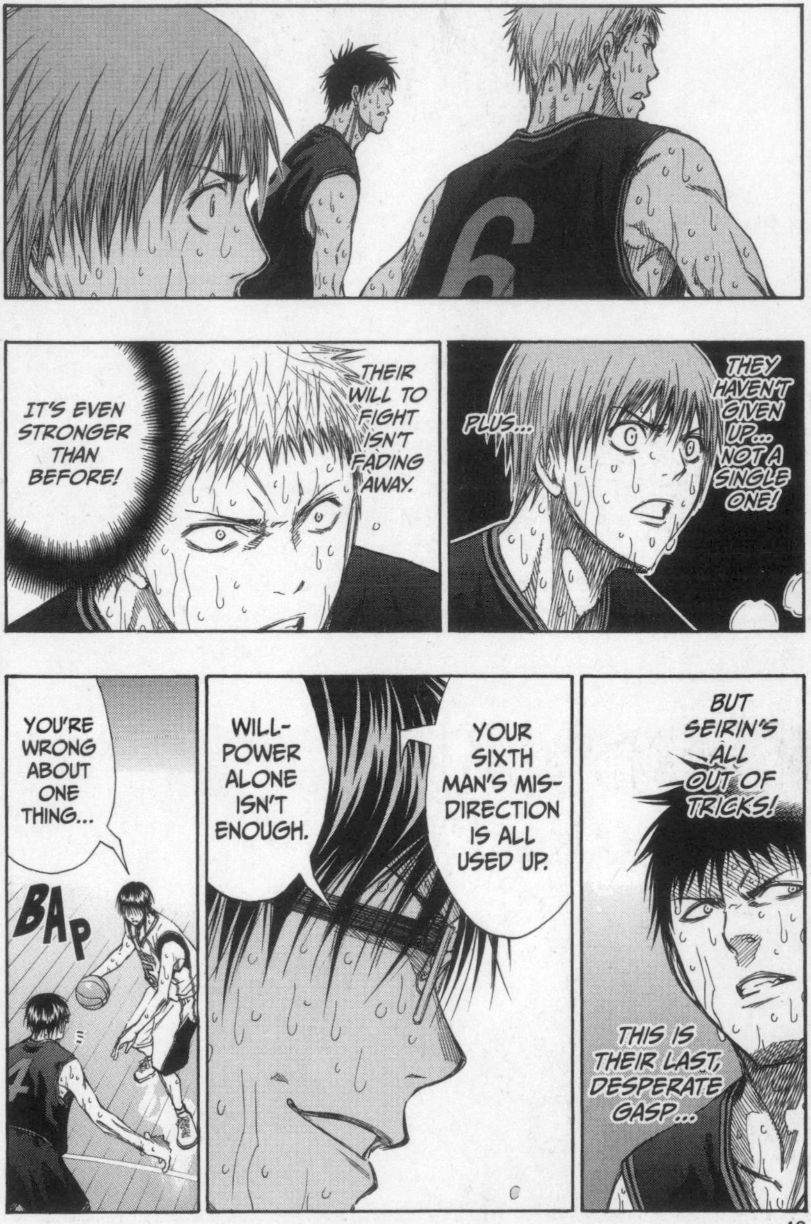
THEY HAVEN'T GIVEN UP... NOT A SINGLE ONE!
PLUS...
THEIR WILL TO FIGHT ISN'T FADING AWAY.
IT'S EVEN STRONGER THAN BEFORE!
BUT SEIRIN'S ALL OUT OF TRICKS!
THIS IS THEIR LAST, DESPERATE GASP...
YOUR SIXTH MAN'S MIS-DIRECTION IS ALL USED UP.
WILL-POWER ALONE ISN'T ENOUGH.
YOU'RE WRONG ABOUT ONE THING...
BAP

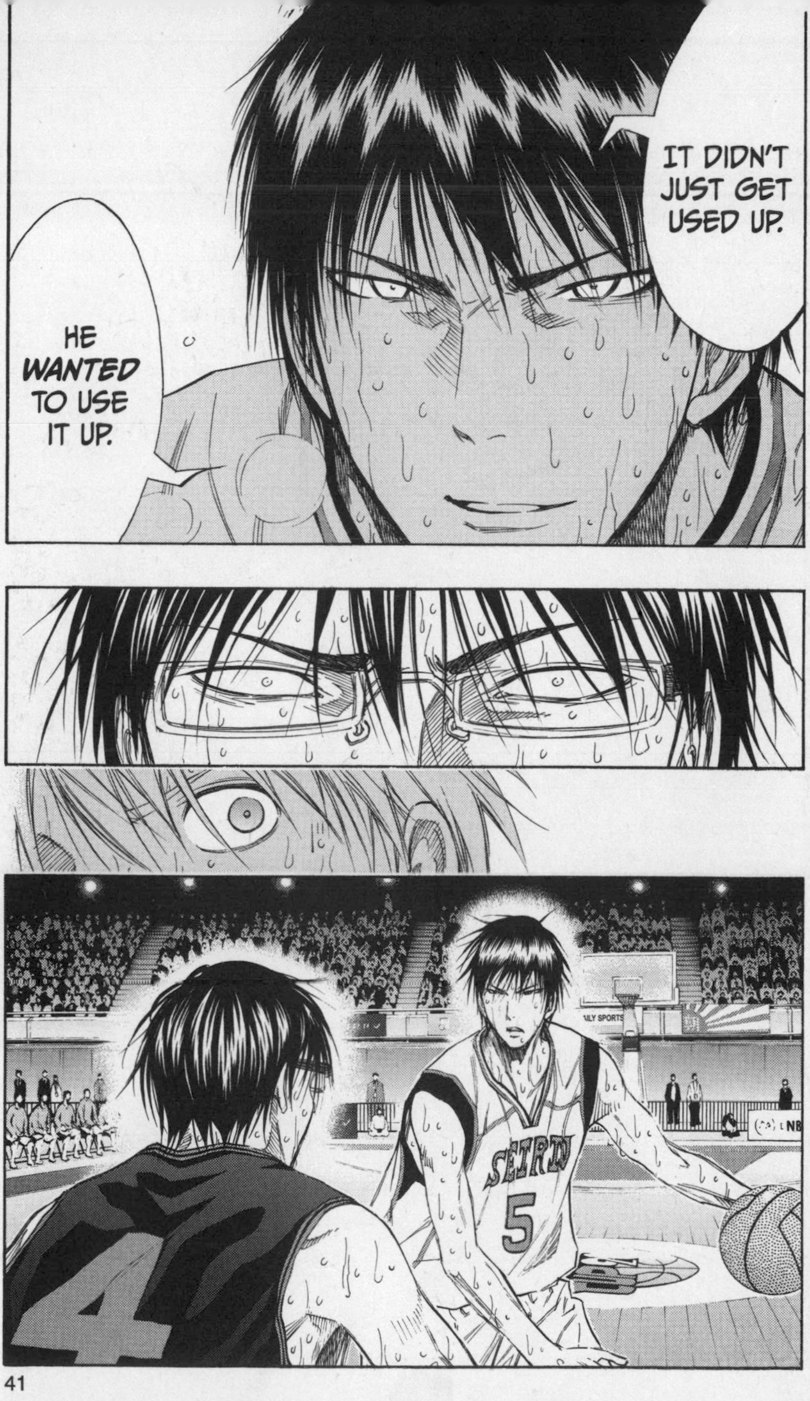
IT DIDN'T JUST GET USED UP.
HE WANTED TO USE IT UP.
SEIRIN
5
4

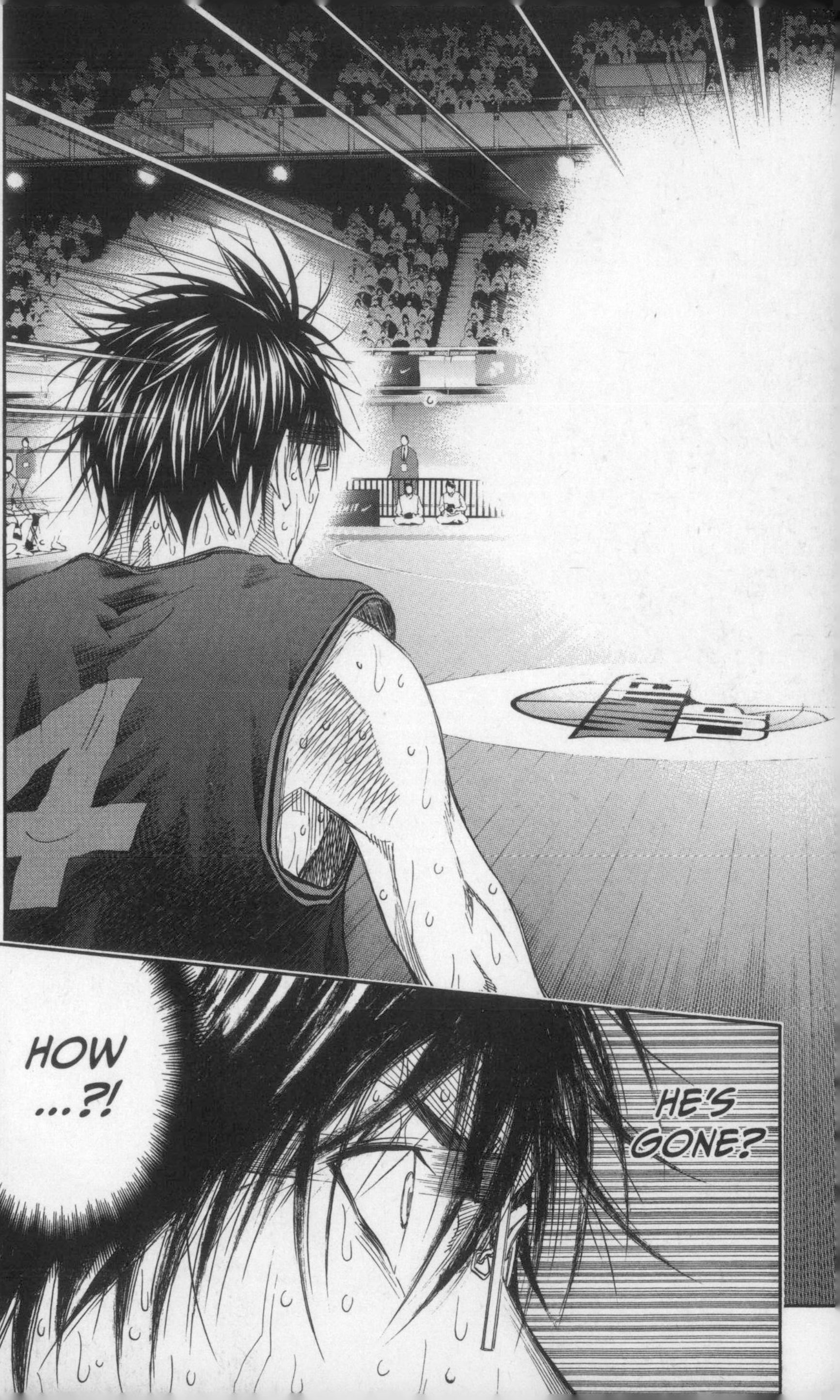
HE'S GONE?
HOW ...?!

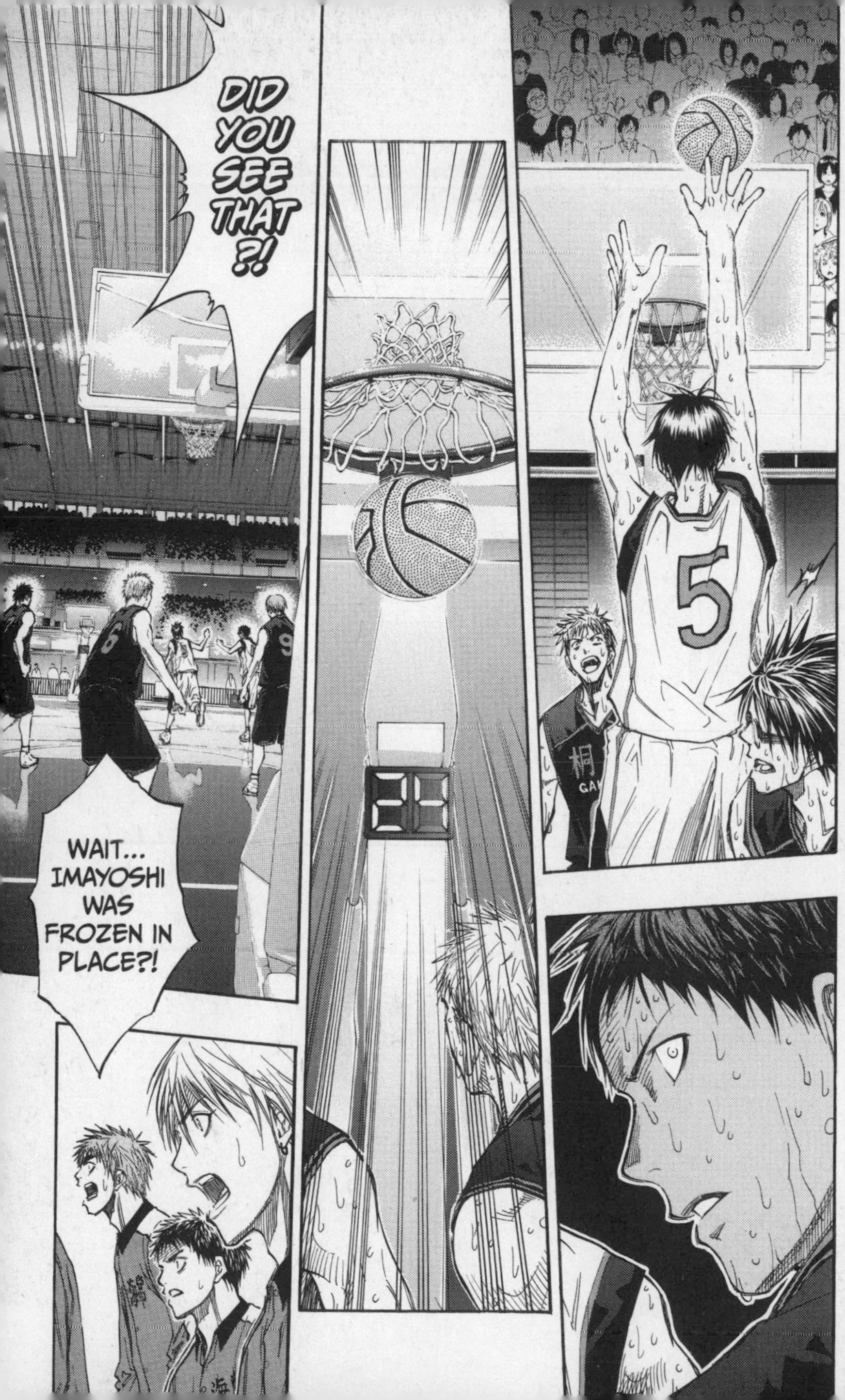
DID YOU SEE THAT?!
WAIT... IMAYOSHI WAS FROZEN IN PLACE?!

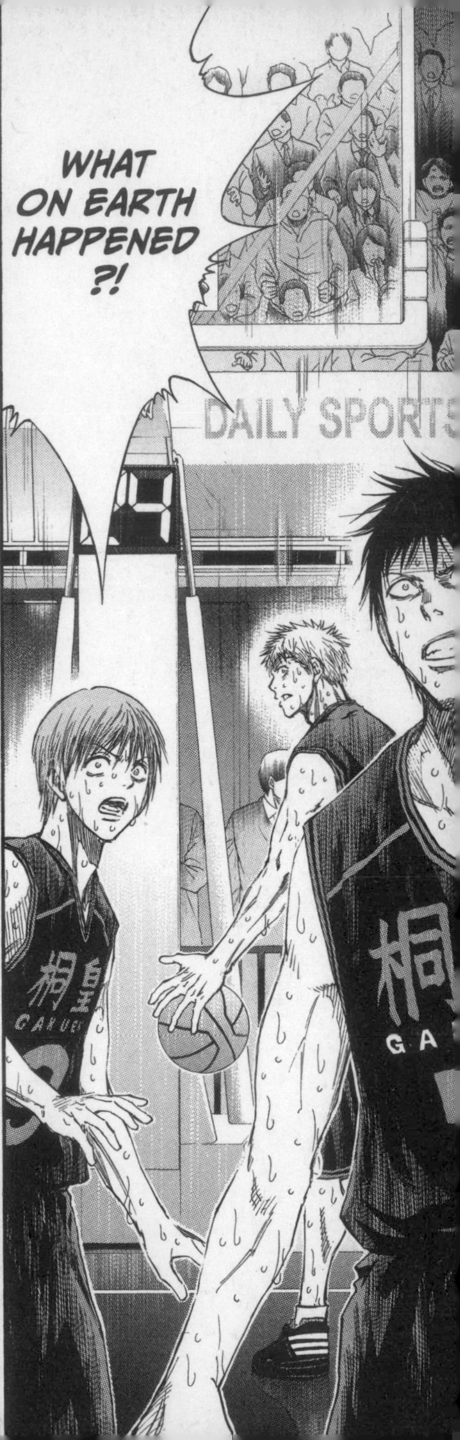
WHAT ON EARTH HAPPENED ?!
DAILY SPORTS
GAKUEN

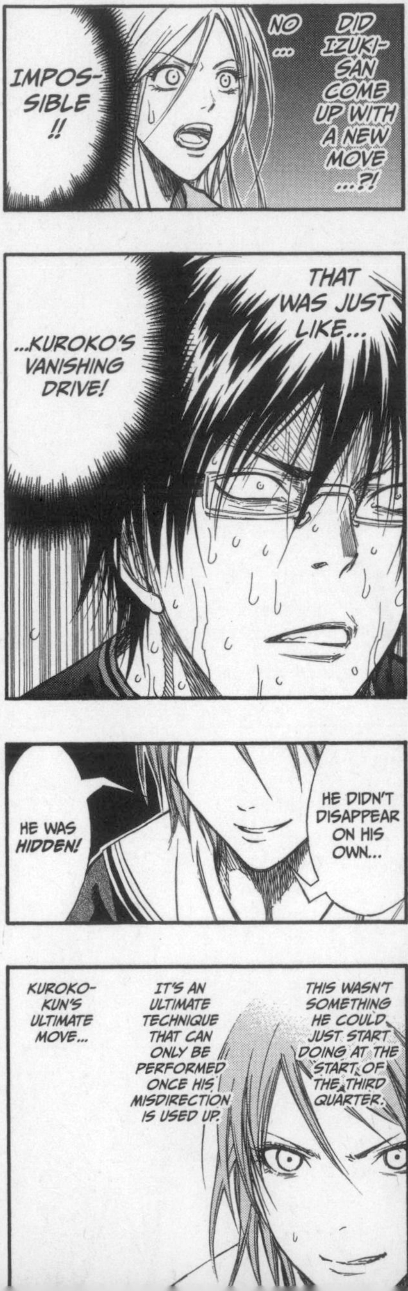
NO ... DID IZUKI-SAN COME UP WITH A NEW MOVE ...?!
IMPOSSIBLE!!
THAT WAS JUST LIKE...
...KUROKO'S VANISHING DRIVE!
HE DIDN'T DISAPPEAR ON HIS OWN...
HE WAS HIDDEN!
THIS WASN'T SOMETHING HE COULD JUST START DOING AT THE START OF THE THIRD QUARTER.
IT'S AN ULTIMATE TECHNIQUE THAT CAN ONLY BE PERFORMED ONCE HIS MISDIRECTION IS USED UP.
KUROKO-KUN'S ULTIMATE MOVE...

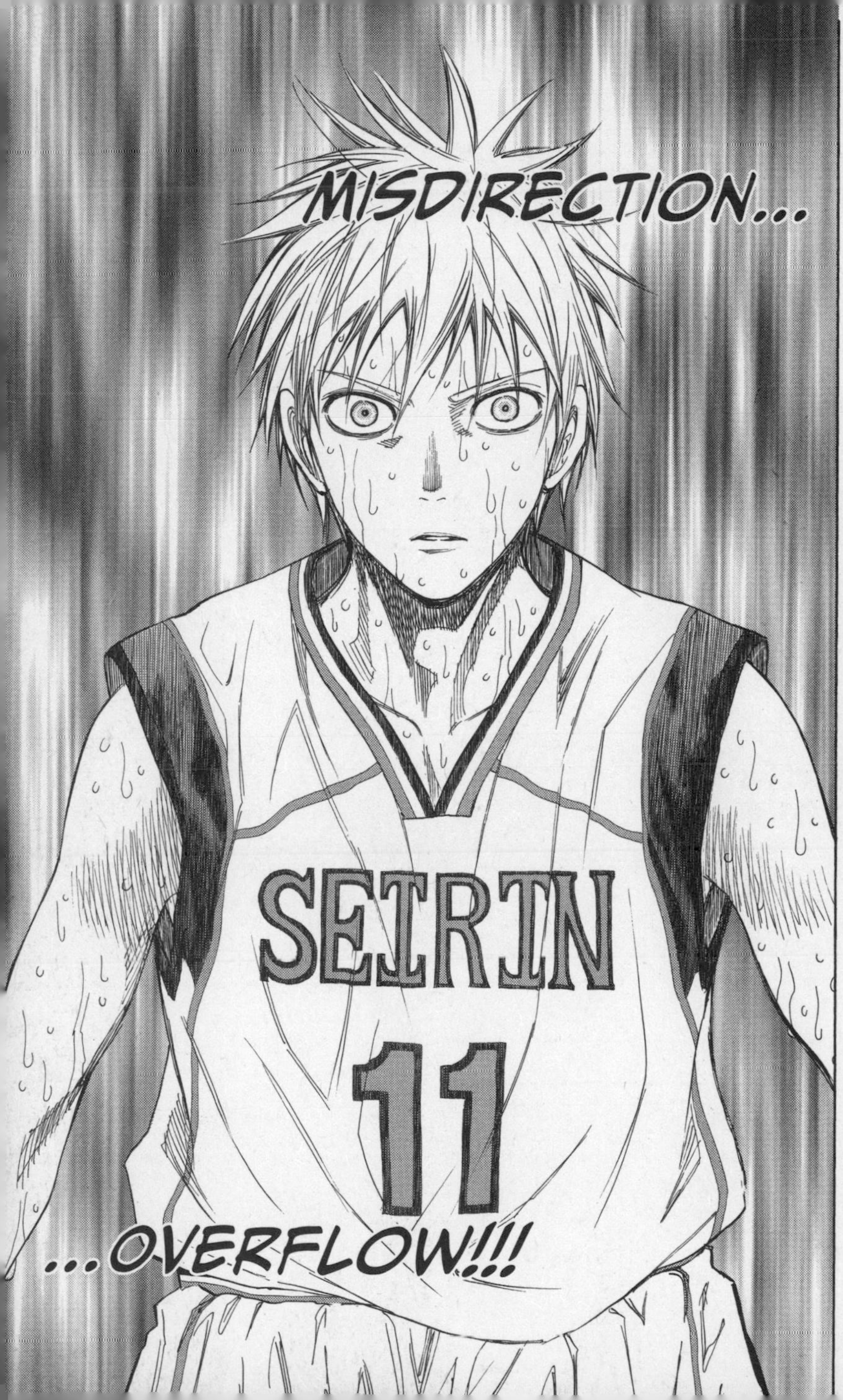
MISDIRECTION...
...OVERFLOW!!!
SEIRIN
11

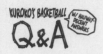

KUROKO'S BASKETBALL
Q&A
W/ HALFWAY-DECENT ANSWERS

Q. IN 110TH QUARTER, TO-OH ACADEMY AND SEIRIN HAVE A SAUNA ENDURANCE BATTLE, BUT WHO ENDED UP WINNING?
(CHISATO SUZUKI from KANAGAWA PREFECTURE)

A. MITOBE LASTED THE LONGEST—THEREFORE, IT'S SEIRIN'S WIN.

KUROKO'S BASKETBALL BLOOPERS
TAKE 1

THIS TOURNAMENT IS THE LAST TIME...
...I GET TO PLAY BASKETBALL WITH YOU GUYS.
SHF
KIYOSHI...
YOU SURE YOU WRAPPED THAT RIGHT?
THAT TAPE.
HM? OH?!
I WAS WONDERING WHY IT WAS SO HARD TO STAND UP!
YOU'RE SLOW TO CATCH ON!

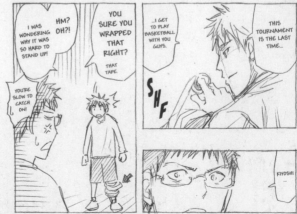

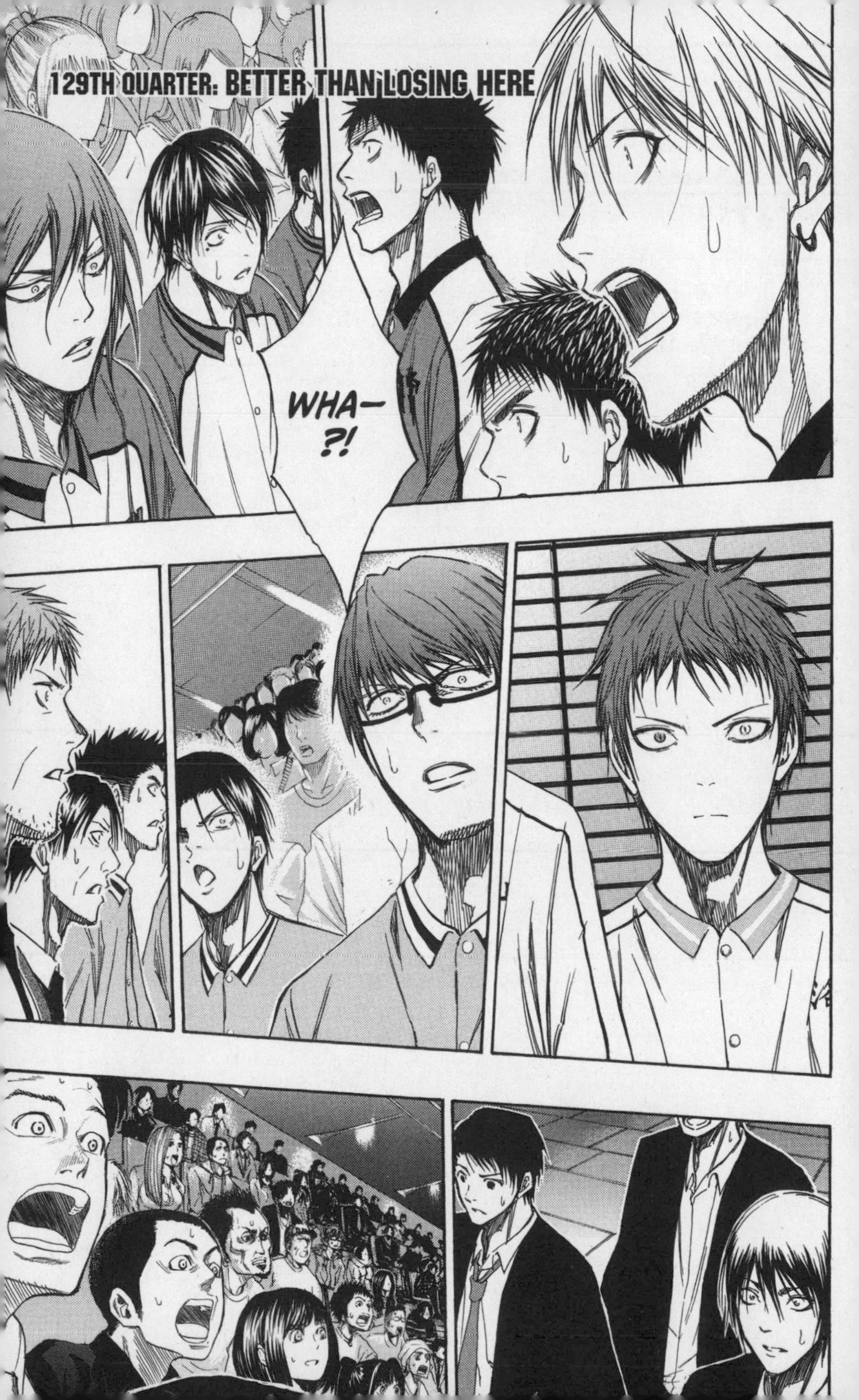
129TH QUARTER: BETTER THAN LOSING HERE
WHA— ?!

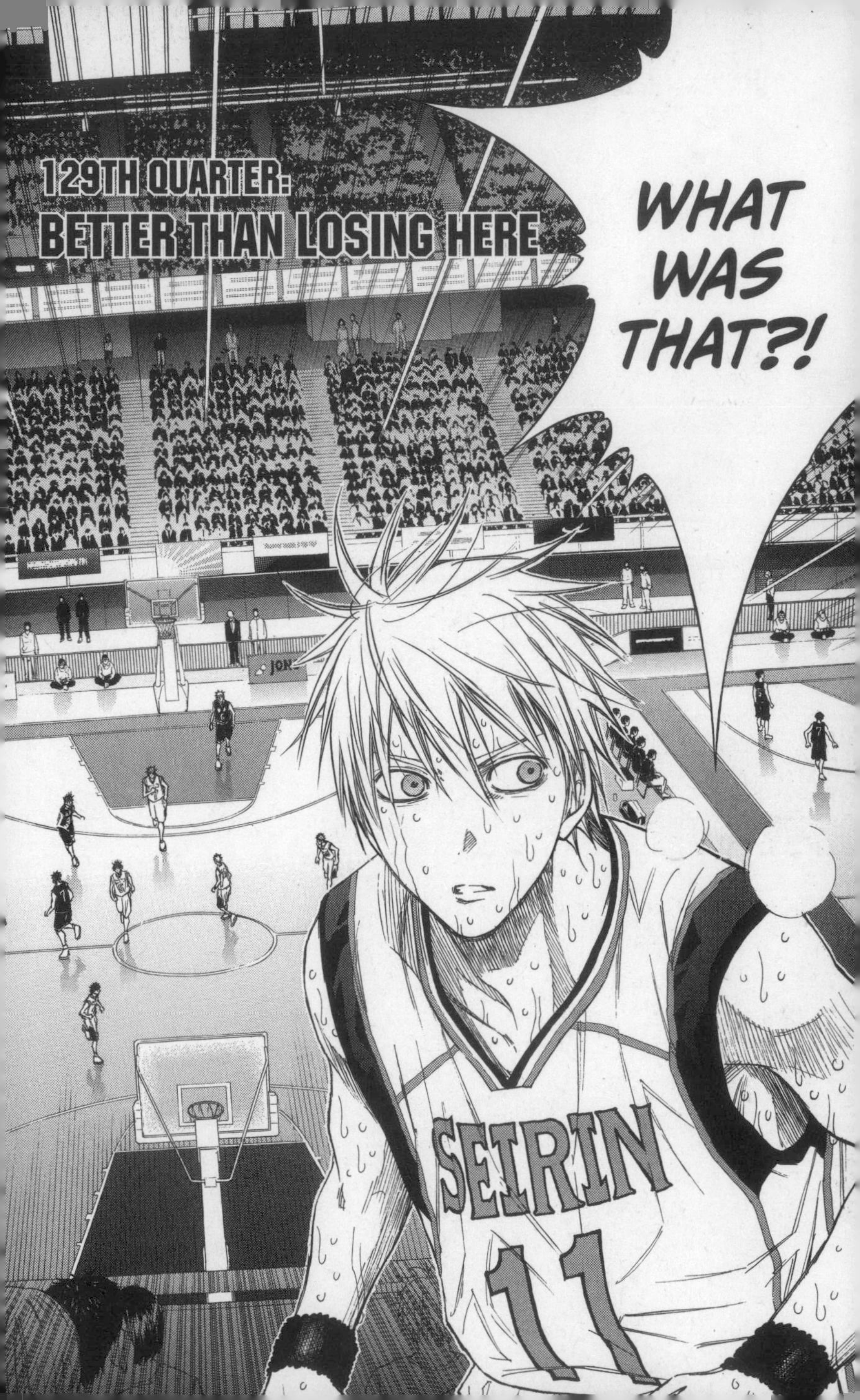
129TH QUARTER:
BETTER THAN LOSING HERE
WHAT WAS THAT?!
SEIRIN
11

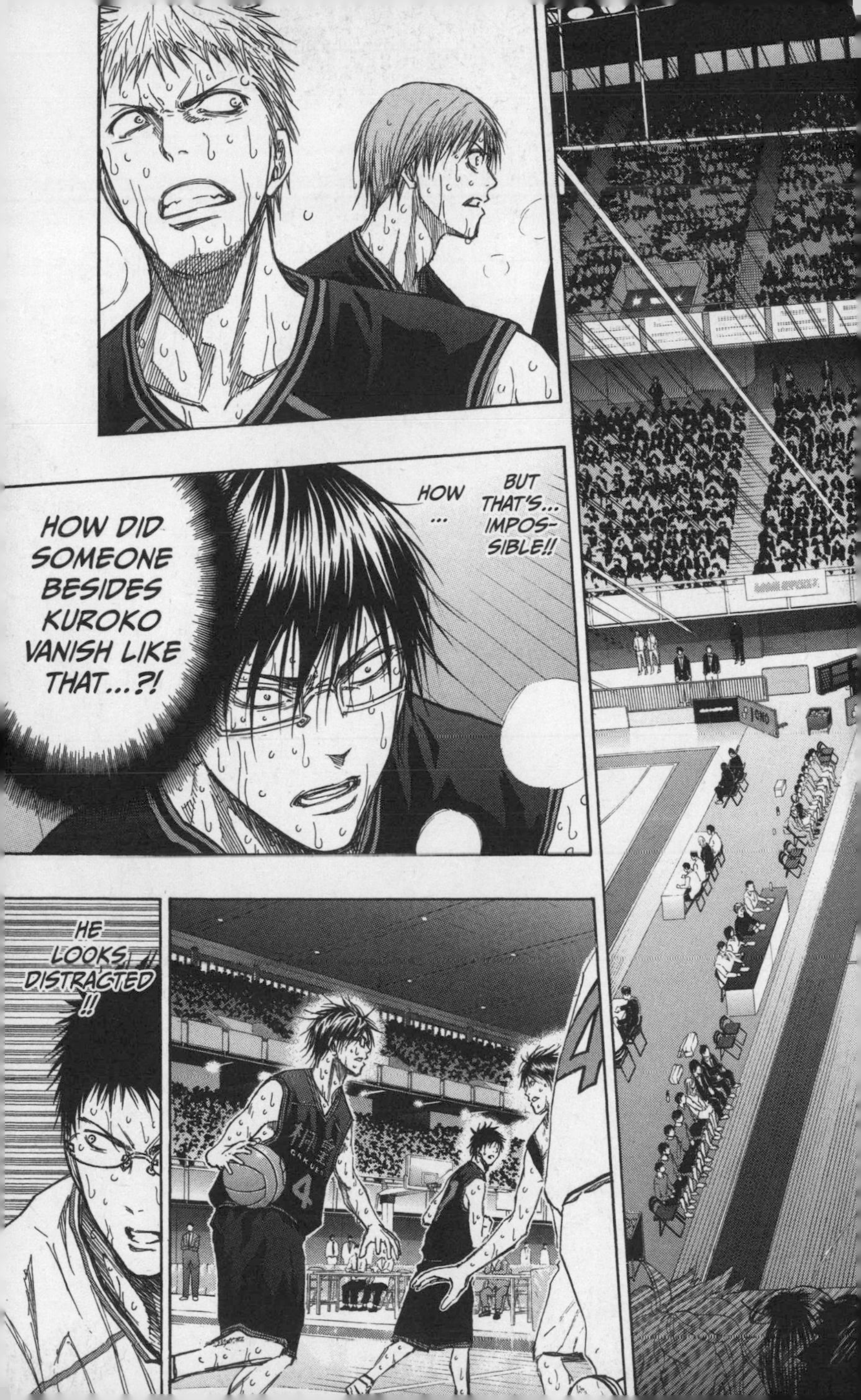
BUT THAT'S... IMPOSSIBLE!!
HOW ...
HOW DID SOMEONE BESIDES KUROKO VANISH LIKE THAT...?!
HE LOOKS DISTRACTED!!

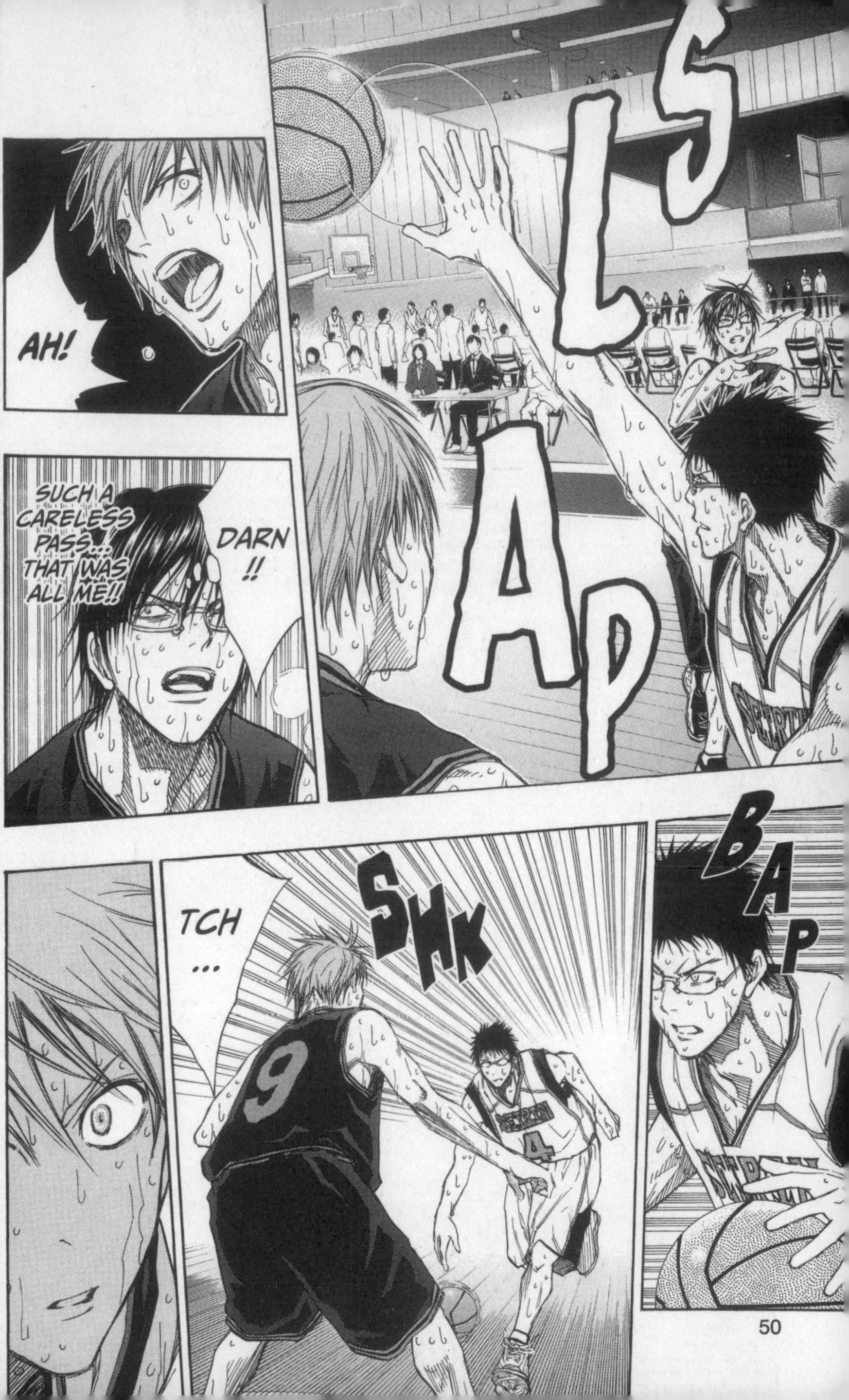
SLAP
AH!
DARN !!
SUCH A CARELESS PASS... THAT WAS ALL ME!!
BAP
SHK
TCH ...

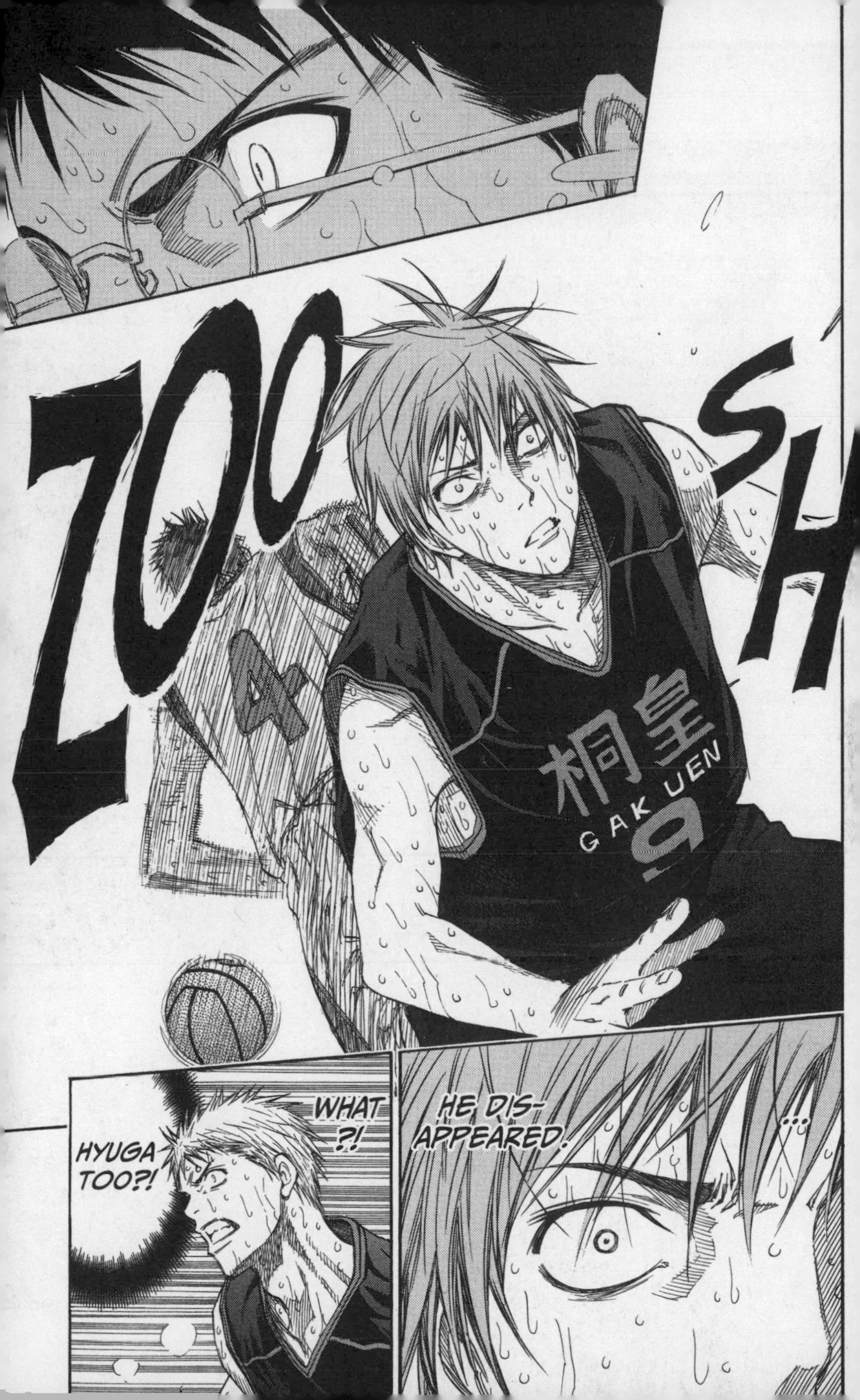

ZOOSH
桐皇
GAKUEN
9
4
HE DIS-APPEARED.
...
WHAT?!
HYUGA TOO?!

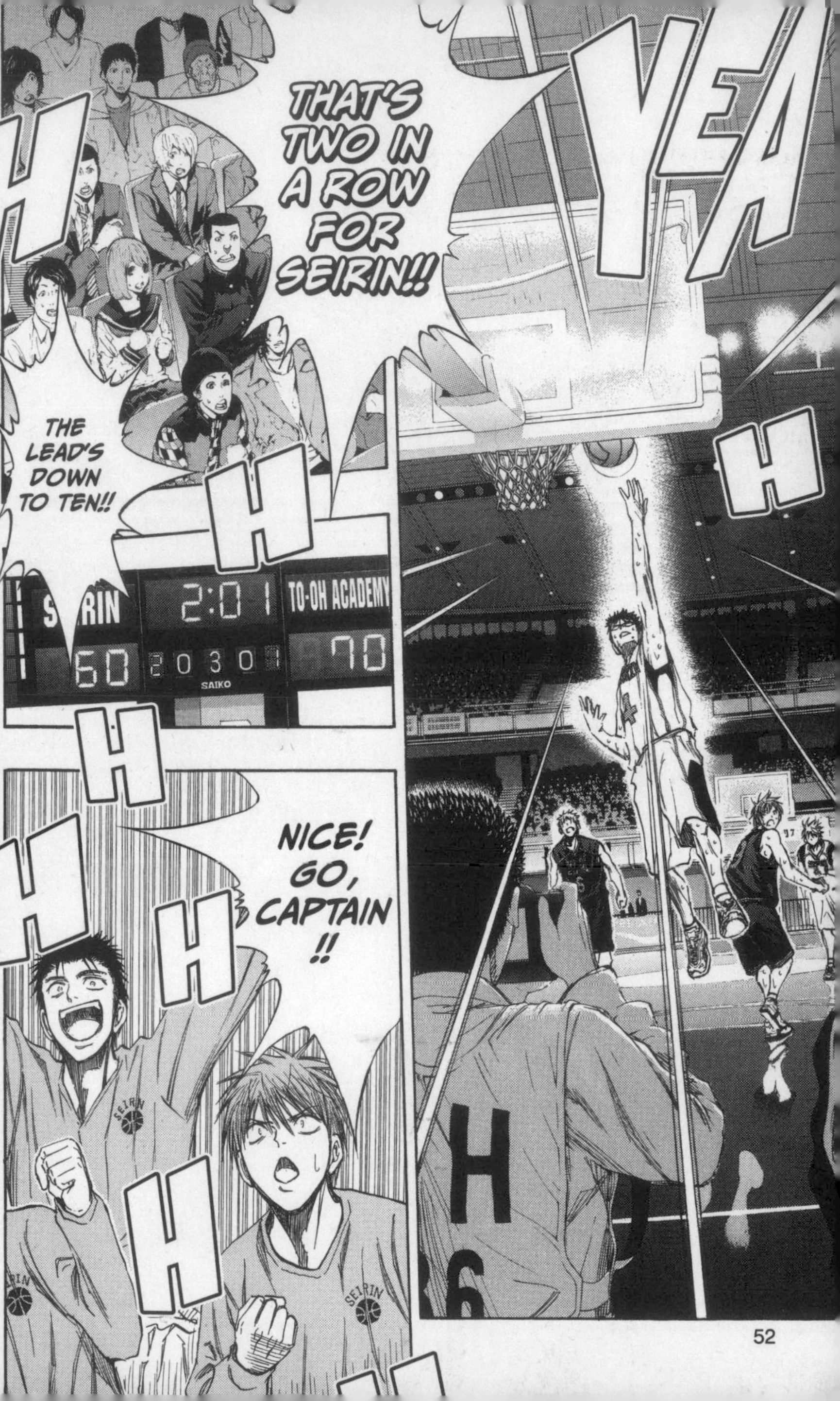
YEAHHHHHHH
THAT'S TWO IN A ROW FOR SEIRIN!!
THE LEAD'S DOWN TO TEN!!
2:01
TO-OH ACADEMY
60
70
SAIKO
NICE! GO, CAPTAIN!!

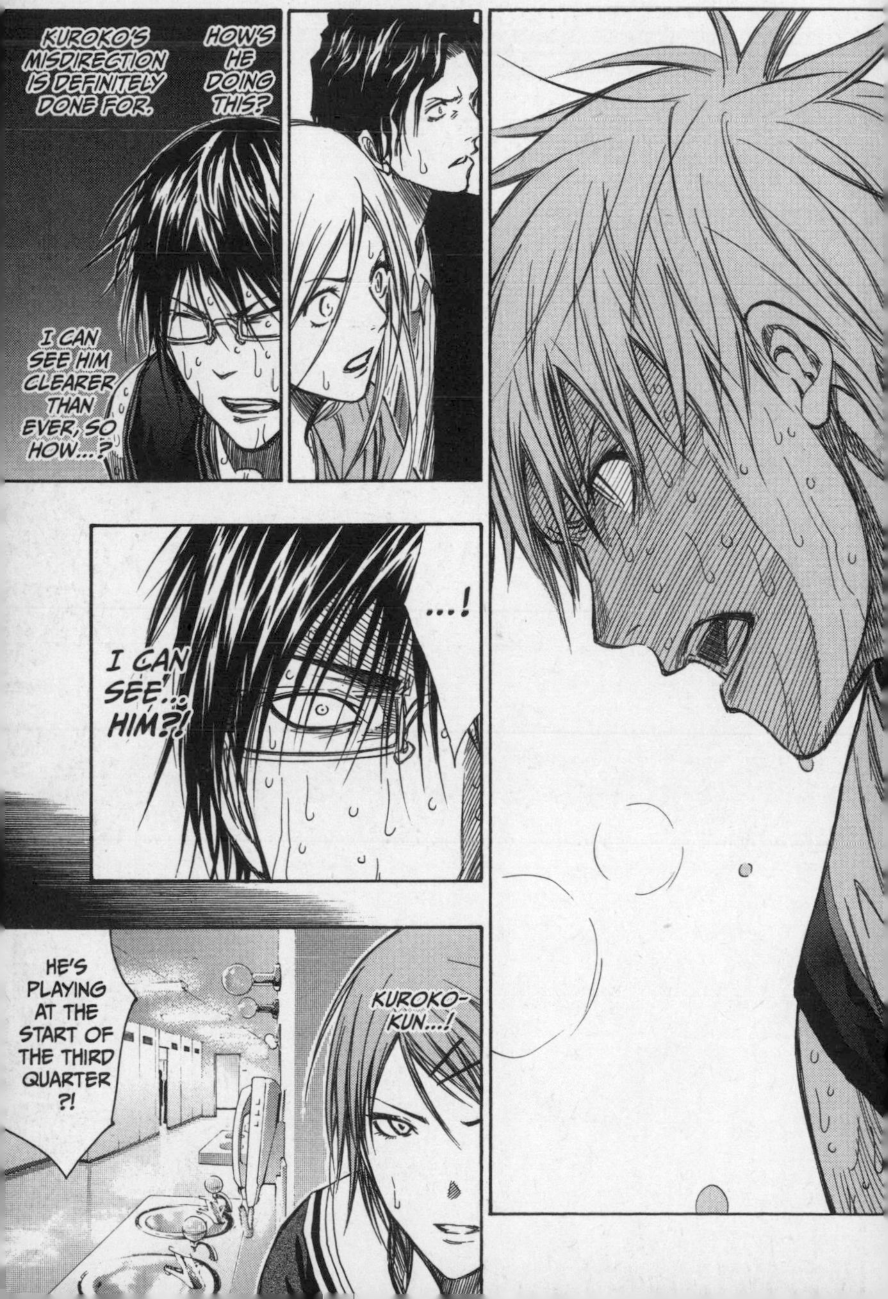
HOW'S HE DOING THIS?
KUROKO'S MISDIRECTION IS DEFINITELY DONE FOR.
I CAN SEE HIM CLEARER THAN EVER, SO HOW...?
...!
I CAN SEE... HIM?!
KUROKO-KUN...!
HE'S PLAYING AT THE START OF THE THIRD QUARTER ?!

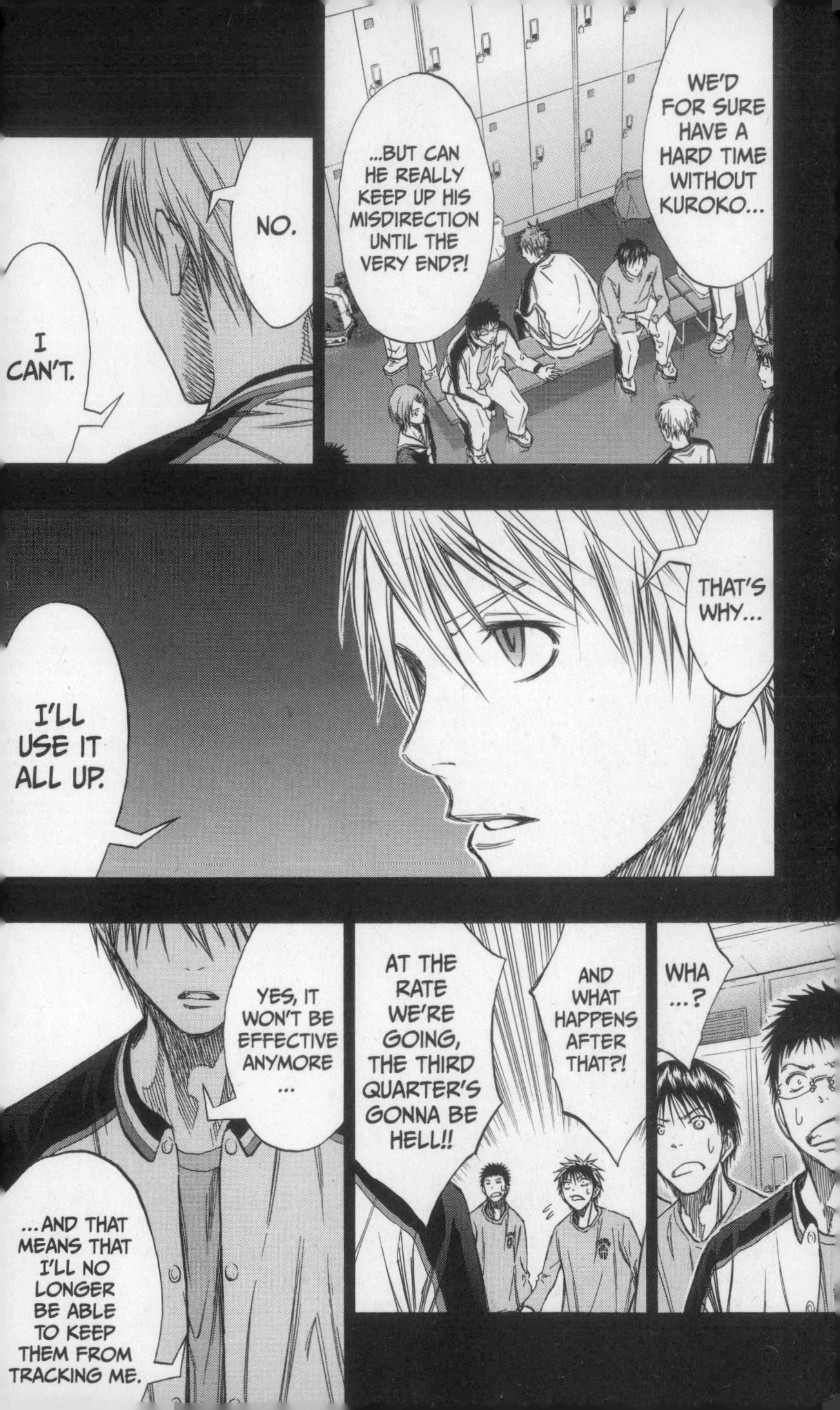
WE'D FOR SURE HAVE A HARD TIME WITHOUT KUROKO...
...BUT CAN HE REALLY KEEP UP HIS MISDIRECTION UNTIL THE VERY END?!
NO.
I CAN'T.
THAT'S WHY...
I'LL USE IT ALL UP.
WHA...?
AND WHAT HAPPENS AFTER THAT?!
AT THE RATE WE'RE GOING, THE THIRD QUARTER'S GONNA BE HELL!!
YES, IT WON'T BE EFFECTIVE ANYMORE...
...AND THAT MEANS THAT I'LL NO LONGER BE ABLE TO KEEP THEM FROM TRACKING ME.

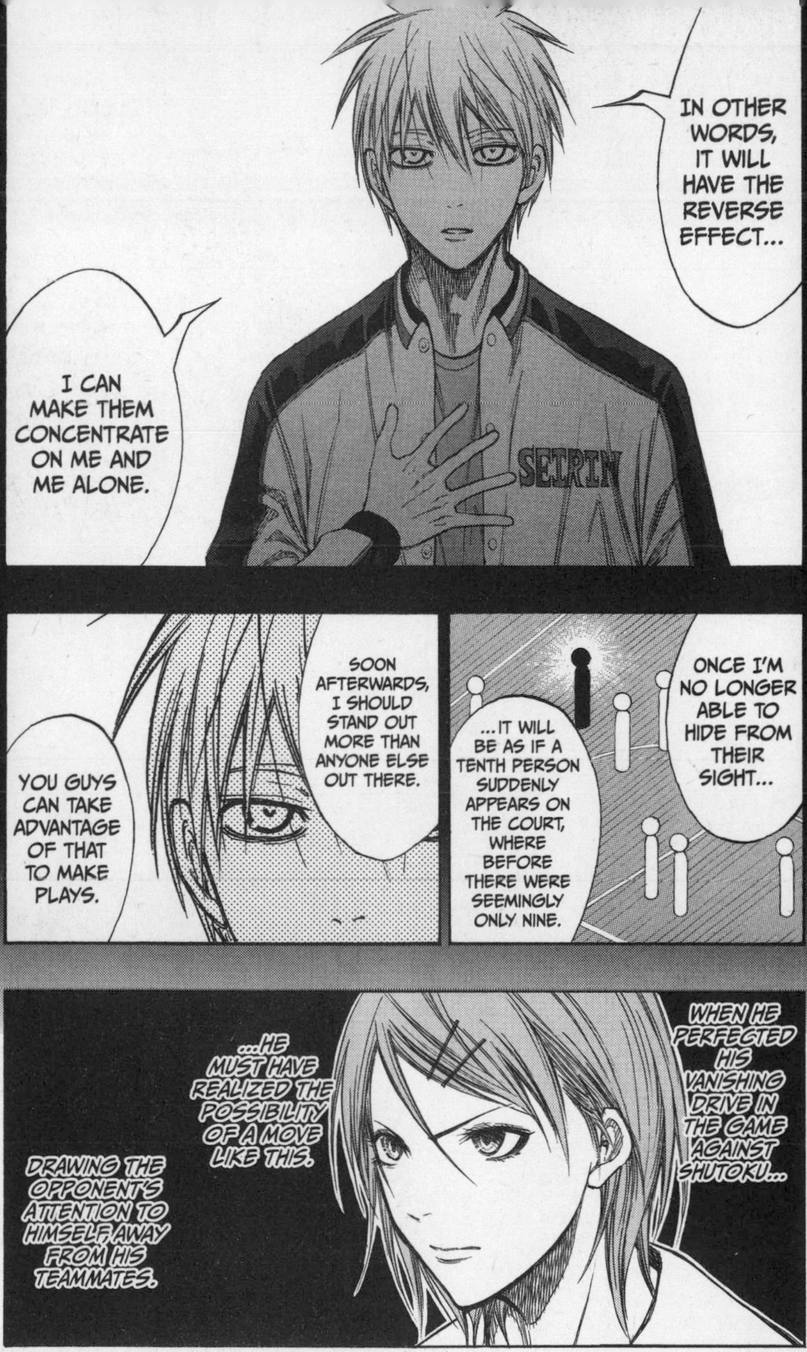
IN OTHER WORDS, IT WILL HAVE THE REVERSE EFFECT...
I CAN MAKE THEM CONCENTRATE ON ME AND ME ALONE.
ONCE I'M NO LONGER ABLE TO HIDE FROM THEIR SIGHT...
...IT WILL BE AS IF A TENTH PERSON SUDDENLY APPEARS ON THE COURT, WHERE BEFORE THERE WERE SEEMINGLY ONLY NINE.
SOON AFTERWARDS, I SHOULD STAND OUT MORE THAN ANYONE ELSE OUT THERE.
YOU GUYS CAN TAKE ADVANTAGE OF THAT TO MAKE PLAYS.
WHEN HE PERFECTED HIS VANISHING DRIVE IN THE GAME AGAINST SHUTOKU...
...HE MUST HAVE REALIZED THE POSSIBILITY OF A MOVE LIKE THIS.
DRAWING THE OPPONENT'S ATTENTION TO HIMSELF, AWAY FROM HIS TEAMMATES.

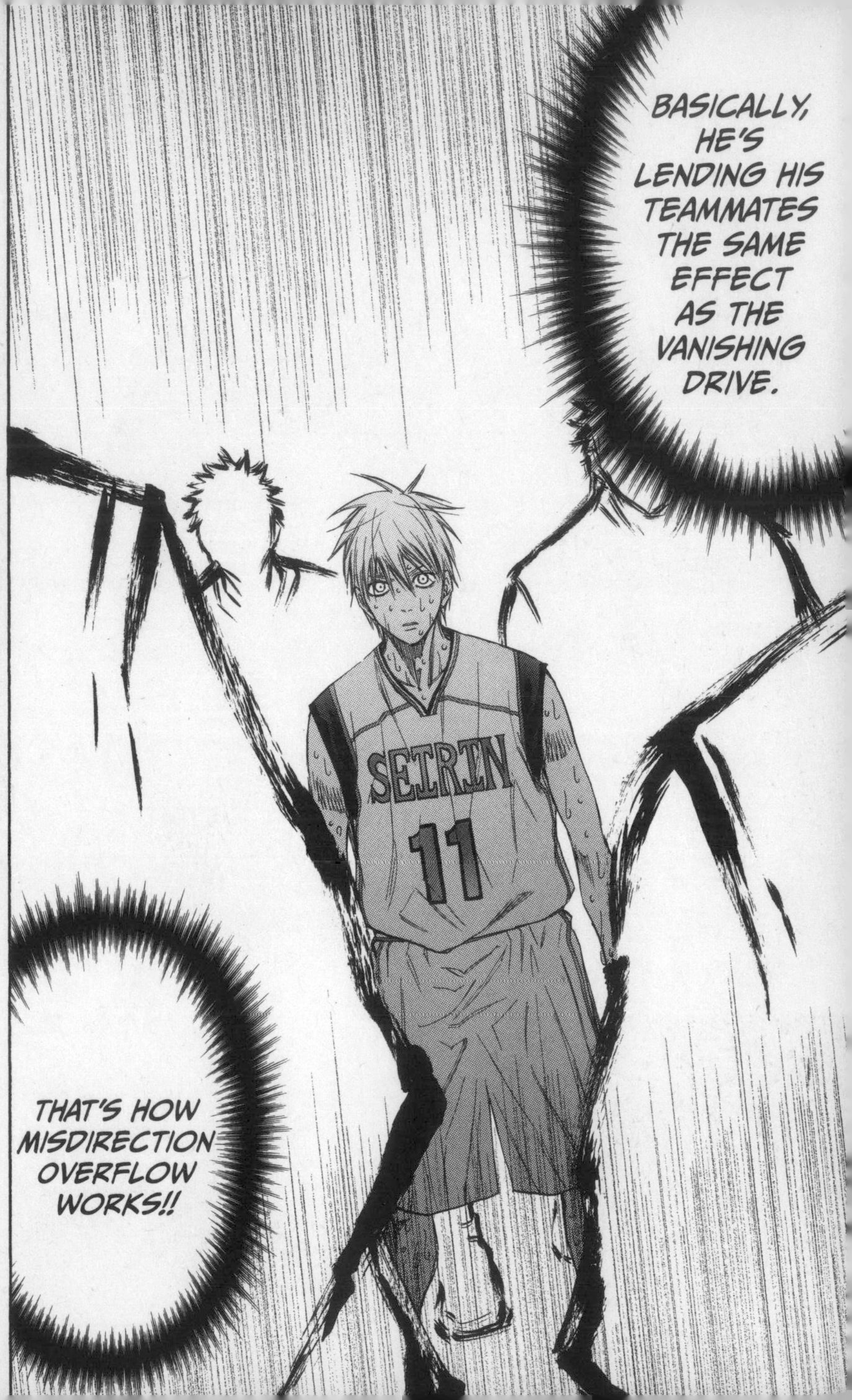
BASICALLY, HE'S LENDING HIS TEAMMATES THE SAME EFFECT AS THE VANISHING DRIVE.
SEIRIN
11
THAT'S HOW MISDIRECTION OVERFLOW WORKS!!

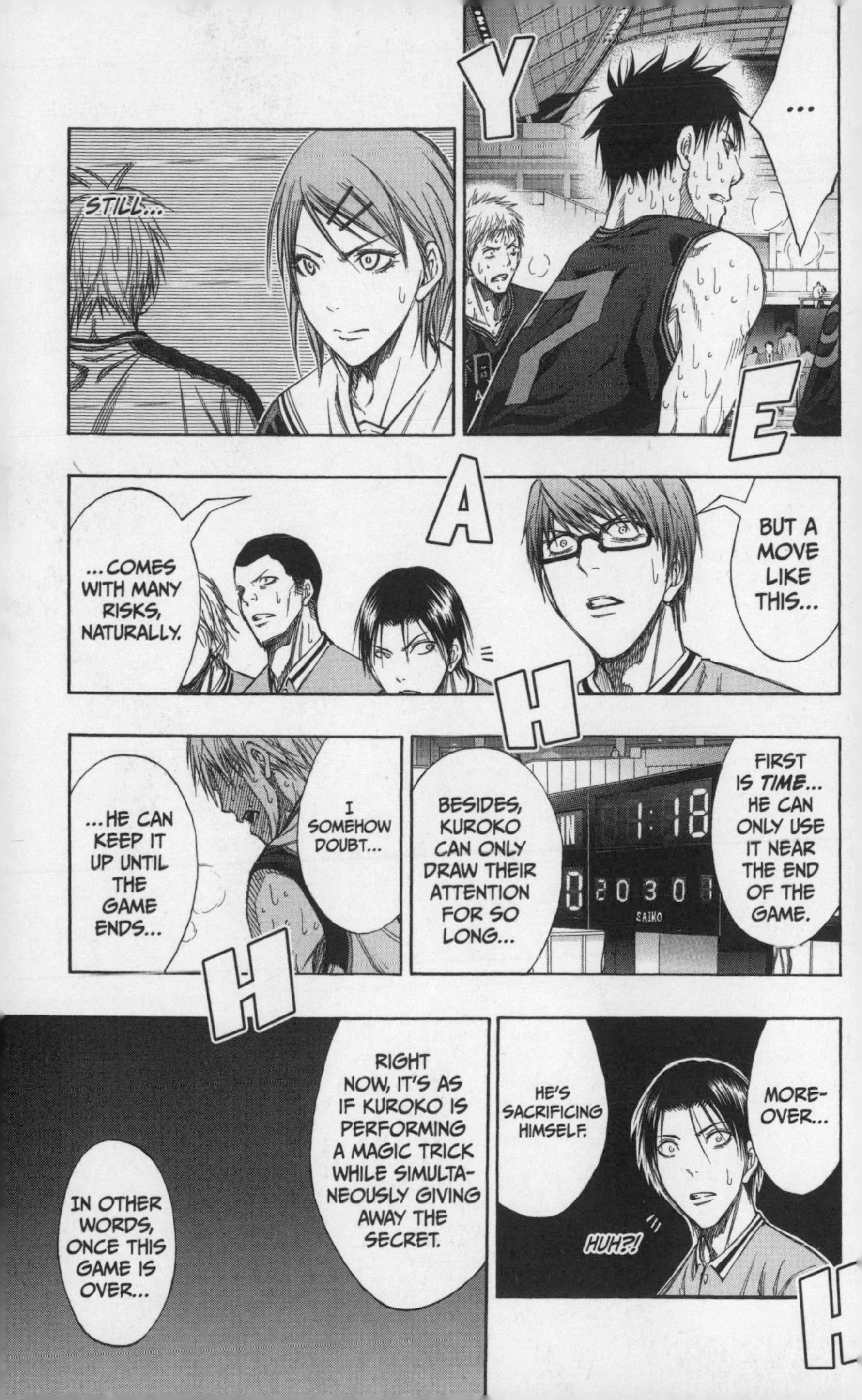

...
YEAHHH
STILL...
BUT A MOVE LIKE THIS...
...COMES WITH MANY RISKS, NATURALLY.
FIRST IS *TIME*... HE CAN ONLY USE IT NEAR THE END OF THE GAME.
BESIDES, KUROKO CAN ONLY DRAW THEIR ATTENTION FOR SO LONG...
I SOMEHOW DOUBT...
...HE CAN KEEP IT UP UNTIL THE GAME ENDS...
MORE-OVER...
HUH?!
HE'S SACRIFICING HIMSELF.
RIGHT NOW, IT'S AS IF KUROKO IS PERFORMING A MAGIC TRICK WHILE SIMULTA-NEOUSLY GIVING AWAY THE SECRET.
IN OTHER WORDS, ONCE THIS GAME IS OVER...

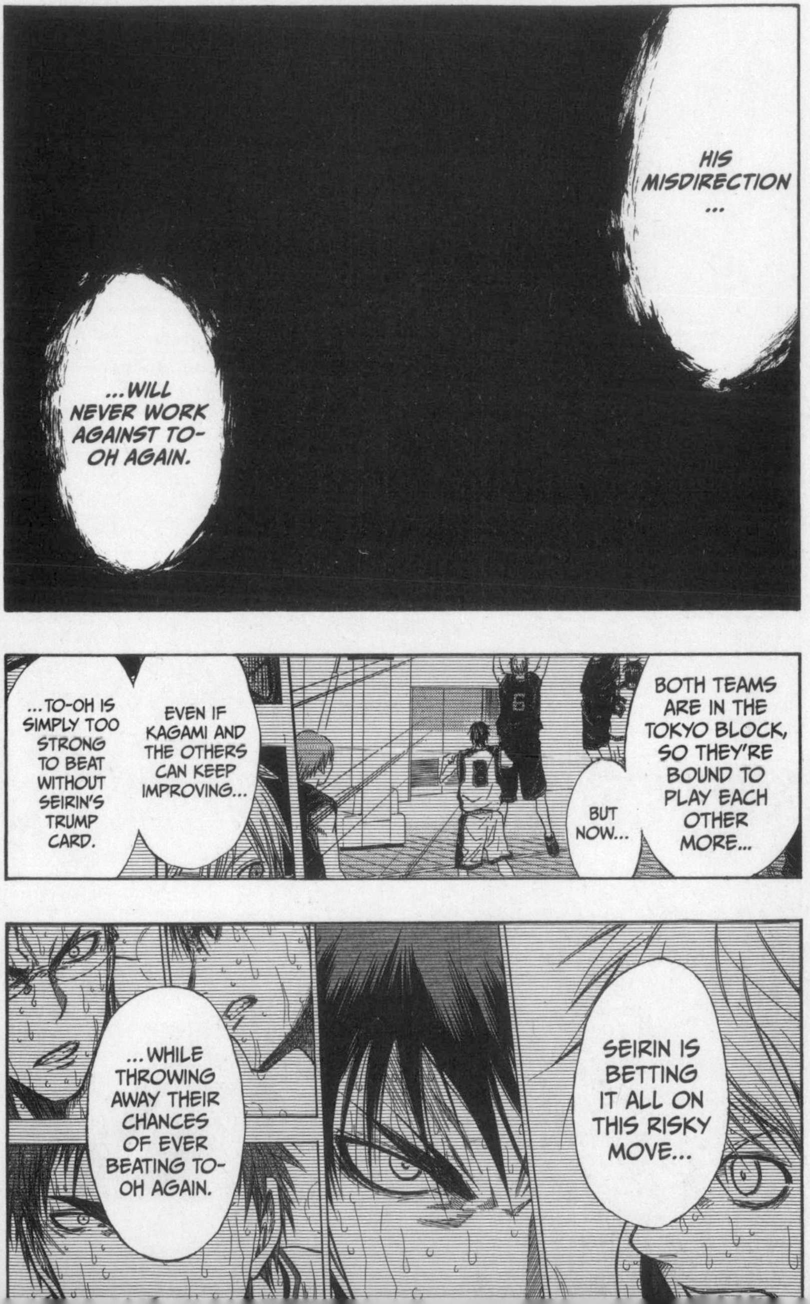
HIS MISDIRECTION...
...WILL NEVER WORK AGAINST TO-OH AGAIN.
BOTH TEAMS ARE IN THE TOKYO BLOCK, SO THEY'RE BOUND TO PLAY EACH OTHER MORE...
BUT NOW...
EVEN IF KAGAMI AND THE OTHERS CAN KEEP IMPROVING...
...TO-OH IS SIMPLY TOO STRONG TO BEAT WITHOUT SEIRIN'S TRUMP CARD.
SEIRIN IS BETTING IT ALL ON THIS RISKY MOVE...
...WHILE THROWING AWAY THEIR CHANCES OF EVER BEATING TO-OH AGAIN.

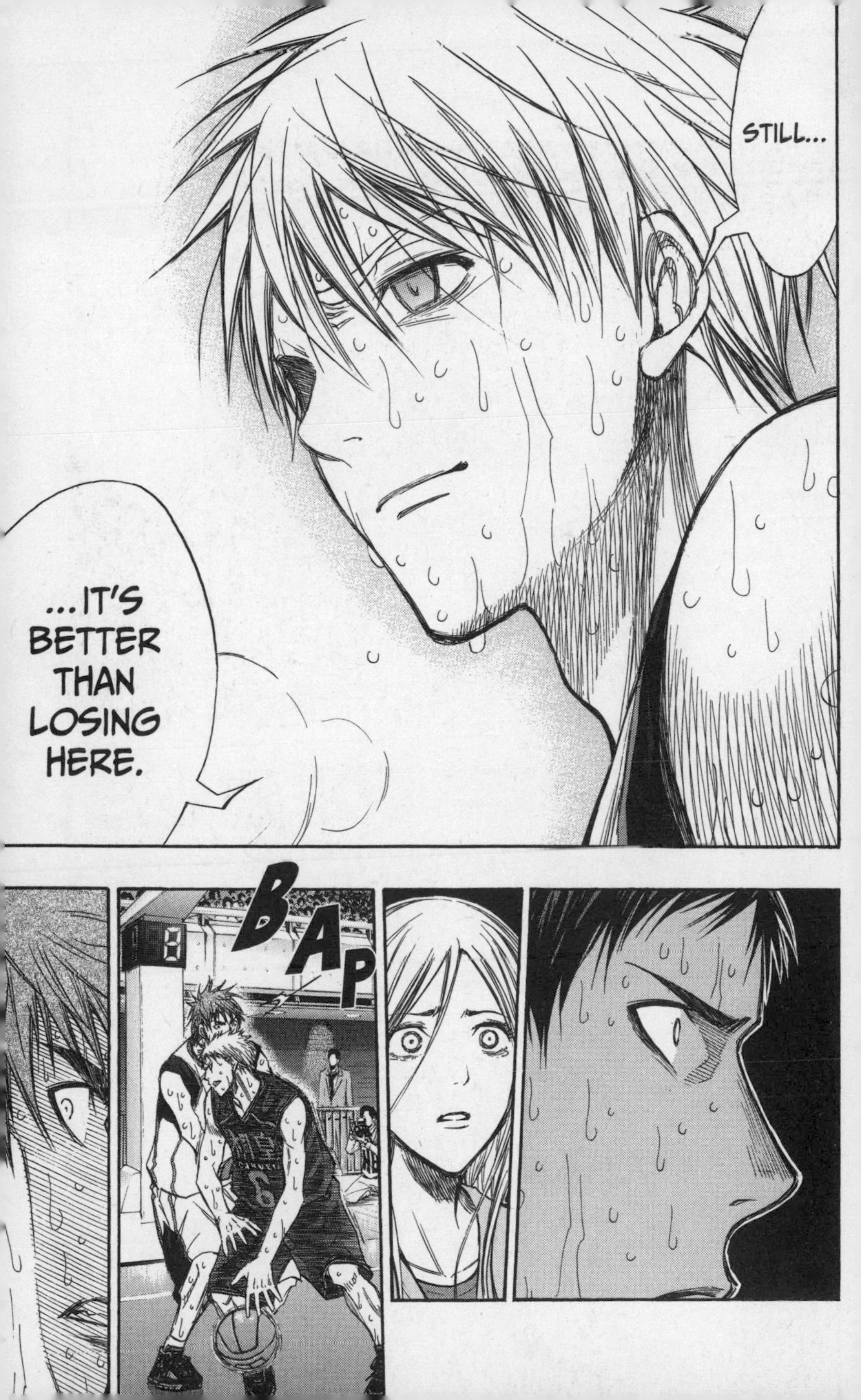
STILL...
...IT'S BETTER THAN LOSING HERE.
BAP

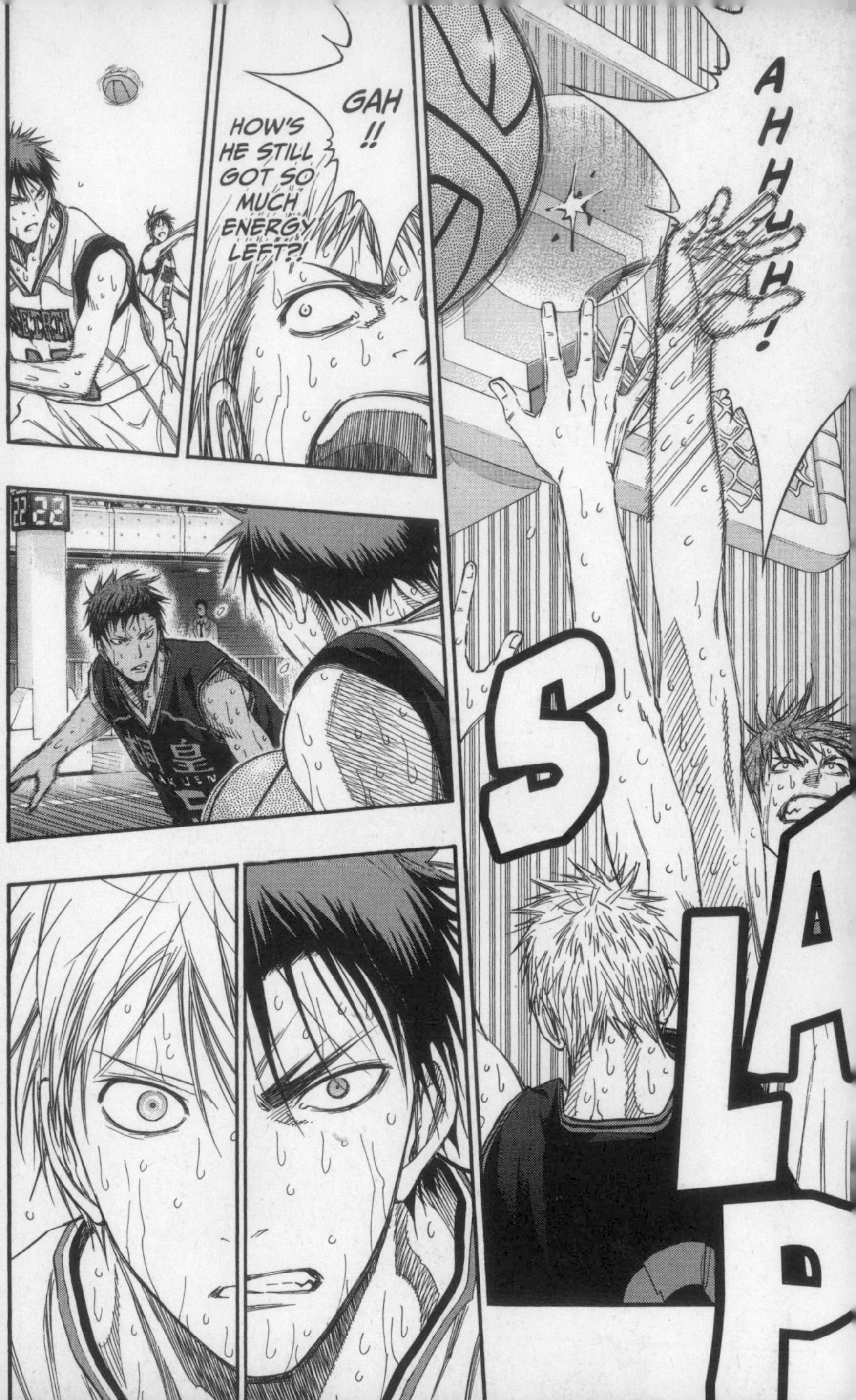
AHHUH!
SLAP
GAH!!
HOW'S HE STILL GOT SO MUCH ENERGY LEFT?!

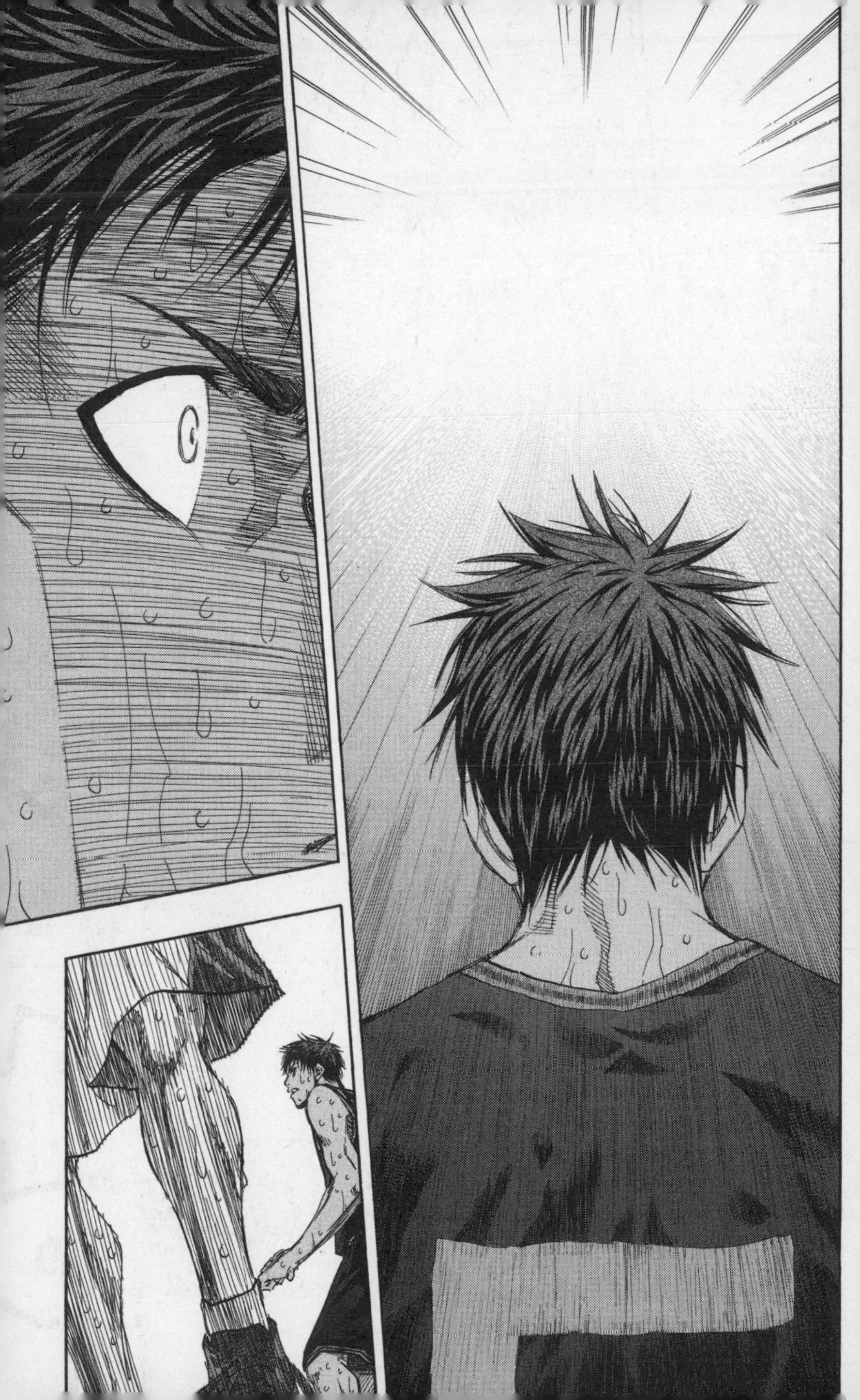

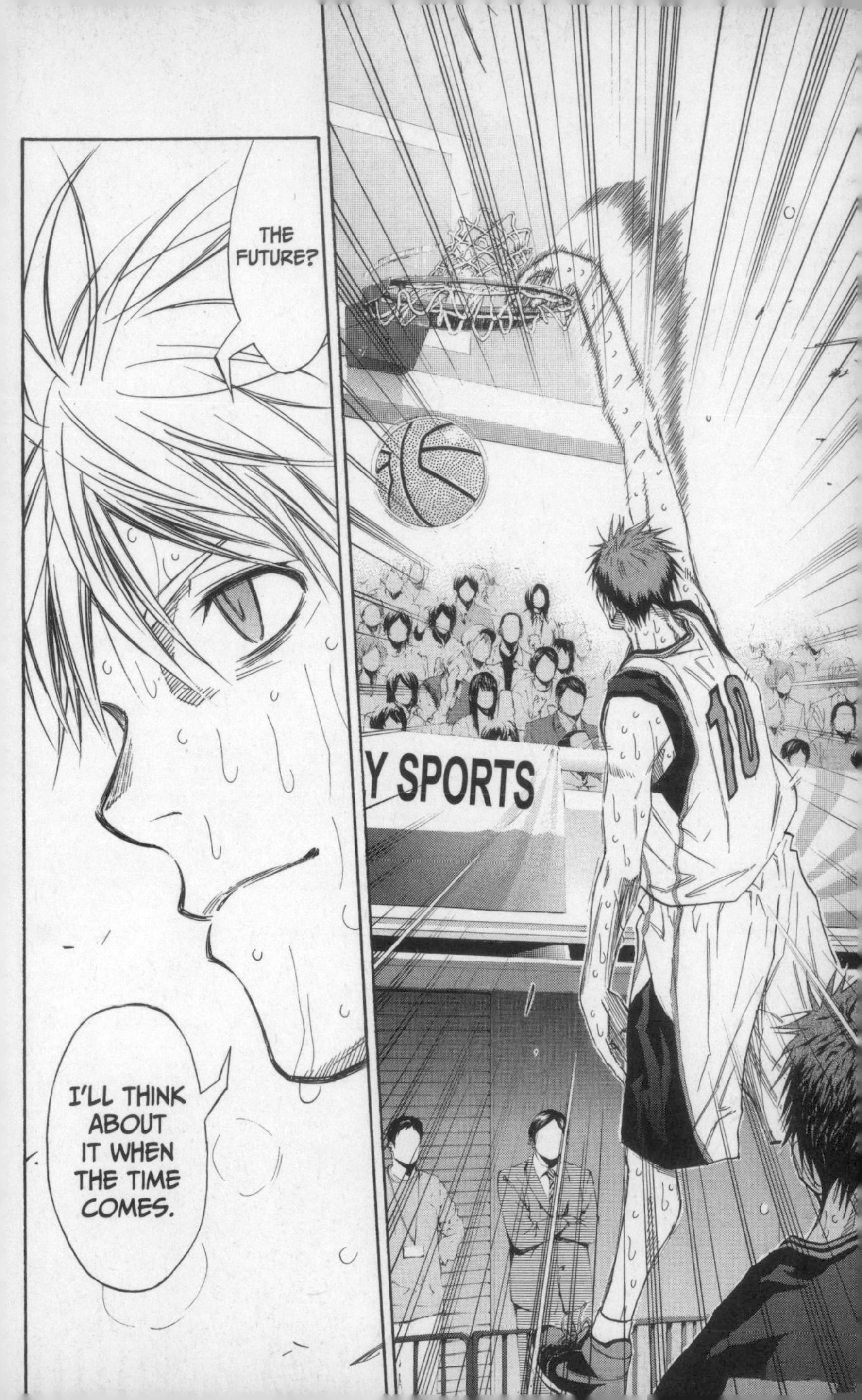
Y SPORTS
THE FUTURE?
I'LL THINK ABOUT IT WHEN THE TIME COMES.

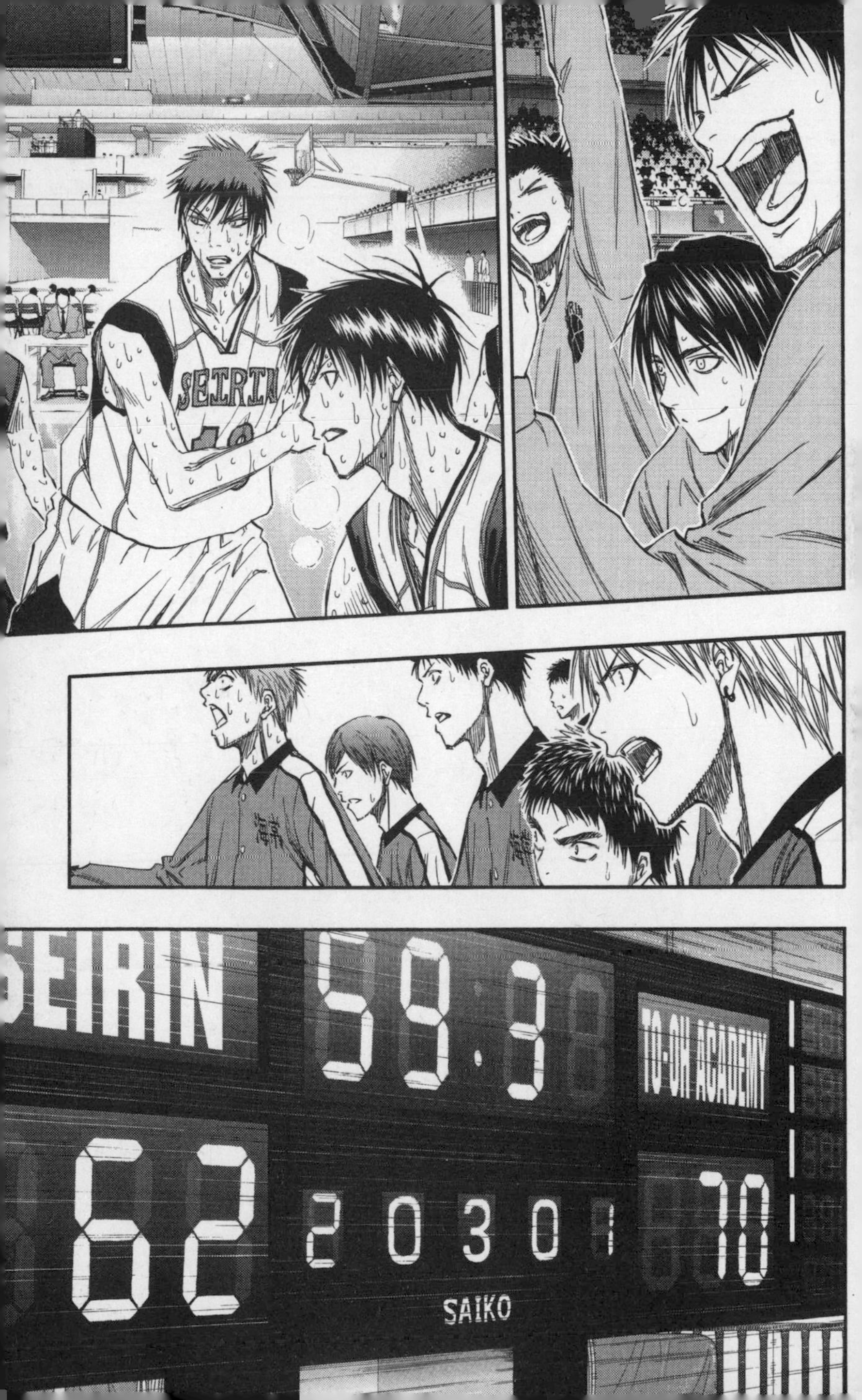
SEIRIN
SEIRIN
59.3
TO-OH ACADEMY
62
2 0 3 0 1
70
SAIKO

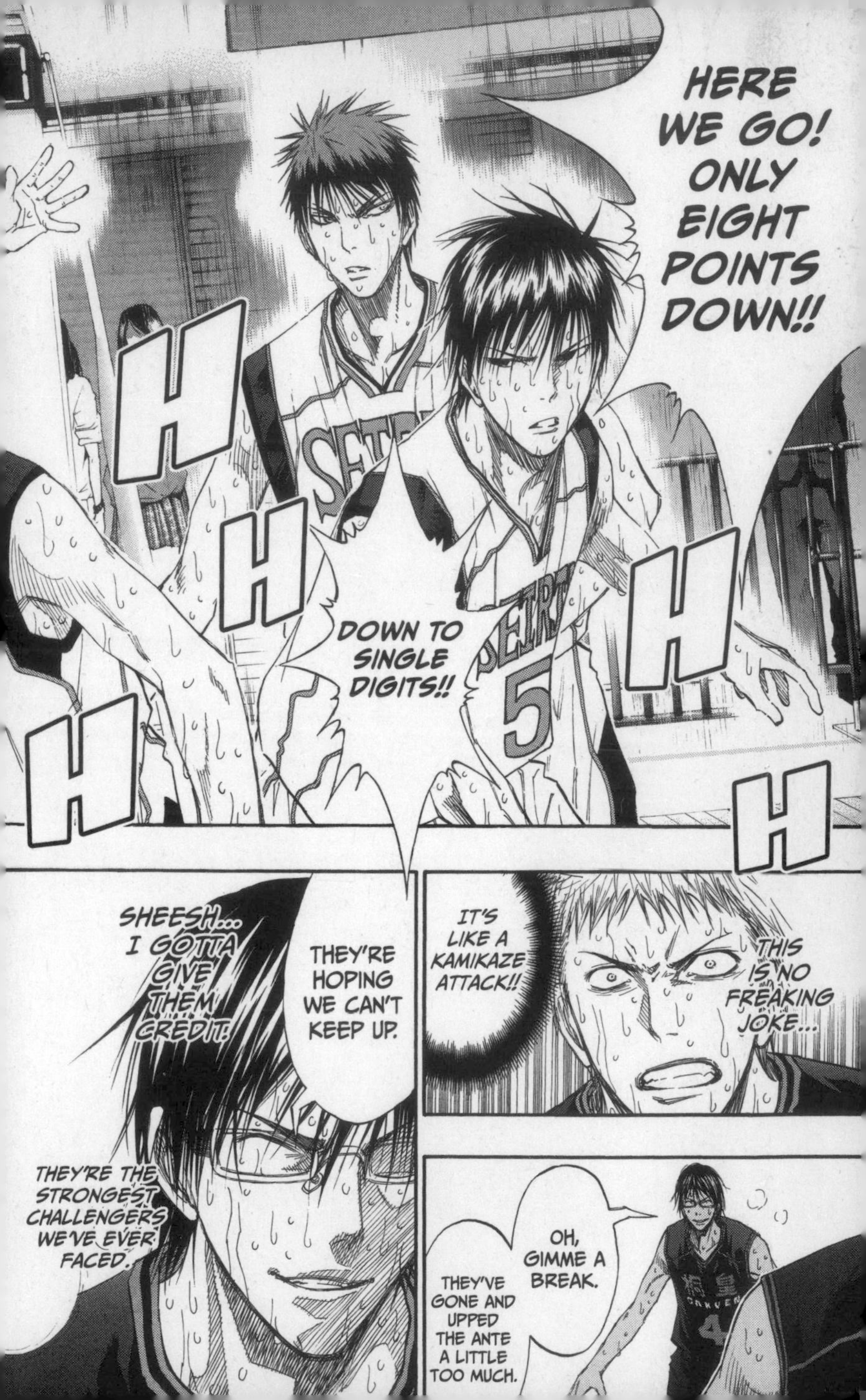
HERE WE GO! ONLY EIGHT POINTS DOWN!!
H
H
H
H
H
DOWN TO SINGLE DIGITS!!
THIS IS NO FREAKING JOKE...
IT'S LIKE A KAMIKAZE ATTACK!!
OH, GIMME A BREAK.
THEY'VE GONE AND UPPED THE ANTE A LITTLE TOO MUCH.
THEY'RE HOPING WE CAN'T KEEP UP.
SHEESH... I GOTTA GIVE THEM CREDIT.
THEY'RE THE STRONGEST CHALLENGERS WE'VE EVER FACED.

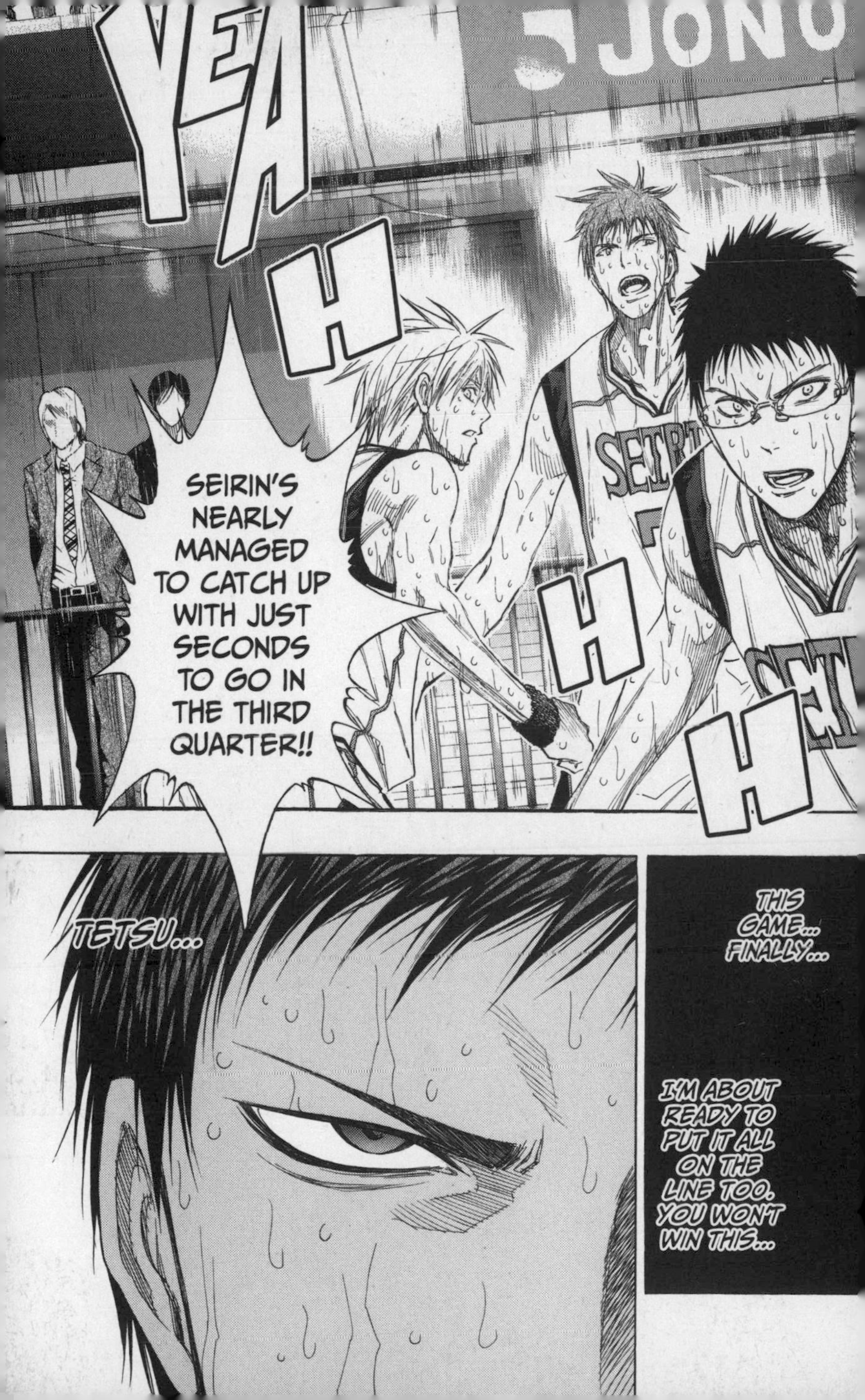
YEAHHH
SEIRIN'S NEARLY MANAGED TO CATCH UP WITH JUST SECONDS TO GO IN THE THIRD QUARTER!!
THIS GAME... FINALLY...
I'M ABOUT READY TO PUT IT ALL ON THE LINE TOO. YOU WON'T WIN THIS...
TETSU...

KUROKO'S BASKETBALL BLOOPERS

TAKE 12

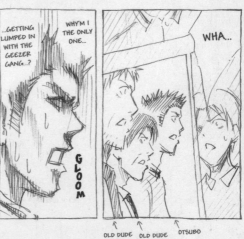

WHA...
OLD DUDE
OLD DUDE
OTSUBO
WHY'M I THE ONLY ONE...
...GETTING LUMPED IN WITH THE GEEZER GANG...?
GLOOM

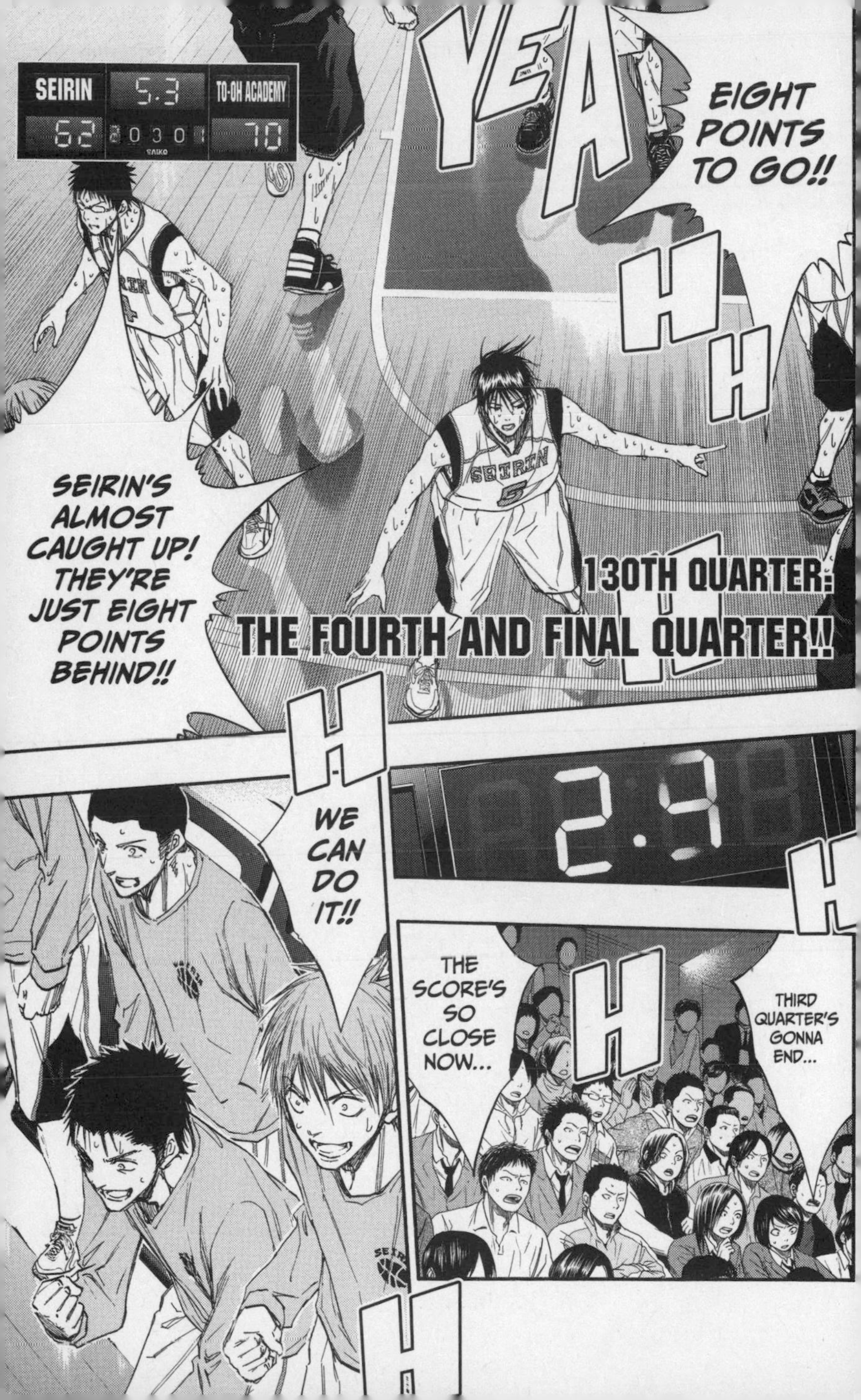
YEA
EIGHT POINTS TO GO!!
HHH
130TH QUARTER:
THE FOURTH AND FINAL QUARTER!!
SEIRIN 5.3 TO-OH ACADEMY
62 70
SEIRIN'S ALMOST CAUGHT UP! THEY'RE JUST EIGHT POINTS BEHIND!!
H
THIRD QUARTER'S GONNA END...
THE SCORE'S SO CLOSE NOW...
H
WE CAN DO IT!!
H

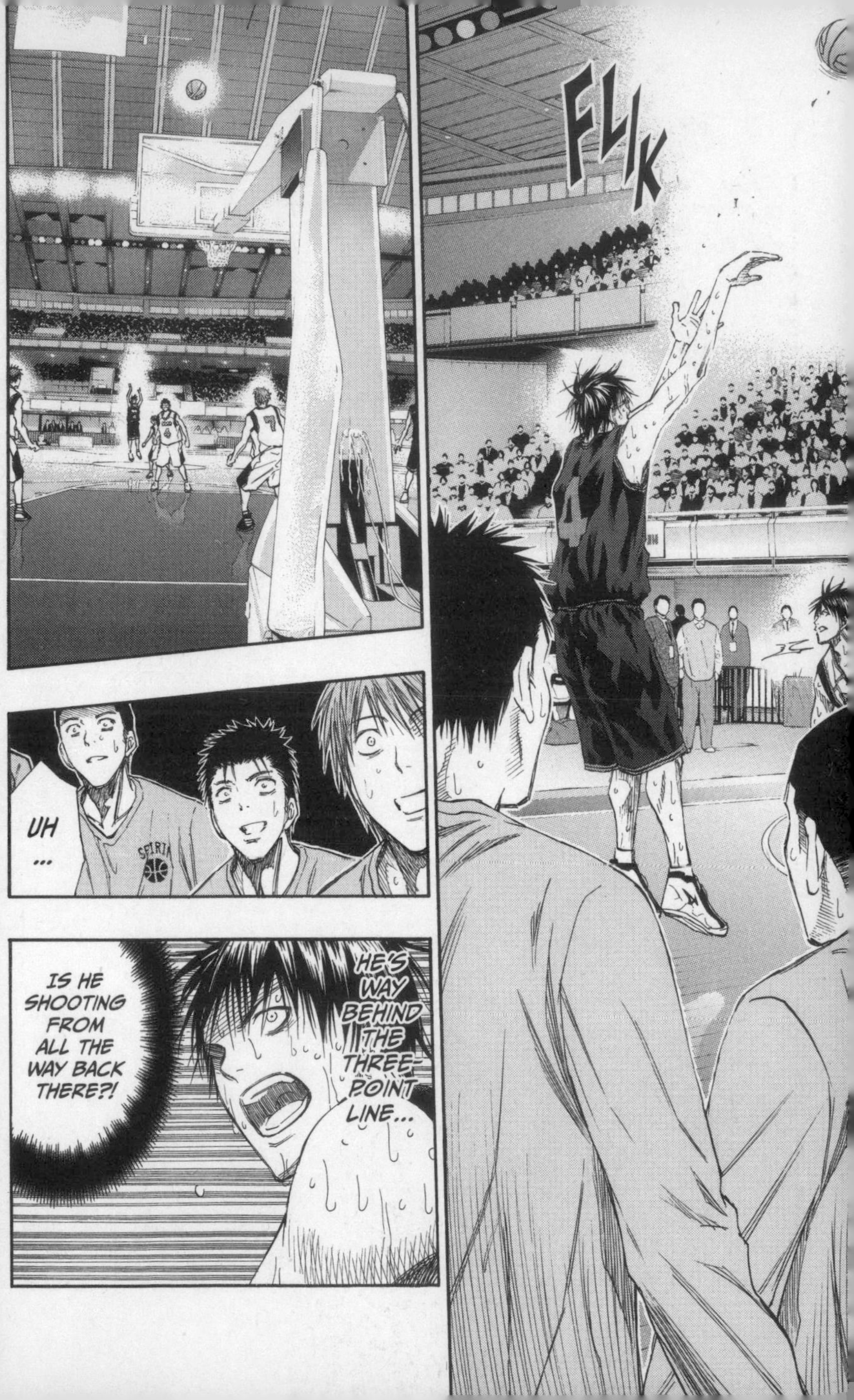
FLIK
UH ...
HE'S WAY BEHIND THE THREE-POINT LINE...
IS HE SHOOTING FROM ALL THE WAY BACK THERE?!

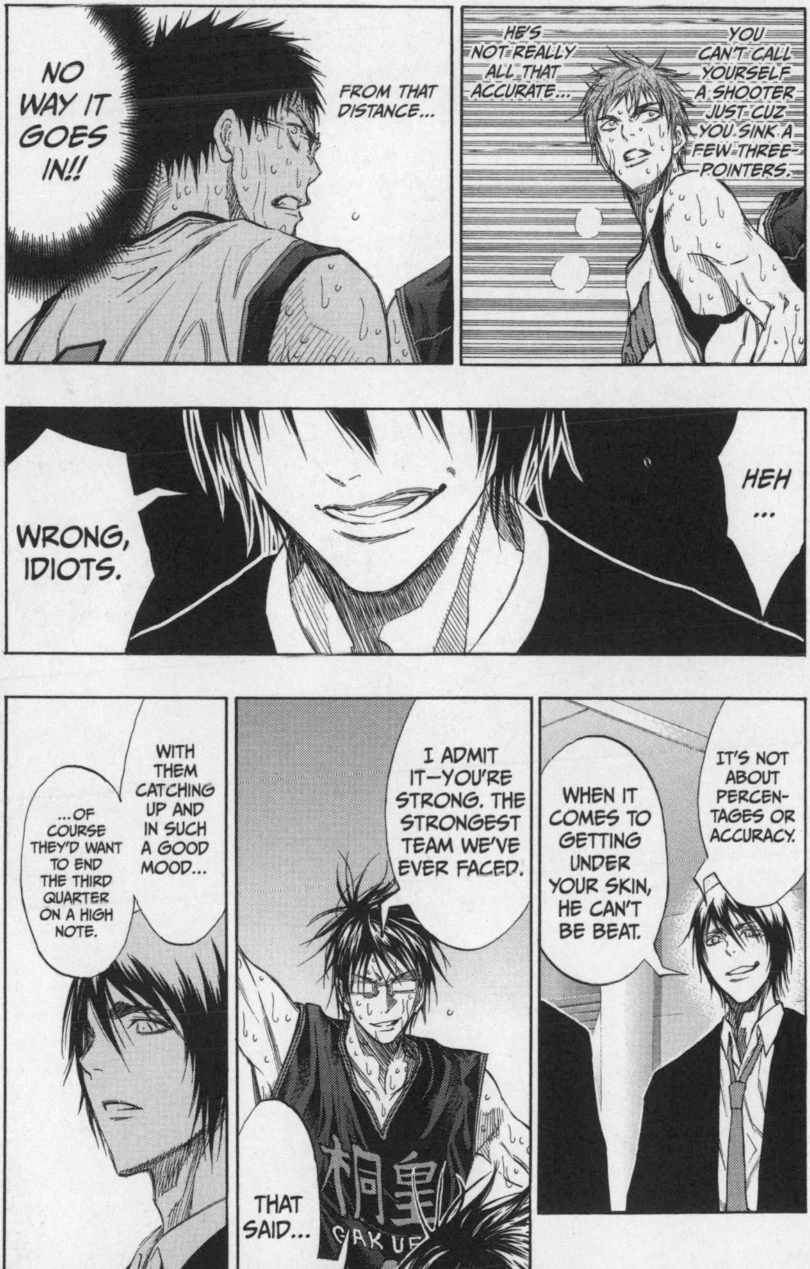
YOU CAN'T CALL YOURSELF A SHOOTER JUST CUZ YOU SINK A FEW THREE-POINTERS.
HE'S NOT REALLY ALL THAT ACCURATE...
FROM THAT DISTANCE...
NO WAY IT GOES IN!!
HEH ...
WRONG, IDIOTS.
IT'S NOT ABOUT PERCEN-TAGES OR ACCURACY.
WHEN IT COMES TO GETTING UNDER YOUR SKIN, HE CAN'T BE BEAT.
I ADMIT IT—YOU'RE STRONG. THE STRONGEST TEAM WE'VE EVER FACED.
THAT SAID...
WITH THEM CATCHING UP AND IN SUCH A GOOD MOOD...
...OF COURSE THEY'D WANT TO END THE THIRD QUARTER ON A HIGH NOTE.

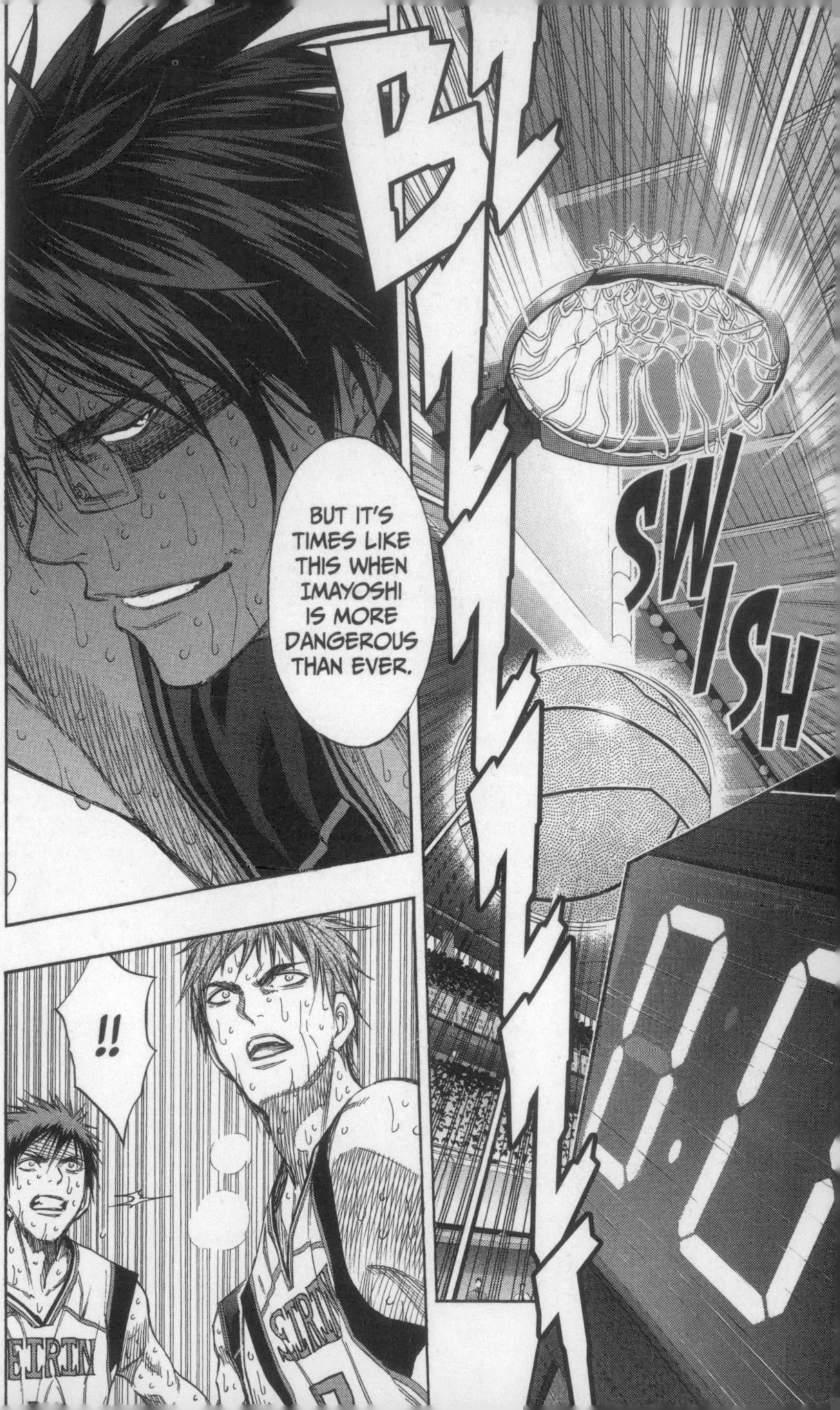
BZZ
SWISH
BUT IT'S TIMES LIKE THIS WHEN IMAYOSHI IS MORE DANGEROUS THAN EVER.
!!

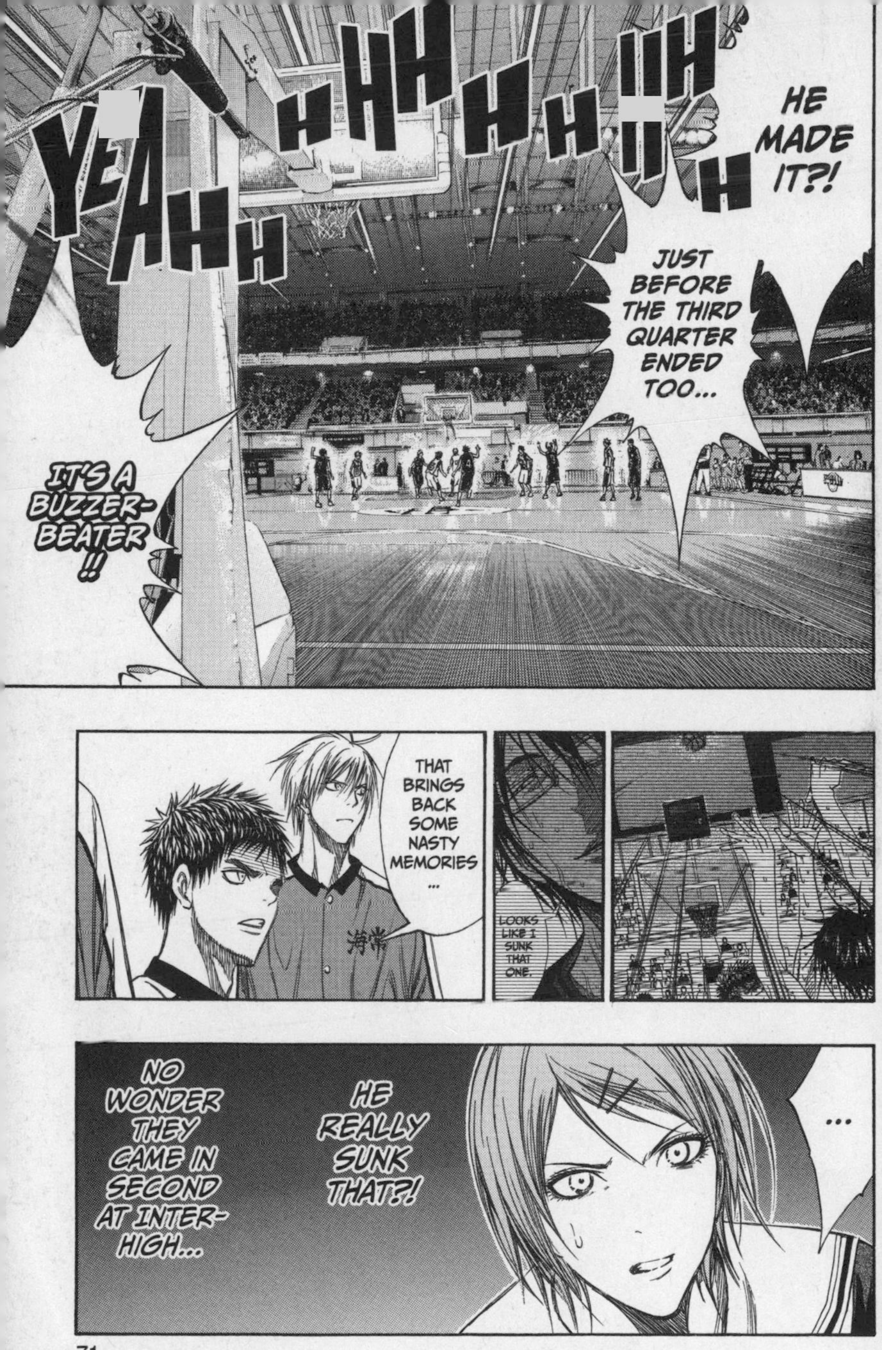
HE MADE IT?!
YEAHHHHHHHHHHH
JUST BEFORE THE THIRD QUARTER ENDED TOO...
IT'S A BUZZER-BEATER!!
LOOKS LIKE I SUNK THAT ONE.
THAT BRINGS BACK SOME NASTY MEMORIES...
...
HE REALLY SUNK THAT?!
NO WONDER THEY CAME IN SECOND AT INTER-HIGH...

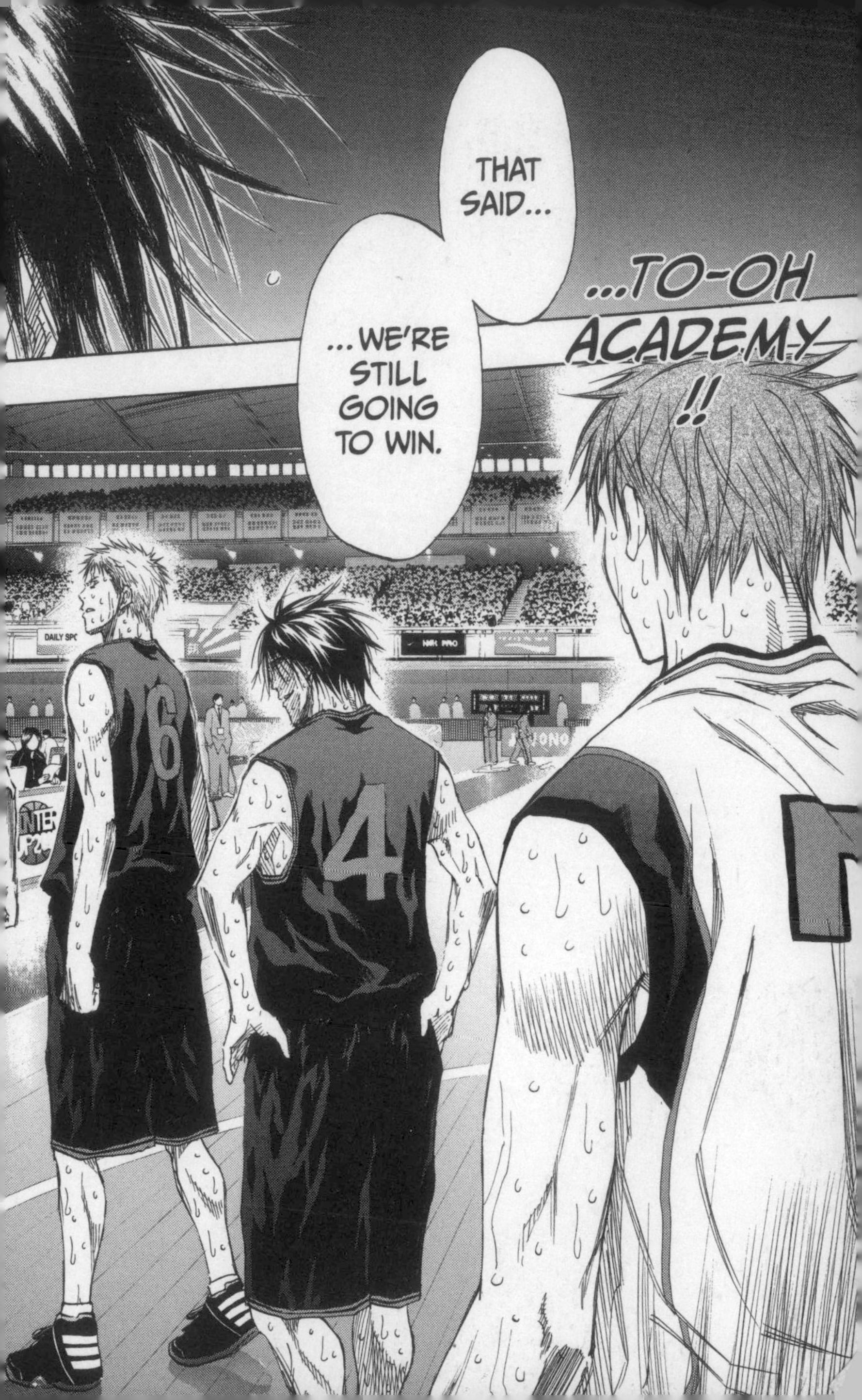
THAT SAID...
...WE'RE STILL GOING TO WIN.
...TO-OH ACADEMY!!

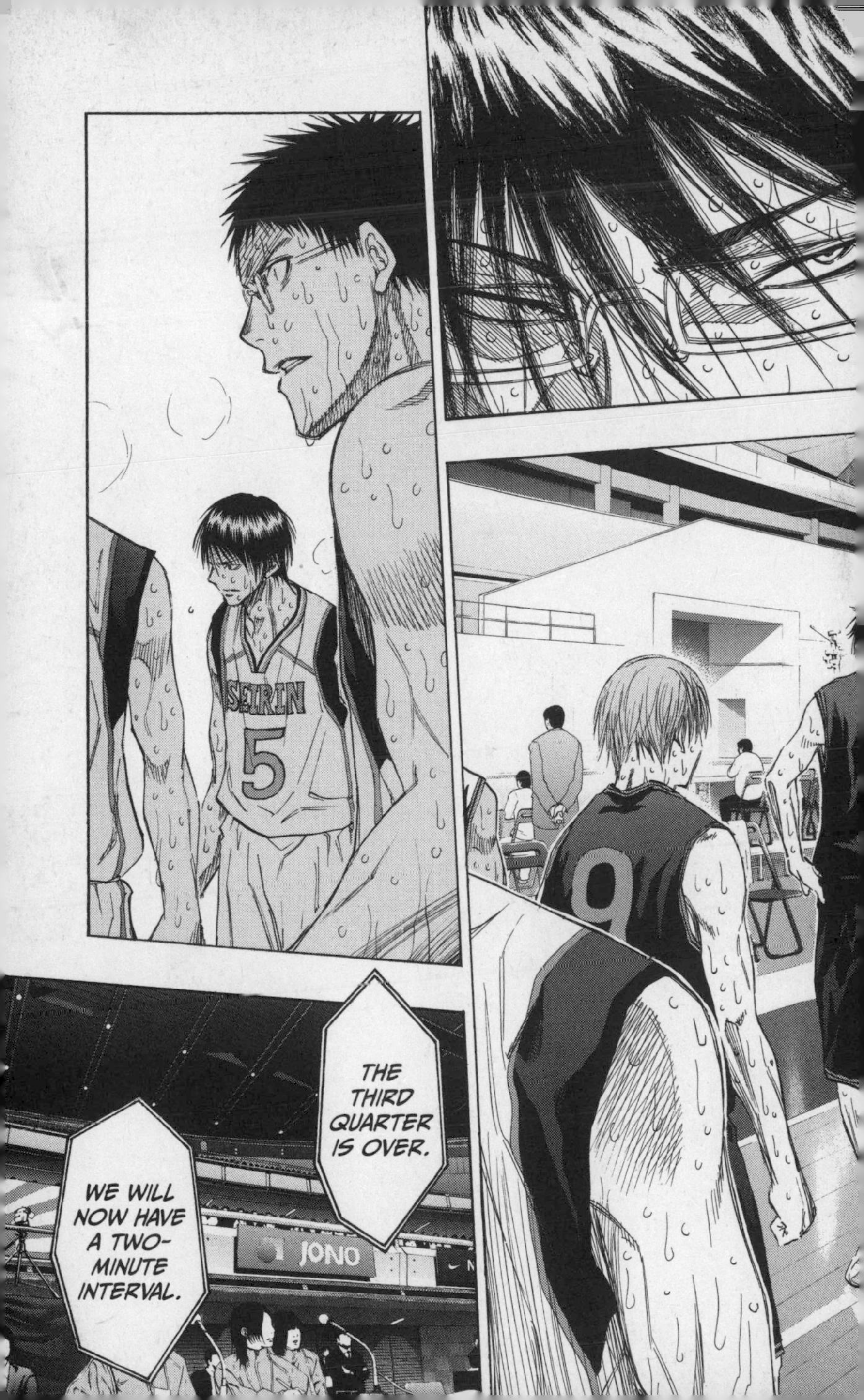
SEIRIN
5
9
THE THIRD QUARTER IS OVER.
WE WILL NOW HAVE A TWO-MINUTE INTERVAL.
JONO

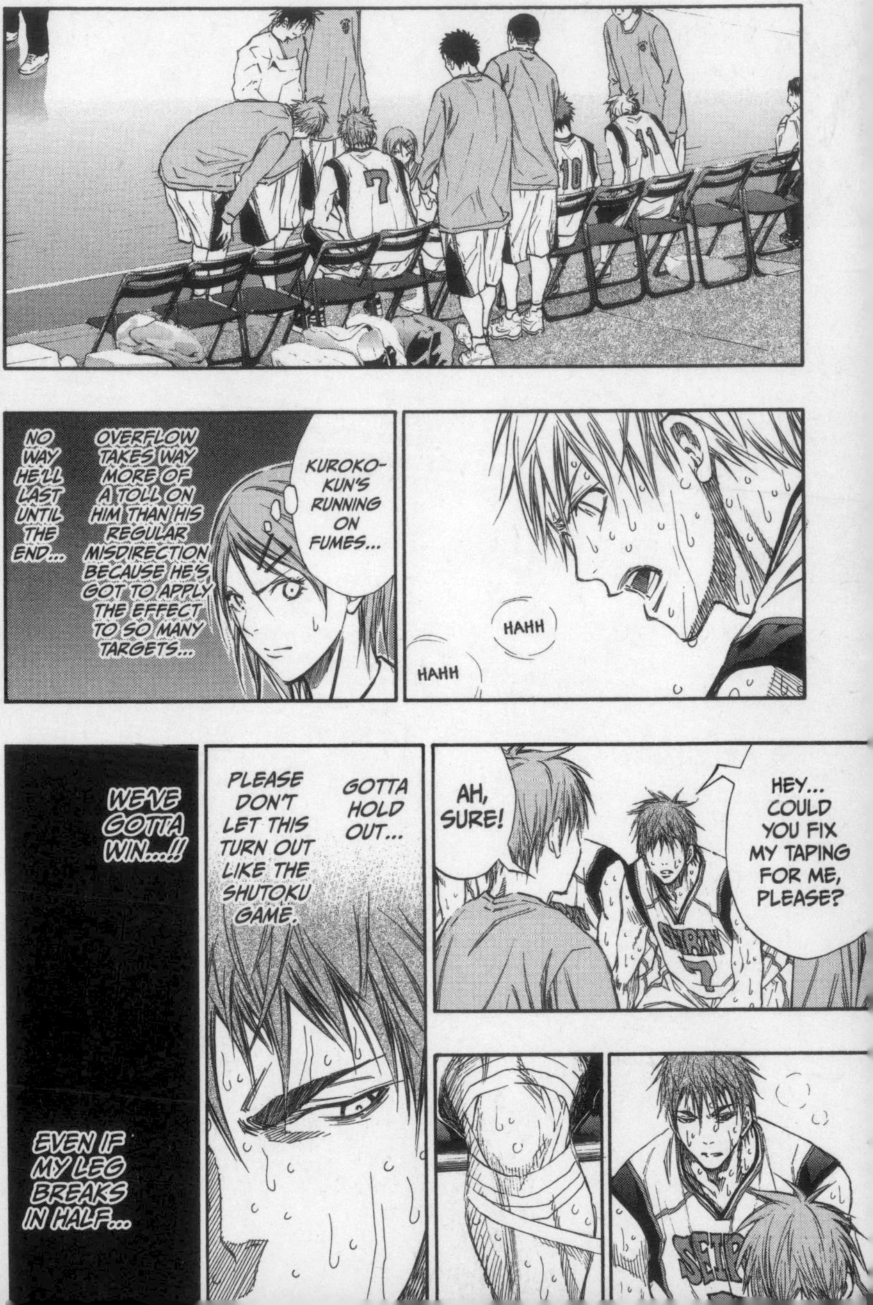
HAHH
HAHH
KUROKO-KUN'S RUNNING ON FUMES...
OVERFLOW TAKES WAY MORE OF A TOLL ON HIM THAN HIS REGULAR MISDIRECTION BECAUSE HE'S GOT TO APPLY THE EFFECT TO SO MANY TARGETS...
NO WAY HE'LL LAST UNTIL THE END...
HEY... COULD YOU FIX MY TAPING FOR ME, PLEASE?
AH, SURE!
GOTTA HOLD OUT...
PLEASE DON'T LET THIS TURN OUT LIKE THE SHUTOKU GAME.
WE'VE GOTTA WIN...!!
EVEN IF MY LEG BREAKS IN HALF...

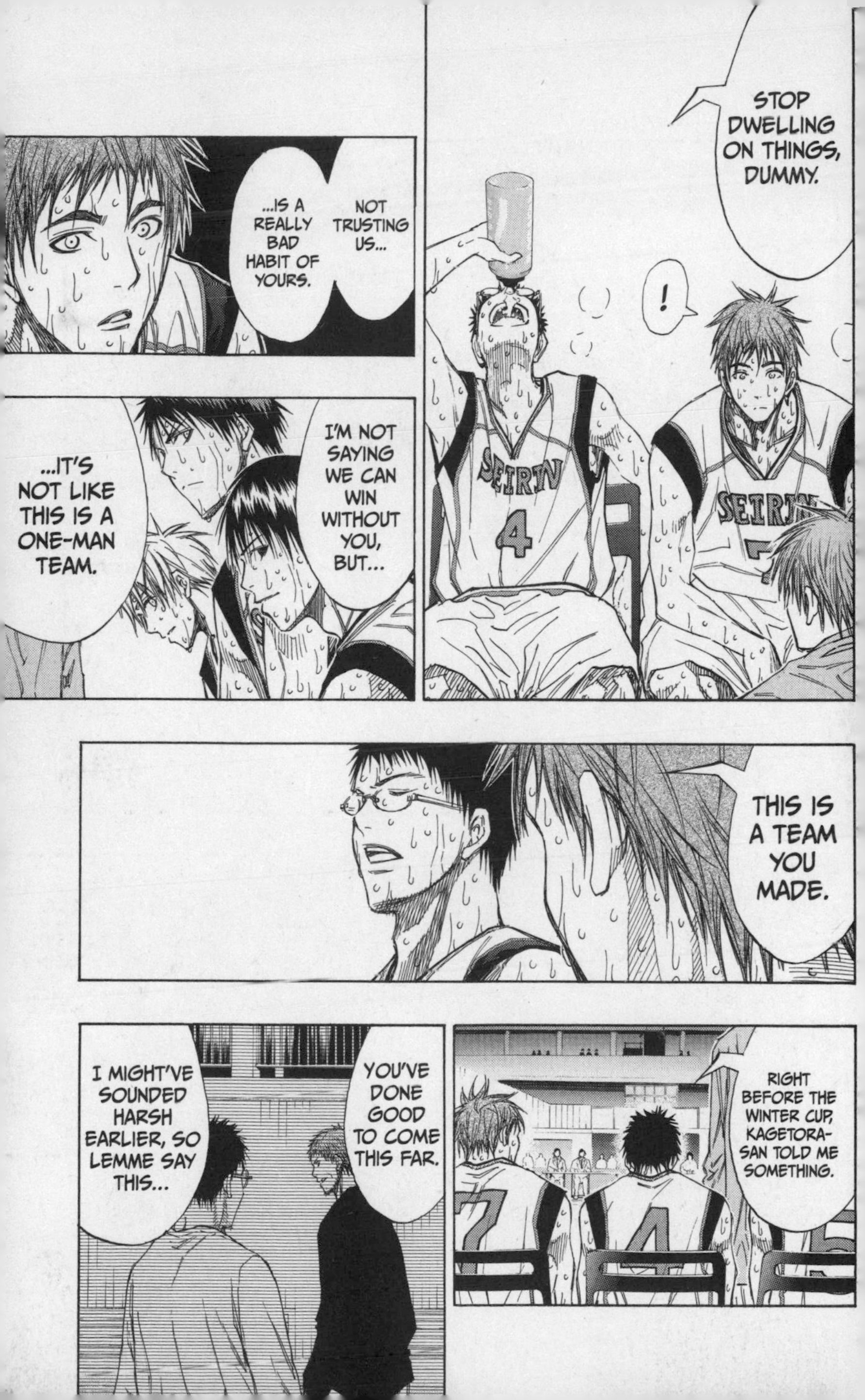
STOP DWELLING ON THINGS, DUMMY.
!
NOT TRUSTING US...
...IS A REALLY BAD HABIT OF YOURS.
I'M NOT SAYING WE CAN WIN WITHOUT YOU, BUT...
...IT'S NOT LIKE THIS IS A ONE-MAN TEAM.
THIS IS A TEAM YOU MADE.
RIGHT BEFORE THE WINTER CUP, KAGETORA-SAN TOLD ME SOMETHING.
I MIGHT'VE SOUNDED HARSH EARLIER, SO LEMME SAY THIS...
YOU'VE DONE GOOD TO COME THIS FAR.

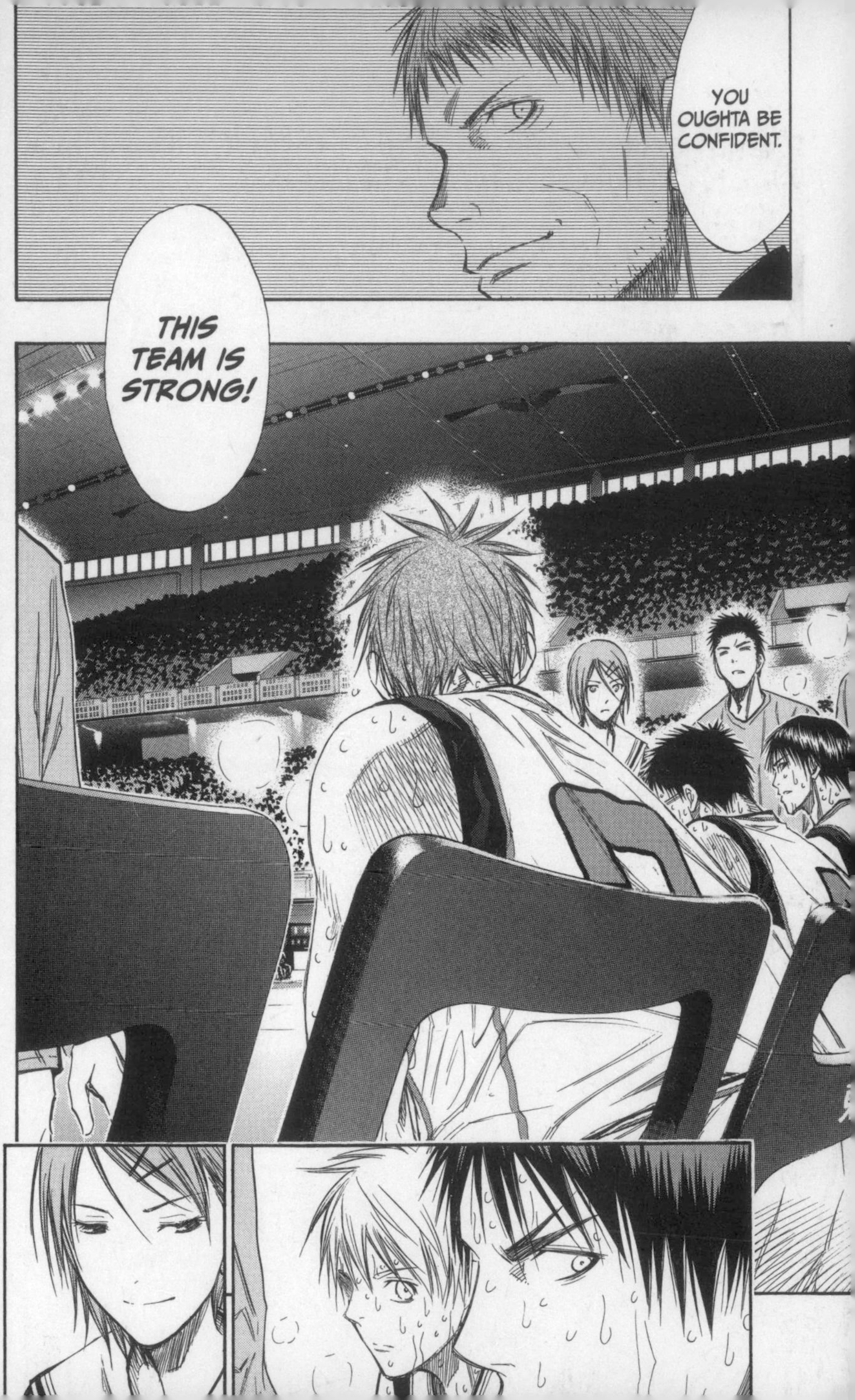
YOU OUGHTA BE CONFIDENT.
THIS TEAM IS STRONG!

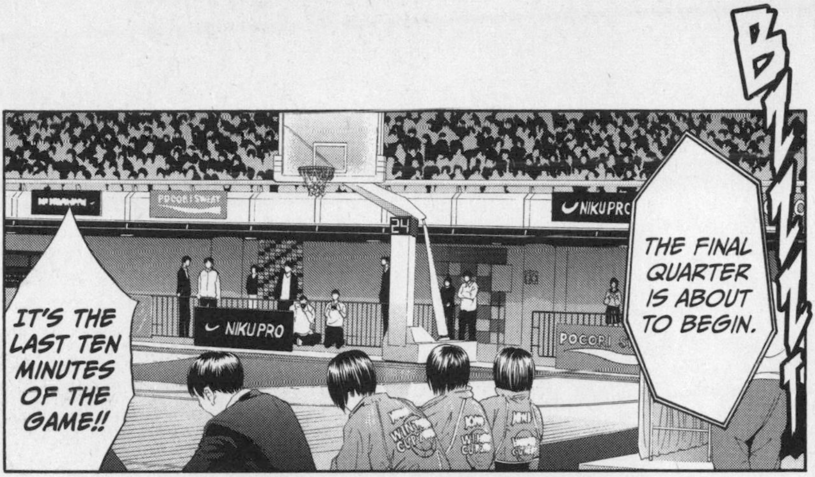
THE FINAL QUARTER IS ABOUT TO BEGIN.
IT'S THE LAST TEN MINUTES OF THE GAME!!
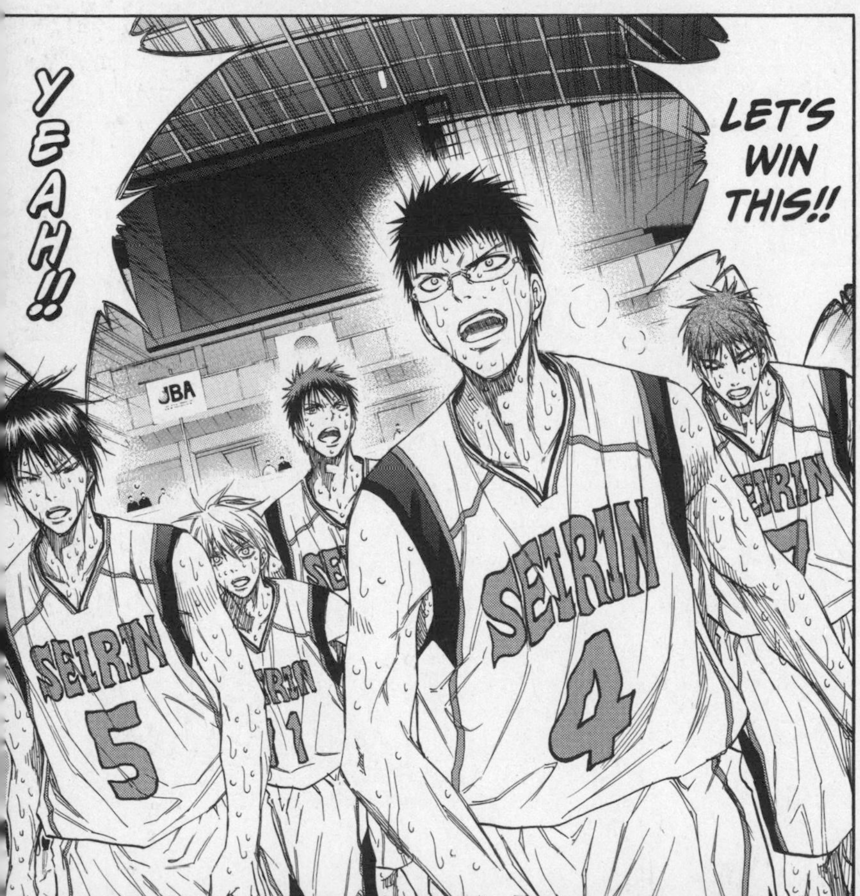
LET'S WIN THIS!!
YEAH!!

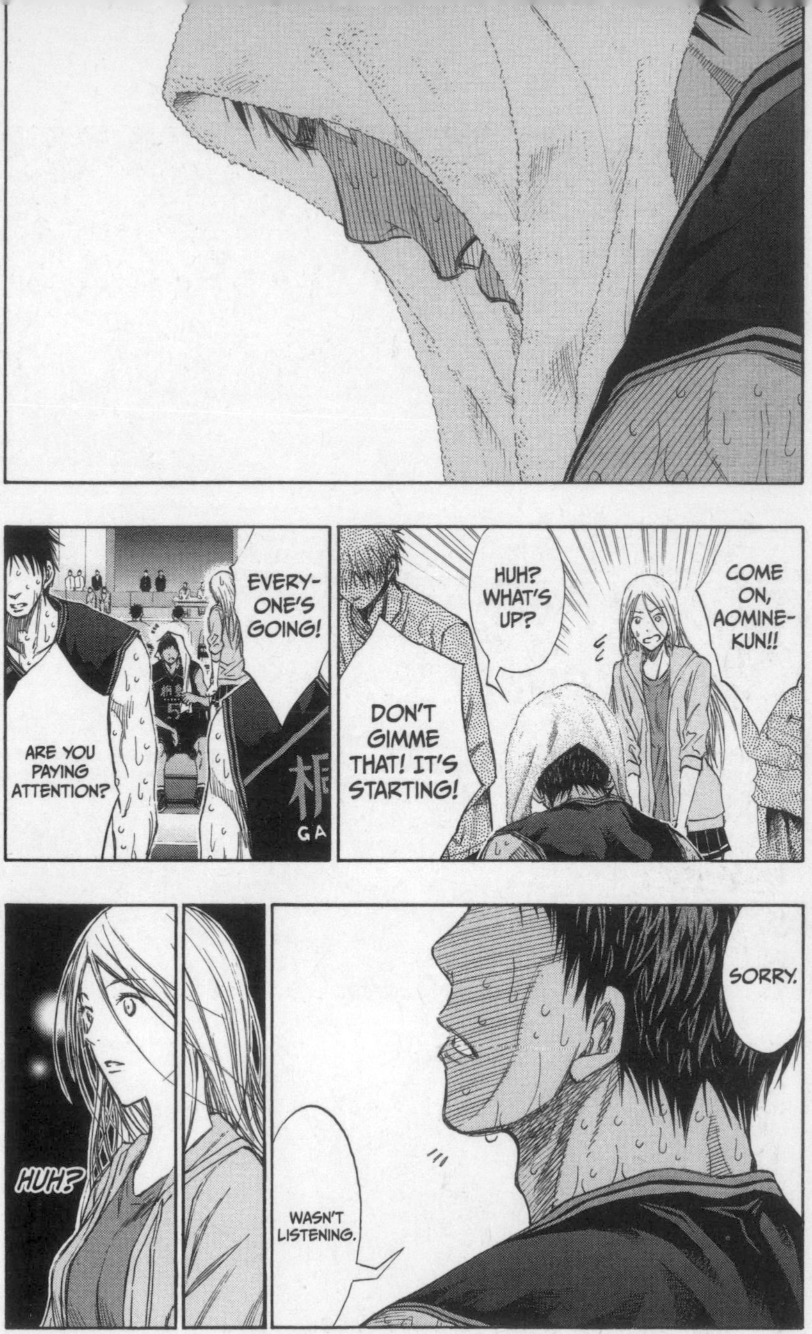
COME ON, AOMINE-KUN!!
HUH? WHAT'S UP?
DON'T GIMME THAT! IT'S STARTING!
EVERY-ONE'S GOING!
ARE YOU PAYING ATTENTION?
SORRY.
WASN'T LISTENING.
HUH?

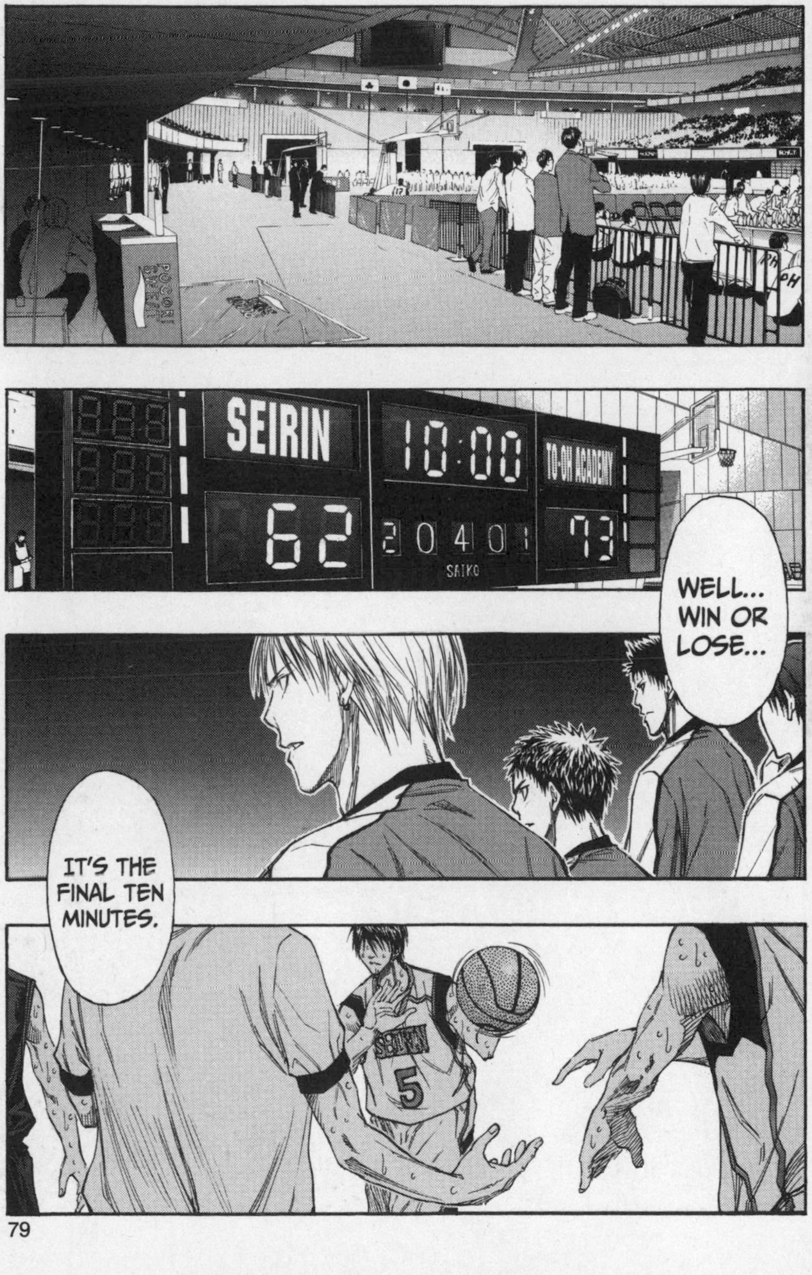
SEIRIN
10:00
TO-OH ACADEMY
62
73
WELL... WIN OR LOSE...
IT'S THE FINAL TEN MINUTES.

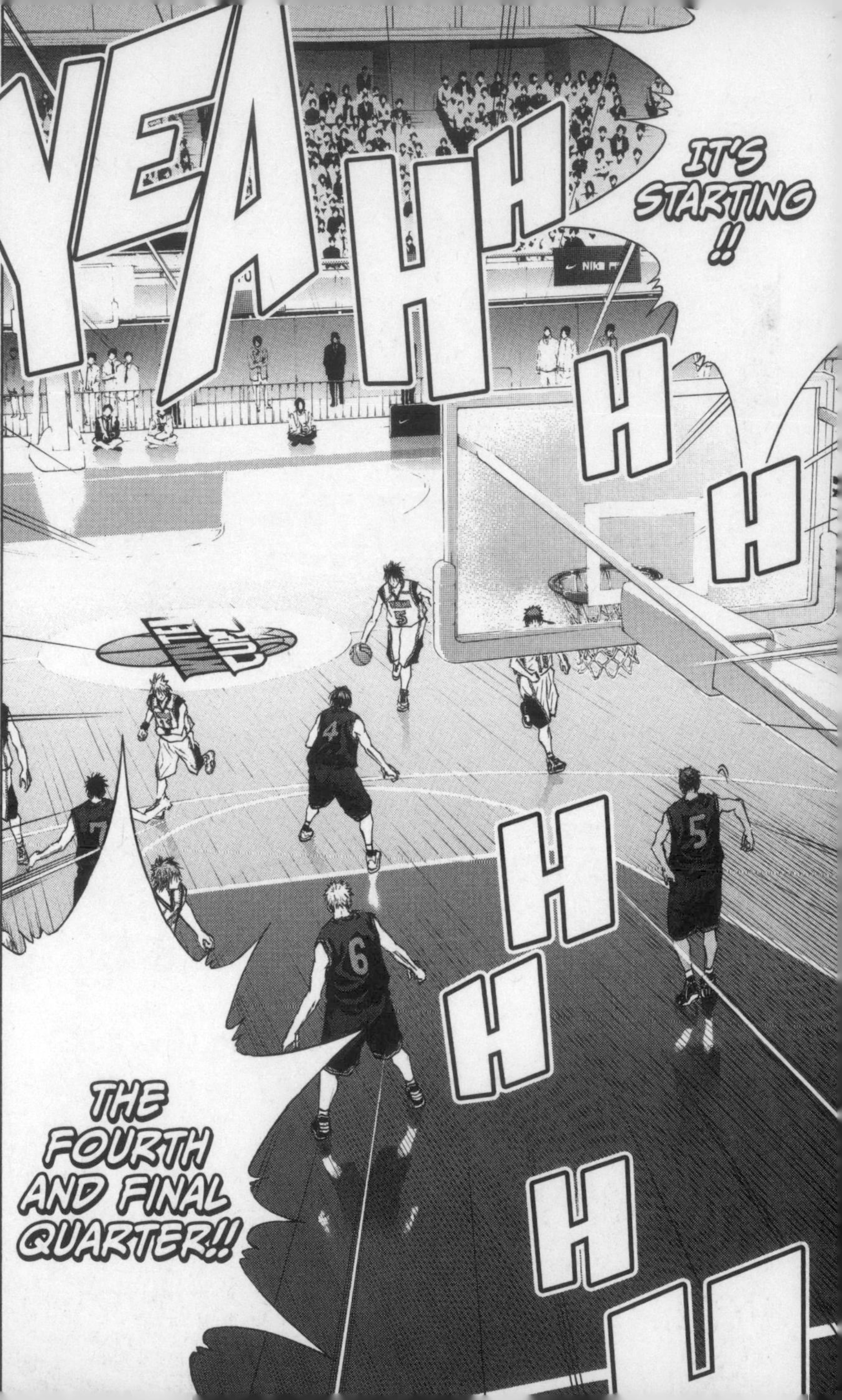
YEAHHHHHHHH
IT'S STARTING!!
THE FOURTH AND FINAL QUARTER!!

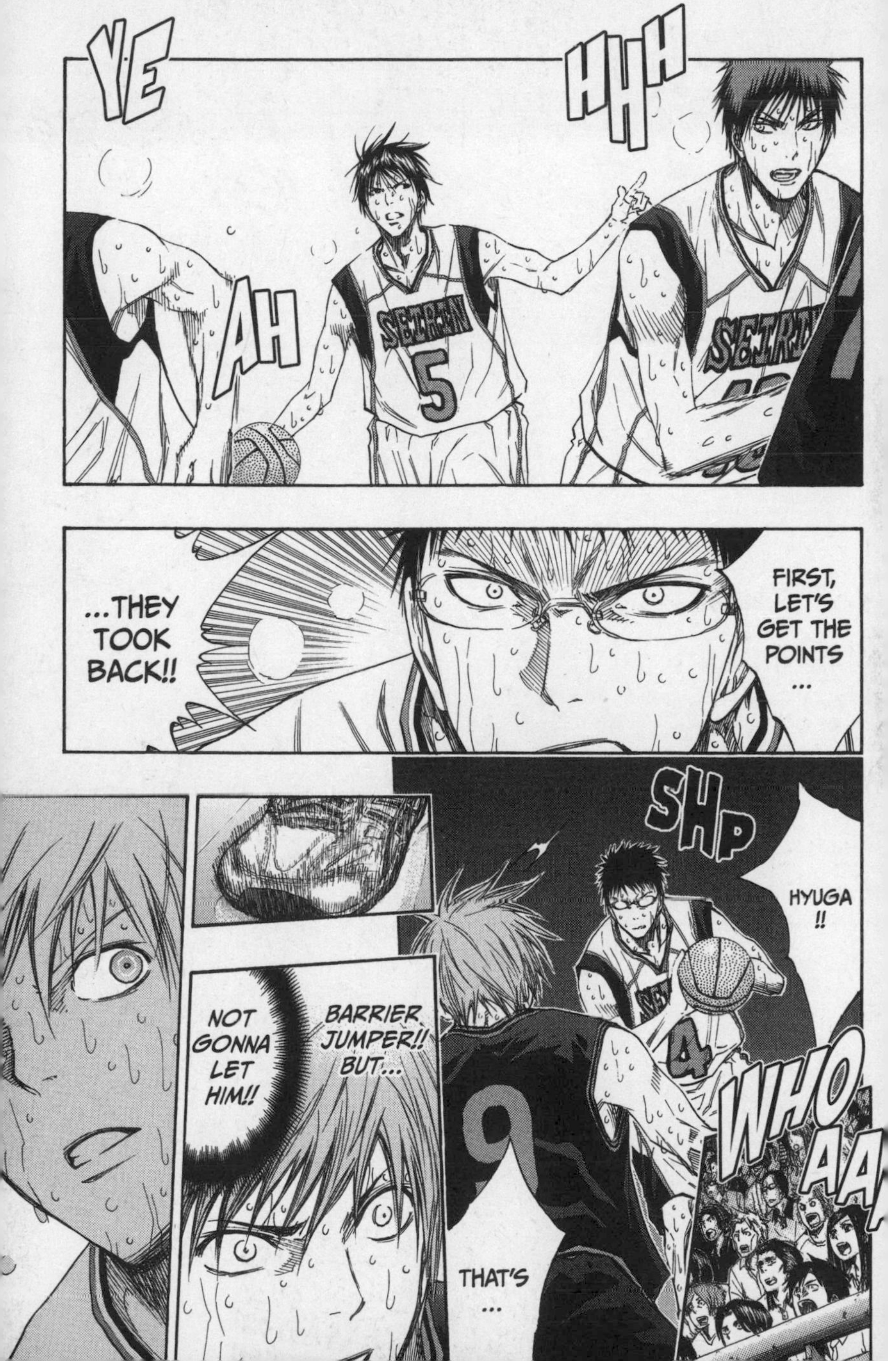
YE
AH
HHH
FIRST, LET'S GET THE POINTS ...
...THEY TOOK BACK!!
SHP
HYUGA !!
WHOAAA
BARRIER JUMPER!! BUT...
NOT GONNA LET HIM!!
THAT'S ...

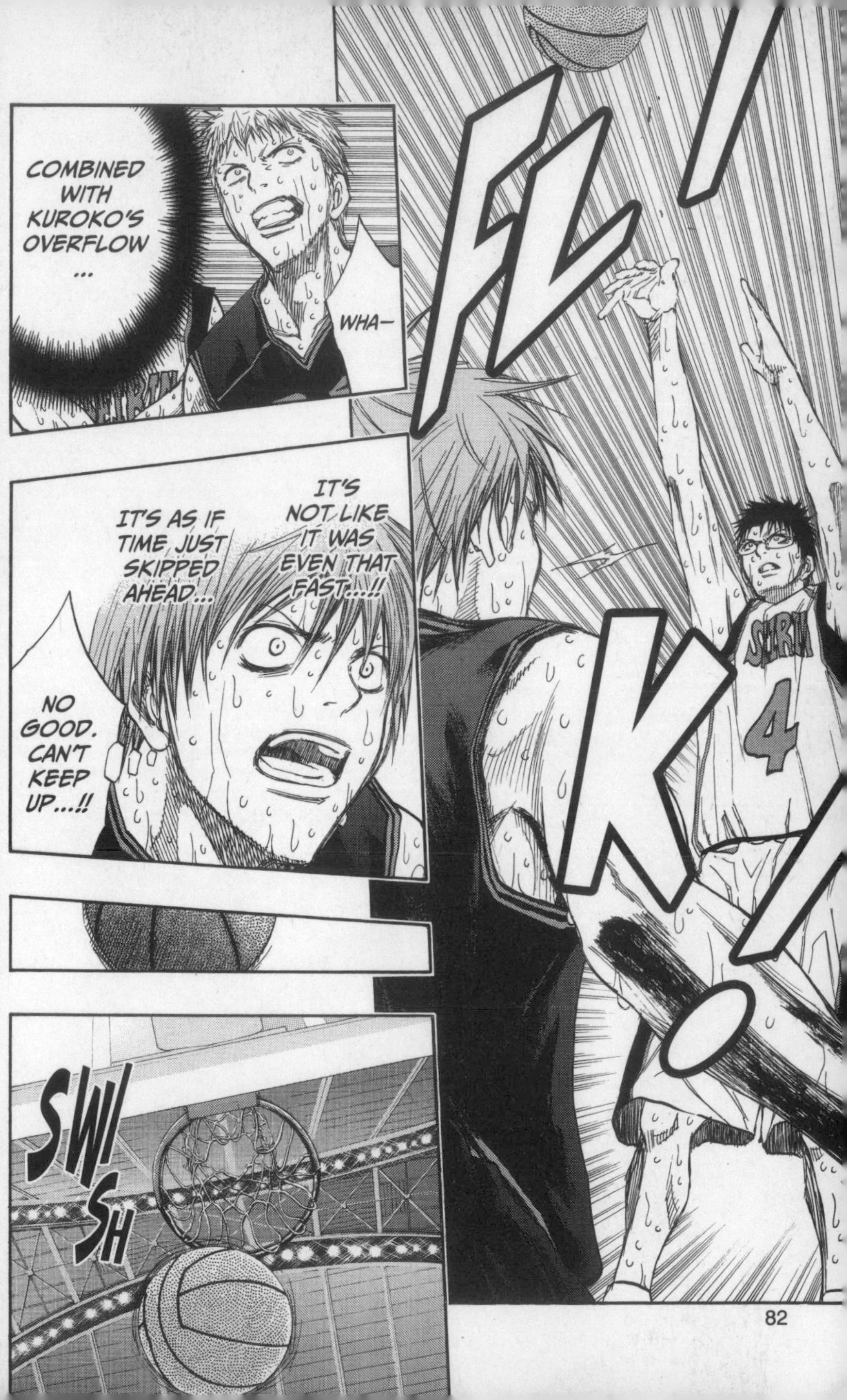
COMBINED WITH KUROKO'S OVERFLOW ...
WHA–
IT'S NOT LIKE IT WAS EVEN THAT FAST...!!
IT'S AS IF TIME JUST SKIPPED AHEAD...
NO GOOD. CAN'T KEEP UP...!!
SWISH

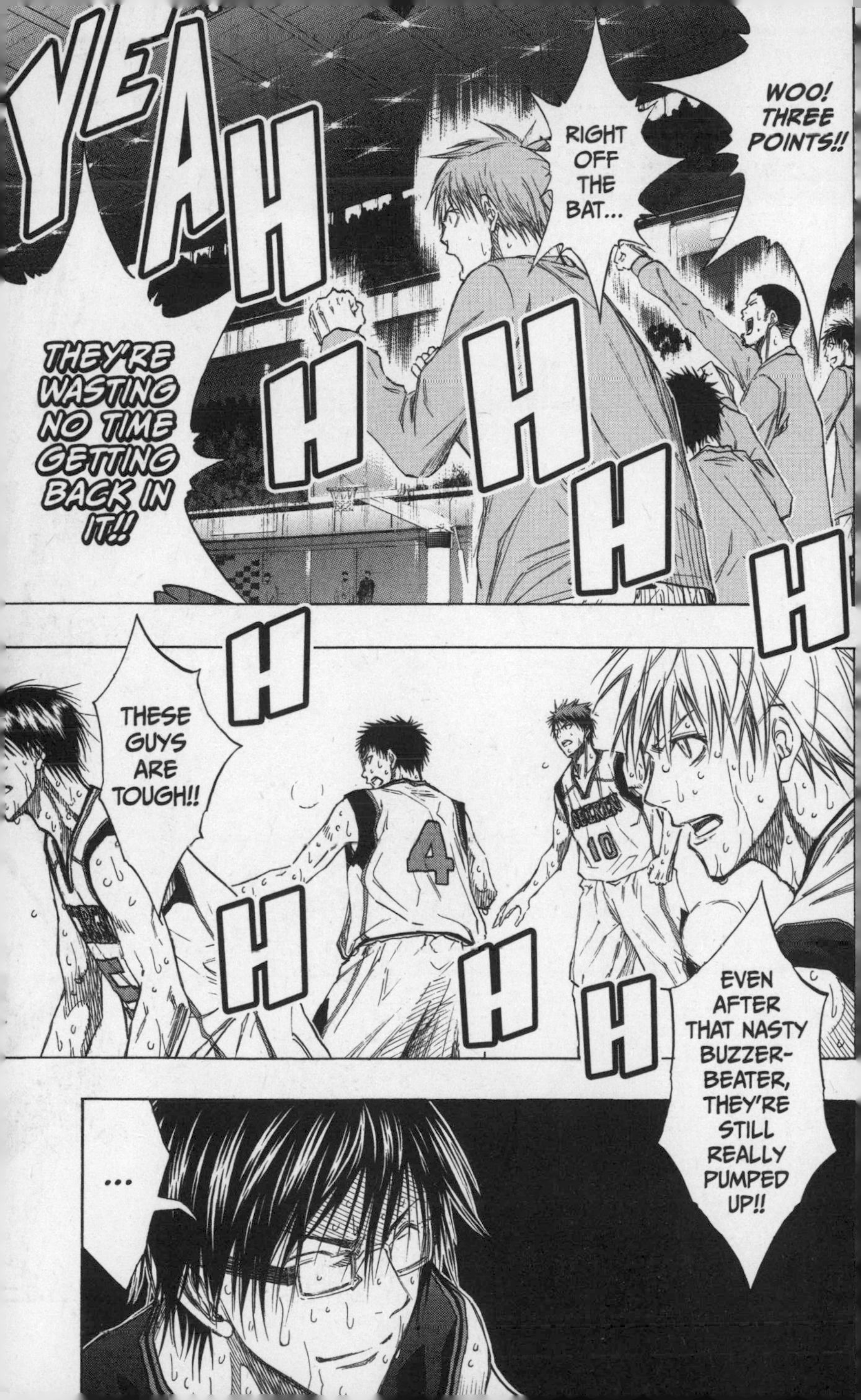
WOO! THREE POINTS!!
RIGHT OFF THE BAT...
YEAHHHHHHHHH
THEY'RE WASTING NO TIME GETTING BACK IN IT!!
EVEN AFTER THAT NASTY BUZZER-BEATER, THEY'RE STILL REALLY PUMPED UP!!
THESE GUYS ARE TOUGH!!
...

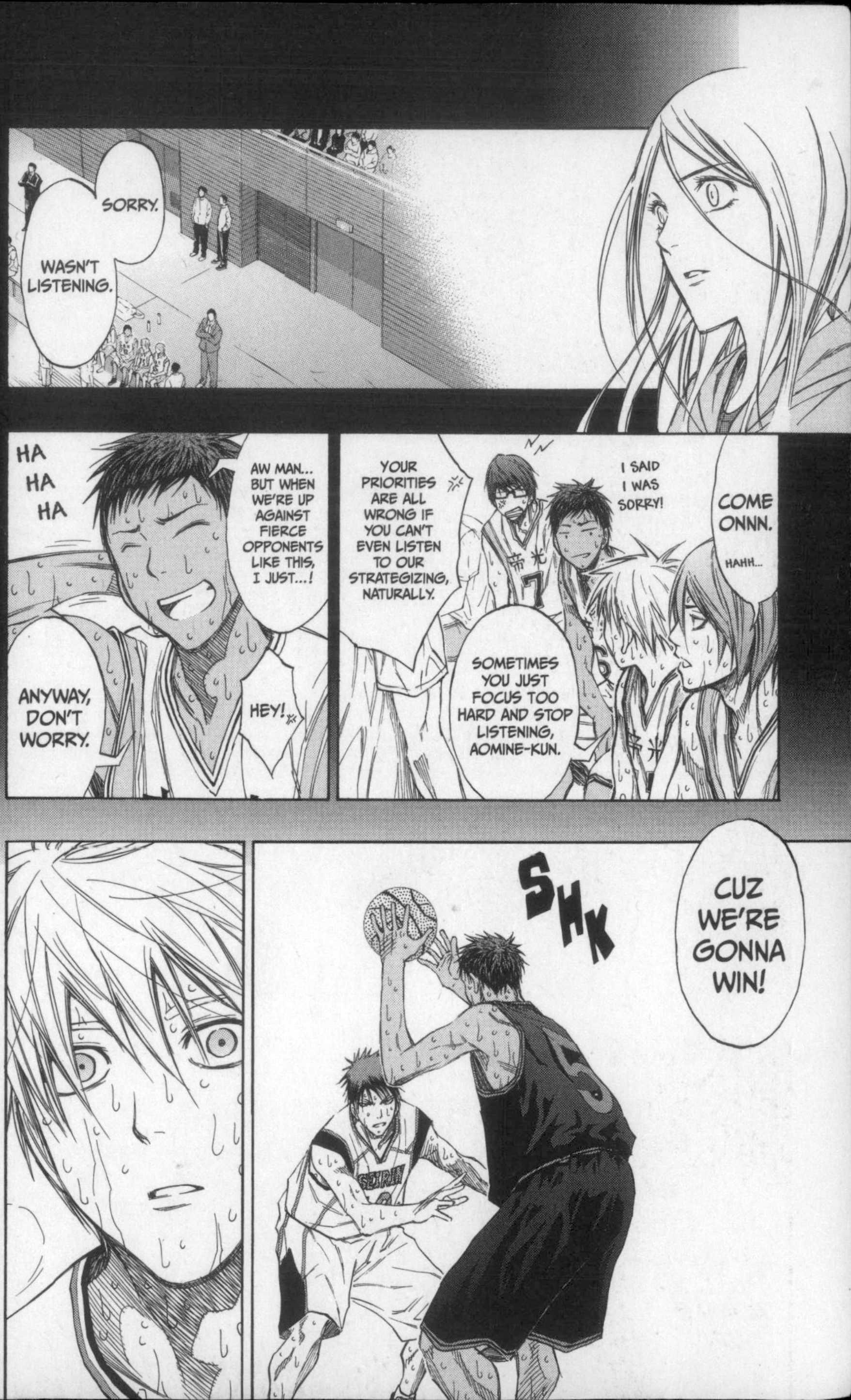
SORRY.
WASN'T LISTENING.
COME ONNN.
HAHH...
I SAID I WAS SORRY!
YOUR PRIORITIES ARE ALL WRONG IF YOU CAN'T EVEN LISTEN TO OUR STRATEGIZING, NATURALLY.
SOMETIMES YOU JUST FOCUS TOO HARD AND STOP LISTENING, AOMINE-KUN.
AW MAN... BUT WHEN WE'RE UP AGAINST FIERCE OPPONENTS LIKE THIS, I JUST...!
HA HA HA
HEY!
ANYWAY, DON'T WORRY.
CUZ WE'RE GONNA WIN!
SHK

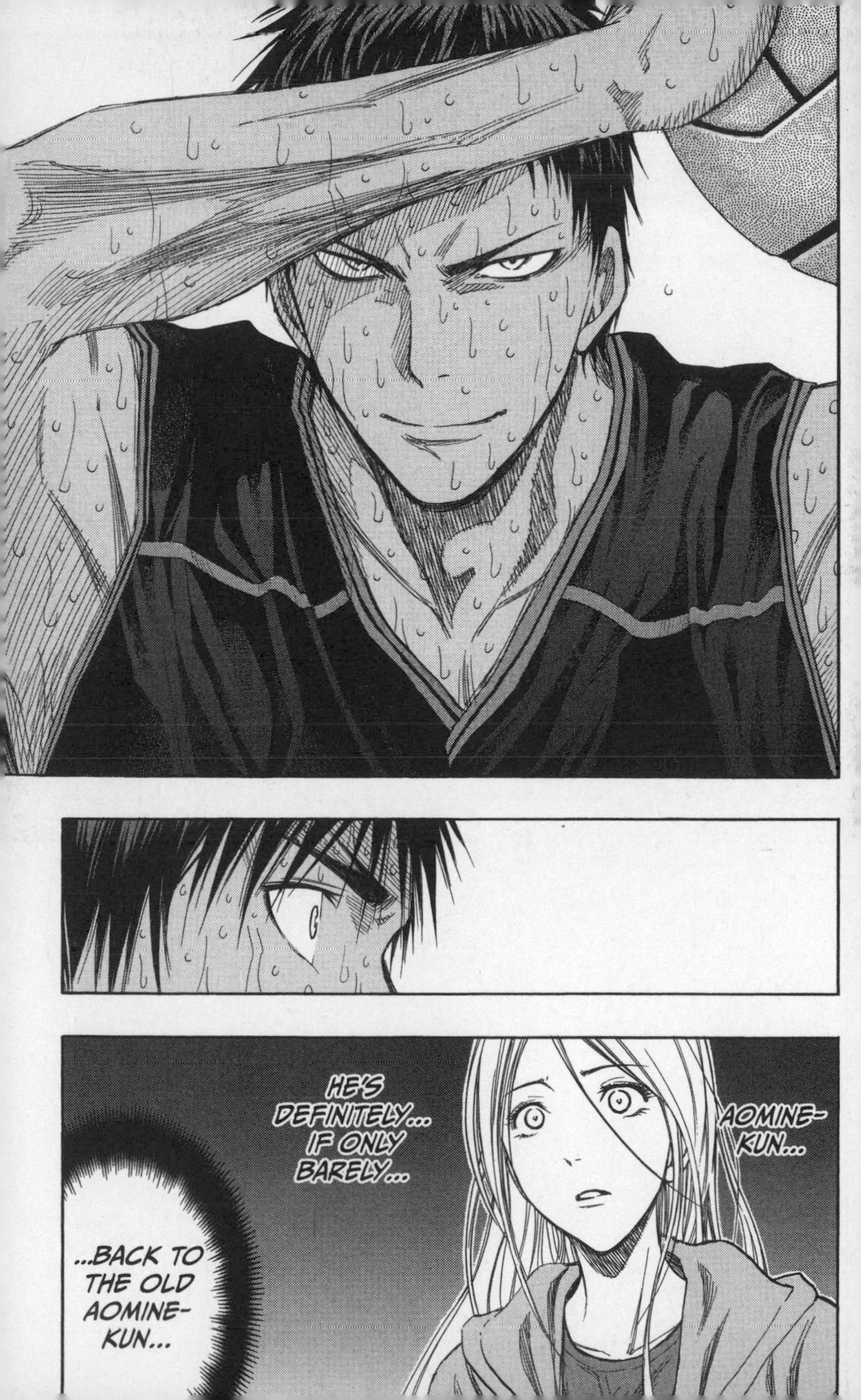
AOMINE-KUN...
HE'S DEFINITELY... IF ONLY BARELY...
...BACK TO THE OLD AOMINE-KUN...

KUROKO'S BASKETBALL Q&A
W/ HALFWAY-DECENT ANSWERS

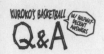

Q. **SINCE KAGAMI IS "DUMMYGAMI," CAN I CALL AOMINE "AOMEANIE"?**
(AKITA PREFECTURE'S KUROKO'S BASKETBALL FAN from AKITA PREFECTURE)

A. SURE!

KUROKO'S BASKETBALL BLOOPERS
TAKE 8

I MODELED THIS GAG OFF A CERTAIN OTHER ONE!

STOP DWELLING ON THINGS, DUM—
BLARRGH?!
KOFF KOFF
SAW THAT COMING!!

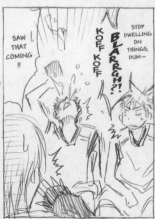

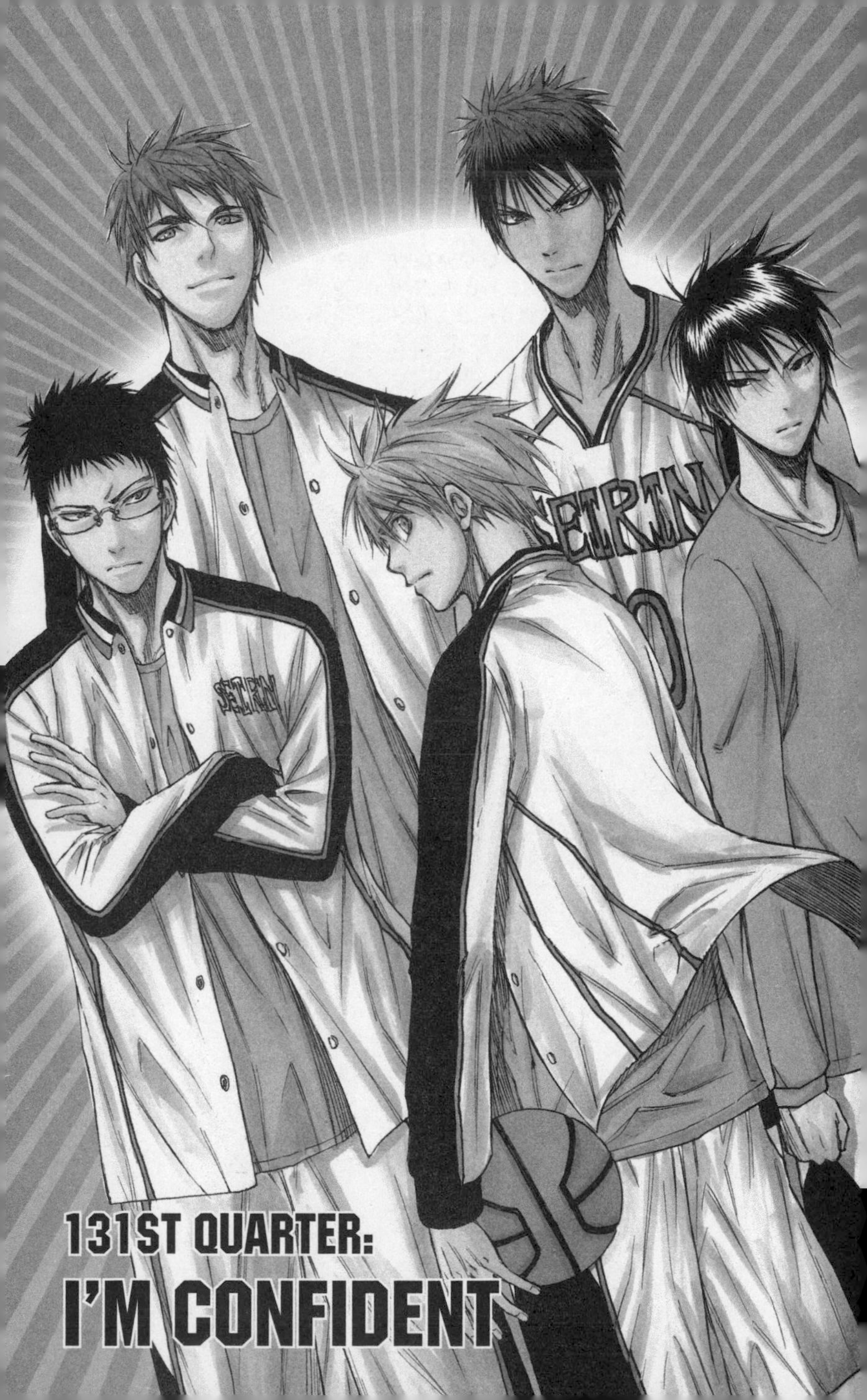
131ST QUARTER:
I'M CONFIDENT

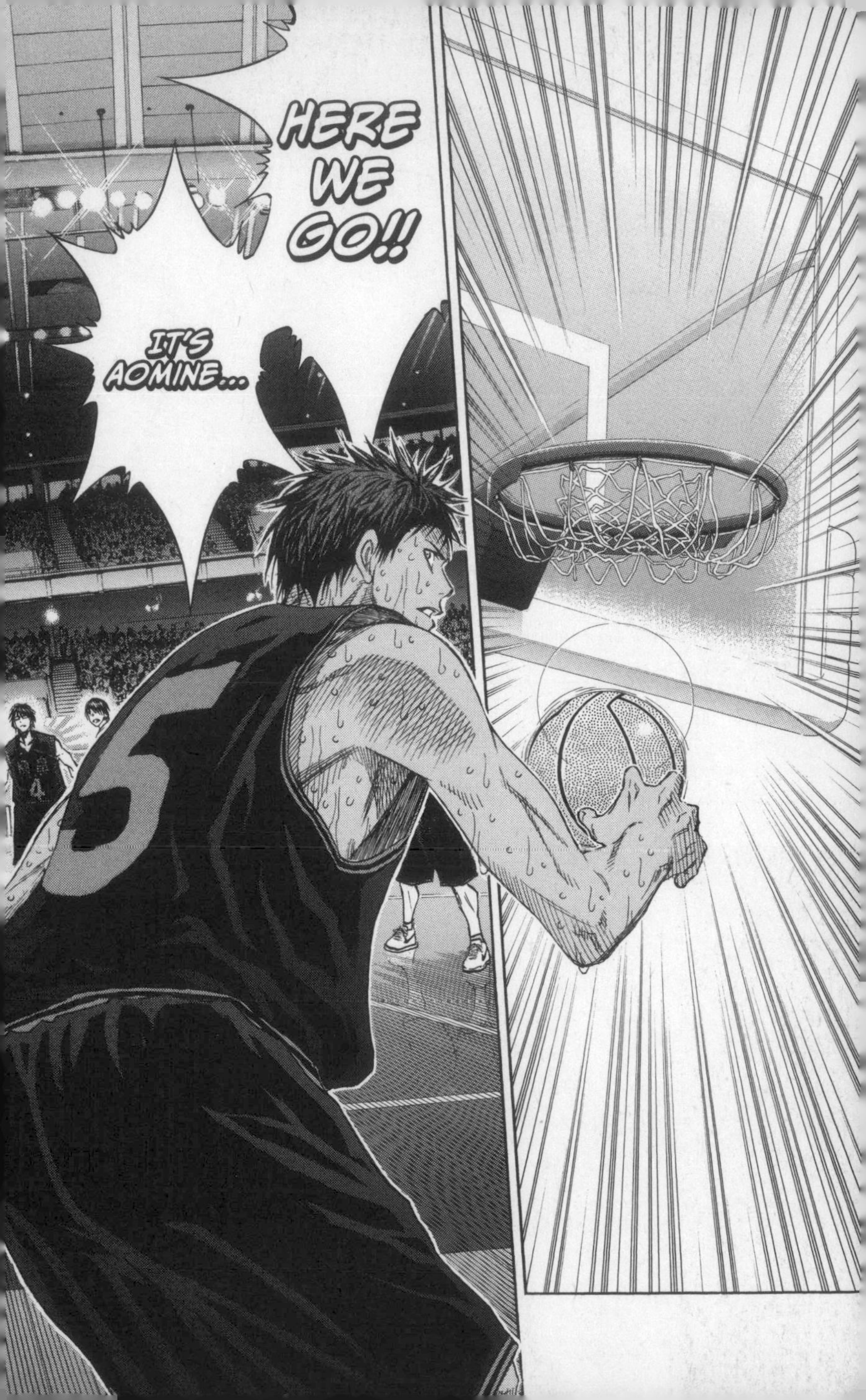
HERE WE GO!!
IT'S AOMINE...

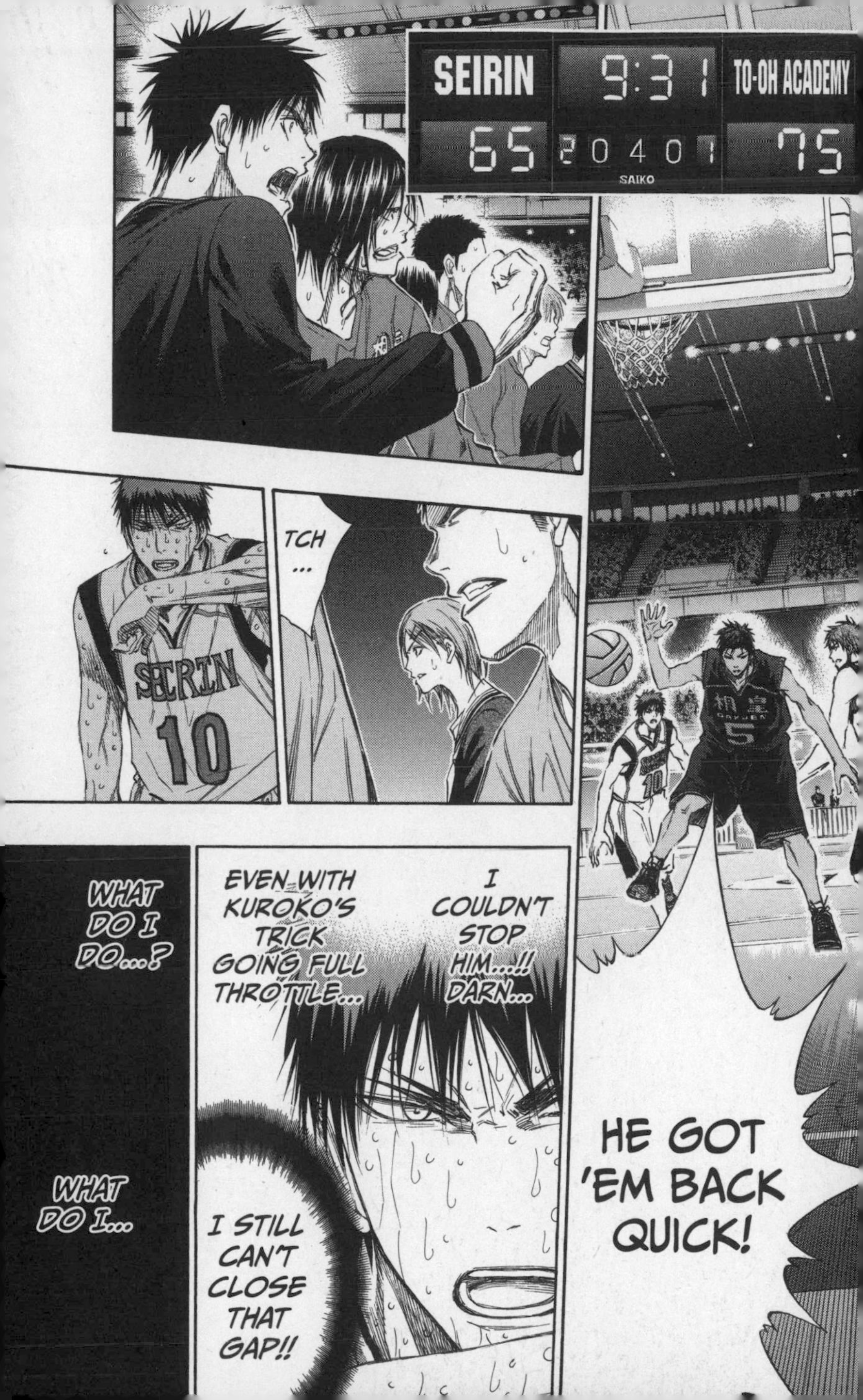
SEIRIN
9:31
TO-OH ACADEMY
65
75
SAIKO
HE GOT 'EM BACK QUICK!
TCH ...
I COULDN'T STOP HIM...!! DARN...
EVEN WITH KUROKO'S TRICK GOING FULL THROTTLE...
I STILL CAN'T CLOSE THAT GAP!!
WHAT DO I DO...?
WHAT DO I...

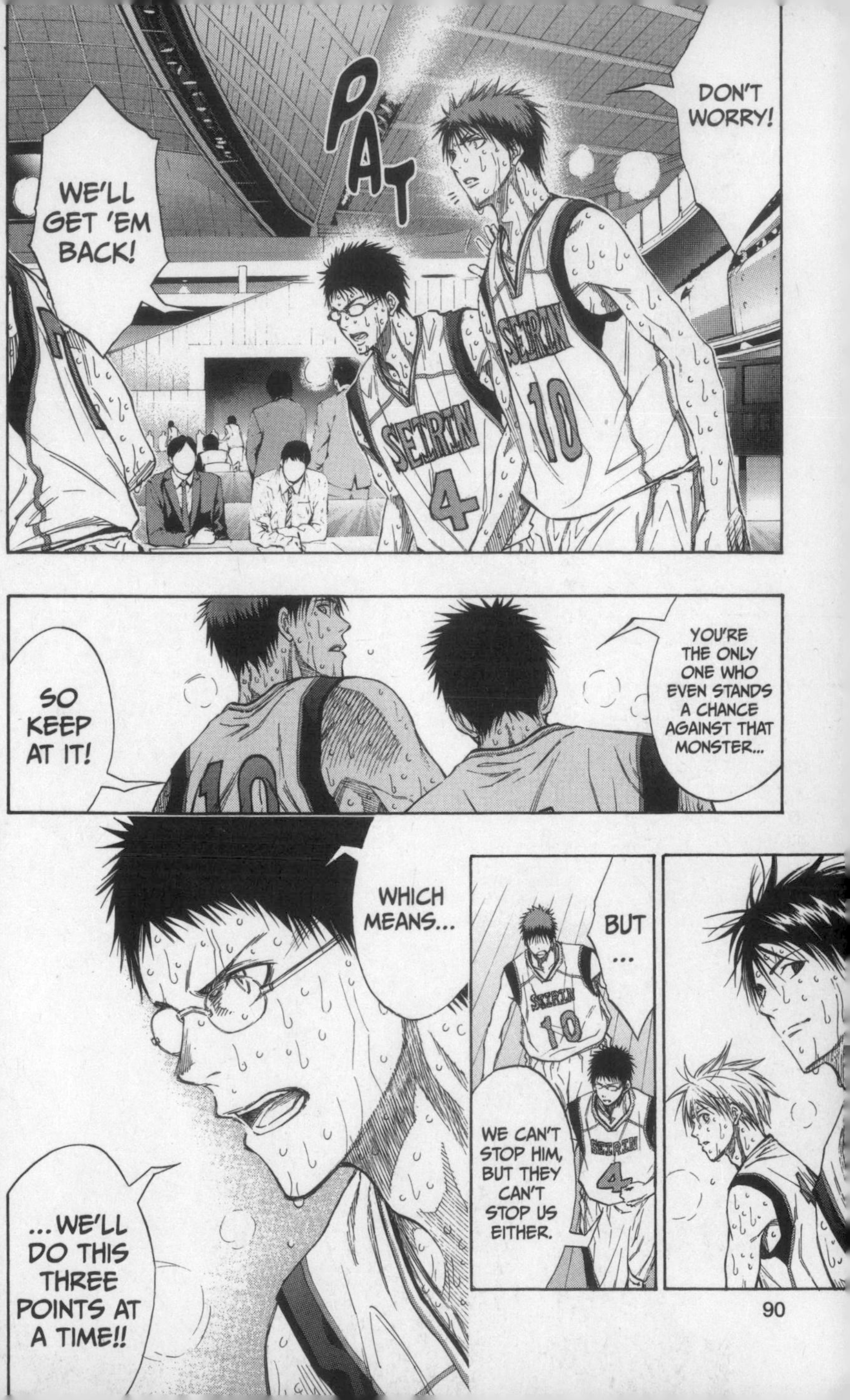
DON'T WORRY!
PAT
WE'LL GET 'EM BACK!
YOU'RE THE ONLY ONE WHO EVEN STANDS A CHANCE AGAINST THAT MONSTER...
SO KEEP AT IT!
BUT ...
WE CAN'T STOP HIM, BUT THEY CAN'T STOP US EITHER.
WHICH MEANS...
...WE'LL DO THIS THREE POINTS AT A TIME!!

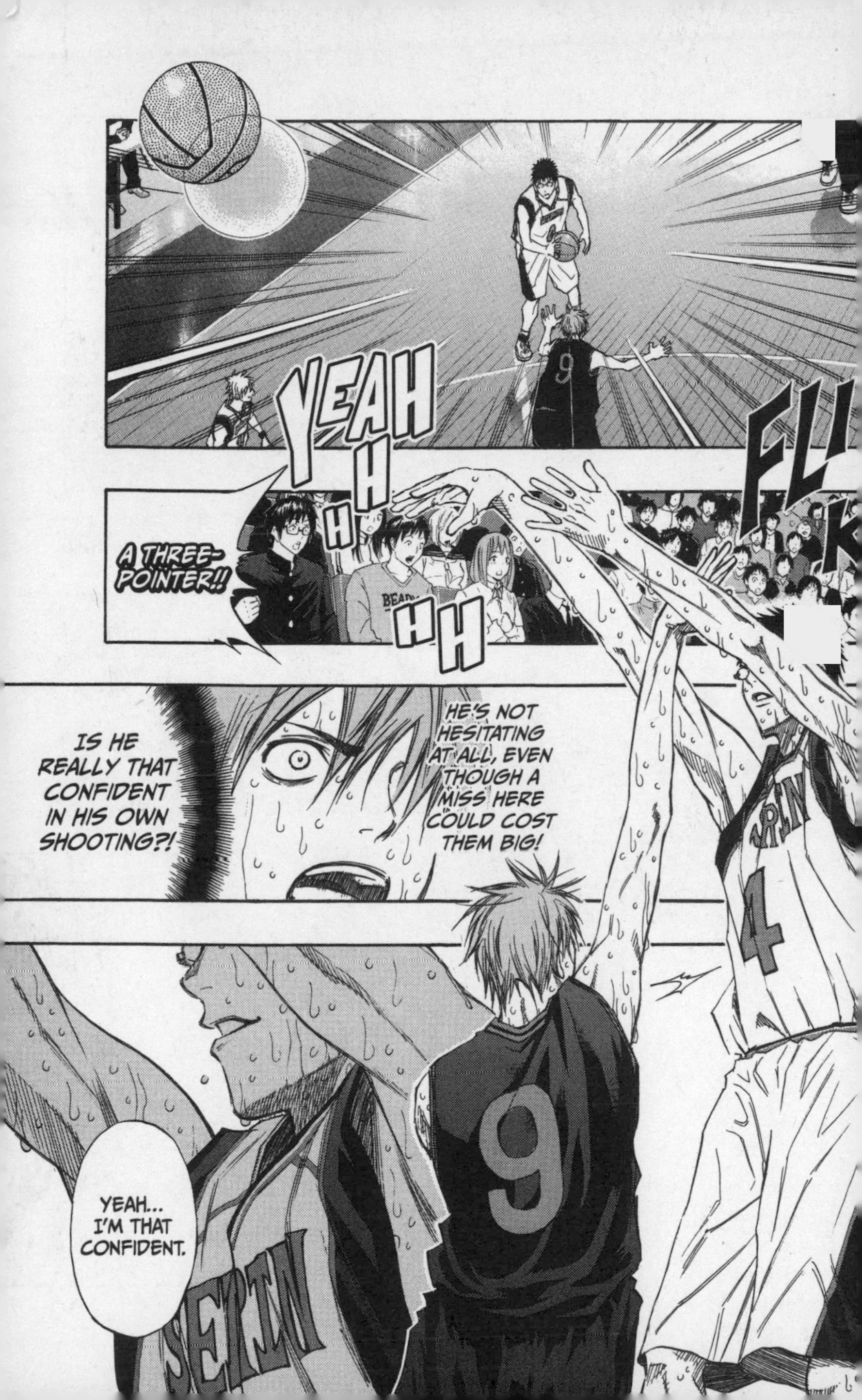
YEAHHHHH
A THREE-POINTER!!
HE'S NOT HESITATING AT ALL, EVEN THOUGH A MISS HERE COULD COST THEM BIG!
IS HE REALLY THAT CONFIDENT IN HIS OWN SHOOTING?!
YEAH... I'M THAT CONFIDENT.

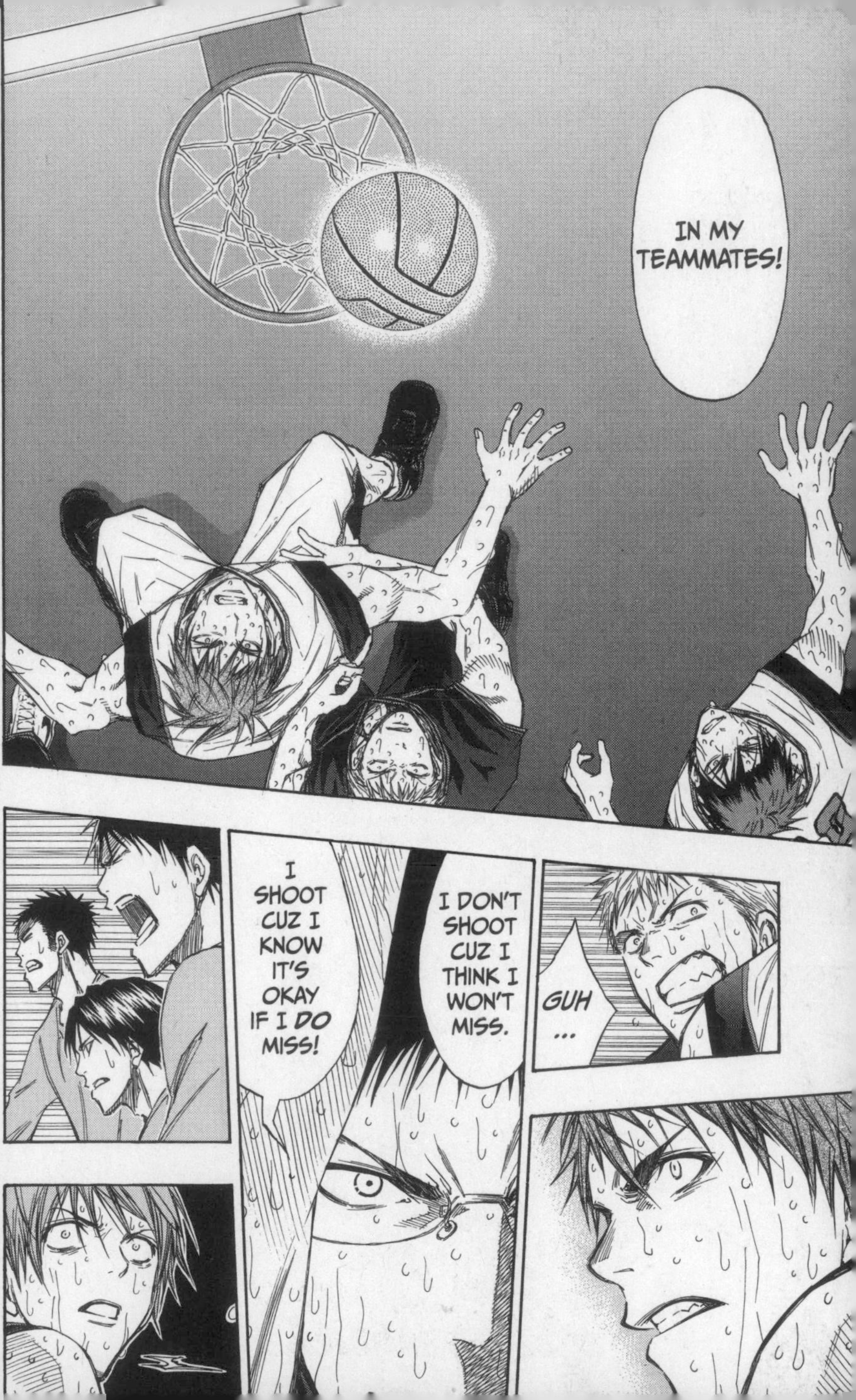
IN MY TEAMMATES!
GUH ...
I DON'T SHOOT CUZ I THINK I WON'T MISS.
I SHOOT CUZ I KNOW IT'S OKAY IF I DO MISS!

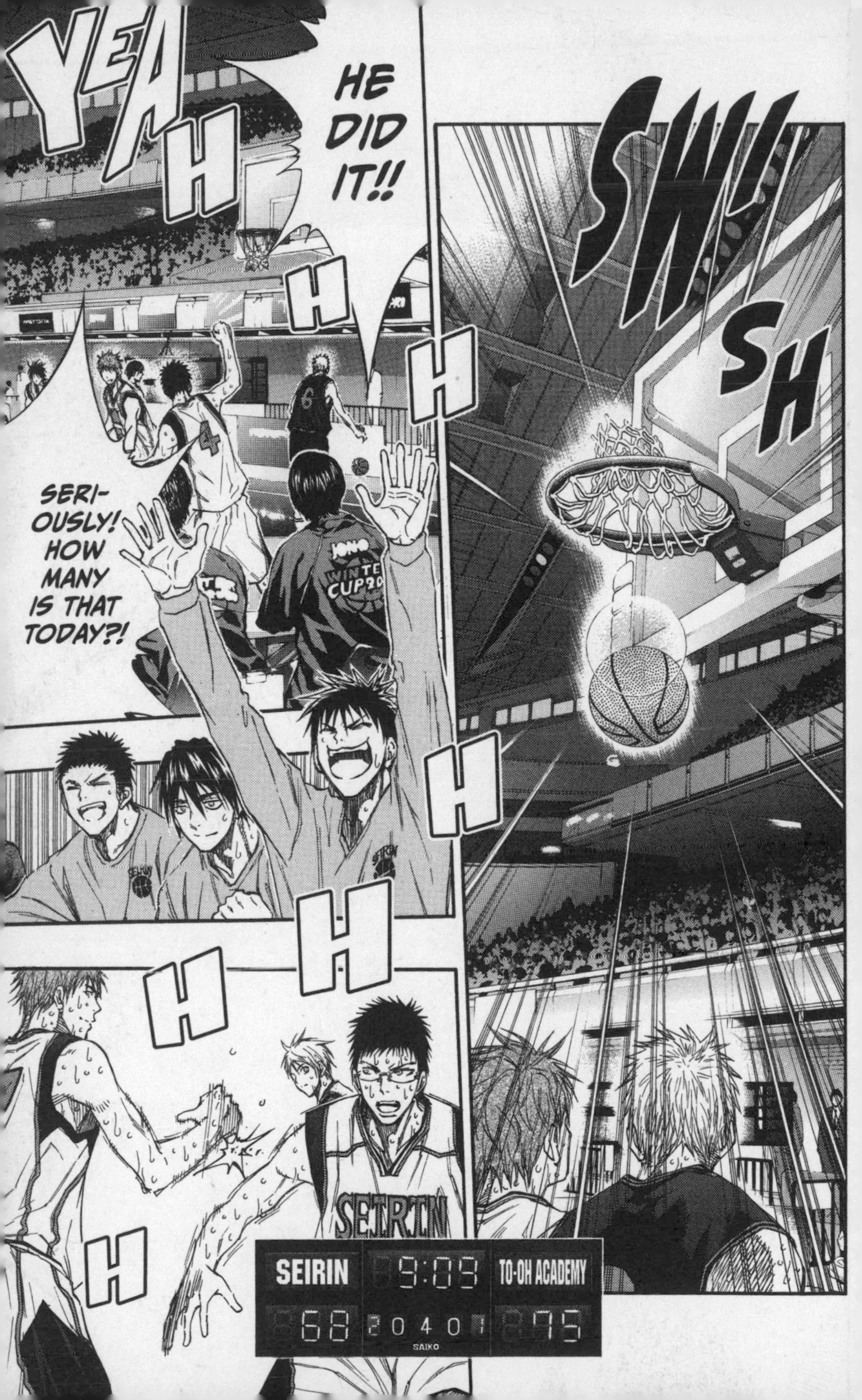
SWISH
YEAHHHHHHHH
HE DID IT!!
SERI-OUSLY! HOW MANY IS THAT TODAY?!
SEIRIN
9:09
TO-OH ACADEMY
68
75
SAIKO

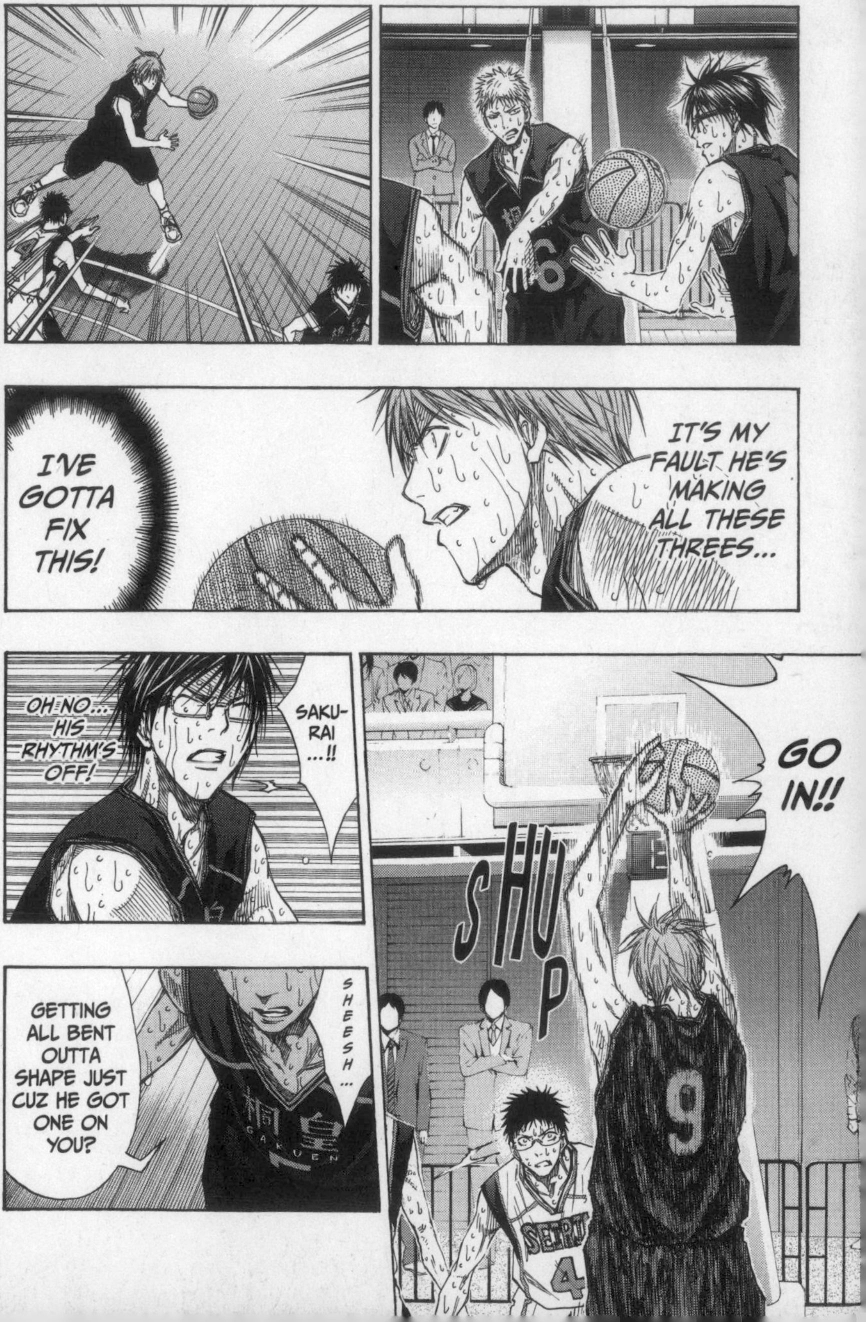
IT'S MY FAULT HE'S MAKING ALL THESE THREES...
I'VE GOTTA FIX THIS!
GO IN!!
SHUP
SAKU-RAI ...!!
OH NO... HIS RHYTHM'S OFF!
SHEESH...
GETTING ALL BENT OUTTA SHAPE JUST CUZ HE GOT ONE ON YOU?

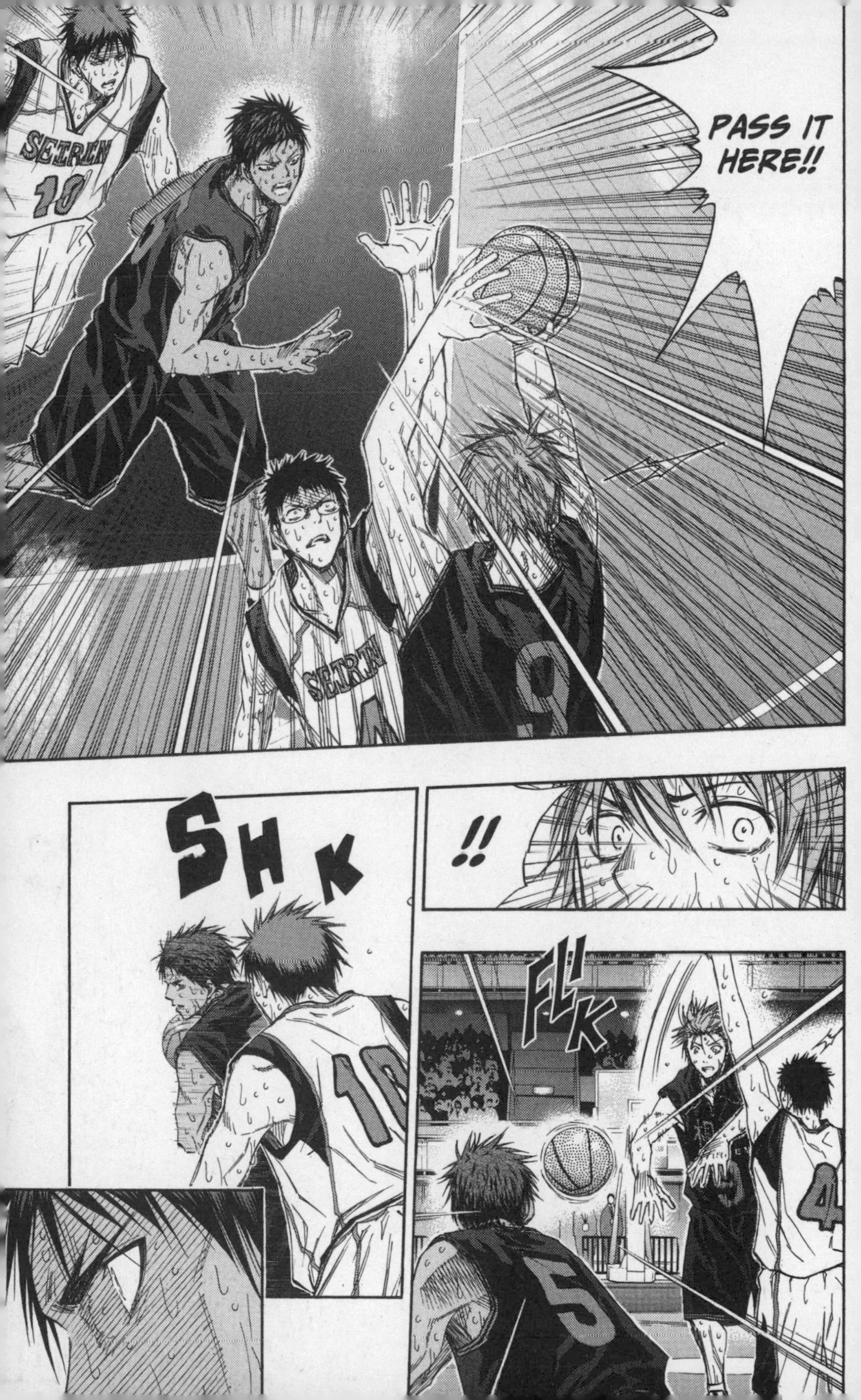
PASS IT HERE!!
!!
SHK
FLIK

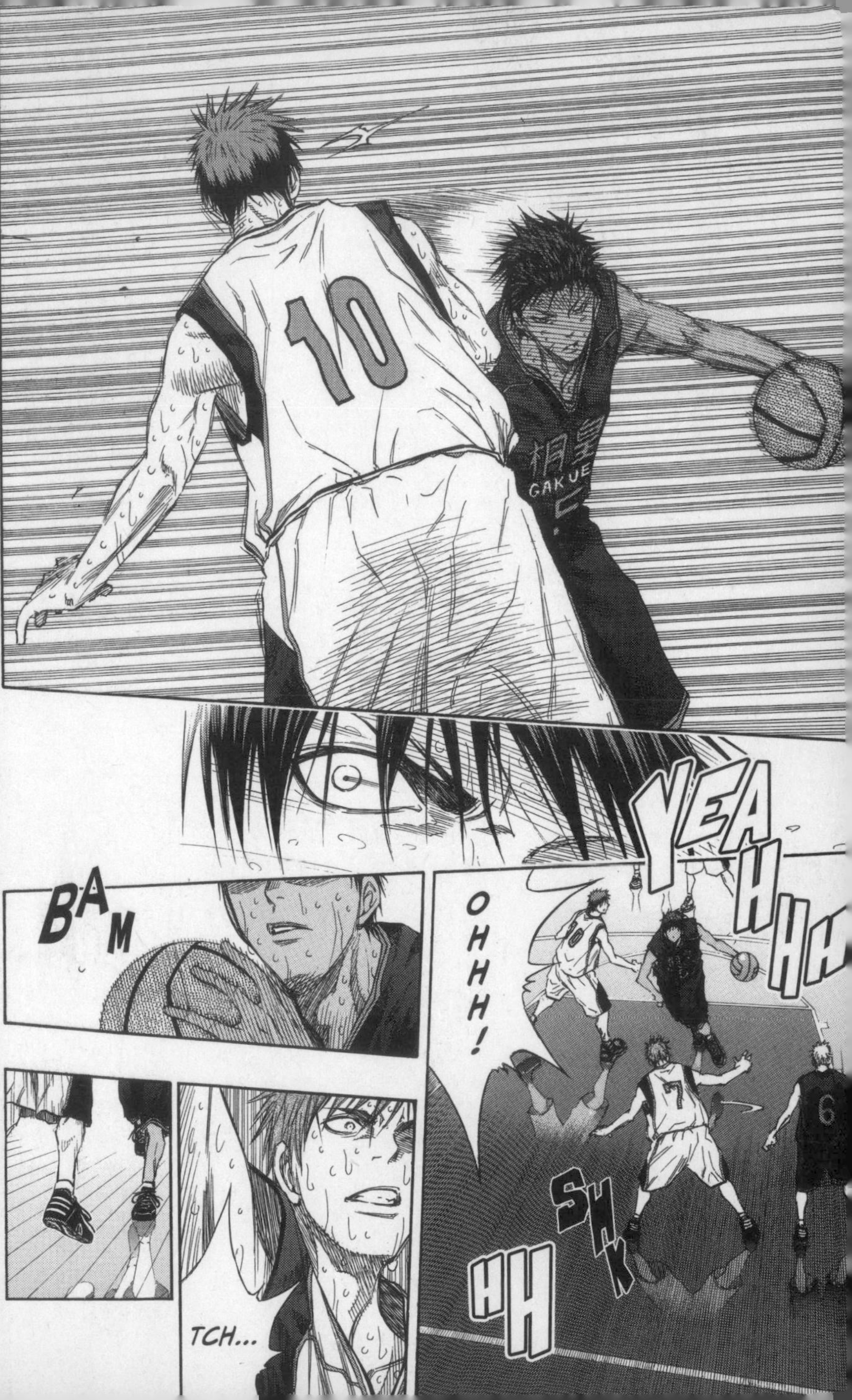
YEAHHHHH
OHHHH!
BAM
SHHHK
TCH...

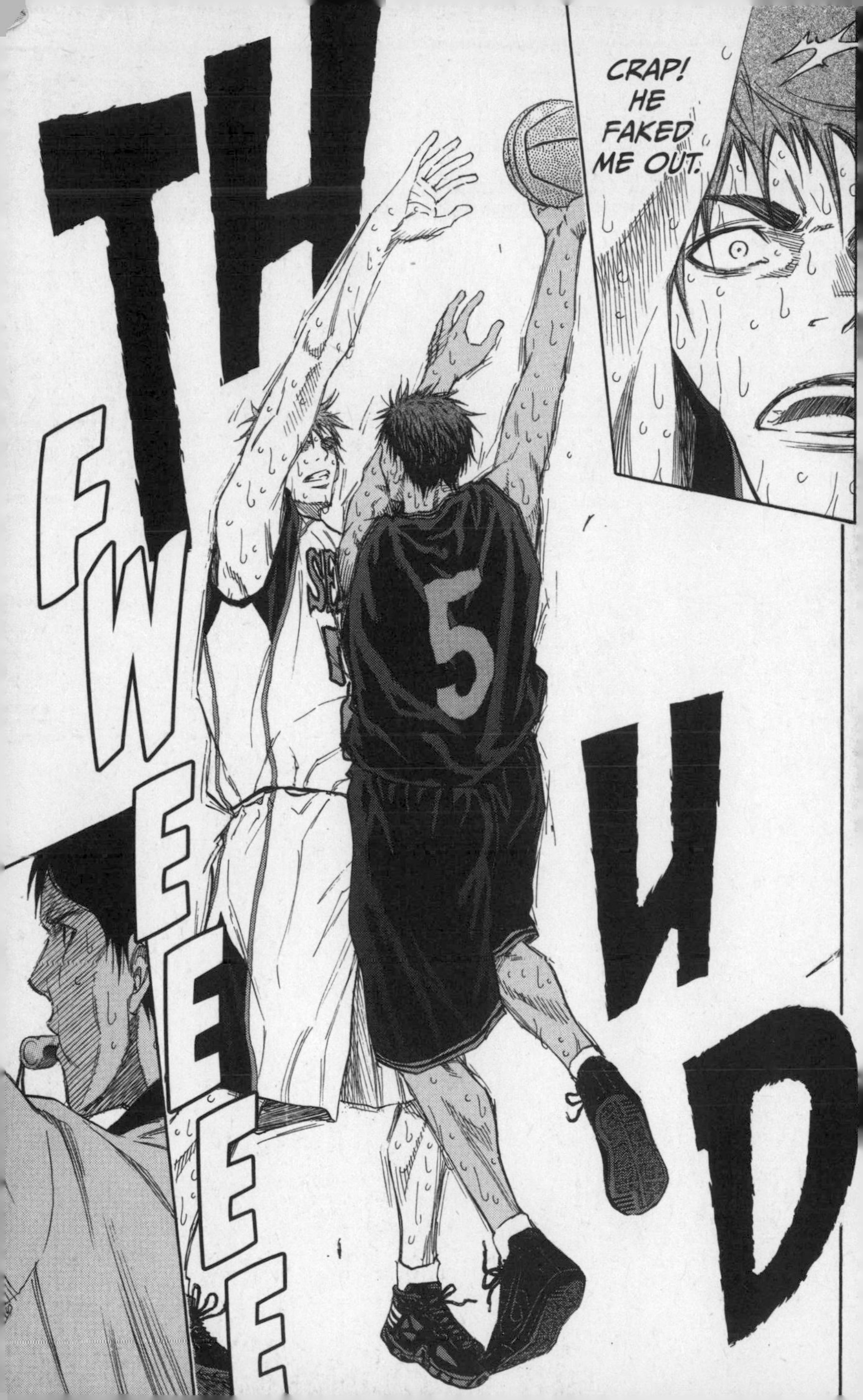
CRAP! HE FAKED ME OUT.
THUD
FWEEEE

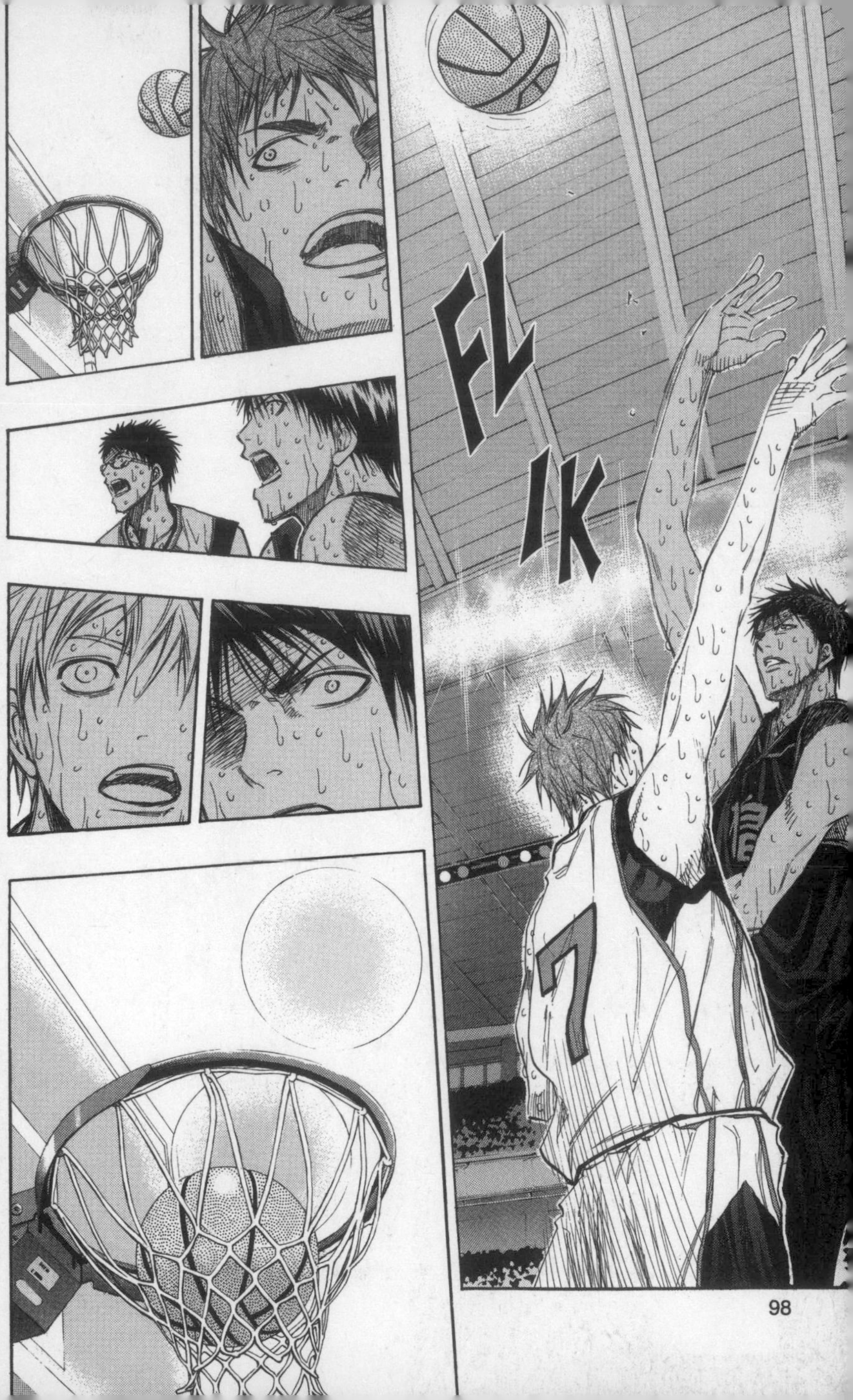
FLIK

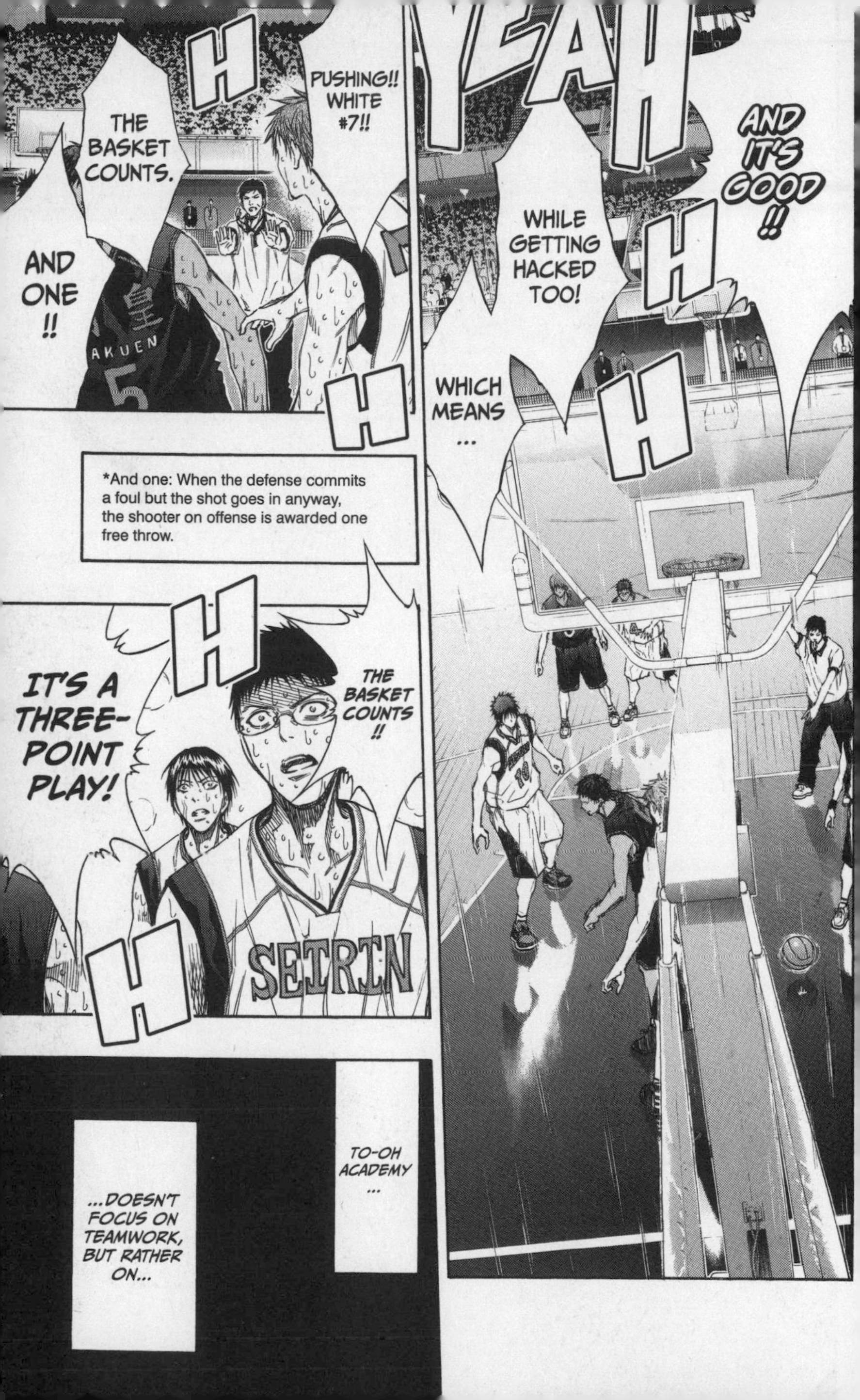
HHHHHHH YEAH
AND IT'S GOOD!!
WHILE GETTING HACKED TOO!
WHICH MEANS ...
PUSHING!! WHITE #7!!
THE BASKET COUNTS.
AND ONE !!
*And one: When the defense commits a foul but the shot goes in anyway, the shooter on offense is awarded one free throw.
THE BASKET COUNTS !!
IT'S A THREE-POINT PLAY!
SEIRIN
TO-OH ACADEMY ...
...DOESN'T FOCUS ON TEAMWORK, BUT RATHER ON...

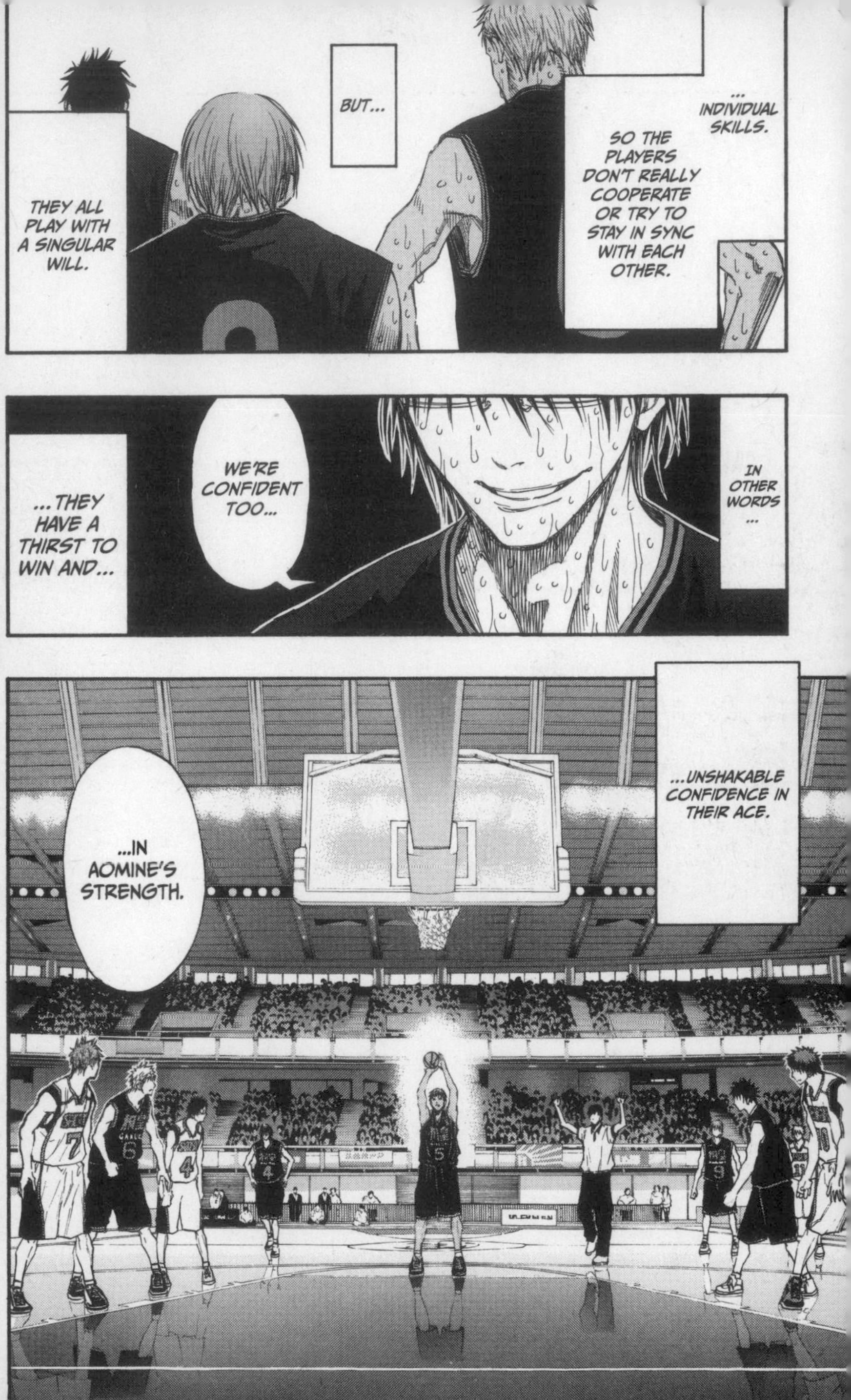
... INDIVIDUAL SKILLS.
SO THE PLAYERS DON'T REALLY COOPERATE OR TRY TO STAY IN SYNC WITH EACH OTHER.
BUT...
THEY ALL PLAY WITH A SINGULAR WILL.
IN OTHER WORDS ...
WE'RE CONFIDENT TOO...
...THEY HAVE A THIRST TO WIN AND...
...UNSHAKABLE CONFIDENCE IN THEIR ACE.
...IN AOMINE'S STRENGTH.

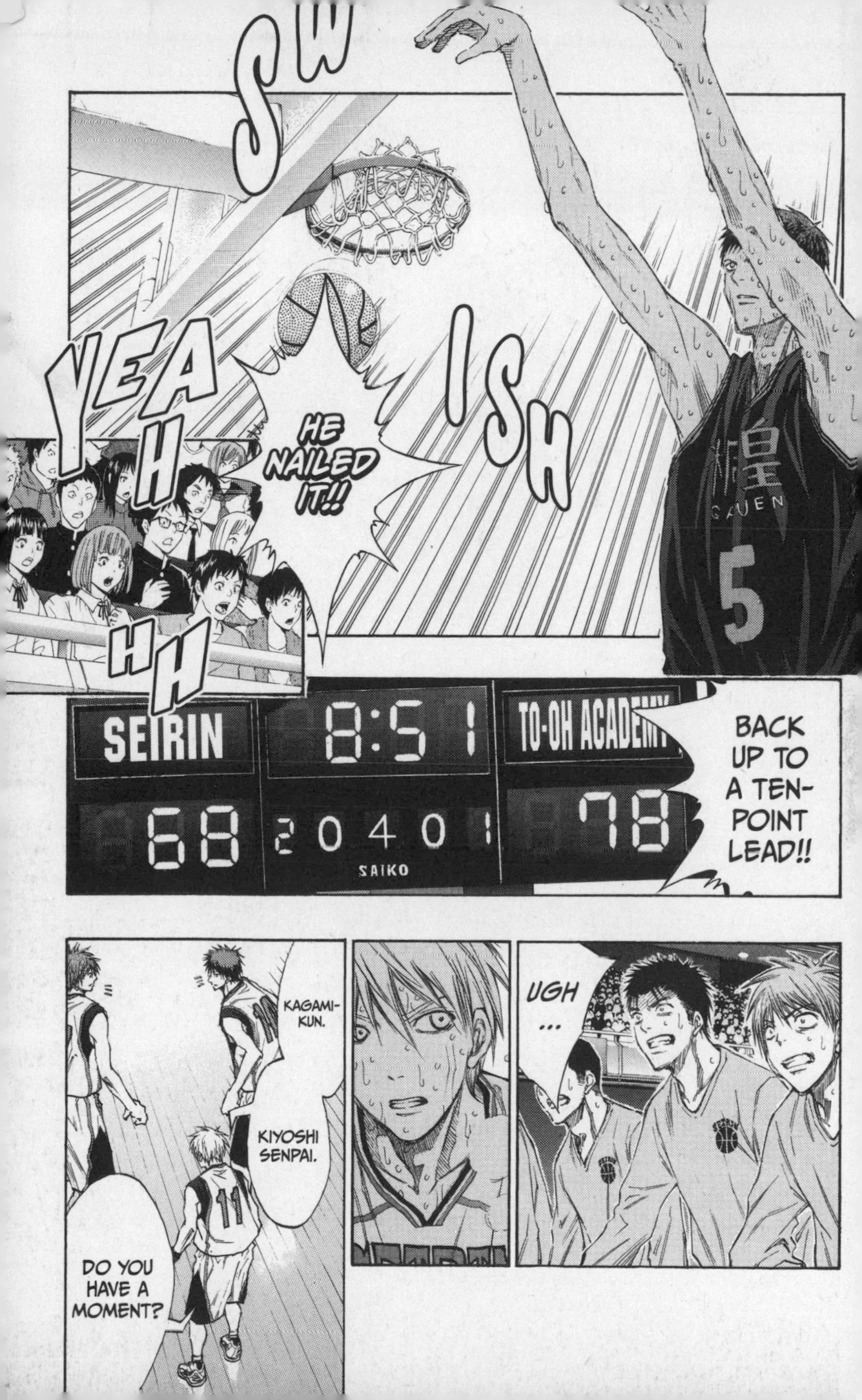

SWISH
HE NAILED IT!!
YEAHHHH
BACK UP TO A TEN-POINT LEAD!!
TO-OH ACADEMY
78
8:51
SEIRIN
68
20401
SAIKO
UGH ...
KAGAMI-KUN.
KIYOSHI SENPAI.
DO YOU HAVE A MOMENT?

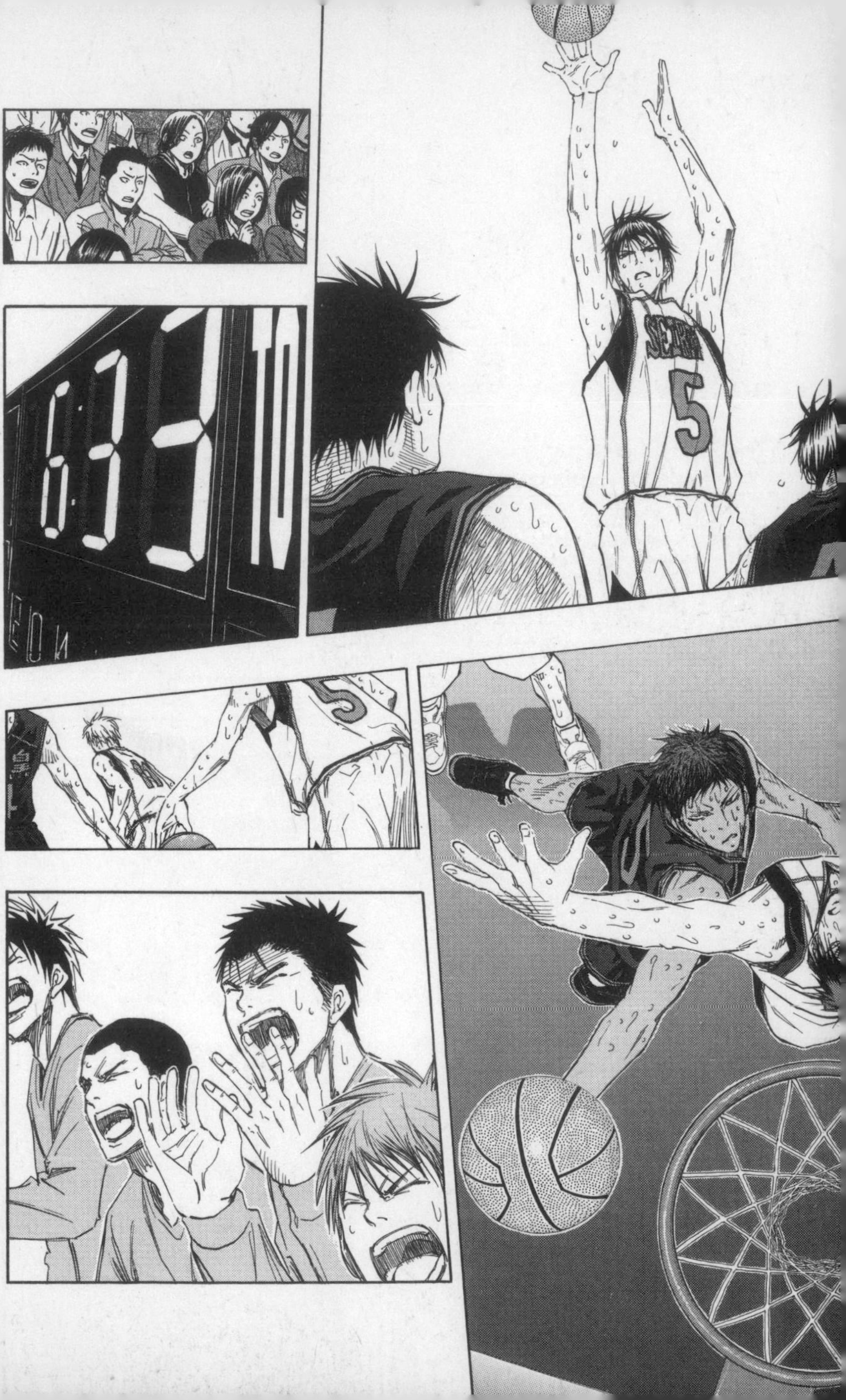

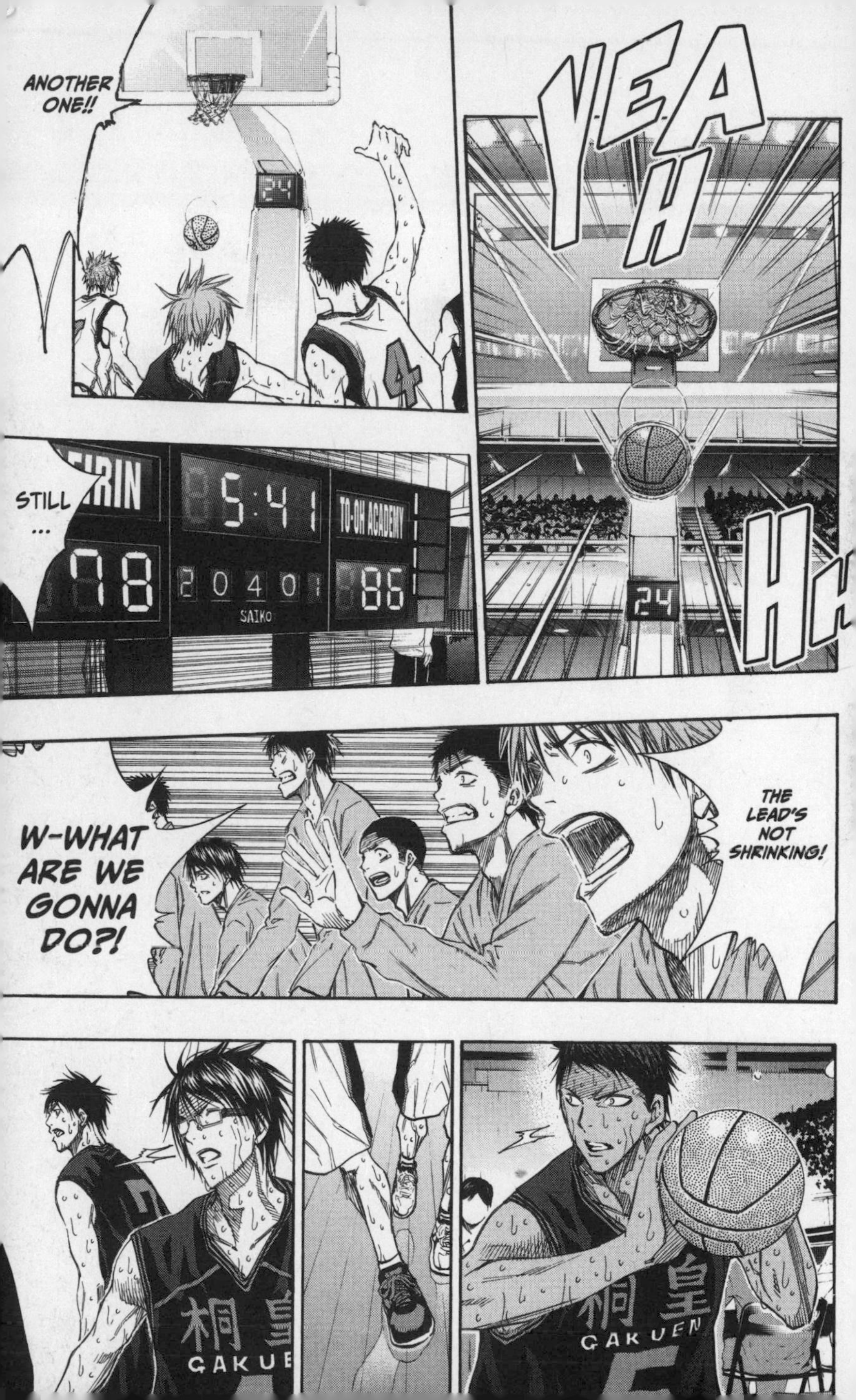
YEAH
HH
ANOTHER ONE!!
STILL ...
TO-OH ACADEMY
5:41
78
86
SAIKO
THE LEAD'S NOT SHRINKING!
W-WHAT ARE WE GONNA DO?!
桐皇
GAKUEN

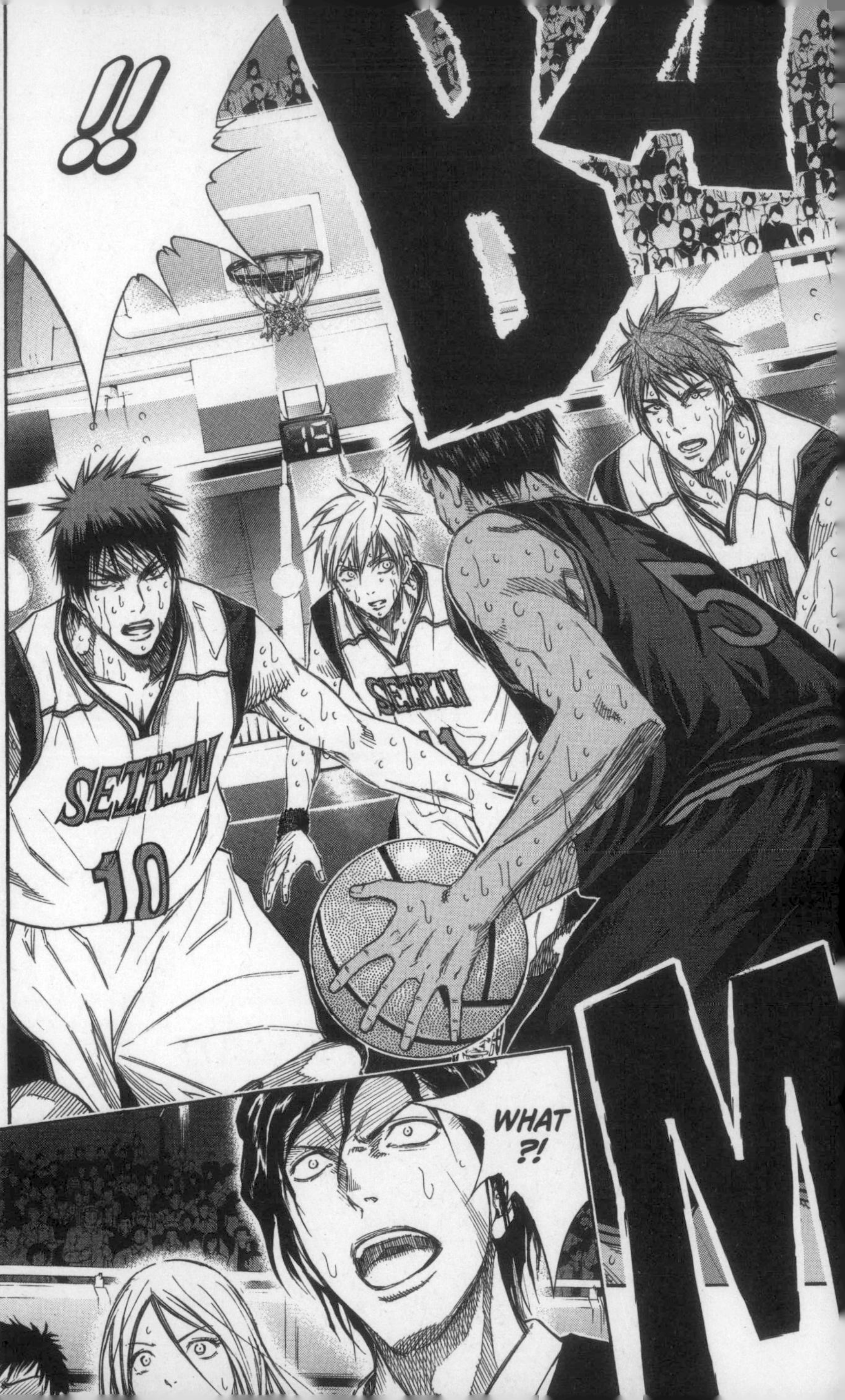
!!
WHAT ?!

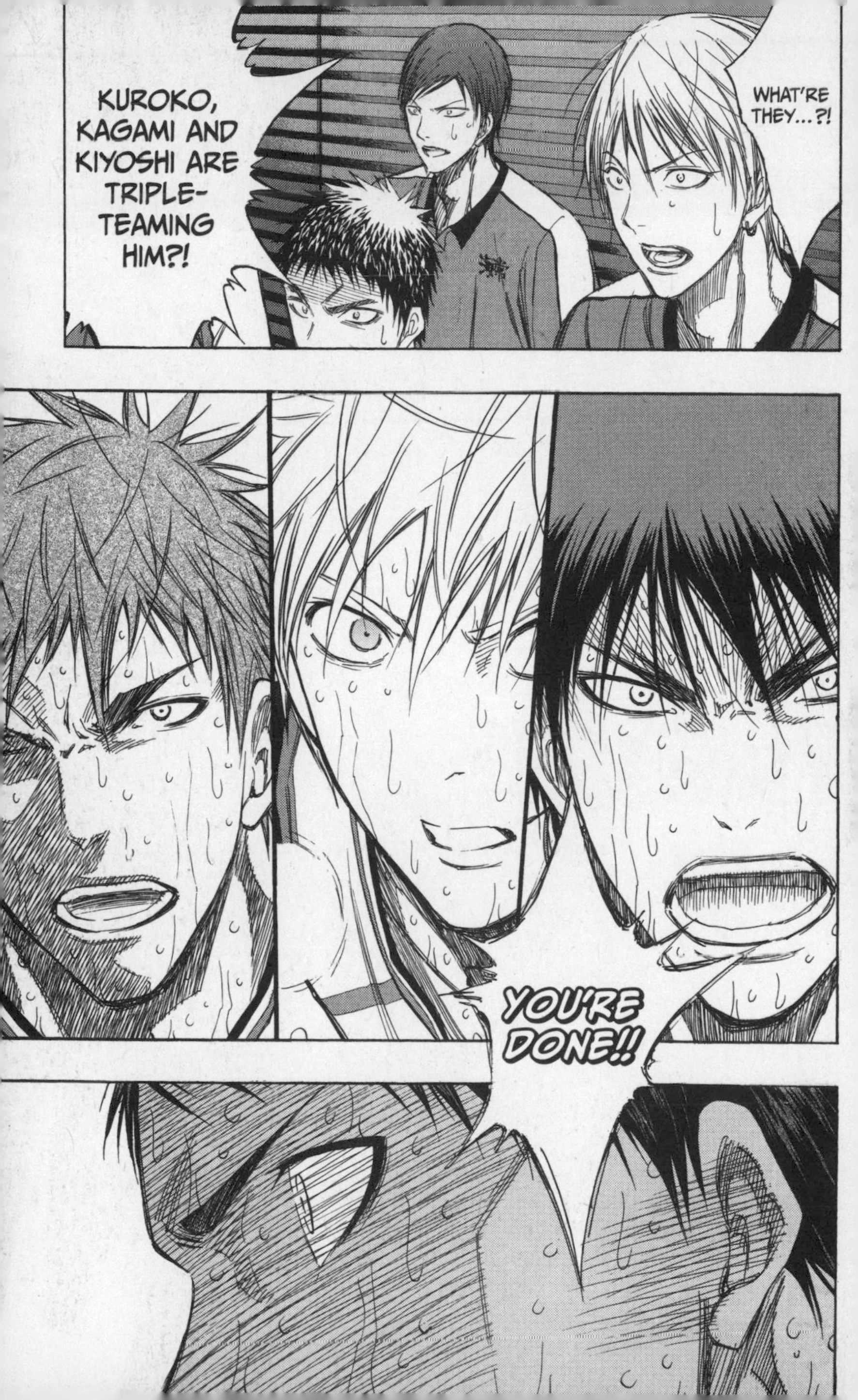
WHAT'RE THEY...?!
KUROKO, KAGAMI AND KIYOSHI ARE TRIPLE-TEAMING HIM?!
YOU'RE DONE!!

KUROKO'S BASKETBALL BLOOPERS TAKE 5

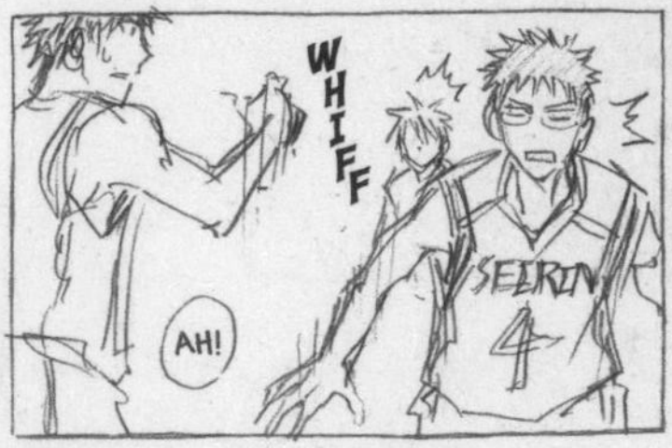
WHIFF
AH!

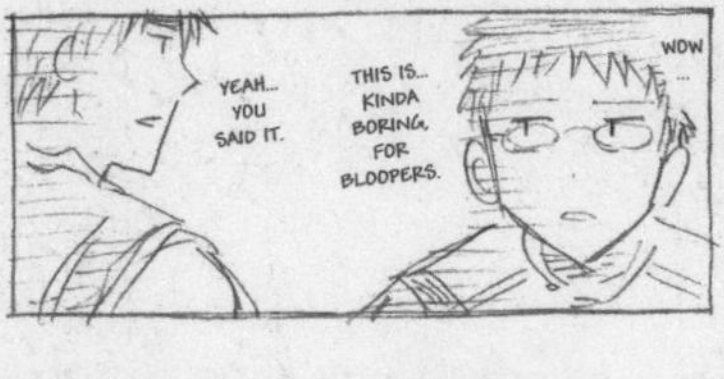
WOW...
THIS IS... KINDA BORING, FOR BLOOPERS.
YEAH... YOU SAID IT.

132ND QUARTER: CAN'T STOP AOMINE-KUN

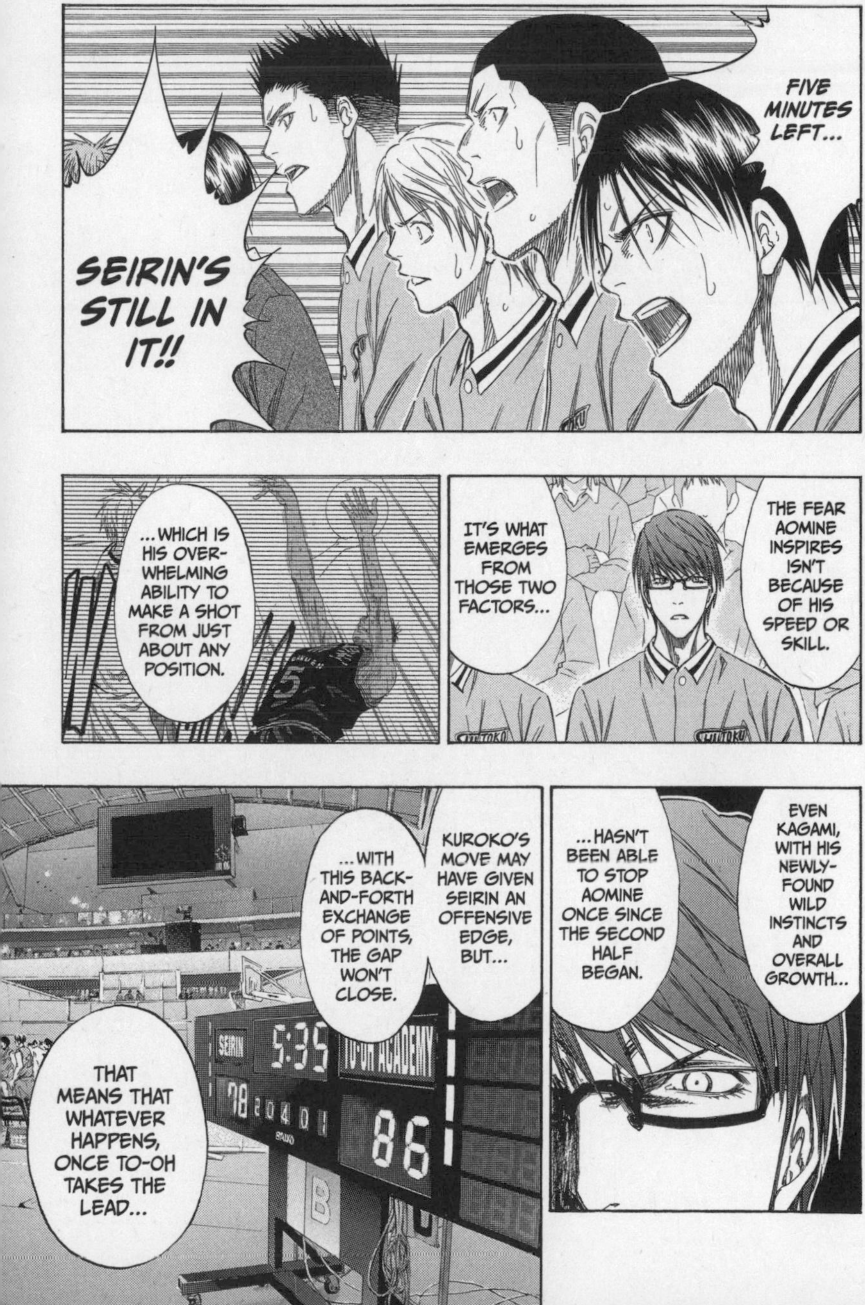
FIVE MINUTES LEFT...
SEIRIN'S STILL IN IT!!
THE FEAR AOMINE INSPIRES ISN'T BECAUSE OF HIS SPEED OR SKILL.
IT'S WHAT EMERGES FROM THOSE TWO FACTORS...
...WHICH IS HIS OVERWHELMING ABILITY TO MAKE A SHOT FROM JUST ABOUT ANY POSITION.
EVEN KAGAMI, WITH HIS NEWLY-FOUND WILD INSTINCTS AND OVERALL GROWTH...
...HASN'T BEEN ABLE TO STOP AOMINE ONCE SINCE THE SECOND HALF BEGAN.
KUROKO'S MOVE MAY HAVE GIVEN SEIRIN AN OFFENSIVE EDGE, BUT...
...WITH THIS BACK-AND-FORTH EXCHANGE OF POINTS, THE GAP WON'T CLOSE.
SEIRIN
5:35
TO-OH ACADEMY
78
86
THAT MEANS THAT WHATEVER HAPPENS, ONCE TO-OH TAKES THE LEAD...

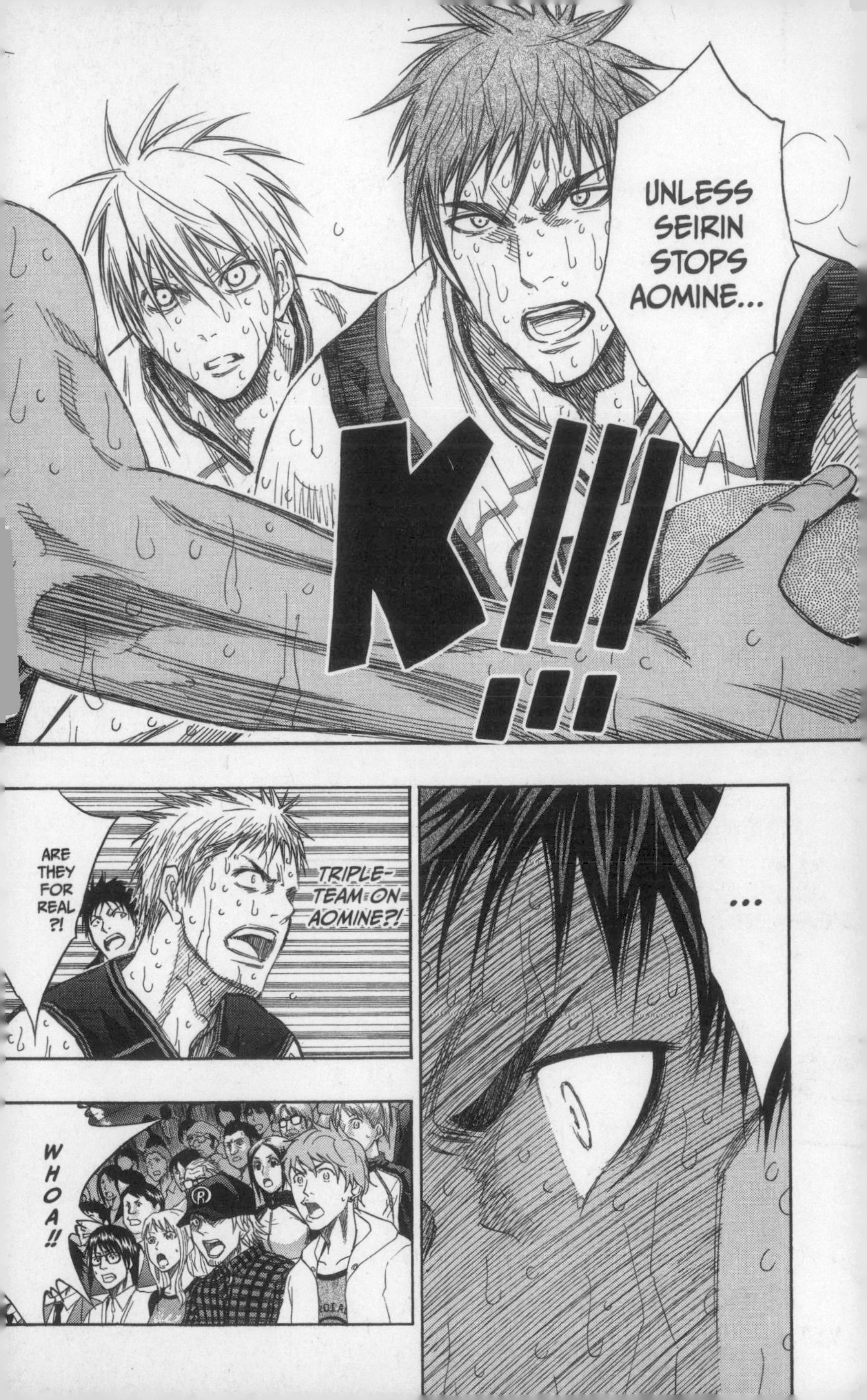
UNLESS SEIRIN STOPS AOMINE...
...
TRIPLE-TEAM ON AOMINE?!
ARE THEY FOR REAL ?!
WHOA!!

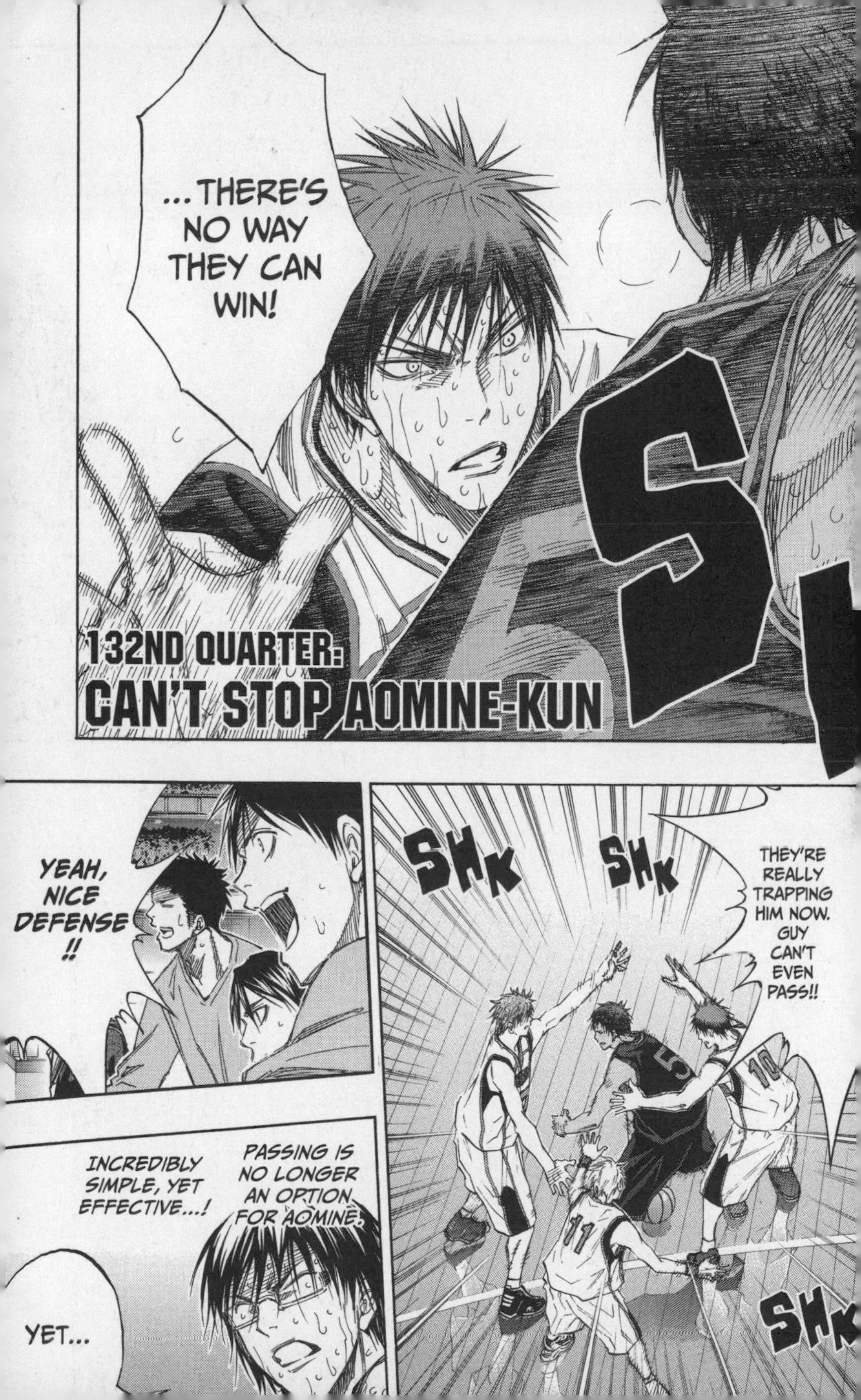
...THERE'S NO WAY THEY CAN WIN!
132ND QUARTER:
CAN'T STOP AOMINE-KUN
THEY'RE REALLY TRAPPING HIM NOW. GUY CAN'T EVEN PASS!!
SHK
SHK
SHK
YEAH, NICE DEFENSE!!
PASSING IS NO LONGER AN OPTION FOR AOMINE.
INCREDIBLY SIMPLE, YET EFFECTIVE...!
YET...

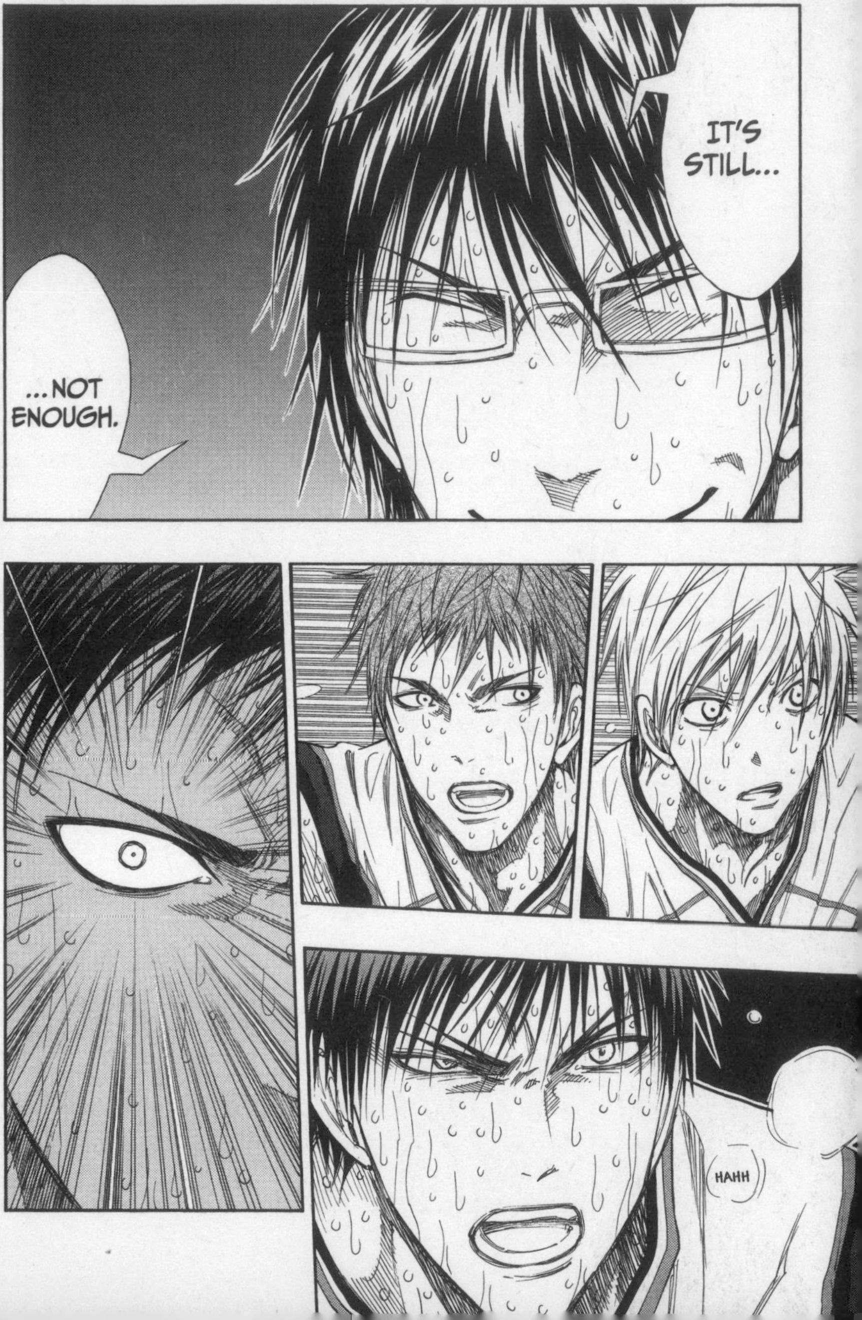
IT'S STILL...
...NOT ENOUGH.
HAHH

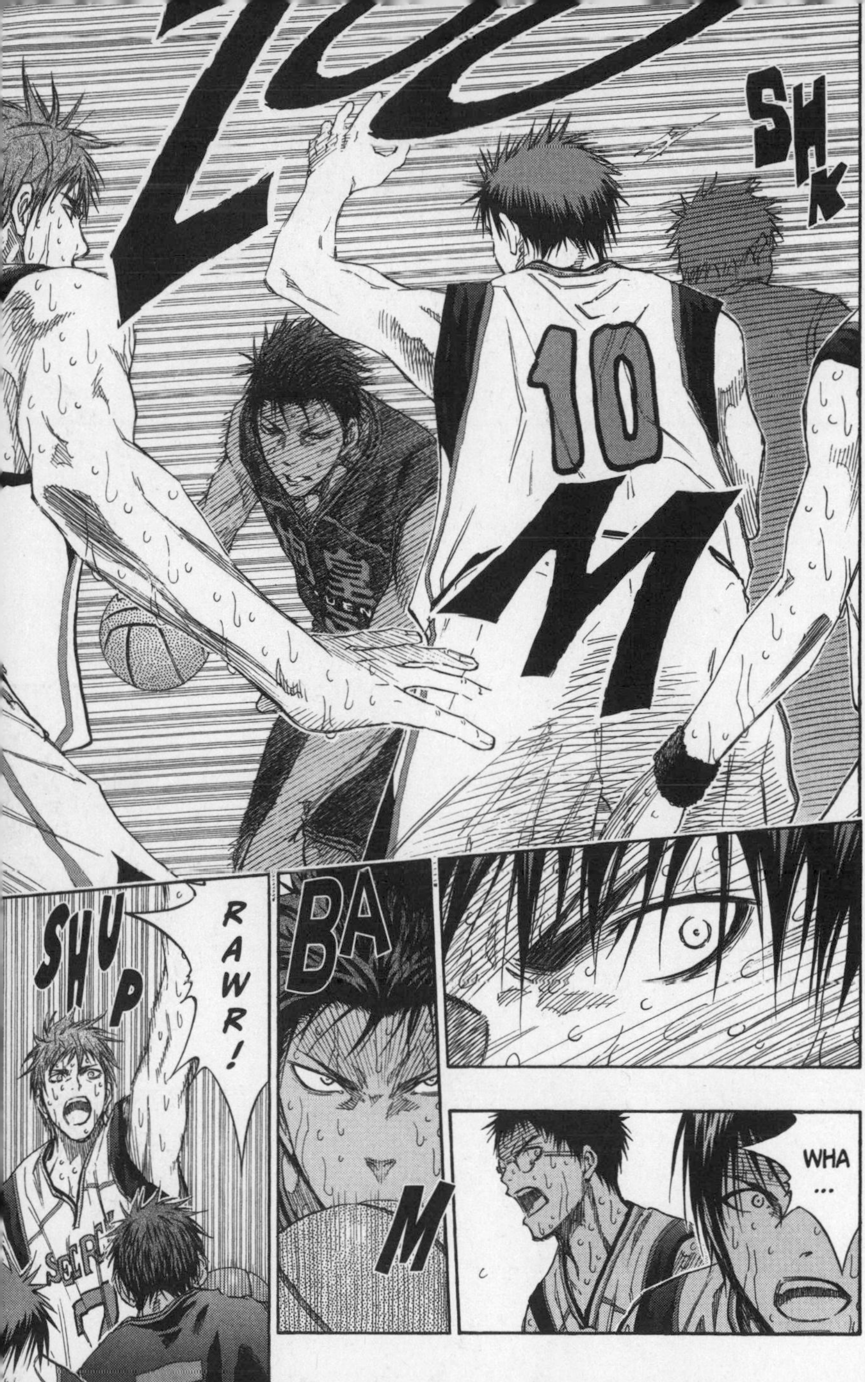
SHK
WHA ...
BAM
RAWR!
SHUP

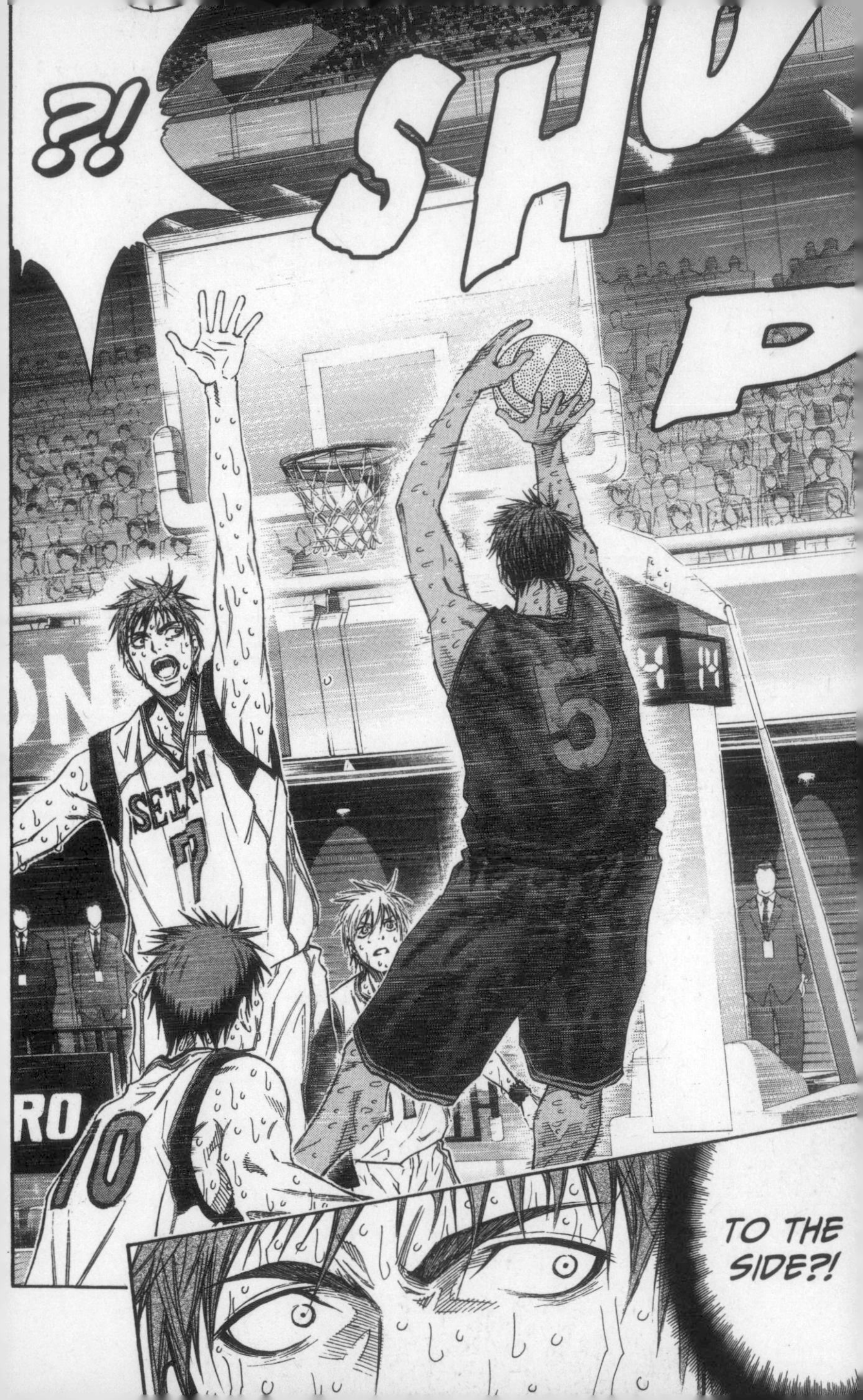
SHUP
?!
TO THE SIDE?!

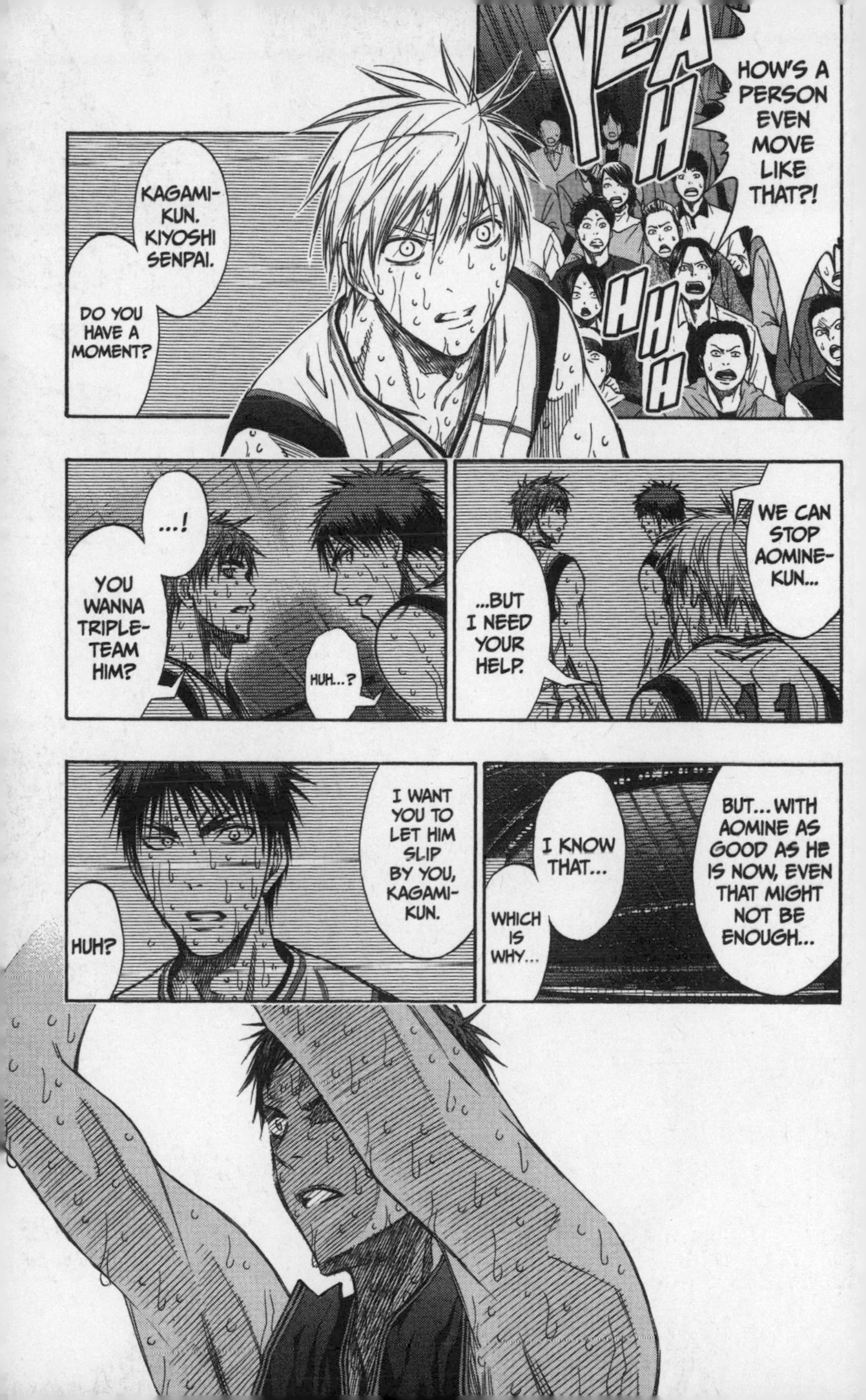
YEAHHHH
HOW'S A PERSON EVEN MOVE LIKE THAT?!
KAGAMI-KUN. KIYOSHI SENPAI.
DO YOU HAVE A MOMENT?
WE CAN STOP AOMINE-KUN...
...BUT I NEED YOUR HELP.
...!
HUH...?
YOU WANNA TRIPLE-TEAM HIM?
BUT... WITH AOMINE AS GOOD AS HE IS NOW, EVEN THAT MIGHT NOT BE ENOUGH...
I KNOW THAT...
WHICH IS WHY...
I WANT YOU TO LET HIM SLIP BY YOU, KAGAMI-KUN.
HUH?

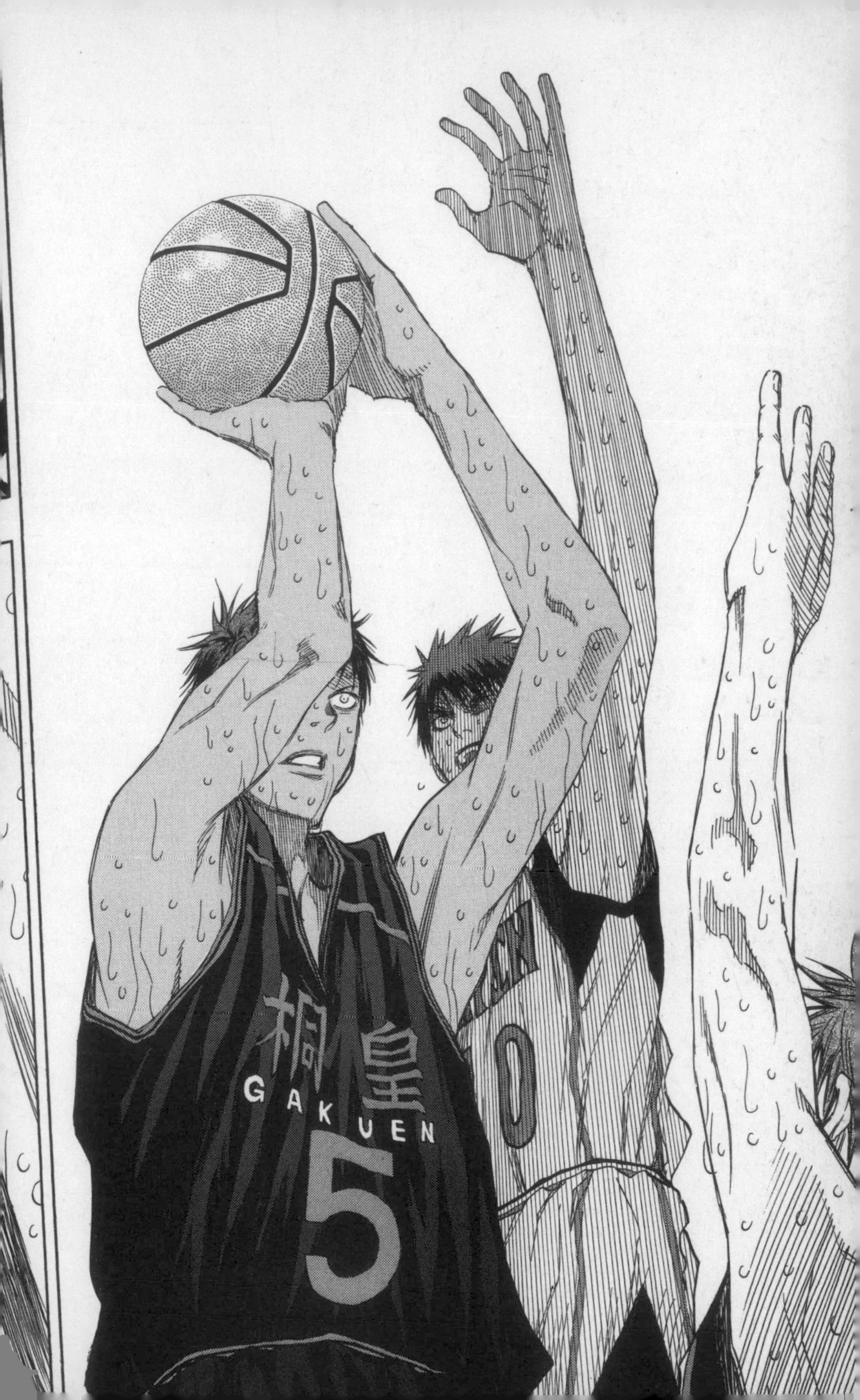
桐皇
GAKUEN
5
0

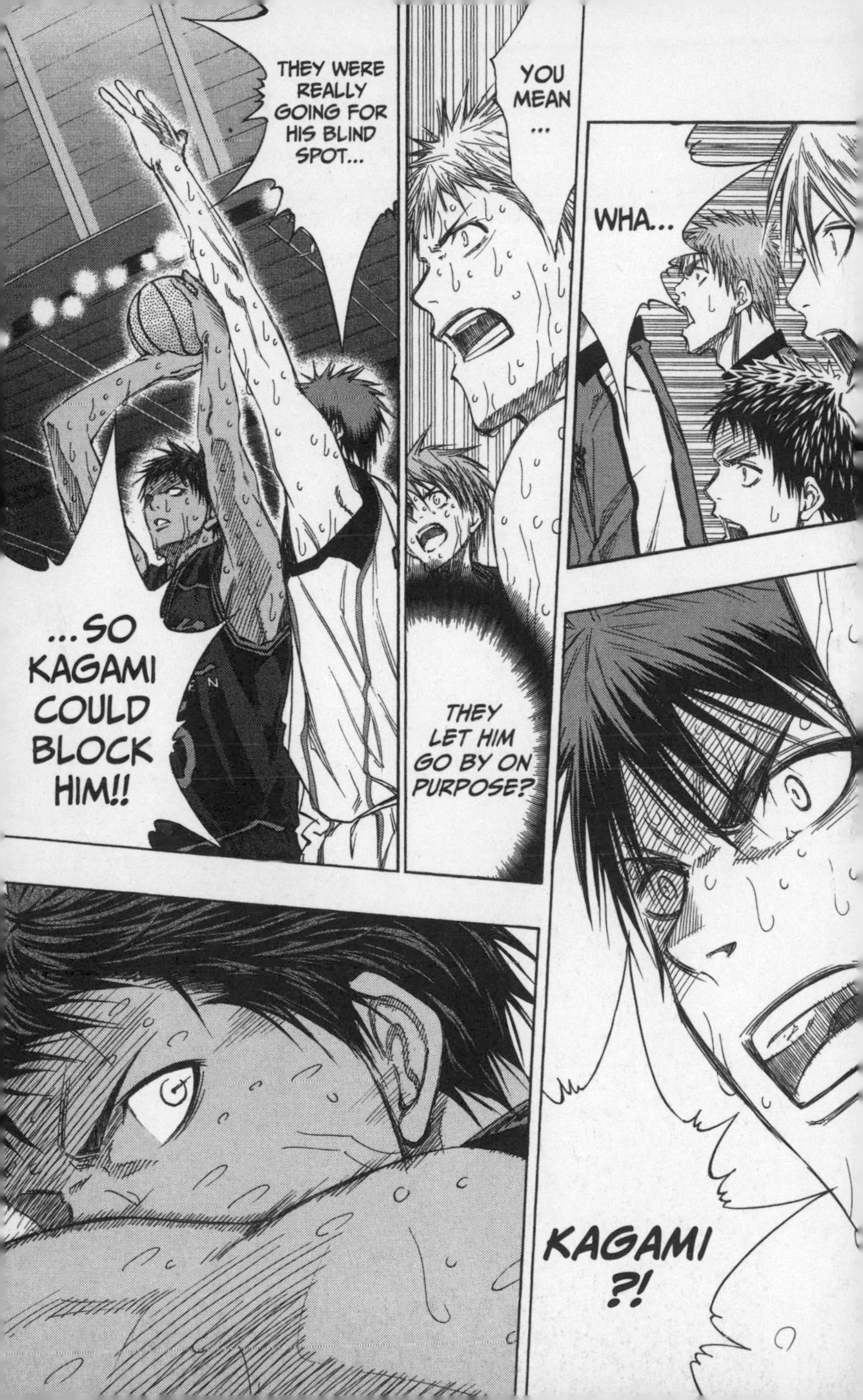
WHA...
YOU MEAN ...
THEY LET HIM GO BY ON PURPOSE?
THEY WERE REALLY GOING FOR HIS BLIND SPOT...
...SO KAGAMI COULD BLOCK HIM!!
KAGAMI ?!

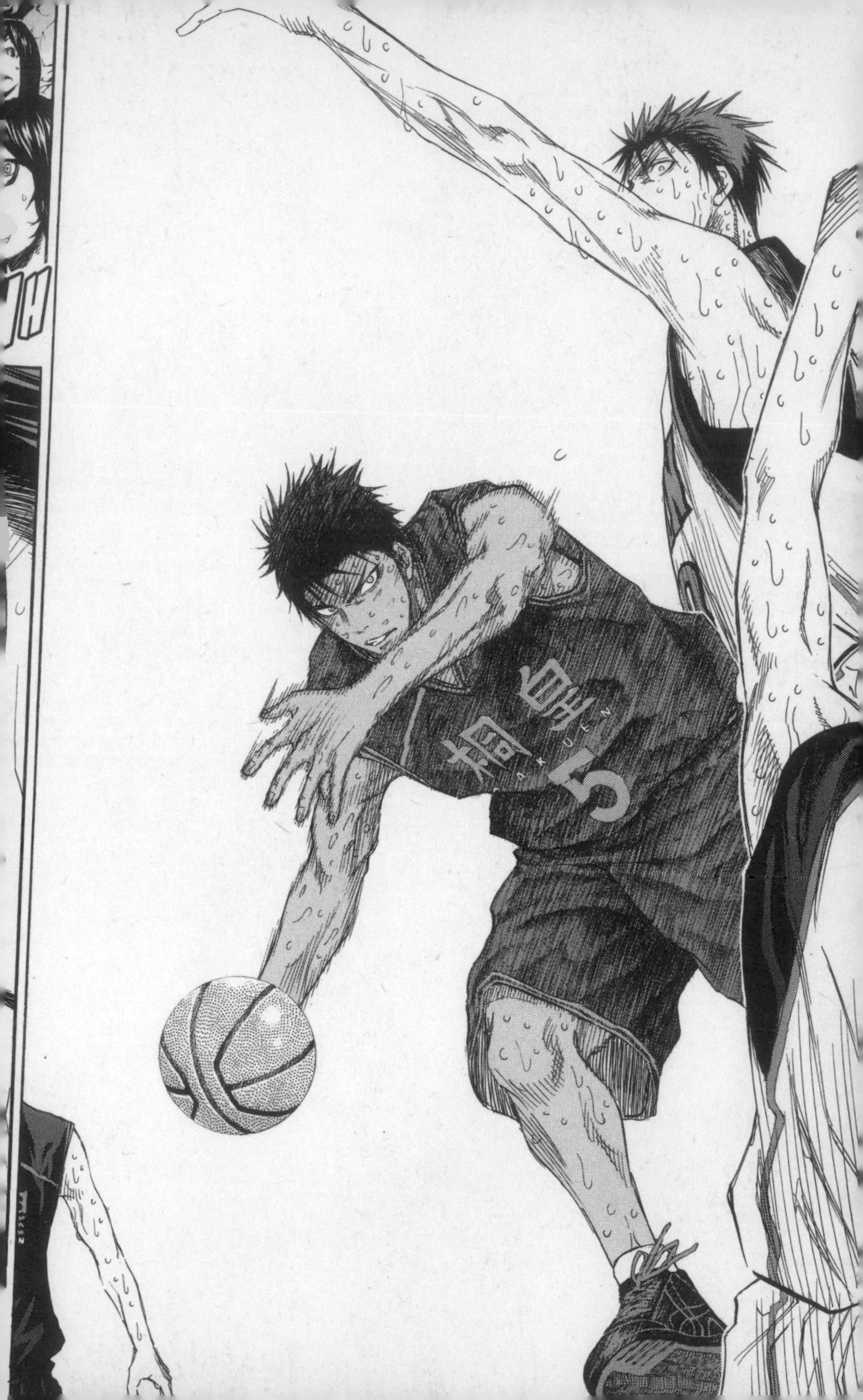

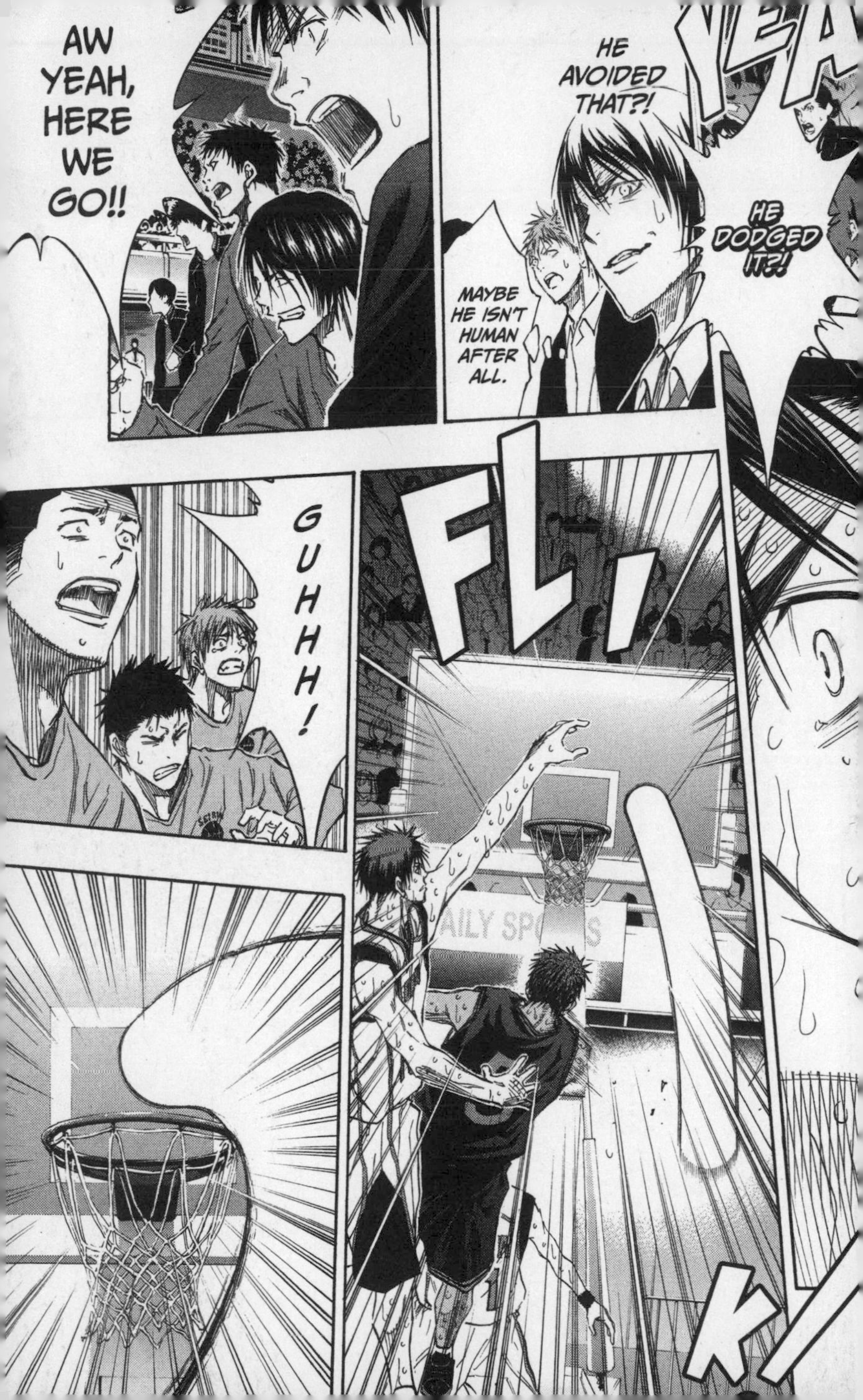
YEA
HE AVOIDED THAT?!
HE DODGED IT?!
MAYBE HE ISN'T HUMAN AFTER ALL.
AW YEAH, HERE WE GO!!
FLI
K
GUHHHH!
AILY SPO S

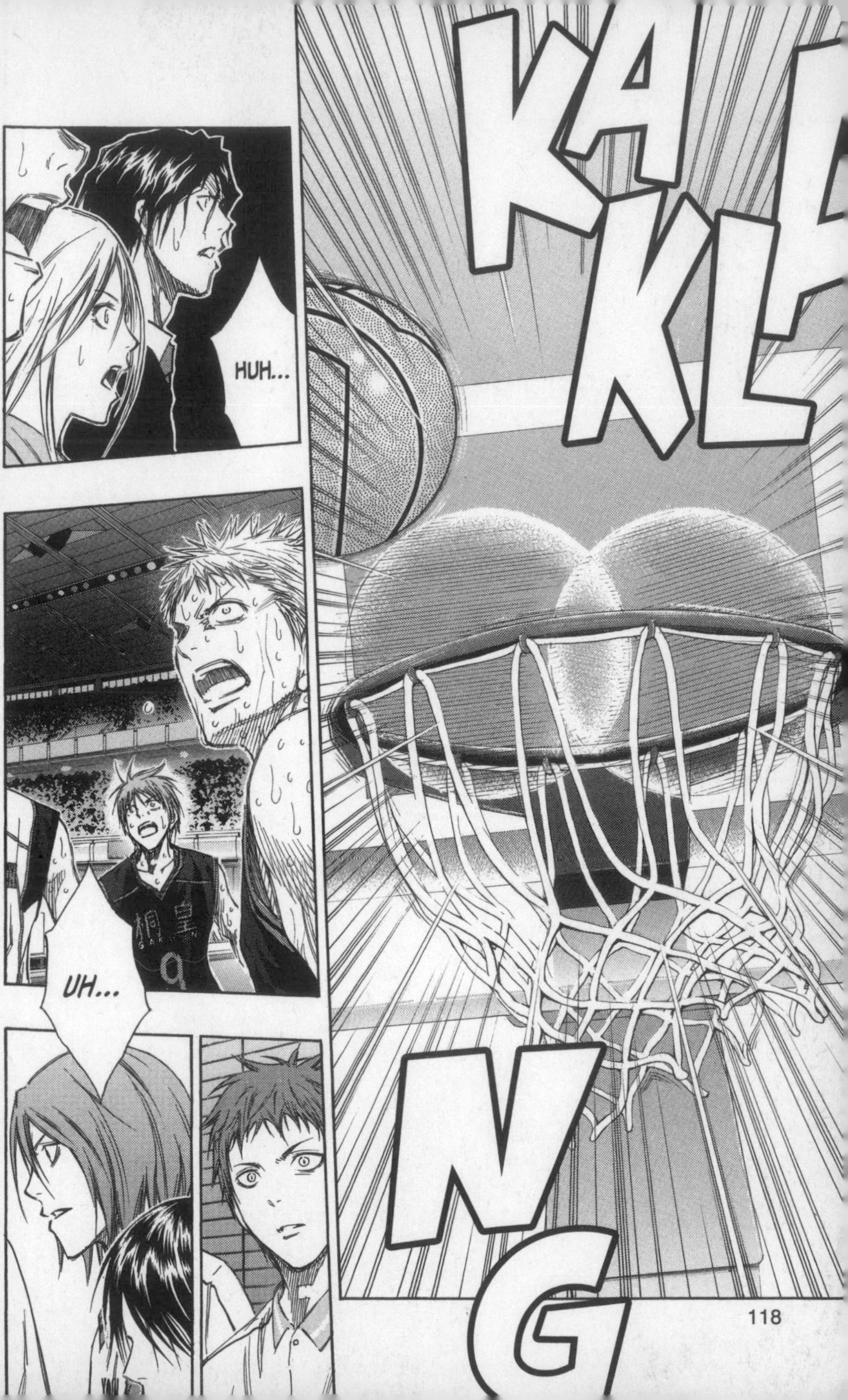
KA
KL
N
G
HUH...
UH...

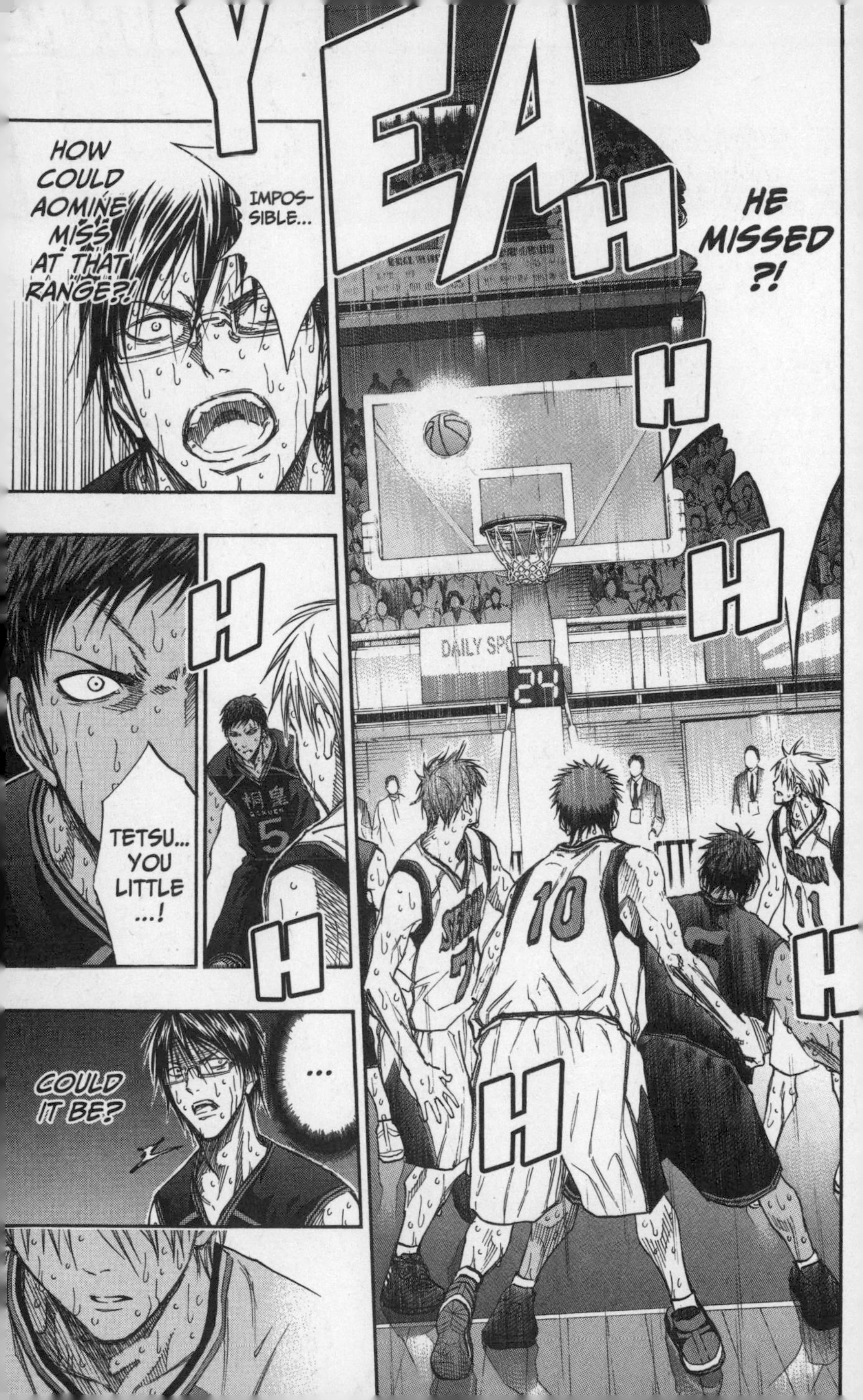
YEAHHHHHHH
HE MISSED ?!
HOW COULD AOMINE MISS AT THAT RANGE?!
IMPOSSIBLE...
TETSU... YOU LITTLE ...!
...
COULD IT BE?

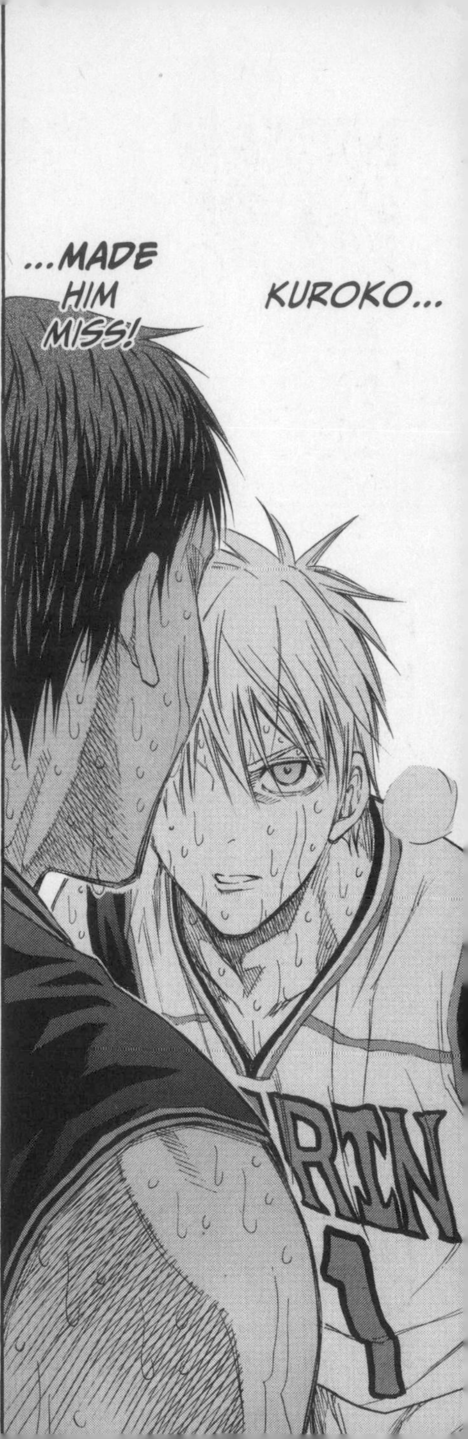
KUROKO...
...MADE HIM MISS!

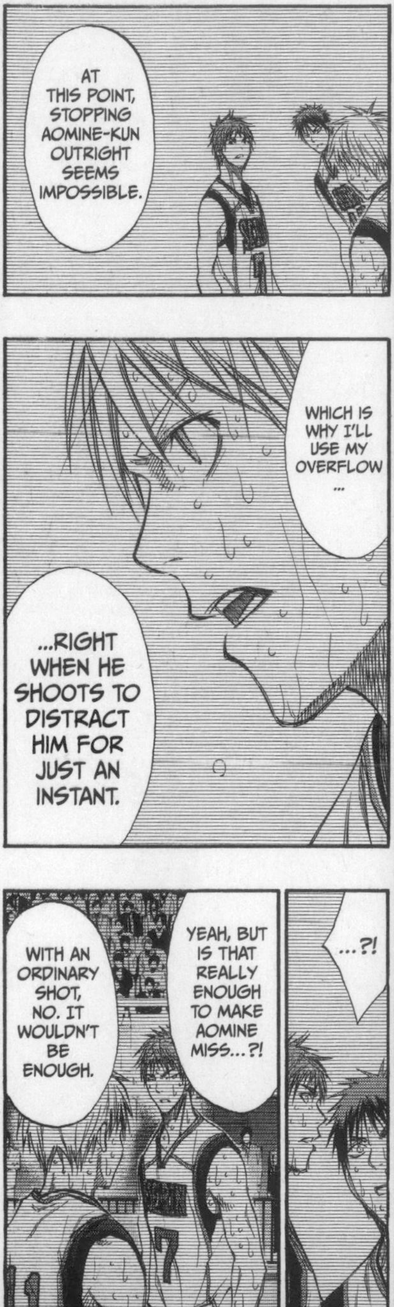
AT THIS POINT, STOPPING AOMINE-KUN OUTRIGHT SEEMS IMPOSSIBLE.
WHICH IS WHY I'LL USE MY OVERFLOW...
...RIGHT WHEN HE SHOOTS TO DISTRACT HIM FOR JUST AN INSTANT.
...?!
YEAH, BUT IS THAT REALLY ENOUGH TO MAKE AOMINE MISS...?!
WITH AN ORDINARY SHOT, NO. IT WOULDN'T BE ENOUGH.

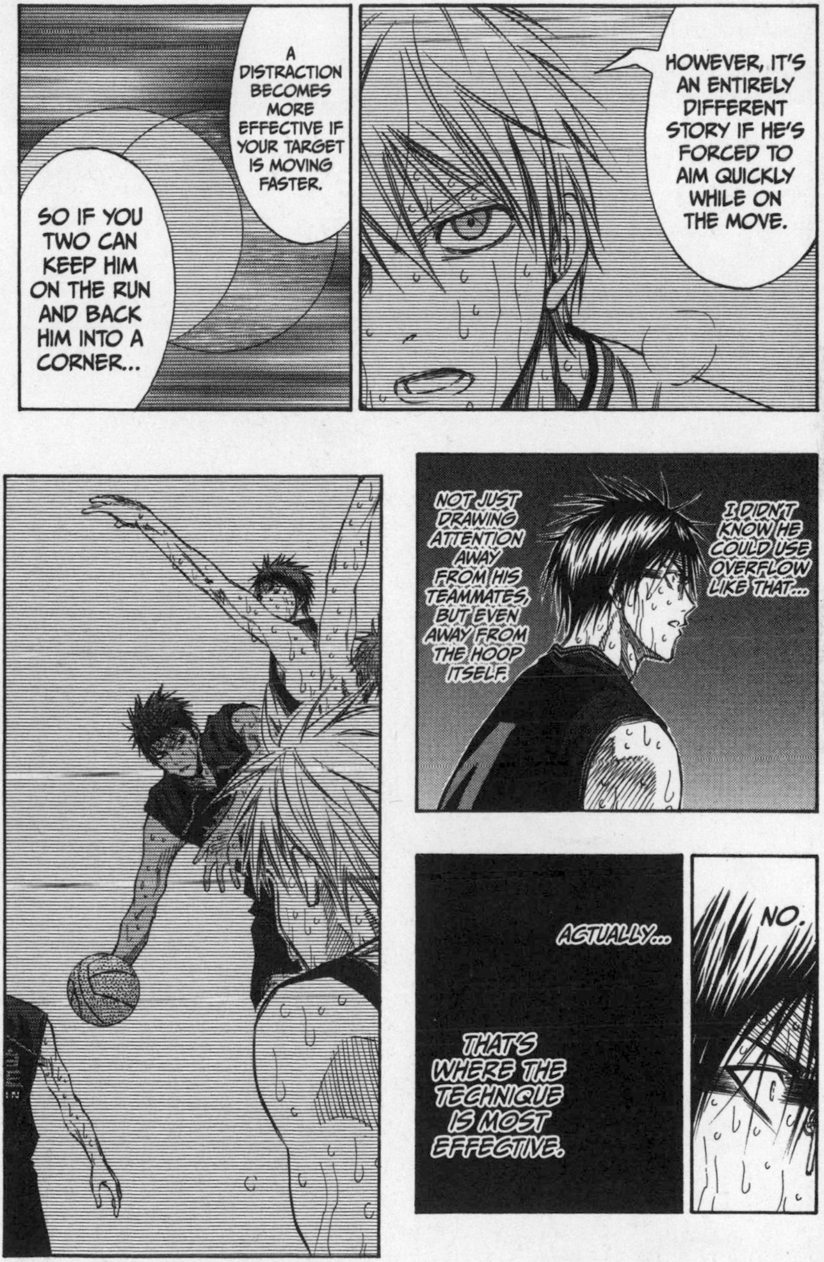
HOWEVER, IT'S AN ENTIRELY DIFFERENT STORY IF HE'S FORCED TO AIM QUICKLY WHILE ON THE MOVE.
A DISTRACTION BECOMES MORE EFFECTIVE IF YOUR TARGET IS MOVING FASTER.
SO IF YOU TWO CAN KEEP HIM ON THE RUN AND BACK HIM INTO A CORNER...
I DIDN'T KNOW HE COULD USE OVERFLOW LIKE THAT...
NOT JUST DRAWING ATTENTION AWAY FROM HIS TEAMMATES, BUT EVEN AWAY FROM THE HOOP ITSELF.
NO.
ACTUALLY...
THAT'S WHERE THE TECHNIQUE IS MOST EFFECTIVE.

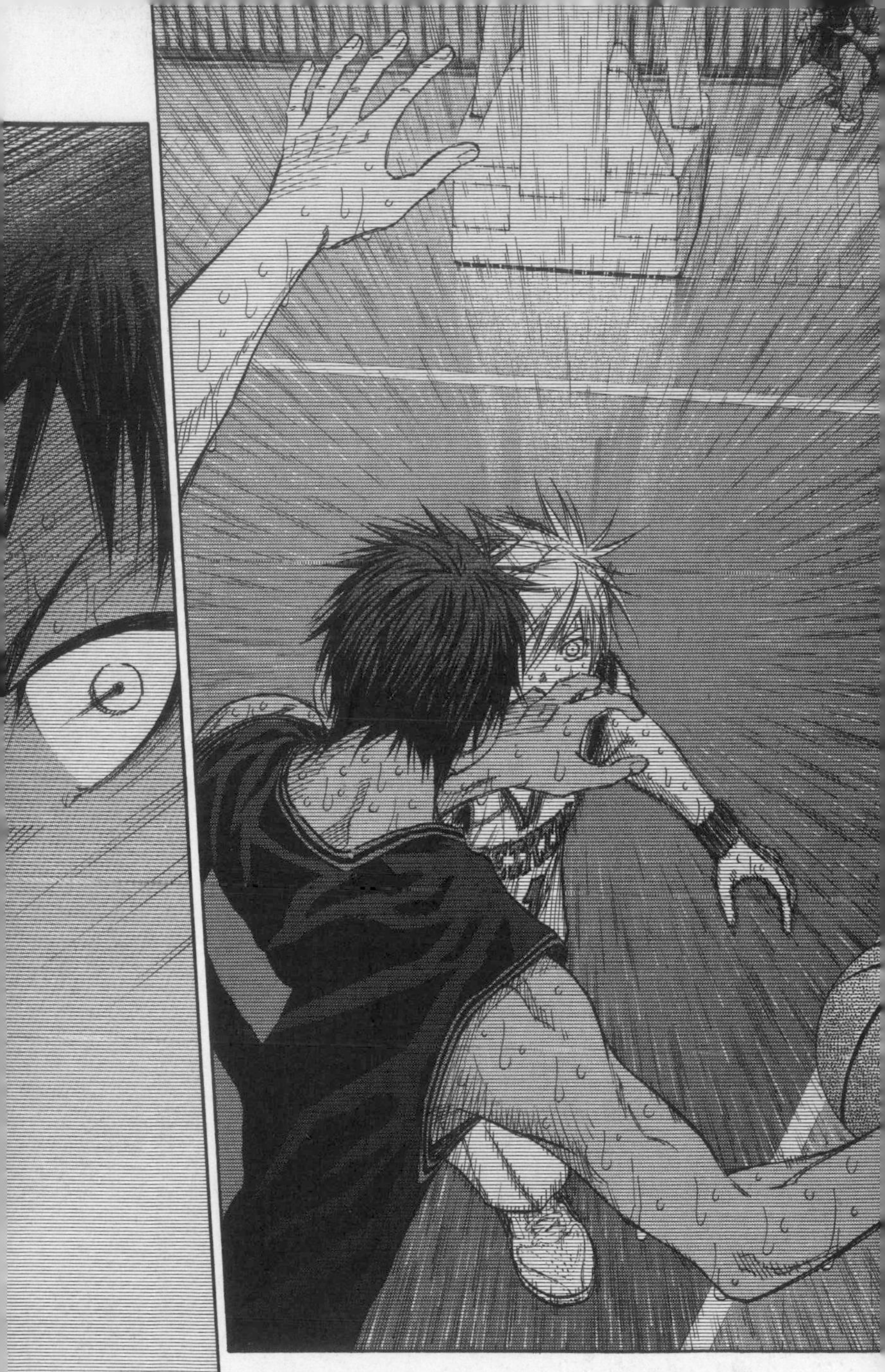

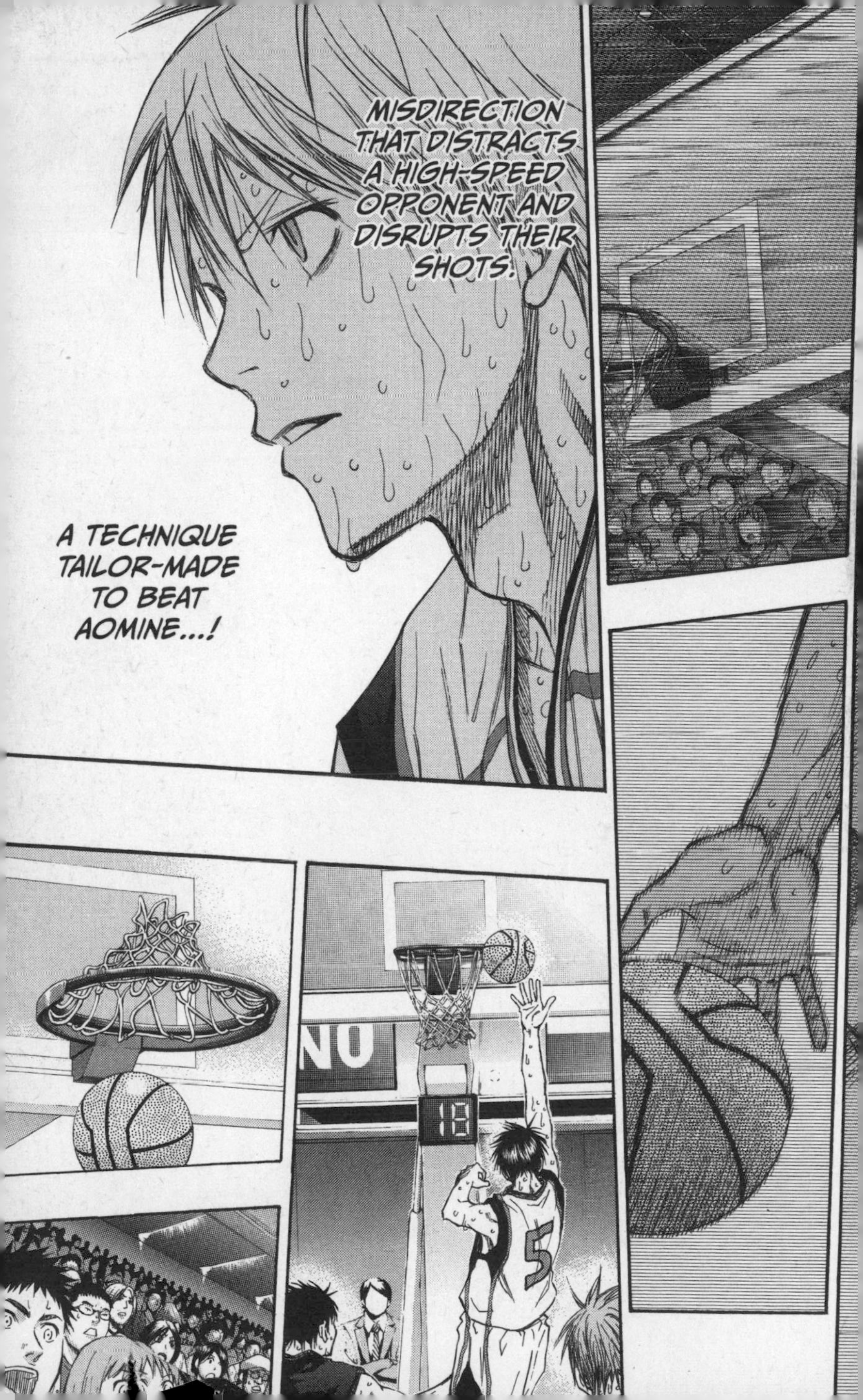
MISDIRECTION THAT DISTRACTS A HIGH-SPEED OPPONENT AND DISRUPTS THEIR SHOTS.
A TECHNIQUE TAILOR-MADE TO BEAT AOMINE...!
NO
18
5

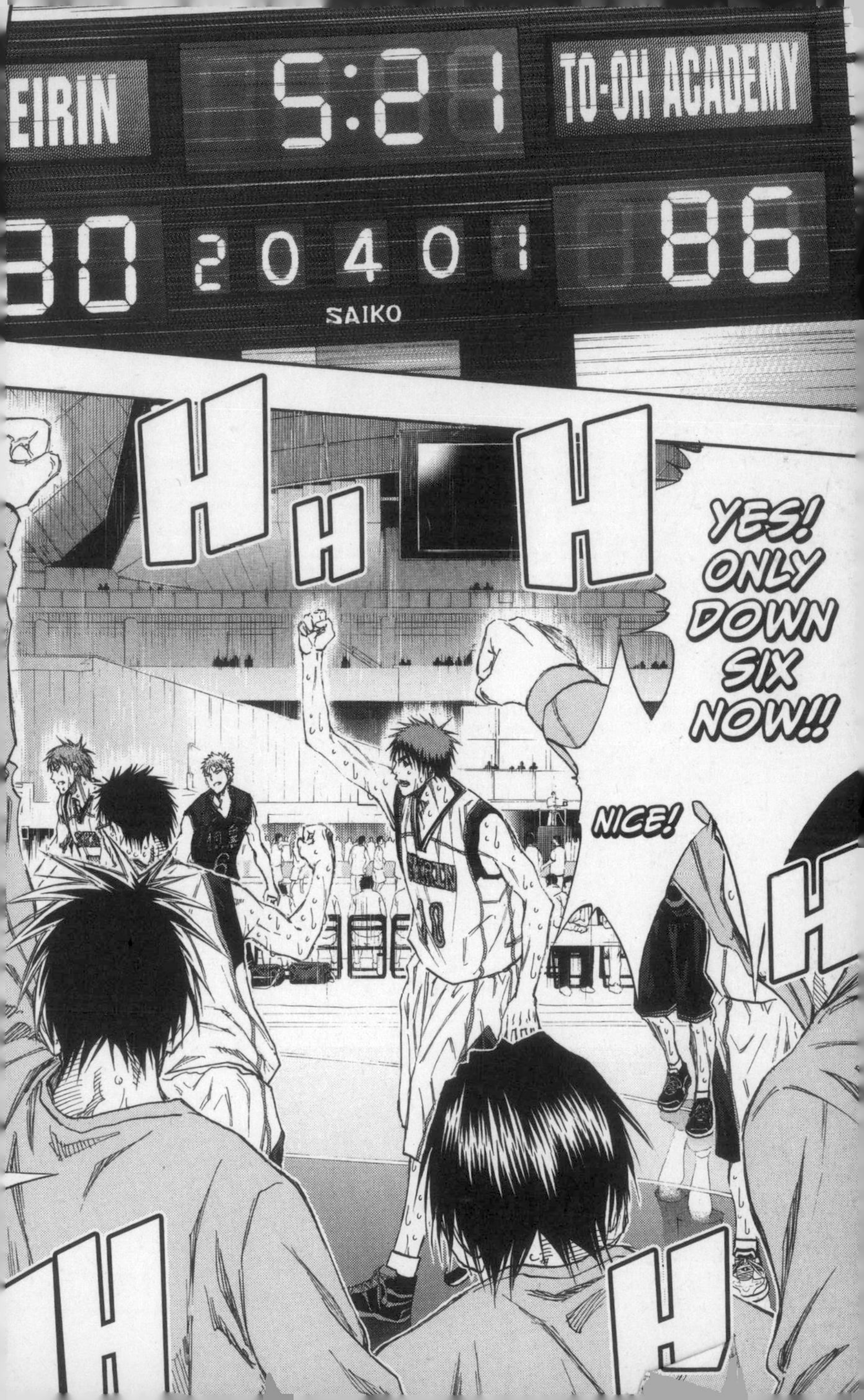
TO-OH ACADEMY
EIRIN
5:21
80
86
SAIKO
YES! ONLY DOWN SIX NOW!!
NICE!
H H H
H
H H

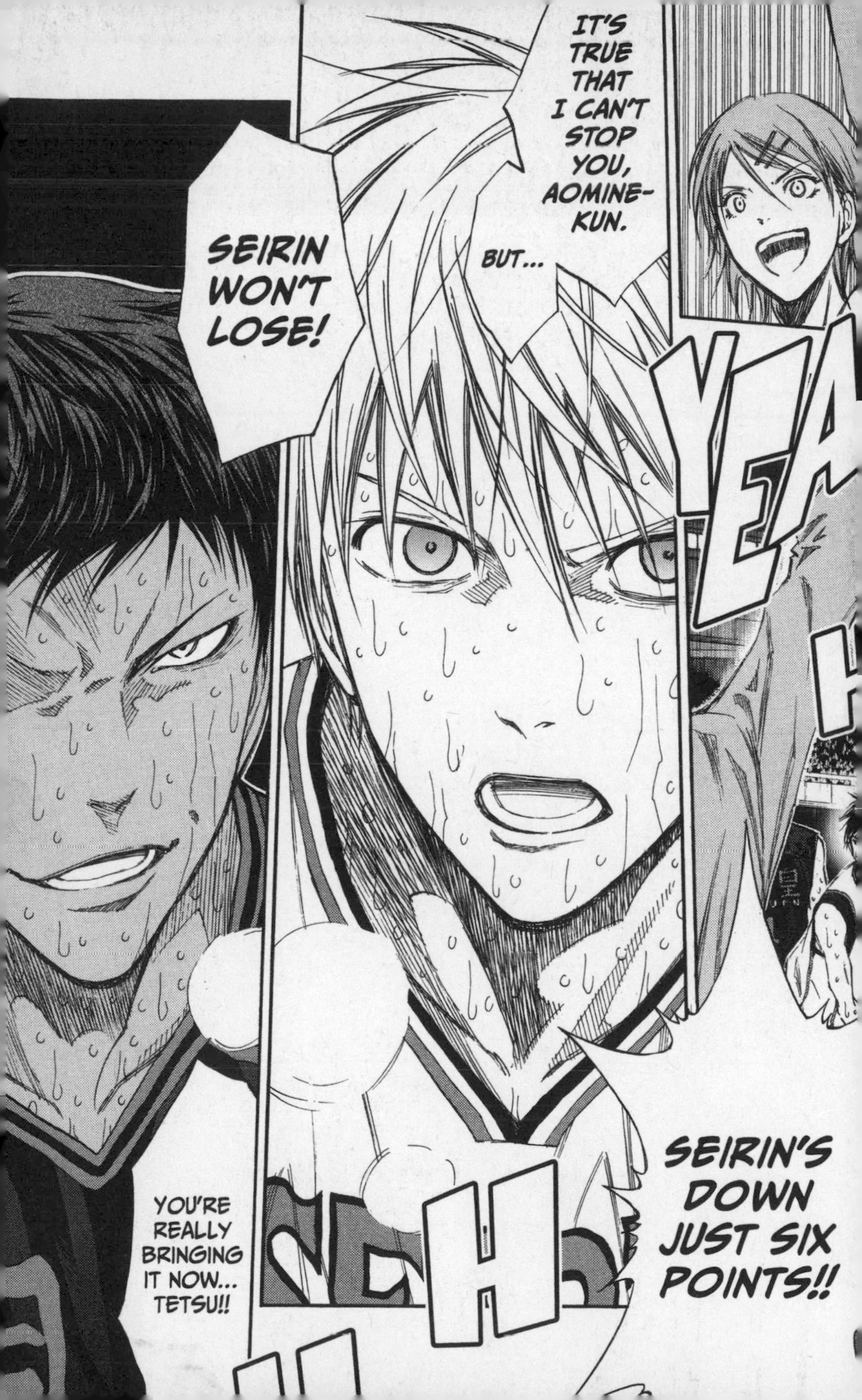
IT'S TRUE THAT I CAN'T STOP YOU, AOMINE-KUN.
BUT...
SEIRIN WON'T LOSE!
YEA
SEIRIN'S DOWN JUST SIX POINTS!!
YOU'RE REALLY BRINGING IT NOW... TETSU!!

KUROKO'S BASKETBALL Q&A (W/ HALFWAY-DECENT ANSWERS)

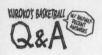

Q. **I WANNA KNOW MORE ABOUT EVERYONE AT SEIRIN! LIKE THEIR BIRTHDAYS AND STUFF... ESPECIALLY KIYOSHI-KUN. ♡ [*LAUGHS*]**
(HANAAME from KAGAWA PREFECTURE)

A. BIRTHDAY / BLOOD TYPE

HYUGA: MAY 16 / A
KIYOSHI: JUN. 10 / O
RIKO: FEB. 5 / A
IZUKI: OCT. 23 / A
KOGANEI: SEP. 11 / B
MITOBE: DEC. 3 / A
TSUCHIDA: MAY 1 / AB
KUROKO: JAN. 31 / A
KAGAMI: AUG. 2 / A
FURIHATA: NOV. 8 / O
KAWAHARA: MAY 18 / B
FUKUDA: APR. 26 / A

KUROKO'S BASKETBALL BLOOPERS
TAKE 8

WHOAAAAA!!

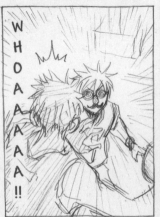

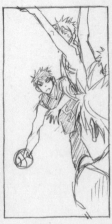

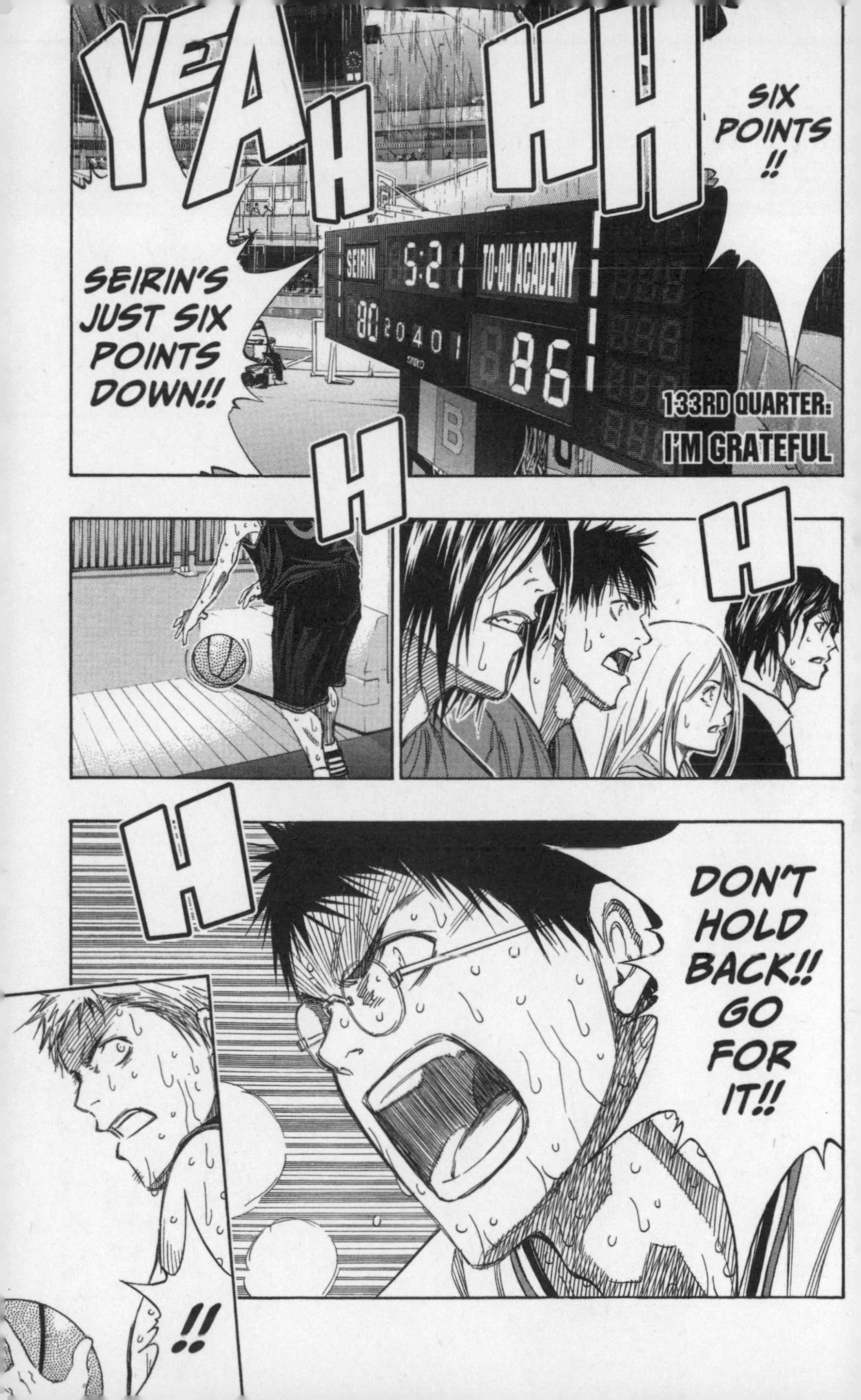
YEAHHHH
SIX POINTS!!
SEIRIN'S JUST SIX POINTS DOWN!!
SEIRIN 5:21 TO-OH ACADEMY
80
86
133RD QUARTER: I'M GRATEFUL
H
H
H
DON'T HOLD BACK!! GO FOR IT!!
!!

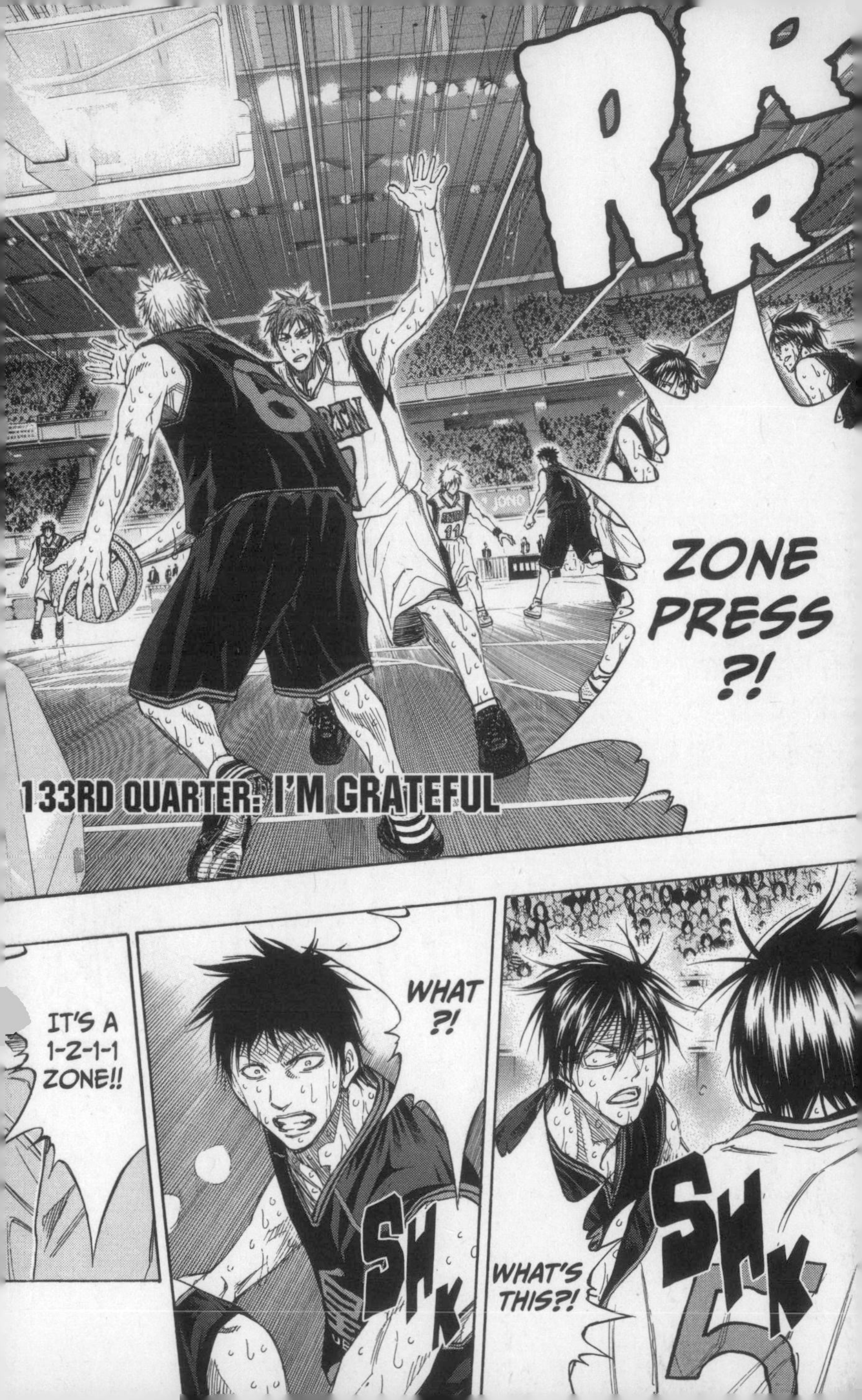
RR
ZONE PRESS ?!
133RD QUARTER: I'M GRATEFUL
WHAT'S THIS?!
SHK
WHAT ?!
SHK
IT'S A 1-2-1-1 ZONE!!

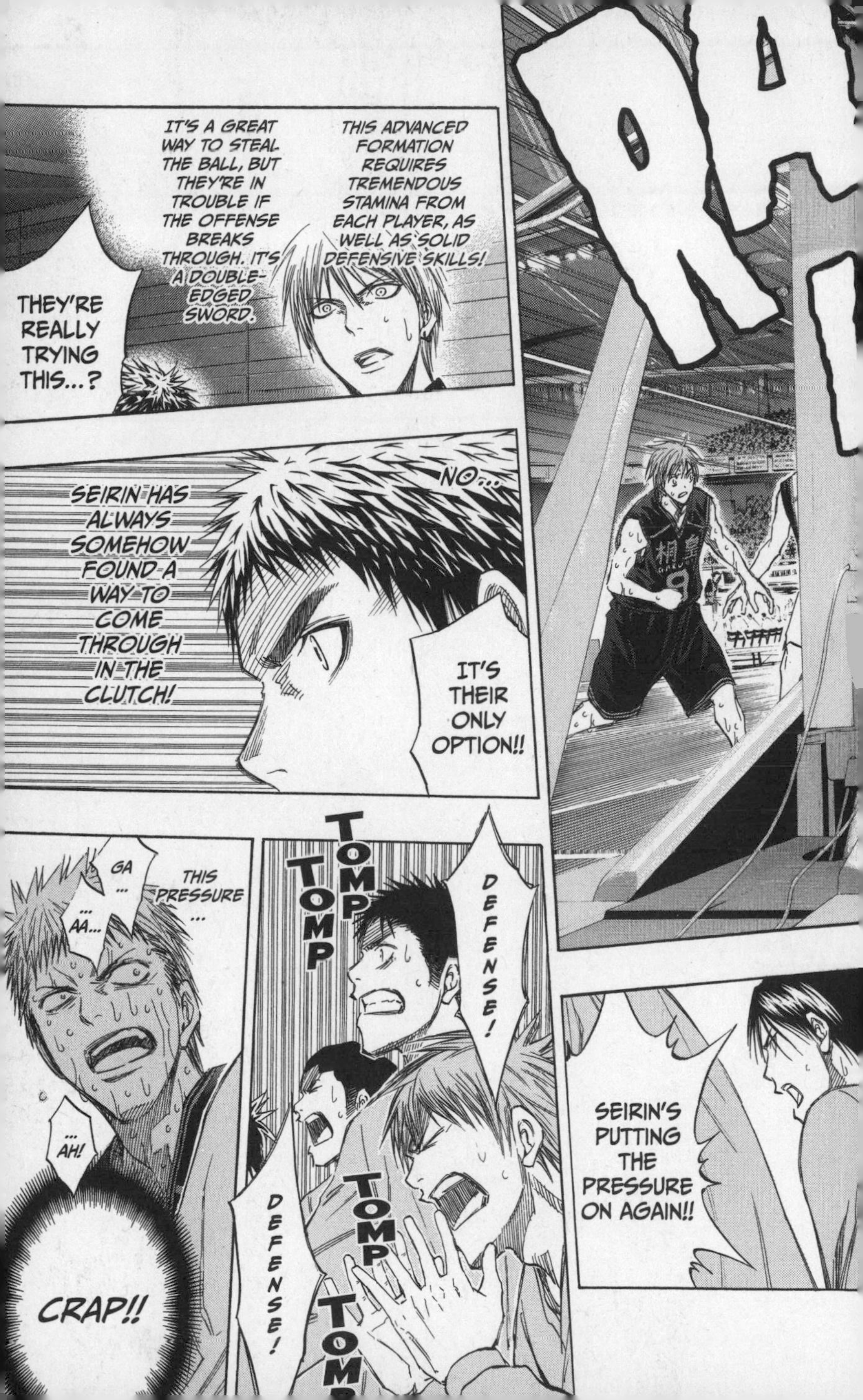
THIS ADVANCED FORMATION REQUIRES TREMENDOUS STAMINA FROM EACH PLAYER, AS WELL AS SOLID DEFENSIVE SKILLS!
IT'S A GREAT WAY TO STEAL THE BALL, BUT THEY'RE IN TROUBLE IF THE OFFENSE BREAKS THROUGH. IT'S A DOUBLE-EDGED SWORD.
THEY'RE REALLY TRYING THIS...?
NO...
SEIRIN HAS ALWAYS SOMEHOW FOUND A WAY TO COME THROUGH IN THE CLUTCH!
IT'S THEIR ONLY OPTION!!
SEIRIN'S PUTTING THE PRESSURE ON AGAIN!!
TOMP TOMP
DEFENSE!
TOMP
DEFENSE!
TOMP
GA... ...AA...
THIS PRESSURE...
...AH!
CRAP!!

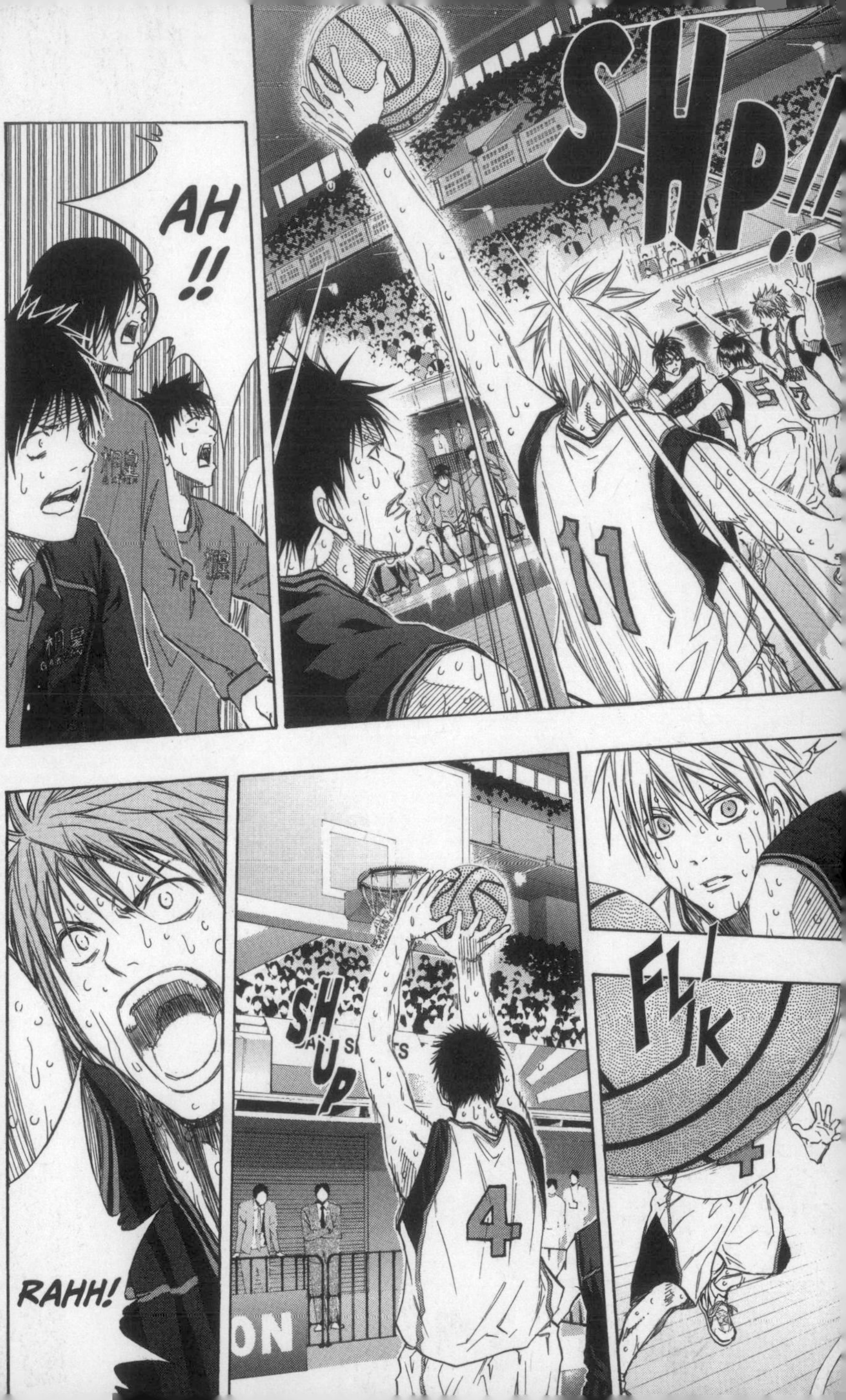
SHP!!
AH!!
FLIK
SHUP
RAHH!

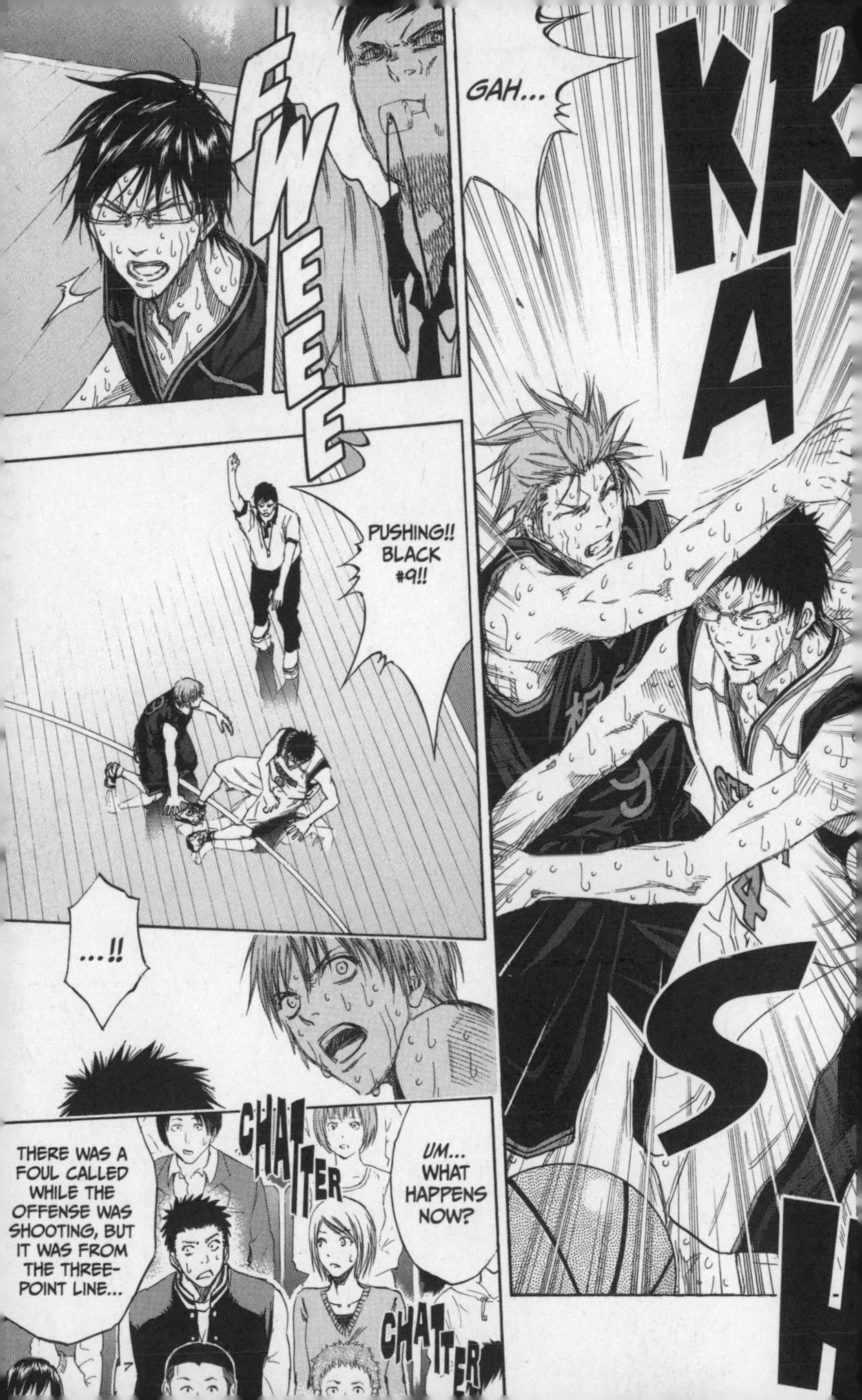
KRASH
GAH...
FWEEE
PUSHING!! BLACK #9!!
...!!
CHATTER
UM... WHAT HAPPENS NOW?
THERE WAS A FOUL CALLED WHILE THE OFFENSE WAS SHOOTING, BUT IT WAS FROM THE THREE-POINT LINE...
CHATTER

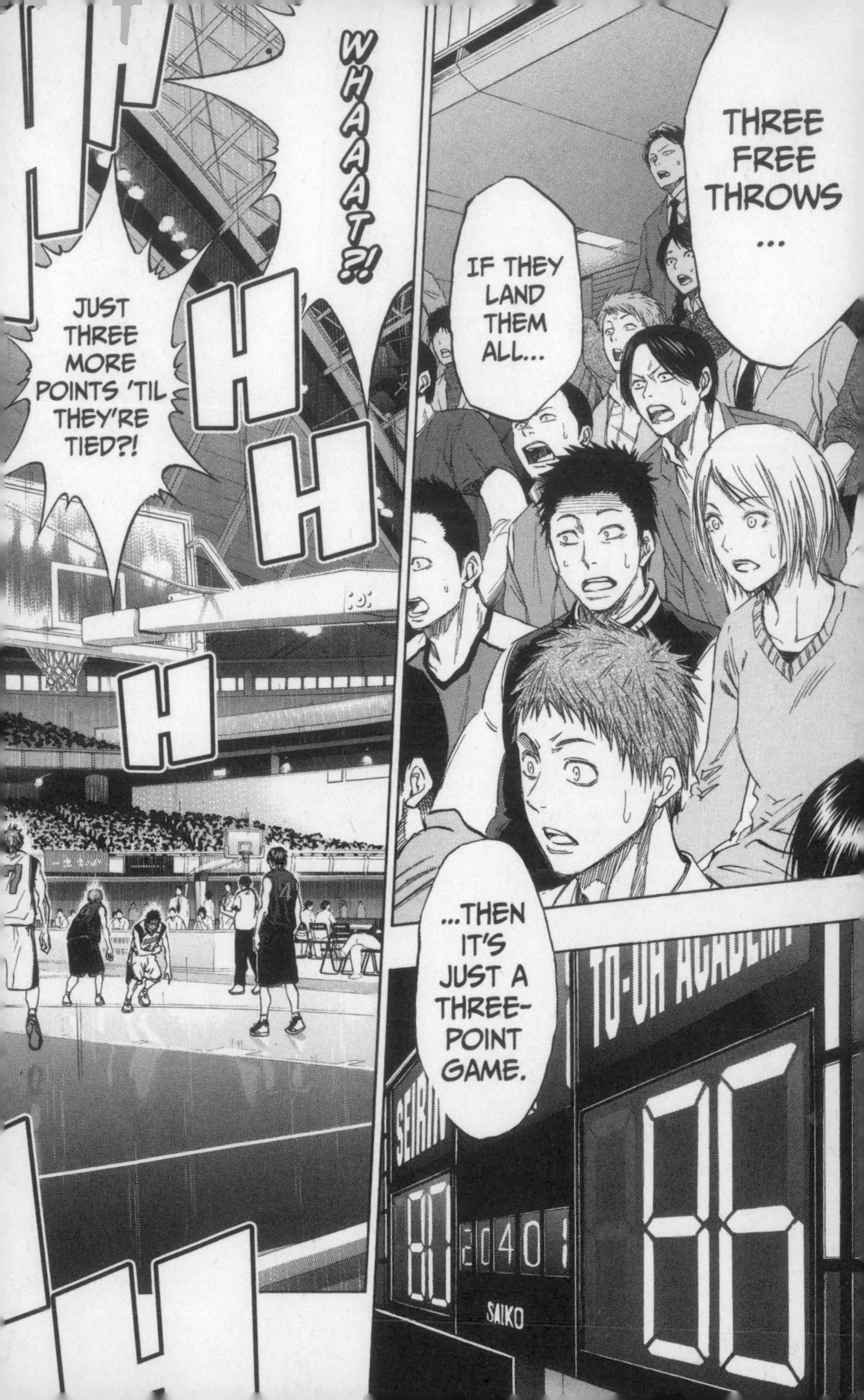
THREE FREE THROWS ...
IF THEY LAND THEM ALL...
...THEN IT'S JUST A THREE-POINT GAME.
TO-OH ACADEMY
SEIRIN
SAIKO
WHAAAAT?!
HHHH
JUST THREE MORE POINTS 'TIL THEY'RE TIED?!

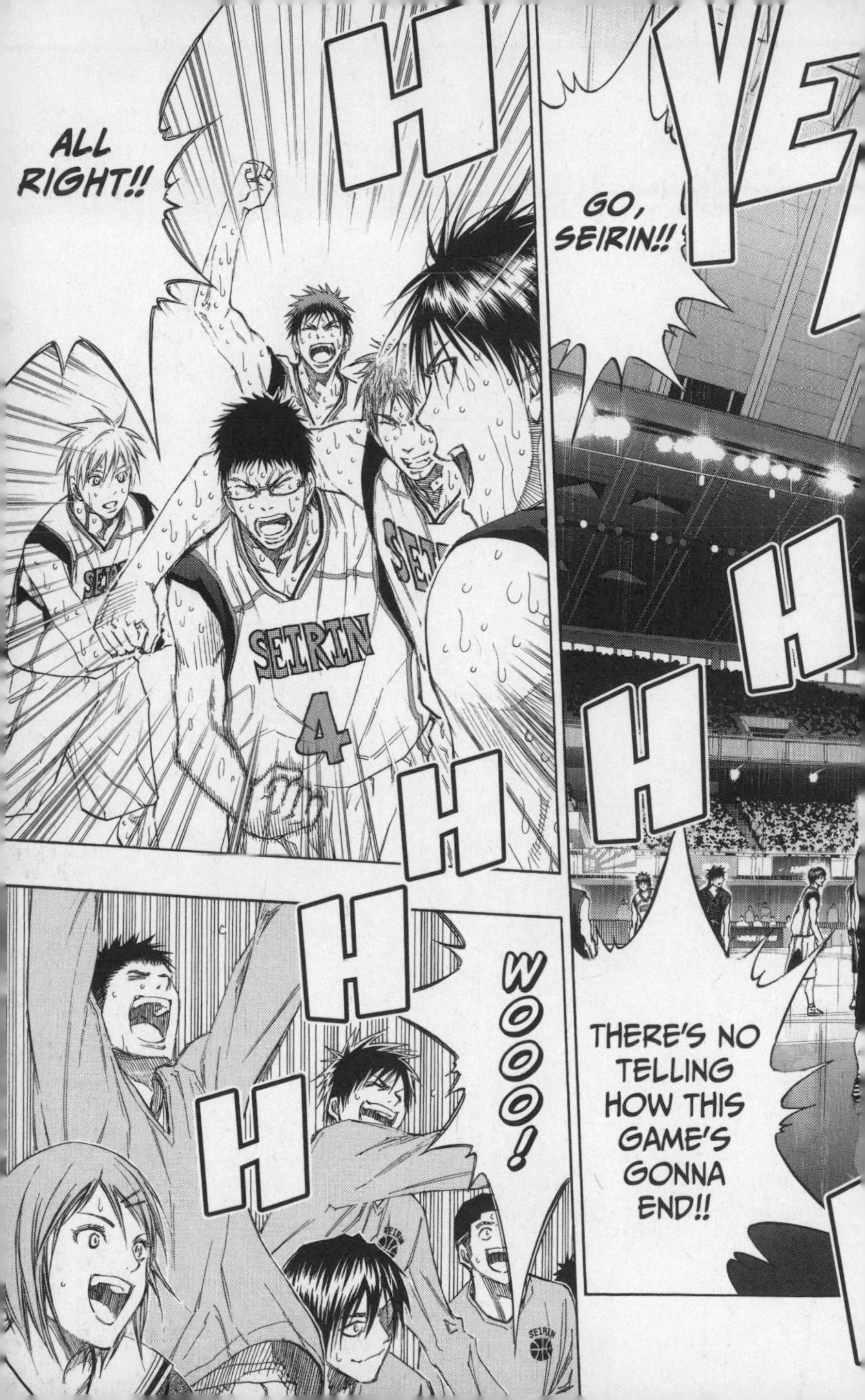
GO, SEIRIN!!
THERE'S NO TELLING HOW THIS GAME'S GONNA END!!
ALL RIGHT!!
WOOOO!

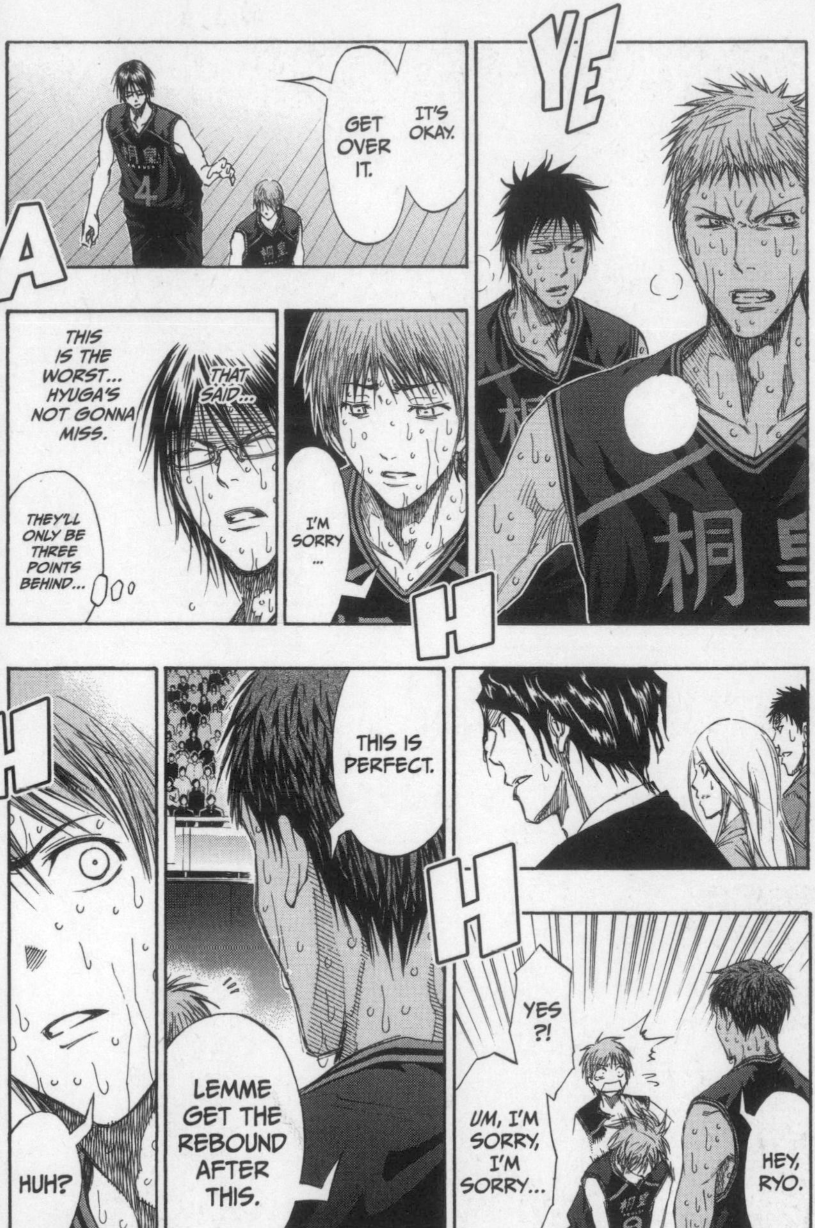
YEAHHH
IT'S OKAY.
GET OVER IT.
I'M SORRY...
THAT SAID...
THIS IS THE WORST... HYUGA'S NOT GONNA MISS.
THEY'LL ONLY BE THREE POINTS BEHIND...
HEY, RYO.
YES?!
UM, I'M SORRY, I'M SORRY...
THIS IS PERFECT.
LEMME GET THE REBOUND AFTER THIS.
HUH?

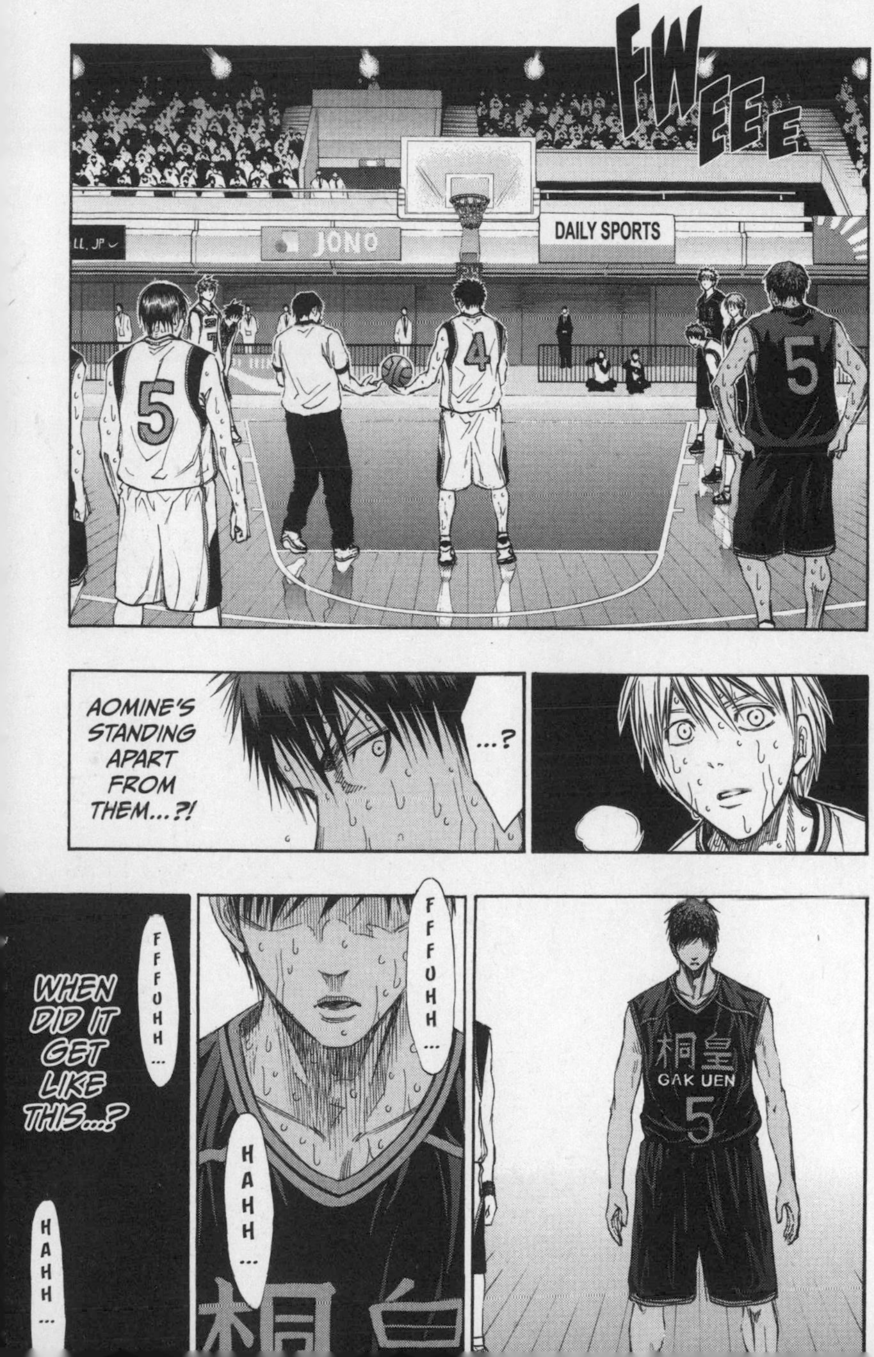
FWEEE
DAILY SPORTS
JONO
...?
AOMINE'S STANDING APART FROM THEM...?!
桐皇
GAK UEN
FFFUHH ...
HAHH ...
FFFUHH ...
WHEN DID IT GET LIKE THIS...?
HAHH ...

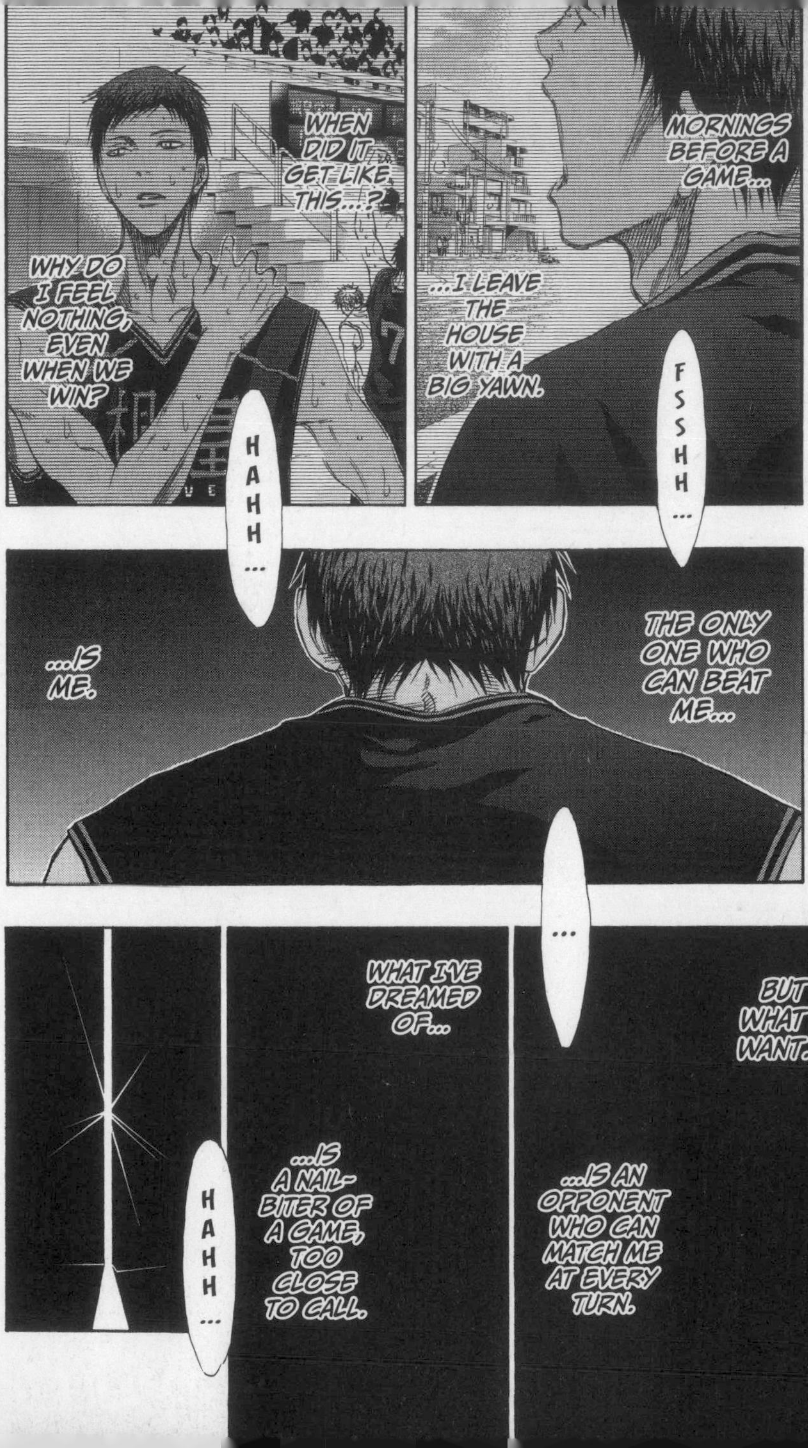
MORNINGS BEFORE A GAME...
...I LEAVE THE HOUSE WITH A BIG YAWN.
FSSHH...
WHEN DID IT GET LIKE THIS...?
WHY DO I FEEL NOTHING, EVEN WHEN WE WIN?
HAHH...
THE ONLY ONE WHO CAN BEAT ME...
...IS ME.
...
BUT WHAT I WANT...
...IS AN OPPONENT WHO CAN MATCH ME AT EVERY TURN.
WHAT I'VE DREAMED OF...
...IS A NAIL-BITER OF A GAME, TOO CLOSE TO CALL.
HAHH...

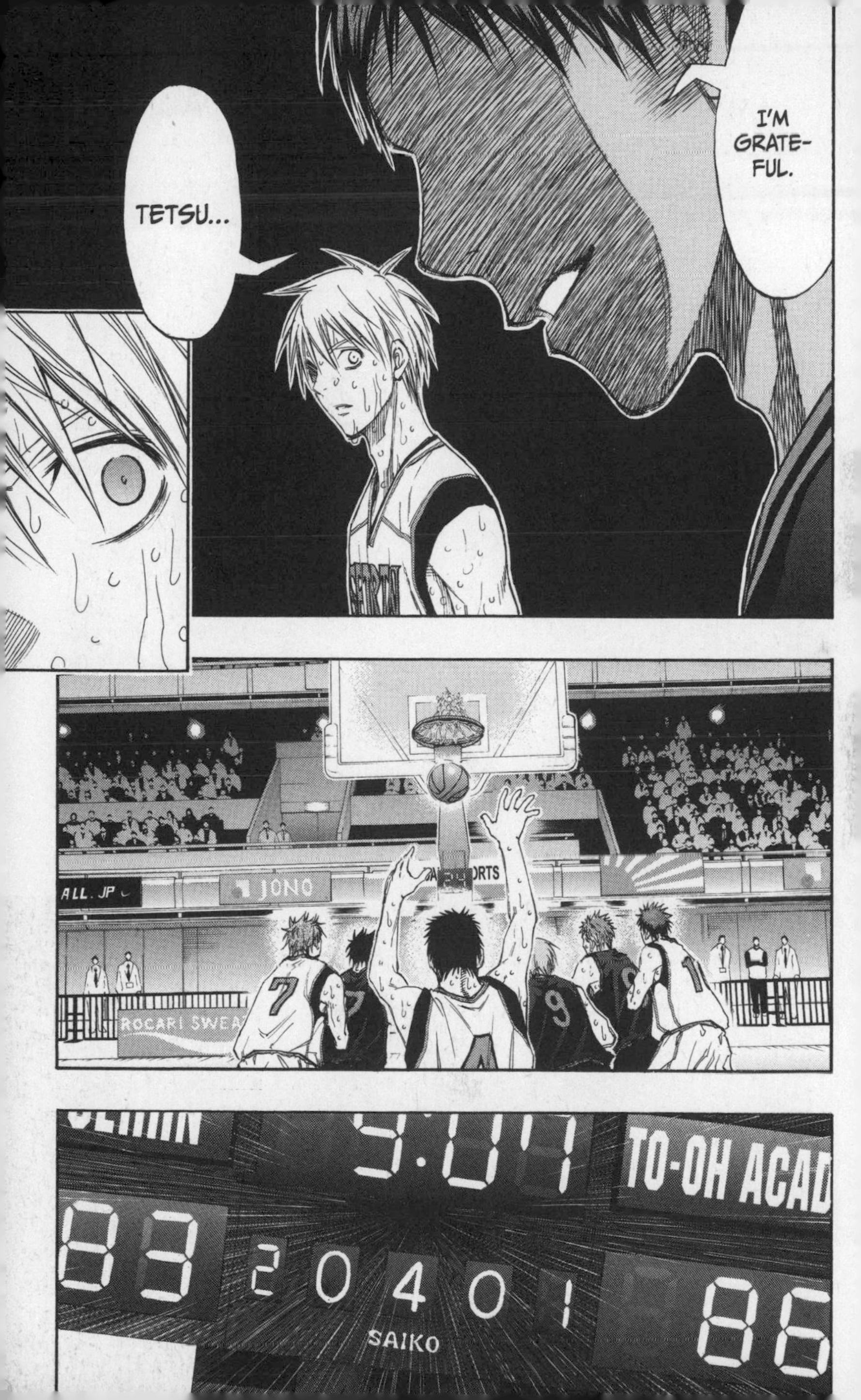
I'M GRATEFUL.
TETSU...
JONO
TO-OH ACAD
SAIKO

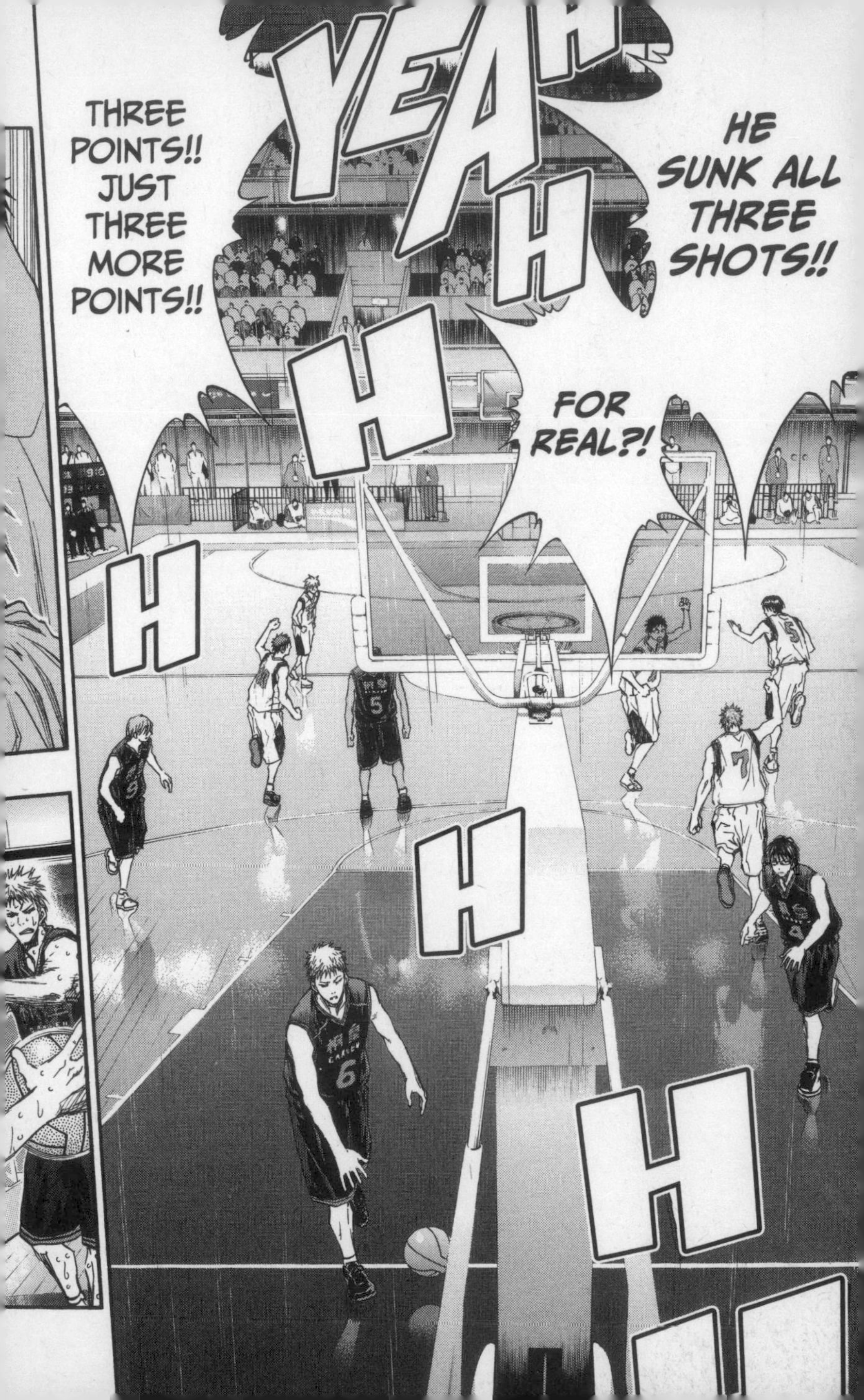
YEAHHHHHH
HE SUNK ALL THREE SHOTS!!
FOR REAL?!
THREE POINTS!! JUST THREE MORE POINTS!!

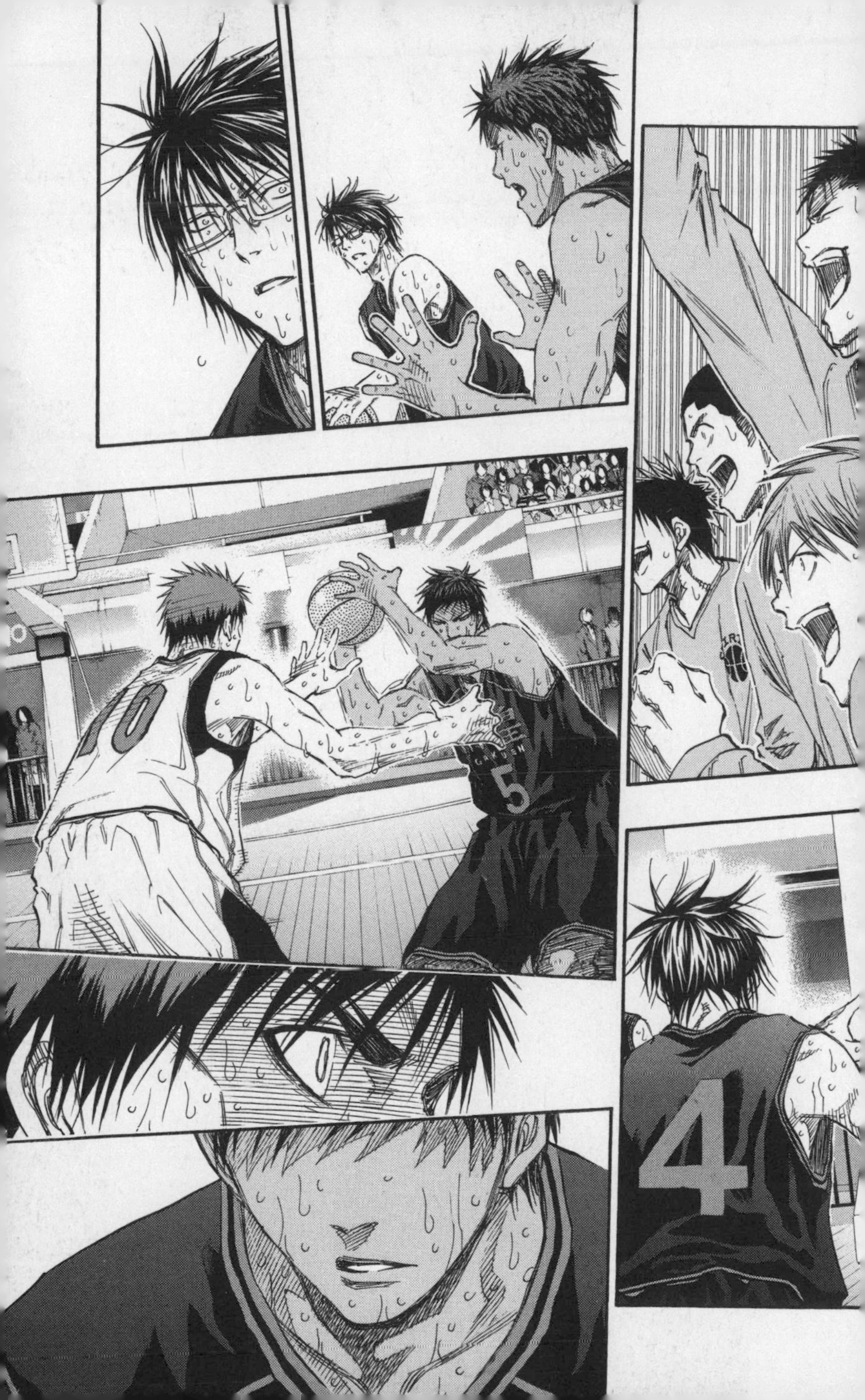

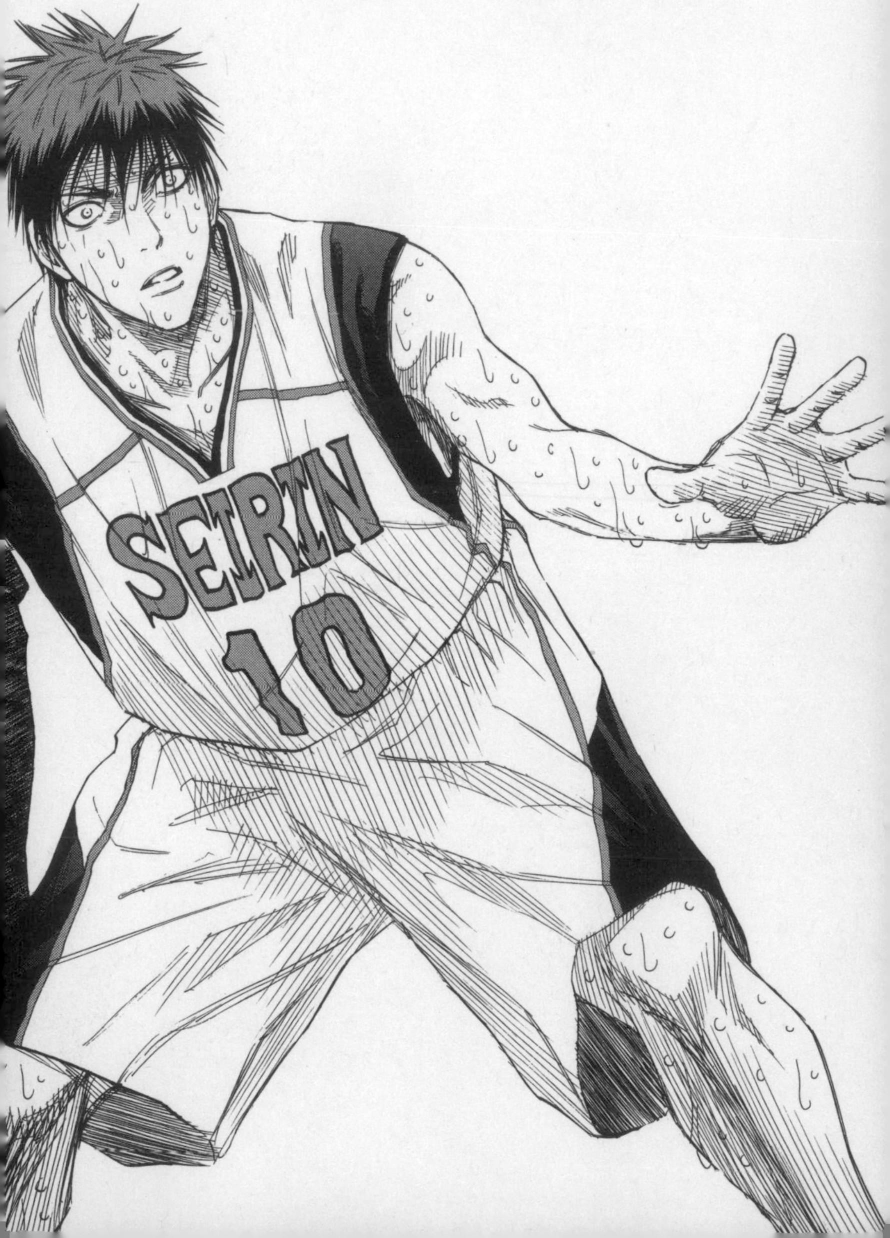
SEIRIN
10

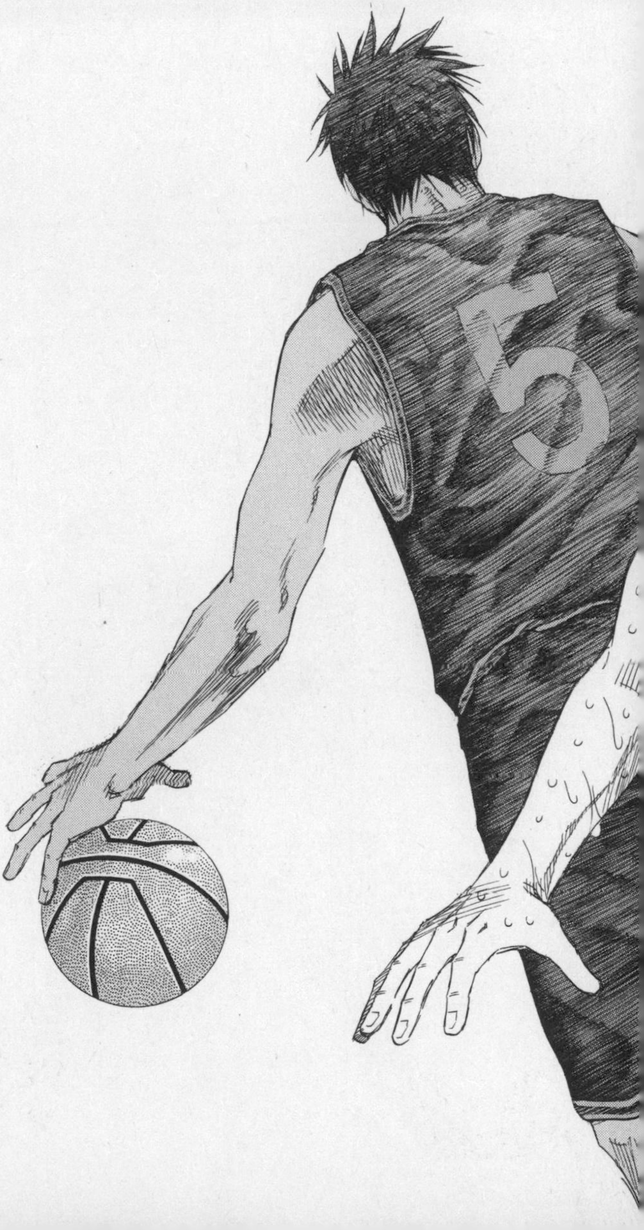

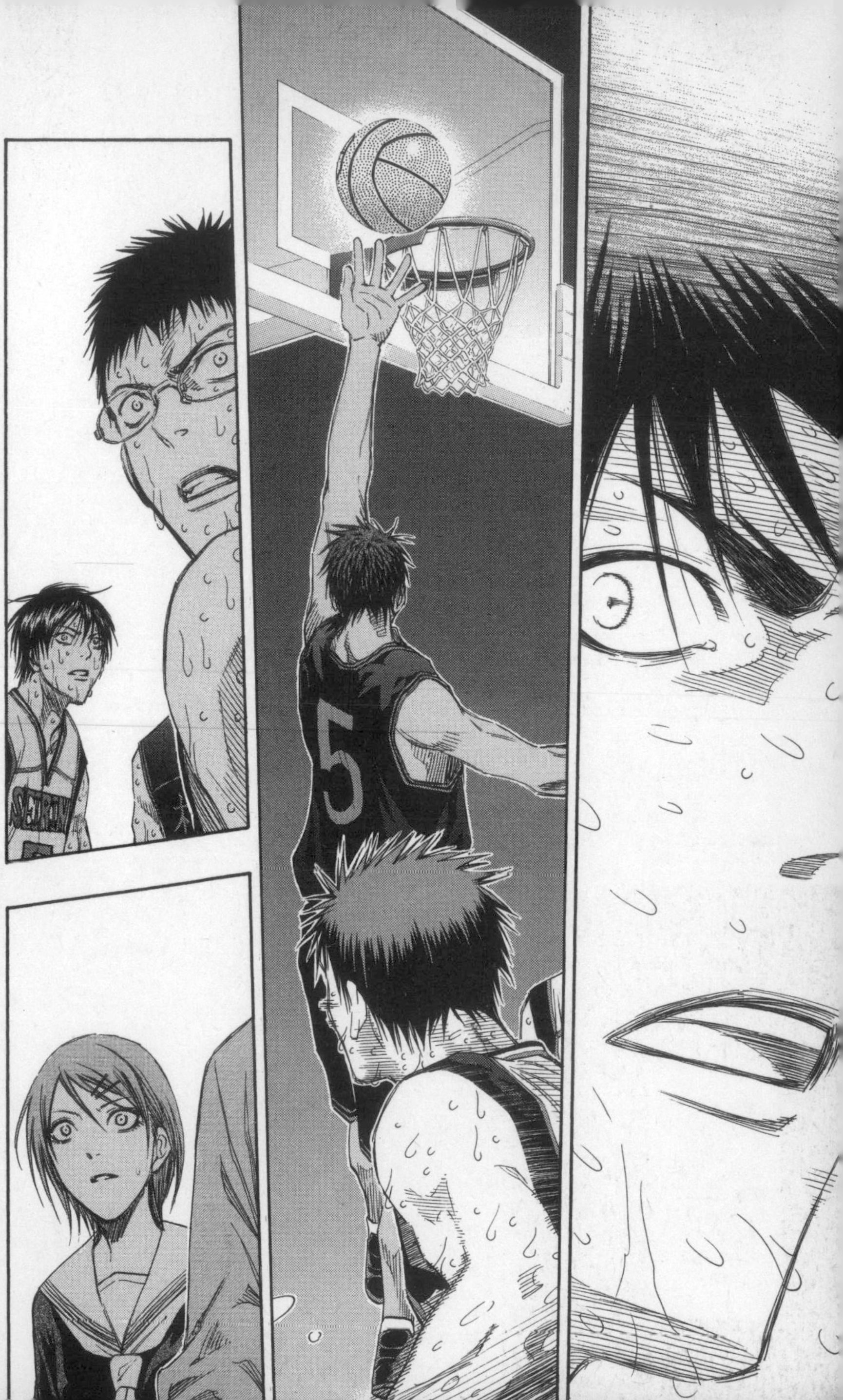

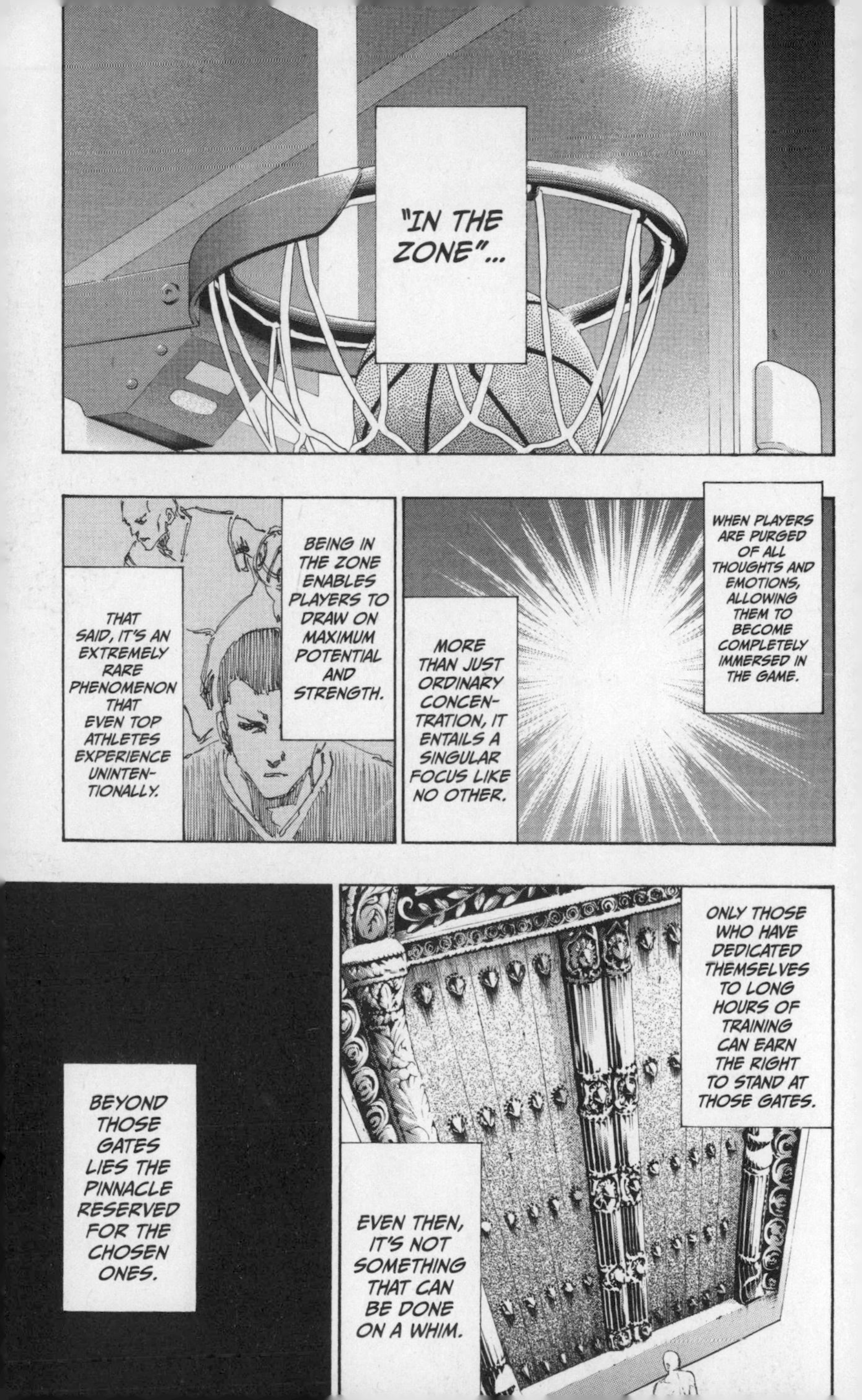
"IN THE ZONE"...
WHEN PLAYERS ARE PURGED OF ALL THOUGHTS AND EMOTIONS, ALLOWING THEM TO BECOME COMPLETELY IMMERSED IN THE GAME.
MORE THAN JUST ORDINARY CONCEN-TRATION, IT ENTAILS A SINGULAR FOCUS LIKE NO OTHER.
BEING IN THE ZONE ENABLES PLAYERS TO DRAW ON MAXIMUM POTENTIAL AND STRENGTH.
THAT SAID, IT'S AN EXTREMELY RARE PHENOMENON THAT EVEN TOP ATHLETES EXPERIENCE UNINTEN-TIONALLY.
ONLY THOSE WHO HAVE DEDICATED THEMSELVES TO LONG HOURS OF TRAINING CAN EARN THE RIGHT TO STAND AT THOSE GATES.
EVEN THEN, IT'S NOT SOMETHING THAT CAN BE DONE ON A WHIM.
BEYOND THOSE GATES LIES THE PINNACLE RESERVED FOR THE CHOSEN ONES.

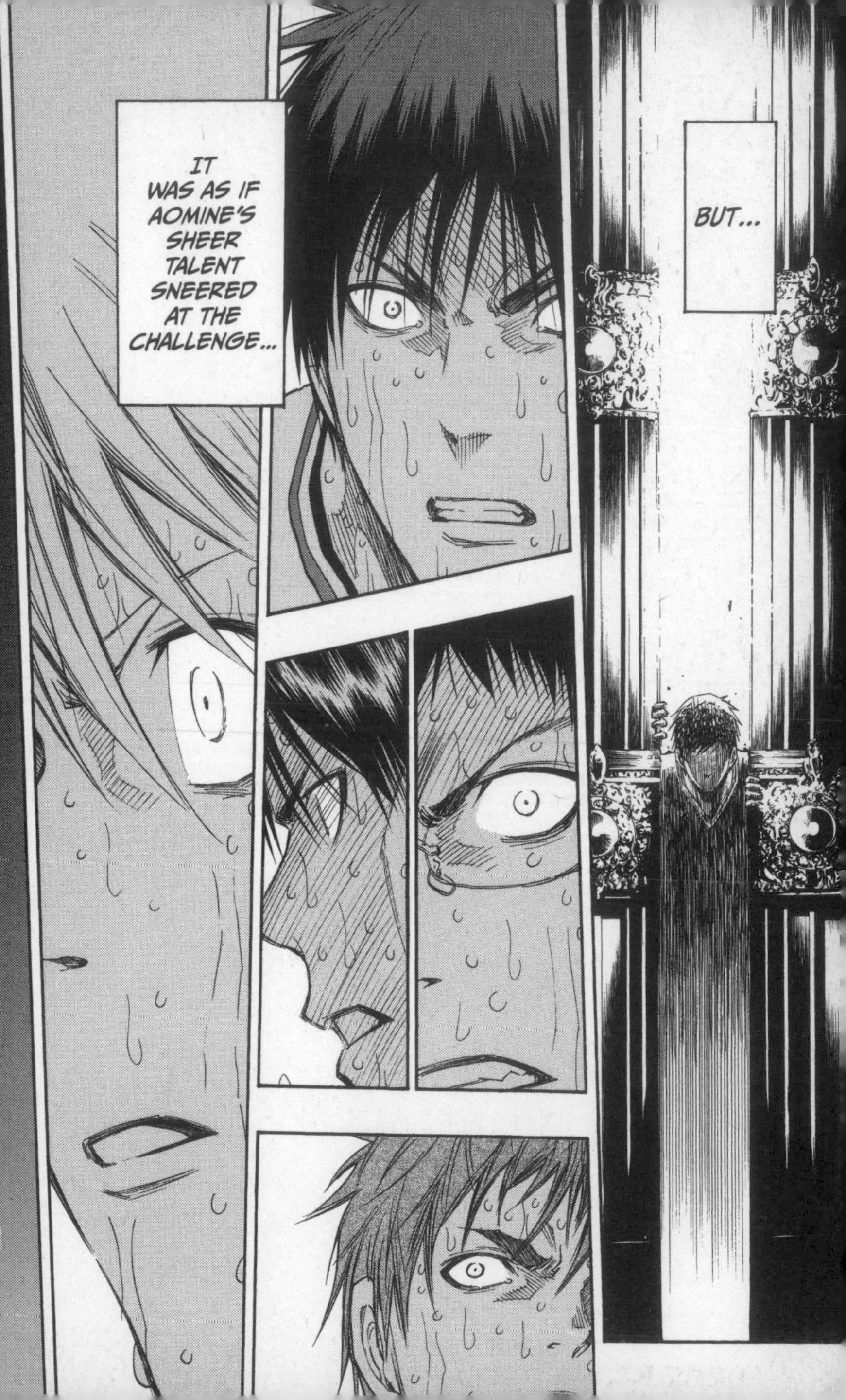
BUT...
IT WAS AS IF AOMINE'S SHEER TALENT SNEERED AT THE CHALLENGE...

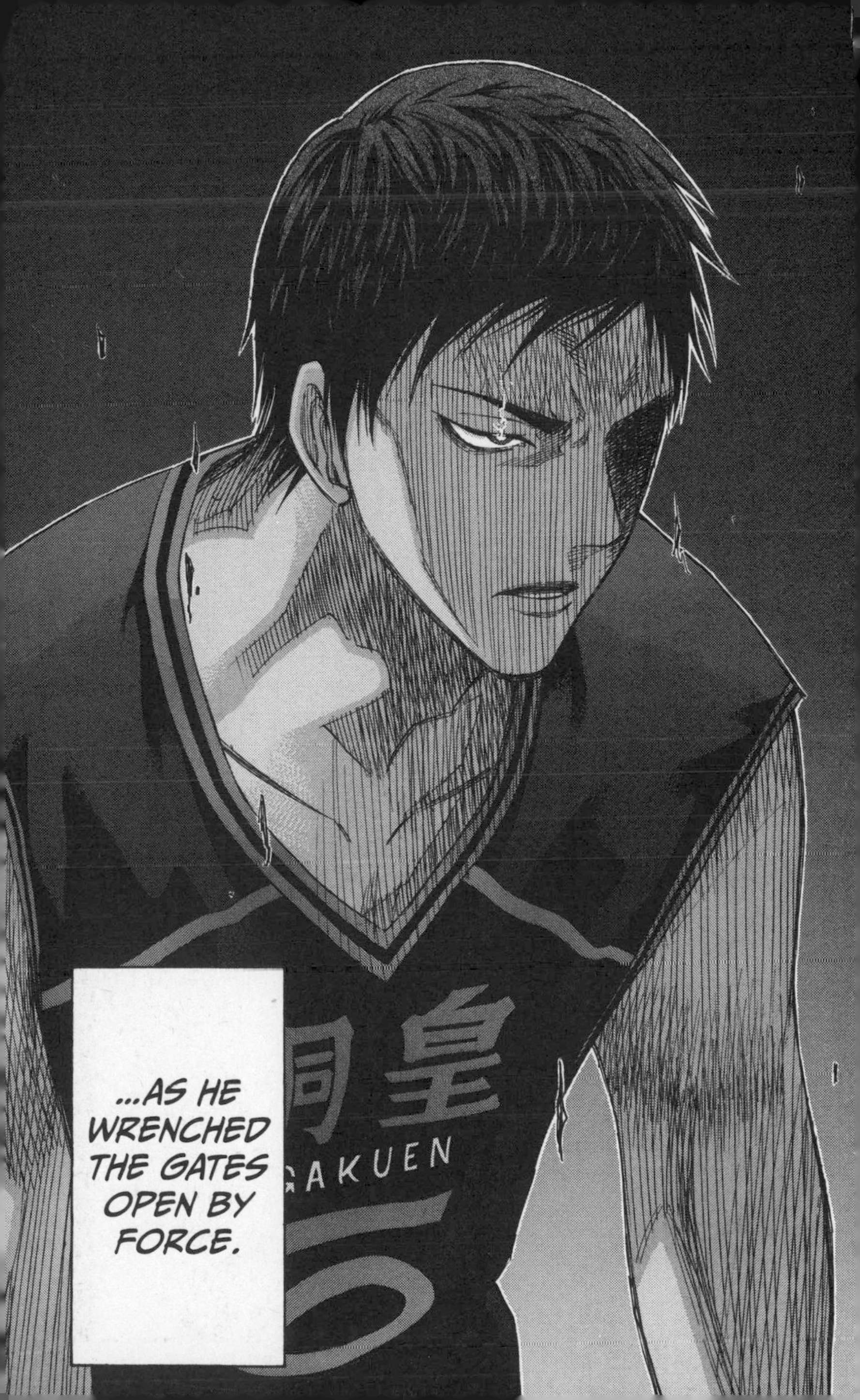
...AS HE WRENCHED THE GATES OPEN BY FORCE.
GAKUEN

KUROKO'S BASKETBALL BLOOPERS
TAKE 4

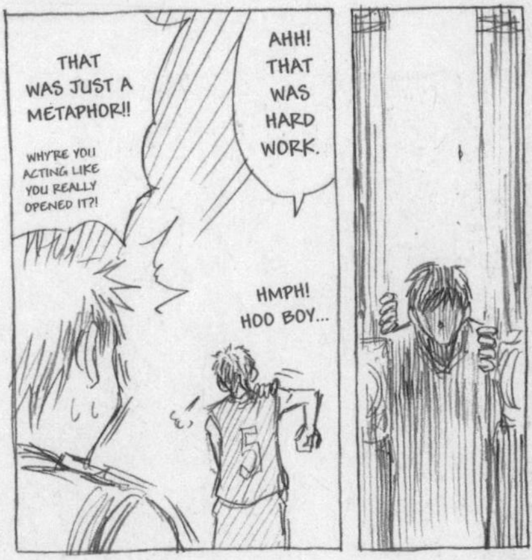
AHH! THAT WAS HARD WORK.
THAT WAS JUST A METAPHOR!!
WHY'RE YOU ACTING LIKE YOU REALLY OPENED IT?!
HMPH! HOO BOY...

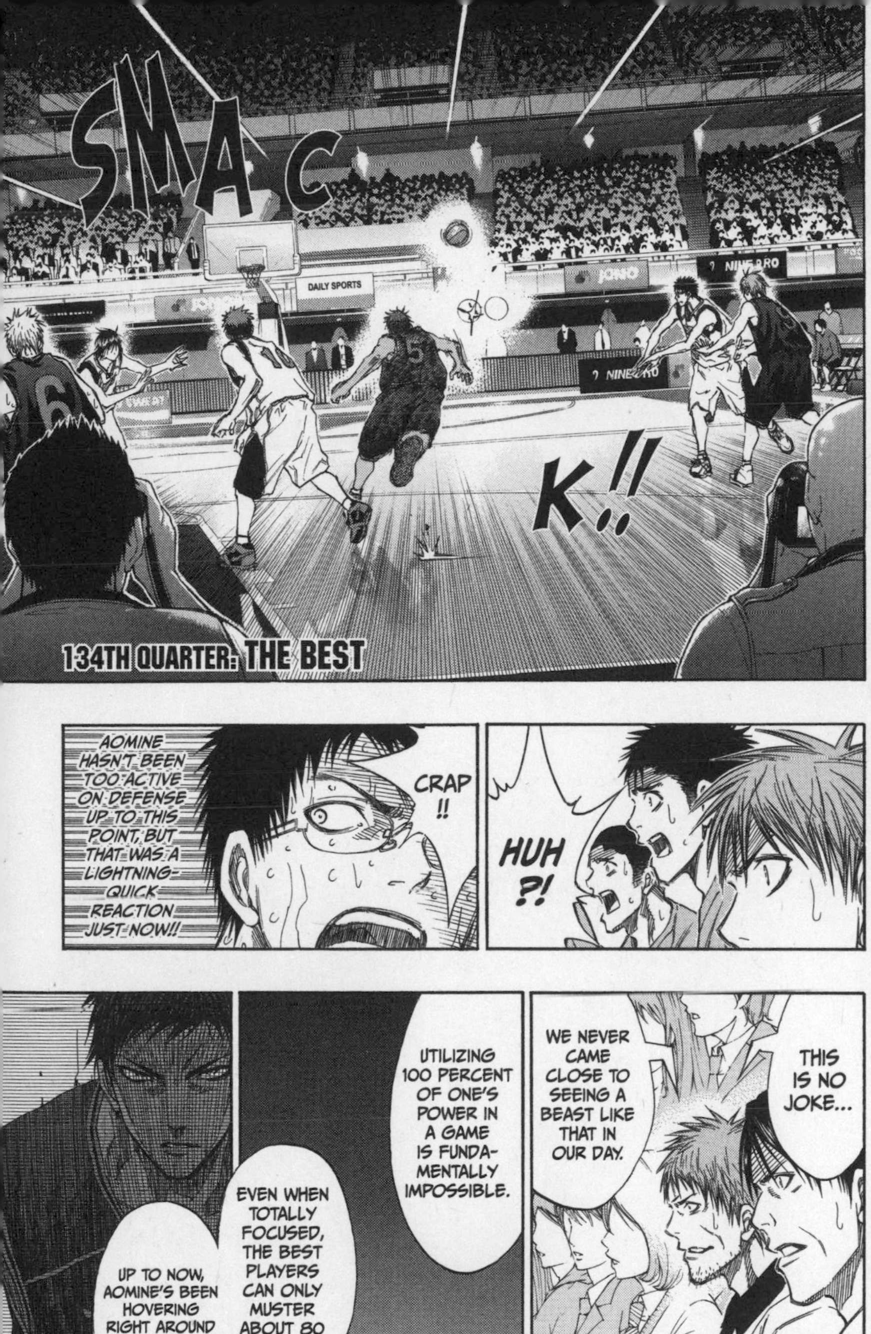

SMACK!!
134TH QUARTER: THE BEST
DAILY SPORTS
HUH ?!
CRAP !!
AOMINE HASN'T BEEN TOO ACTIVE ON DEFENSE UP TO THIS POINT, BUT THAT WAS A LIGHTNING-QUICK REACTION JUST NOW!!
THIS IS NO JOKE...
WE NEVER CAME CLOSE TO SEEING A BEAST LIKE THAT IN OUR DAY.
UTILIZING 100 PERCENT OF ONE'S POWER IN A GAME IS FUNDAMENTALLY IMPOSSIBLE.
EVEN WHEN TOTALLY FOCUSED, THE BEST PLAYERS CAN ONLY MUSTER ABOUT 80 PERCENT.
UP TO NOW, AOMINE'S BEEN HOVERING RIGHT AROUND THAT 80 PERCENT BENCHMARK.

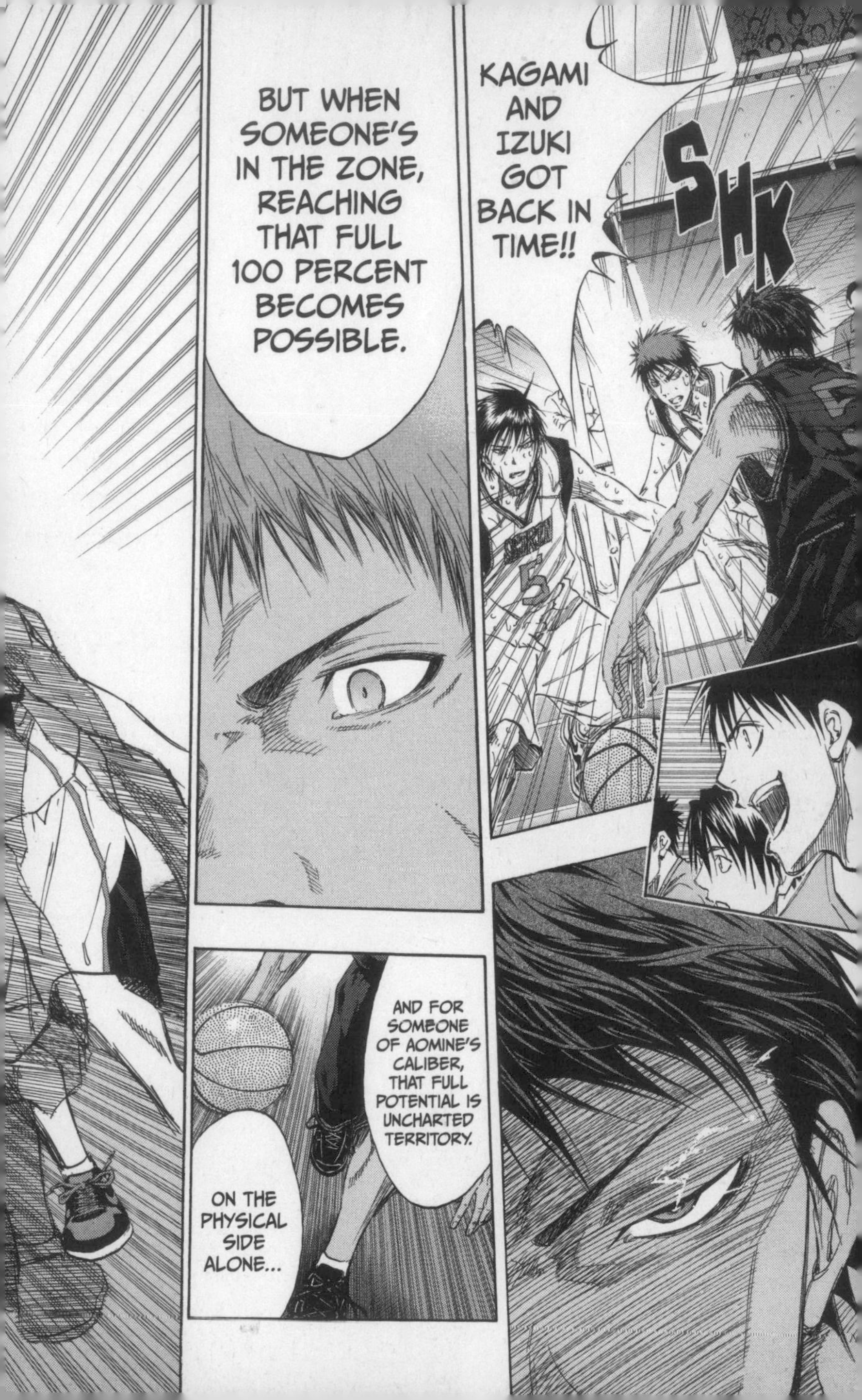
KAGAMI AND IZUKI GOT BACK IN TIME!!
SHK
BUT WHEN SOMEONE'S IN THE ZONE, REACHING THAT FULL 100 PERCENT BECOMES POSSIBLE.
AND FOR SOMEONE OF AOMINE'S CALIBER, THAT FULL POTENTIAL IS UNCHARTED TERRITORY.
ON THE PHYSICAL SIDE ALONE...

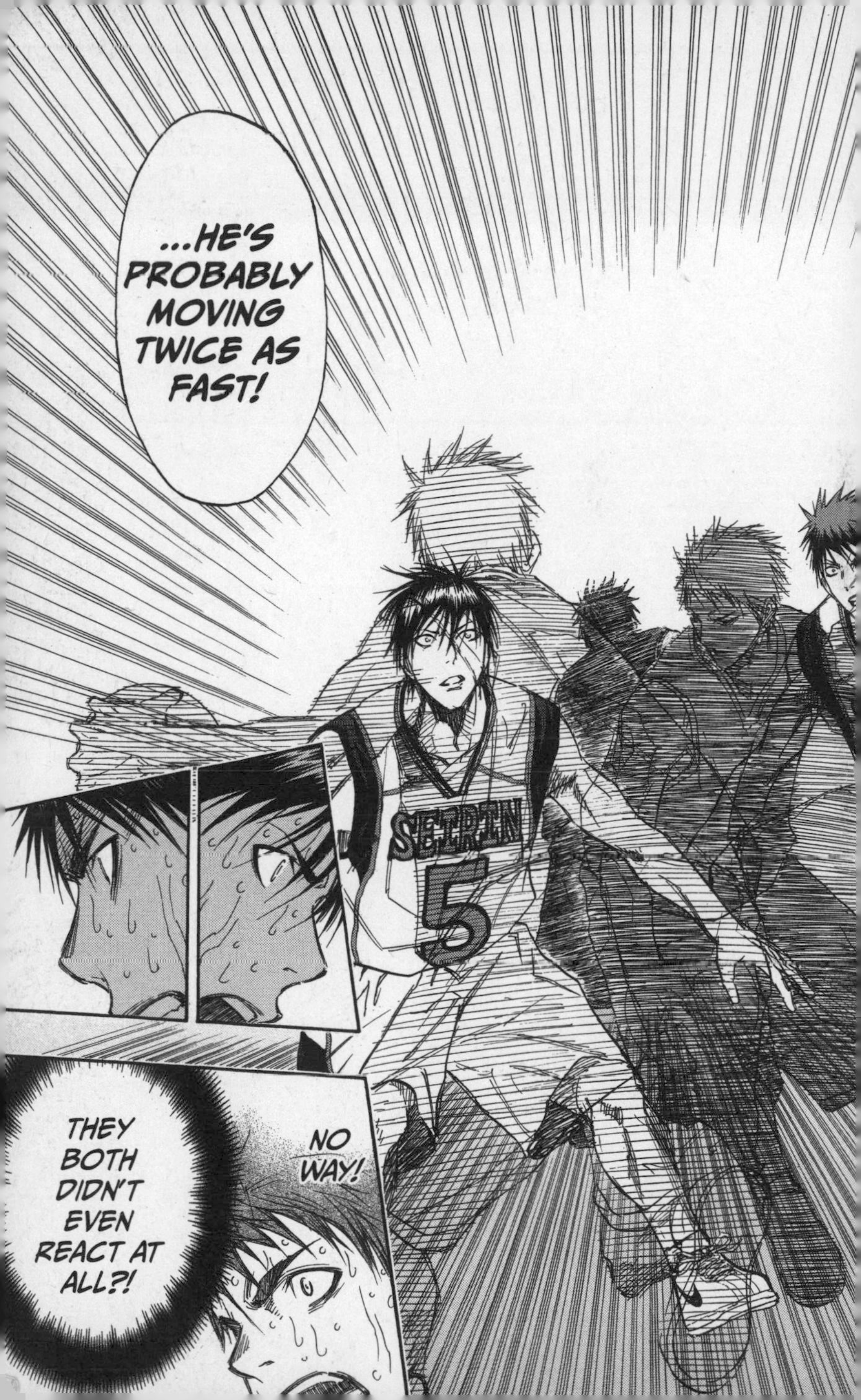
...HE'S PROBABLY MOVING TWICE AS FAST!
NO WAY!
THEY BOTH DIDN'T EVEN REACT AT ALL?!

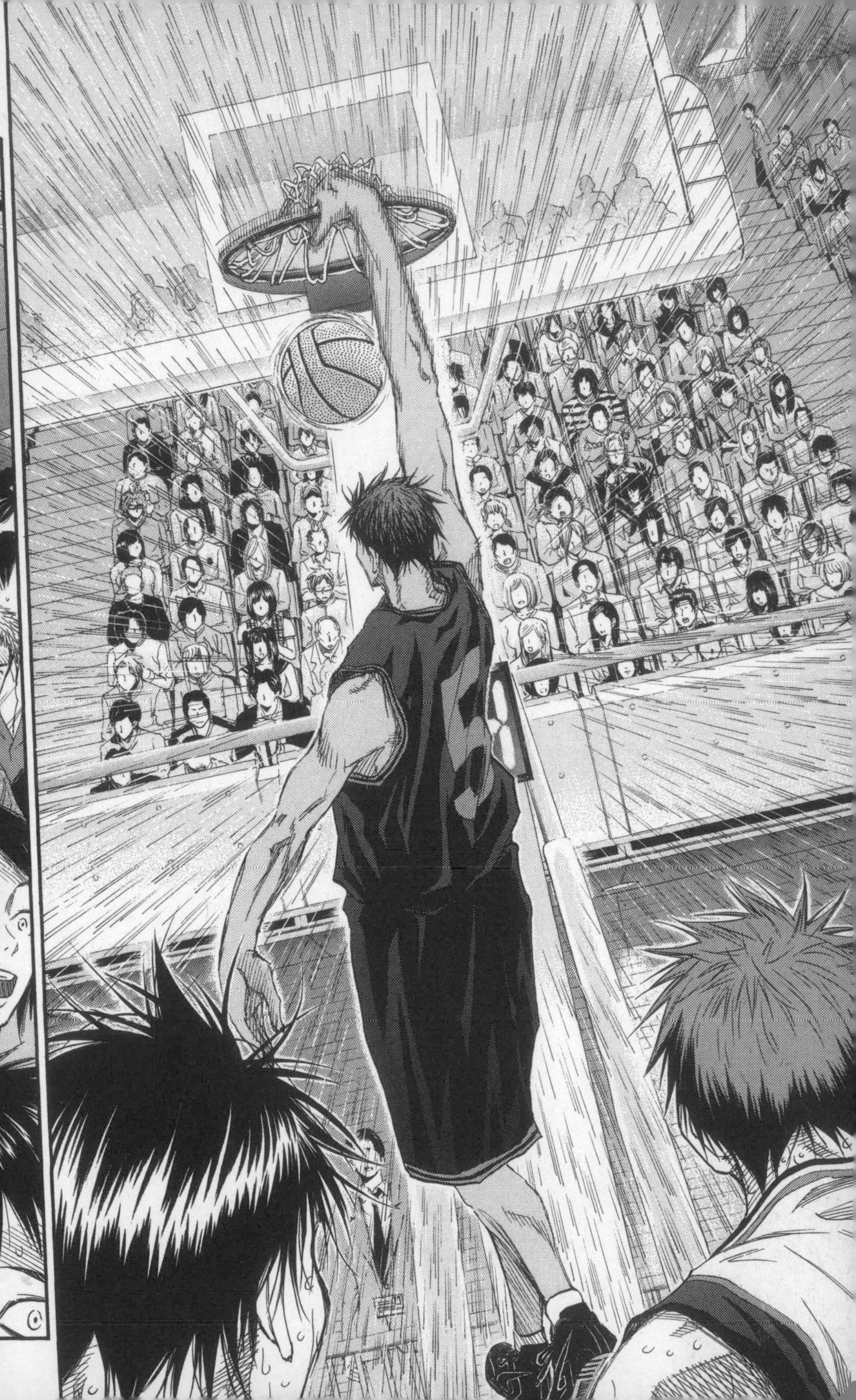

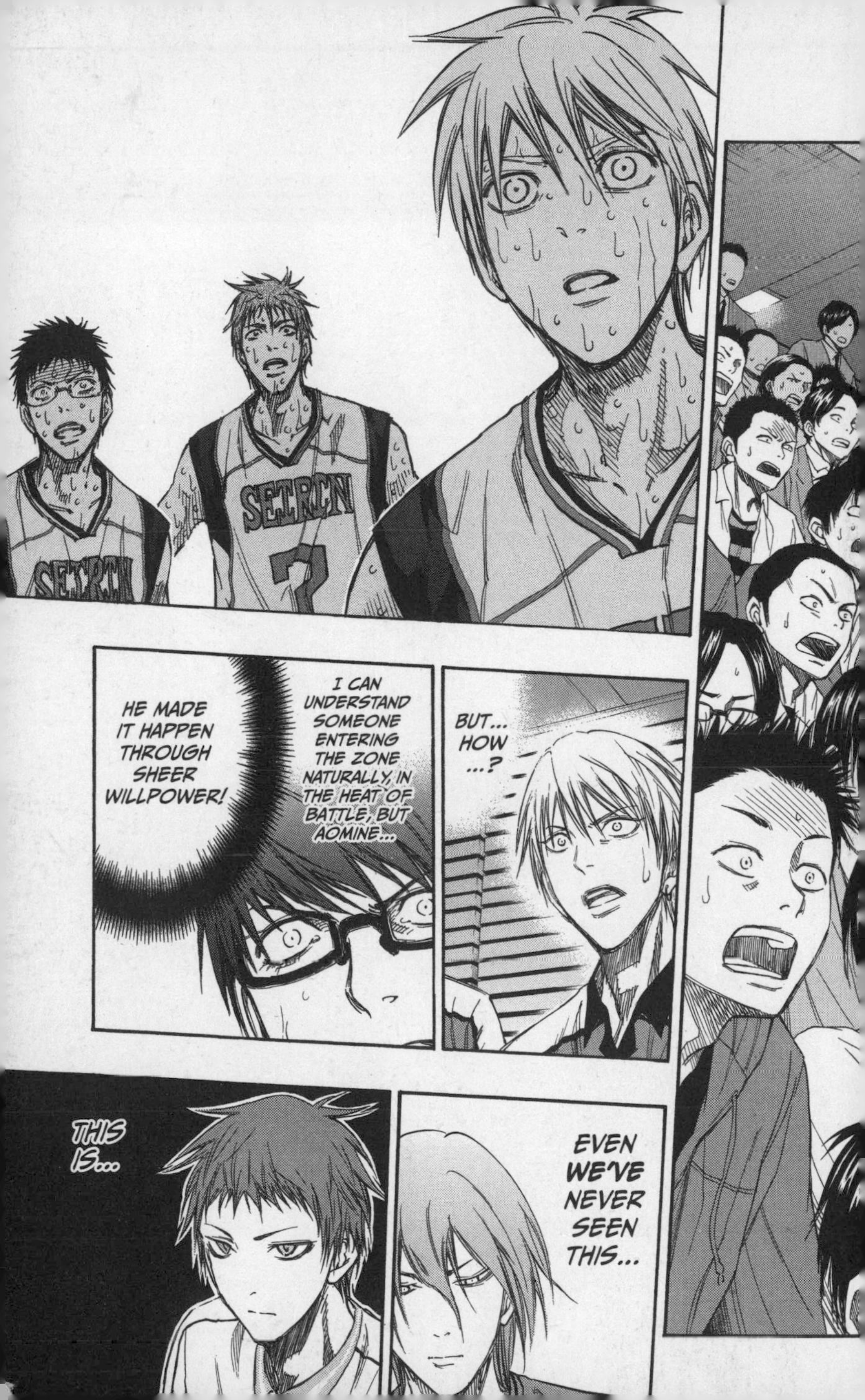
BUT... HOW ...?
I CAN UNDERSTAND SOMEONE ENTERING THE ZONE NATURALLY, IN THE HEAT OF BATTLE, BUT AOMINE...
HE MADE IT HAPPEN THROUGH SHEER WILLPOWER!
EVEN WE'VE NEVER SEEN THIS...
THIS IS...

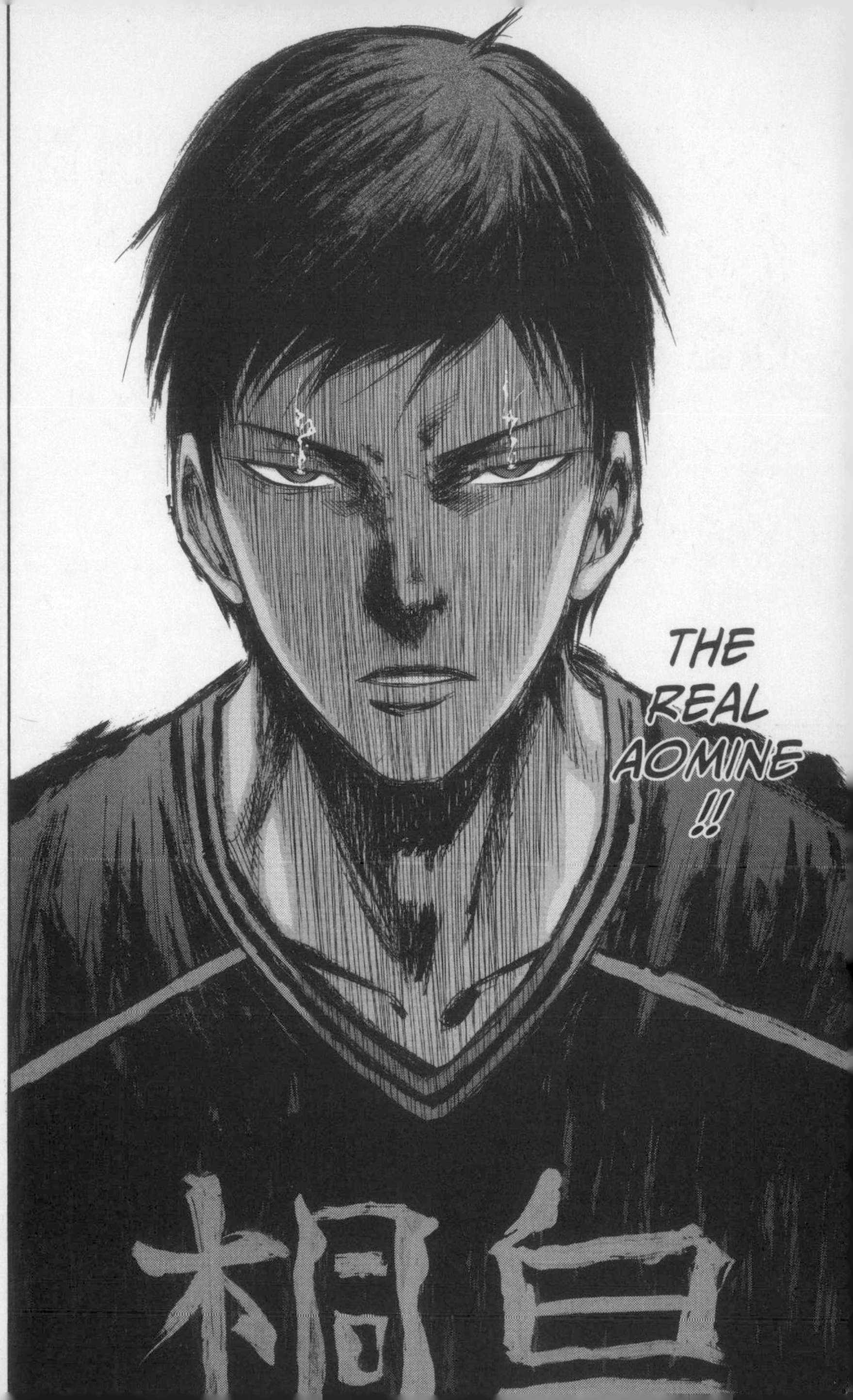
THE REAL AOMINE !!

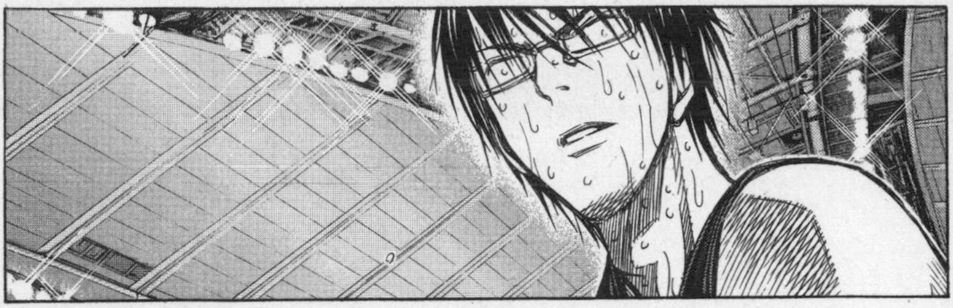

134TH QUARTER:
THE BEST

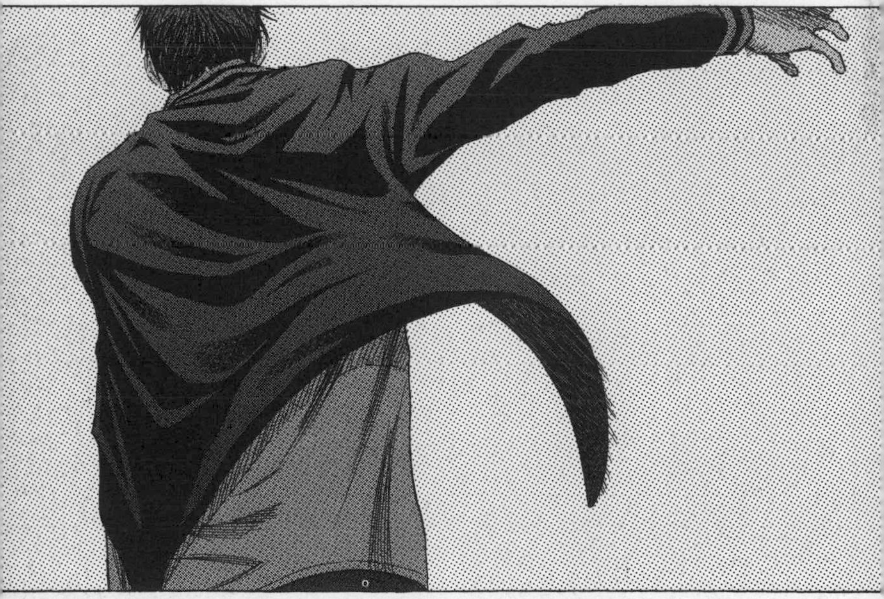

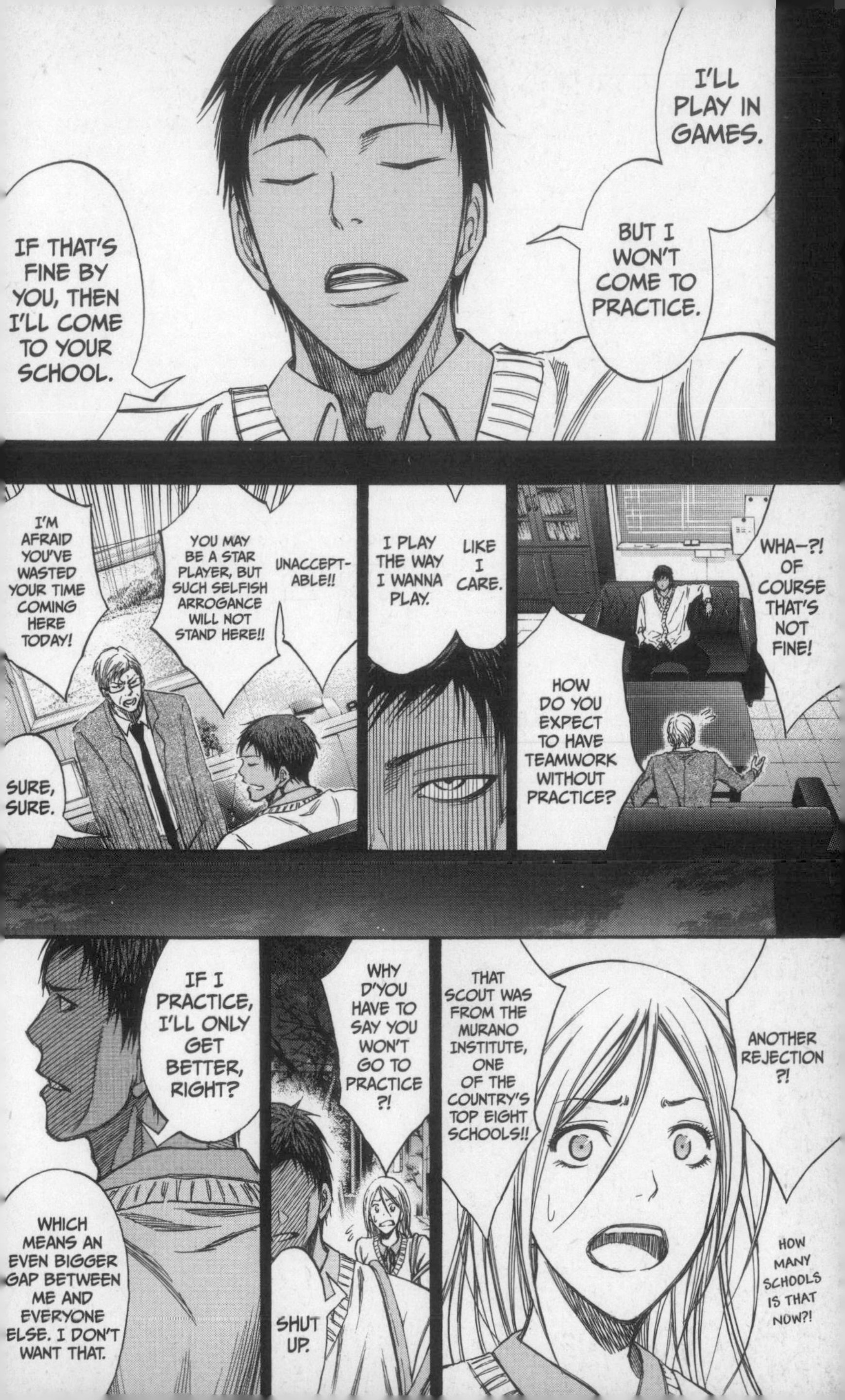
I'LL PLAY IN GAMES.
BUT I WON'T COME TO PRACTICE.
IF THAT'S FINE BY YOU, THEN I'LL COME TO YOUR SCHOOL.
WHA—?! OF COURSE THAT'S NOT FINE!
HOW DO YOU EXPECT TO HAVE TEAMWORK WITHOUT PRACTICE?
LIKE I CARE.
I PLAY THE WAY I WANNA PLAY.
UNACCEPTABLE!!
YOU MAY BE A STAR PLAYER, BUT SUCH SELFISH ARROGANCE WILL NOT STAND HERE!!
I'M AFRAID YOU'VE WASTED YOUR TIME COMING HERE TODAY!
SURE, SURE.
ANOTHER REJECTION?!
THAT SCOUT WAS FROM THE MURANO INSTITUTE, ONE OF THE COUNTRY'S TOP EIGHT SCHOOLS!!
HOW MANY SCHOOLS IS THAT NOW?!
WHY D'YOU HAVE TO SAY YOU WON'T GO TO PRACTICE?!
SHUT UP.
IF I PRACTICE, I'LL ONLY GET BETTER, RIGHT?
WHICH MEANS AN EVEN BIGGER GAP BETWEEN ME AND EVERYONE ELSE. I DON'T WANT THAT.

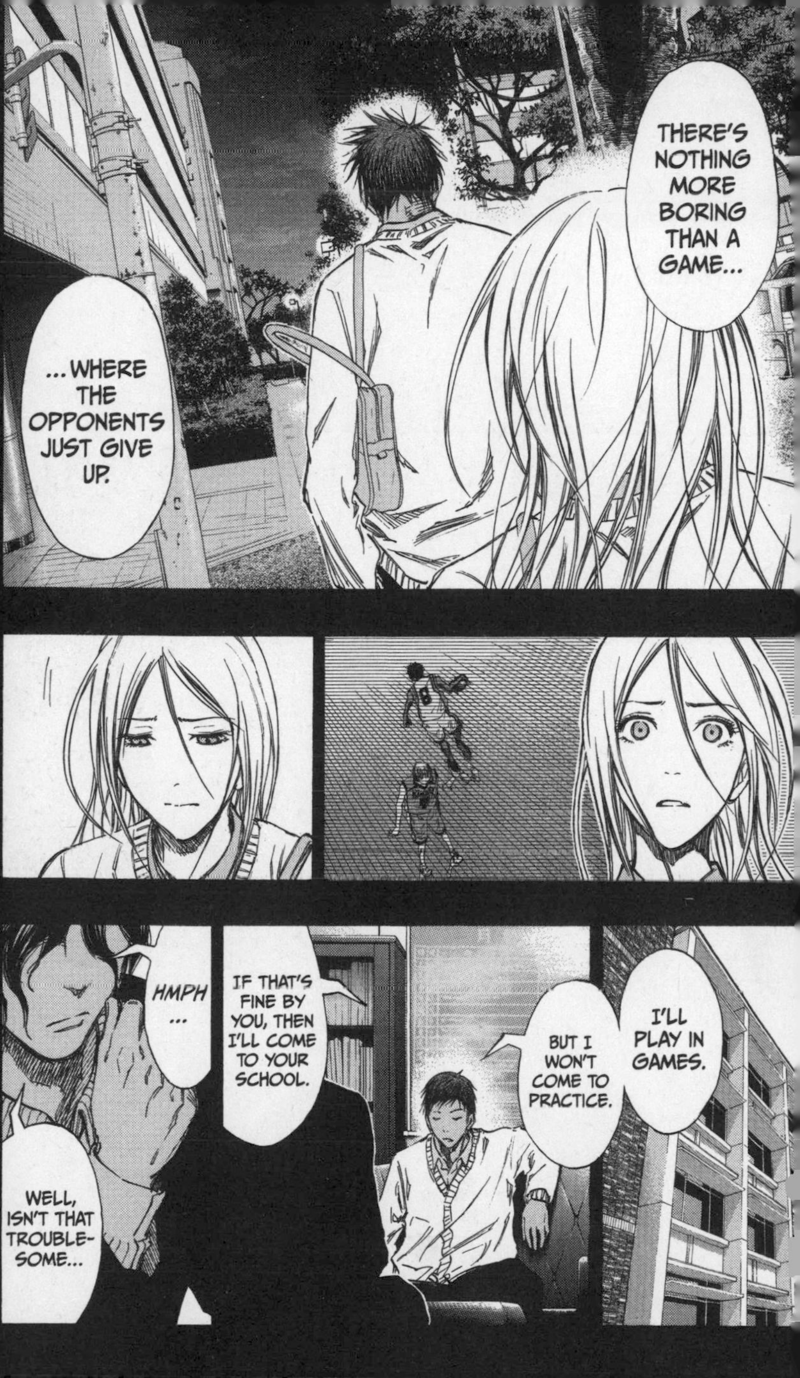
THERE'S NOTHING MORE BORING THAN A GAME...
...WHERE THE OPPONENTS JUST GIVE UP.
I'LL PLAY IN GAMES.
BUT I WON'T COME TO PRACTICE.
IF THAT'S FINE BY YOU, THEN I'LL COME TO YOUR SCHOOL.
HMPH...
WELL, ISN'T THAT TROUBLESOME...

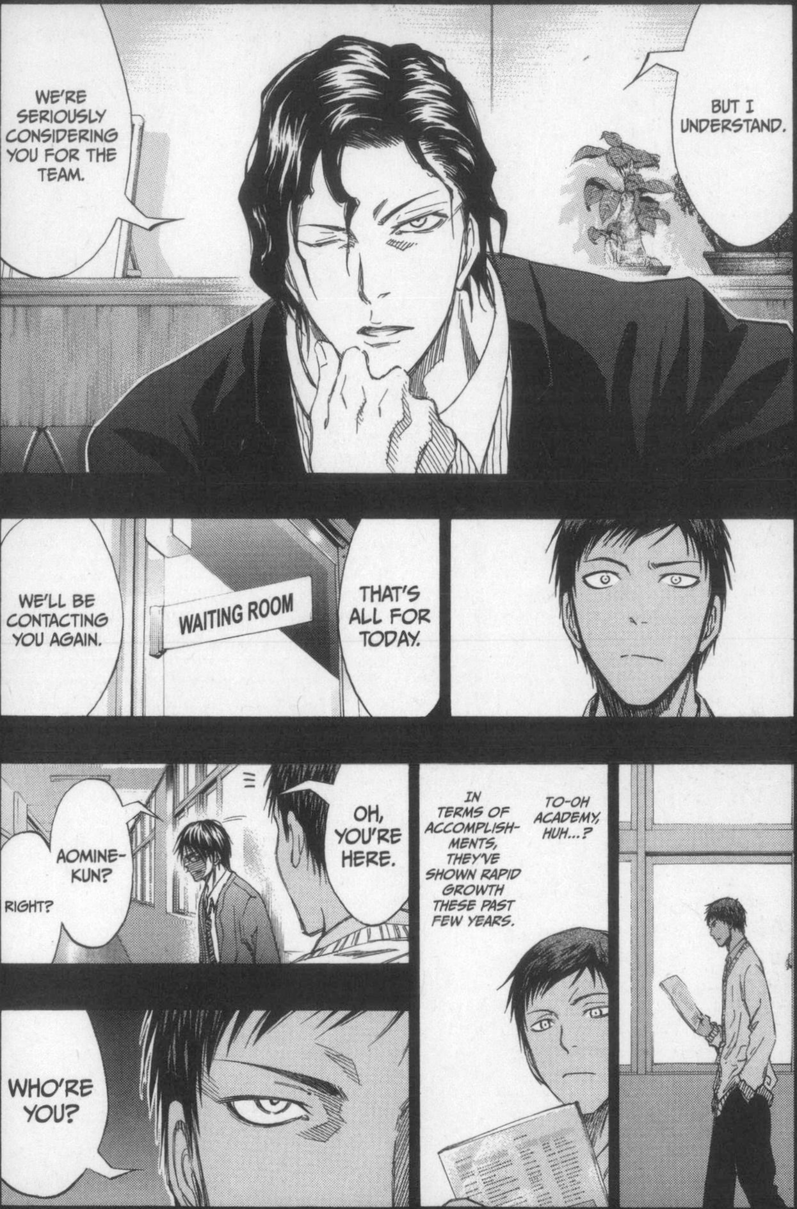
BUT I UNDERSTAND.
WE'RE SERIOUSLY CONSIDERING YOU FOR THE TEAM.
THAT'S ALL FOR TODAY.
WAITING ROOM
WE'LL BE CONTACTING YOU AGAIN.
TO-OH ACADEMY, HUH...?
IN TERMS OF ACCOMPLISH-MENTS, THEY'VE SHOWN RAPID GROWTH THESE PAST FEW YEARS.
OH, YOU'RE HERE.
AOMINE-KUN?
RIGHT?
WHO'RE YOU?

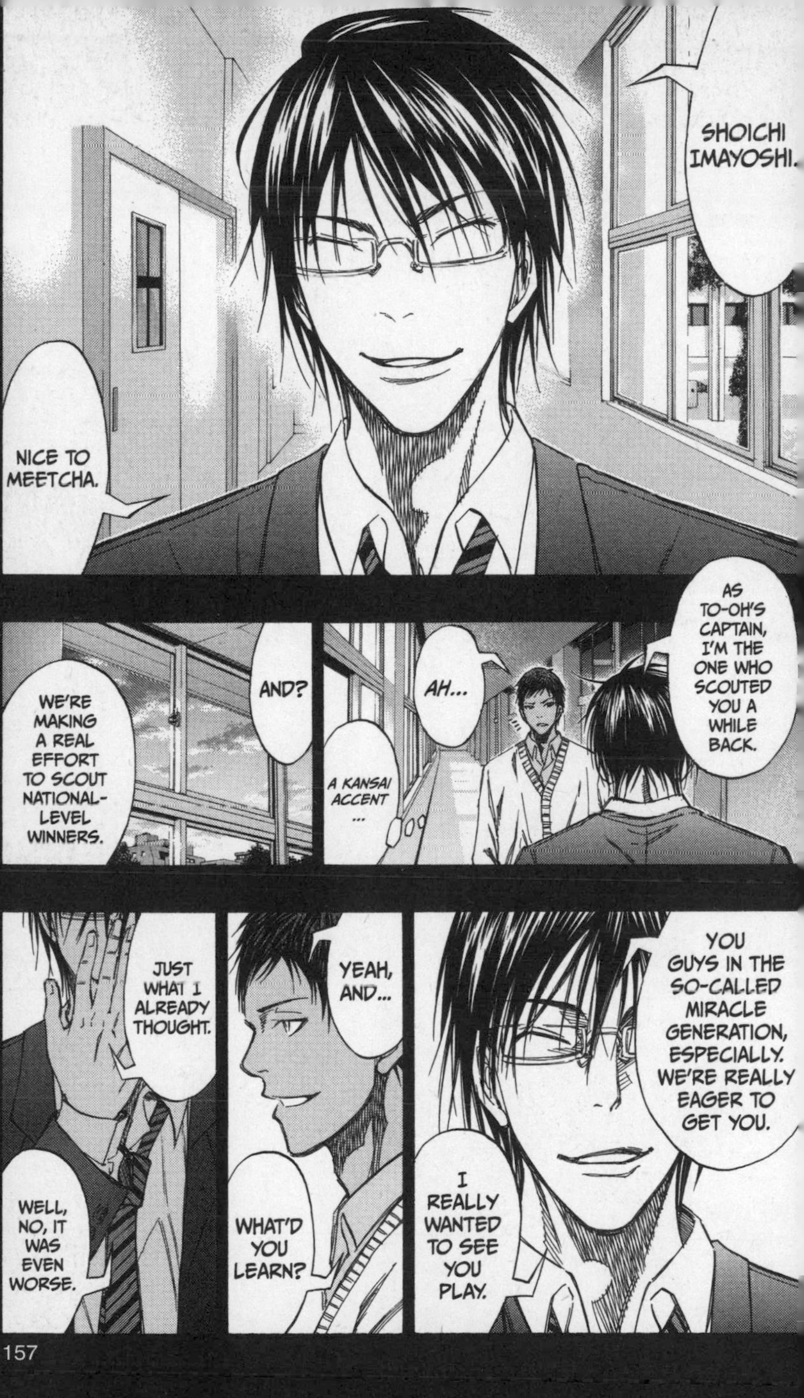
SHOICHI IMAYOSHI.
NICE TO MEETCHA.
AS TO-OH'S CAPTAIN, I'M THE ONE WHO SCOUTED YOU A WHILE BACK.
AH...
A KANSAI ACCENT ...
AND?
WE'RE MAKING A REAL EFFORT TO SCOUT NATIONAL-LEVEL WINNERS.
YOU GUYS IN THE SO-CALLED MIRACLE GENERATION, ESPECIALLY. WE'RE REALLY EAGER TO GET YOU.
I REALLY WANTED TO SEE YOU PLAY.
YEAH, AND...
WHAT'D YOU LEARN?
JUST WHAT I ALREADY THOUGHT.
WELL, NO, IT WAS EVEN WORSE.

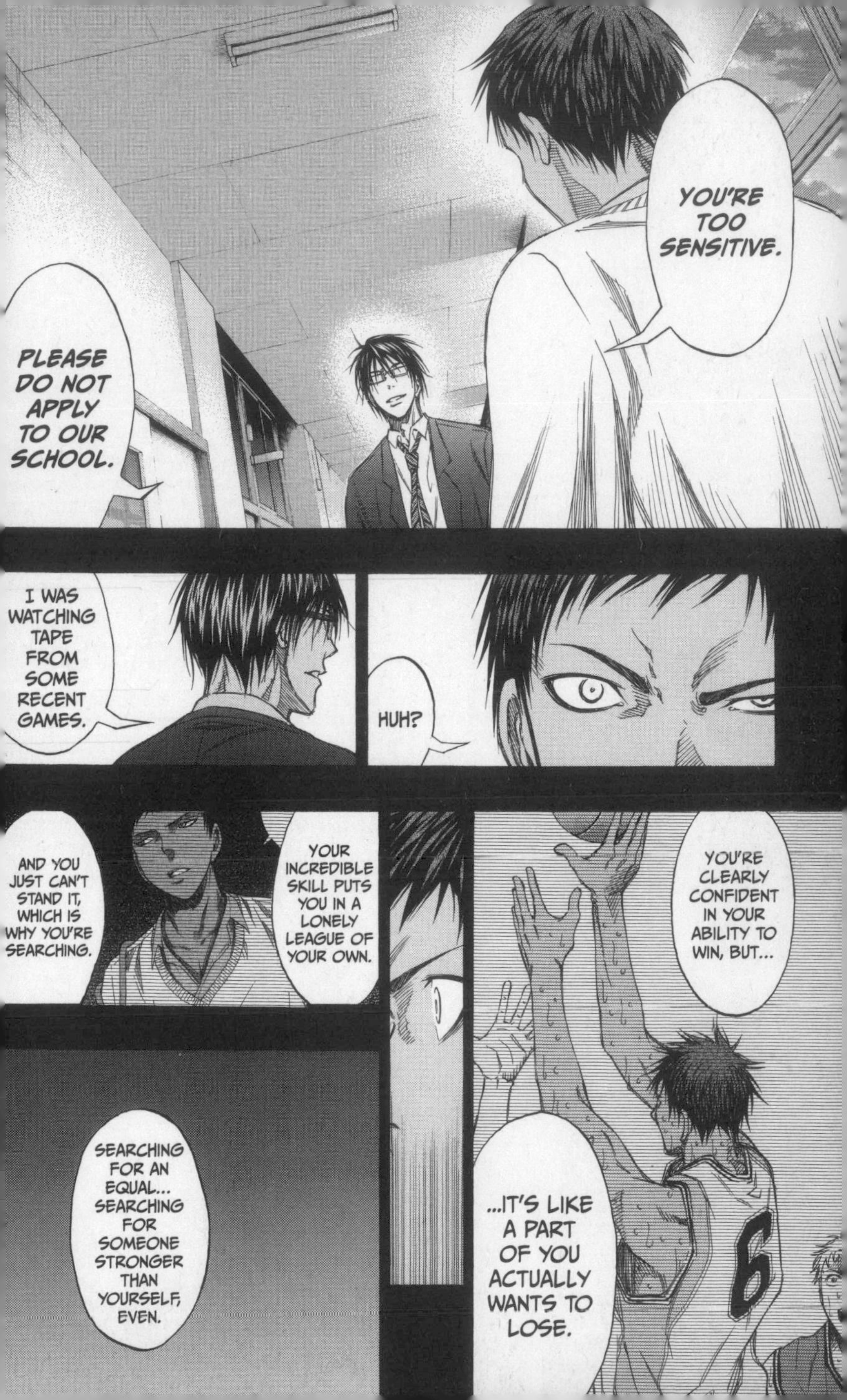
YOU'RE TOO SENSITIVE.
PLEASE DO NOT APPLY TO OUR SCHOOL.
HUH?
I WAS WATCHING TAPE FROM SOME RECENT GAMES.
YOU'RE CLEARLY CONFIDENT IN YOUR ABILITY TO WIN, BUT...
...IT'S LIKE A PART OF YOU ACTUALLY WANTS TO LOSE.
YOUR INCREDIBLE SKILL PUTS YOU IN A LONELY LEAGUE OF YOUR OWN.
AND YOU JUST CAN'T STAND IT, WHICH IS WHY YOU'RE SEARCHING.
SEARCHING FOR AN EQUAL... SEARCHING FOR SOMEONE STRONGER THAN YOURSELF, EVEN.

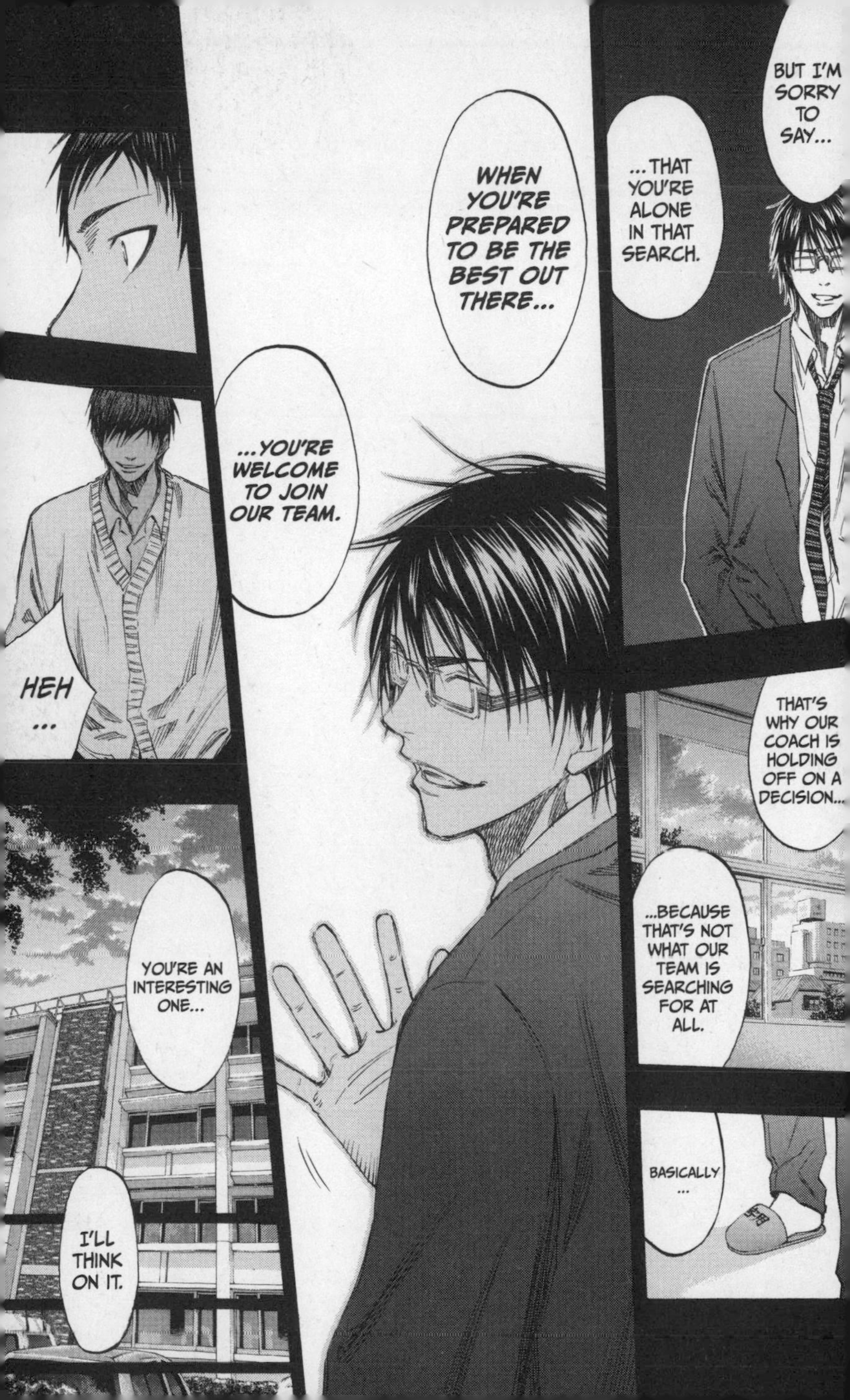
BUT I'M SORRY TO SAY...
...THAT YOU'RE ALONE IN THAT SEARCH.
THAT'S WHY OUR COACH IS HOLDING OFF ON A DECISION...
...BECAUSE THAT'S NOT WHAT OUR TEAM IS SEARCHING FOR AT ALL.
BASICALLY...
WHEN YOU'RE PREPARED TO BE THE BEST OUT THERE...
...YOU'RE WELCOME TO JOIN OUR TEAM.
HEH...
YOU'RE AN INTERESTING ONE...
I'LL THINK ON IT.

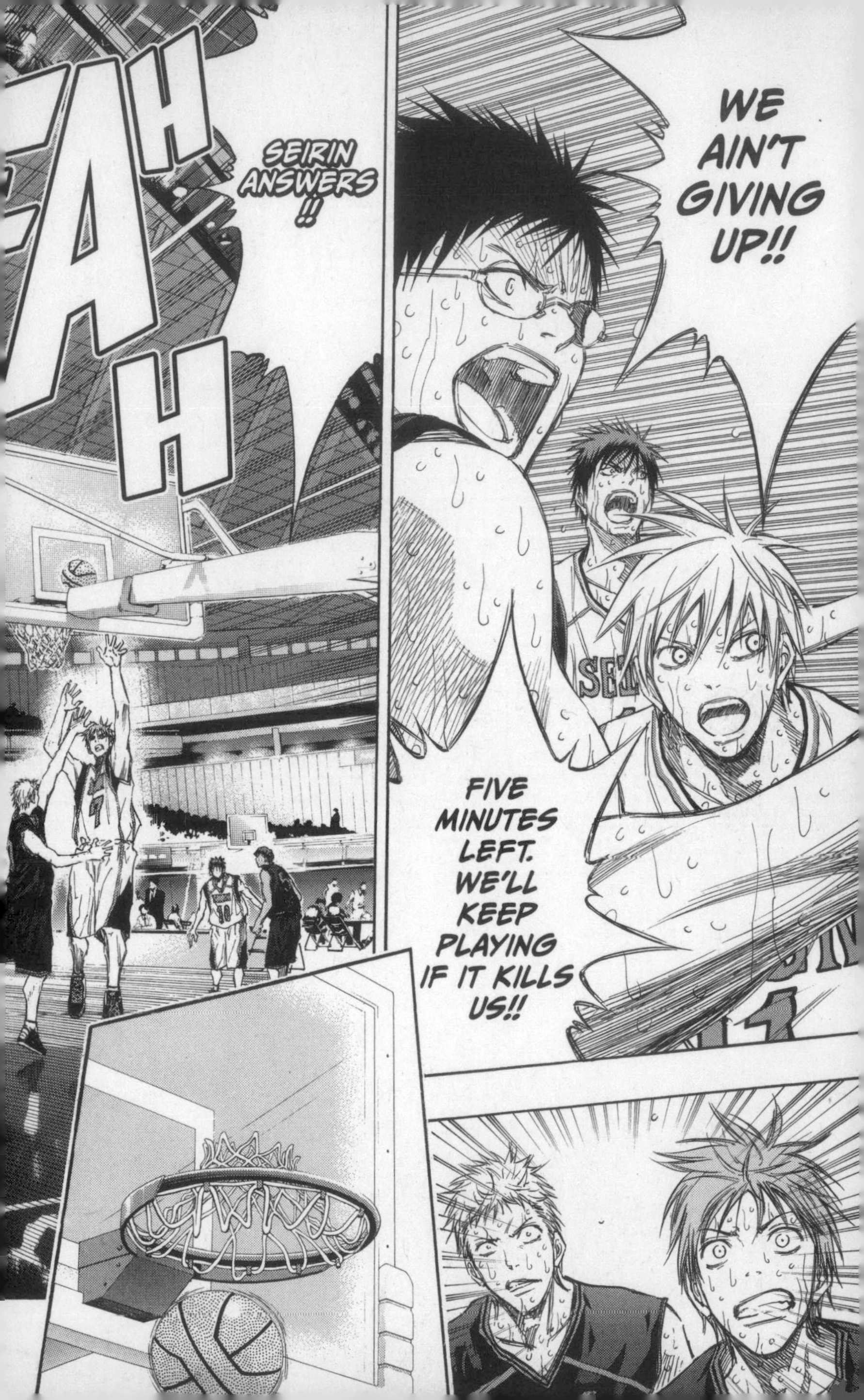

WE AIN'T GIVING UP!!
FIVE MINUTES LEFT. WE'LL KEEP PLAYING IF IT KILLS US!!
EAHH
SEIRIN ANSWERS!!

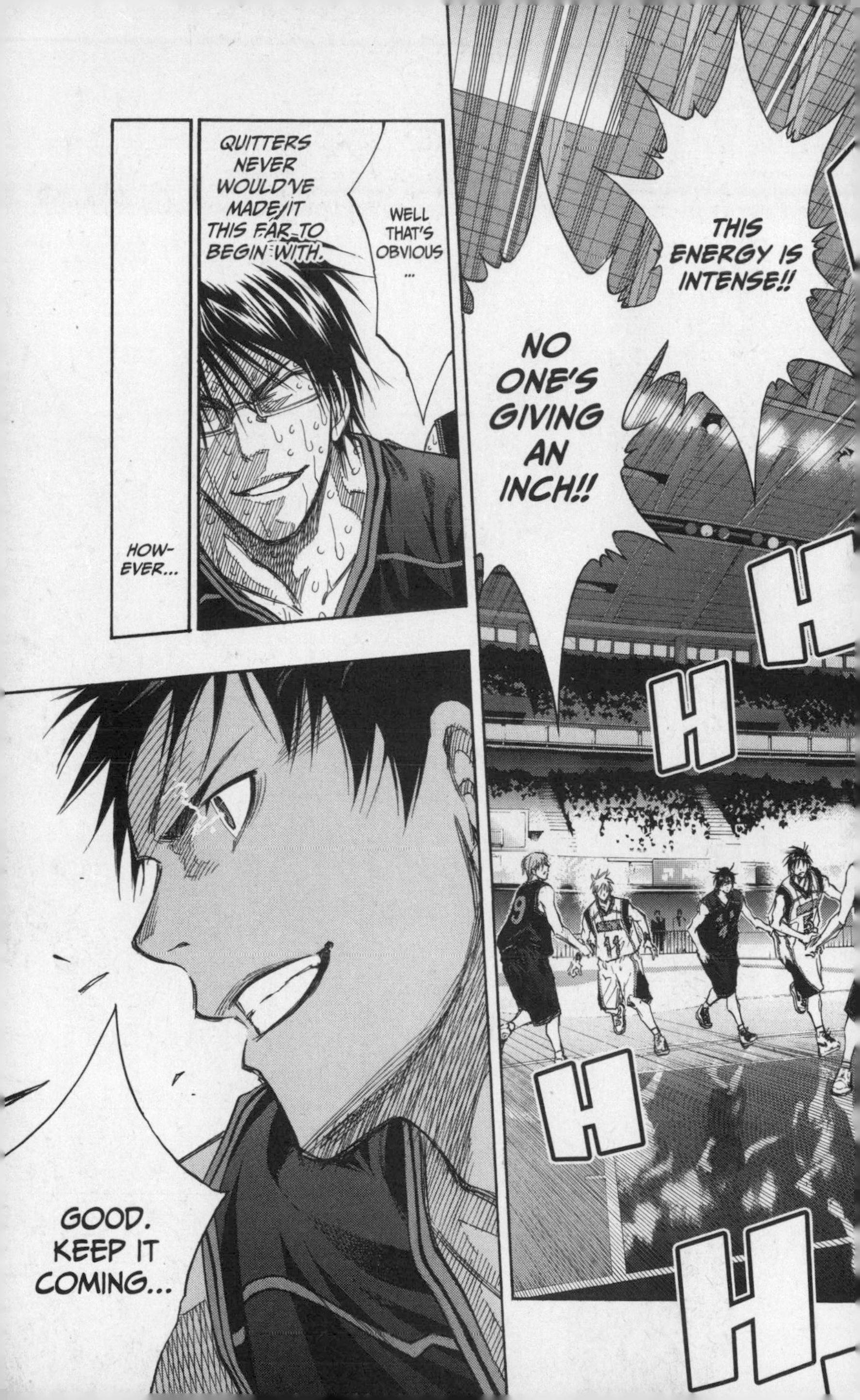

THIS ENERGY IS INTENSE!!
NO ONE'S GIVING AN INCH!!
H H H H H
WELL THAT'S OBVIOUS...
QUITTERS NEVER WOULD'VE MADE IT THIS FAR TO BEGIN WITH.
HOW-EVER...
GOOD. KEEP IT COMING...

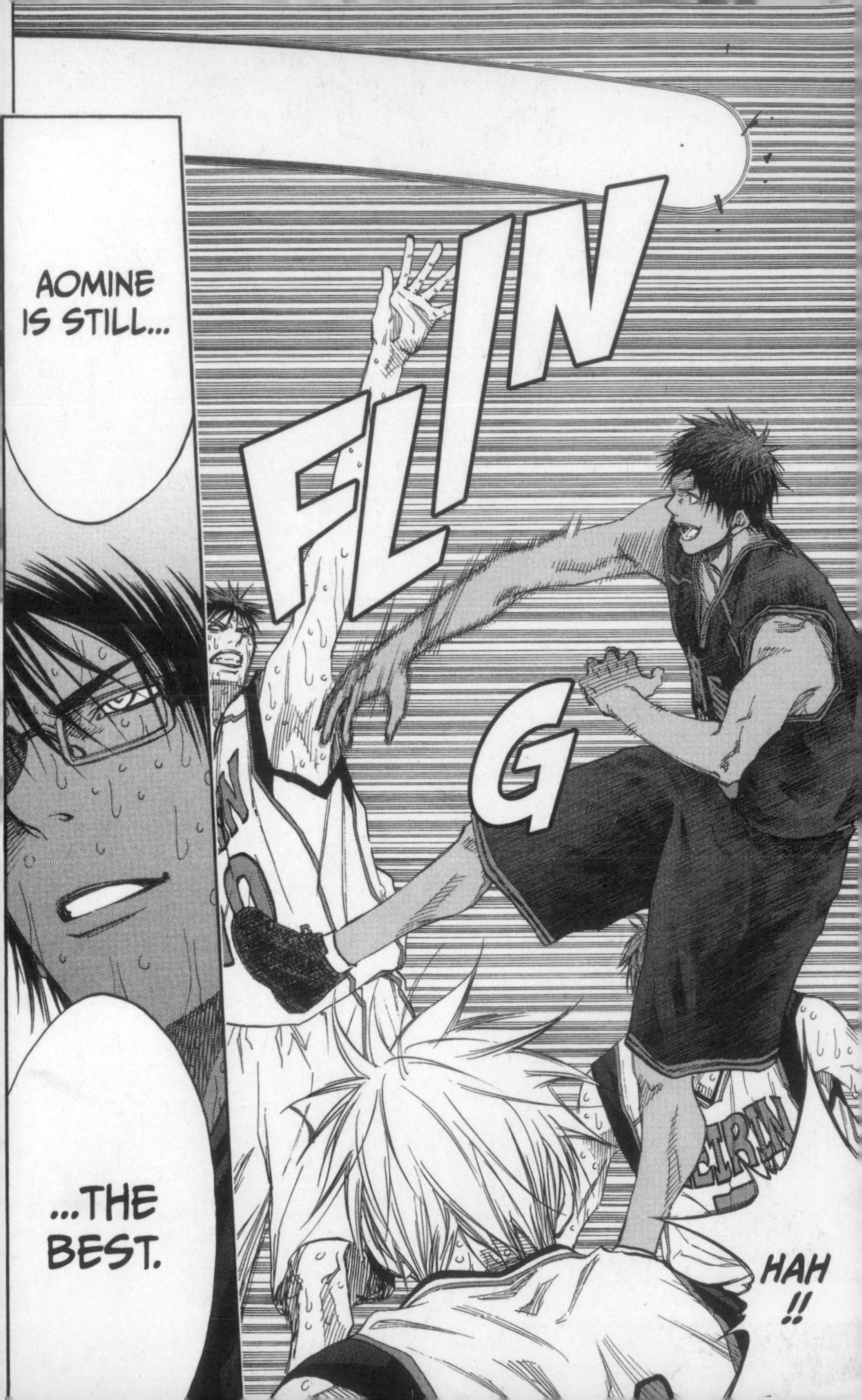
FLIIN
G
HAH!!
AOMINE IS STILL...
...THE BEST.

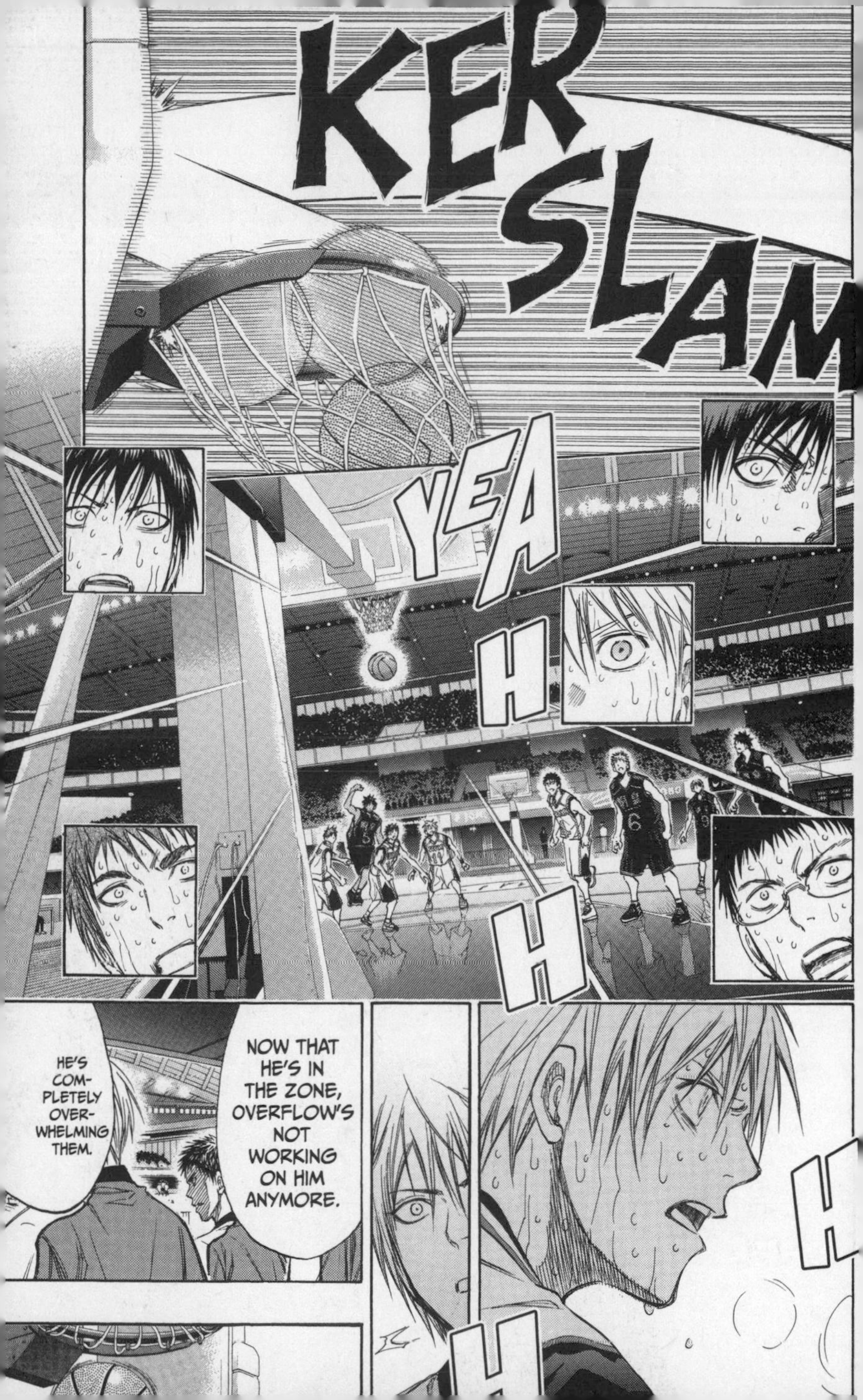
KER
SLAM
YEAH
HH
NOW THAT HE'S IN THE ZONE, OVERFLOW'S NOT WORKING ON HIM ANYMORE.
HE'S COMPLETELY OVERWHELMING THEM.
HHH

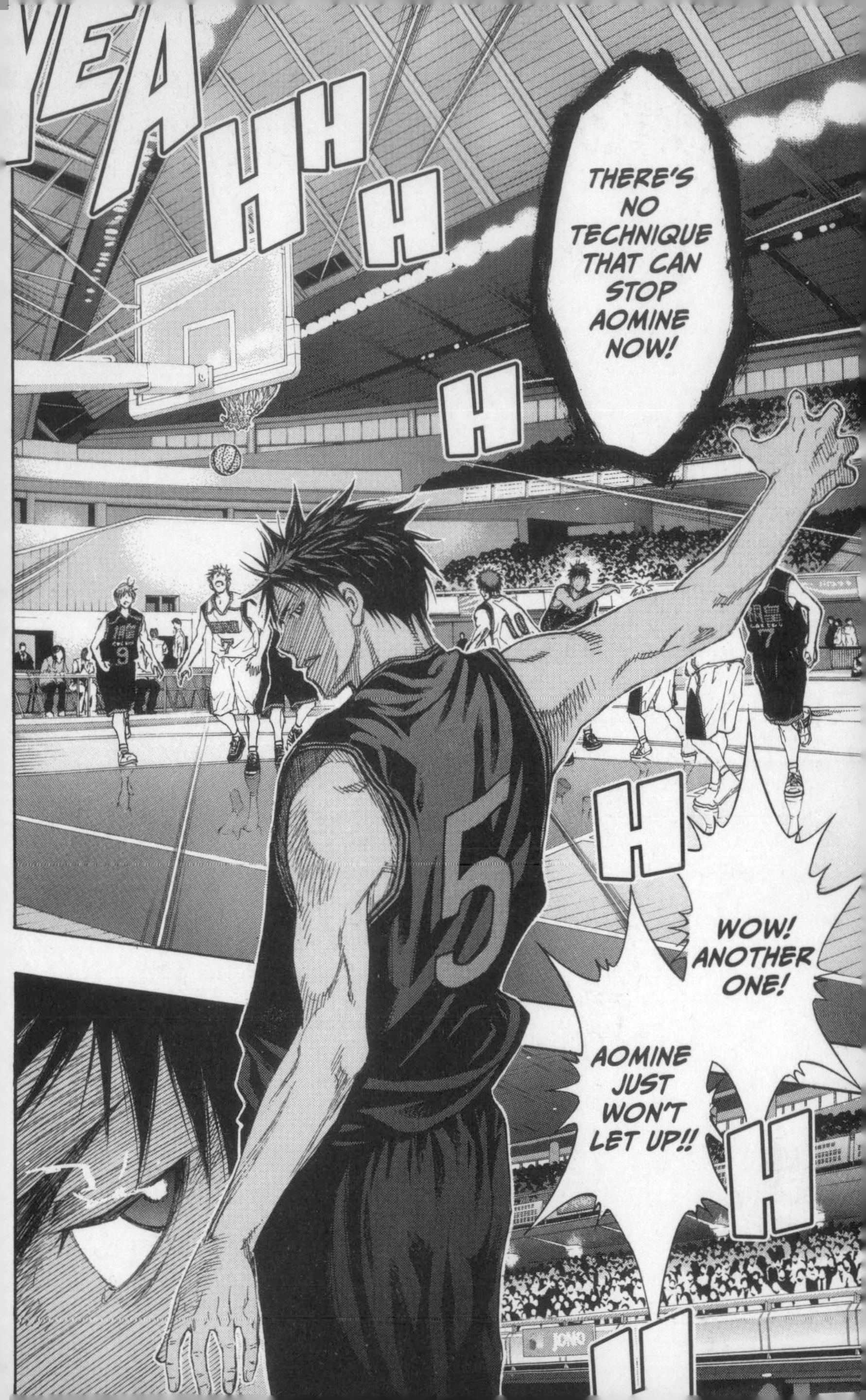
THERE'S NO TECHNIQUE THAT CAN STOP AOMINE NOW!
YEAHHHHHH
WOW! ANOTHER ONE!
AOMINE JUST WON'T LET UP!!

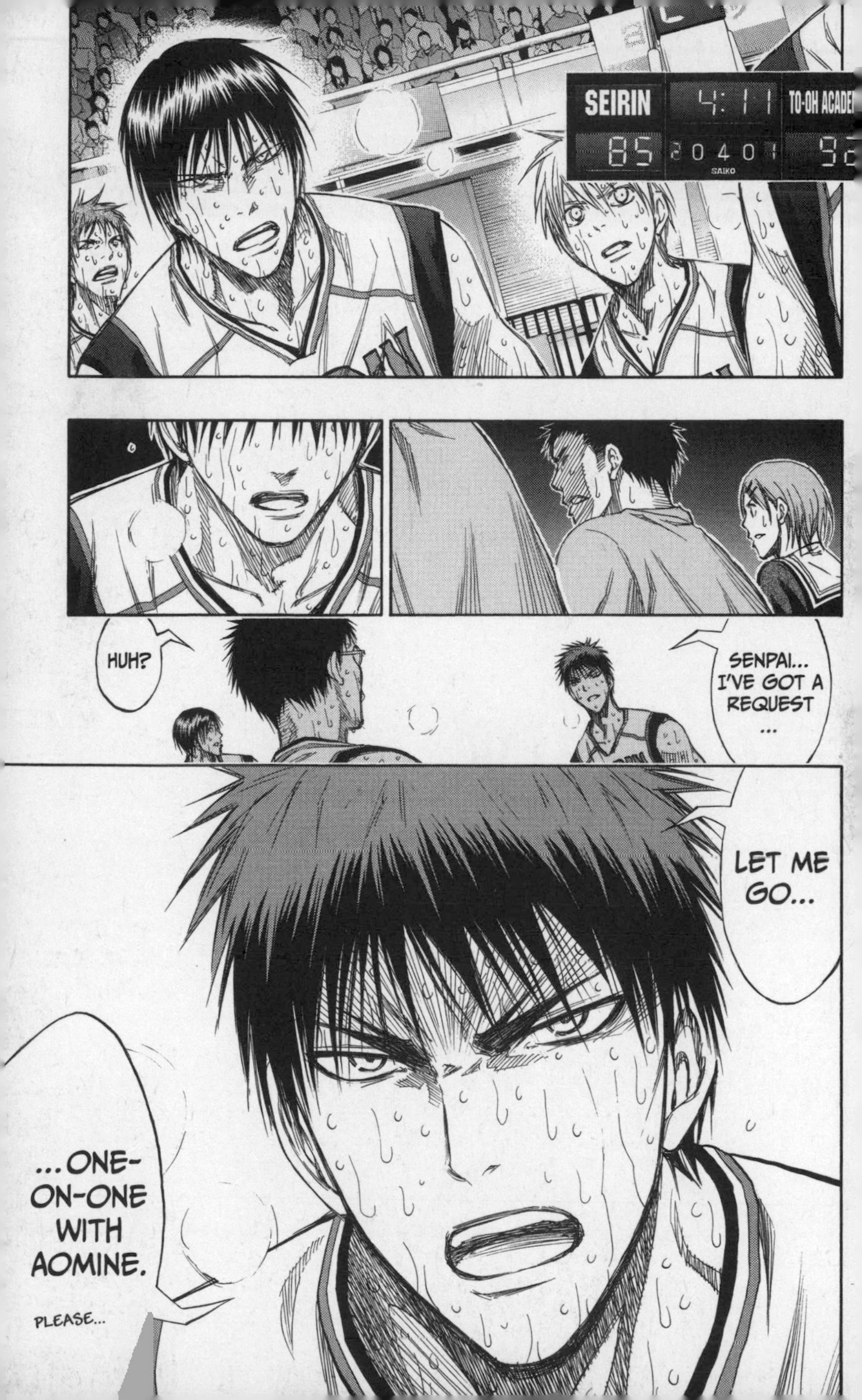
SEIRIN
4:11
85
SENPAI... I'VE GOT A REQUEST ...
HUH?
LET ME GO...
...ONE-ON-ONE WITH AOMINE.
PLEASE...

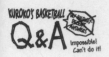

KUROKO'S BASKETBALL Q&A

Impossible! Can't do it!

Q. **WHEN IT COMES TO MOMOI AND THE SIX MIRACLE GENERATION BOYS, IS THAT THEIR NATURAL HAIR COLOR?**
(POPII from AICHI PREFECTURE)

A. I DON'T KNOW.

KUROKO'S BASKETBALL BLOOPERS

TAKE 2

TO-OH ACADEMY, HUH...?
IN TERMS OF ACCOMPLISHMENTS, THEY'VE SHOWN RAPID GROWTH THESE PAST FEW YEARS.
PAMPHLET
TO-OH ACADEMY
JOIN US, WON'T YOU?
I'LL DO IT...!
HOLD ON. WHEN'D WE START USING THOSE PAMPHLETS?
SHP
ONE-TRACK MIND, HUH?

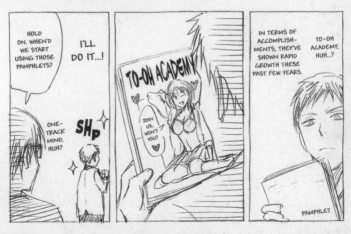

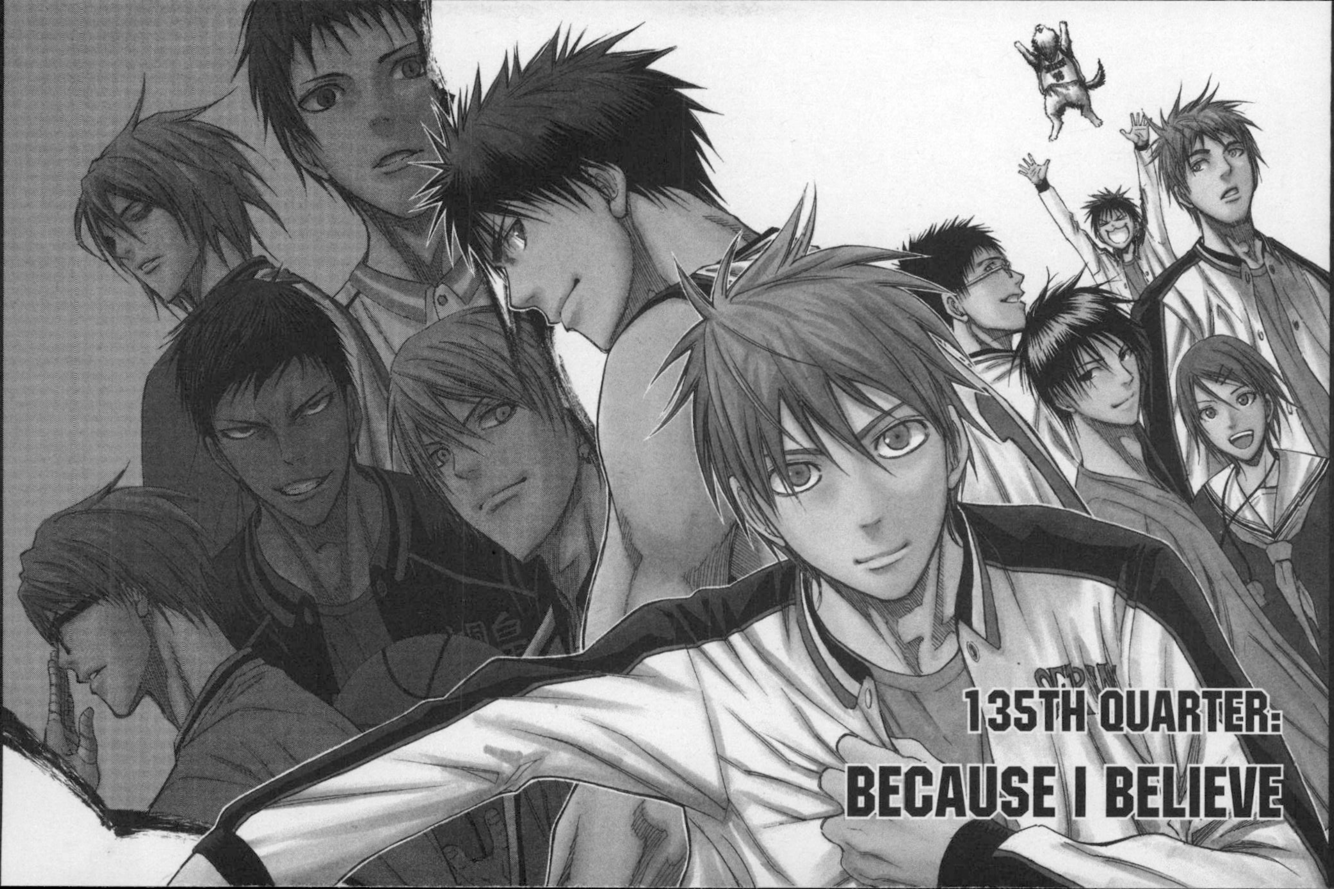
135TH QUARTER:
BECAUSE I BELIEVE

Kuroko's
BASKETBALL

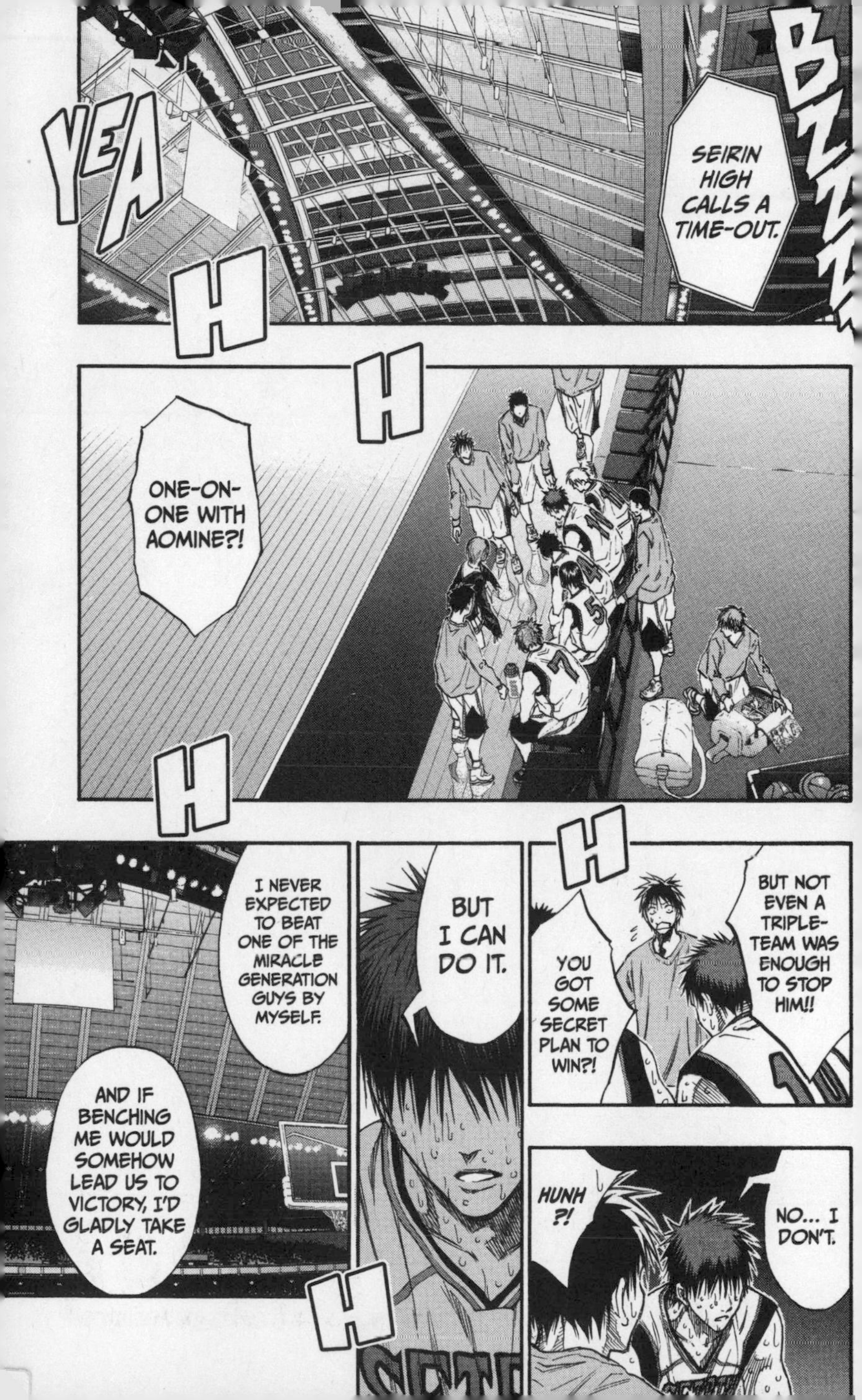
BZZZ
SEIRIN HIGH CALLS A TIME-OUT.
YEA
H
H
ONE-ON-ONE WITH AOMINE?!
H
H
BUT NOT EVEN A TRIPLE-TEAM WAS ENOUGH TO STOP HIM!!
YOU GOT SOME SECRET PLAN TO WIN?!
NO... I DON'T.
HUNH ?!
BUT I CAN DO IT.
H
I NEVER EXPECTED TO BEAT ONE OF THE MIRACLE GENERATION GUYS BY MYSELF.
AND IF BENCHING ME WOULD SOMEHOW LEAD US TO VICTORY, I'D GLADLY TAKE A SEAT.

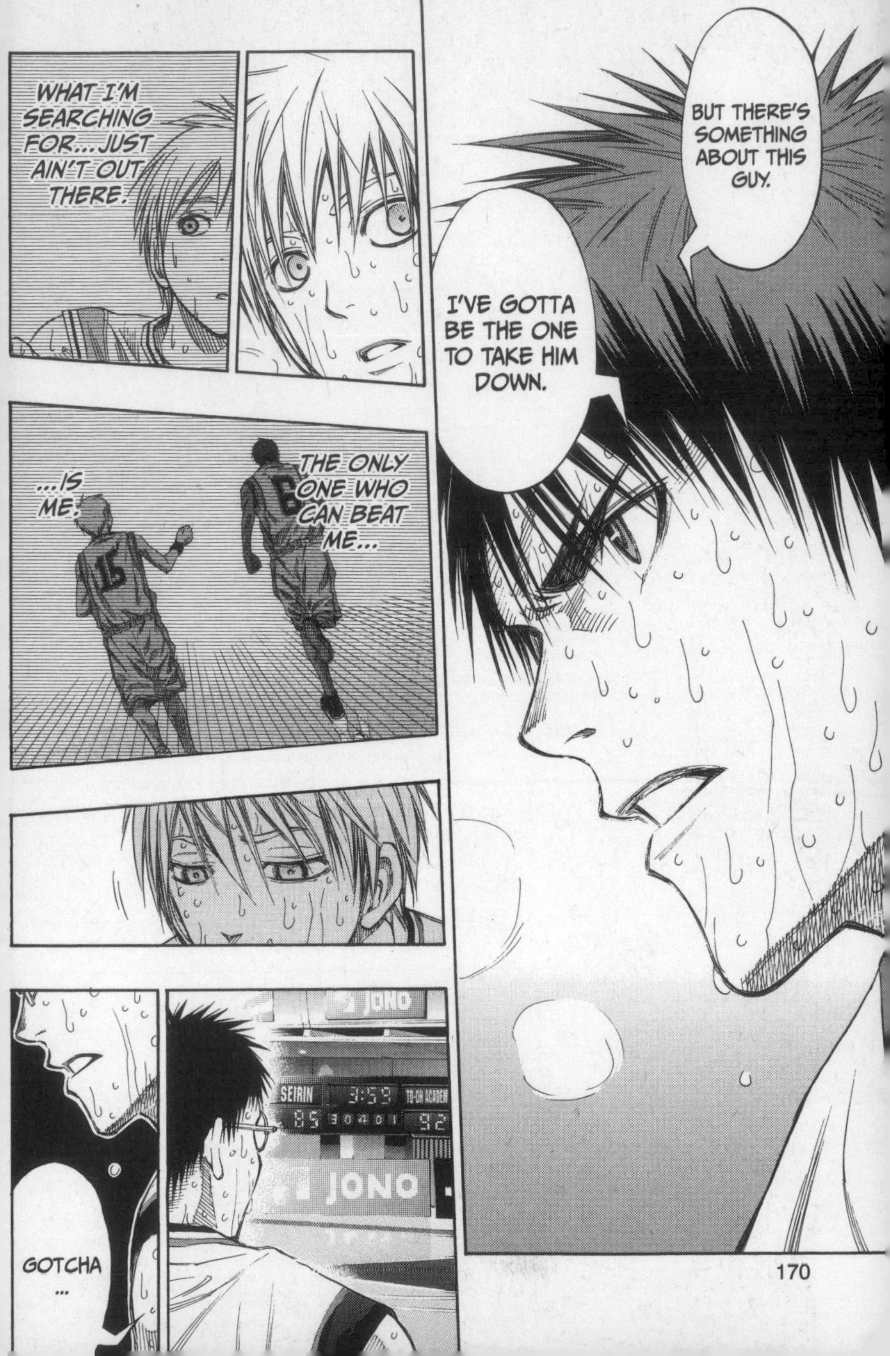
BUT THERE'S SOMETHING ABOUT THIS GUY.
I'VE GOTTA BE THE ONE TO TAKE HIM DOWN.
WHAT I'M SEARCHING FOR... JUST AIN'T OUT THERE.
THE ONLY ONE WHO CAN BEAT ME...
...IS ME.
JONO
SEIRIN
3:59
85
92
JONO
GOTCHA ...

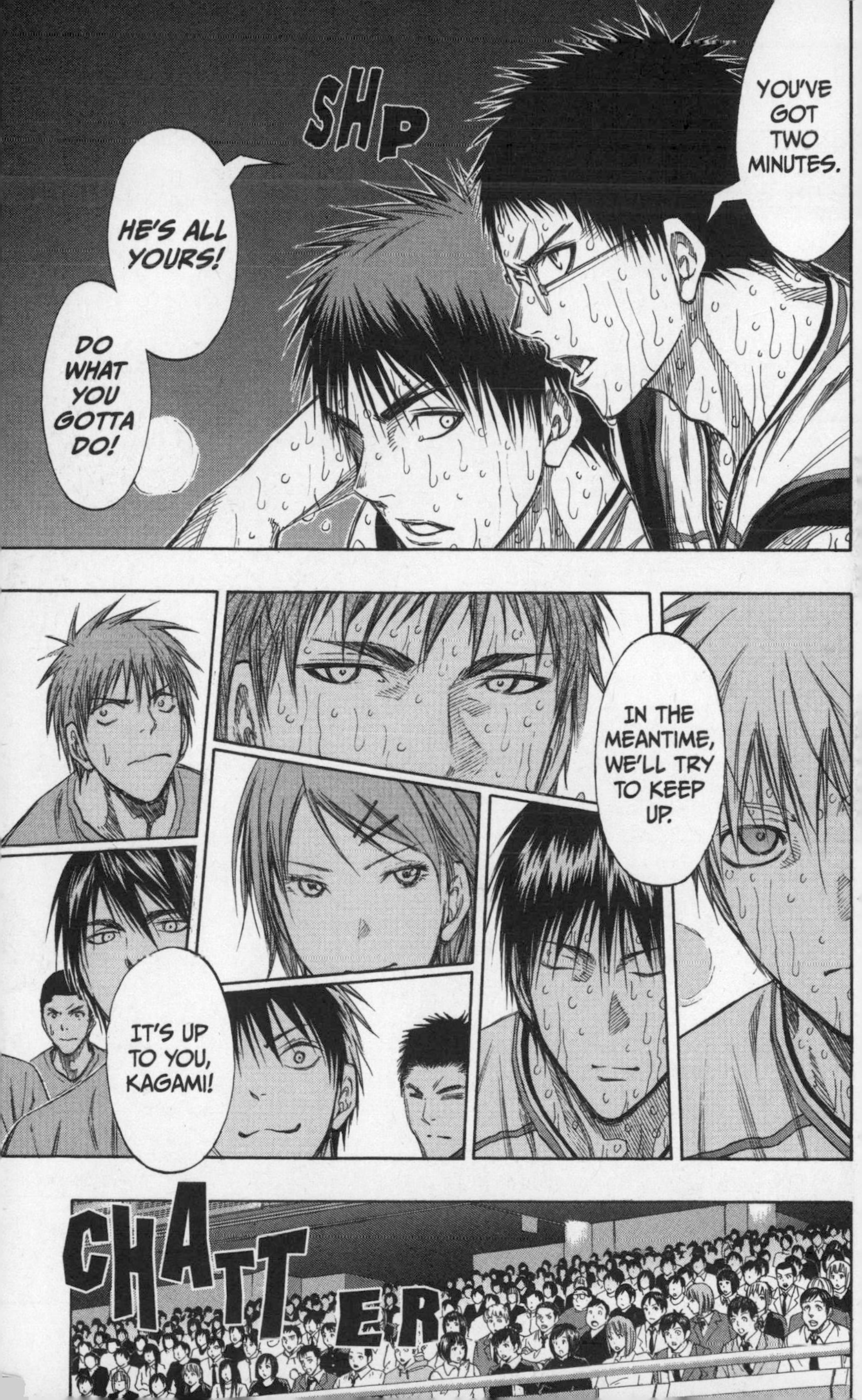
YOU'VE GOT TWO MINUTES.
SHP
HE'S ALL YOURS!
DO WHAT YOU GOTTA DO!
IN THE MEANTIME, WE'LL TRY TO KEEP UP.
IT'S UP TO YOU, KAGAMI!
CHATTER

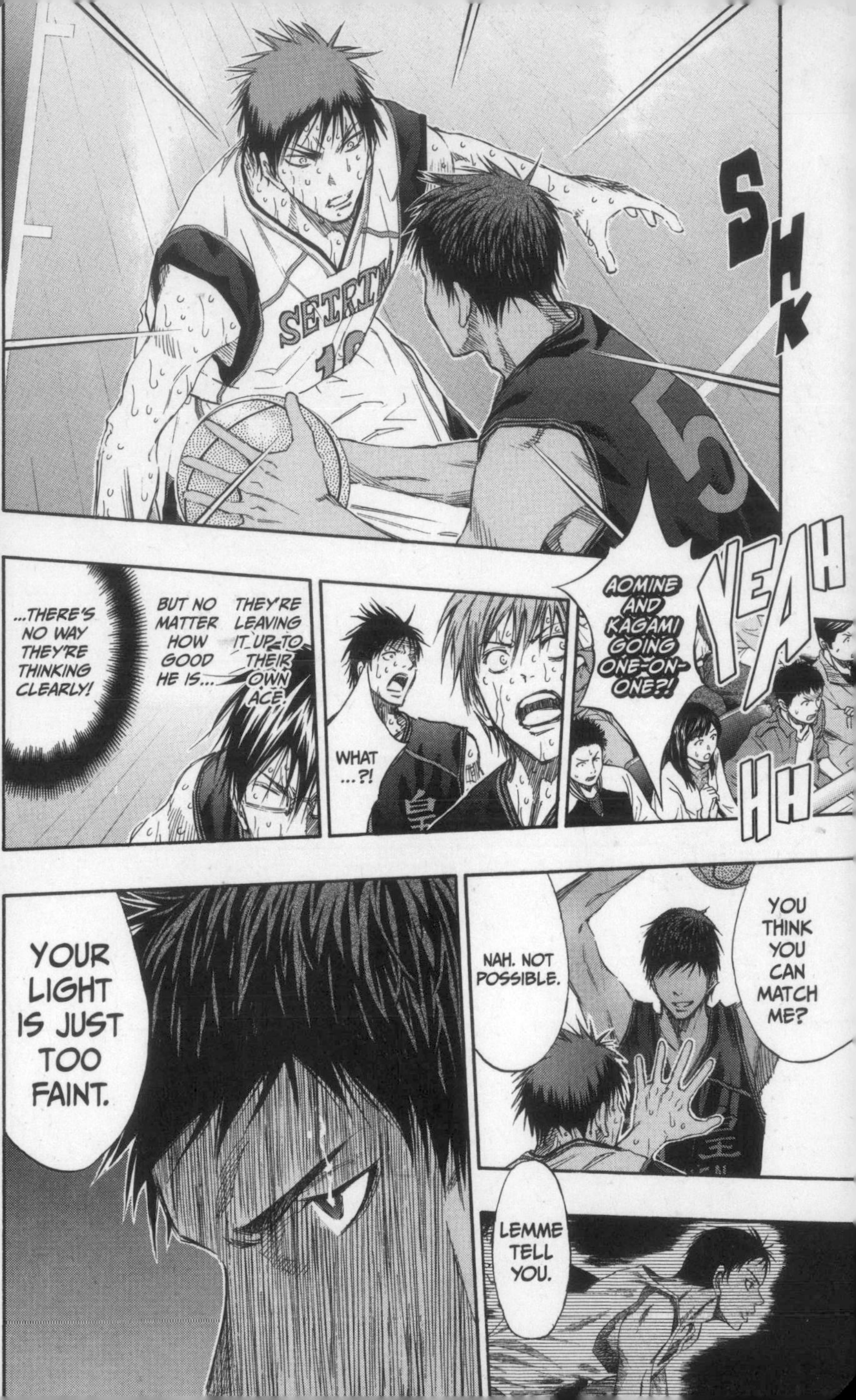
SHHK
AOMINE AND KAGAMI GOING ONE-ON-ONE?!
YEAHHH
WHAT ...?!
THEY'RE LEAVING IT UP TO THEIR OWN ACE.
BUT NO MATTER HOW GOOD HE IS...
...THERE'S NO WAY THEY'RE THINKING CLEARLY!
YOU THINK YOU CAN MATCH ME?
NAH. NOT POSSIBLE.
LEMME TELL YOU.
YOUR LIGHT IS JUST TOO FAINT.

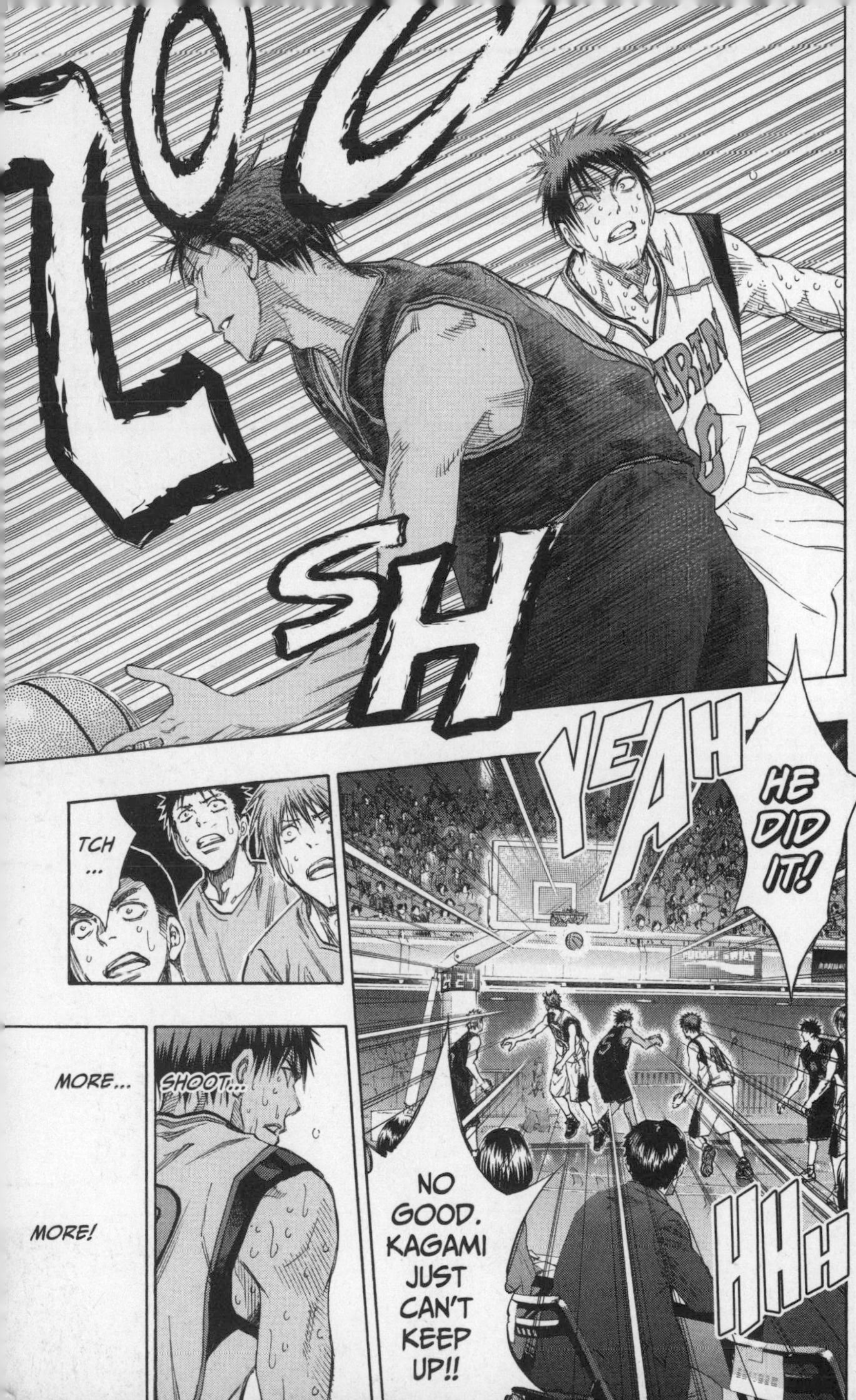
SH
YEAH
HE DID IT!
HHH
NO GOOD. KAGAMI JUST CAN'T KEEP UP!!
TCH ...
SHOOT...
MORE...
MORE!

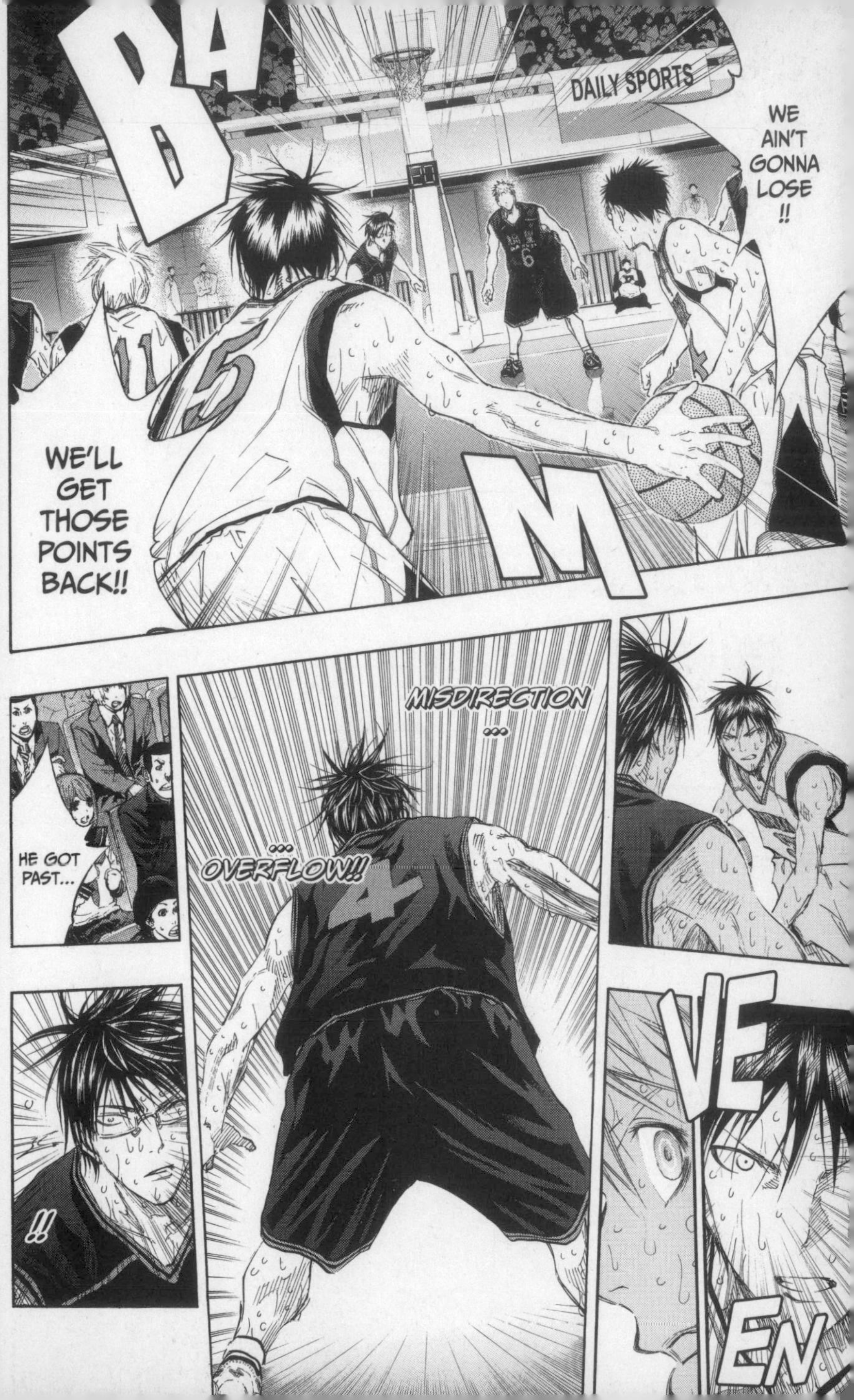
DAILY SPORTS
WE AIN'T GONNA LOSE!!
BAM
WE'LL GET THOSE POINTS BACK!!
VEEN
MISDIRECTION...
...OVERFLOW!!
HE GOT PAST...
!!

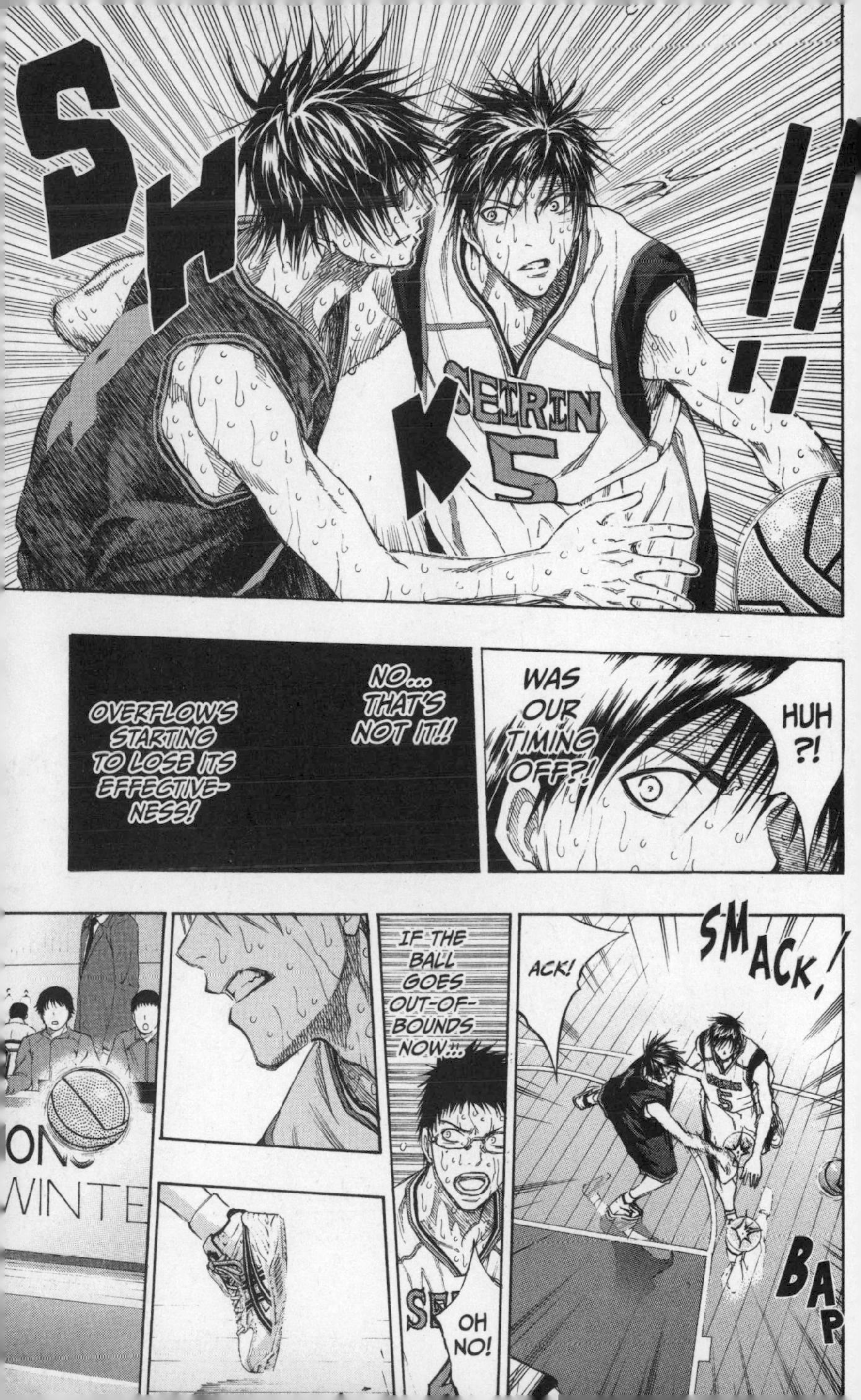
SHK!!
HUH ?!
WAS OUR TIMING OFF?!
NO... THAT'S NOT IT!!
OVERFLOW'S STARTING TO LOSE ITS EFFECTIVE-NESS!
SMACK!
ACK!
BAP
IF THE BALL GOES OUT-OF-BOUNDS NOW...!
OH NO!

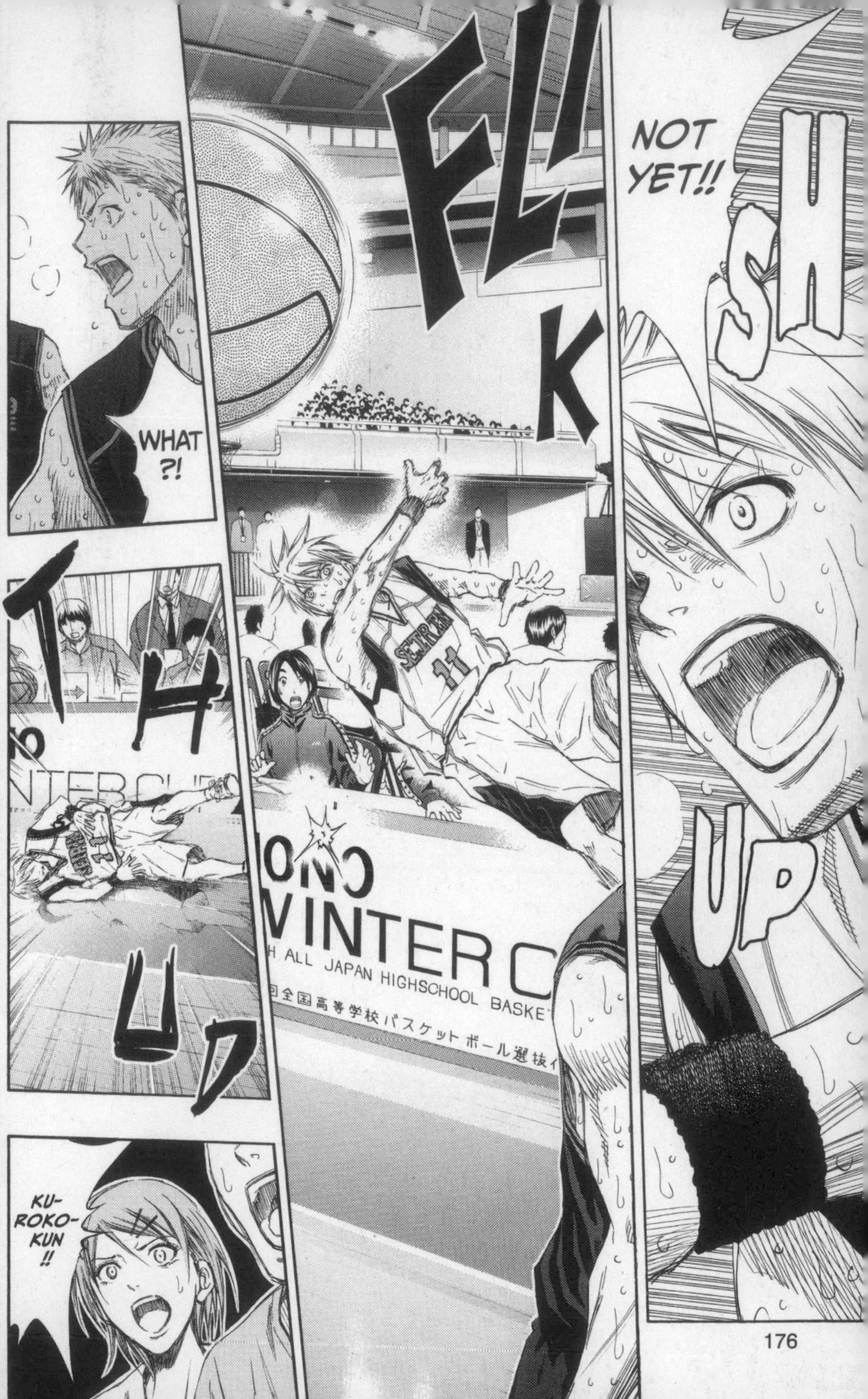
NOT YET!!
SHUP
FLIK
WHAT ?!
THUD
KU-ROKO-KUN !!

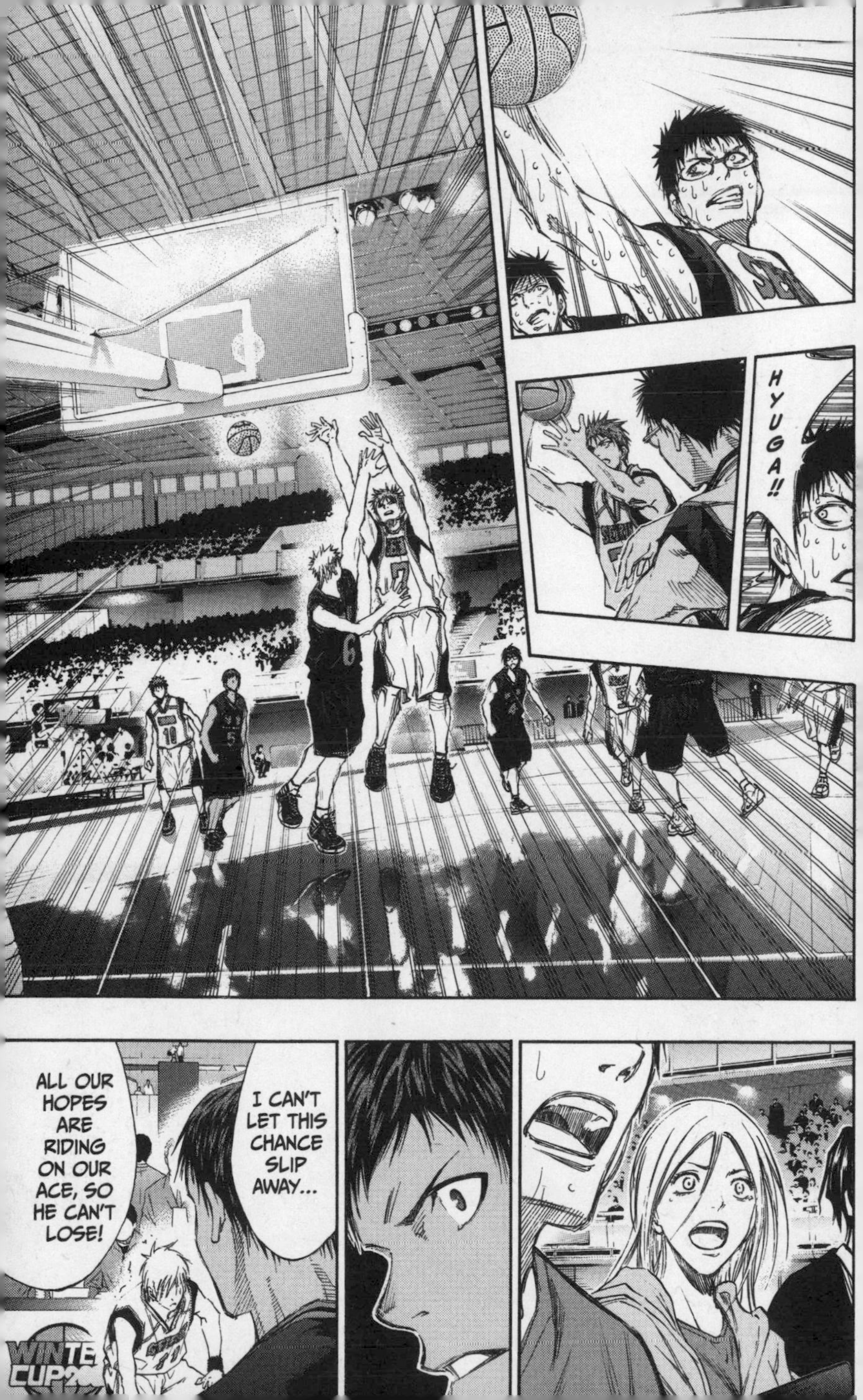
HYUGA!!
I CAN'T LET THIS CHANCE SLIP AWAY...
ALL OUR HOPES ARE RIDING ON OUR ACE, SO HE CAN'T LOSE!

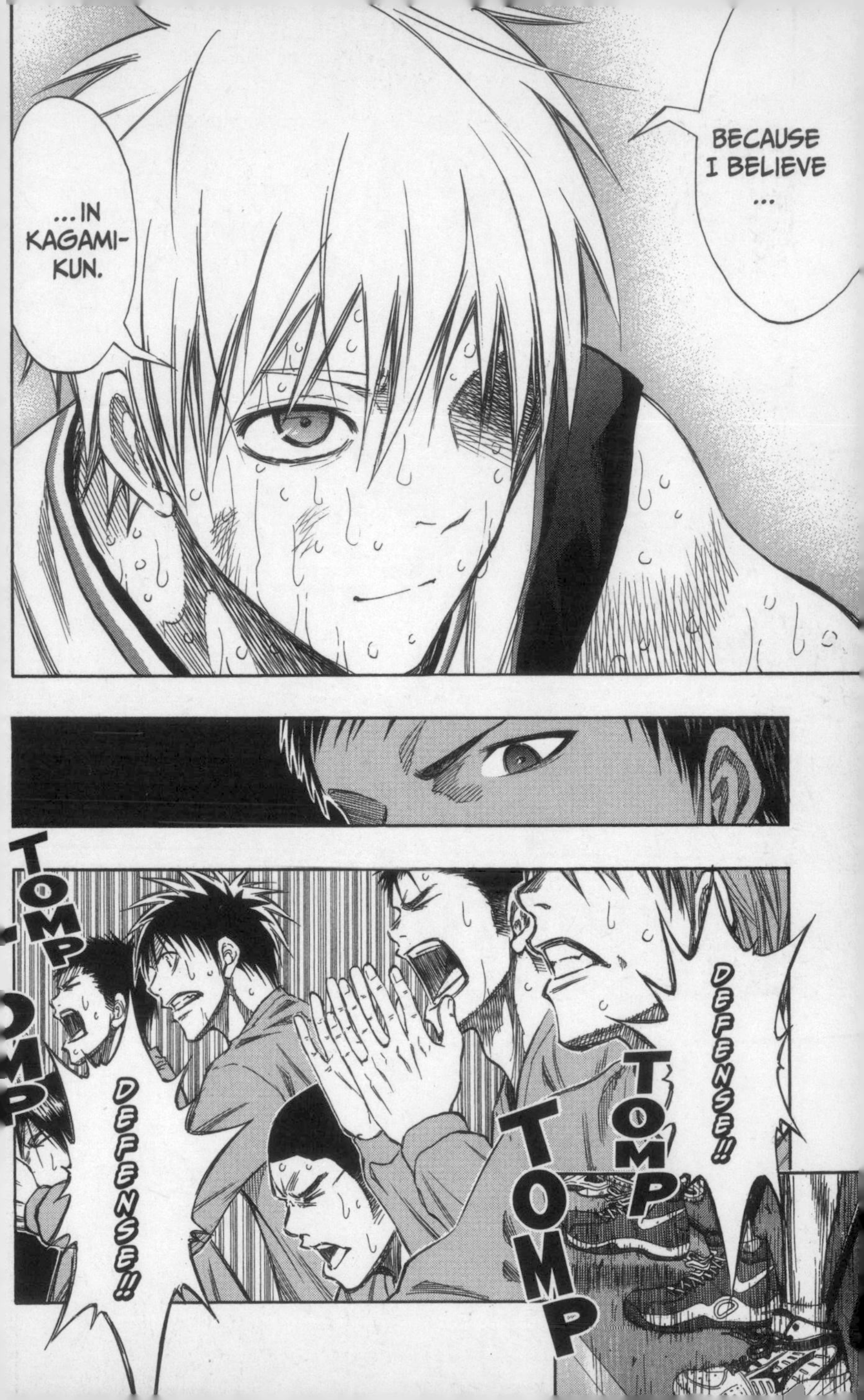

BECAUSE I BELIEVE ...
...IN KAGAMI-KUN.
DEFENSE!!
TOMP
TOMP
DEFENSE!!
TOMP

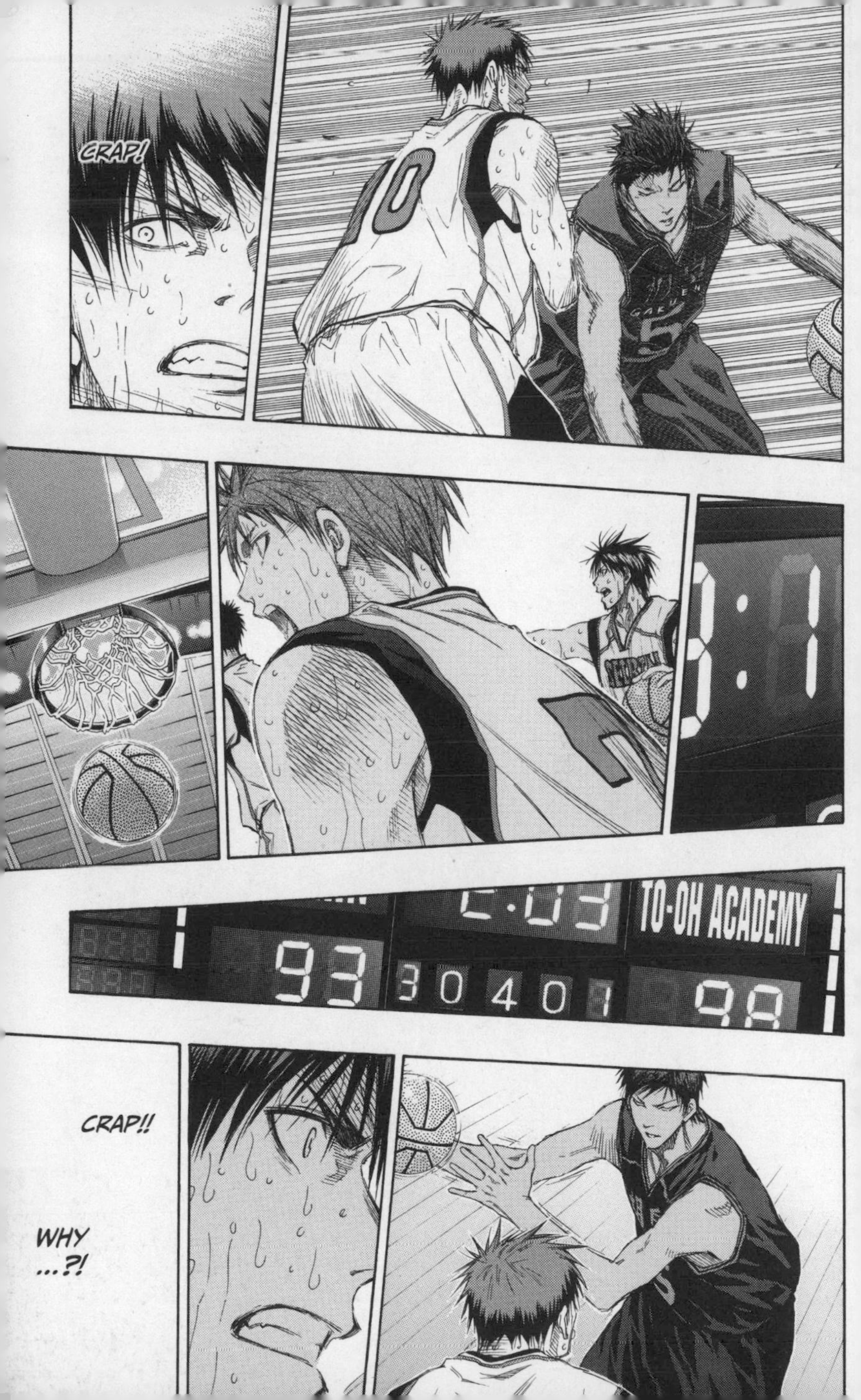
CRAP!
TO-OH ACADEMY
93
CRAP!!
WHY ...?!

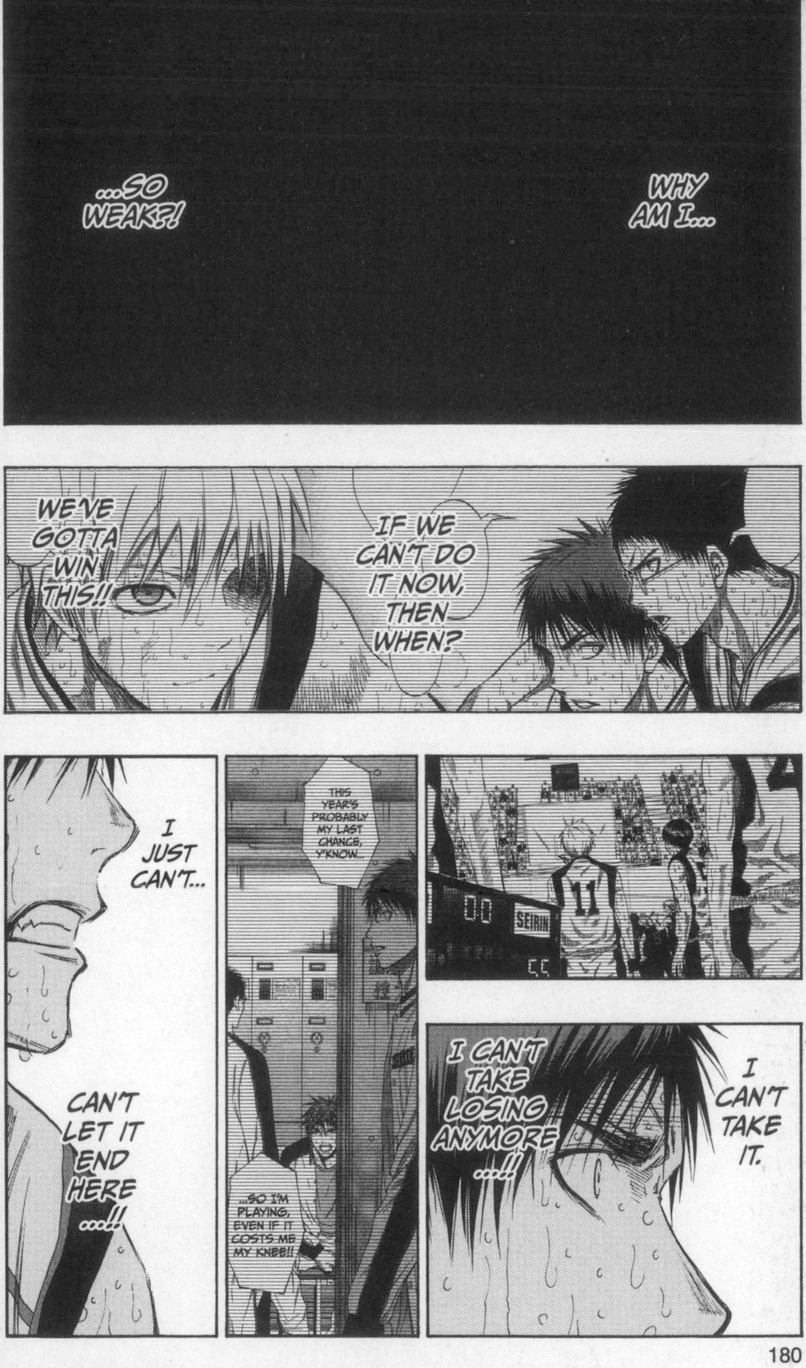
WHY AM I...
...SO WEAK?!
IF WE CAN'T DO IT NOW, THEN WHEN?
WE'VE GOTTA WIN THIS!!
I CAN'T TAKE IT.
I CAN'T TAKE LOSING ANYMORE ...!!
SEIRIN
THIS YEAR'S PROBABLY MY LAST CHANCE, Y'KNOW...
...SO I'M PLAYING, EVEN IF IT COSTS ME MY KNEE!!
I JUST CAN'T...
CAN'T LET IT END HERE ...!!

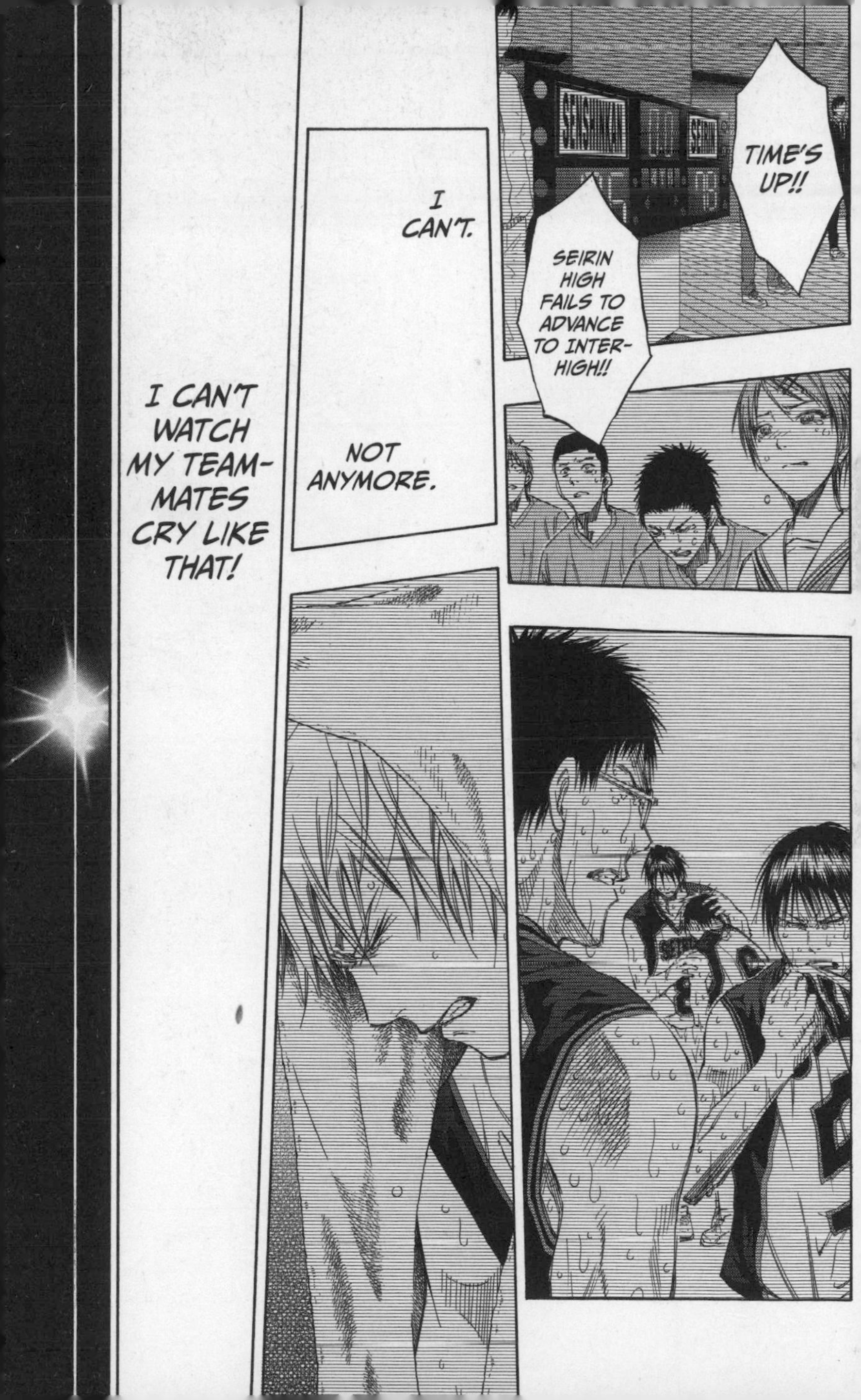
SENSHINKAN
SEIRIN
TIME'S UP!!
SEIRIN HIGH FAILS TO ADVANCE TO INTER-HIGH!!
I CAN'T.
NOT ANYMORE.
I CAN'T WATCH MY TEAM-MATES CRY LIKE THAT!

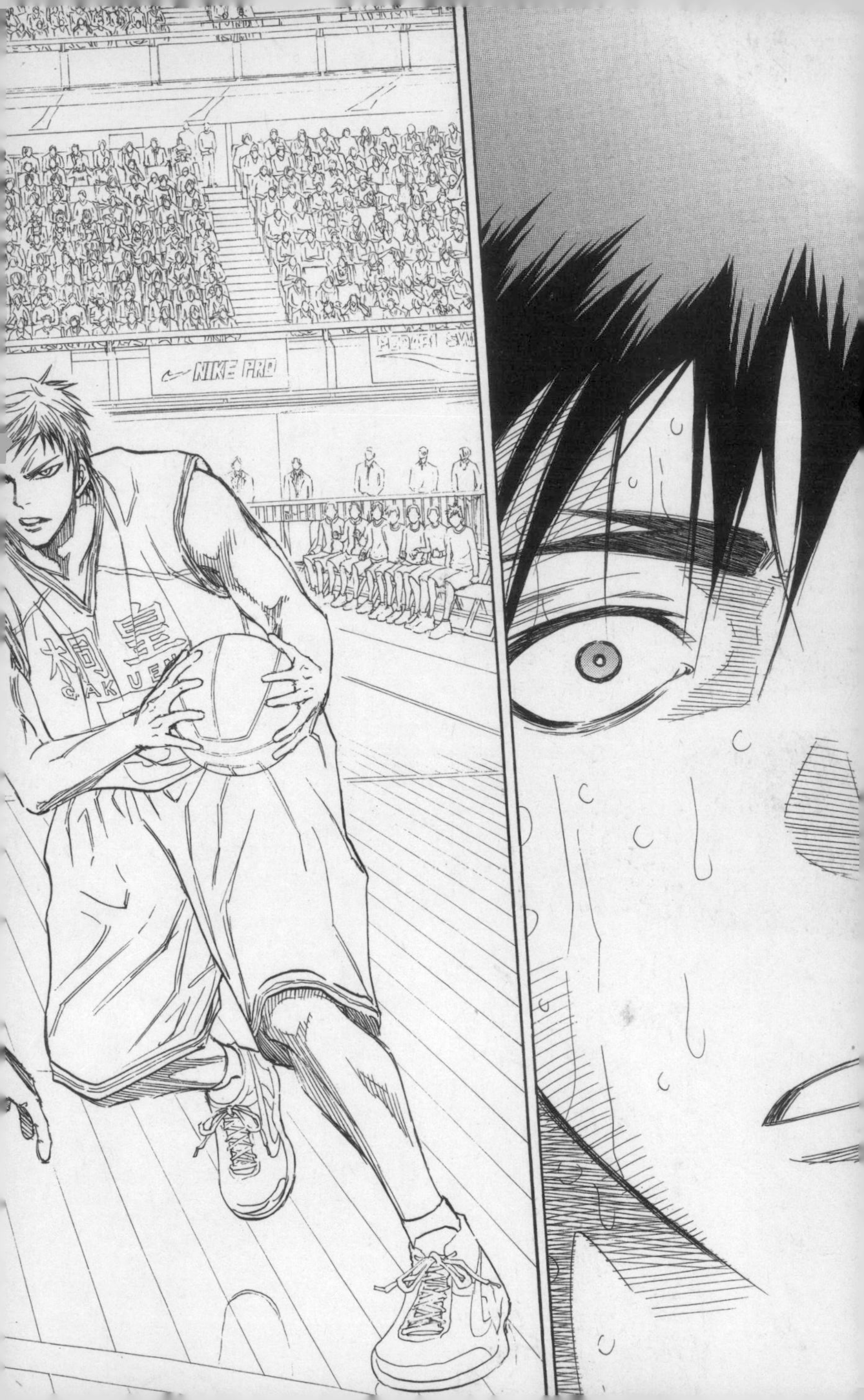
NIKE PRO
桐皇

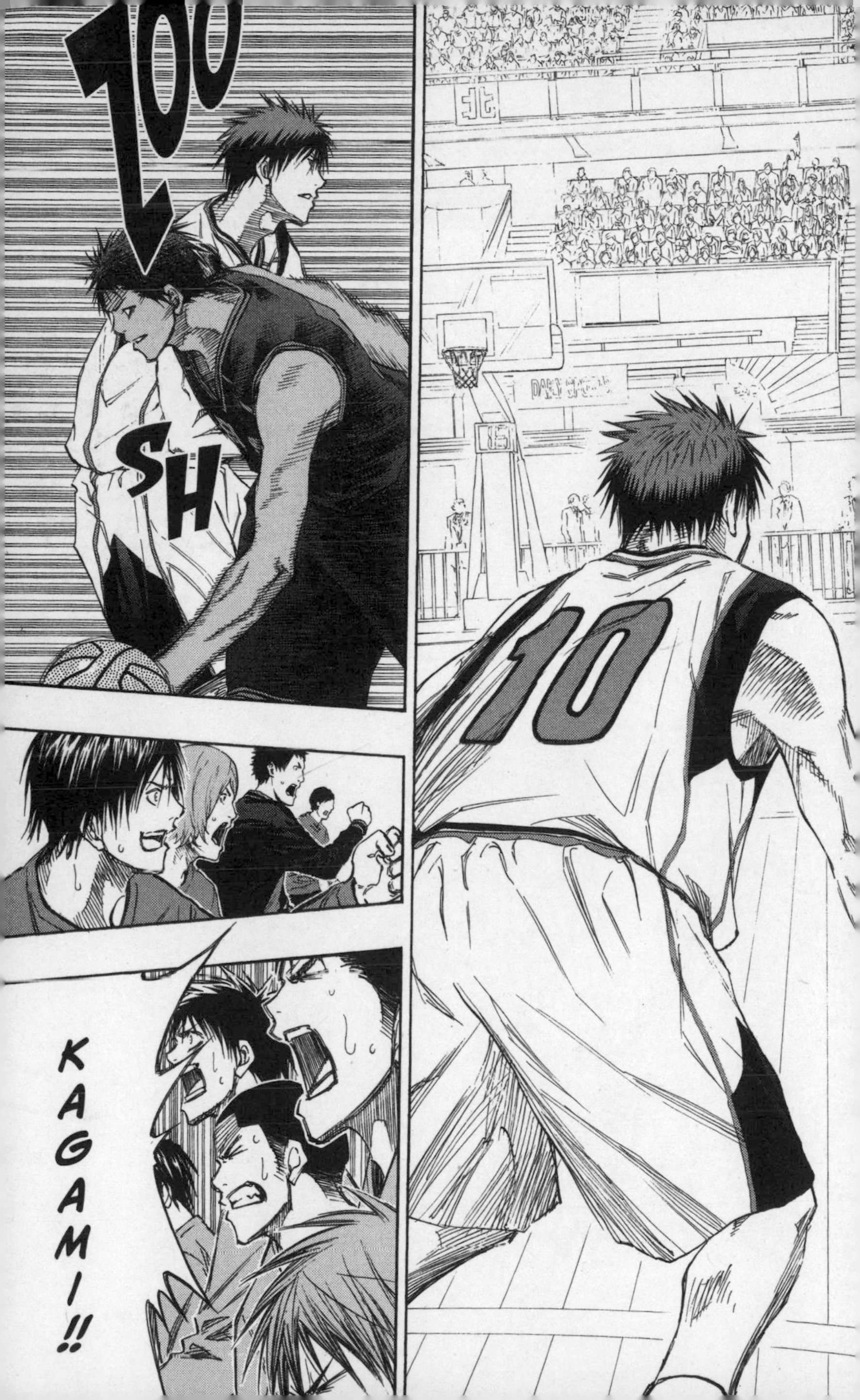
TOO
SH
KAGAMI!!

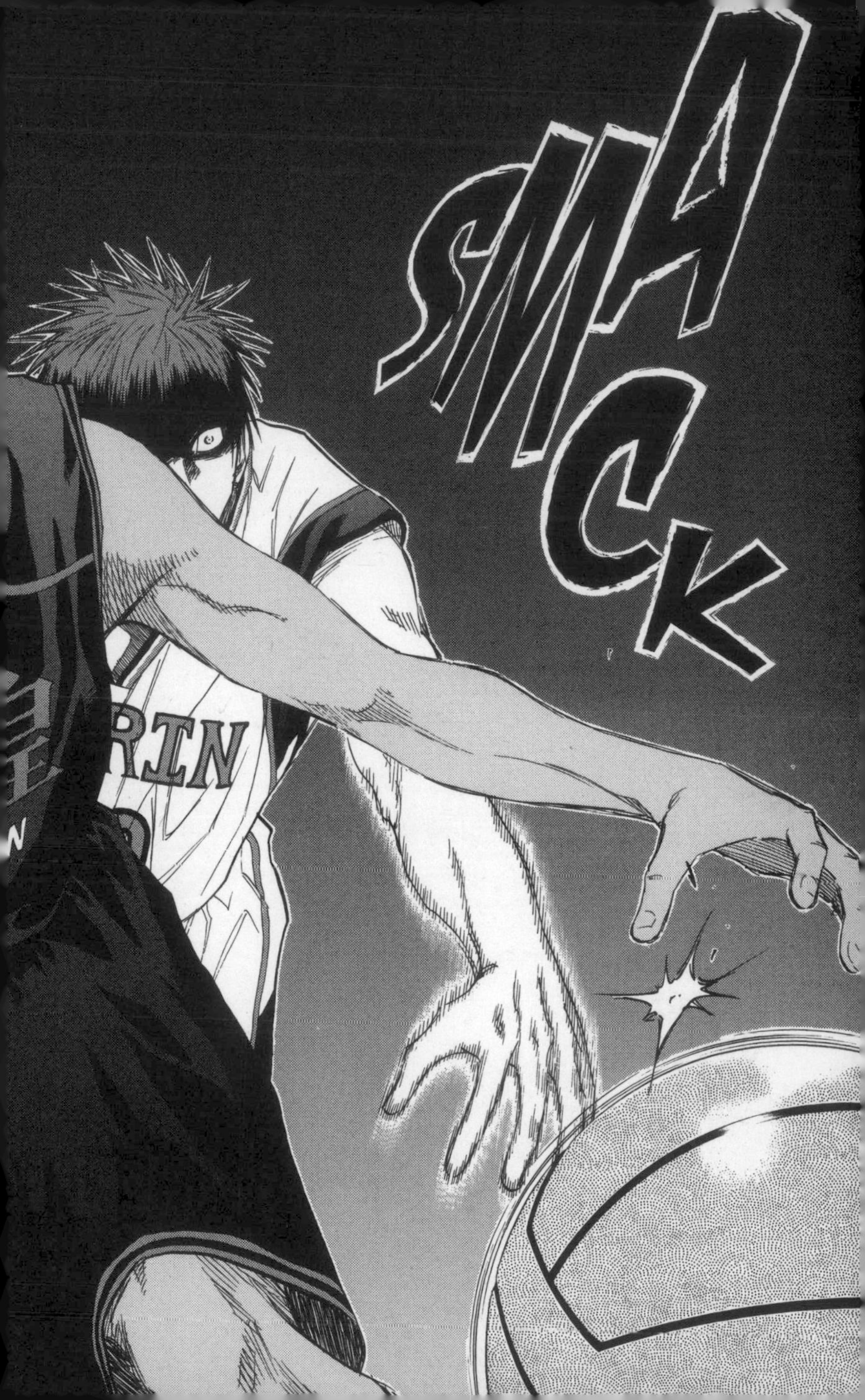
SMACK

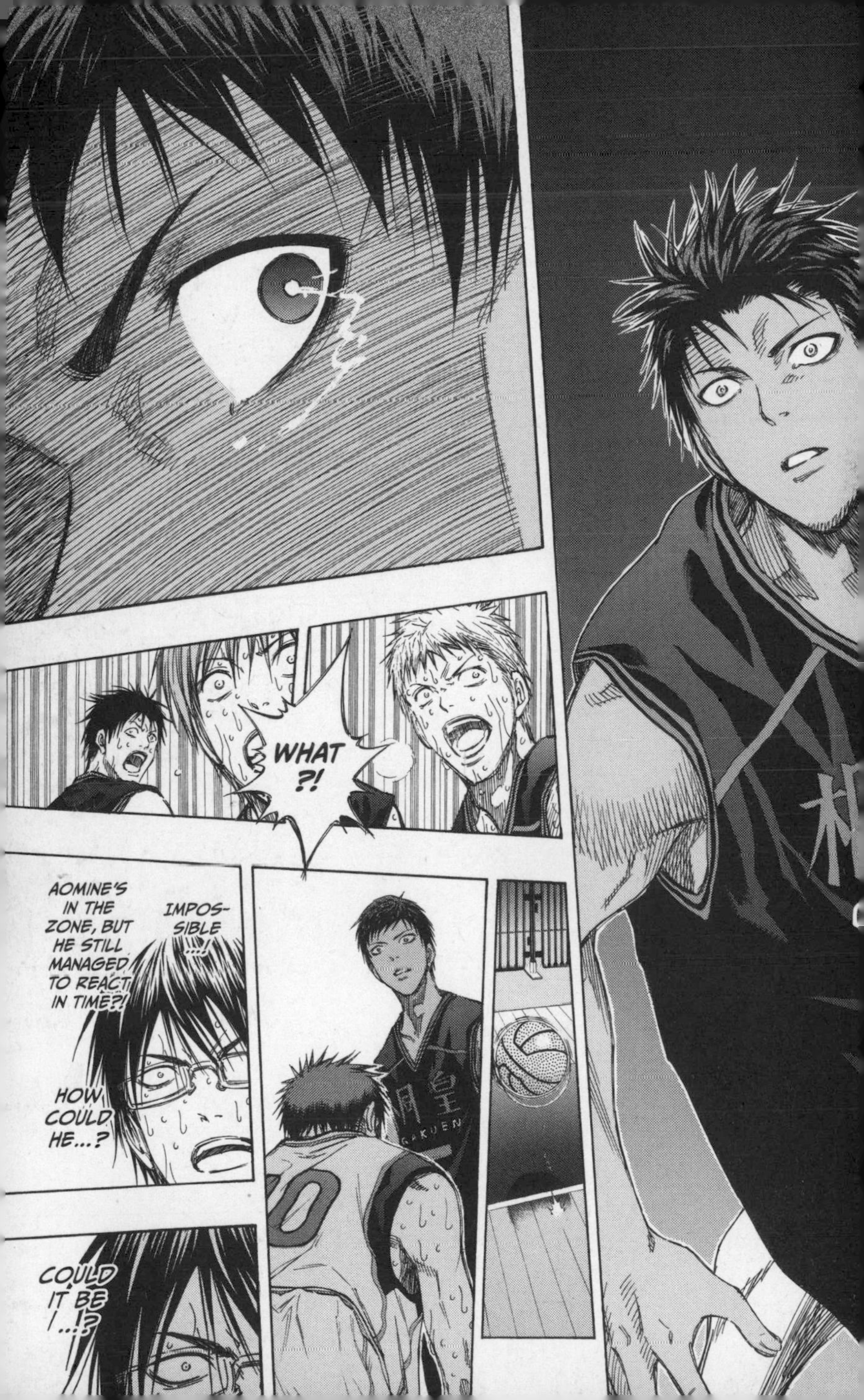
WHAT ?!
IMPOS-SIBLE ...!
AOMINE'S IN THE ZONE, BUT HE STILL MANAGED TO REACT IN TIME?!
HOW COULD HE...?
COULD IT BE ...!?

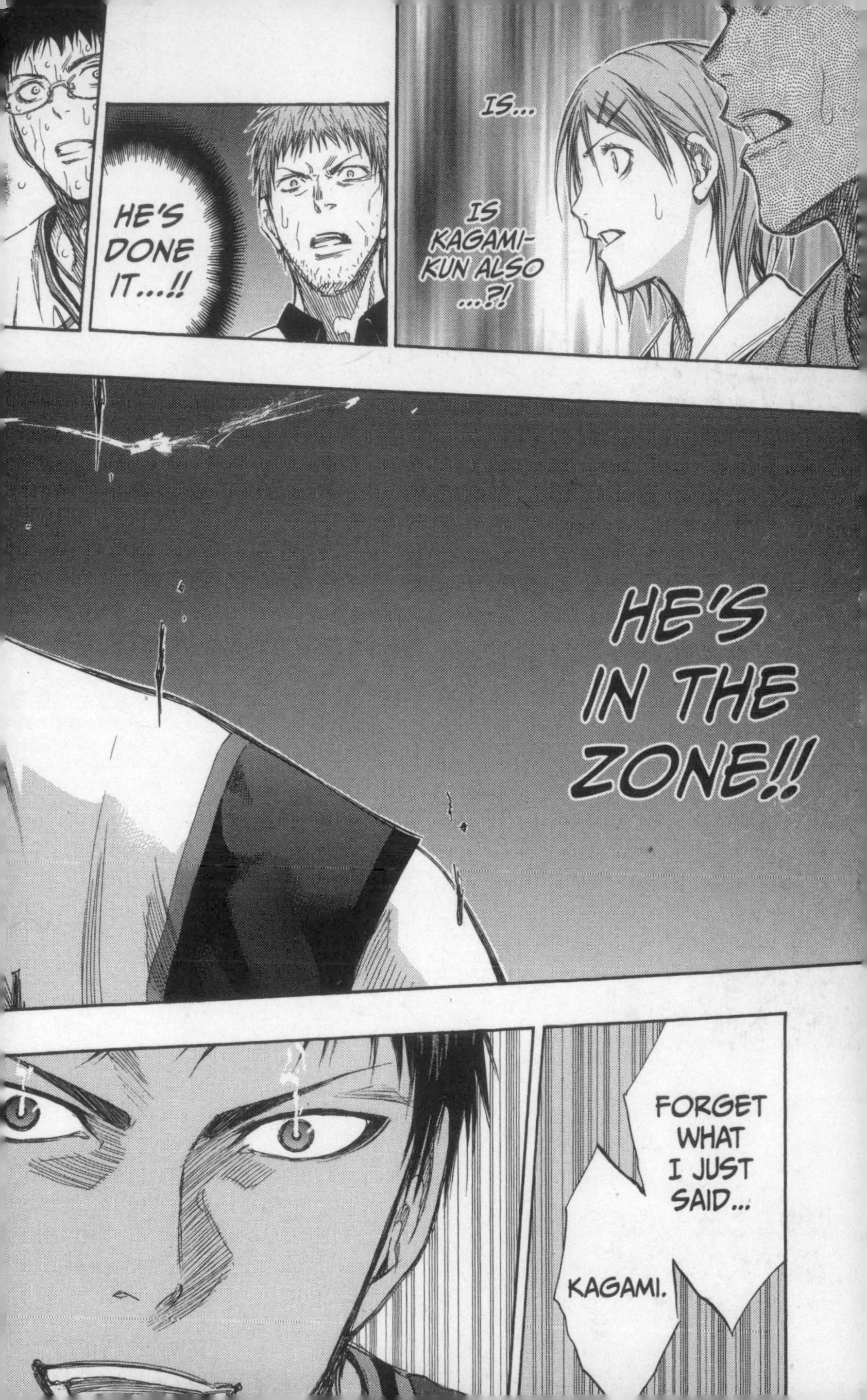
IS...
IS KAGAMI-KUN ALSO ...?!
HE'S DONE IT...!!
HE'S IN THE ZONE!!
FORGET WHAT I JUST SAID...
KAGAMI.

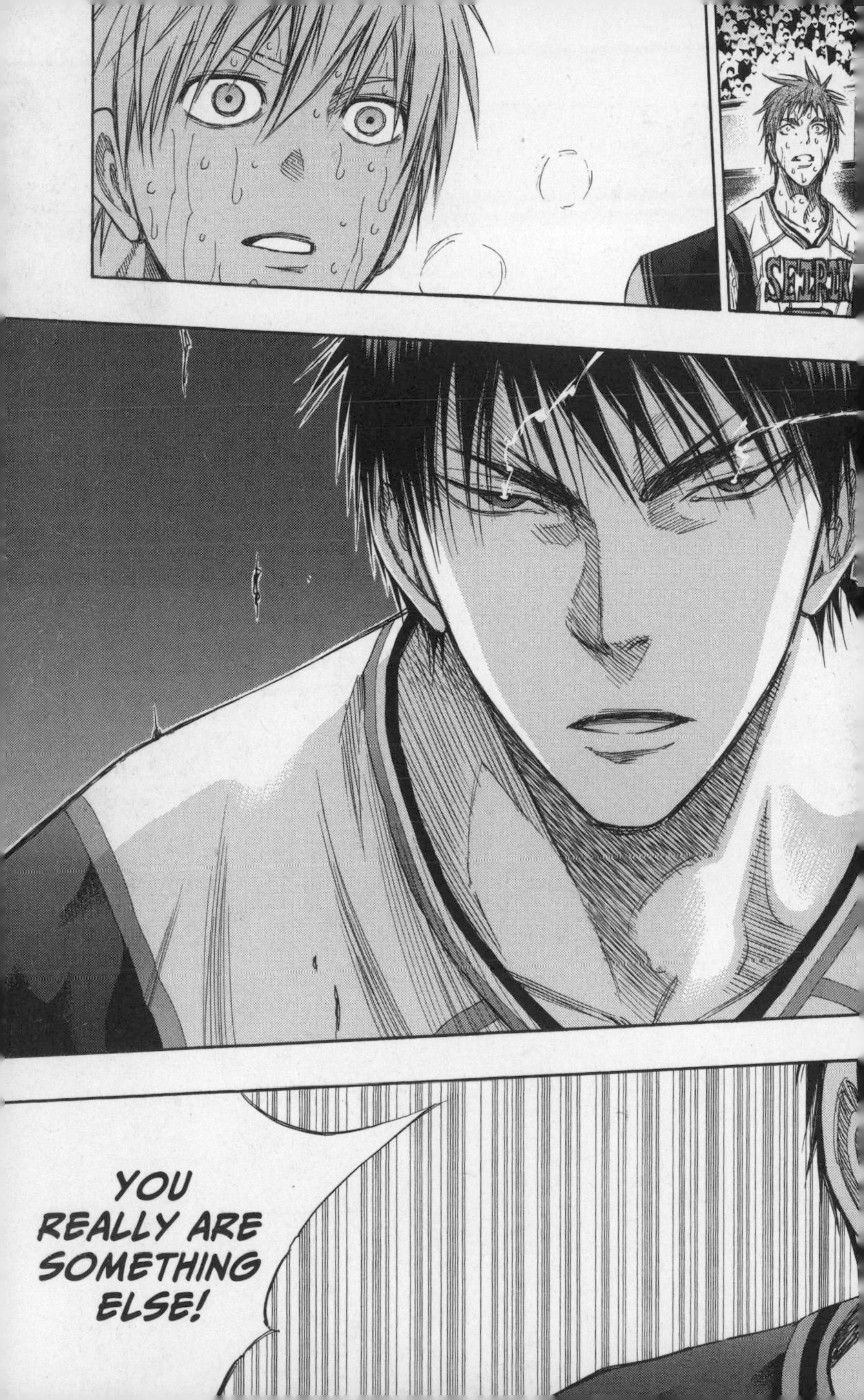
YOU REALLY ARE SOMETHING ELSE!

KUROKO'S BASKETBALL BLOOPERS TAKE 1

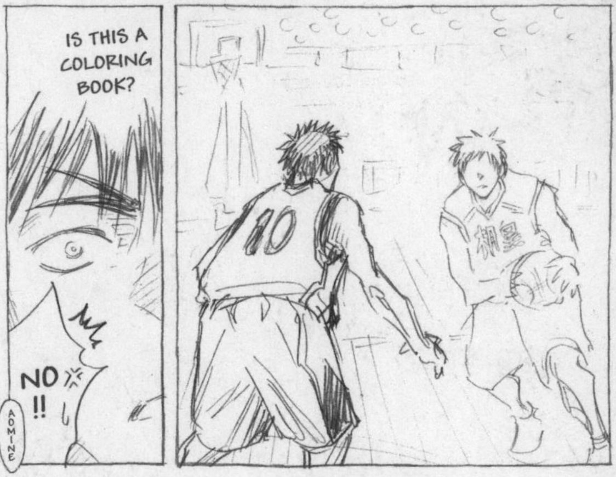
IS THIS A COLORING BOOK?
NO!!
AOMINE

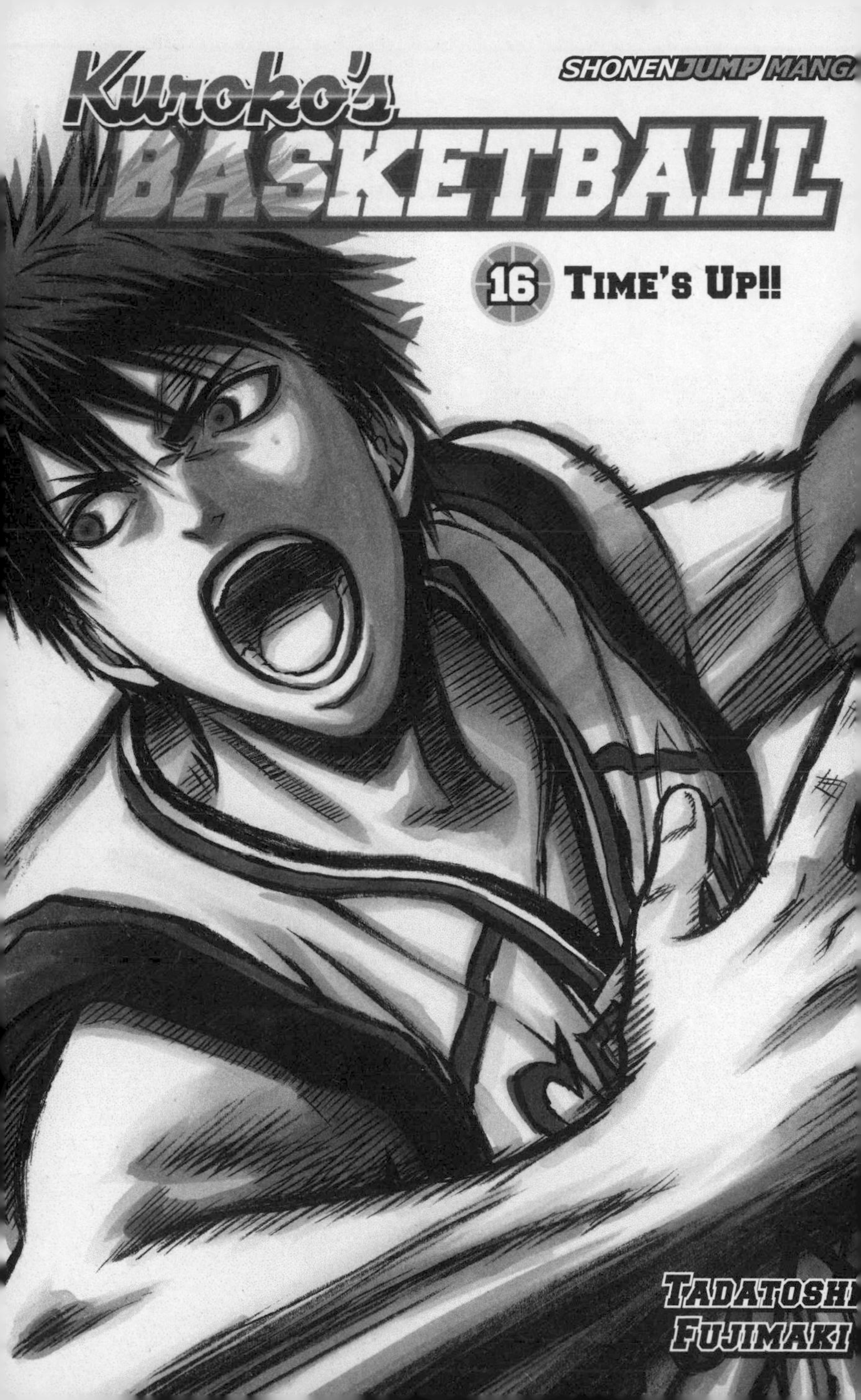
Kuroko's
BASKETBALL
SHONEN JUMP MANG
16 TIME'S UP!!
TADATOSHI
FUJIMAKI

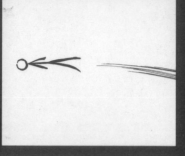

TADATOSHI FUJIMAKI

Whenever I'm thinking up the plot, I always go for a walk. Walking just feels good, and it makes it easier for me to get my thoughts in order. On the flip side, I often get writer's block when sitting around at home. So if it's raining when I need to come up with ideas, I find myself in a bit of trouble.

—2012

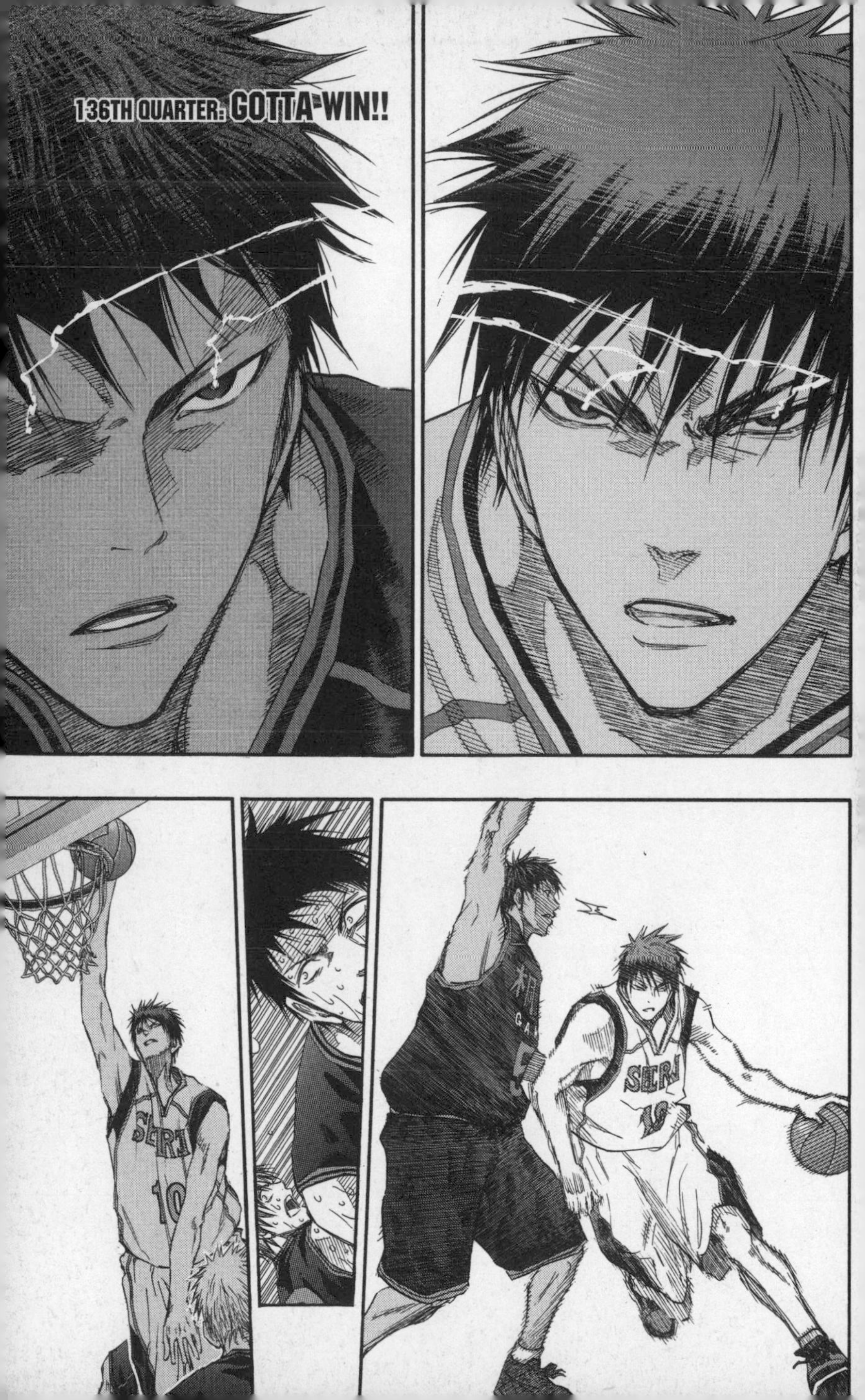
136TH QUARTER: GOTTA WIN!!

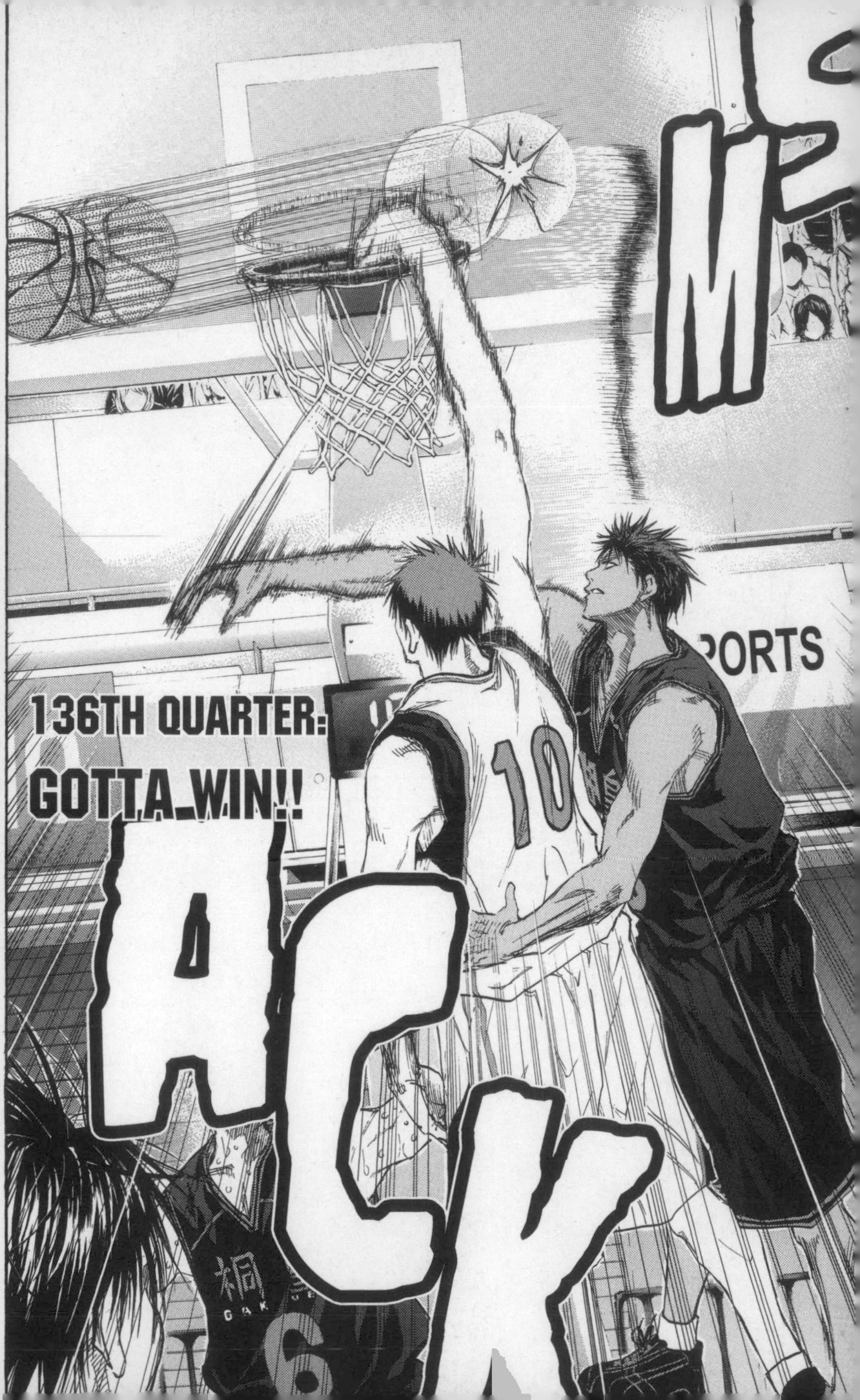
M
PORTS
ACK

136TH QUARTER: GOTTA WIN!!

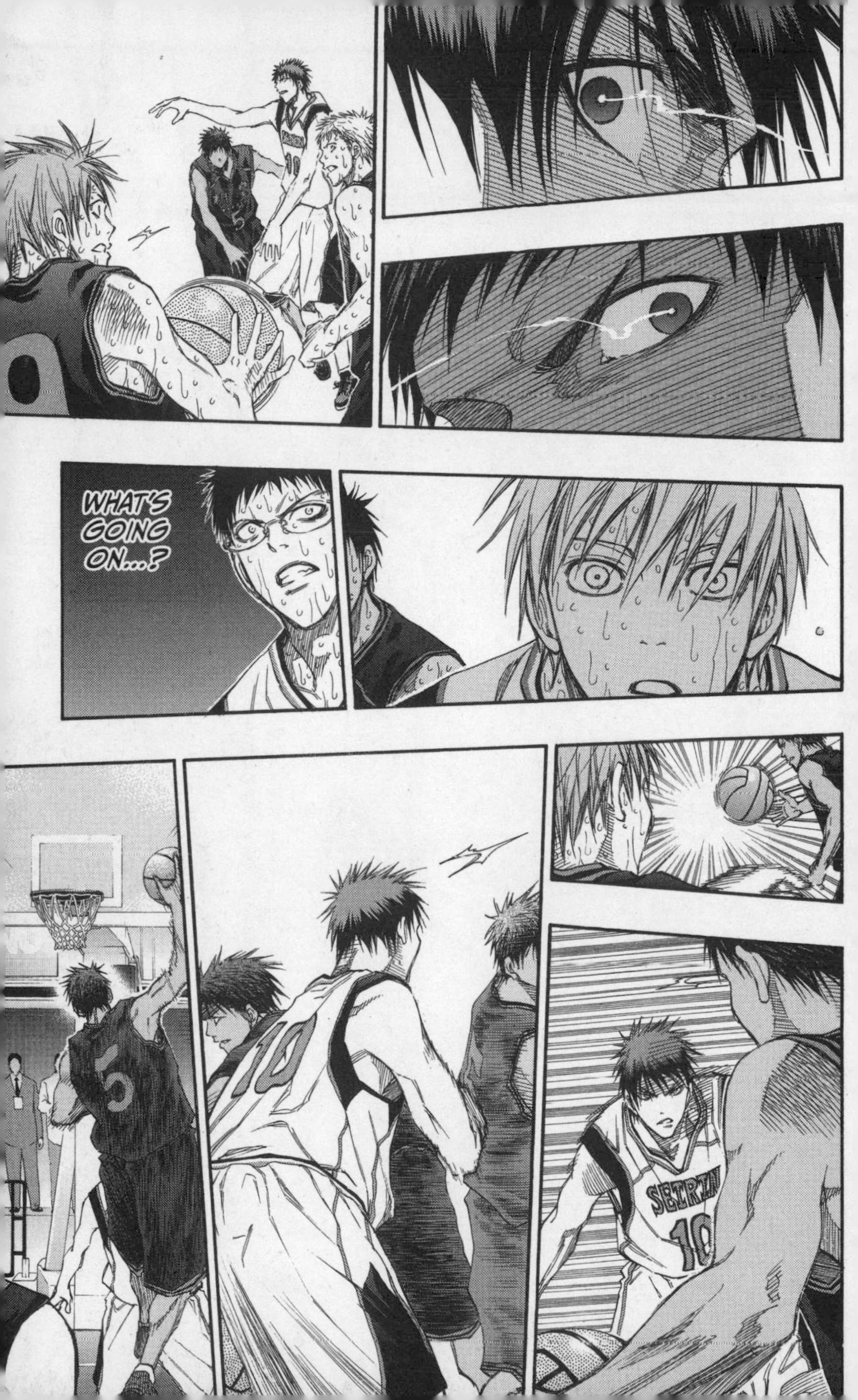
WHAT'S GOING ON...?

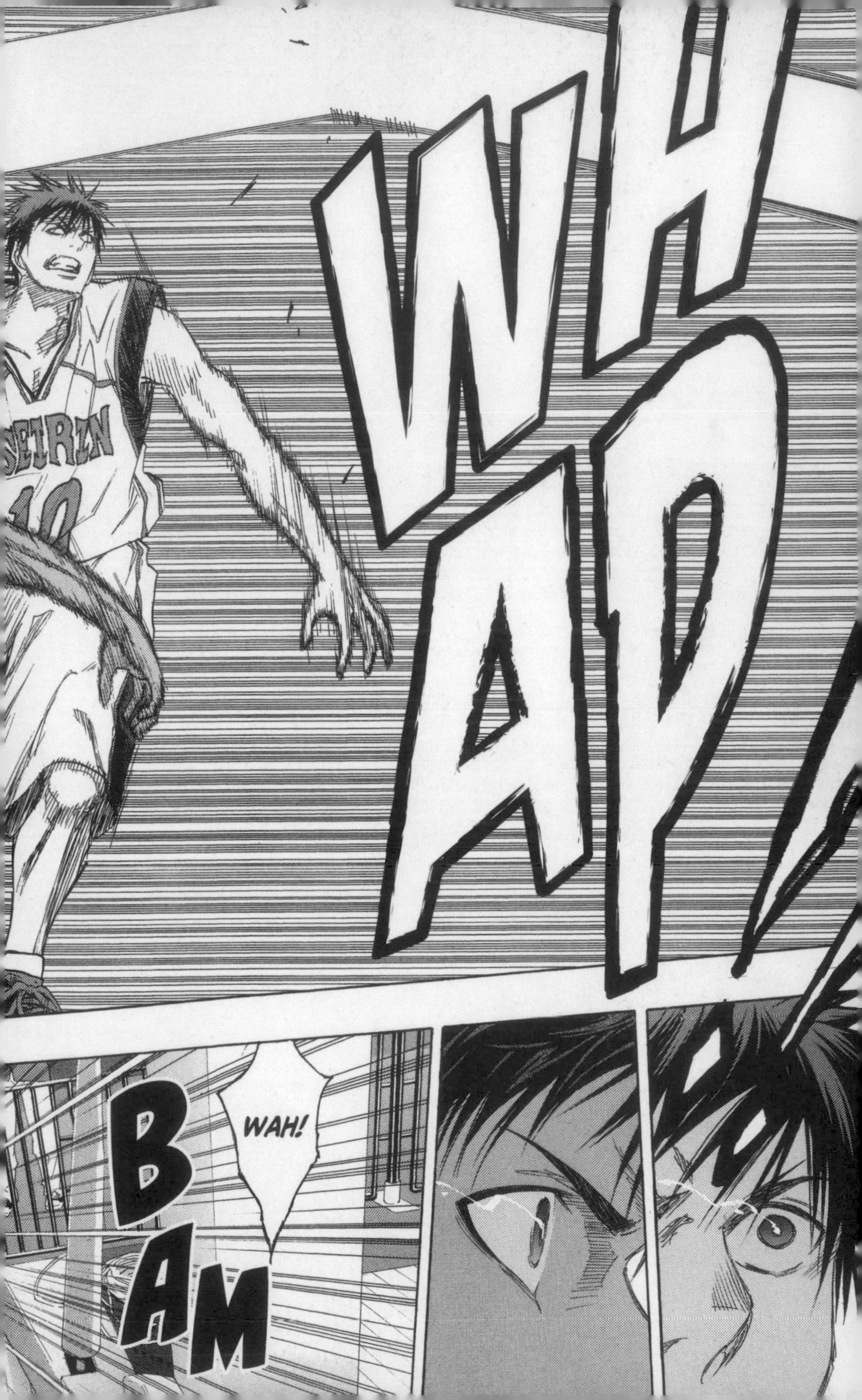
WHAP!!
WAH!
BAM

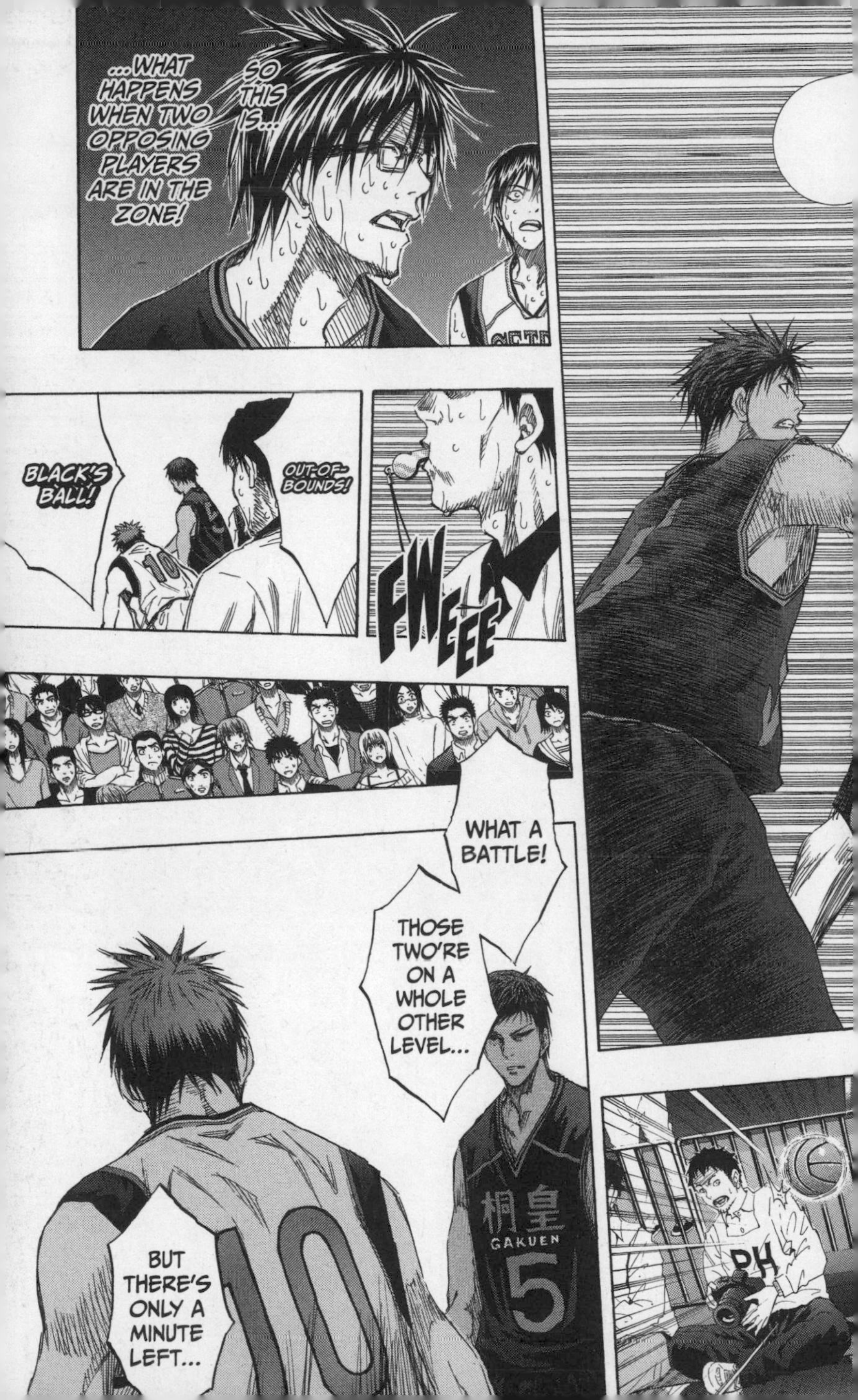
SO THIS IS...
...WHAT HAPPENS WHEN TWO OPPOSING PLAYERS ARE IN THE ZONE!
OUT-OF-BOUNDS!
FWEEE
BLACK'S BALL!
WHAT A BATTLE!
THOSE TWO'RE ON A WHOLE OTHER LEVEL...
桐皇 GAKUEN 5
BUT THERE'S ONLY A MINUTE LEFT...

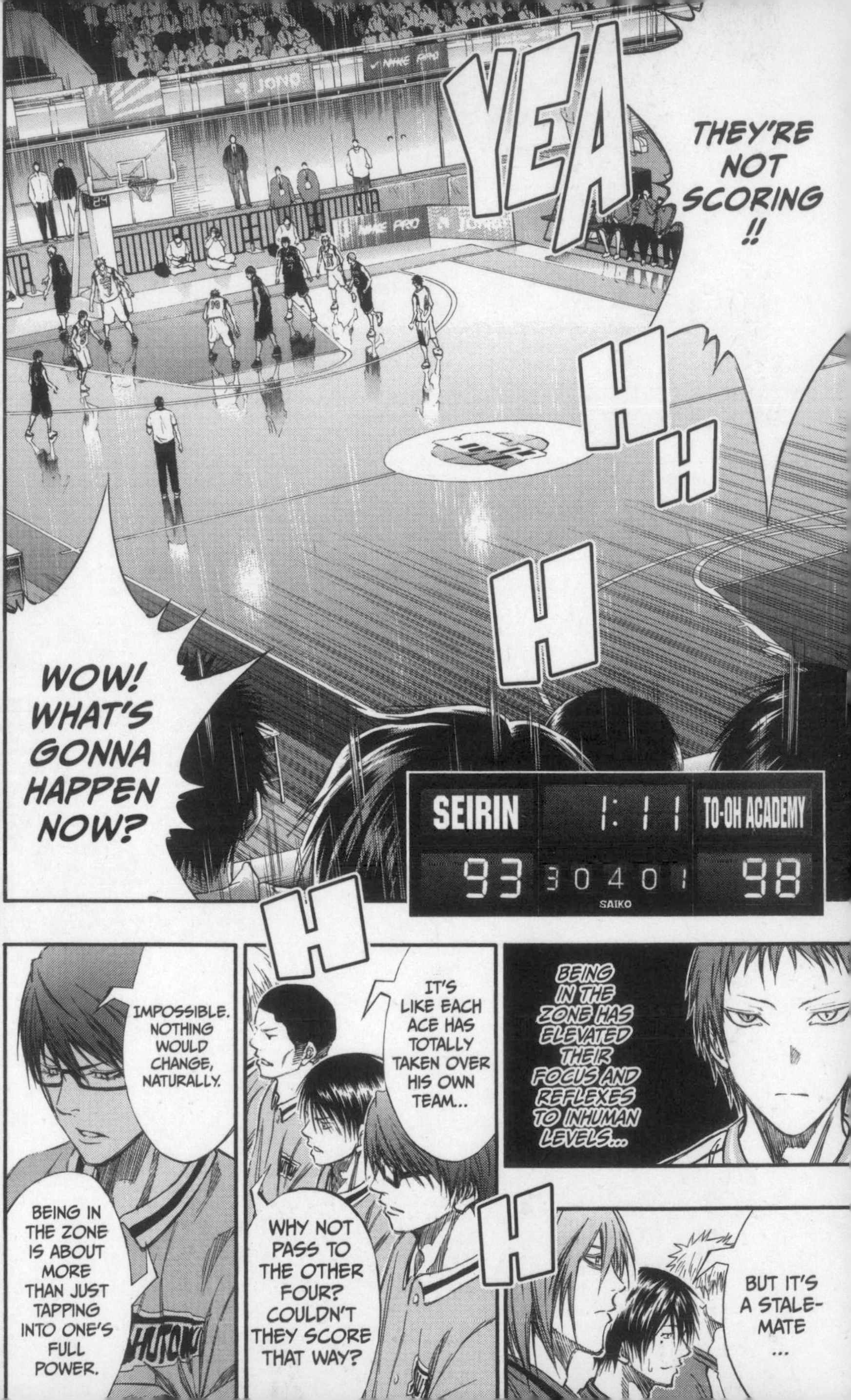
YEA
THEY'RE NOT SCORING !!
HHHH
WOW! WHAT'S GONNA HAPPEN NOW?
SEIRIN
1:11
TO-OH ACADEMY
93
98
SAIKO
H
BEING IN THE ZONE HAS ELEVATED THEIR FOCUS AND REFLEXES TO INHUMAN LEVELS...
H
BUT IT'S A STALE-MATE ...
IT'S LIKE EACH ACE HAS TOTALLY TAKEN OVER HIS OWN TEAM...
WHY NOT PASS TO THE OTHER FOUR? COULDN'T THEY SCORE THAT WAY?
IMPOSSIBLE. NOTHING WOULD CHANGE, NATURALLY.
BEING IN THE ZONE IS ABOUT MORE THAN JUST TAPPING INTO ONE'S FULL POWER.

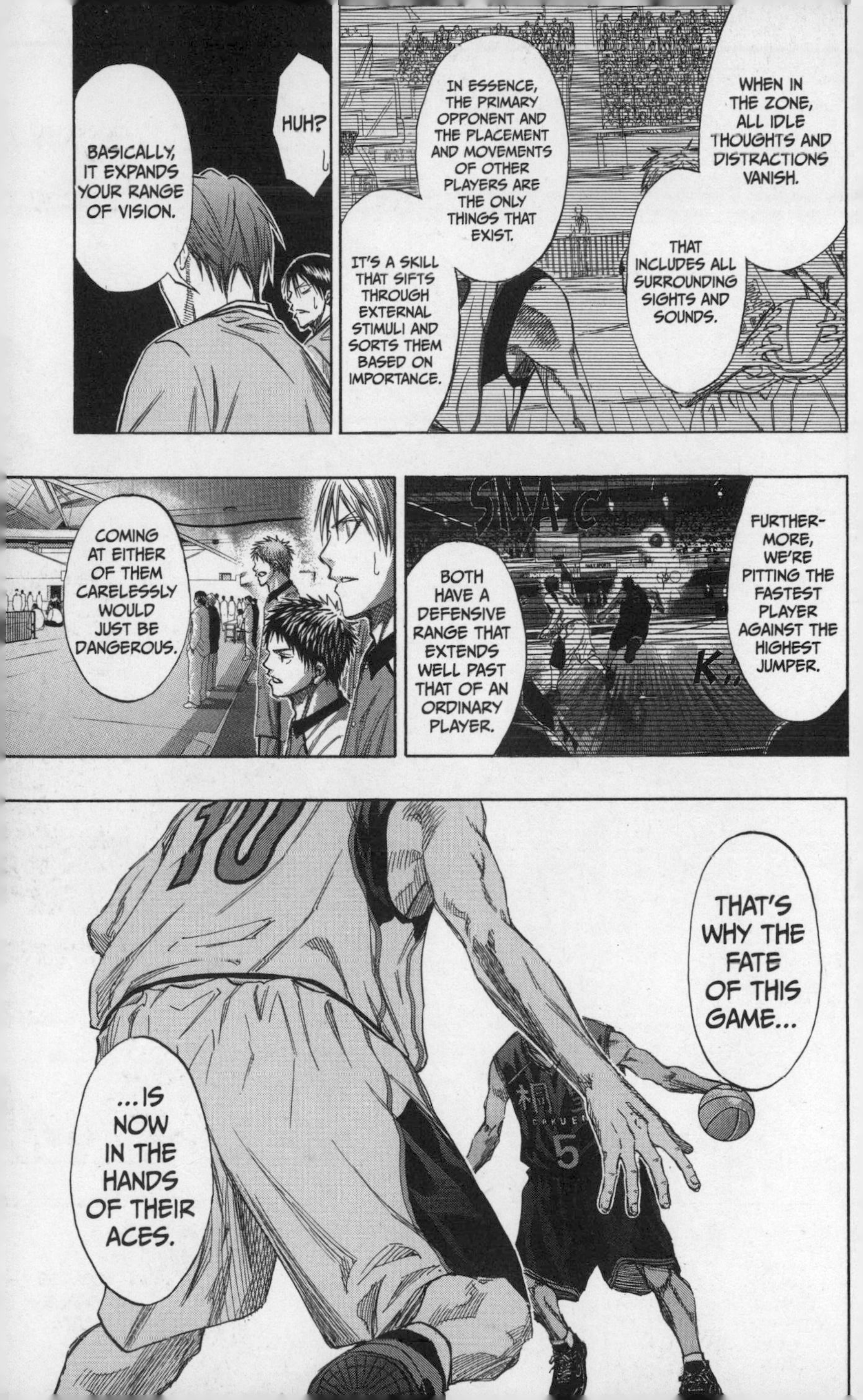
WHEN IN THE ZONE, ALL IDLE THOUGHTS AND DISTRACTIONS VANISH.
THAT INCLUDES ALL SURROUNDING SIGHTS AND SOUNDS.
IN ESSENCE, THE PRIMARY OPPONENT AND THE PLACEMENT AND MOVEMENTS OF OTHER PLAYERS ARE THE ONLY THINGS THAT EXIST.
IT'S A SKILL THAT SIFTS THROUGH EXTERNAL STIMULI AND SORTS THEM BASED ON IMPORTANCE.
HUH?
BASICALLY, IT EXPANDS YOUR RANGE OF VISION.
FURTHER-MORE, WE'RE PITTING THE FASTEST PLAYER AGAINST THE HIGHEST JUMPER.
BOTH HAVE A DEFENSIVE RANGE THAT EXTENDS WELL PAST THAT OF AN ORDINARY PLAYER.
COMING AT EITHER OF THEM CARELESSLY WOULD JUST BE DANGEROUS.
THAT'S WHY THE FATE OF THIS GAME...
...IS NOW IN THE HANDS OF THEIR ACES.

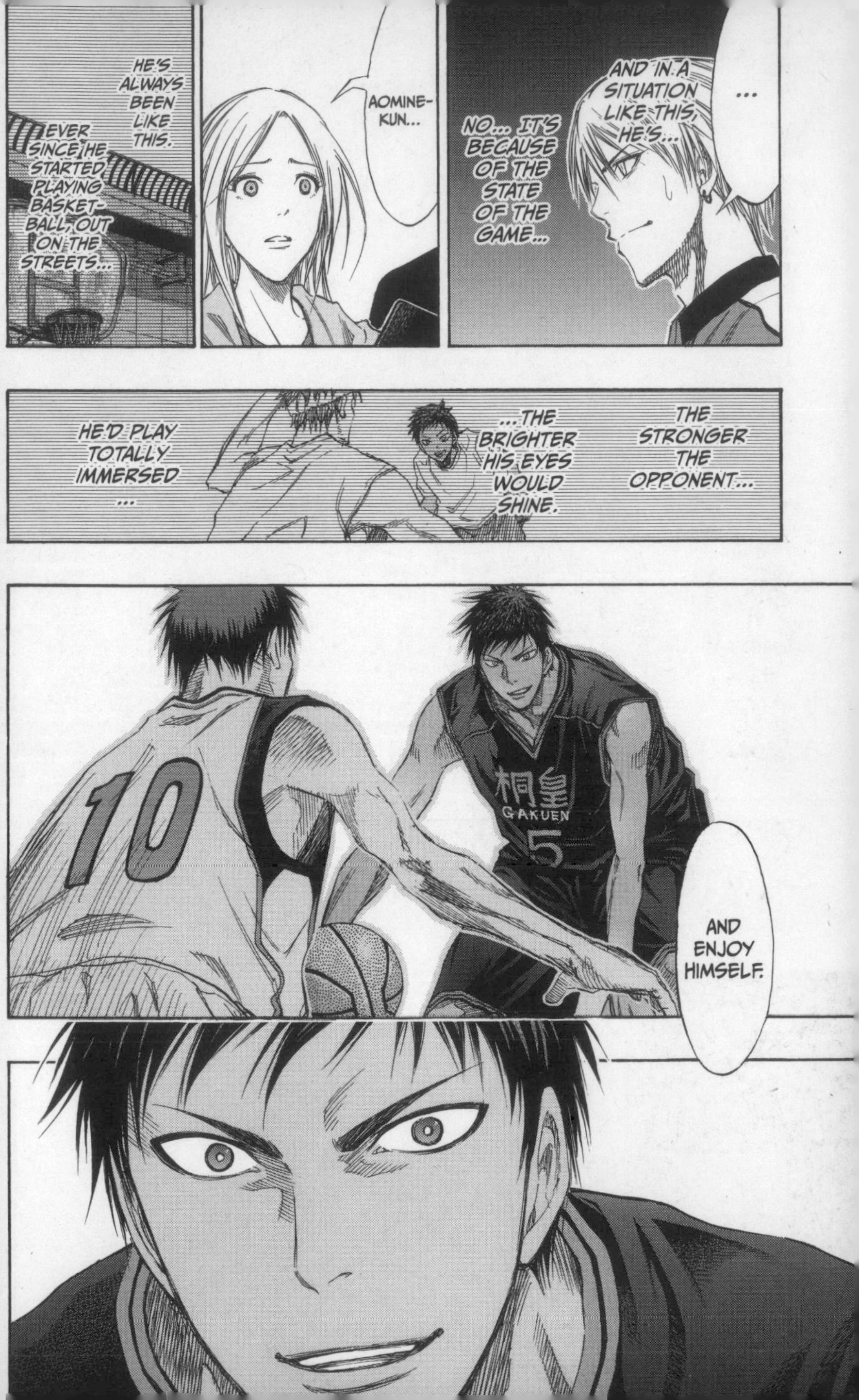
...
AND IN A SITUATION LIKE THIS, HE'S...
NO... IT'S BECAUSE OF THE STATE OF THE GAME...
AOMINE-KUN...
HE'S ALWAYS BEEN LIKE THIS.
EVER SINCE HE STARTED PLAYING BASKET-BALL, OUT ON THE STREETS...
THE STRONGER THE OPPONENT...
...THE BRIGHTER HIS EYES WOULD SHINE.
HE'D PLAY TOTALLY IMMERSED...
10
桐皇
GAKUEN
5
AND ENJOY HIMSELF.

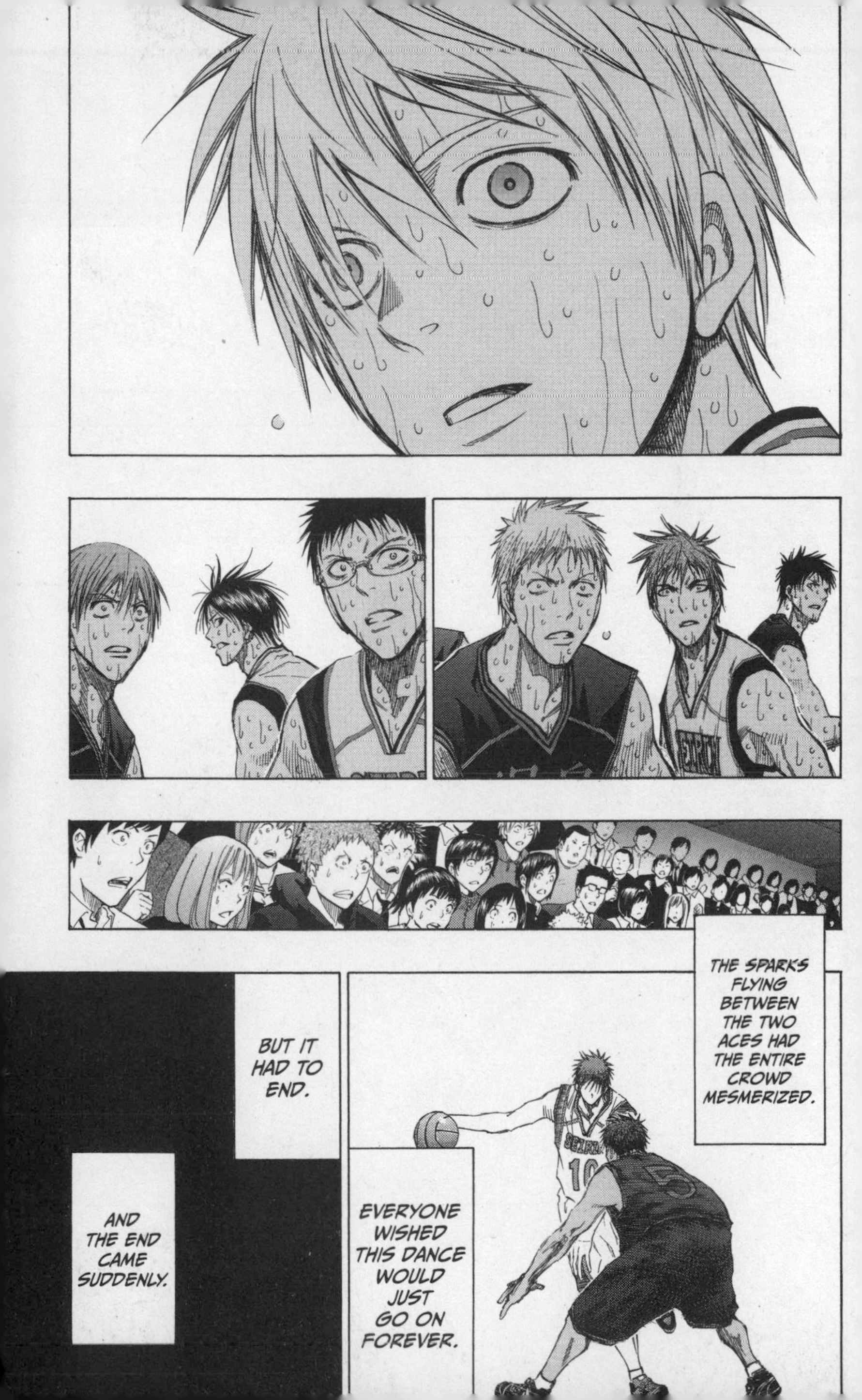
THE SPARKS FLYING BETWEEN THE TWO ACES HAD THE ENTIRE CROWD MESMERIZED.
EVERYONE WISHED THIS DANCE WOULD JUST GO ON FOREVER.
BUT IT HAD TO END.
AND THE END CAME SUDDENLY.

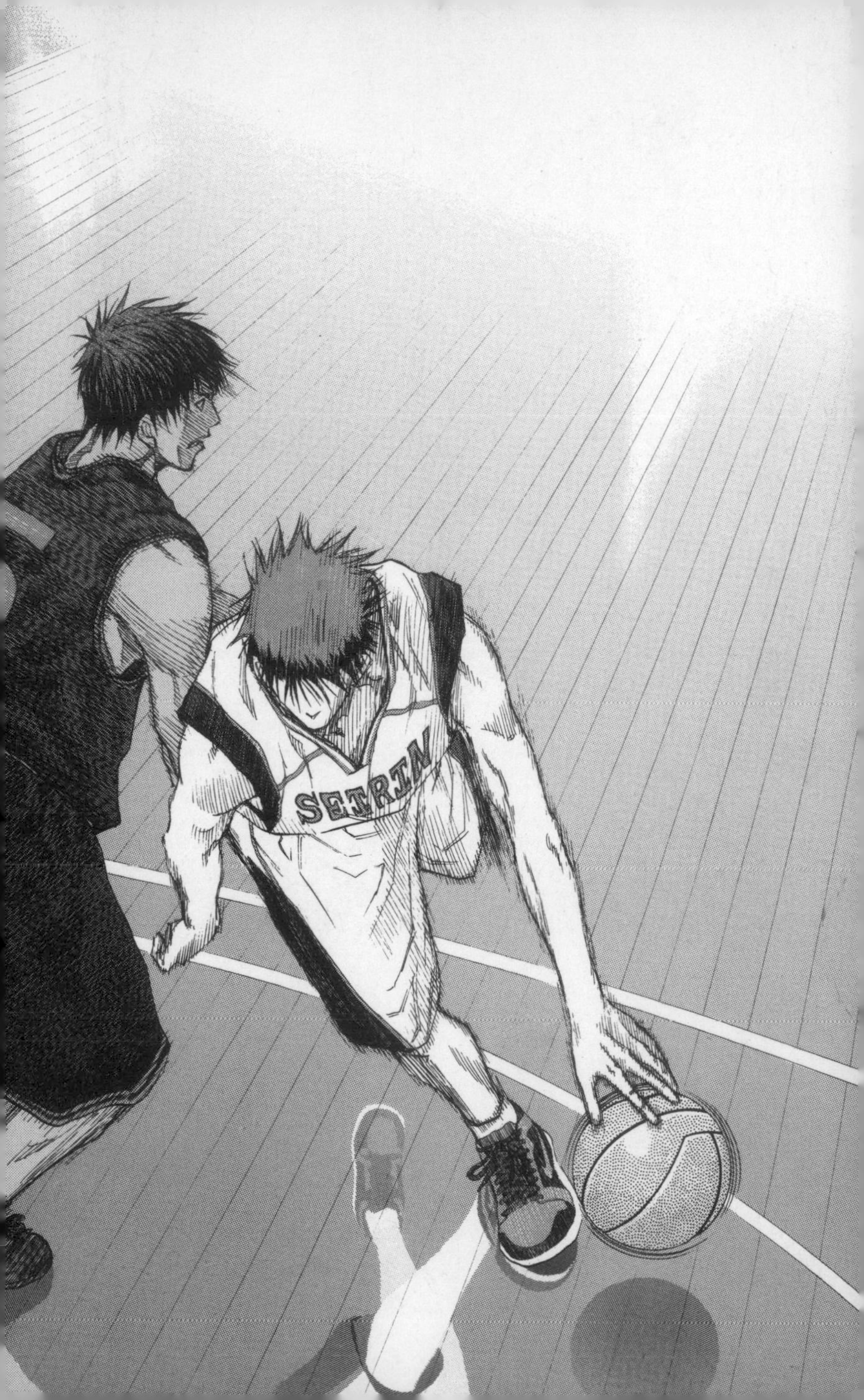
SEIRIN

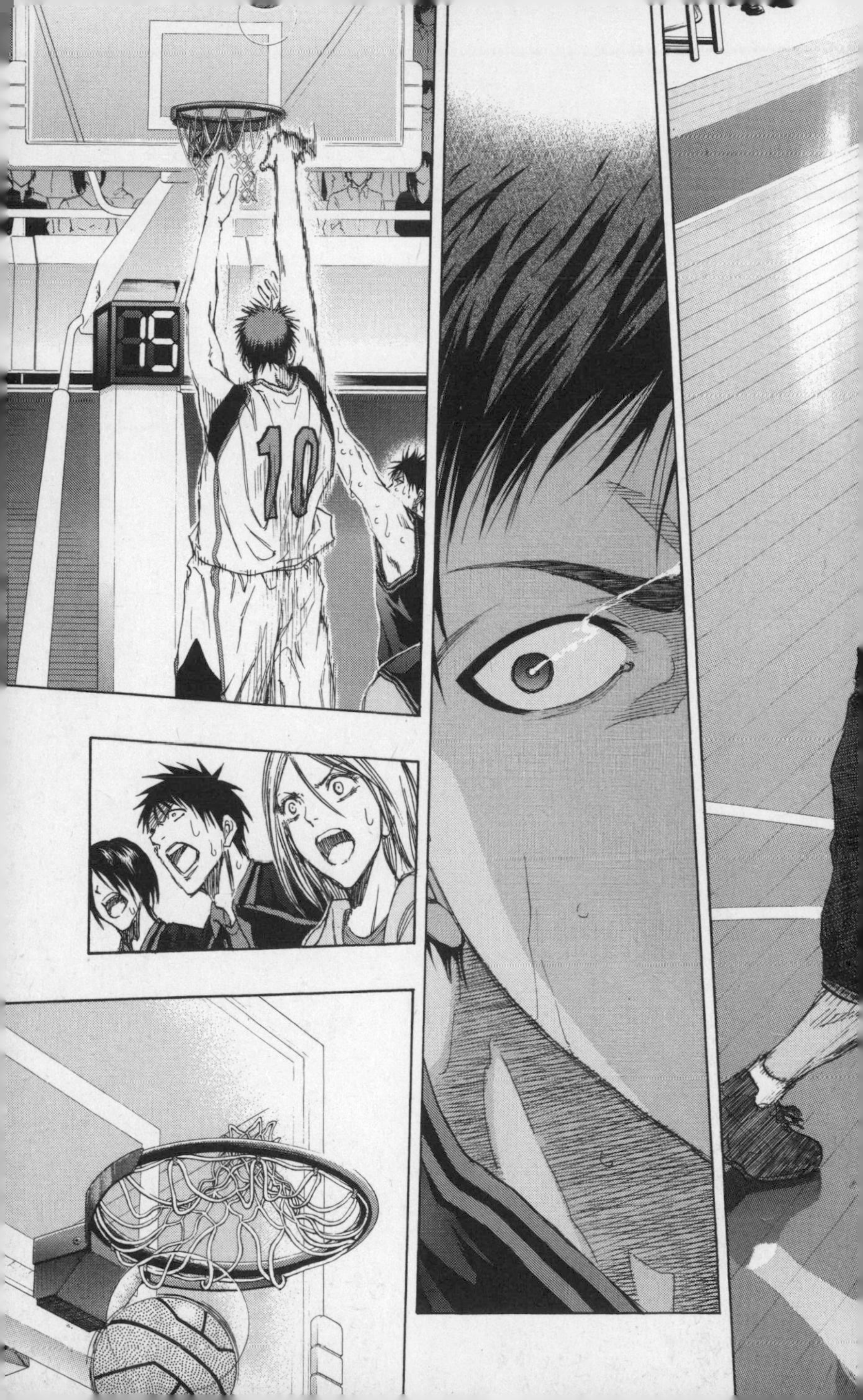

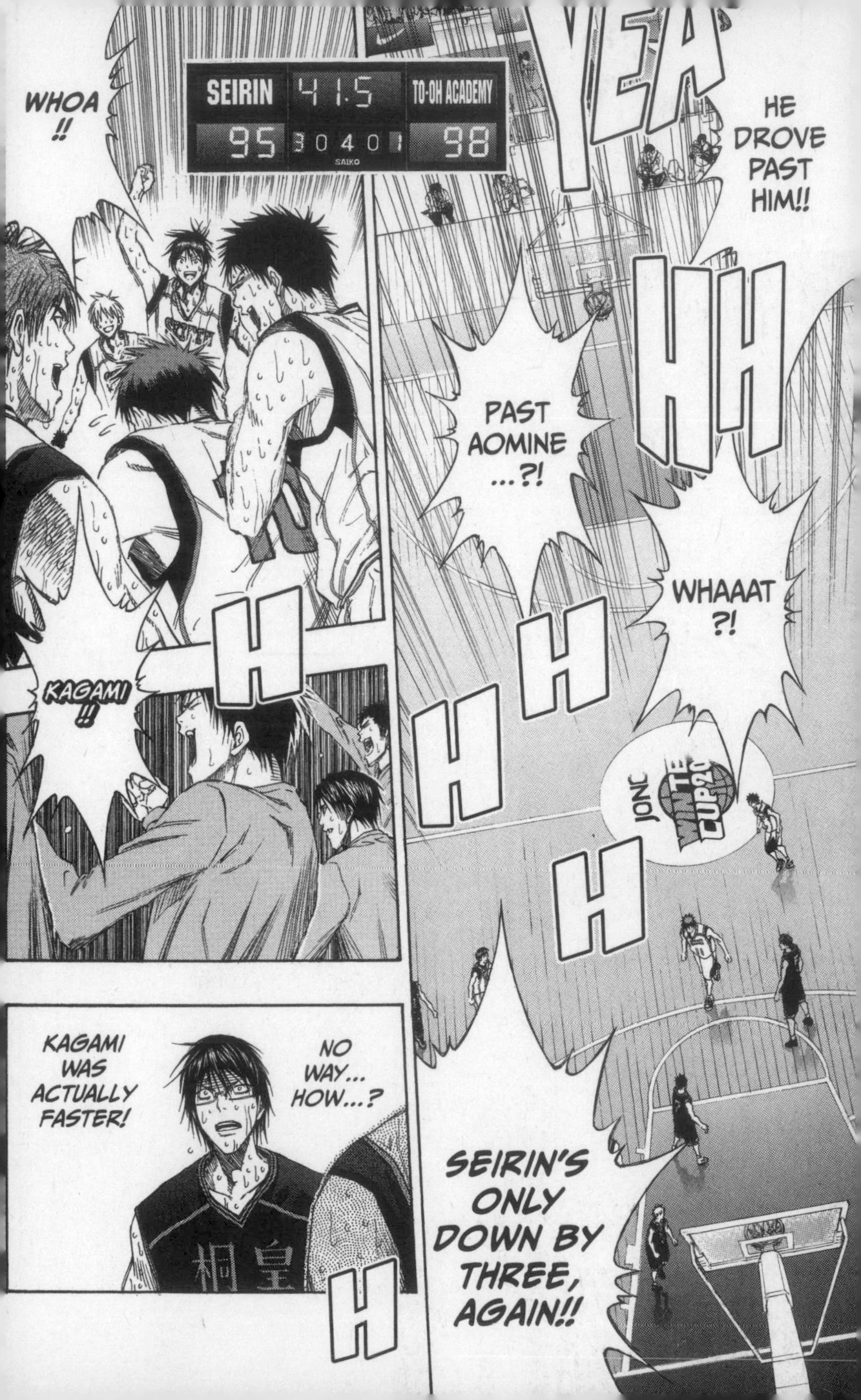
YEAHHHHHHH
HE DROVE PAST HIM!!
PAST AOMINE ...?!
WHAAAT ?!
SEIRIN'S ONLY DOWN BY THREE, AGAIN!!
SEIRIN 41.5 TO-OH ACADEMY
95 98
WHOA !!
KAGAMI !!
NO WAY... HOW...?
KAGAMI WAS ACTUALLY FASTER!

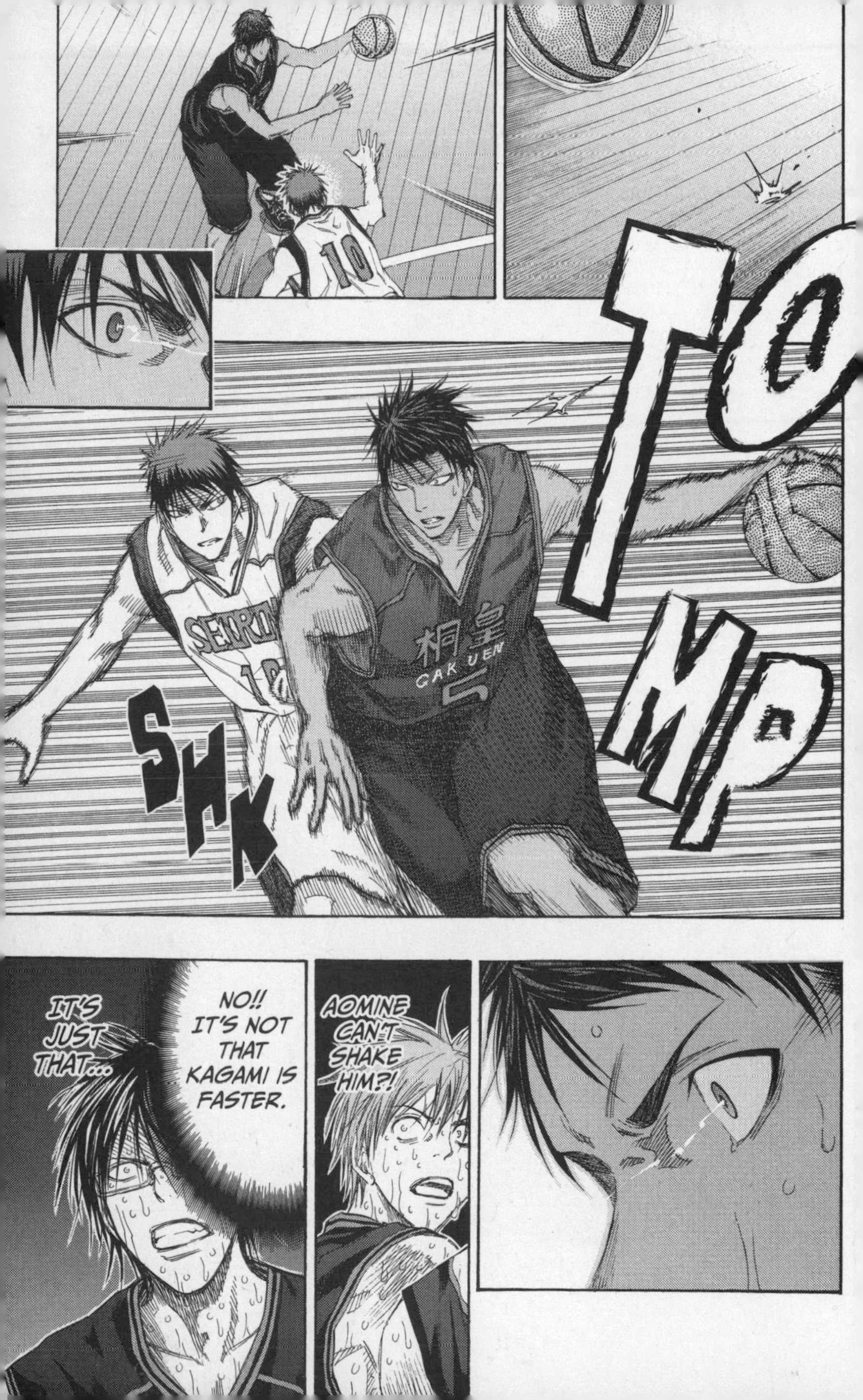
TOMP
SHK
AOMINE CAN'T SHAKE HIM?!
NO!! IT'S NOT THAT KAGAMI IS FASTER.
IT'S JUST THAT...

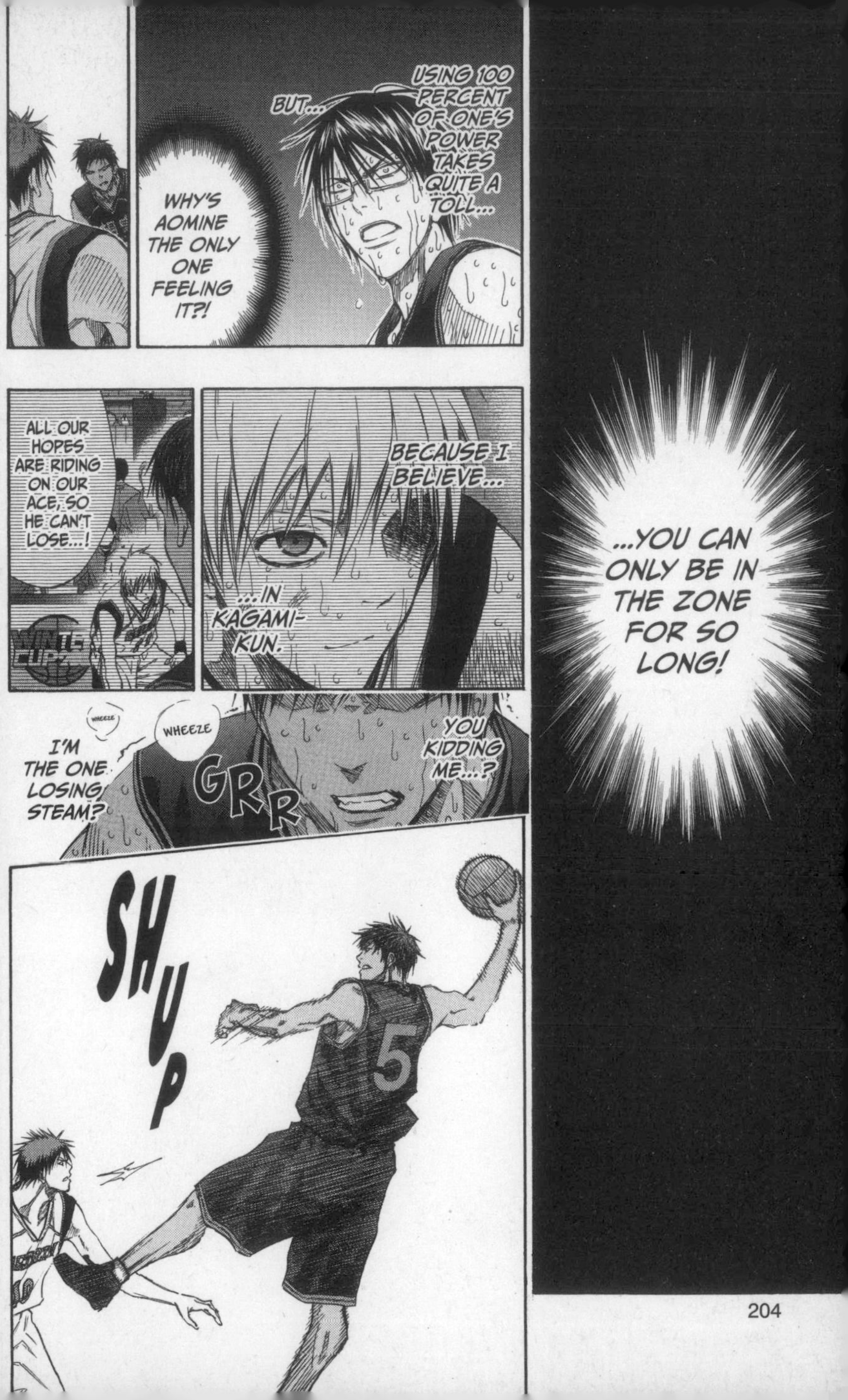
...YOU CAN ONLY BE IN THE ZONE FOR SO LONG!
USING 100 PERCENT OF ONE'S POWER TAKES QUITE A TOLL...
BUT...
WHY'S AOMINE THE ONLY ONE FEELING IT?!
BECAUSE I BELIEVE...
...IN KAGAMI-KUN.
ALL OUR HOPES ARE RIDING ON OUR ACE, SO HE CAN'T LOSE...!
YOU KIDDING ME...?
WHEEZE
WHEEZE
GRR
I'M THE ONE LOSING STEAM?
SHUP

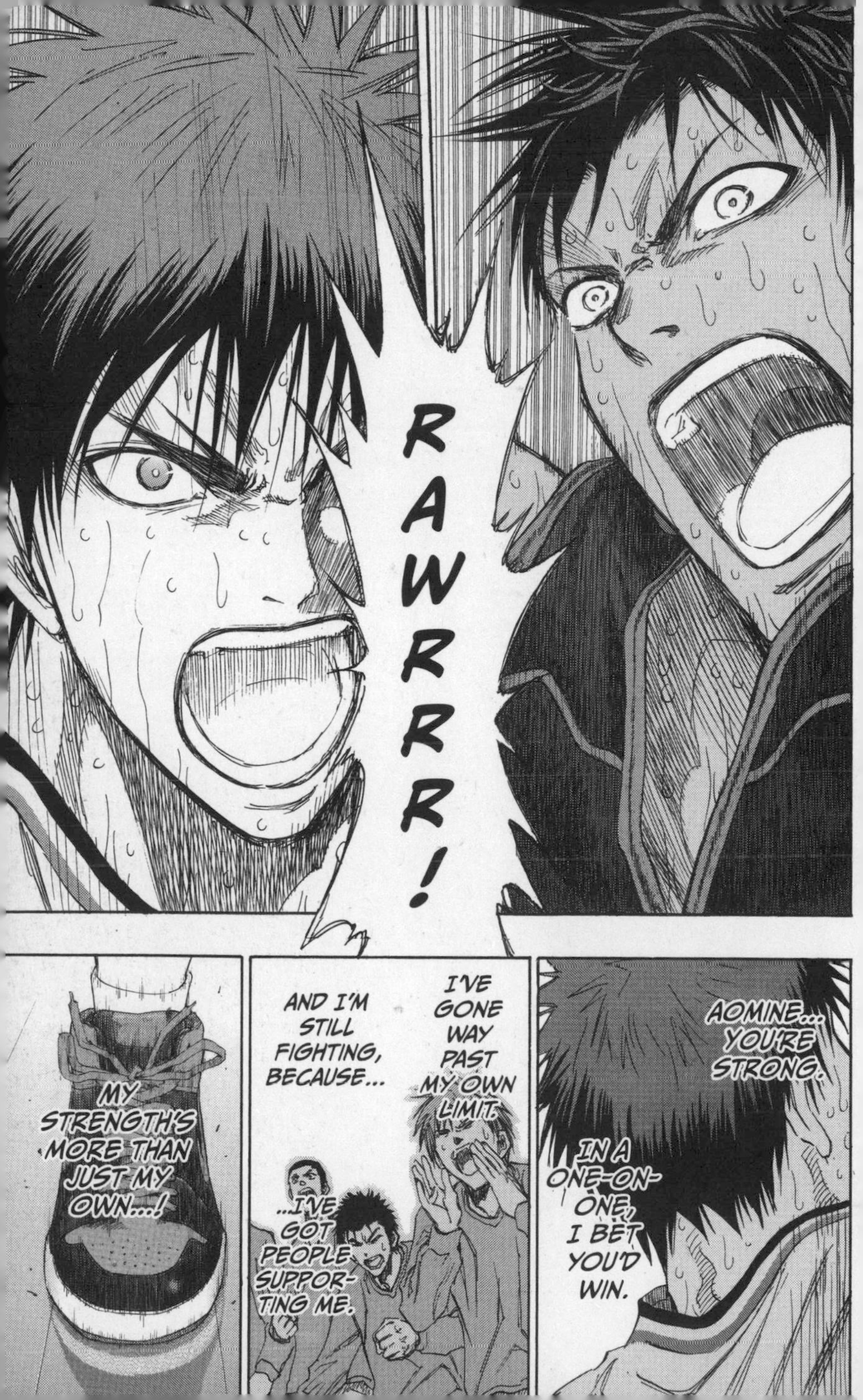
RAWRRR!
AOMINE... YOU'RE STRONG.
IN A ONE-ON-ONE, I BET YOU'D WIN.
I'VE GONE WAY PAST MY OWN LIMIT.
AND I'M STILL FIGHTING, BECAUSE...
...I'VE GOT PEOPLE SUPPORTING ME.
MY STRENGTH'S MORE THAN JUST MY OWN...!

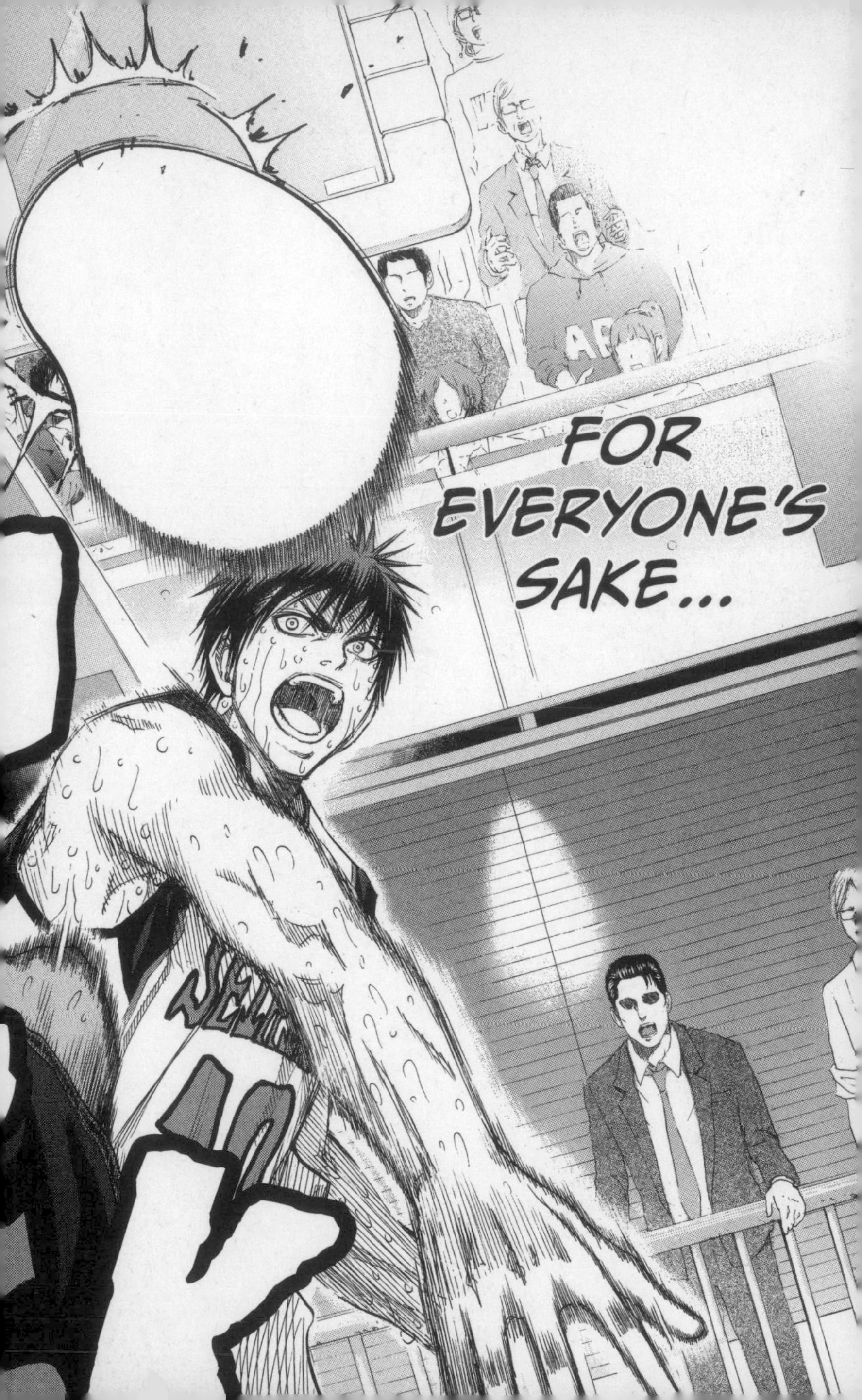
FOR EVERYONE'S SAKE...

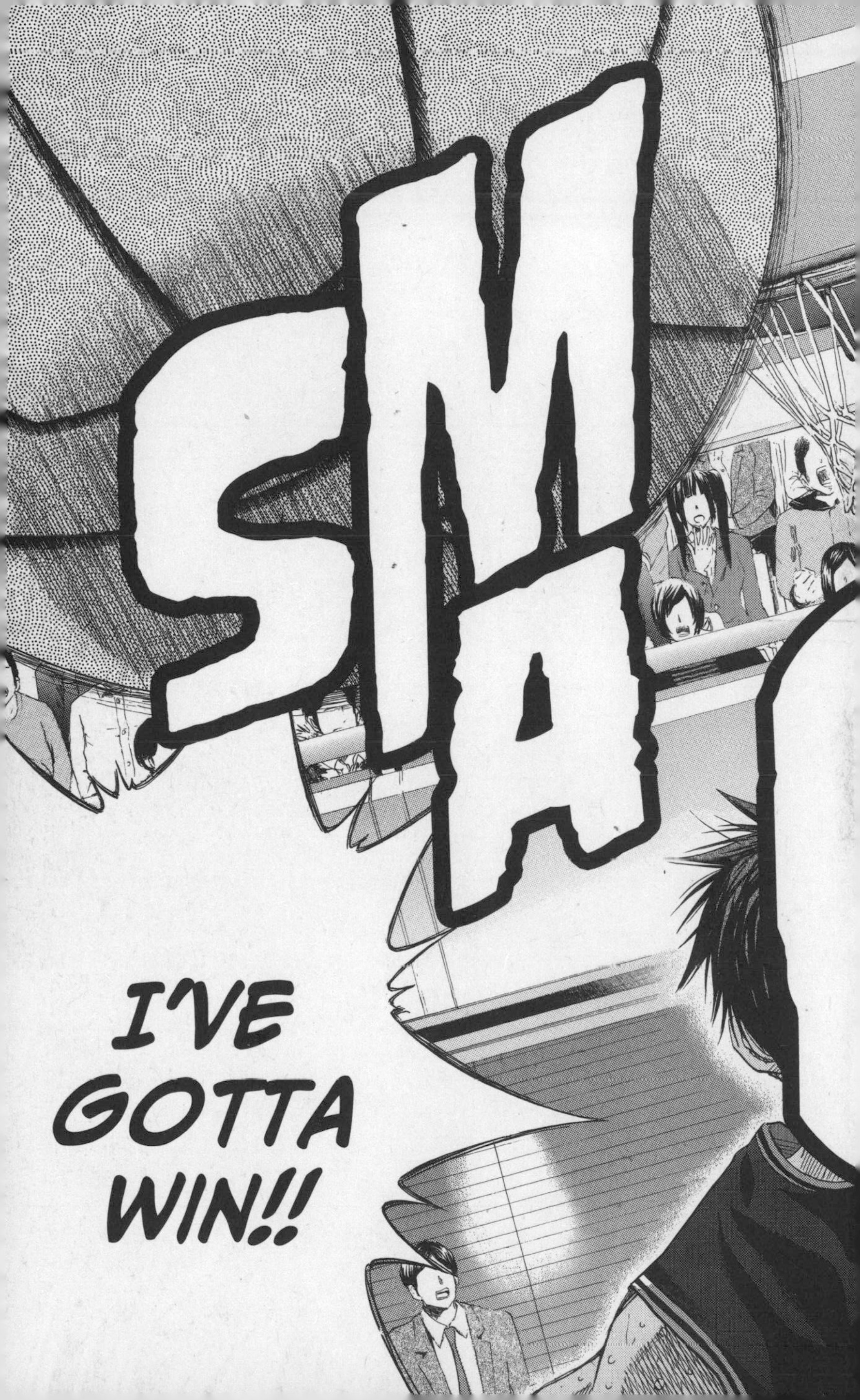
SMA
I'VE GOTTA WIN!!

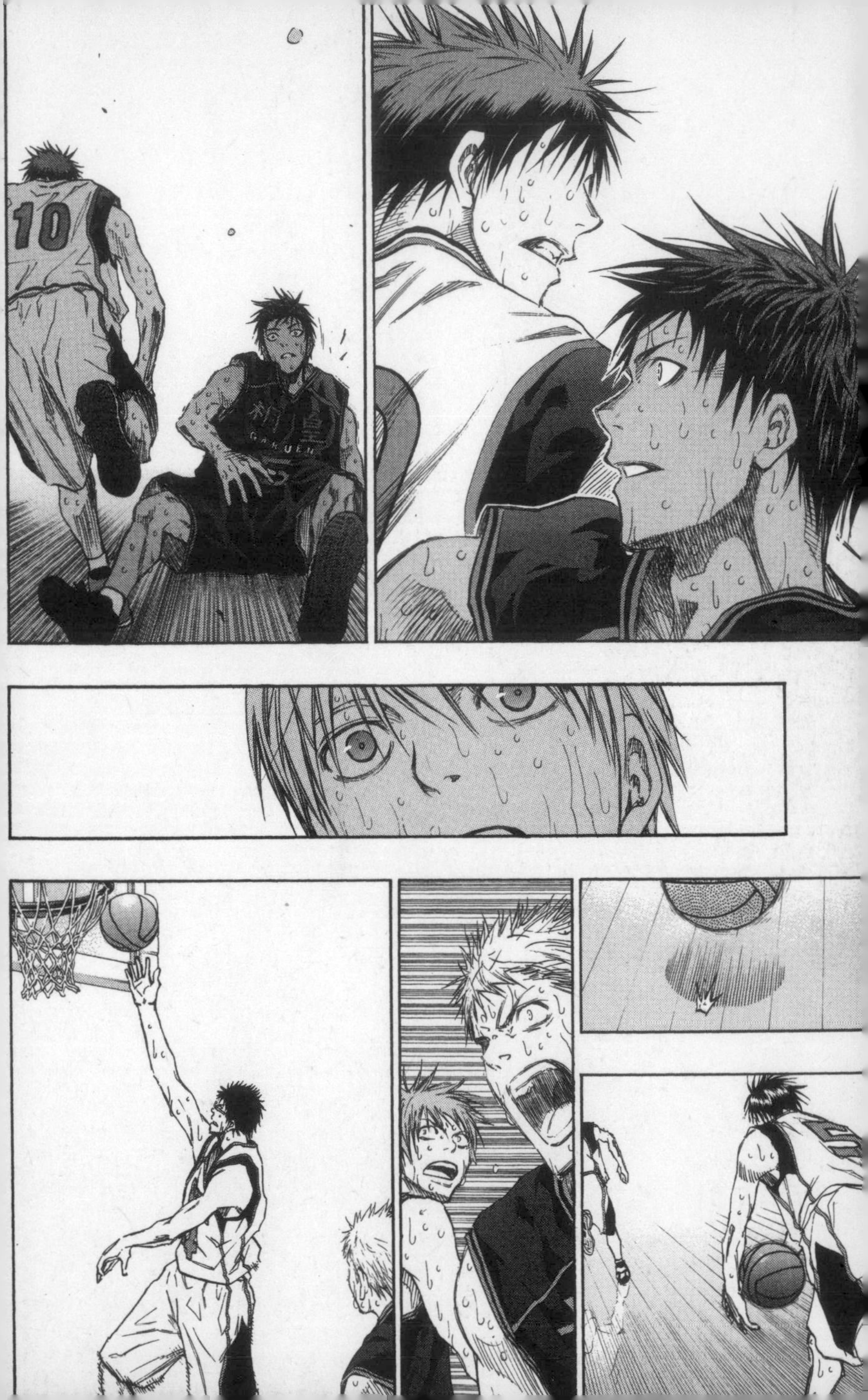

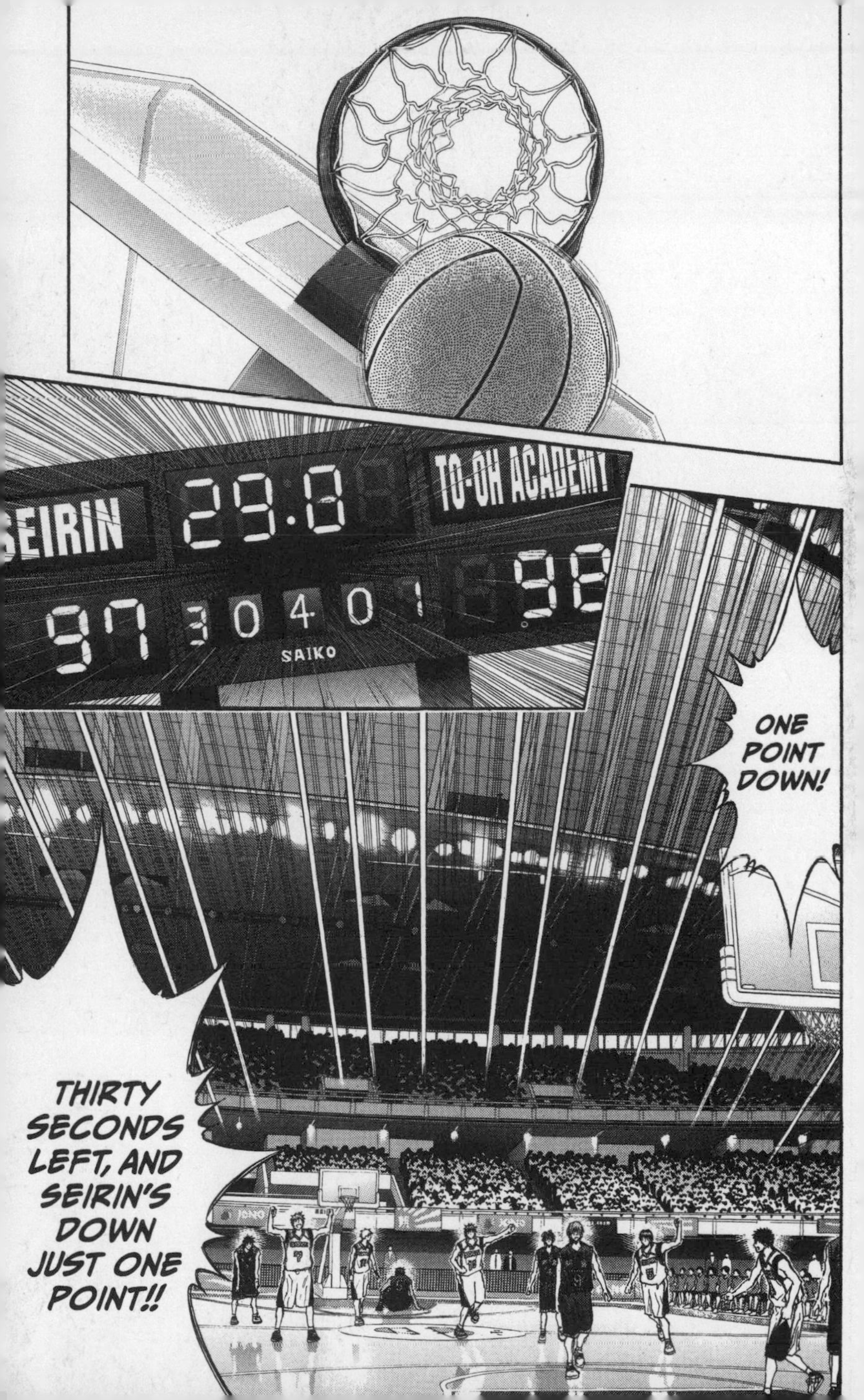
SEIRIN
TO-OH ACADEMY
97
98
SAIKO
ONE POINT DOWN!
THIRTY SECONDS LEFT, AND SEIRIN'S DOWN JUST ONE POINT!!

KUROKO'S BASKETBALL BLOOPERS

TAKE 4

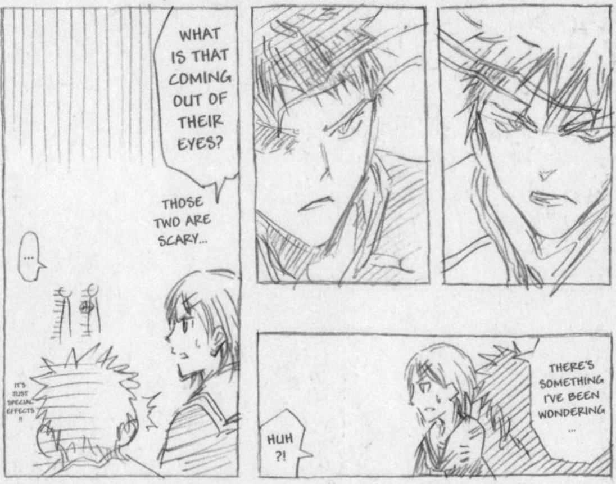
THERE'S SOMETHING I'VE BEEN WONDERING...
HUH?!
WHAT IS THAT COMING OUT OF THEIR EYES?
THOSE TWO ARE SCARY...
...
IT'S JUST SPECIAL EFFECTS!!

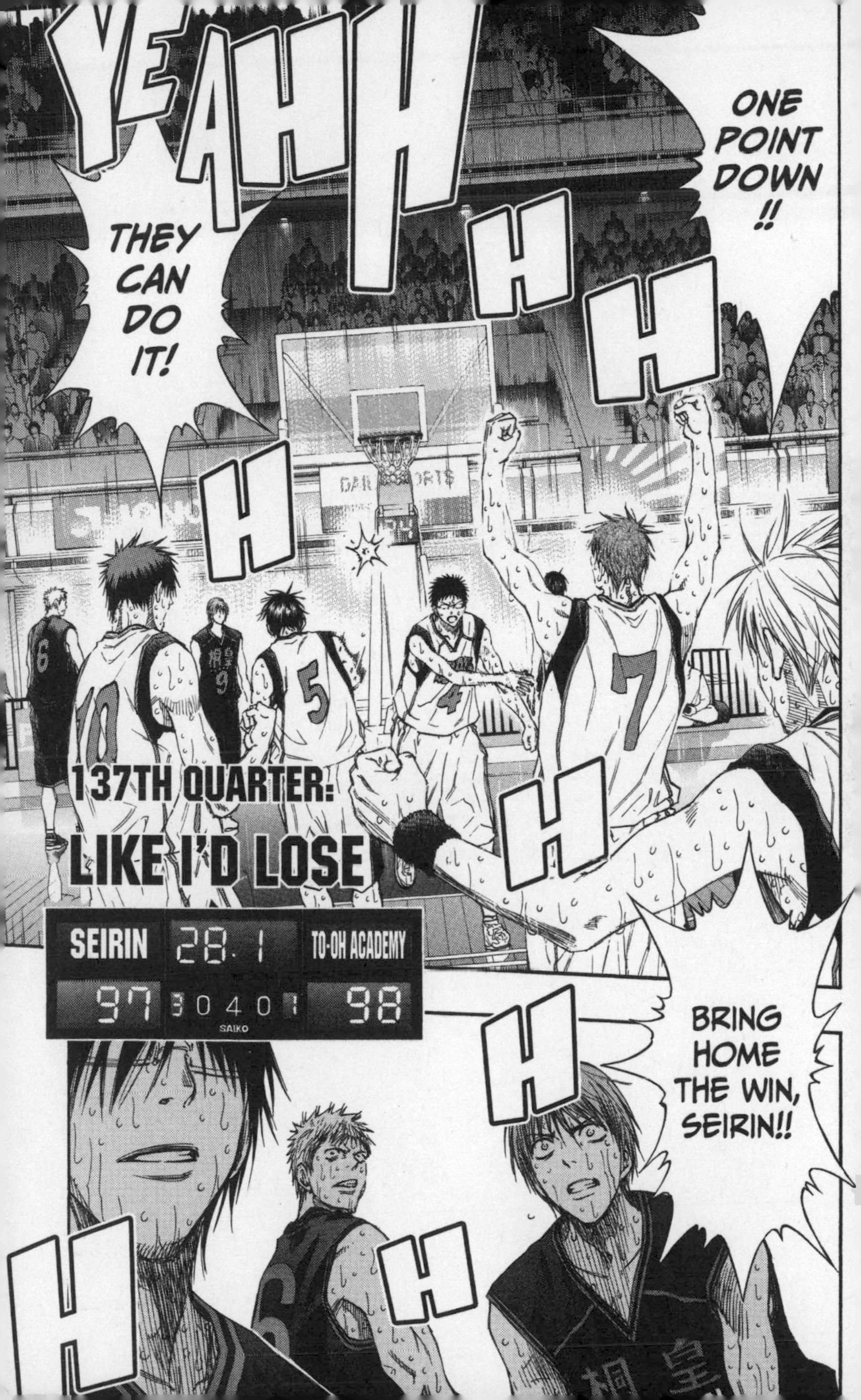
ONE POINT DOWN!!
YEAHHHHHH
THEY CAN DO IT!
137TH QUARTER:
LIKE I'D LOSE
SEIRIN 97
TO-OH ACADEMY 98
28.1
BRING HOME THE WIN, SEIRIN!!
HHH

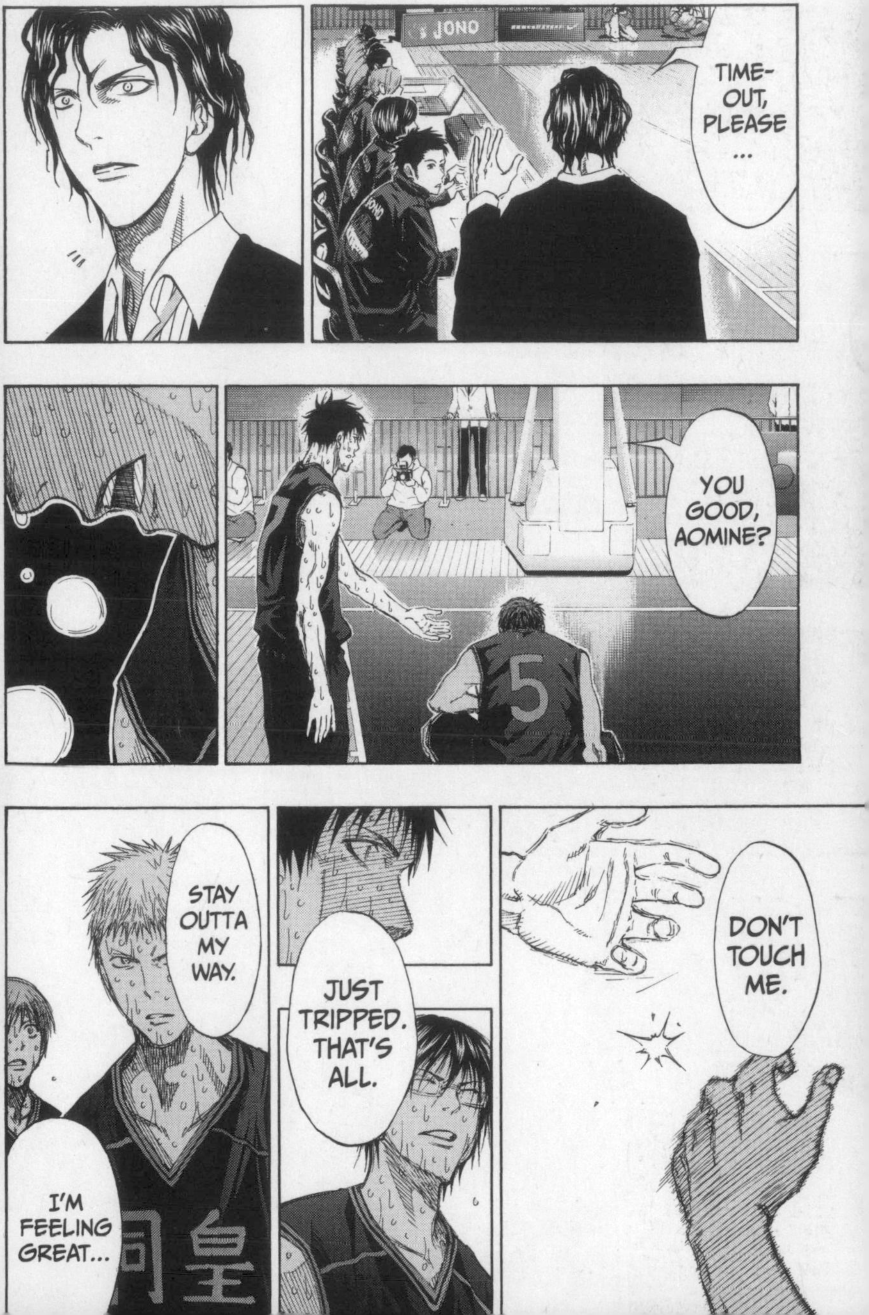
TIME-OUT, PLEASE ...
YOU GOOD, AOMINE?
DON'T TOUCH ME.
JUST TRIPPED. THAT'S ALL.
STAY OUTTA MY WAY.
I'M FEELING GREAT...

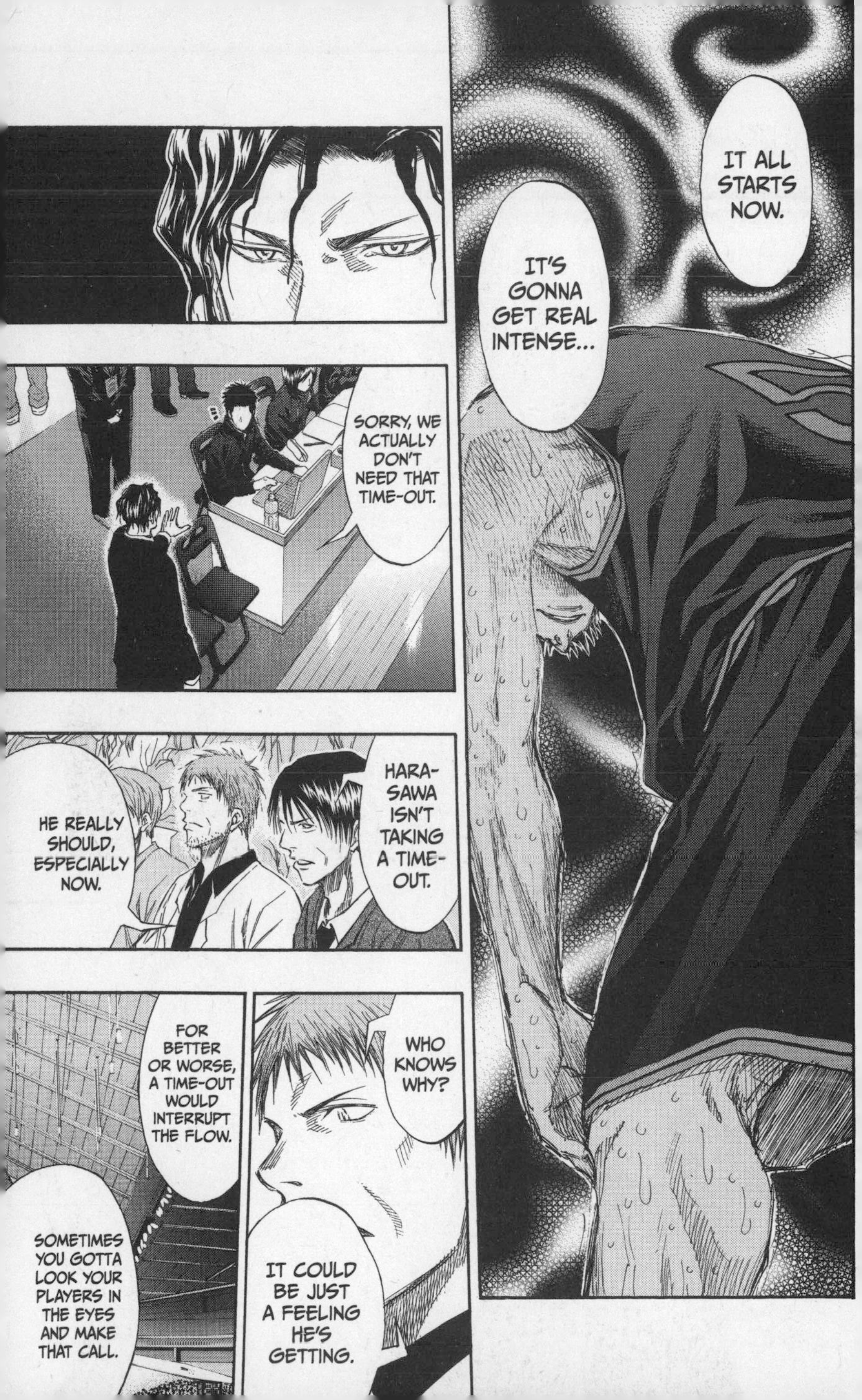

IT ALL STARTS NOW.
IT'S GONNA GET REAL INTENSE...
SORRY, WE ACTUALLY DON'T NEED THAT TIME-OUT.
HARA-SAWA ISN'T TAKING A TIME-OUT.
HE REALLY SHOULD, ESPECIALLY NOW.
WHO KNOWS WHY?
IT COULD BE JUST A FEELING HE'S GETTING.
FOR BETTER OR WORSE, A TIME-OUT WOULD INTERRUPT THE FLOW.
SOMETIMES YOU GOTTA LOOK YOUR PLAYERS IN THE EYES AND MAKE THAT CALL.

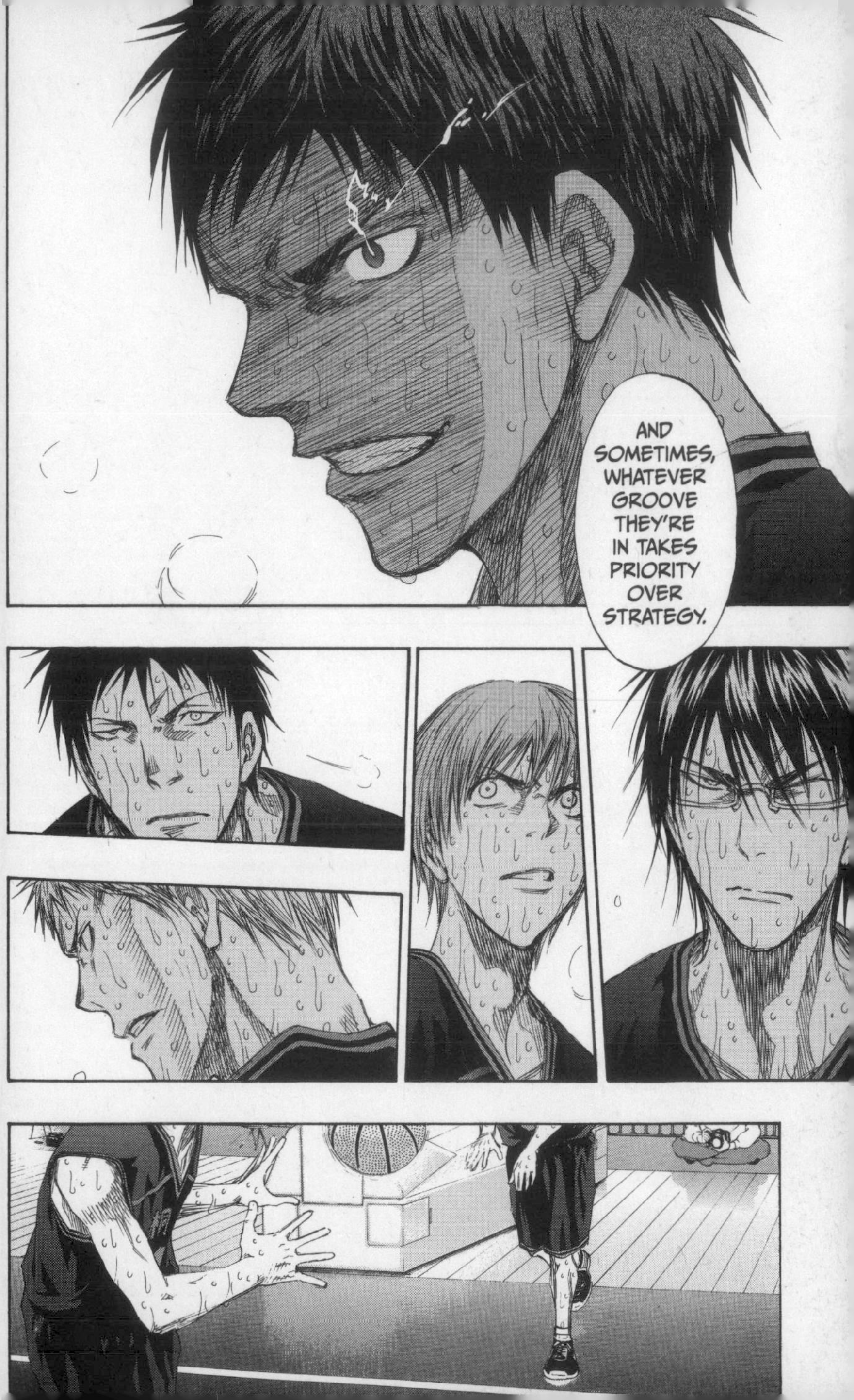
AND SOMETIMES, WHATEVER GROOVE THEY'RE IN TAKES PRIORITY OVER STRATEGY.

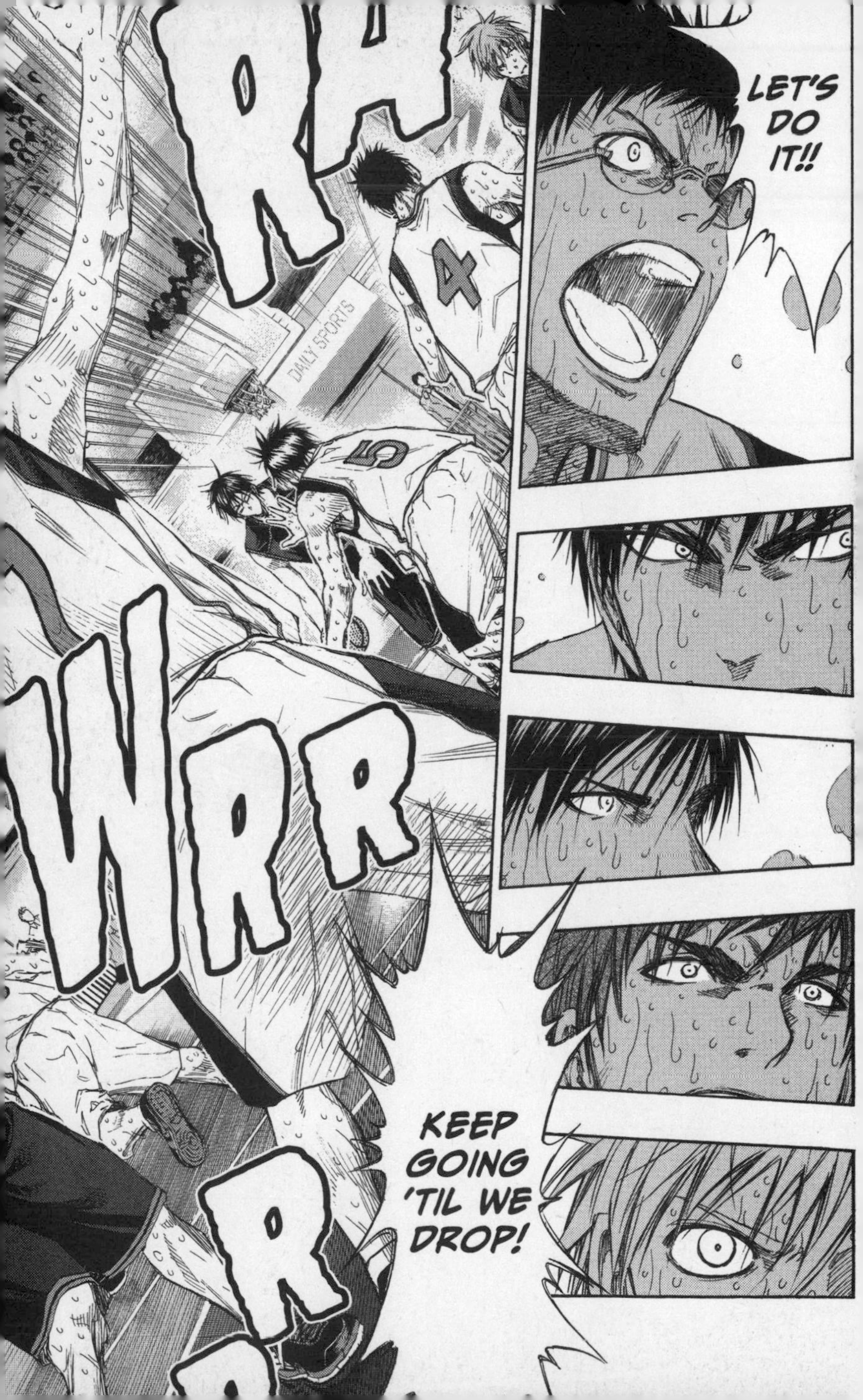
LET'S DO IT!!
KEEP GOING 'TIL WE DROP!

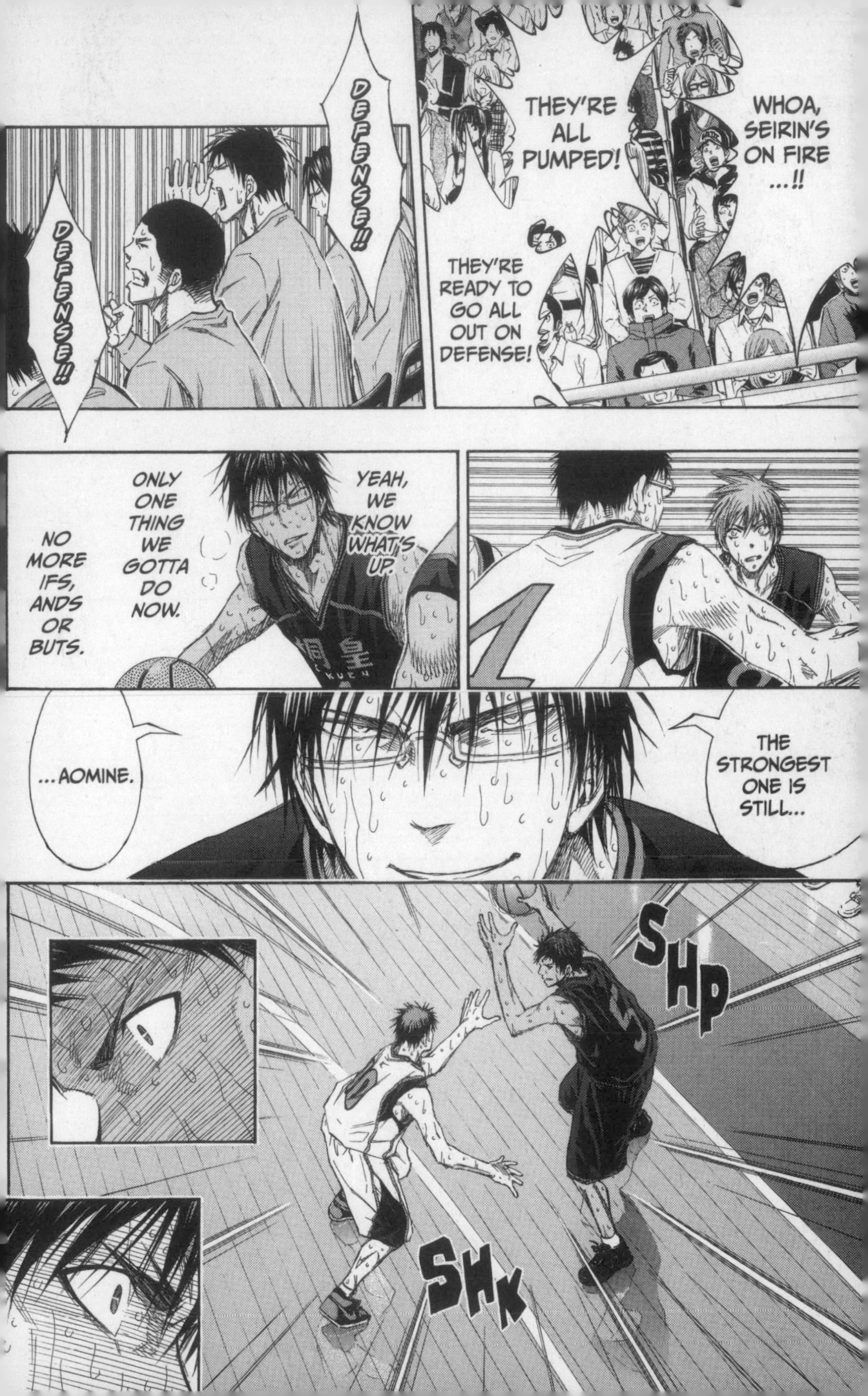
WHOA, SEIRIN'S ON FIRE ...!!
THEY'RE ALL PUMPED!
THEY'RE READY TO GO ALL OUT ON DEFENSE!
DEFENSE!!
DEFENSE!!
YEAH, WE KNOW WHAT'S UP.
ONLY ONE THING WE GOTTA DO NOW.
NO MORE IFS, ANDS OR BUTS.
THE STRONGEST ONE IS STILL...
...AOMINE.
SHP
SHK

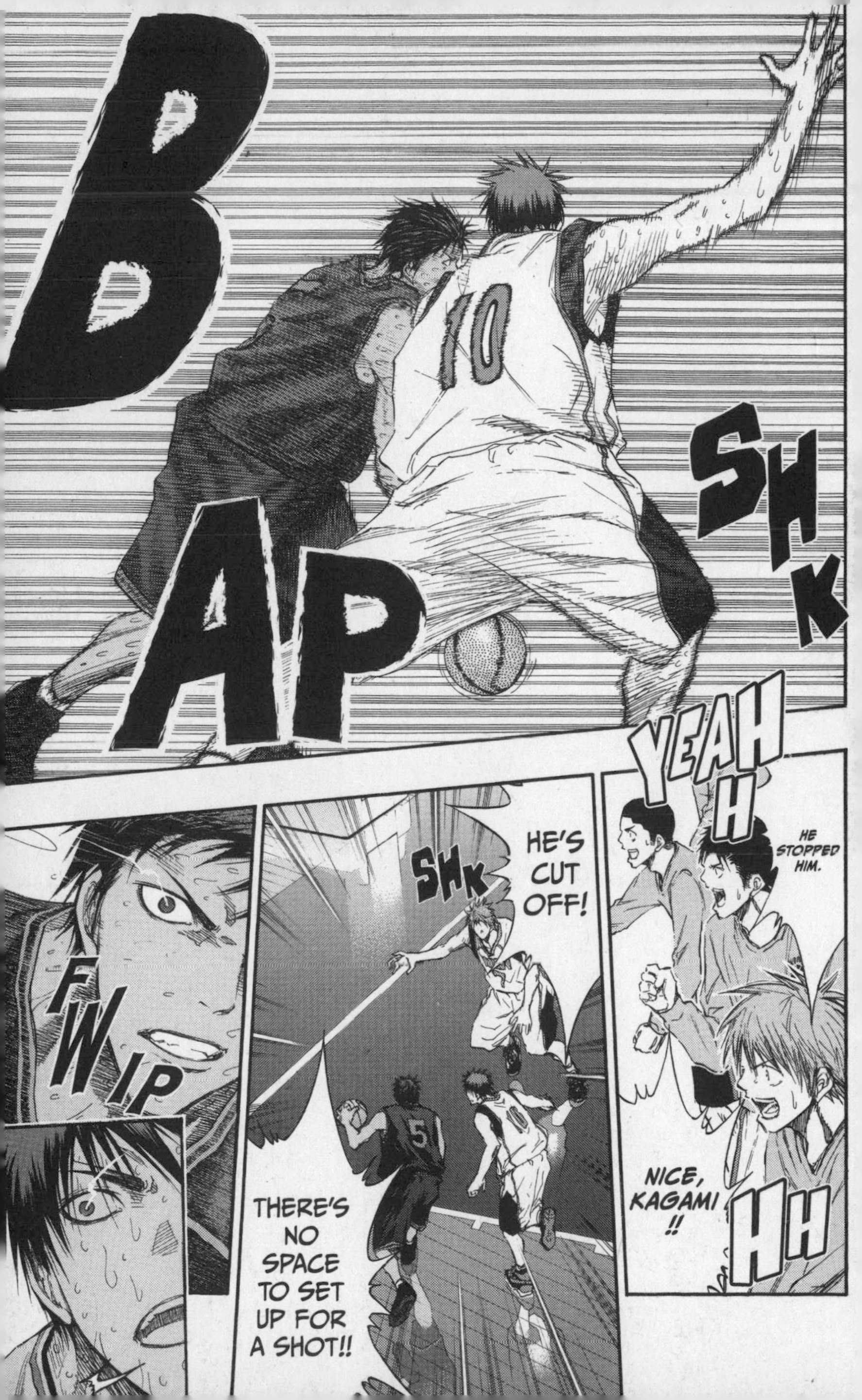
BAP
SHK
YEAHHHH
HE STOPPED HIM.
NICE, KAGAMI!!
SHK
HE'S CUT OFF!
THERE'S NO SPACE TO SET UP FOR A SHOT!!
FWIP

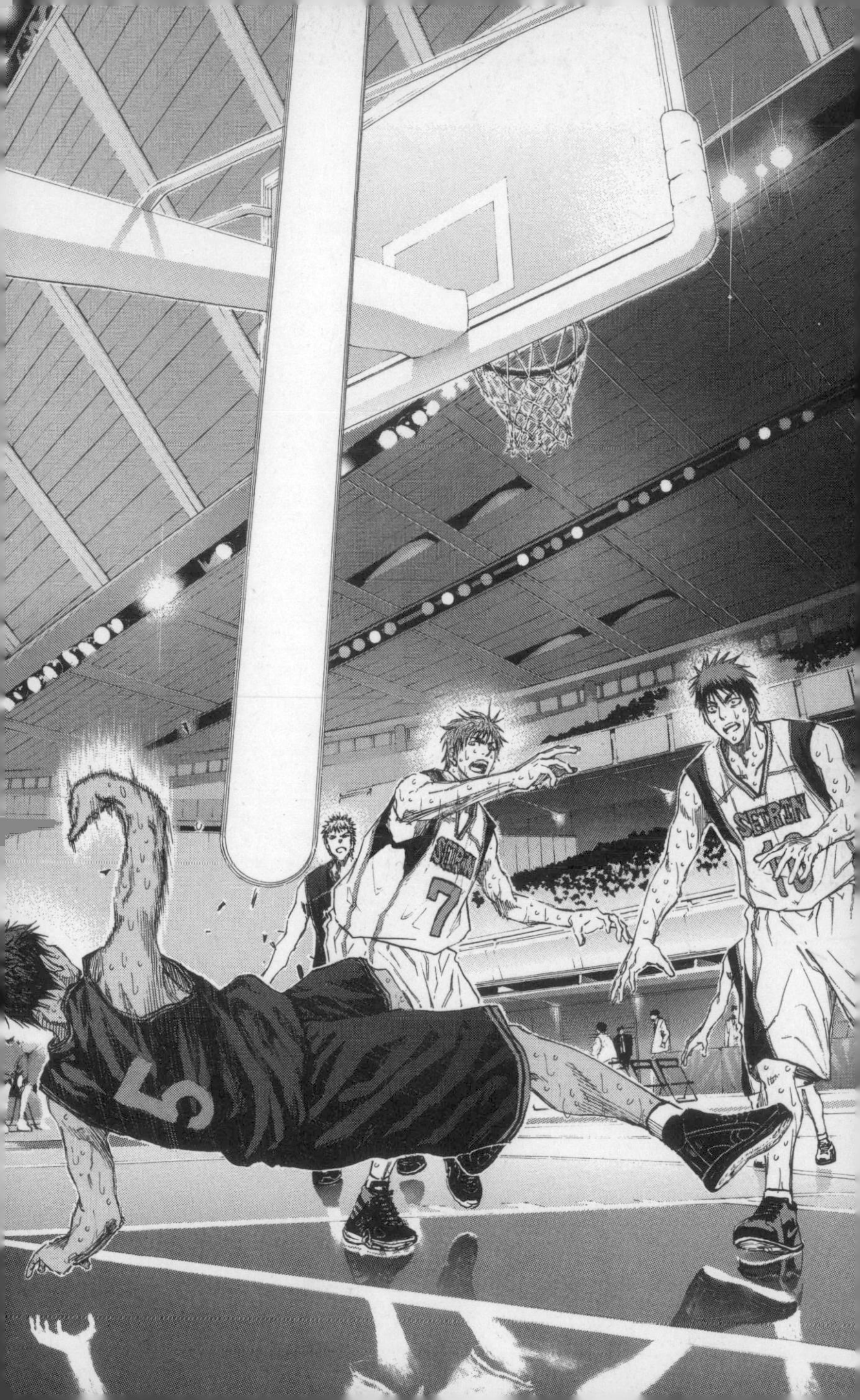

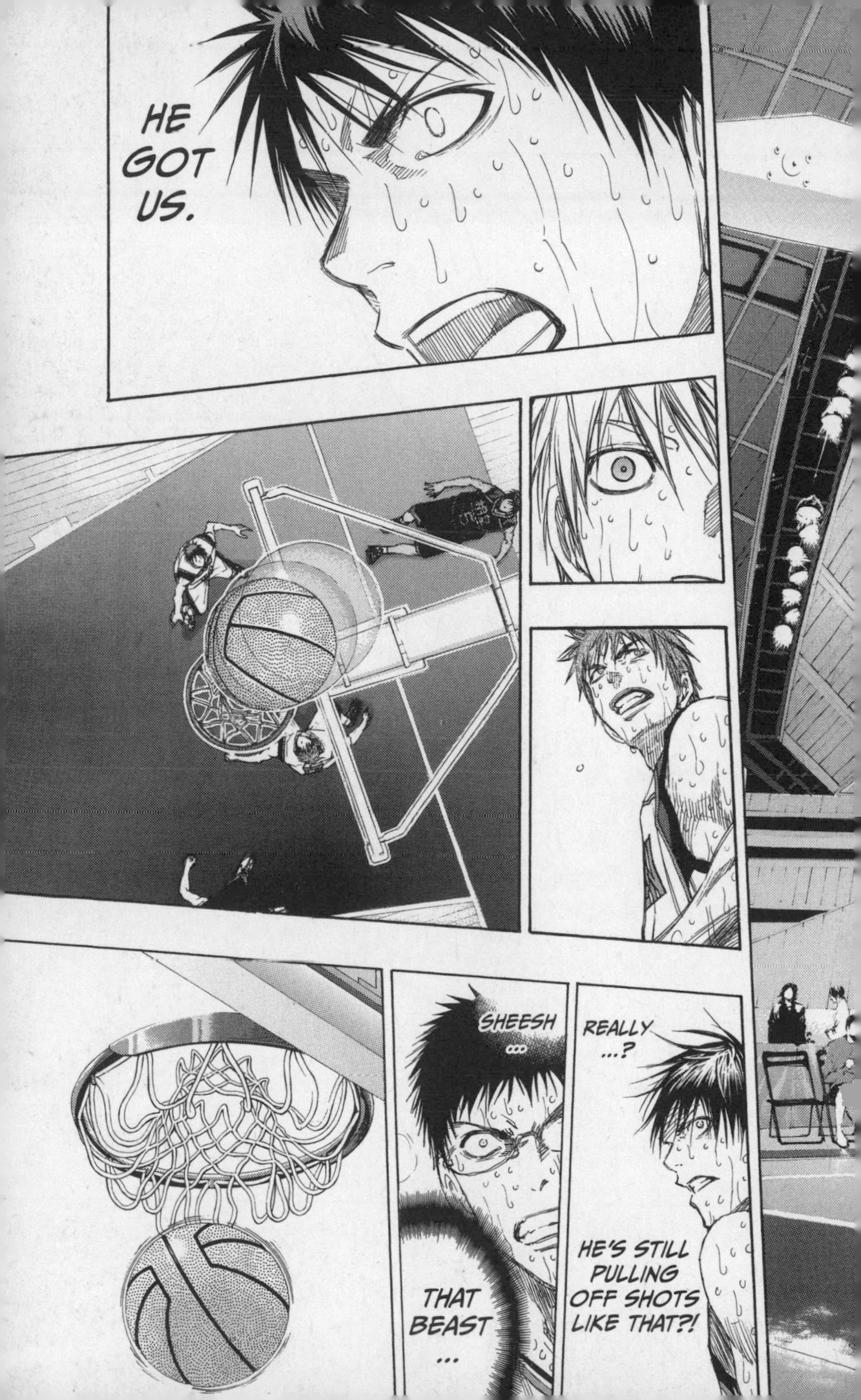
HE GOT US.
REALLY ...?
HE'S STILL PULLING OFF SHOTS LIKE THAT?!
SHEESH ...
THAT BEAST ...

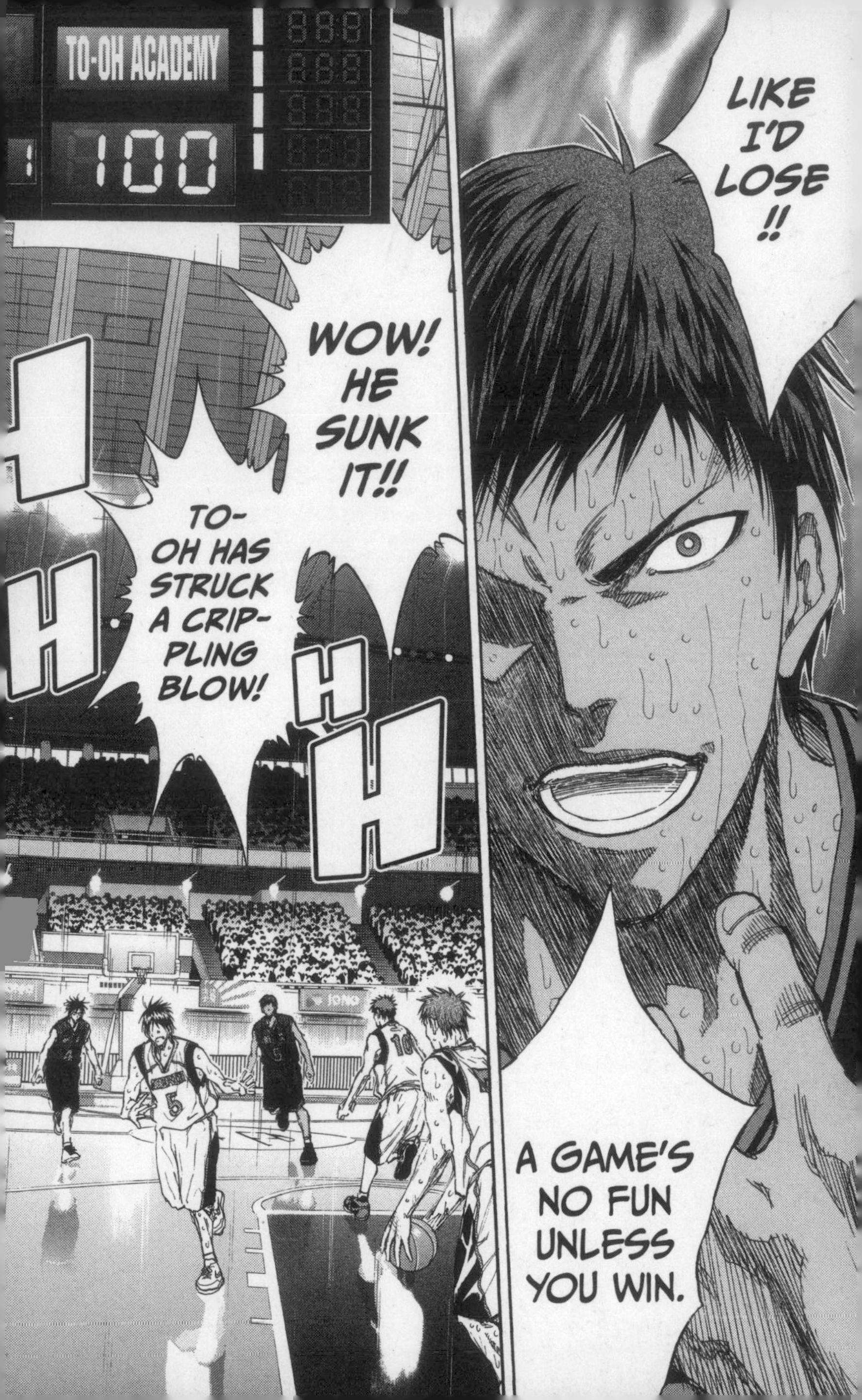
LIKE I'D LOSE!!
A GAME'S NO FUN UNLESS YOU WIN.
TO-OH ACADEMY
100
WOW! HE SUNK IT!!
TO-OH HAS STRUCK A CRIP-PLING BLOW!
H
H
H
H

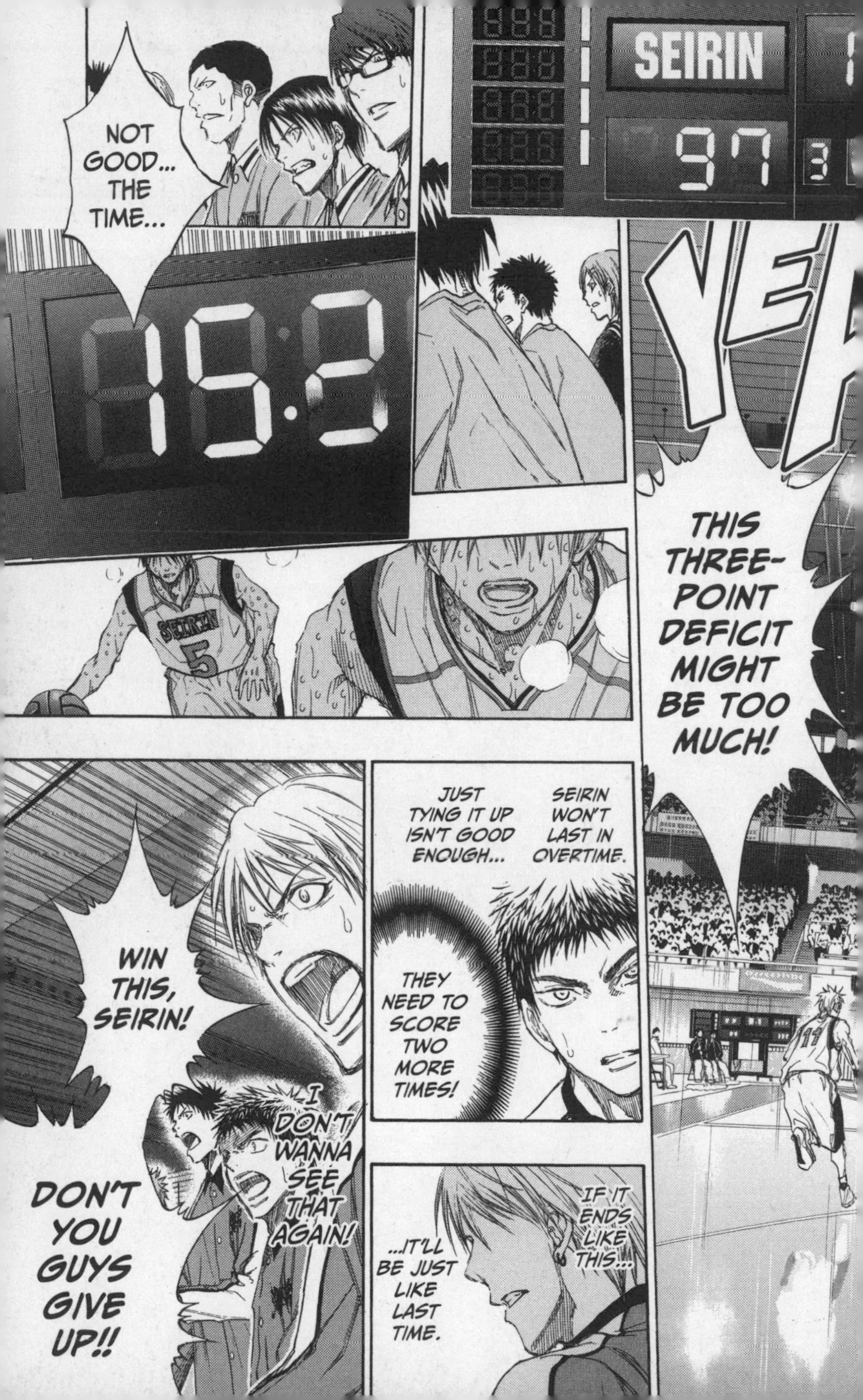

SEIRIN
97
NOT GOOD... THE TIME...
15.2
THIS THREE-POINT DEFICIT MIGHT BE TOO MUCH!
SEIRIN WON'T LAST IN OVERTIME.
JUST TYING IT UP ISN'T GOOD ENOUGH...
THEY NEED TO SCORE TWO MORE TIMES!
IF IT ENDS LIKE THIS...
...IT'LL BE JUST LIKE LAST TIME.
WIN THIS, SEIRIN!
I DON'T WANNA SEE THAT AGAIN!
DON'T YOU GUYS GIVE UP!!

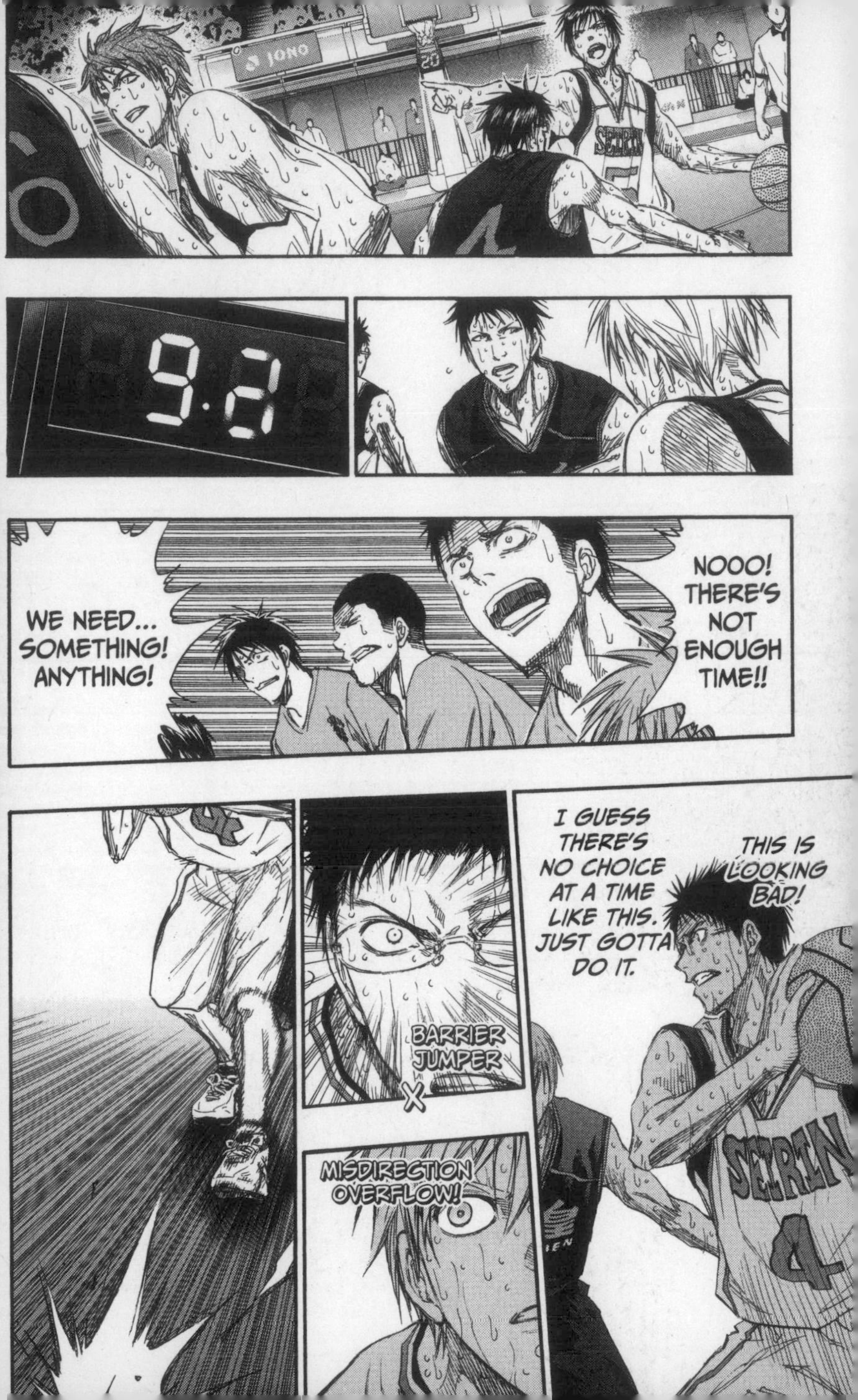

JONO
9.2
NOOO! THERE'S NOT ENOUGH TIME!!
WE NEED... SOMETHING! ANYTHING!
THIS IS LOOKING BAD!
I GUESS THERE'S NO CHOICE AT A TIME LIKE THIS. JUST GOTTA DO IT.
BARRIER JUMPER
X
MISDIRECTION OVERFLOW!

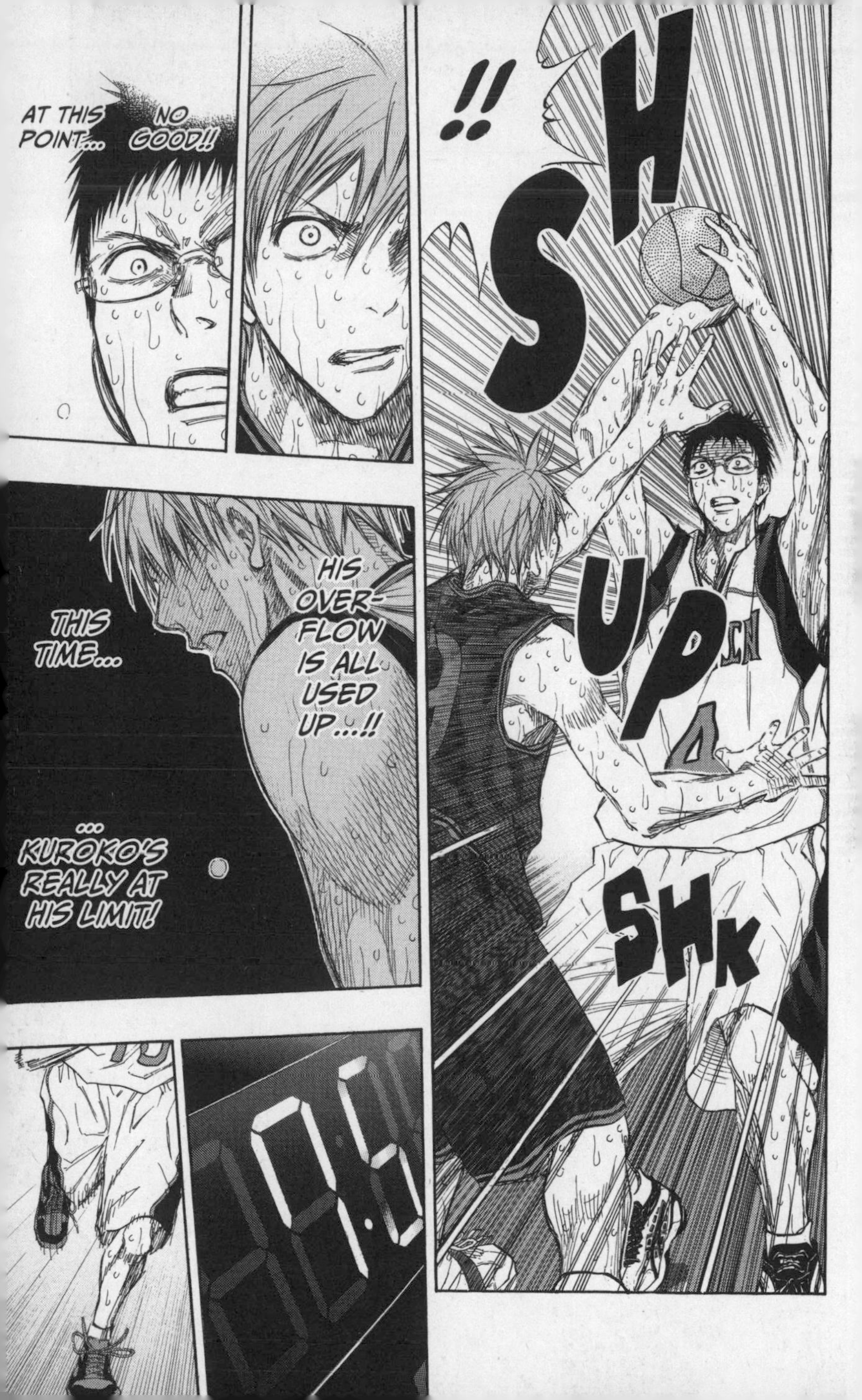
!!
SHH
SHUP
SHK
NO GOOD!!
AT THIS POINT...
HIS OVER-FLOW IS ALL USED UP...!!
THIS TIME...
...KUROKO'S REALLY AT HIS LIMIT!

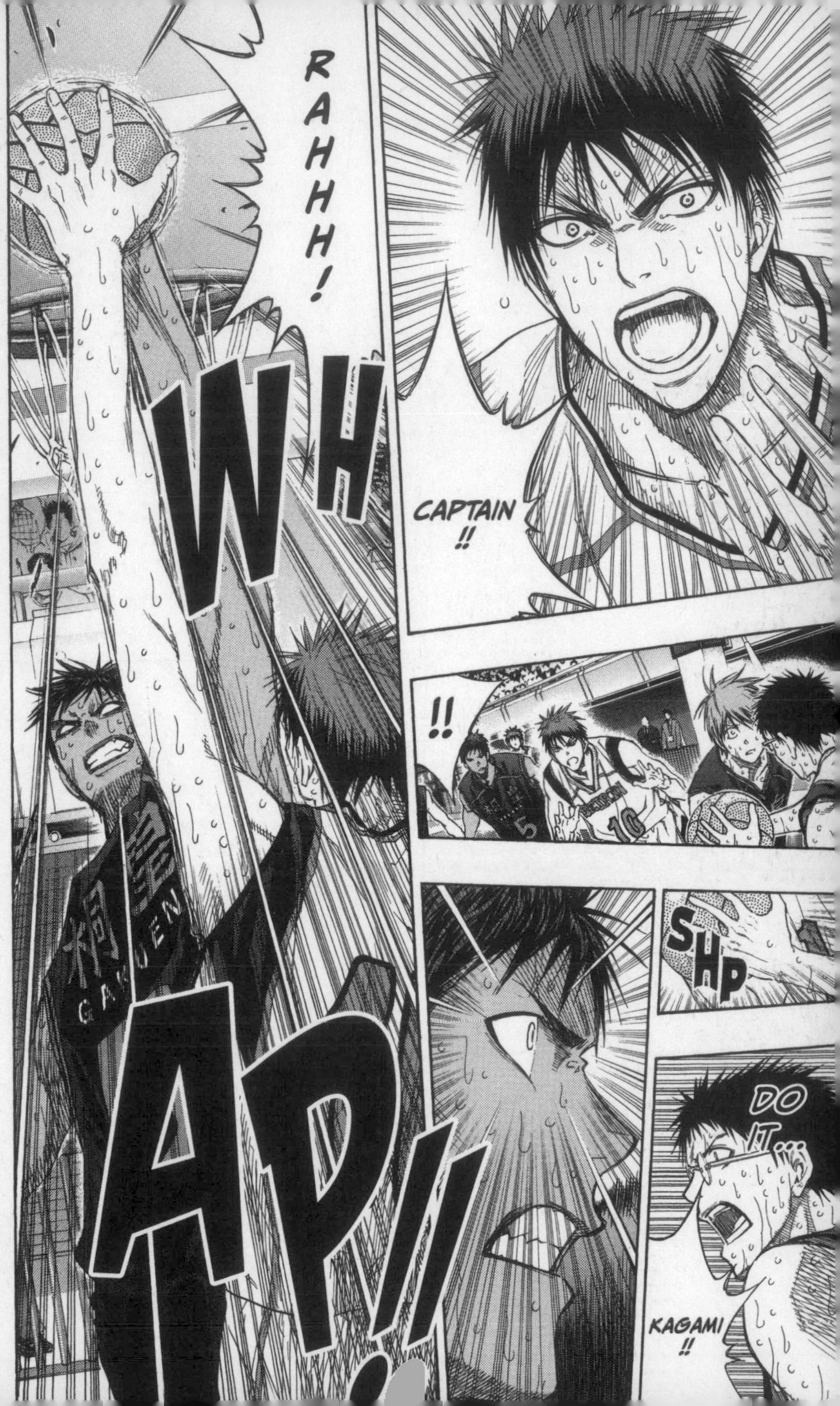
CAPTAIN !!
!!
SHP
DO IT...
KAGAMI !!
RAHHHH!
WHAP!!

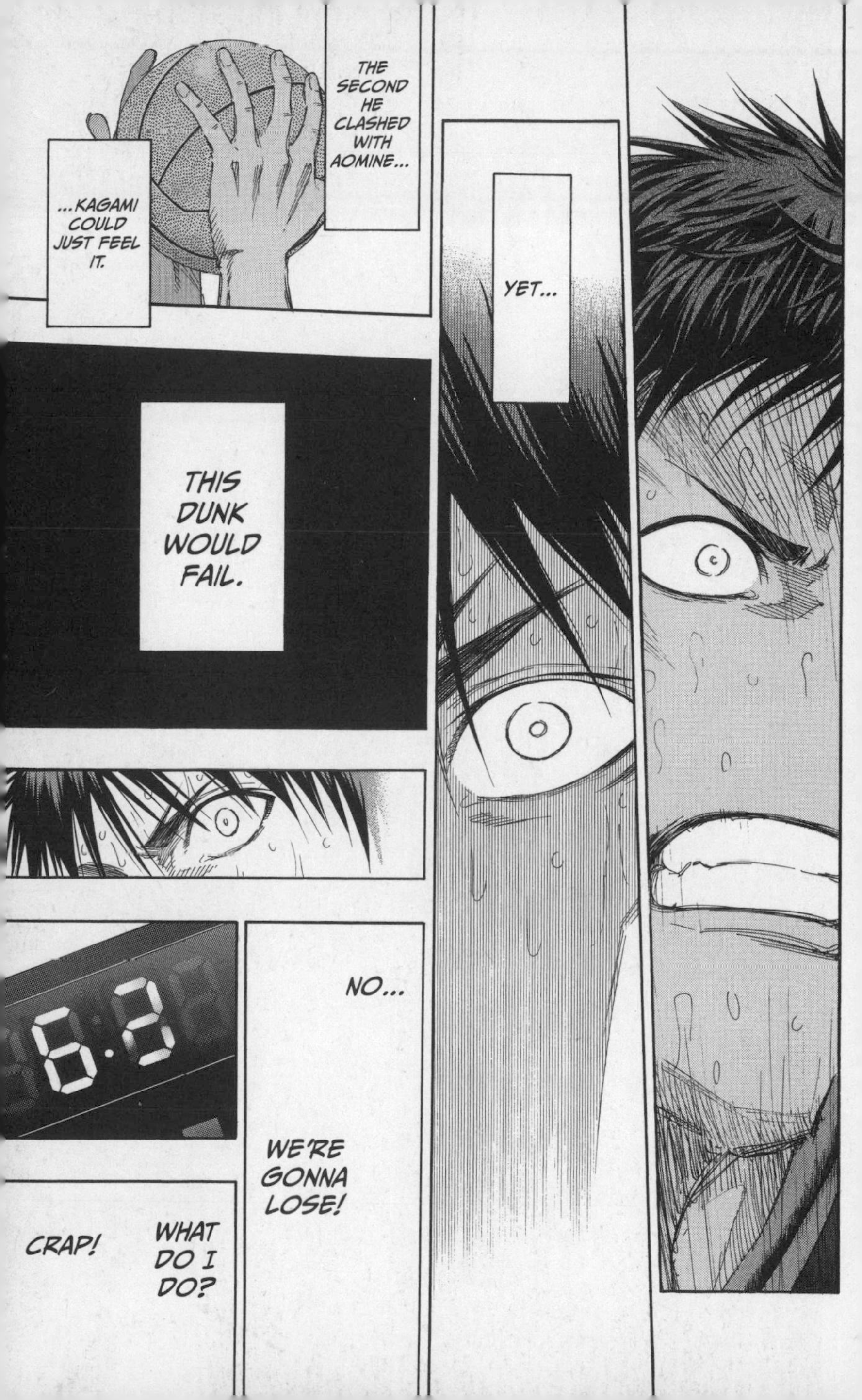
YET...
THE SECOND HE CLASHED WITH AOMINE...
...KAGAMI COULD JUST FEEL IT.
THIS DUNK WOULD FAIL.
6.2
NO...
WE'RE GONNA LOSE!
WHAT DO I DO?
CRAP!

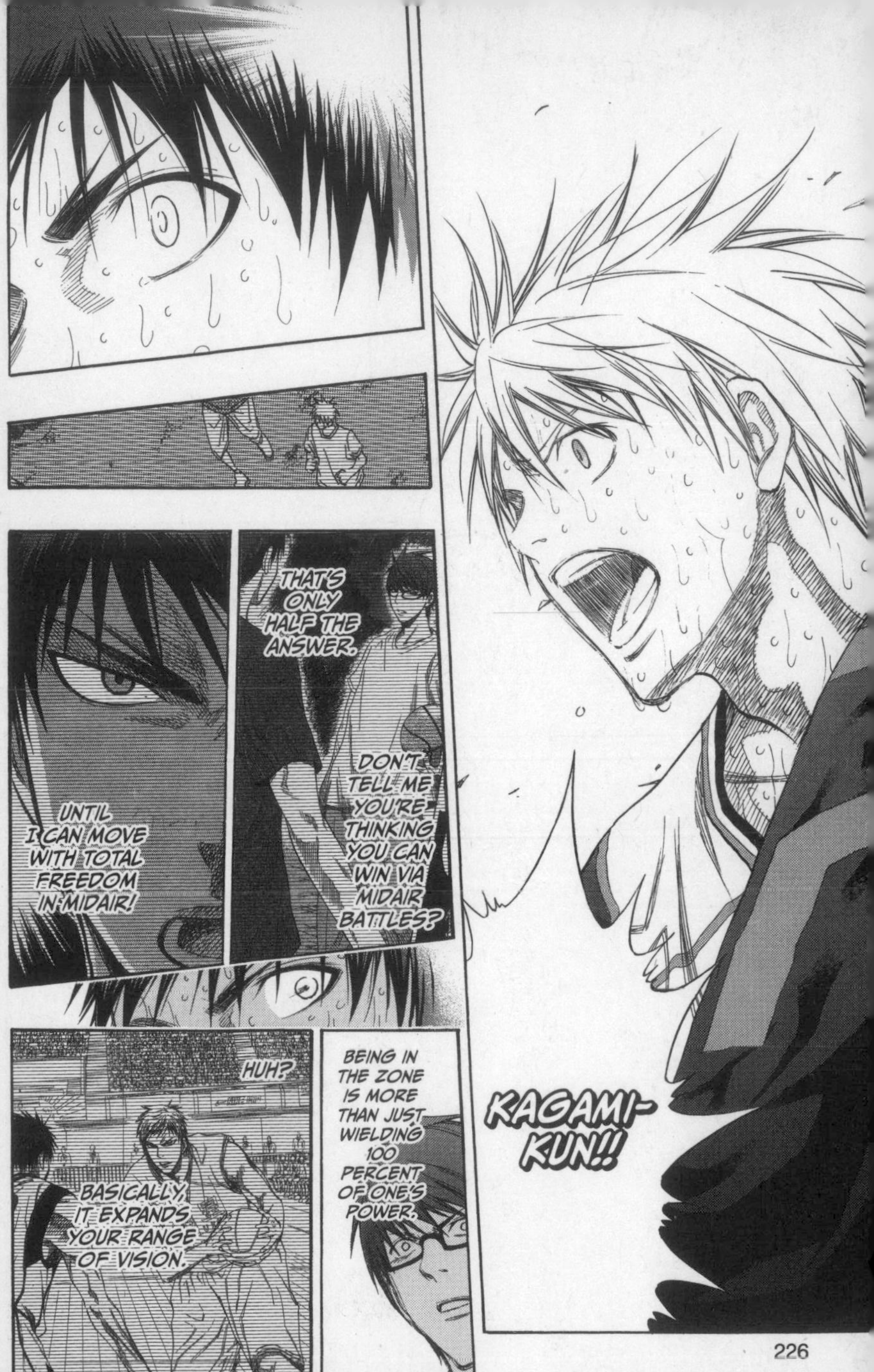
THAT'S ONLY HALF THE ANSWER.
DON'T TELL ME YOU'RE THINKING YOU CAN WIN VIA MIDAIR BATTLES?
UNTIL I CAN MOVE WITH TOTAL FREEDOM IN MIDAIR!
BEING IN THE ZONE IS MORE THAN JUST WIELDING 100 PERCENT OF ONE'S POWER.
HUH?
BASICALLY, IT EXPANDS YOUR RANGE OF VISION.
KAGAMI-KUN!!

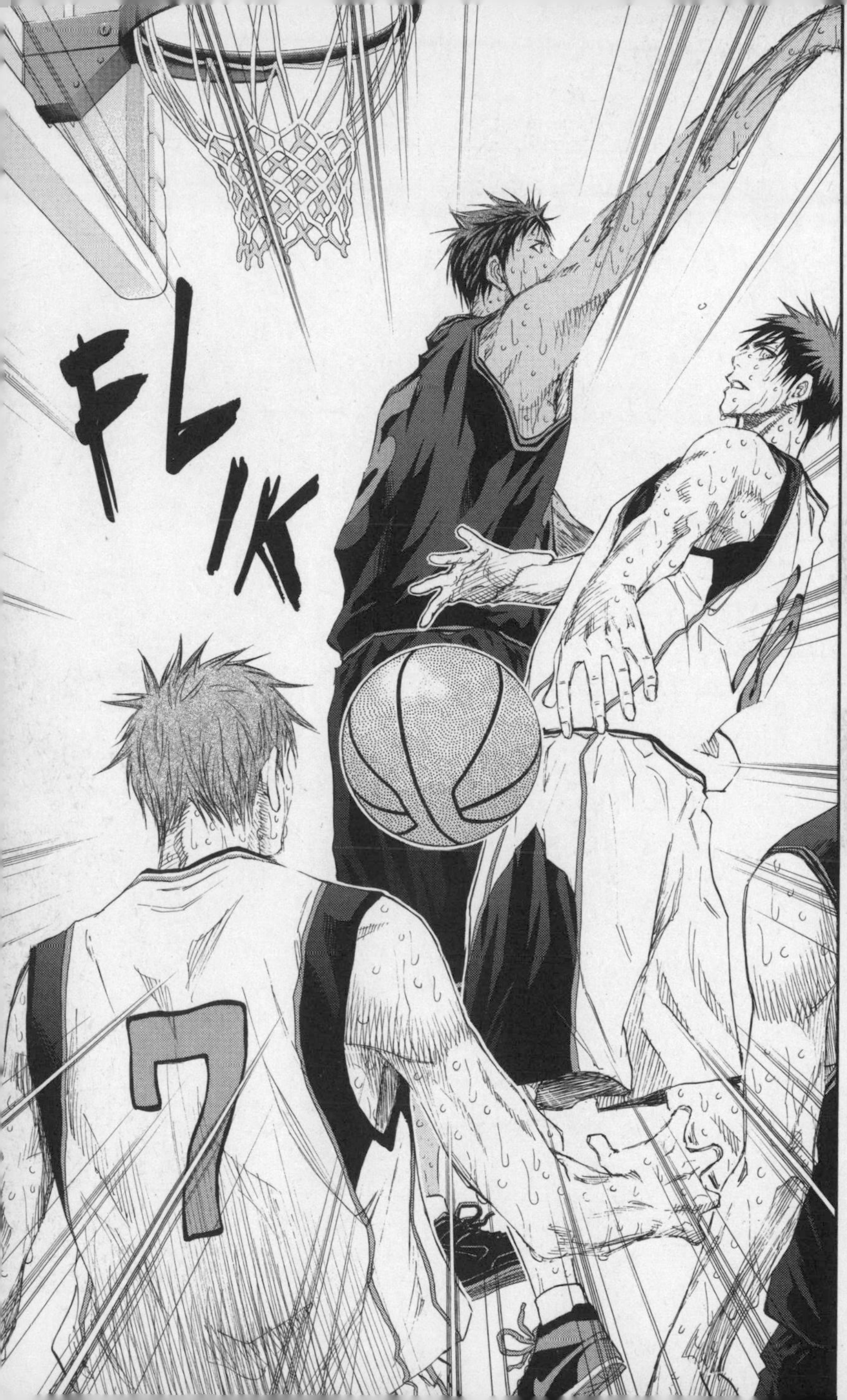
FLIK

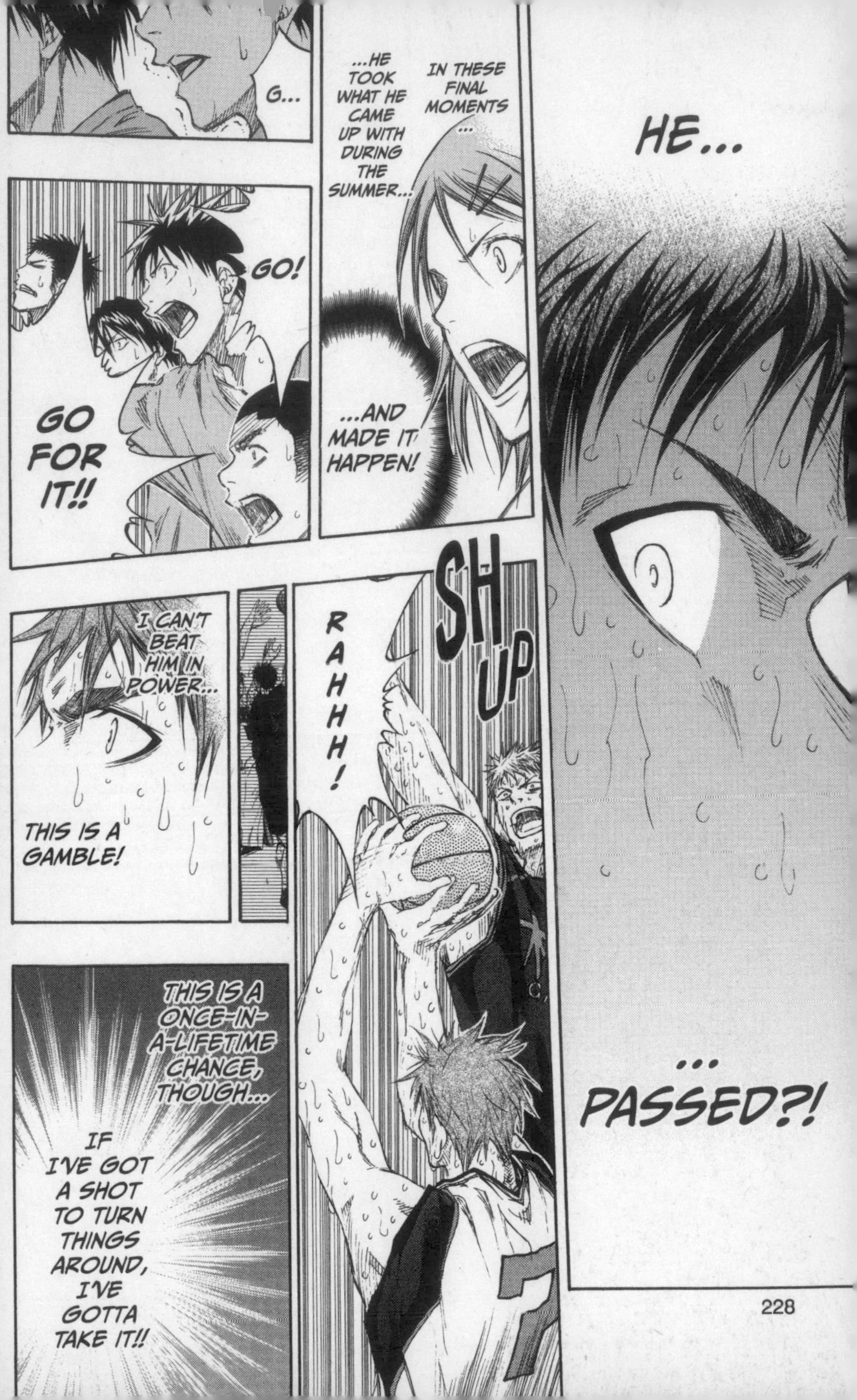
HE...
...PASSED?!
IN THESE FINAL MOMENTS...
...HE TOOK WHAT HE CAME UP WITH DURING THE SUMMER...
...AND MADE IT HAPPEN!
G...
GO!
GO FOR IT!!
SHUP
RAHHHH!
I CAN'T BEAT HIM IN POWER...
THIS IS A GAMBLE!
THIS IS A ONCE-IN-A-LIFETIME CHANCE, THOUGH...
IF I'VE GOT A SHOT TO TURN THINGS AROUND, I'VE GOTTA TAKE IT!!

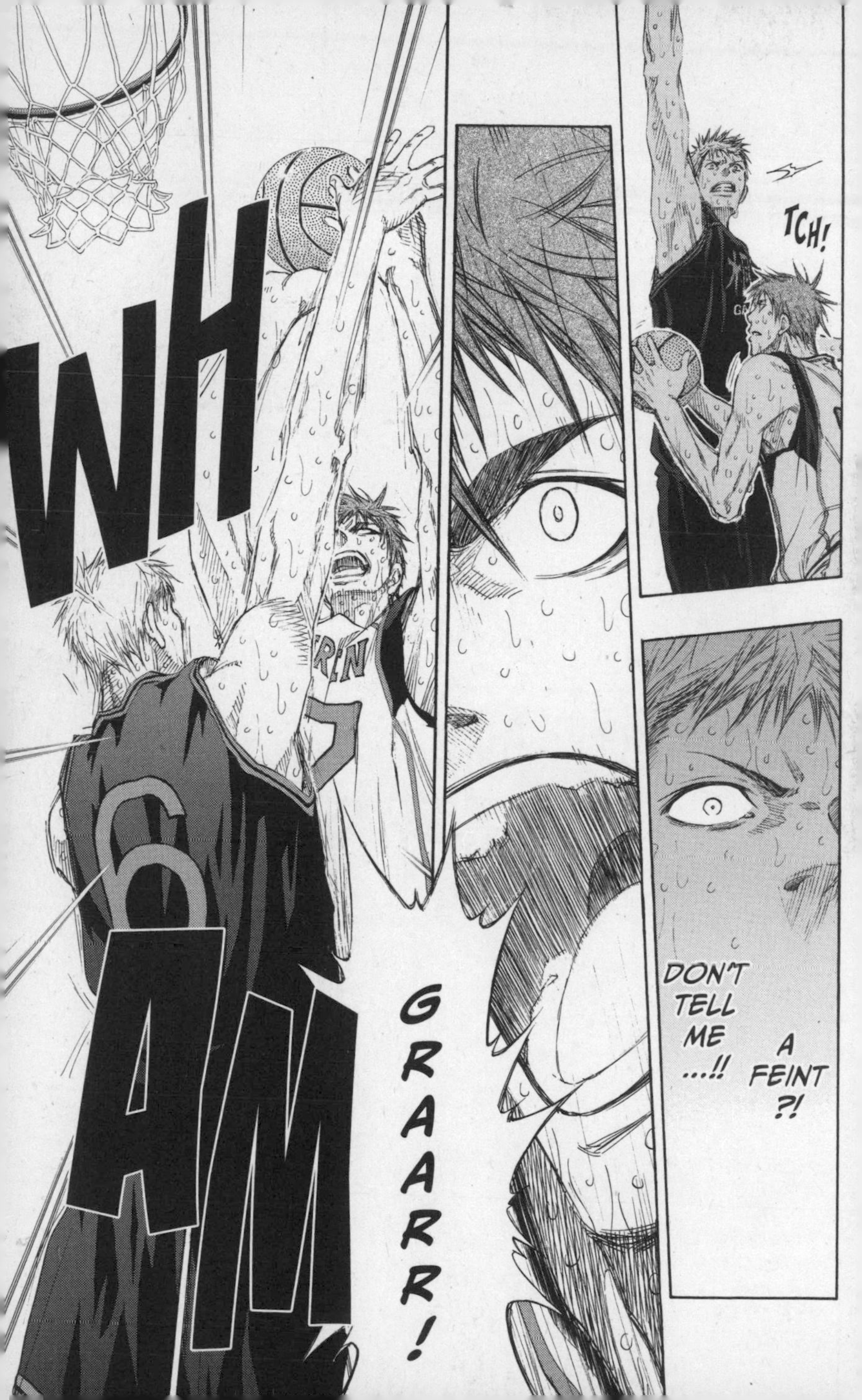
TCH!
DON'T TELL ME ...!!
A FEINT ?!
WHAM
GRAARR!

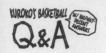

KUROKO'S BASKETBALL Q&A

W/ HALFWAY-DECENT ANSWERS

Q. HOW MUCH MONEY DOES MURASAKIBARA SPEND ON SNACKS?!
(BLUE WATER DROP from SAITAMA PREFECTURE)

A. ALL THE MONEY HE'S GOT.

KUROKO'S BASKETBALL BLOOPERS

TAKE 5

CAMERAMAN
?!
BONK
UGH ?!
AOMINE...
MISSED...
FWISH
OUCH
AOMINE!!
BAP
SHAKA SHAKA

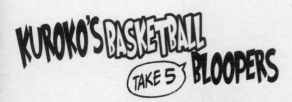

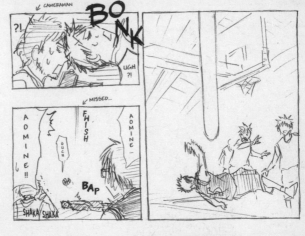

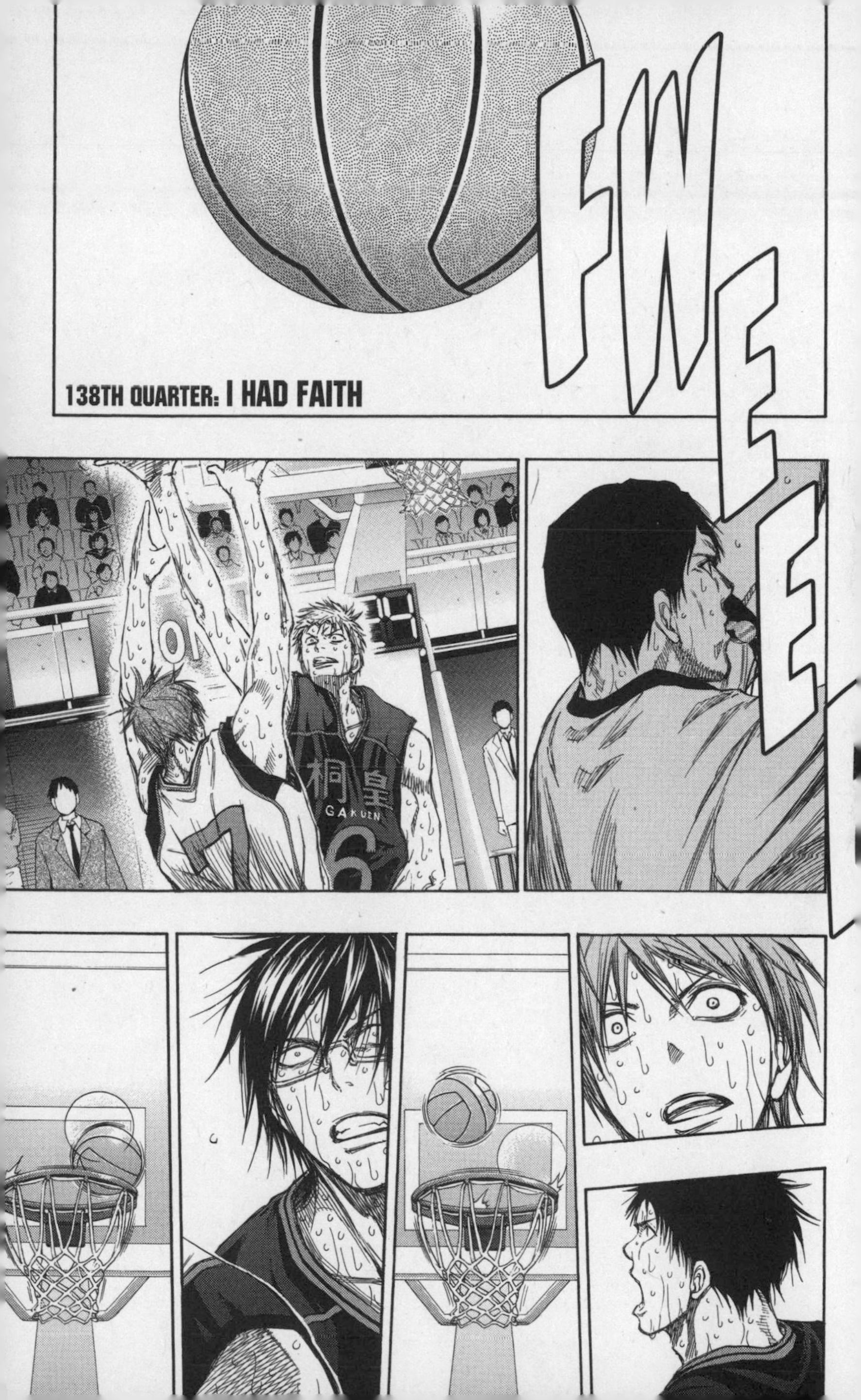
FWEEE
138TH QUARTER: I HAD FAITH

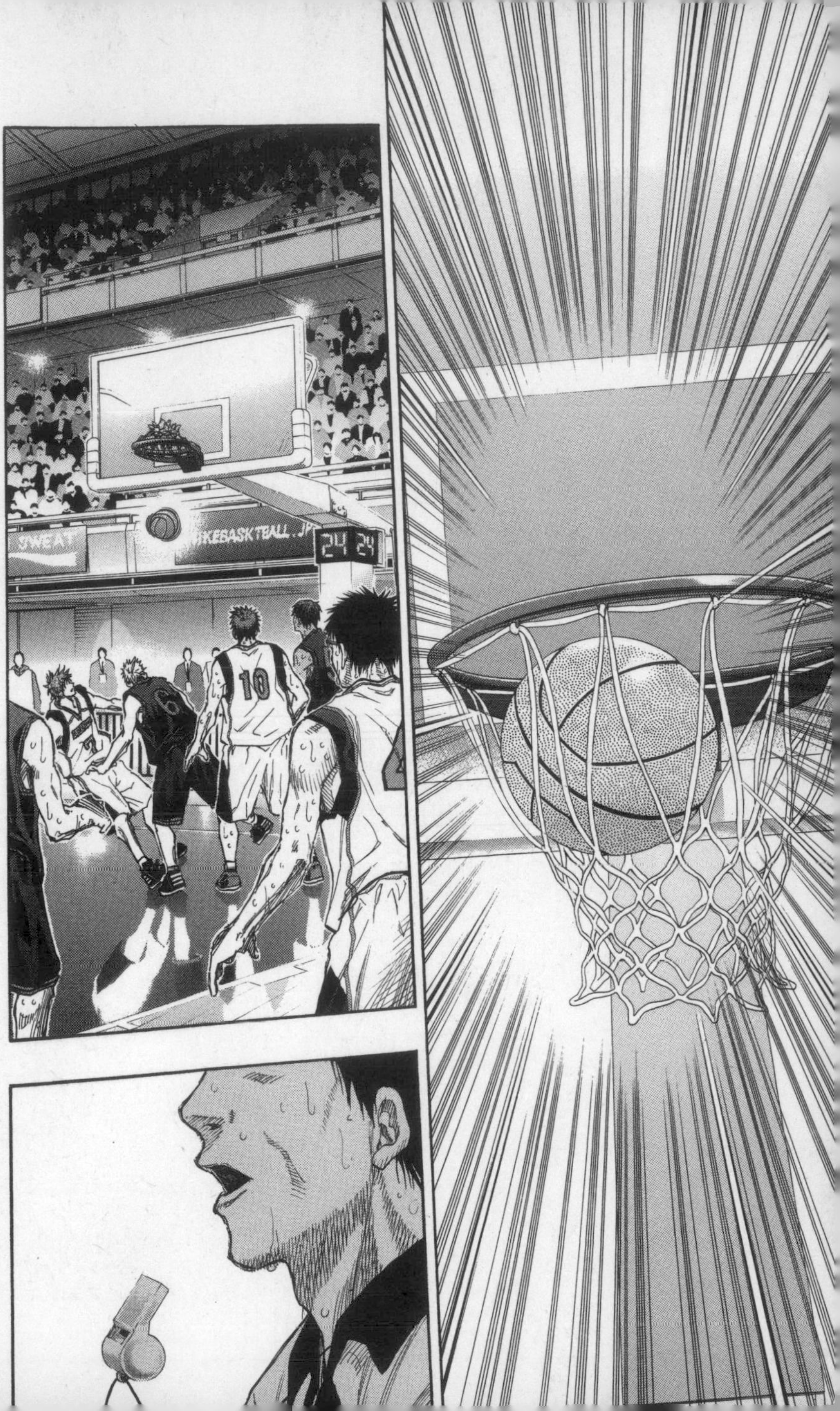
SWEAT
24 24
10

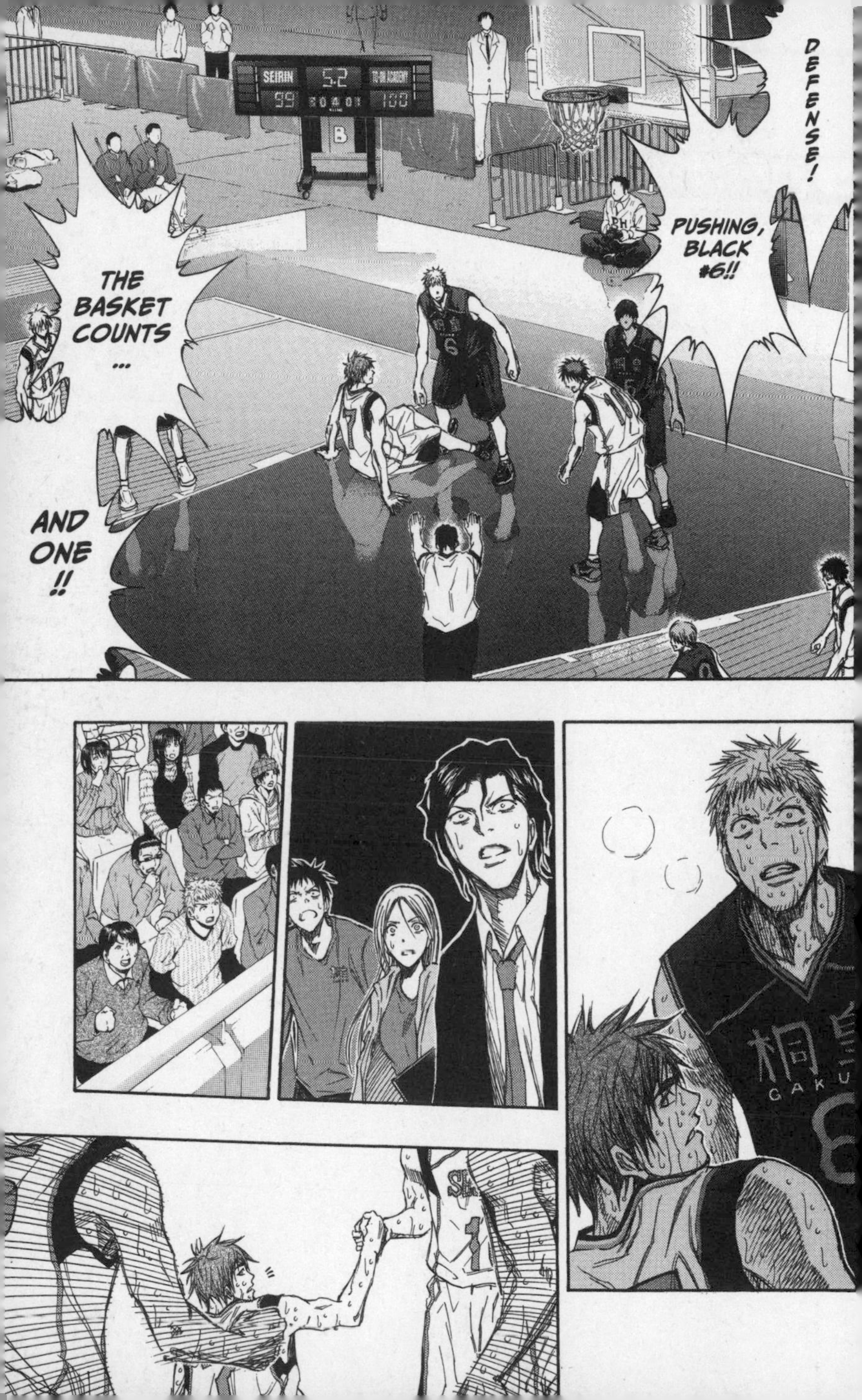
DEFENSE!
PUSHING, BLACK #6!!
THE BASKET COUNTS ...
AND ONE !!

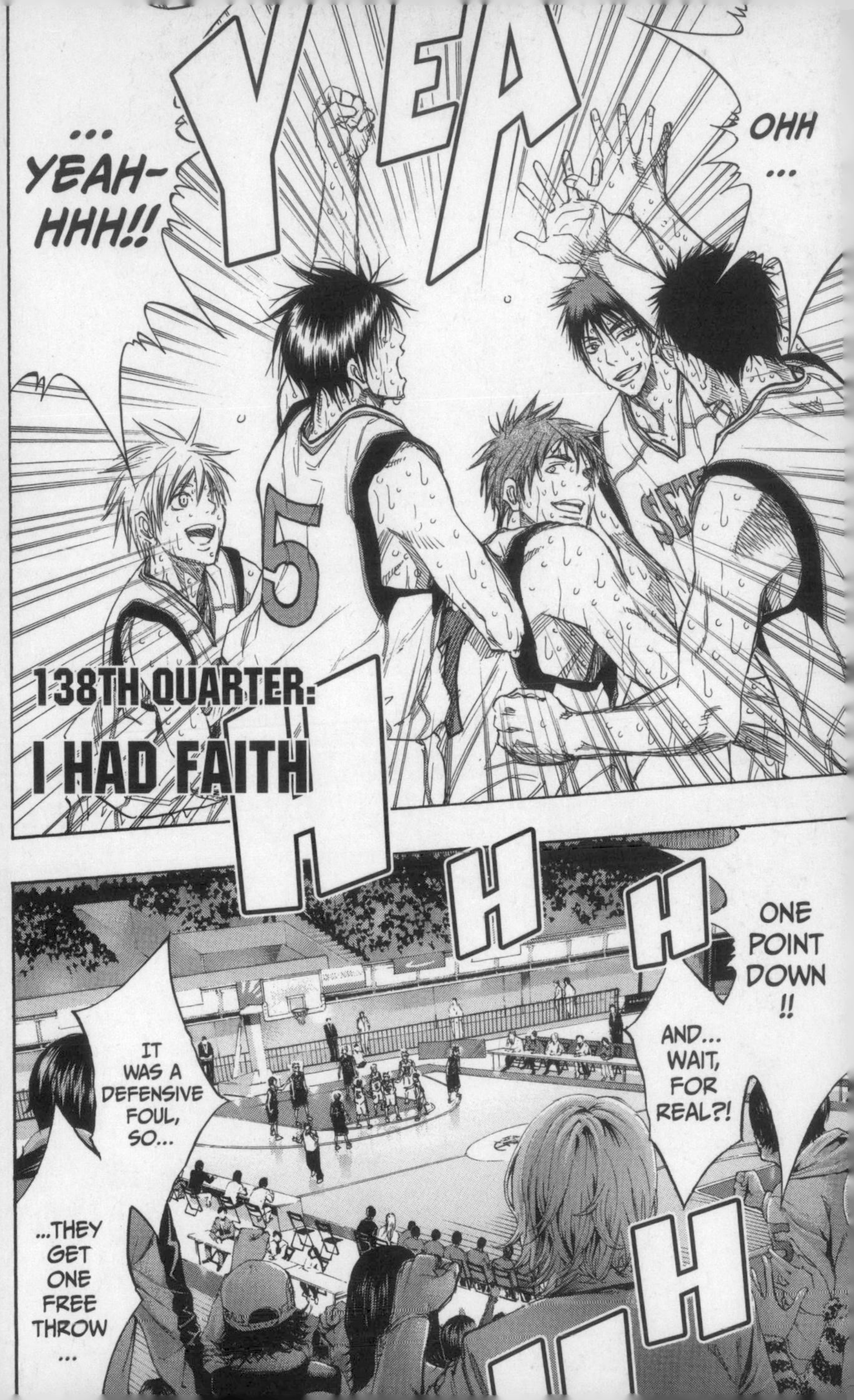
OHH ...
YEA
... YEAH-HHH!!
138TH QUARTER:
I HAD FAITH
H H H
ONE POINT DOWN !!
AND... WAIT, FOR REAL?!
IT WAS A DEFENSIVE FOUL, SO...
...THEY GET ONE FREE THROW ...
H

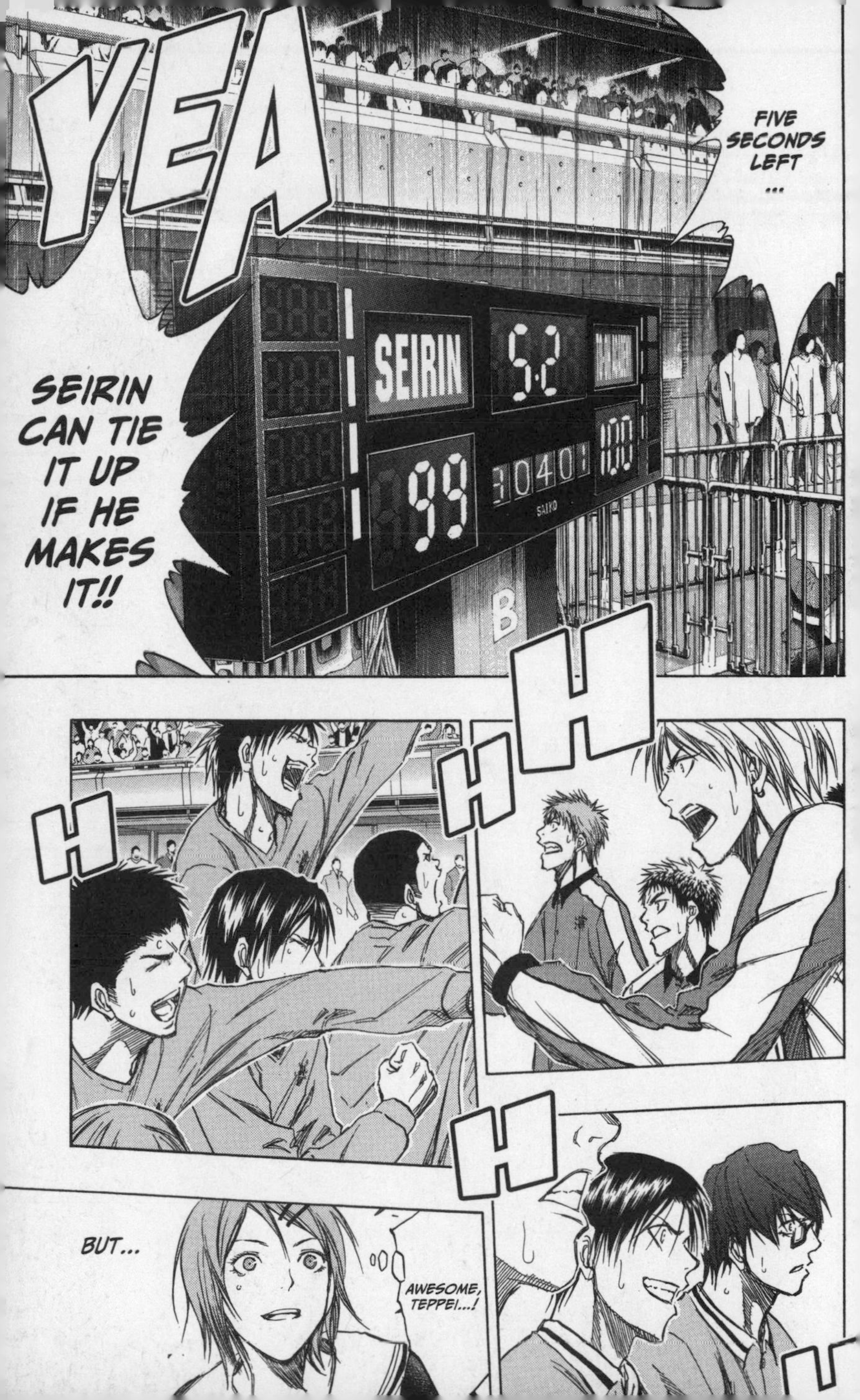

FIVE SECONDS LEFT ...
YEA
SEIRIN
99
100
SEIRIN CAN TIE IT UP IF HE MAKES IT!!
H
H
H
H
AWESOME, TEPPEI...!
BUT...

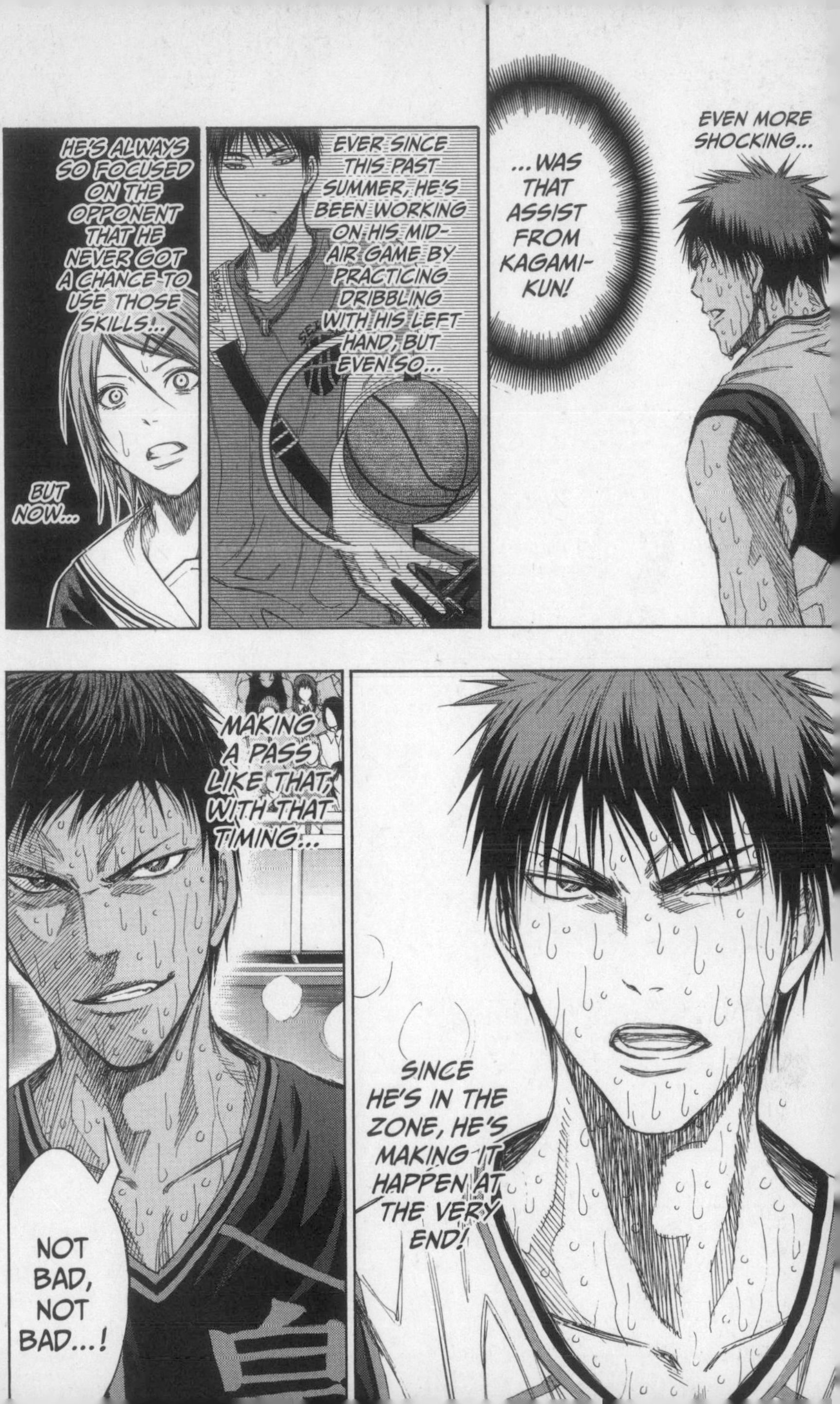
EVEN MORE SHOCKING...
...WAS THAT ASSIST FROM KAGAMI-KUN!
EVER SINCE THIS PAST SUMMER, HE'S BEEN WORKING ON HIS MID-AIR GAME BY PRACTICING DRIBBLING WITH HIS LEFT HAND, BUT EVEN SO...
HE'S ALWAYS SO FOCUSED ON THE OPPONENT THAT HE NEVER GOT A CHANCE TO USE THOSE SKILLS...
BUT NOW...
SINCE HE'S IN THE ZONE, HE'S MAKING IT HAPPEN AT THE VERY END!
MAKING A PASS LIKE THAT, WITH THAT TIMING...
NOT BAD, NOT BAD...!

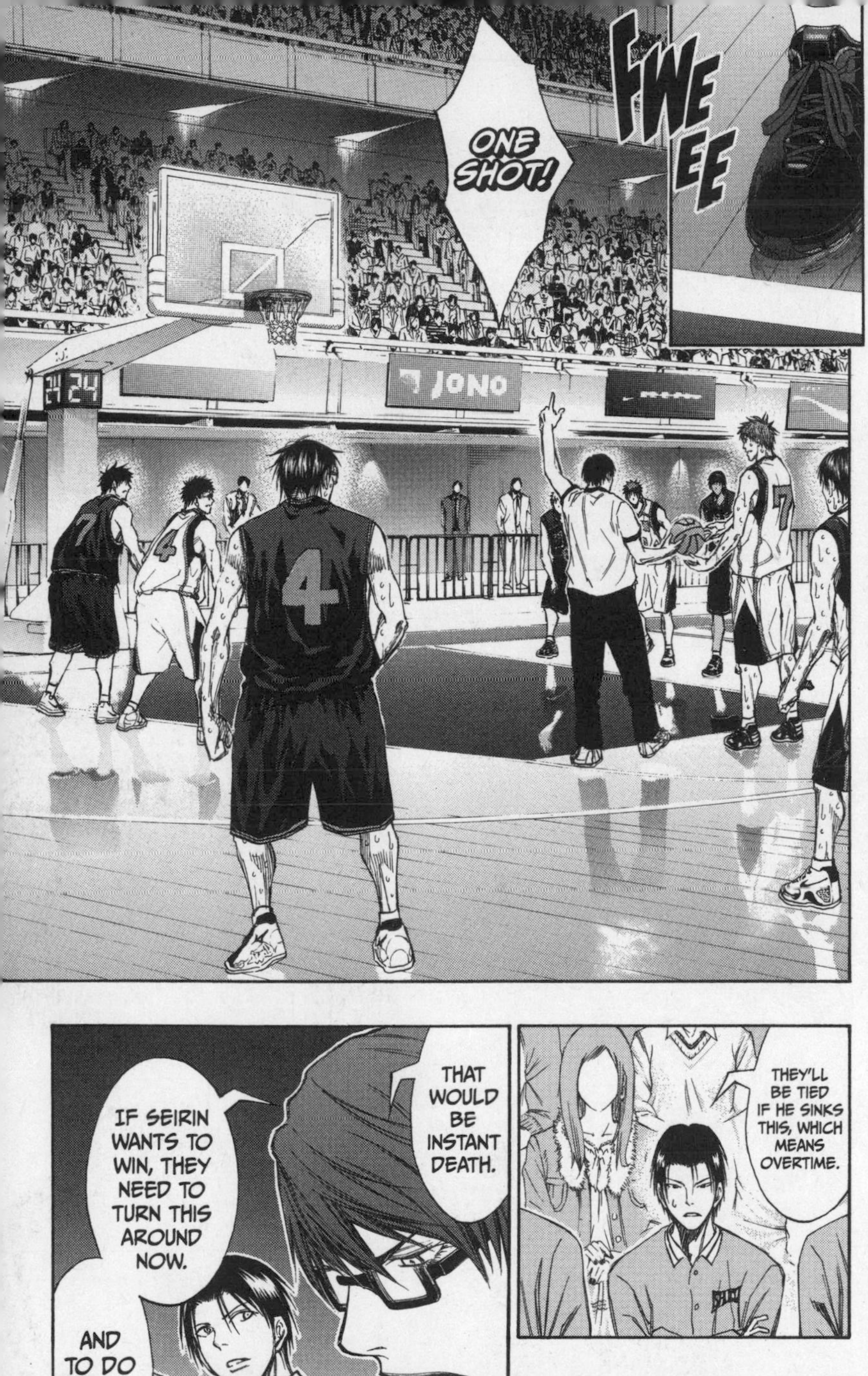
FWEEE
ONE SHOT!
JONO
THEY'LL BE TIED IF HE SINKS THIS, WHICH MEANS OVERTIME.
THAT WOULD BE INSTANT DEATH.
IF SEIRIN WANTS TO WIN, THEY NEED TO TURN THIS AROUND NOW.
AND TO DO THAT...

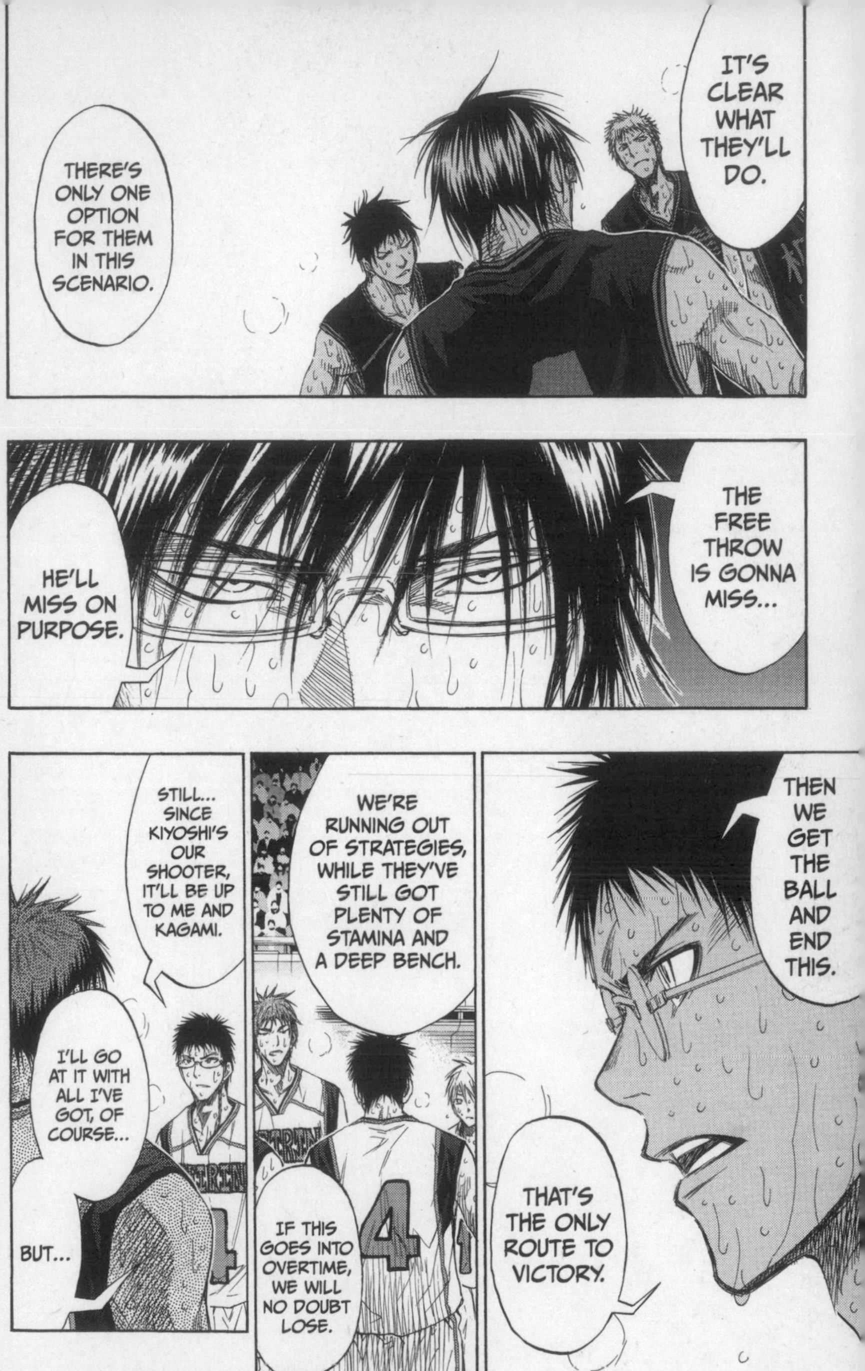
IT'S CLEAR WHAT THEY'LL DO.
THERE'S ONLY ONE OPTION FOR THEM IN THIS SCENARIO.
THE FREE THROW IS GONNA MISS...
HE'LL MISS ON PURPOSE.
THEN WE GET THE BALL AND END THIS.
THAT'S THE ONLY ROUTE TO VICTORY.
WE'RE RUNNING OUT OF STRATEGIES, WHILE THEY'VE STILL GOT PLENTY OF STAMINA AND A DEEP BENCH.
IF THIS GOES INTO OVERTIME, WE WILL NO DOUBT LOSE.
STILL... SINCE KIYOSHI'S OUR SHOOTER, IT'LL BE UP TO ME AND KAGAMI.
I'LL GO AT IT WITH ALL I'VE GOT, OF COURSE...
BUT...

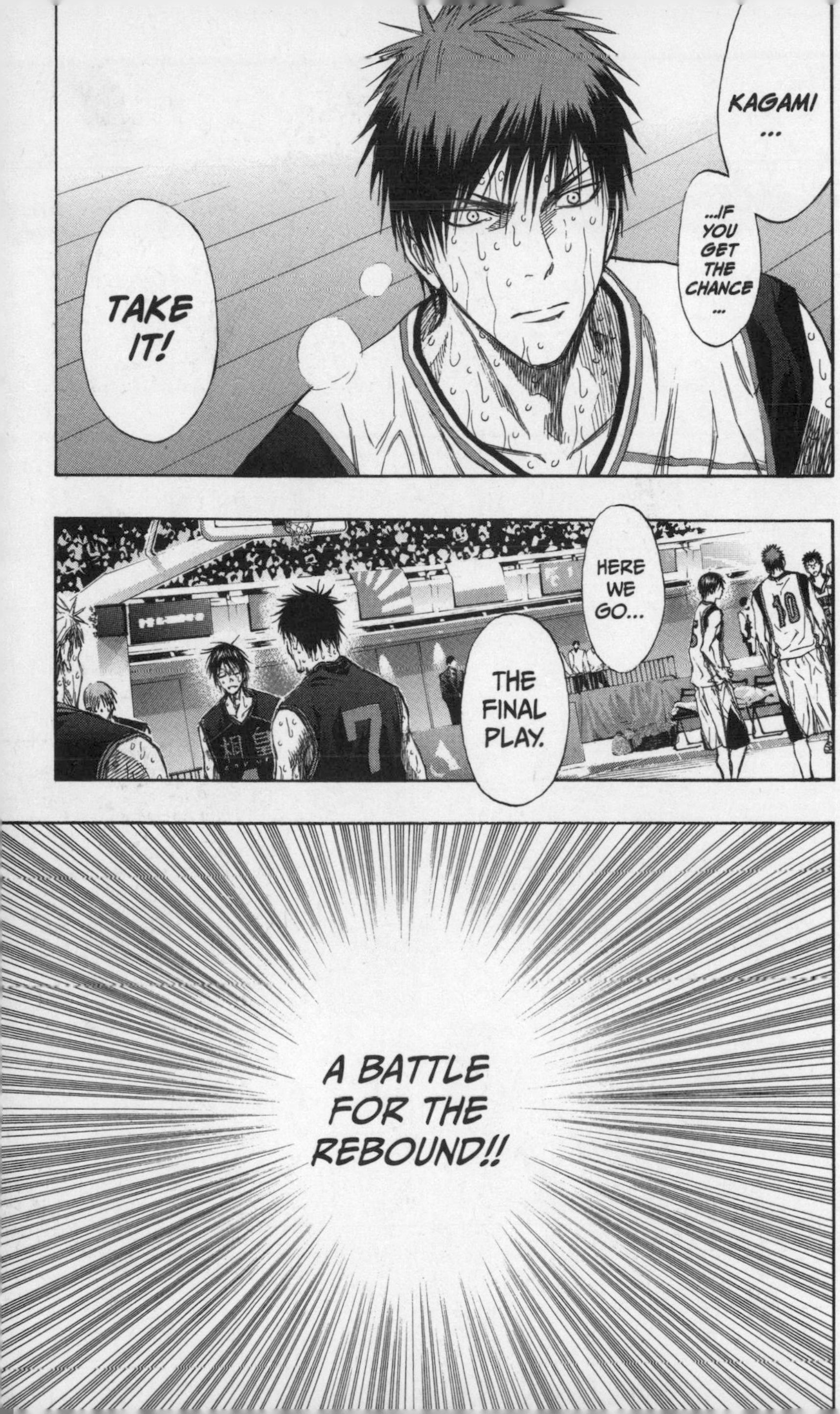
KAGAMI ...
...IF YOU GET THE CHANCE ...
TAKE IT!
HERE WE GO...
THE FINAL PLAY.
A BATTLE FOR THE REBOUND!!

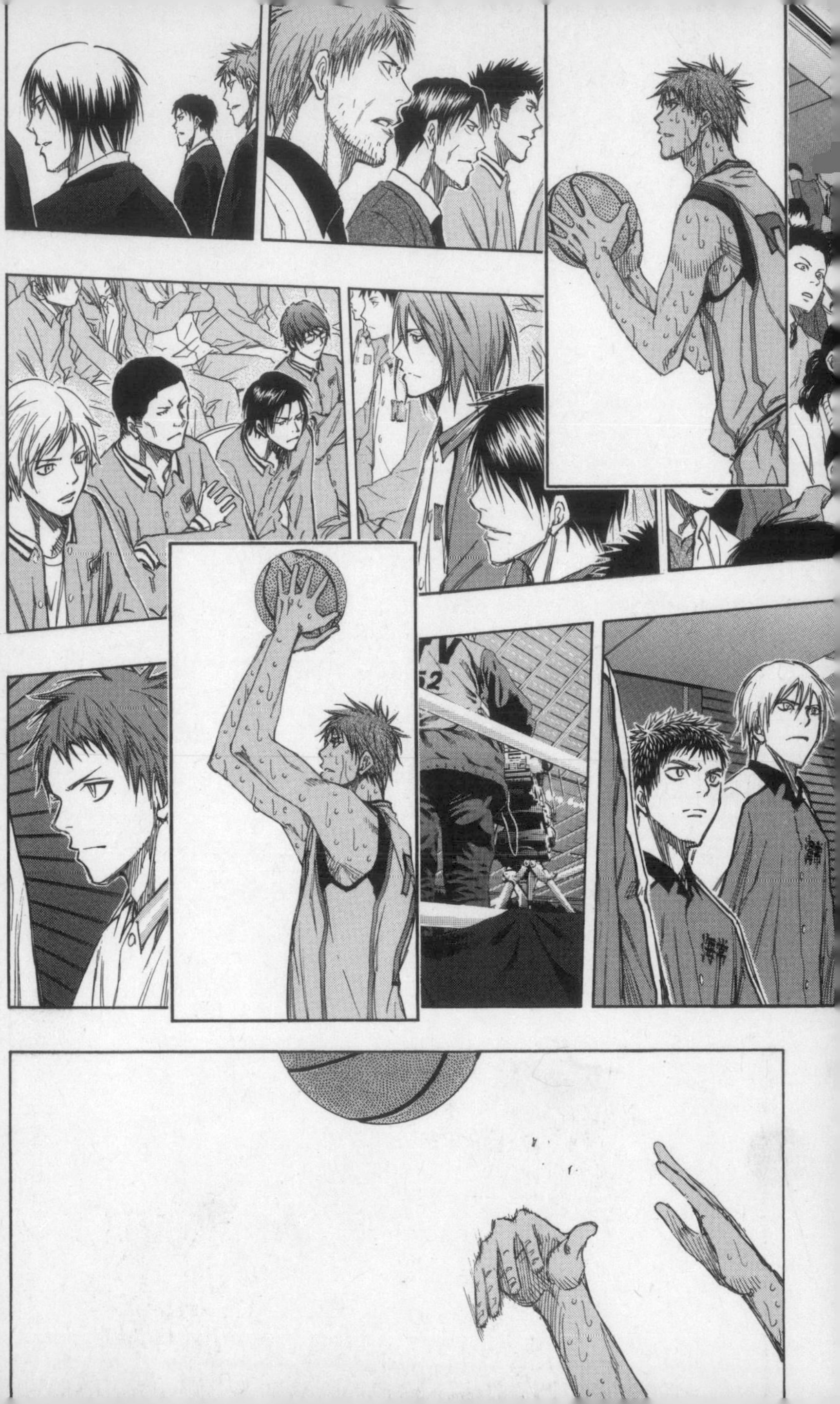

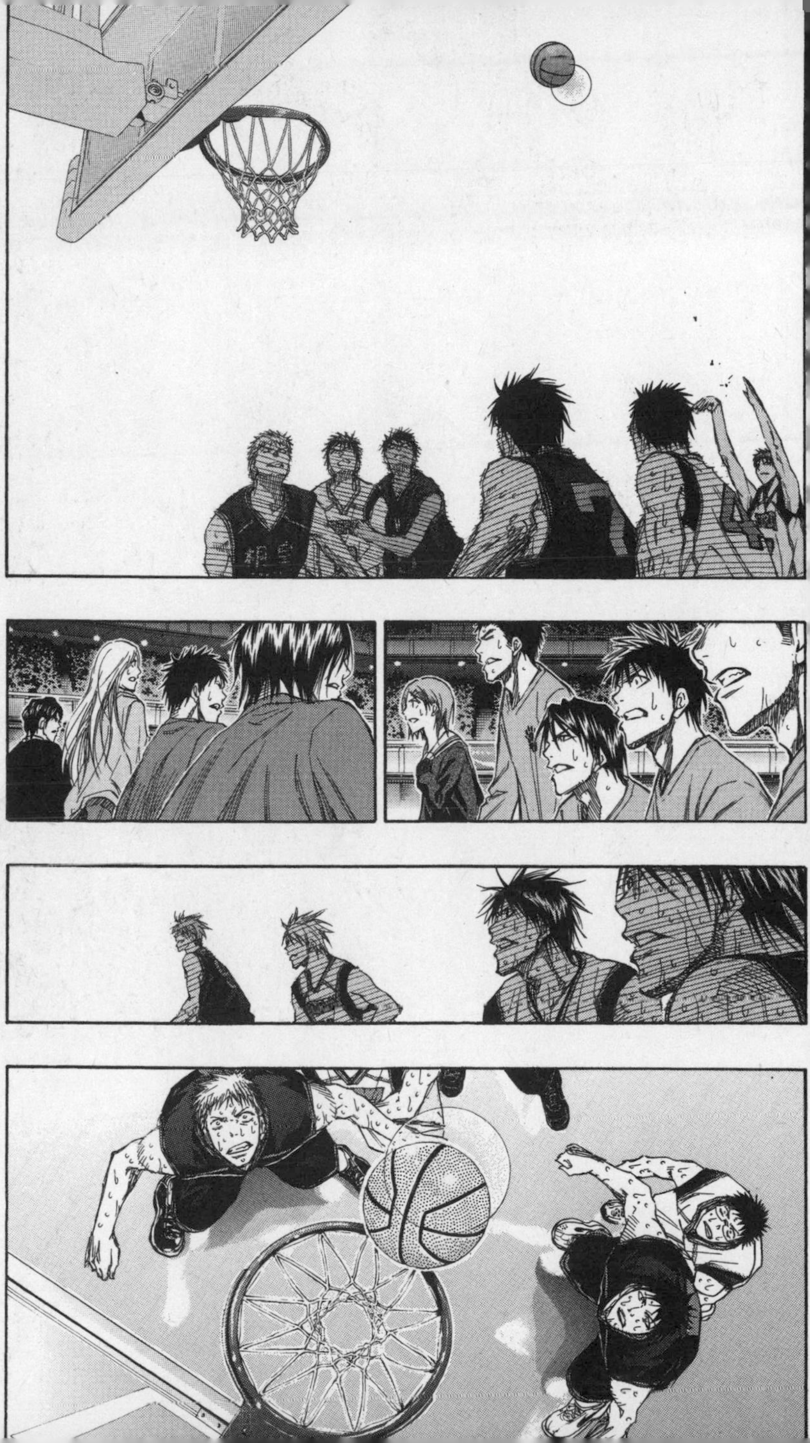

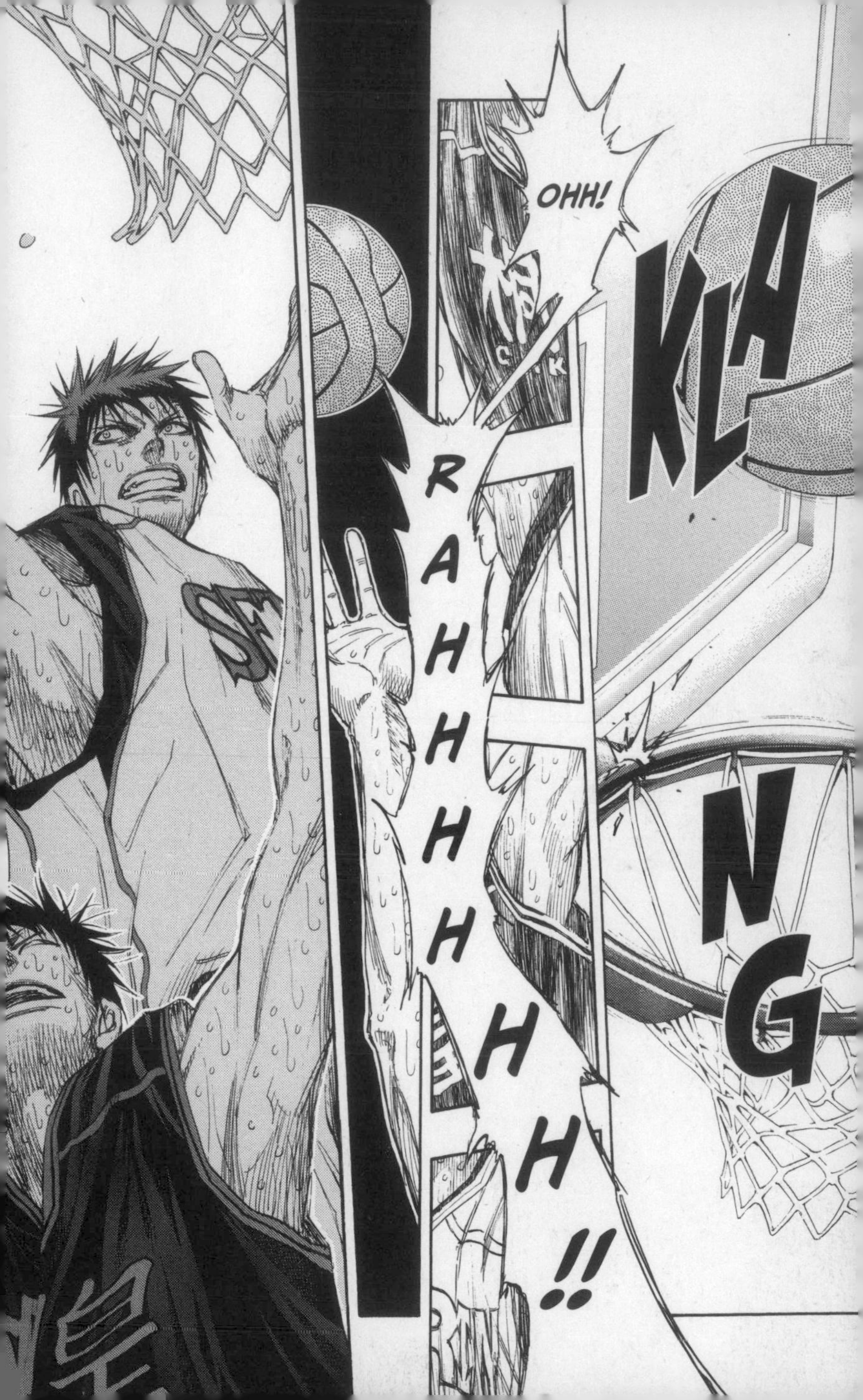
KLANNG
OHH!
RAHHHHHH!!

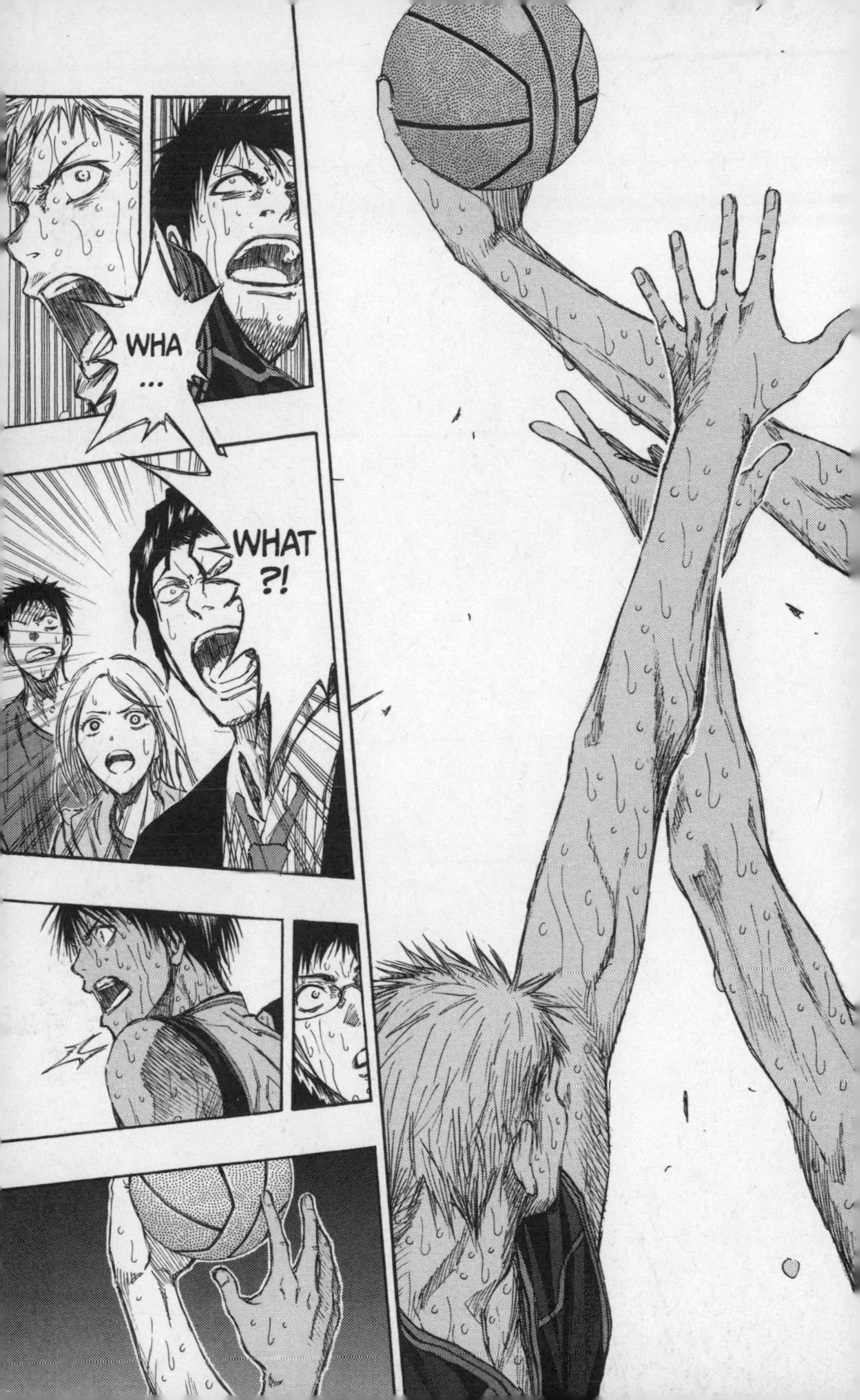
WHA ...
WHAT ?!

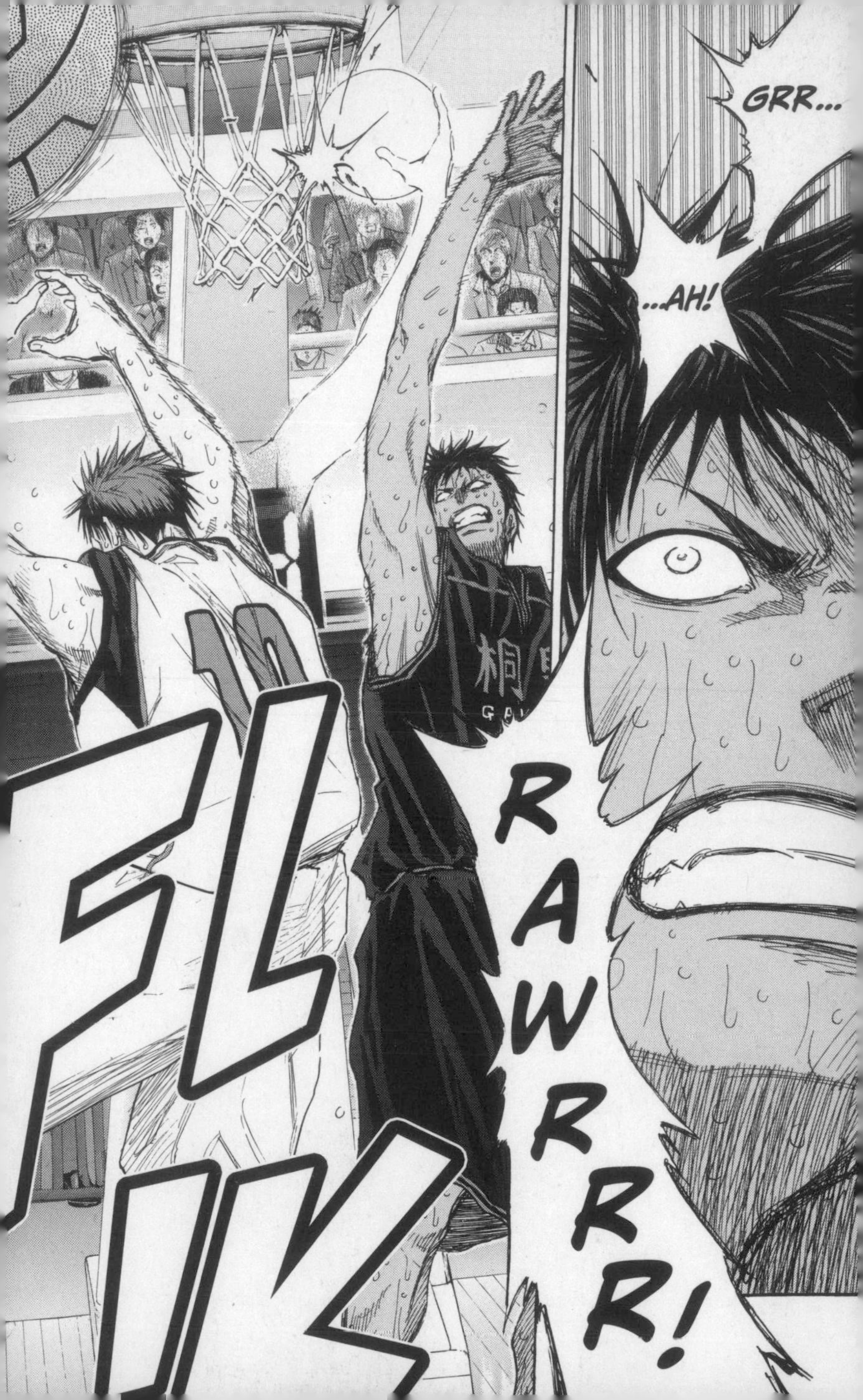
GRR...
...AH!
RAWRRR!

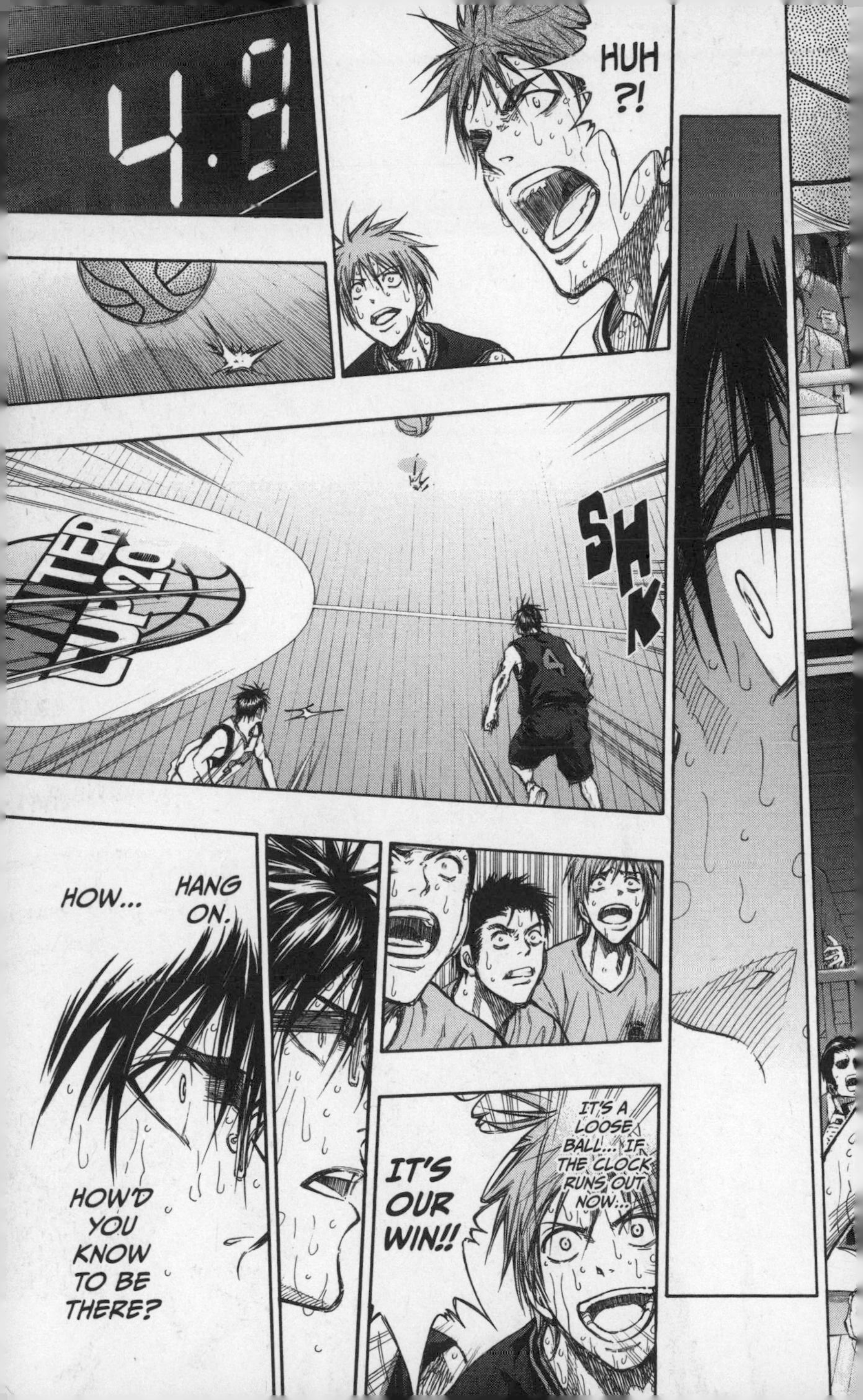
HUH ?!
SHK
IT'S A LOOSE BALL... IF THE CLOCK RUNS OUT NOW...
IT'S OUR WIN!!
HANG ON.
HOW...
HOW'D YOU KNOW TO BE THERE?

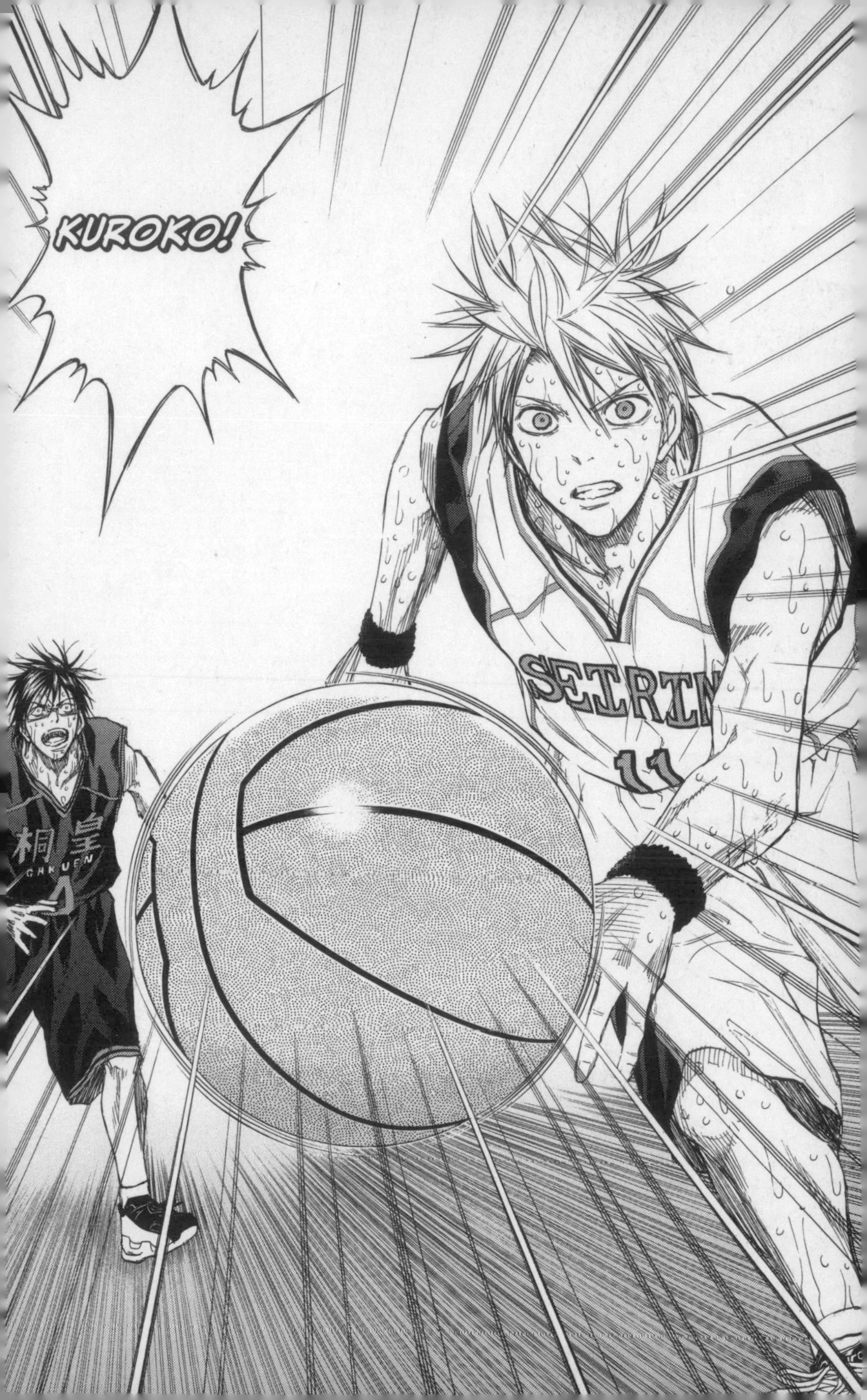
KUROKO!
SEIRIN
11
桐皇
GAKUEN

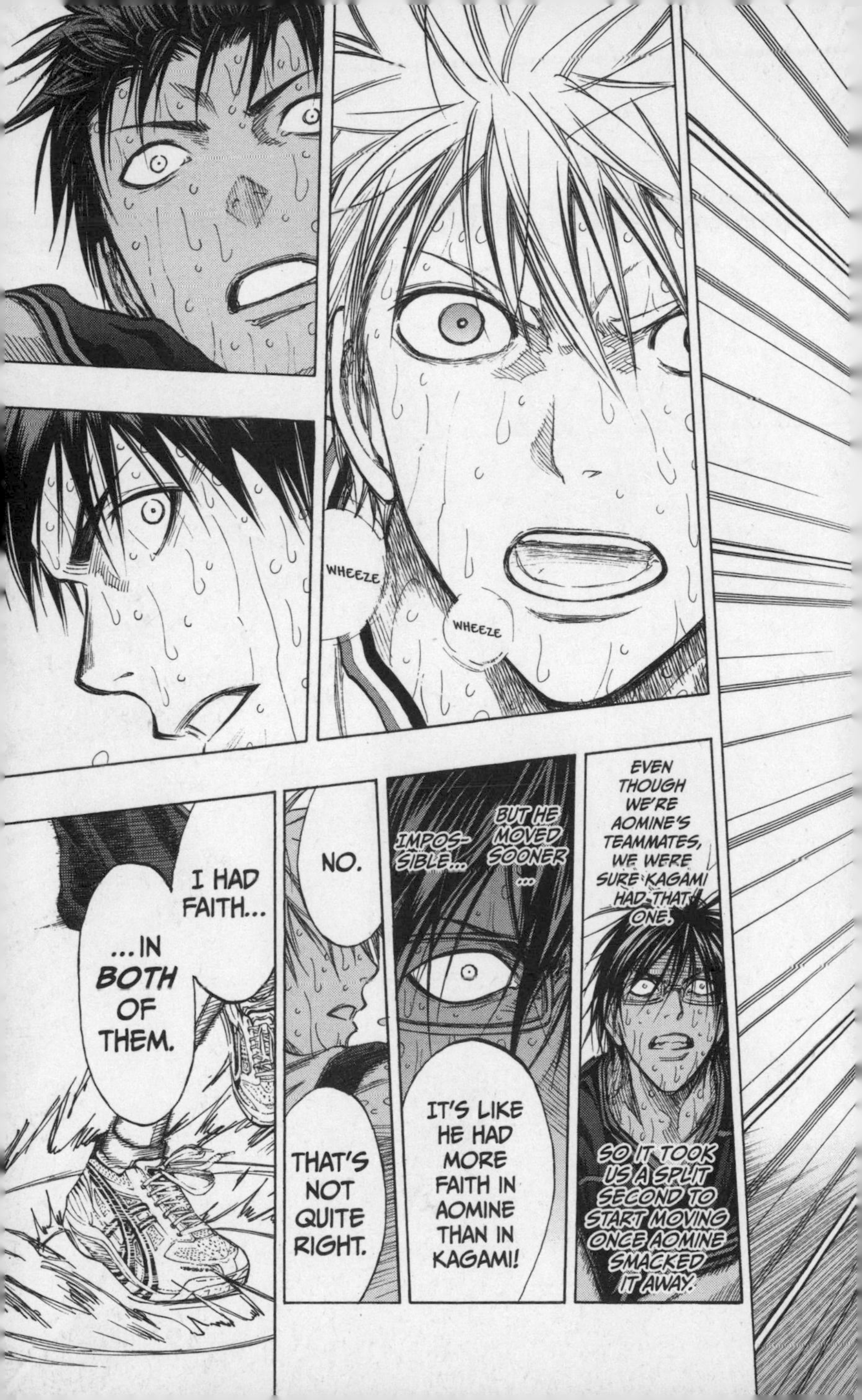
WHEEZE
WHEEZE
EVEN THOUGH WE'RE AOMINE'S TEAMMATES, WE WERE SURE KAGAMI HAD THAT ONE.
SO IT TOOK US A SPLIT SECOND TO START MOVING ONCE AOMINE SMACKED IT AWAY.
BUT HE MOVED SOONER...
IMPOSSIBLE...
IT'S LIKE HE HAD MORE FAITH IN AOMINE THAN IN KAGAMI!
NO.
THAT'S NOT QUITE RIGHT.
I HAD FAITH...
...IN **BOTH** OF THEM.

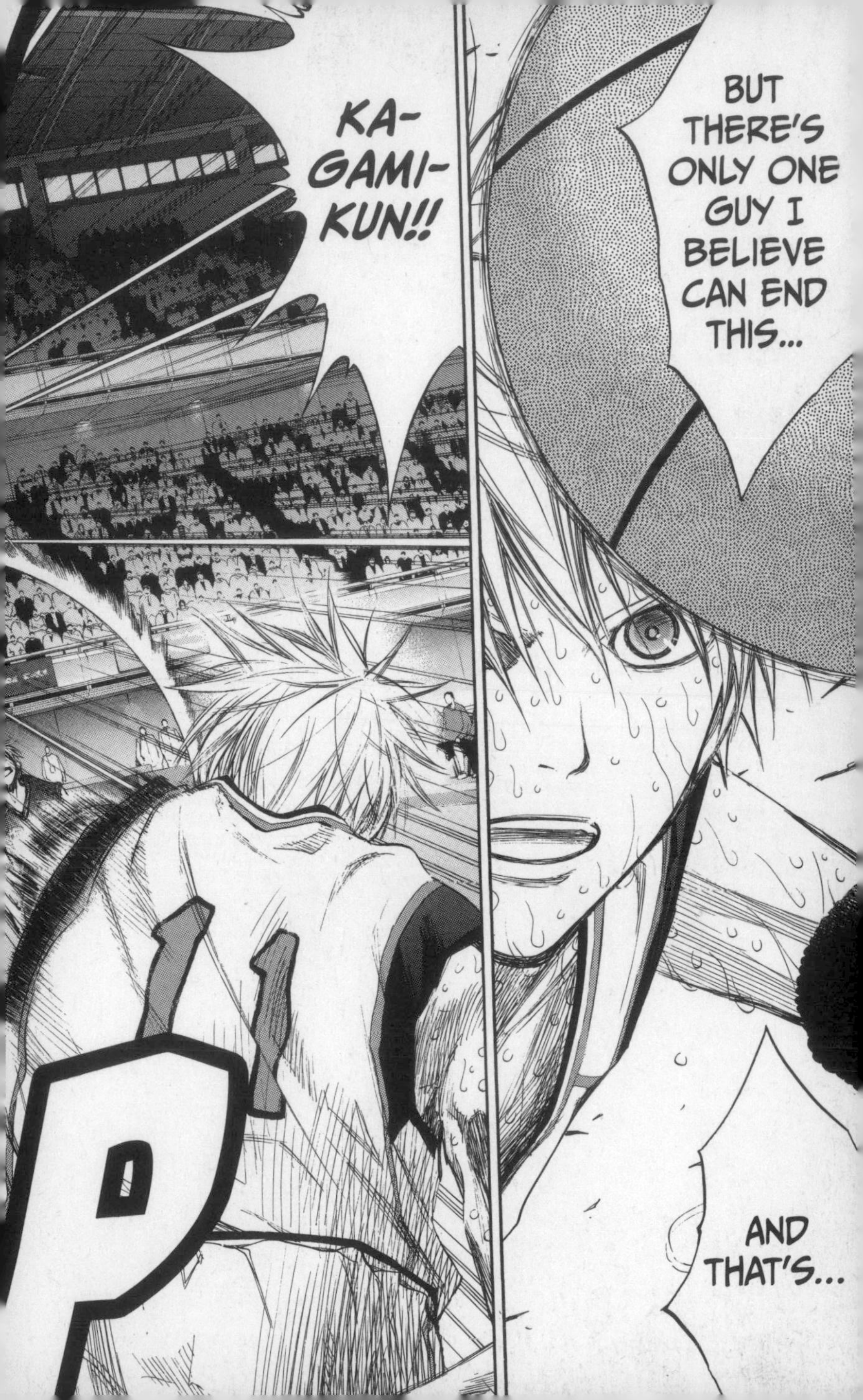
BUT THERE'S ONLY ONE GUY I BELIEVE CAN END THIS...
AND THAT'S...
KA-GAMI-KUN!!

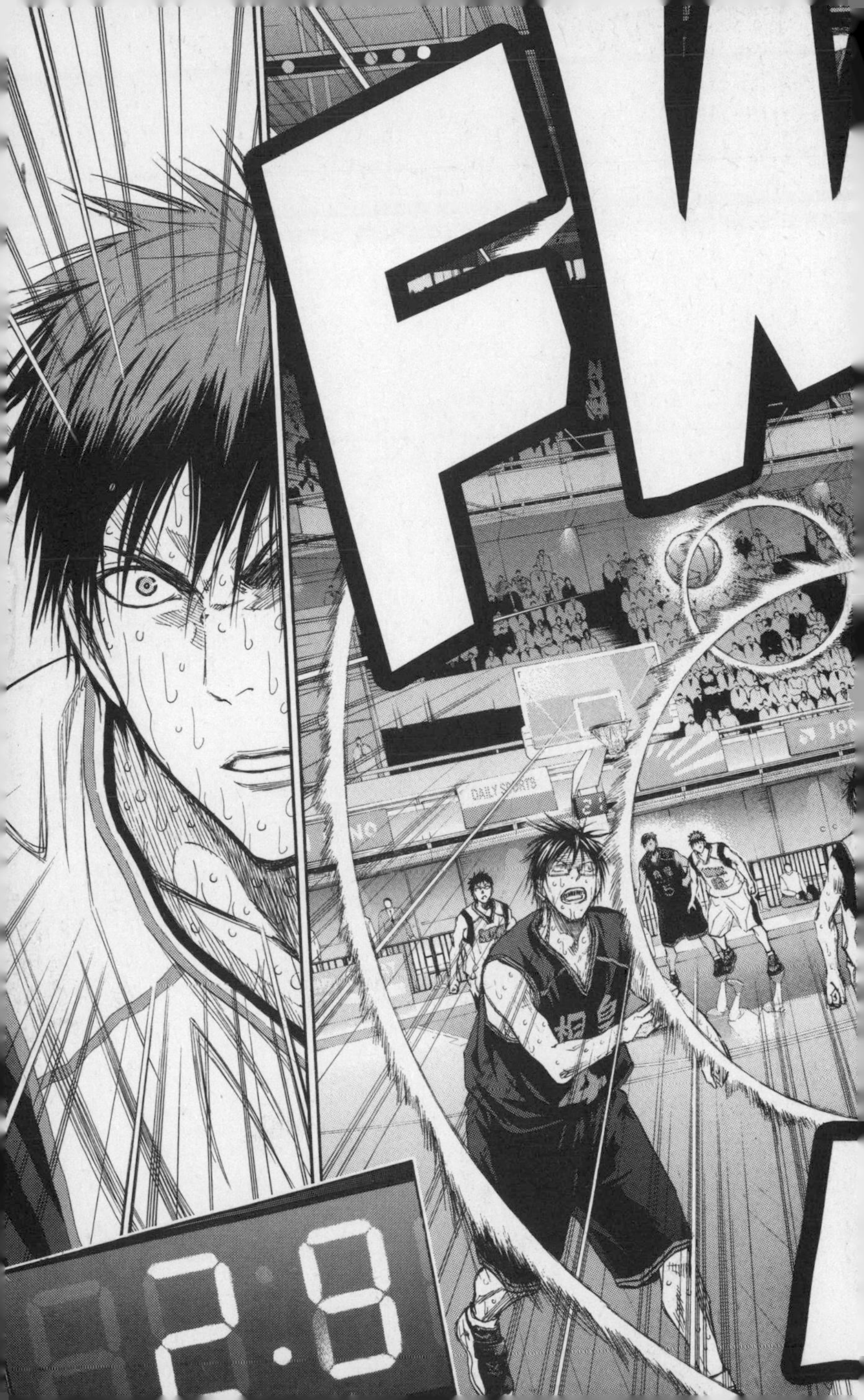
DAILY SPORTS
2.9

KUROKO'S BASKETBALL BLOOPERS

TAKE 12

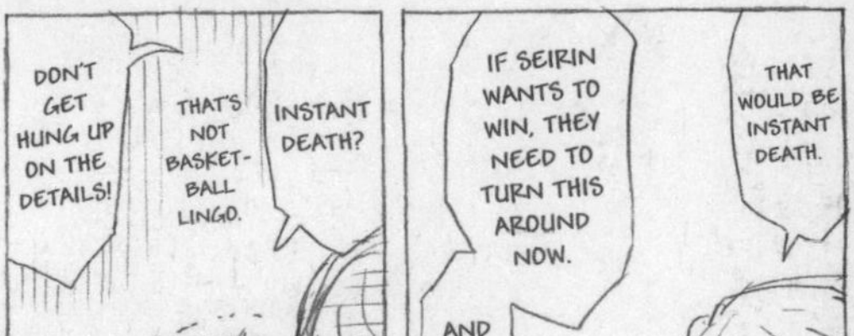
THAT WOULD BE INSTANT DEATH.
IF SEIRIN WANTS TO WIN, THEY NEED TO TURN THIS AROUND NOW.
AND TO DO THAT...
WAIT... HUH?!
SHIN-CHAN!
?
INSTANT DEATH?
THAT'S NOT BASKET-BALL LINGO.
DON'T GET HUNG UP ON THE DETAILS!
PON
SHAKA SHAKA
PFFFT.

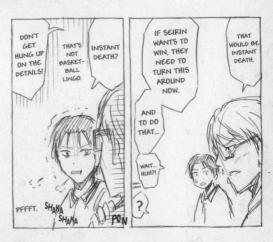

139TH QUARTER: TIME'S UP!!

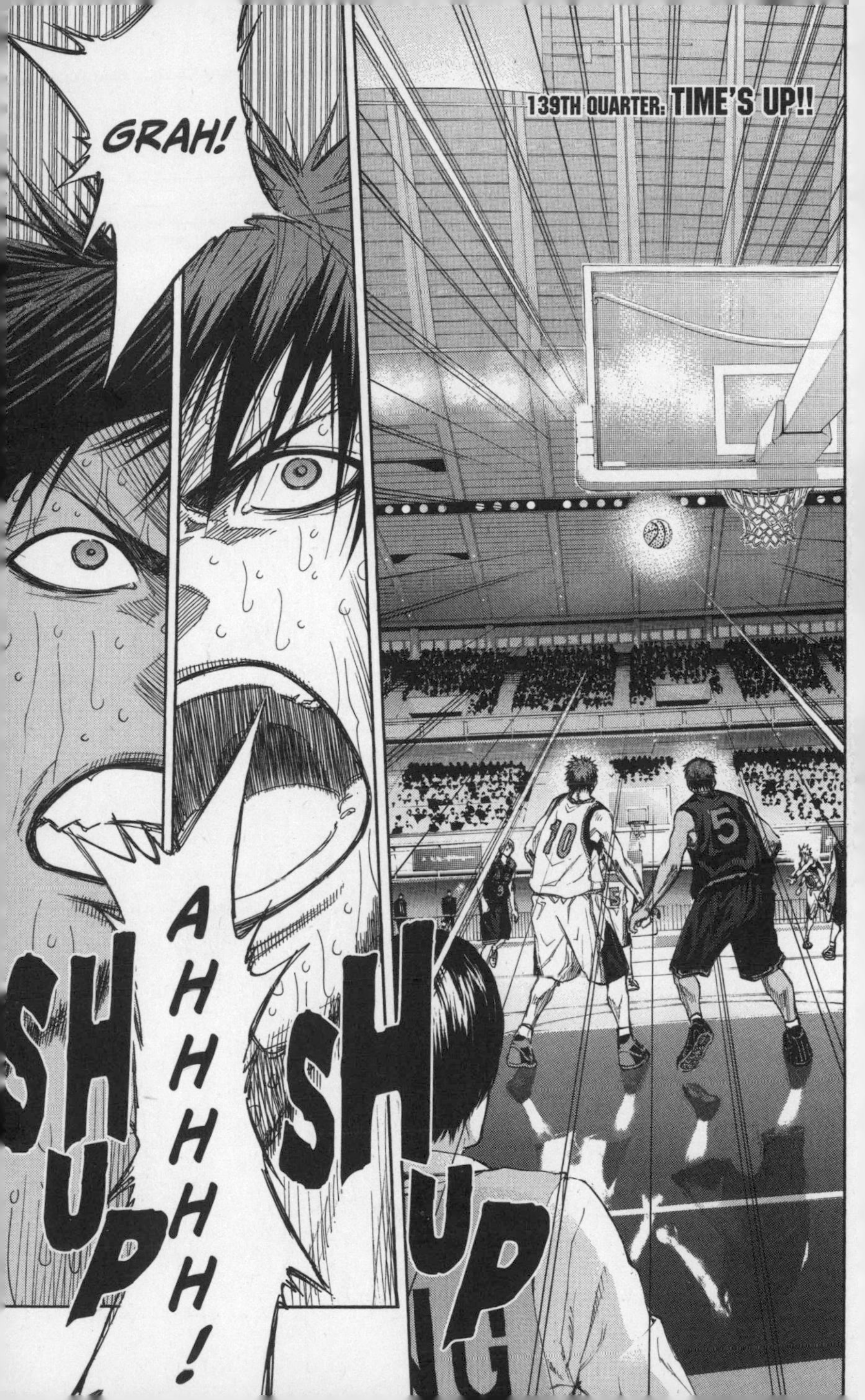
GRAH!
AHHHHHHH!
SHUP
SHUP

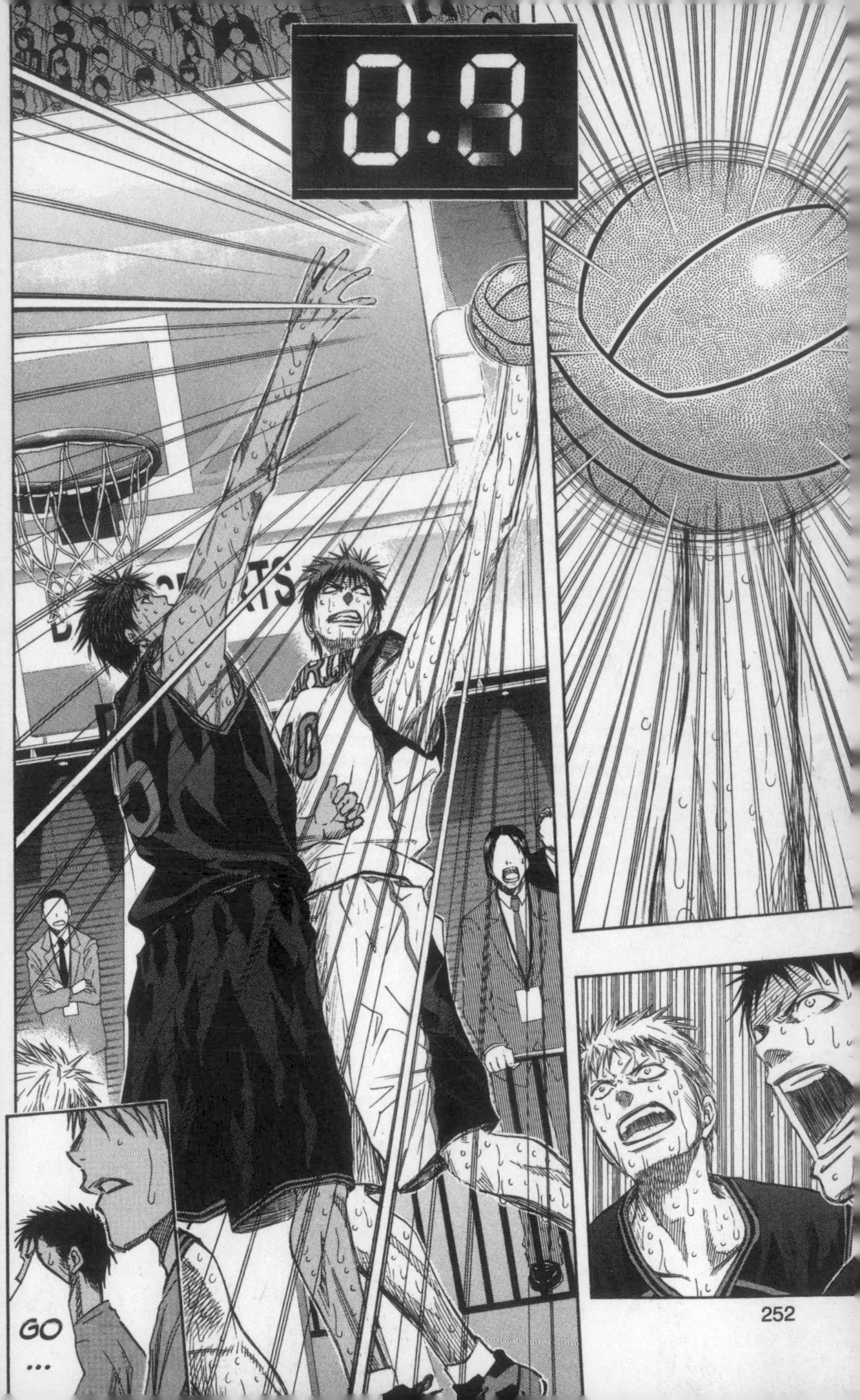
GO
...

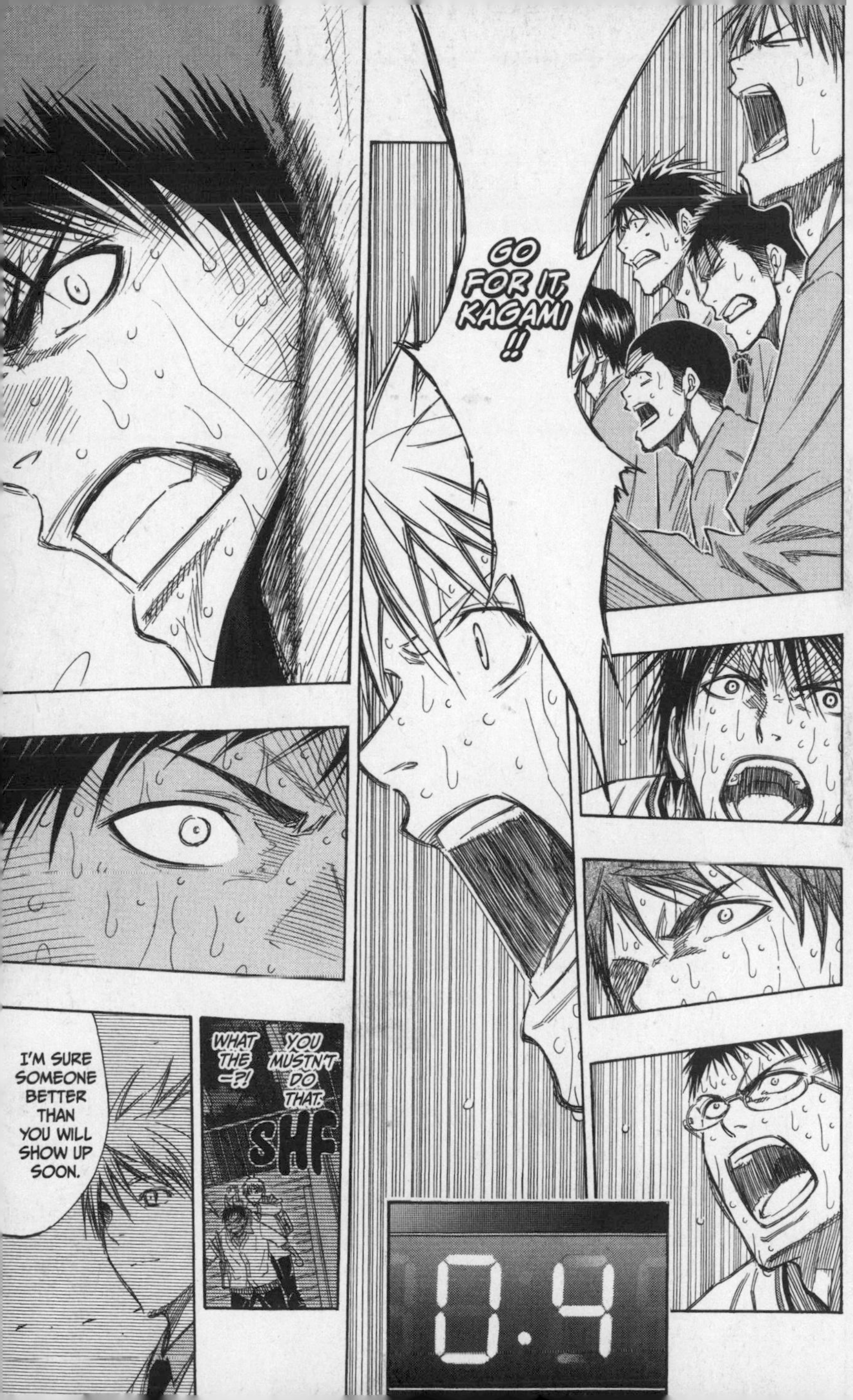
GO FOR IT, KAGAMI!!
0.4
YOU MUSTN'T DO THAT.
WHAT THE—?!
SHF
I'M SURE SOMEONE BETTER THAN YOU WILL SHOW UP SOON.

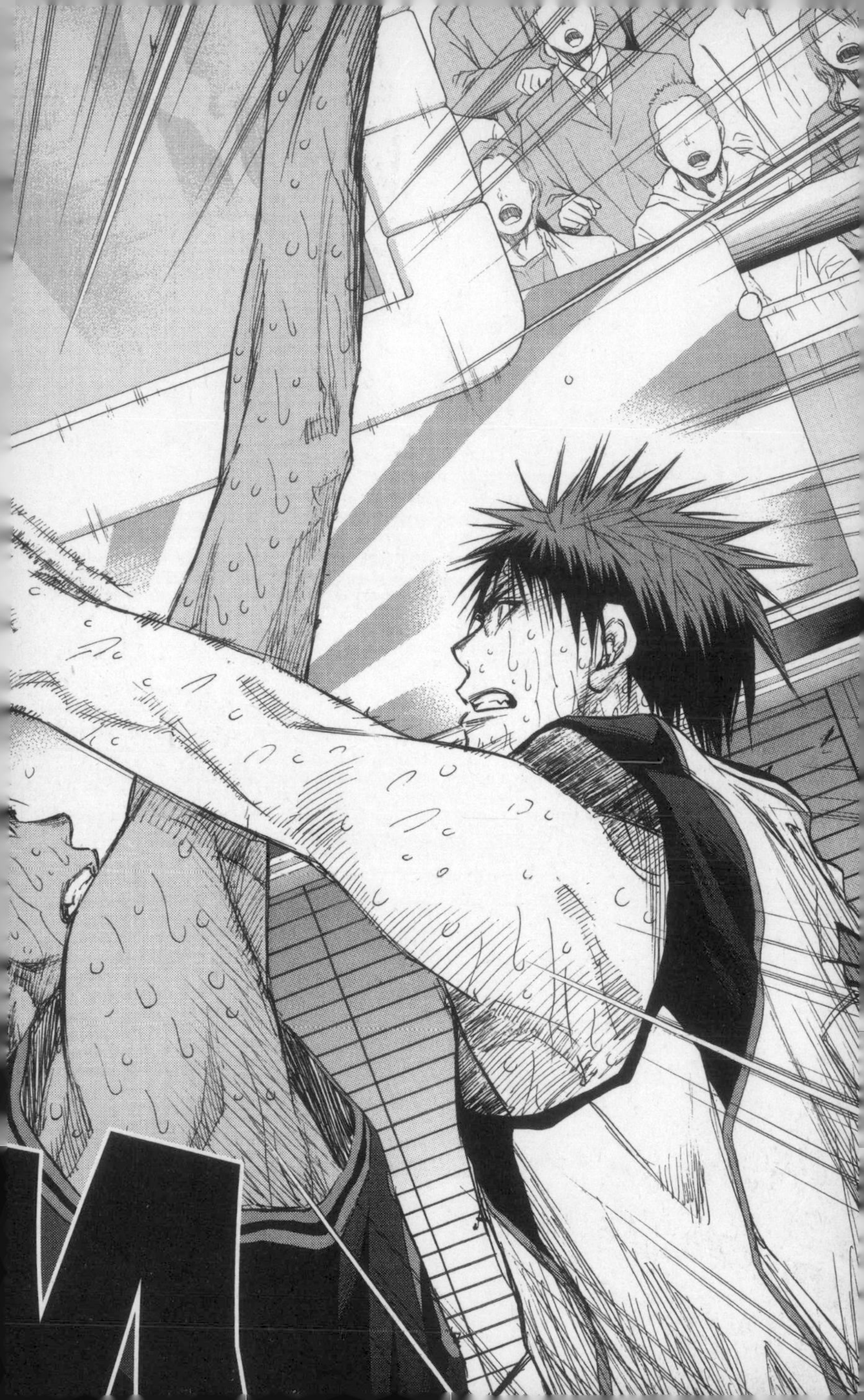
M

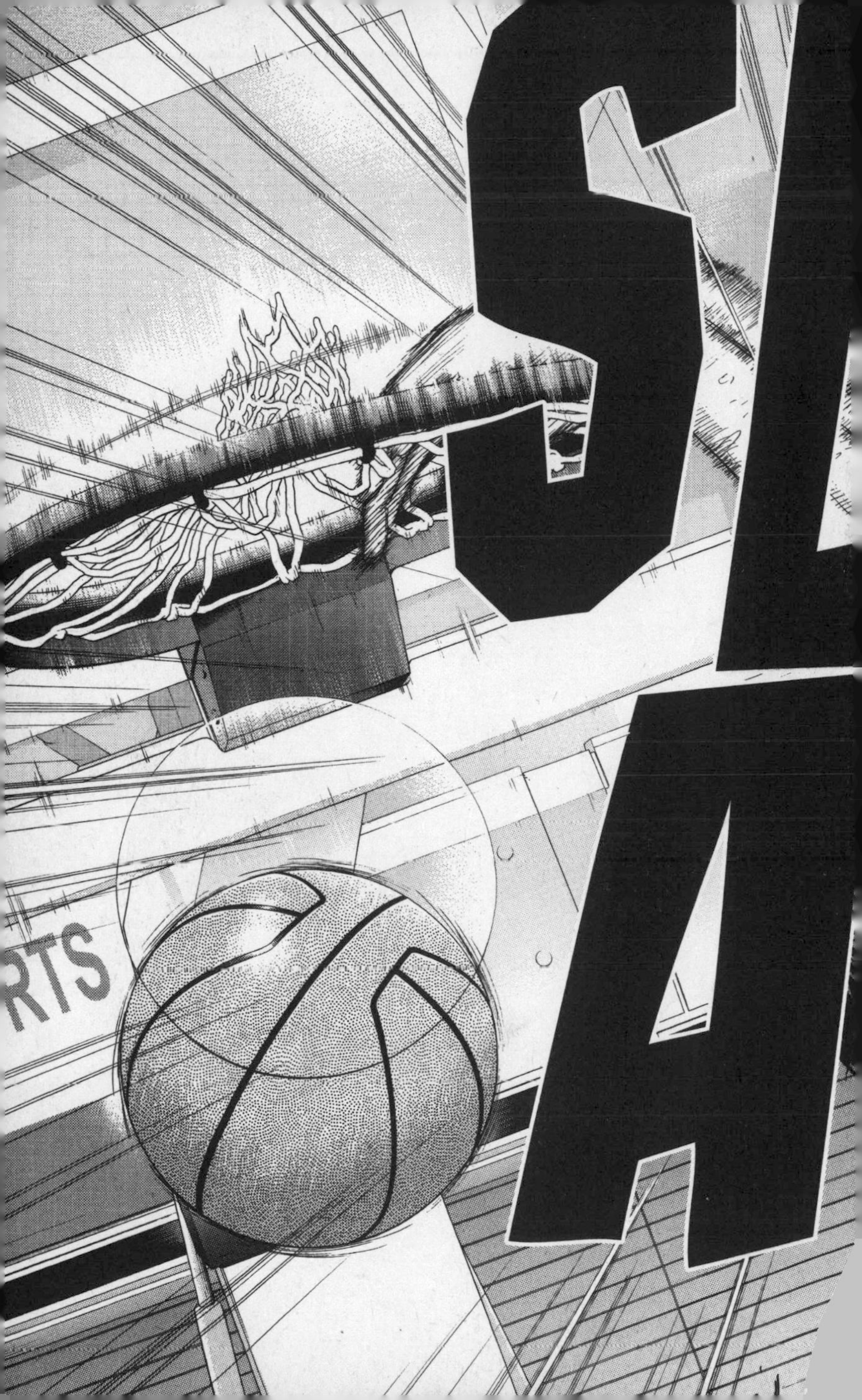
RTS

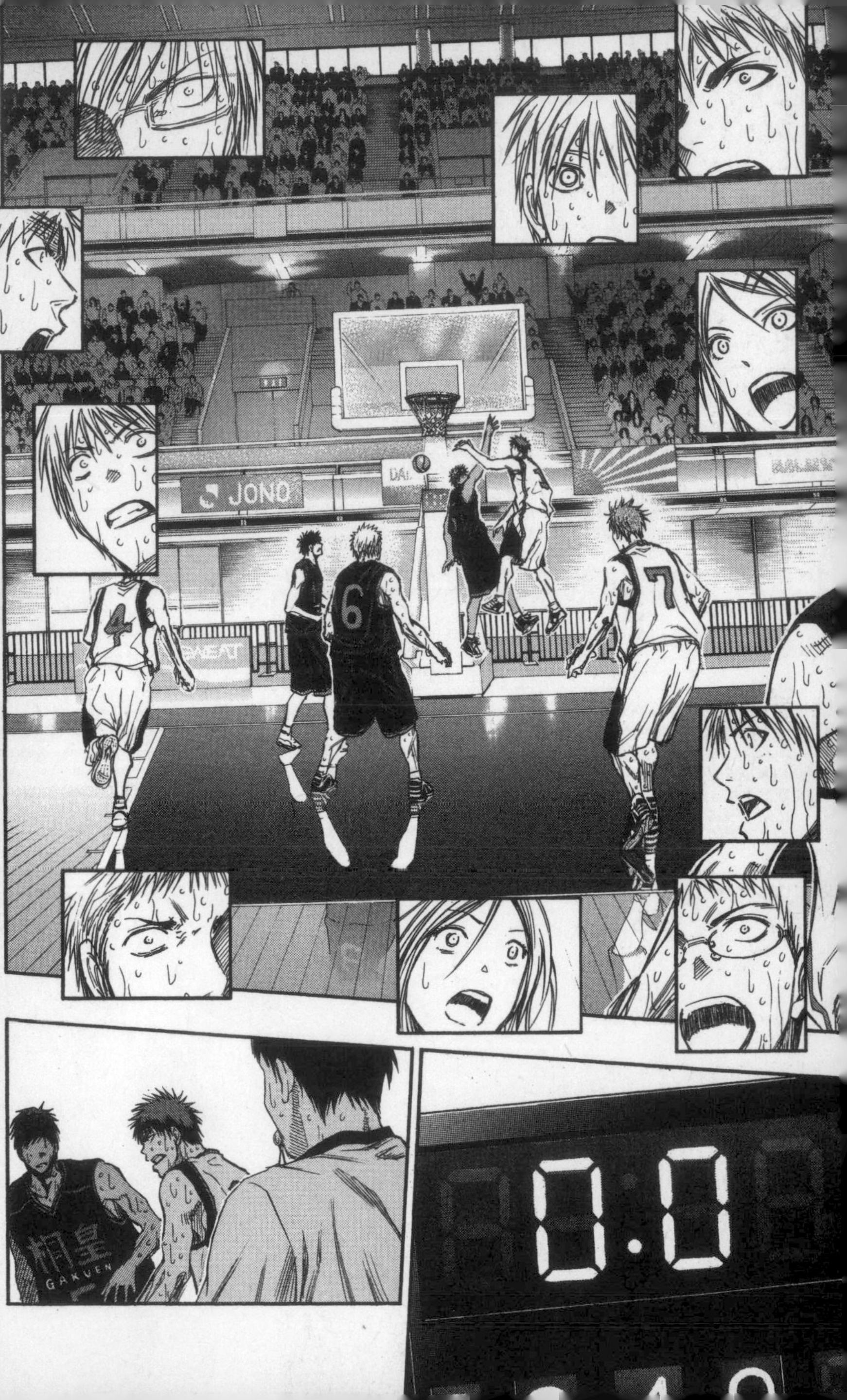
JONO
桐皇
GAKUEN

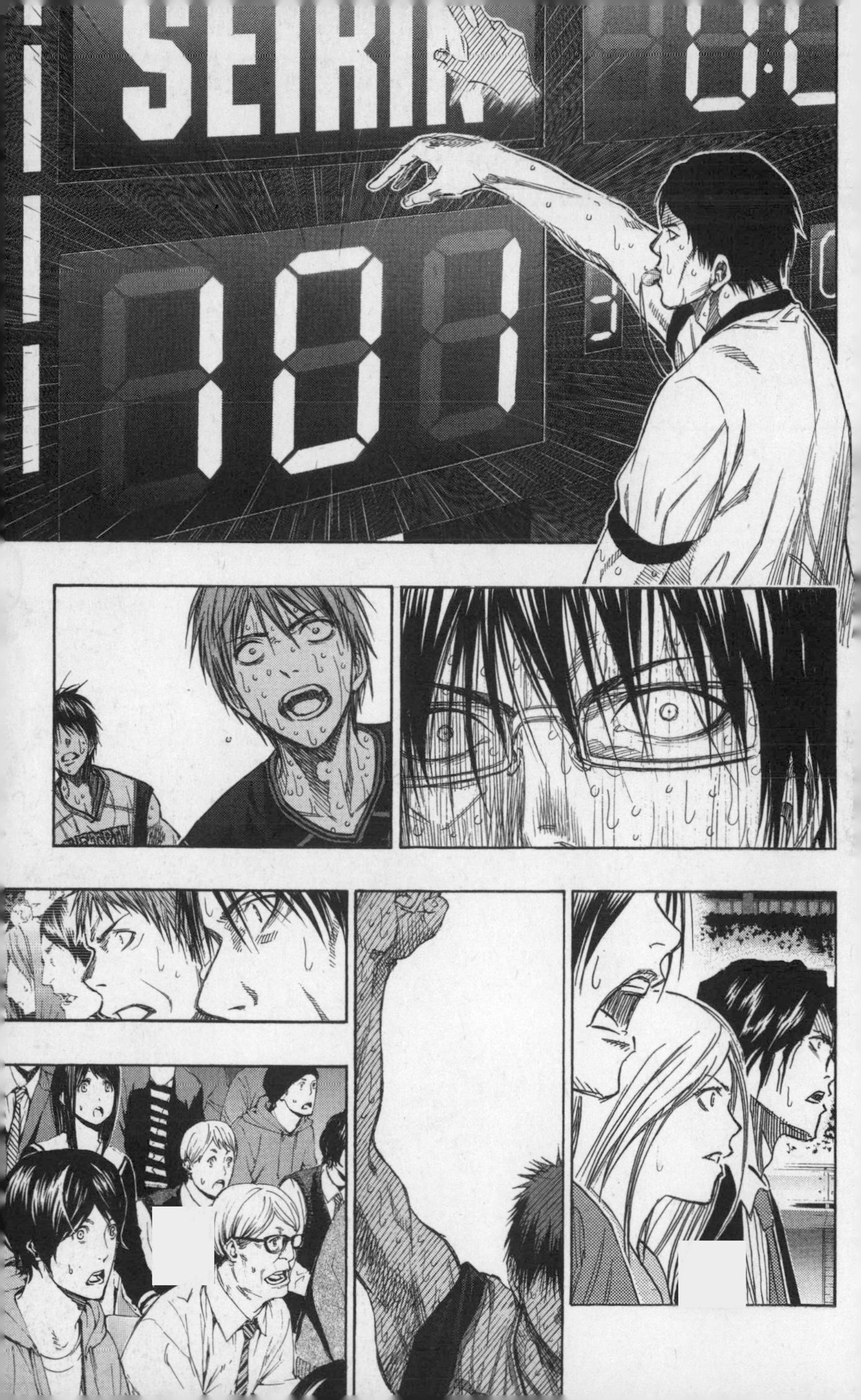
SEIRIN
101

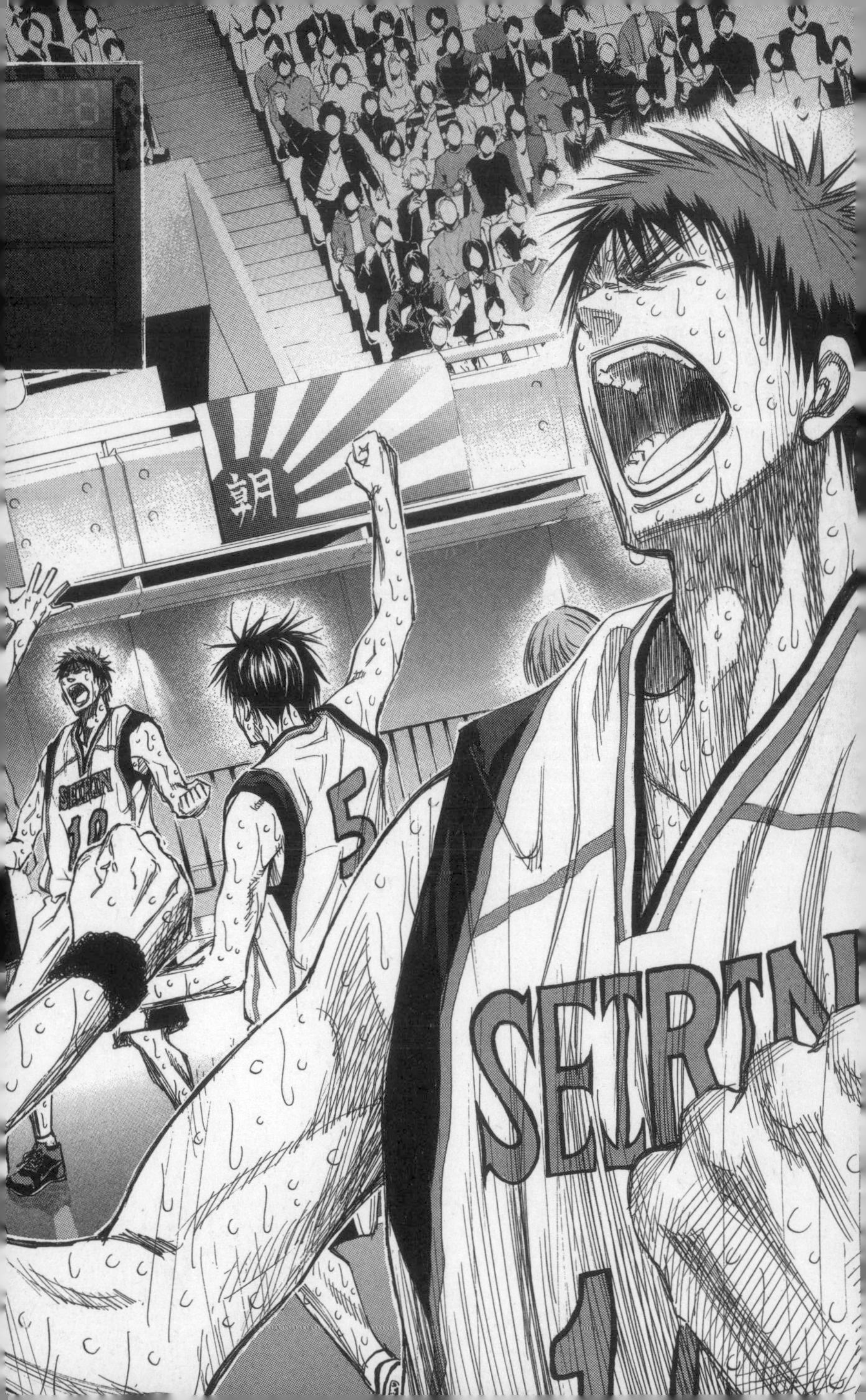
朝

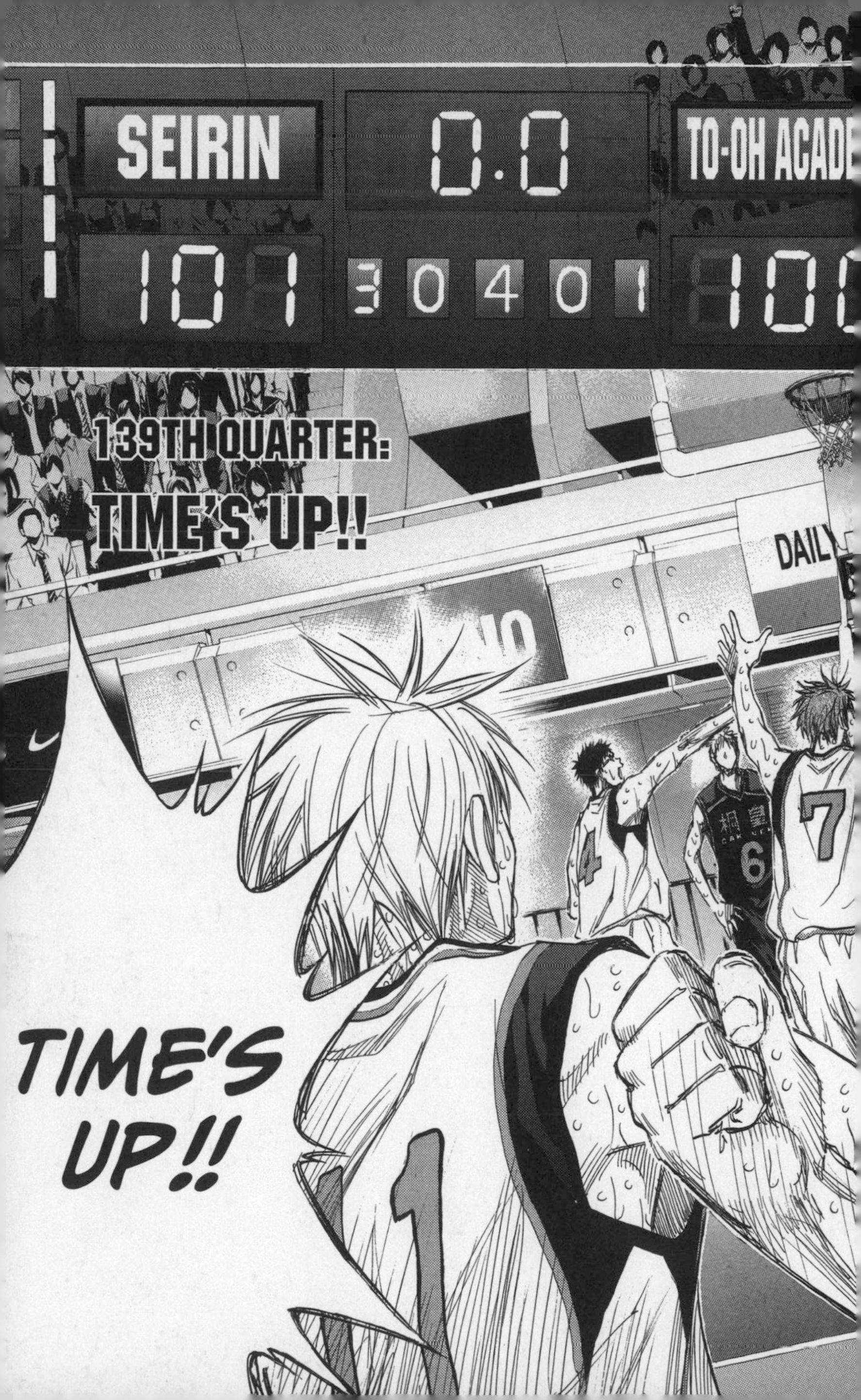
SEIRIN
0.0
TO-OH ACADE
101
139TH QUARTER:
TIME'S UP!!
DAILY
TIME'S UP!!

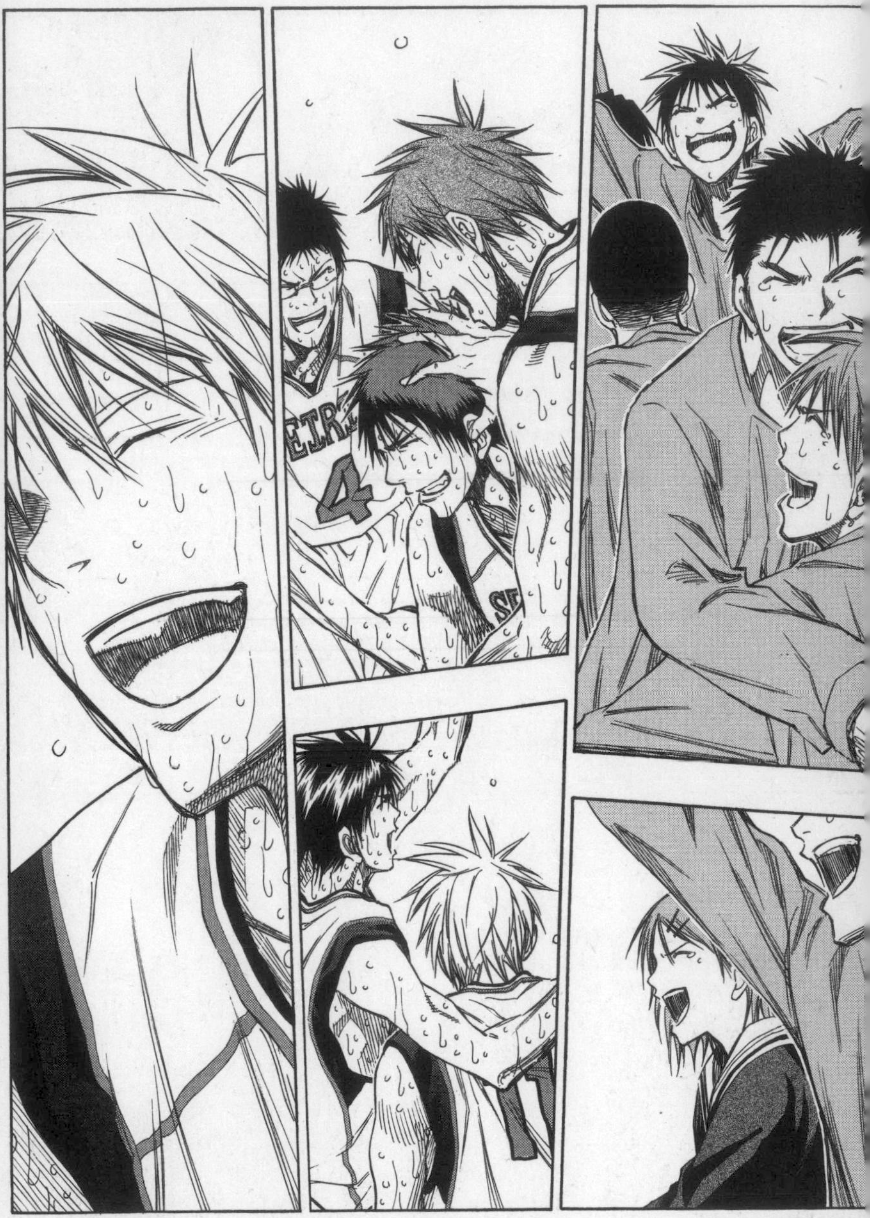

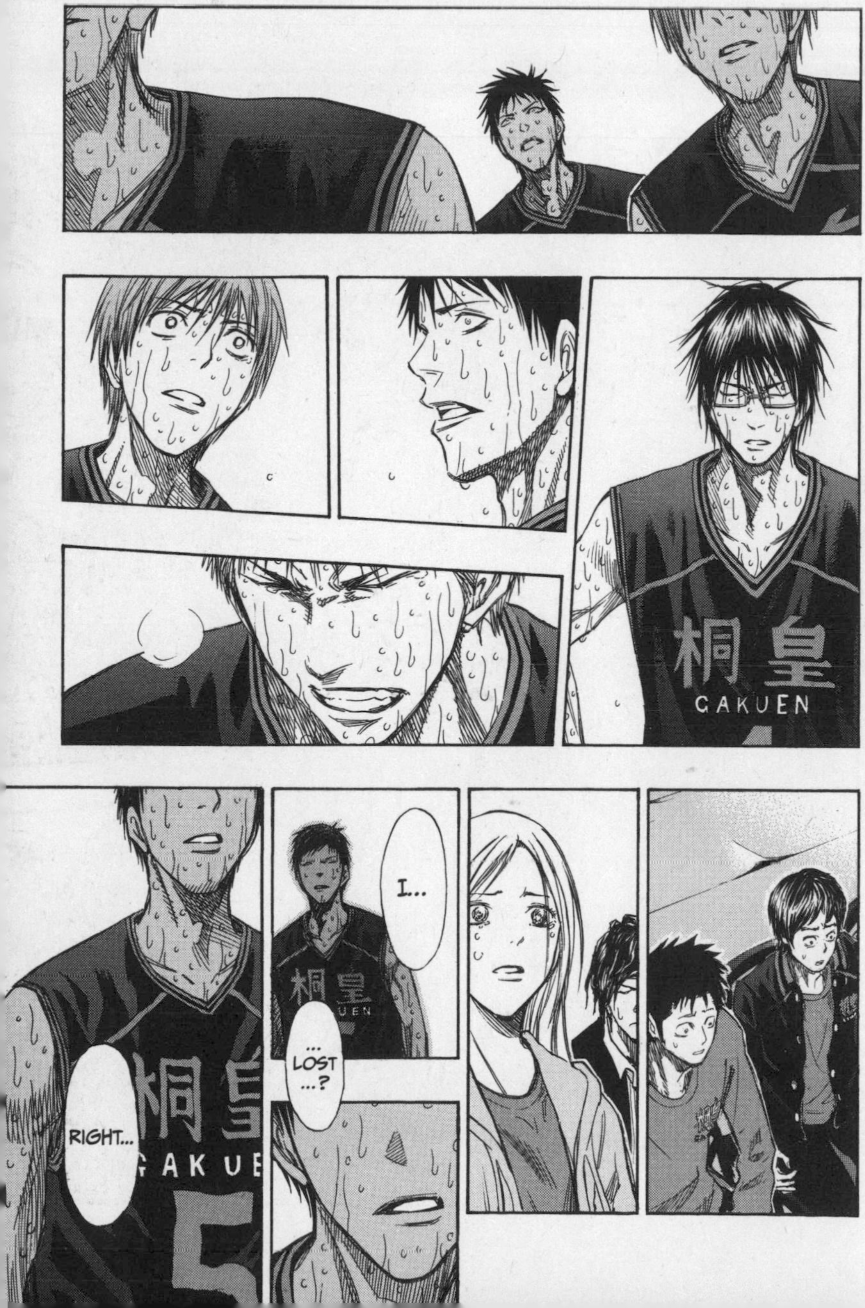
I...
...LOST ...?
RIGHT...

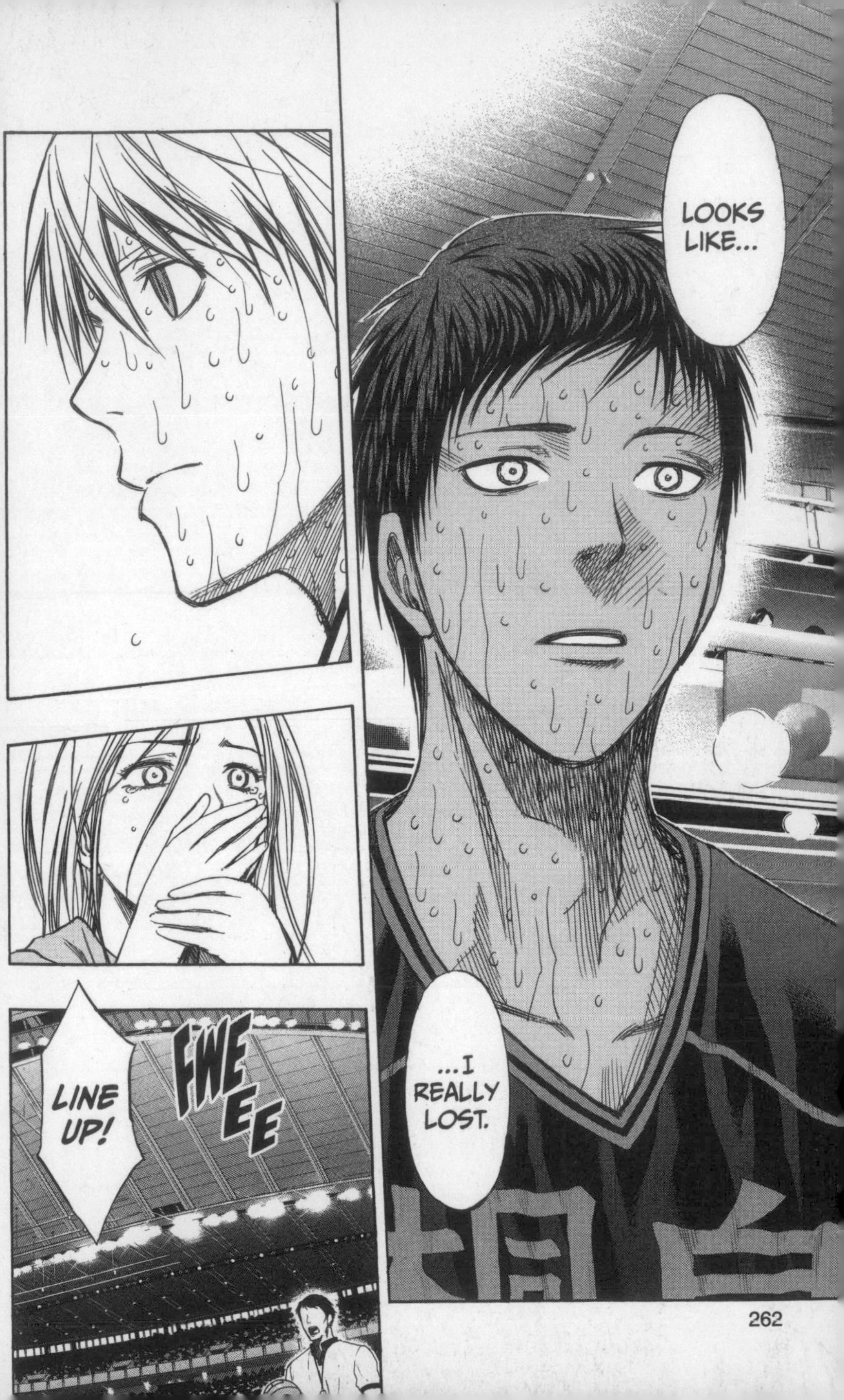

LOOKS LIKE...
...I REALLY LOST.
LINE UP!
FWEEE

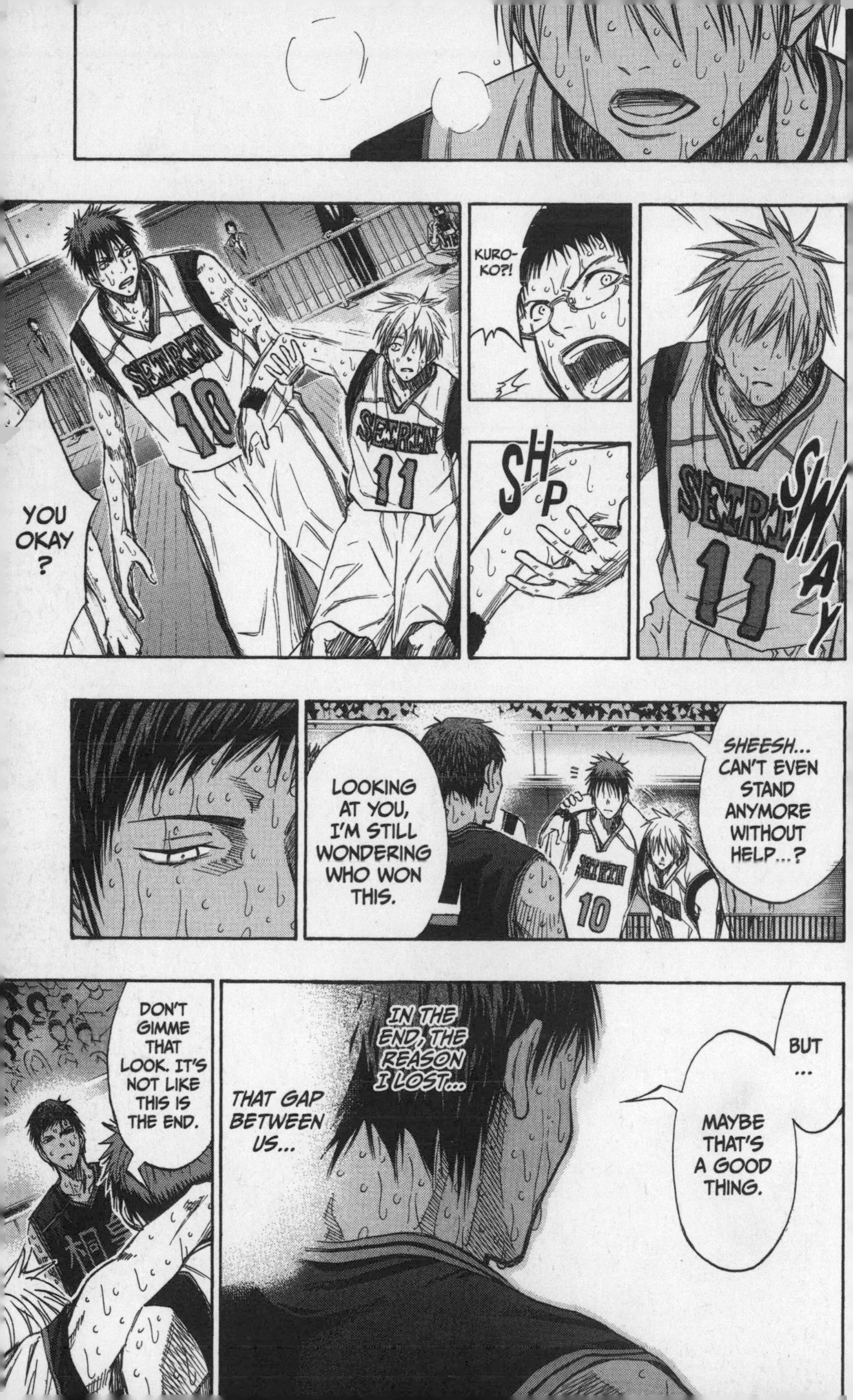
SWAY
KURO-KO?!
SHP
YOU OKAY?
SHEESH... CAN'T EVEN STAND ANYMORE WITHOUT HELP...?
LOOKING AT YOU, I'M STILL WONDERING WHO WON THIS.
BUT ...
MAYBE THAT'S A GOOD THING.
IN THE END, THE REASON I LOST...
THAT GAP BETWEEN US...
DON'T GIMME THAT LOOK. IT'S NOT LIKE THIS IS THE END.

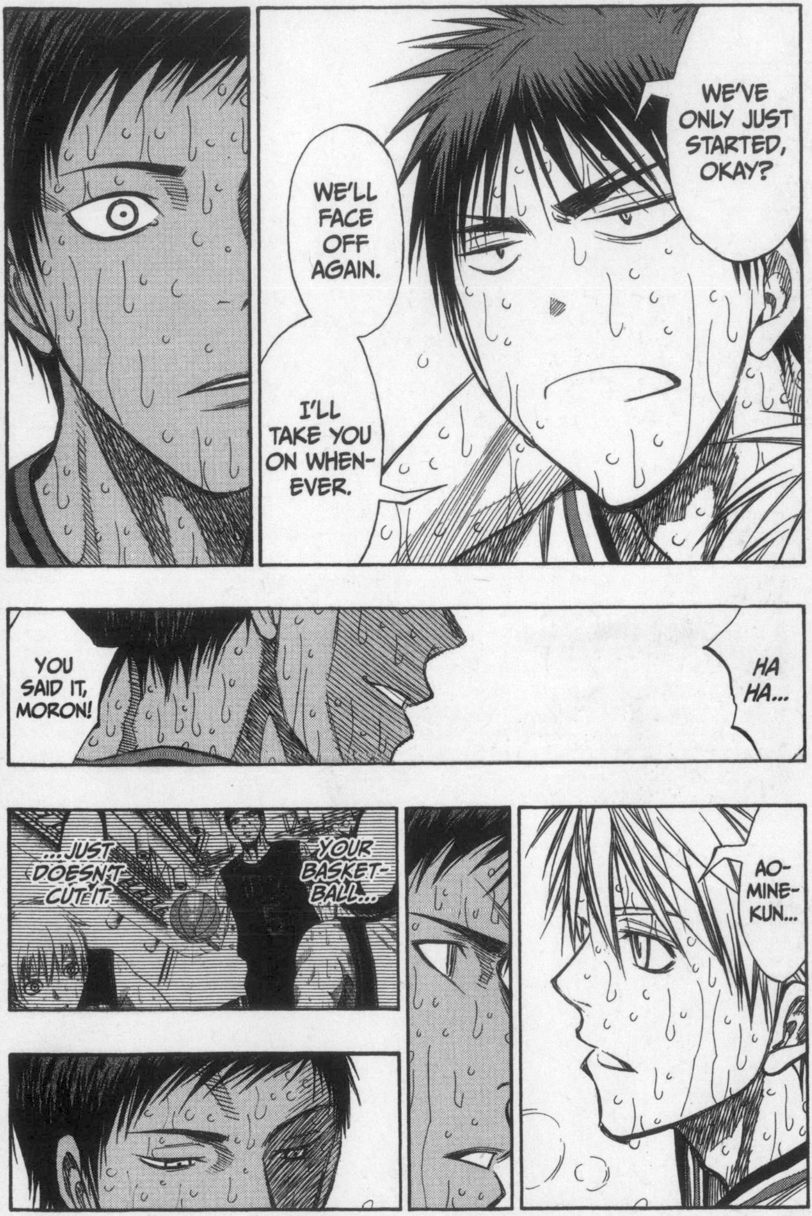
WE'VE ONLY JUST STARTED, OKAY?
WE'LL FACE OFF AGAIN.
I'LL TAKE YOU ON WHEN-EVER.
HA HA...
YOU SAID IT, MORON!
AO-MINE-KUN...
YOUR BASKET-BALL...
...JUST DOESN'T CUT IT.

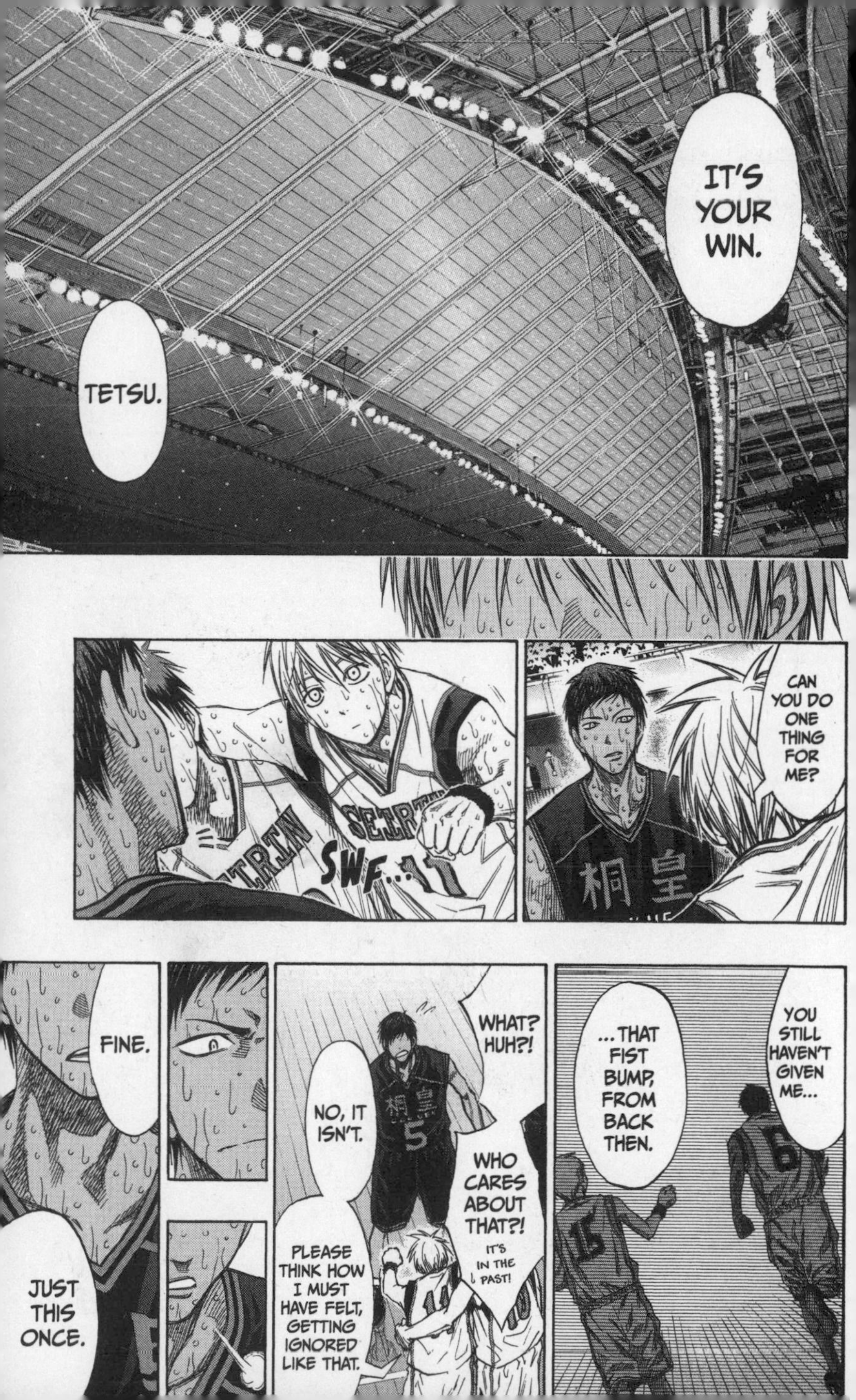
IT'S YOUR WIN.
TETSU.
CAN YOU DO ONE THING FOR ME?
SWF...
YOU STILL HAVEN'T GIVEN ME...
...THAT FIST BUMP, FROM BACK THEN.
WHAT? HUH?!
WHO CARES ABOUT THAT?!
IT'S IN THE PAST!
NO, IT ISN'T.
PLEASE THINK HOW I MUST HAVE FELT, GETTING IGNORED LIKE THAT.
FINE.
JUST THIS ONCE.

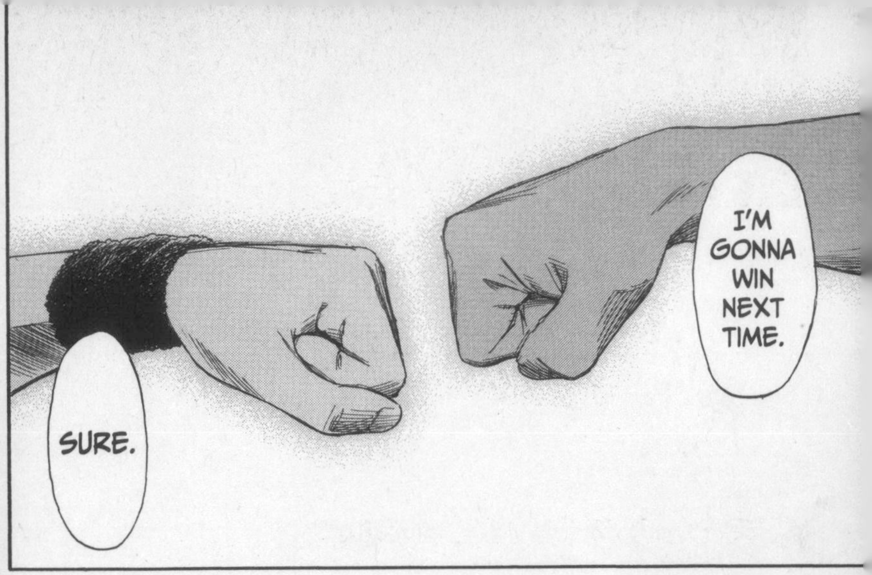
I'M GONNA WIN NEXT TIME.
SURE.

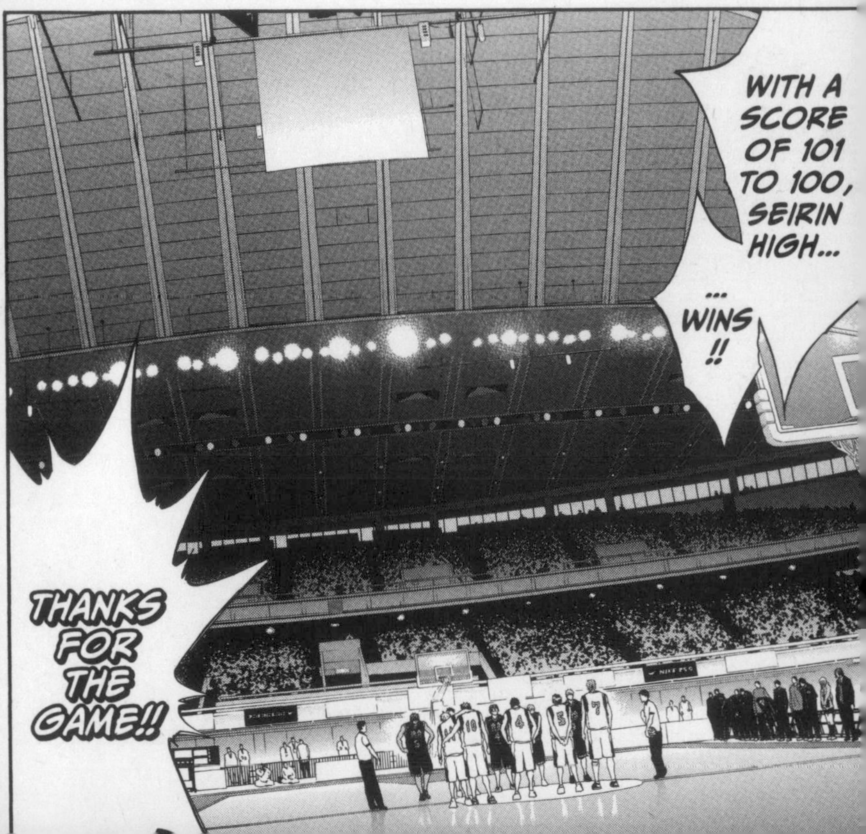
WITH A SCORE OF 101 TO 100, SEIRIN HIGH...
... WINS!!
THANKS FOR THE GAME!!

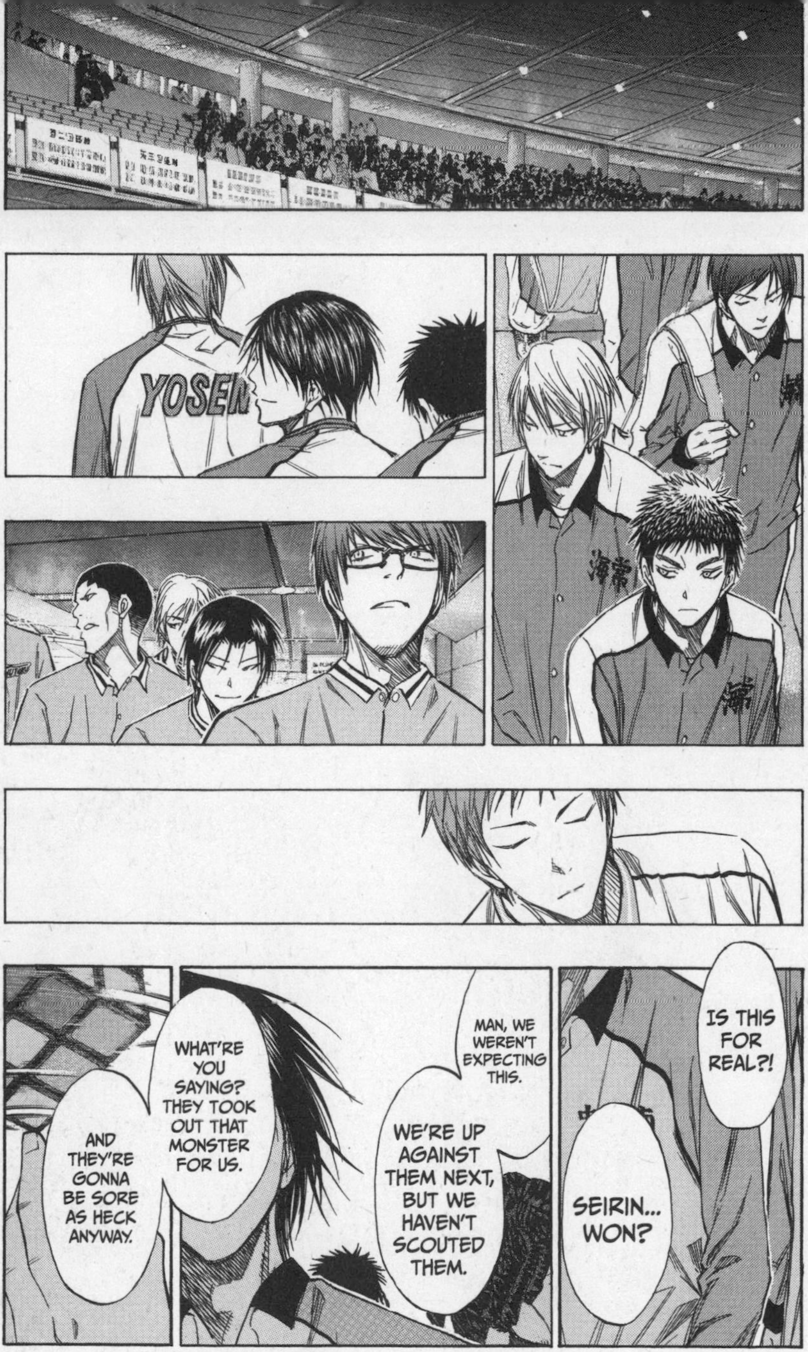
YOSEN
IS THIS FOR REAL?!
SEIRIN... WON?
MAN, WE WEREN'T EXPECTING THIS.
WE'RE UP AGAINST THEM NEXT, BUT WE HAVEN'T SCOUTED THEM.
WHAT'RE YOU SAYING? THEY TOOK OUT THAT MONSTER FOR US.
AND THEY'RE GONNA BE SORE AS HECK ANYWAY.

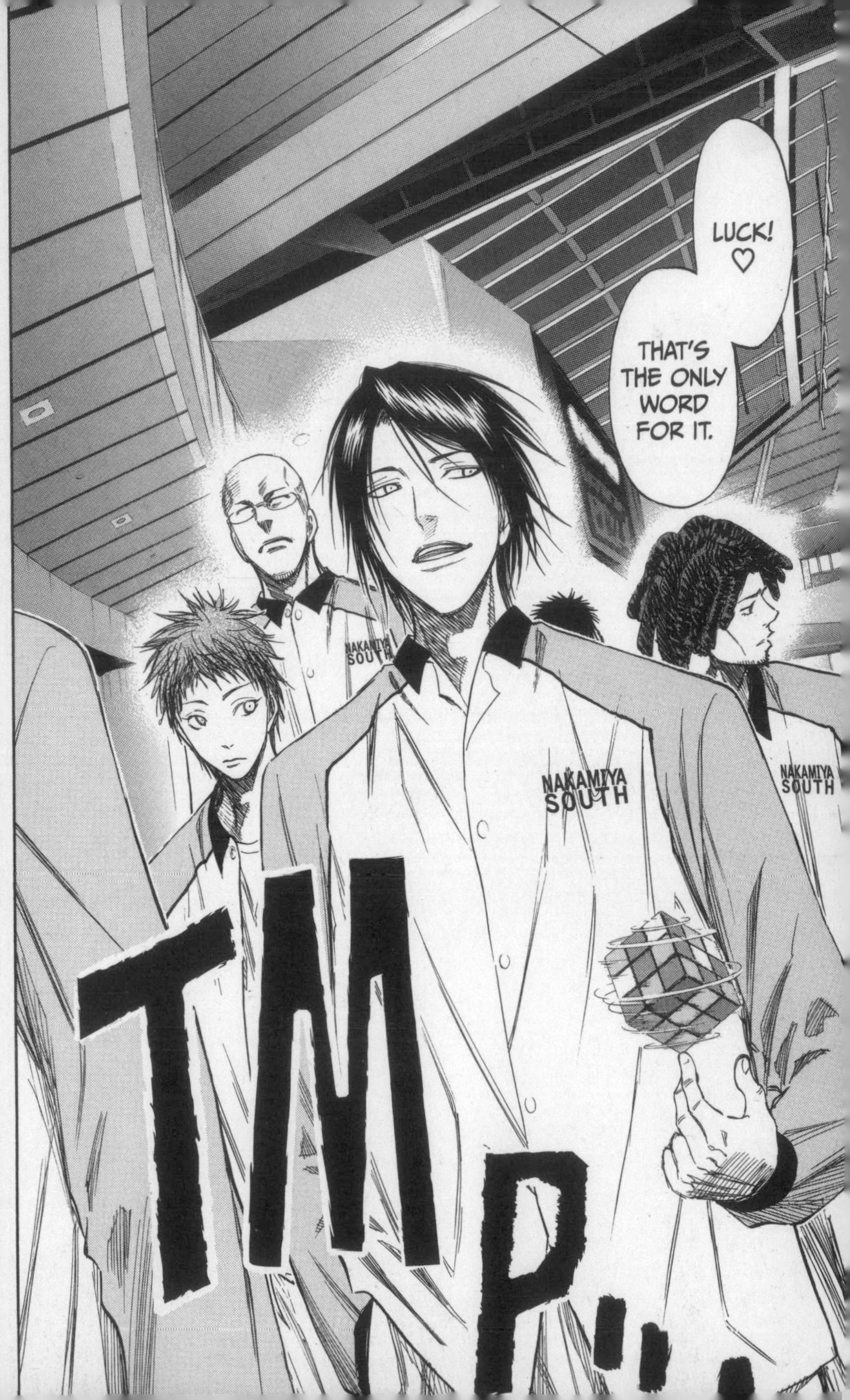
LUCK! ♡
THAT'S THE ONLY WORD FOR IT.
NAKAMIYA SOUTH
NAKAMIYA SOUTH
NAKAMIYA SOUTH
TMP...

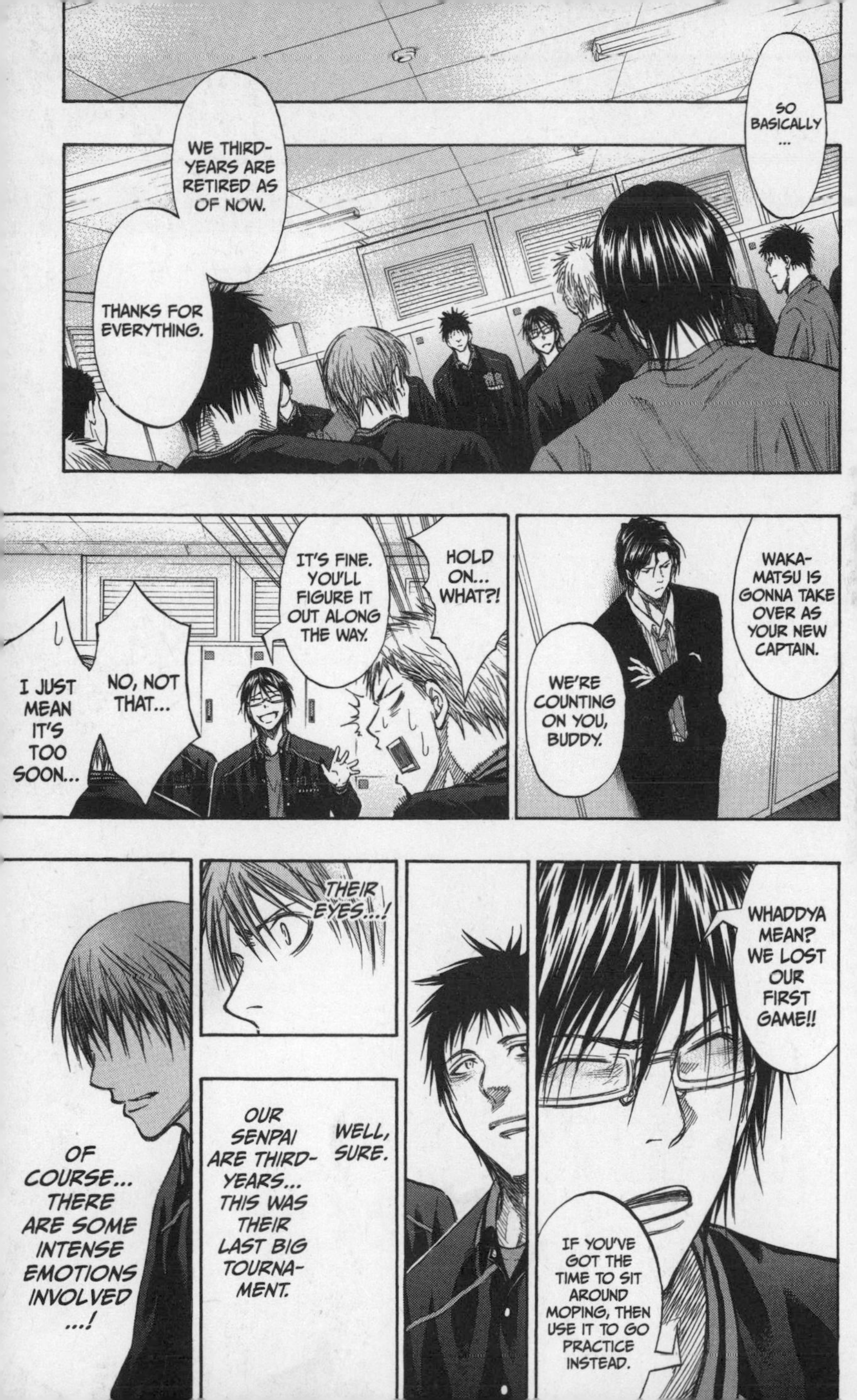
SO BASICALLY...
WE THIRD-YEARS ARE RETIRED AS OF NOW.
THANKS FOR EVERYTHING.
WAKA-MATSU IS GONNA TAKE OVER AS YOUR NEW CAPTAIN.
WE'RE COUNTING ON YOU, BUDDY.
HOLD ON... WHAT?!
IT'S FINE. YOU'LL FIGURE IT OUT ALONG THE WAY.
NO, NOT THAT...
I JUST MEAN IT'S TOO SOON...
WHADDYA MEAN? WE LOST OUR FIRST GAME!!
IF YOU'VE GOT THE TIME TO SIT AROUND MOPING, THEN USE IT TO GO PRACTICE INSTEAD.
THEIR EYES...!
WELL, SURE.
OUR SENPAI ARE THIRD-YEARS... THIS WAS THEIR LAST BIG TOURNA-MENT.
OF COURSE... THERE ARE SOME INTENSE EMOTIONS INVOLVED...!

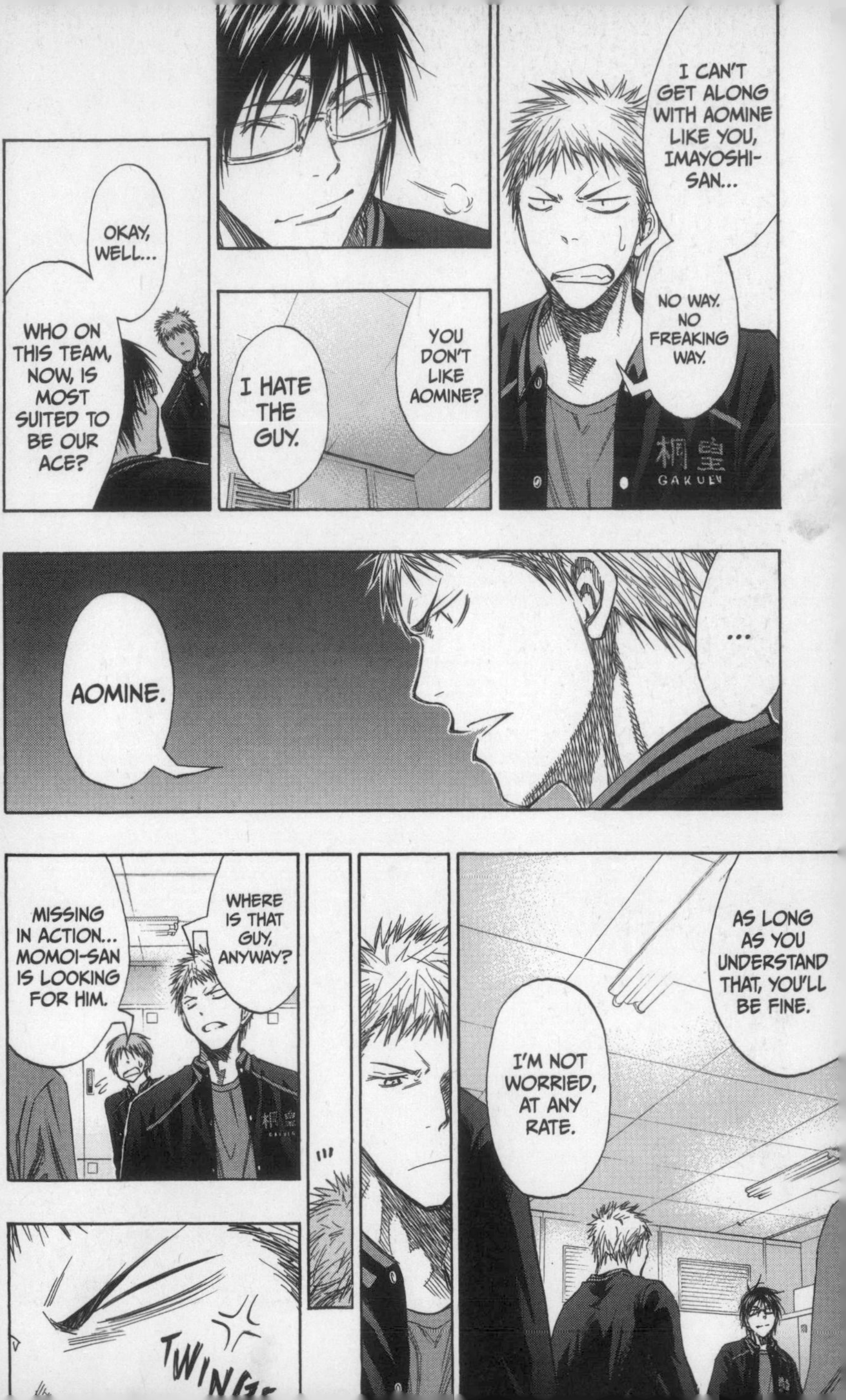
I CAN'T GET ALONG WITH AOMINE LIKE YOU, IMAYOSHI-SAN...
NO WAY. NO FREAKING WAY.
桐皇 GAKUEN
YOU DON'T LIKE AOMINE?
I HATE THE GUY.
OKAY, WELL...
WHO ON THIS TEAM, NOW, IS MOST SUITED TO BE OUR ACE?
...
AOMINE.
AS LONG AS YOU UNDERSTAND THAT, YOU'LL BE FINE.
I'M NOT WORRIED, AT ANY RATE.
WHERE IS THAT GUY, ANYWAY?
MISSING IN ACTION... MOMOI-SAN IS LOOKING FOR HIM.
TWING

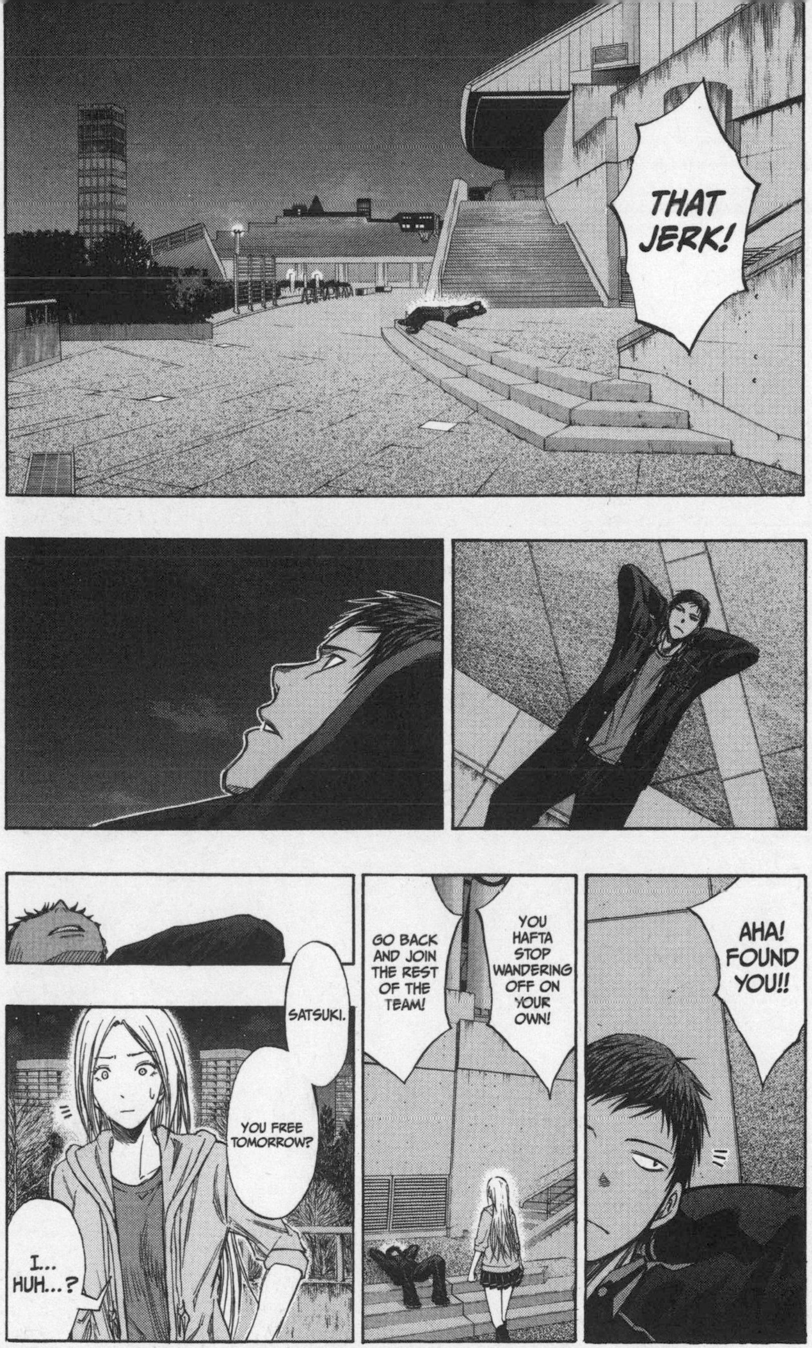
THAT JERK!
AHA! FOUND YOU!!
YOU HAFTA STOP WANDERING OFF ON YOUR OWN!
GO BACK AND JOIN THE REST OF THE TEAM!
SATSUKI.
YOU FREE TOMORROW?
I... HUH...?

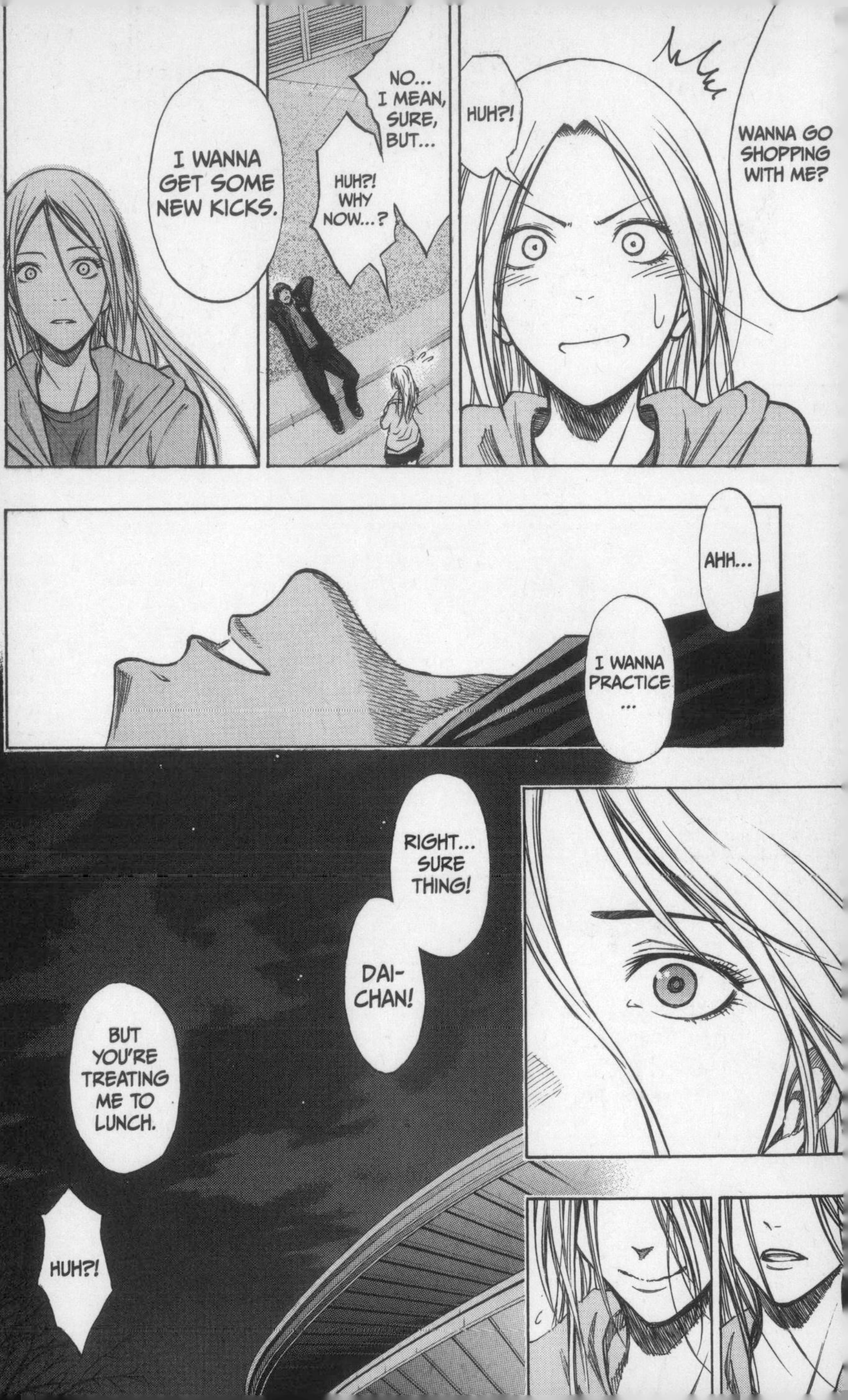
WANNA GO SHOPPING WITH ME?
HUH?!
NO... I MEAN, SURE, BUT...
HUH?! WHY NOW...?
I WANNA GET SOME NEW KICKS.
AHH...
I WANNA PRACTICE...
RIGHT... SURE THING!
DAI-CHAN!
BUT YOU'RE TREATING ME TO LUNCH.
HUH?!

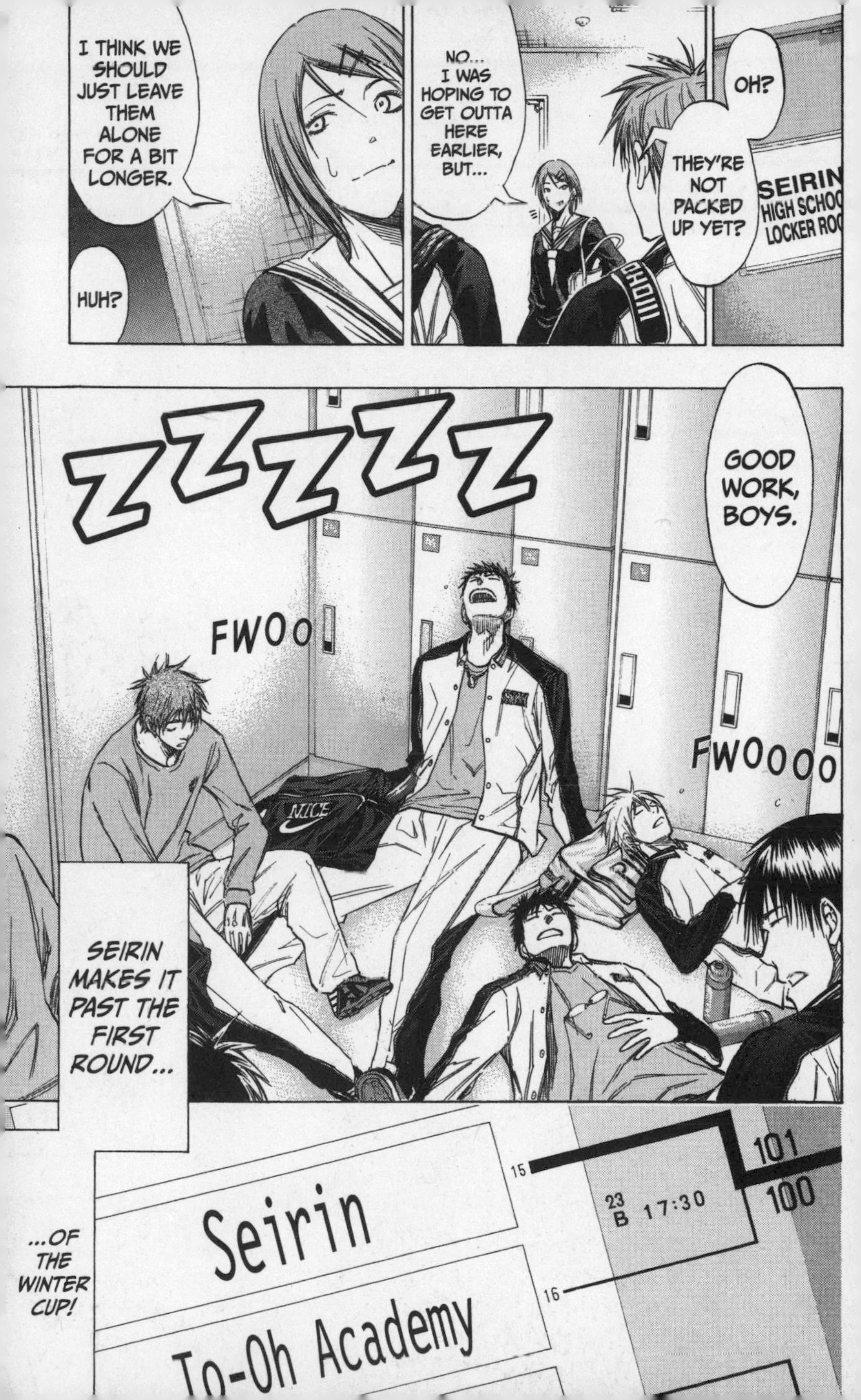
OH?
THEY'RE NOT PACKED UP YET?
SEIRIN HIGH SCHOO LOCKER ROO
NO... I WAS HOPING TO GET OUTTA HERE EARLIER, BUT...
I THINK WE SHOULD JUST LEAVE THEM ALONE FOR A BIT LONGER.
HUH?
GOOD WORK, BOYS.
ZZZZZ
FWOOOOO
FWOO
SEIRIN MAKES IT PAST THE FIRST ROUND...
101
100
15
23 B 17:30
Seirin
16
To-Oh Academy
...OF THE WINTER CUP!

KUROKO'S BASKETBALL Q&A (W/ HALFWAY DECENT ANSWERS)

Q. **I WANT TO KNOW THE NICKNAMES KAGETORA-SAN GAVE ALL THE SEIRIN BASKETBALL CLUB MEMBERS DURING THEIR TRAINING CAMP. PLEASE. DON'T FORGET #2.**
(MASAKI SAKANOUE from FUKUOKA PREFECTURE)

A.

HYUGA → RAGING FOUR-EYES

KIYOSHI → AIRHEAD GUY

RIKO → RIKO-TAN ♡

IZUKI → BOWL CUT

KOGANEI → KITTY-CAT BOY

MITOBE → QUIET DUDE

TSUCHIDA → TAKESHI

KUROKO → THE INVISIBLE ONE

KAGAMI → THE RED ONE

FURIHATA → BROWN HAIR

KAWAHARA → BLACK BEAN

FUKUDA → FUKUSUKE

#2 → DOGGY

THAT WAS A LOT...

PHEW.

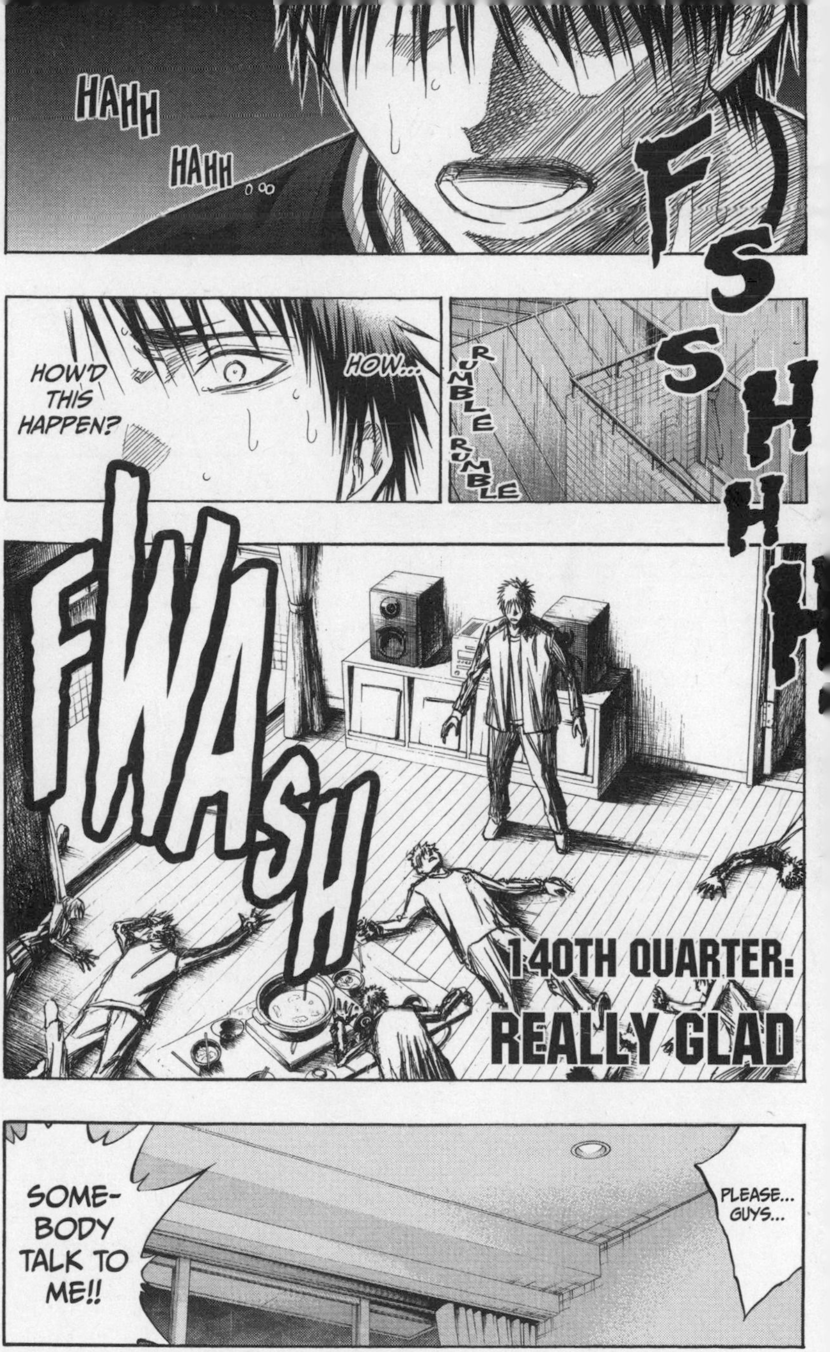
HAHH
HAHH
FSSHHHH
RUMBLE RUMBLE
HOW...
HOW'D THIS HAPPEN?
FWASH
140TH QUARTER: REALLY GLAD
PLEASE... GUYS...
SOME-BODY TALK TO ME!!

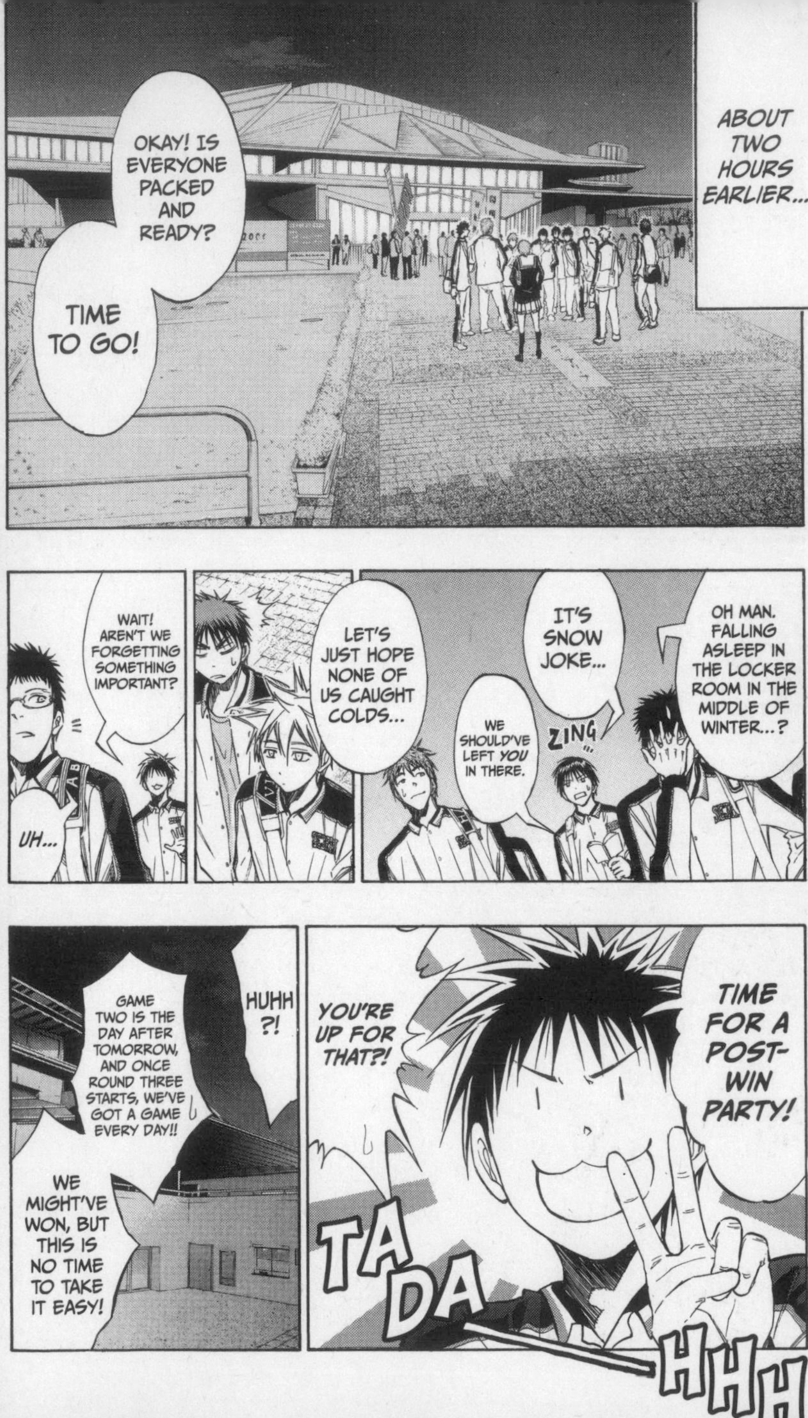
ABOUT TWO HOURS EARLIER...
OKAY! IS EVERYONE PACKED AND READY?
TIME TO GO!
OH MAN. FALLING ASLEEP IN THE LOCKER ROOM IN THE MIDDLE OF WINTER...?
IT'S SNOW JOKE...
ZING
WE SHOULD'VE LEFT YOU IN THERE.
LET'S JUST HOPE NONE OF US CAUGHT COLDS...
WAIT! AREN'T WE FORGETTING SOMETHING IMPORTANT?
UH...
TIME FOR A POST-WIN PARTY!
YOU'RE UP FOR THAT?!
TA DA HHH
HUHH ?!
GAME TWO IS THE DAY AFTER TOMORROW, AND ONCE ROUND THREE STARTS, WE'VE GOT A GAME EVERY DAY!!
WE MIGHT'VE WON, BUT THIS IS NO TIME TO TAKE IT EASY!

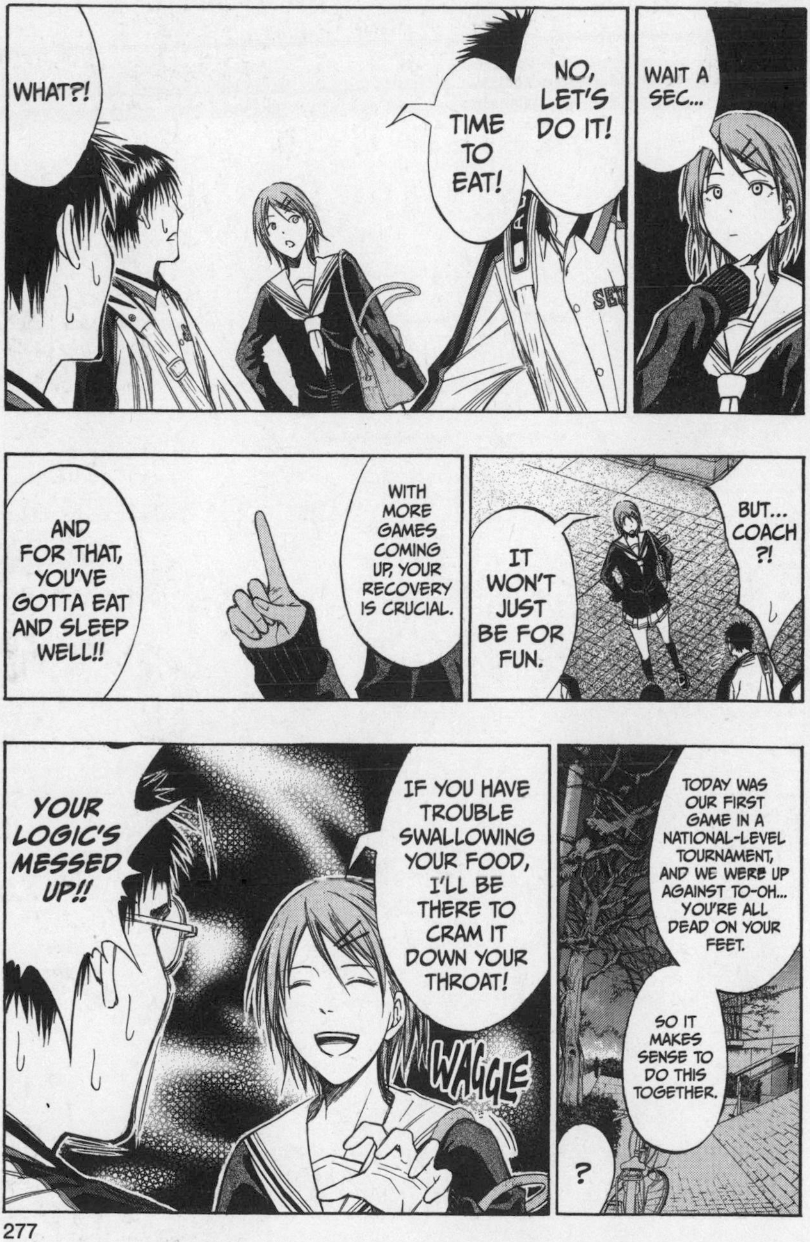

WAIT A SEC...
NO, LET'S DO IT!
TIME TO EAT!
WHAT?!
BUT... COACH?!
IT WON'T JUST BE FOR FUN.
WITH MORE GAMES COMING UP, YOUR RECOVERY IS CRUCIAL.
AND FOR THAT, YOU'VE GOTTA EAT AND SLEEP WELL!!
TODAY WAS OUR FIRST GAME IN A NATIONAL-LEVEL TOURNAMENT, AND WE WERE UP AGAINST TO-OH... YOU'RE ALL DEAD ON YOUR FEET.
SO IT MAKES SENSE TO DO THIS TOGETHER.
?
IF YOU HAVE TROUBLE SWALLOWING YOUR FOOD, I'LL BE THERE TO CRAM IT DOWN YOUR THROAT!
WAGGLE
YOUR LOGIC'S MESSED UP!!

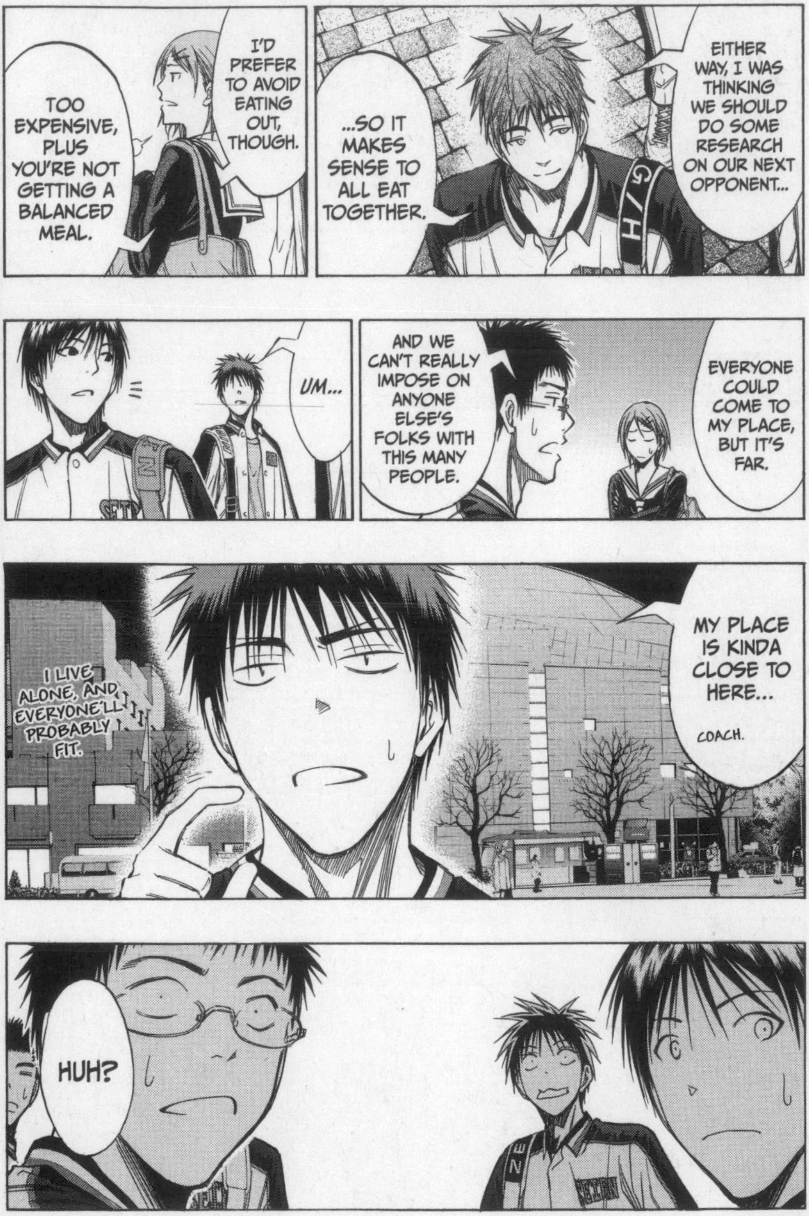
EITHER WAY, I WAS THINKING WE SHOULD DO SOME RESEARCH ON OUR NEXT OPPONENT...
...SO IT MAKES SENSE TO ALL EAT TOGETHER.
I'D PREFER TO AVOID EATING OUT, THOUGH.
TOO EXPENSIVE, PLUS YOU'RE NOT GETTING A BALANCED MEAL.
EVERYONE COULD COME TO MY PLACE, BUT IT'S FAR.
AND WE CAN'T REALLY IMPOSE ON ANYONE ELSE'S FOLKS WITH THIS MANY PEOPLE.
UM...
MY PLACE IS KINDA CLOSE TO HERE...
COACH.
I LIVE ALONE, AND EVERYONE'LL PROBABLY FIT.
HUH?

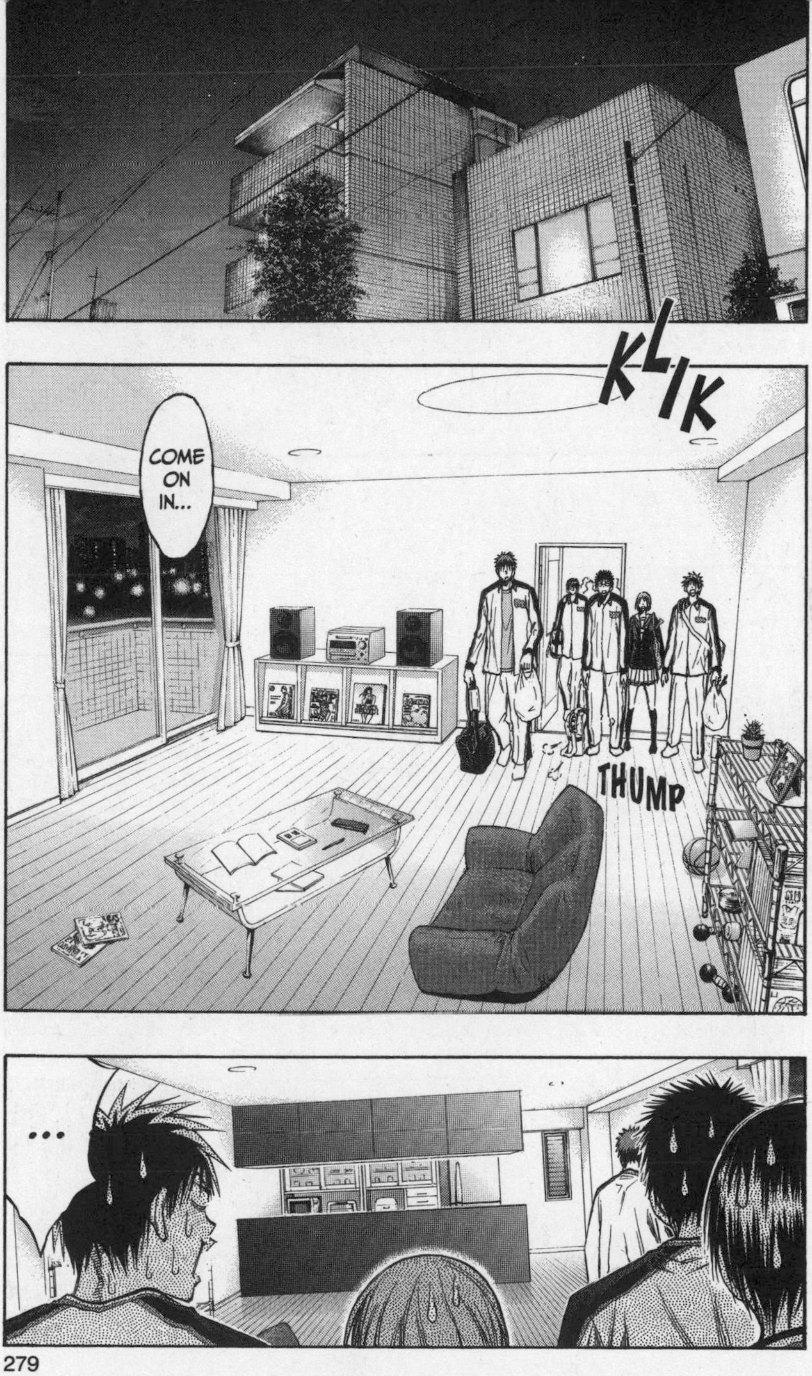
KLIK
COME ON IN...
THUMP
...

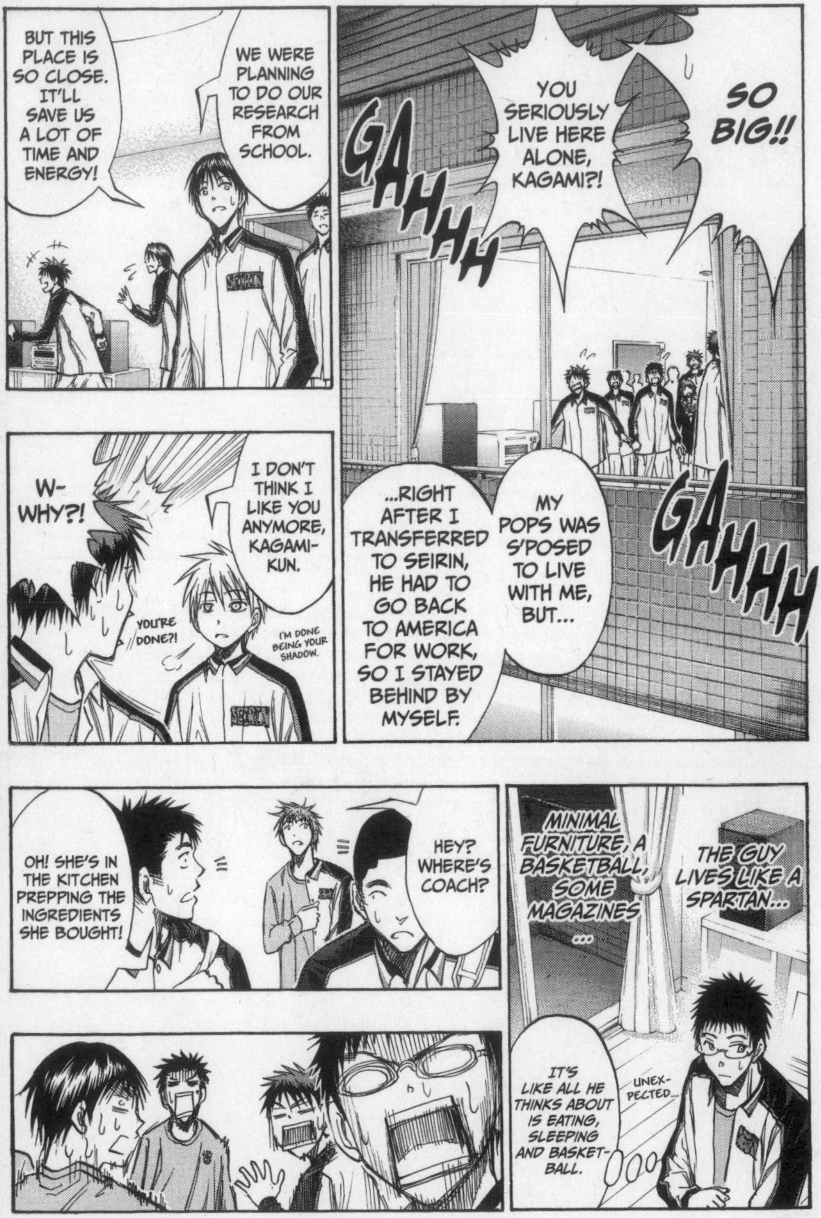
SO BIG!!
YOU SERIOUSLY LIVE HERE ALONE, KAGAMI?!
GAHHHH
GAHHHH
MY POPS WAS S'POSED TO LIVE WITH ME, BUT...
...RIGHT AFTER I TRANSFERRED TO SEIRIN, HE HAD TO GO BACK TO AMERICA FOR WORK, SO I STAYED BEHIND BY MYSELF.
WE WERE PLANNING TO DO OUR RESEARCH FROM SCHOOL.
BUT THIS PLACE IS SO CLOSE. IT'LL SAVE US A LOT OF TIME AND ENERGY!
I DON'T THINK I LIKE YOU ANYMORE, KAGAMI-KUN.
I'M DONE BEING YOUR SHADOW.
W-WHY?!
YOU'RE DONE?!
THE GUY LIVES LIKE A SPARTAN...
MINIMAL FURNITURE, A BASKETBALL, SOME MAGAZINES...
UNEX-PECTED...
IT'S LIKE ALL HE THINKS ABOUT IS EATING, SLEEPING AND BASKET-BALL.
HEY? WHERE'S COACH?
OH! SHE'S IN THE KITCHEN PREPPING THE INGREDIENTS SHE BOUGHT!

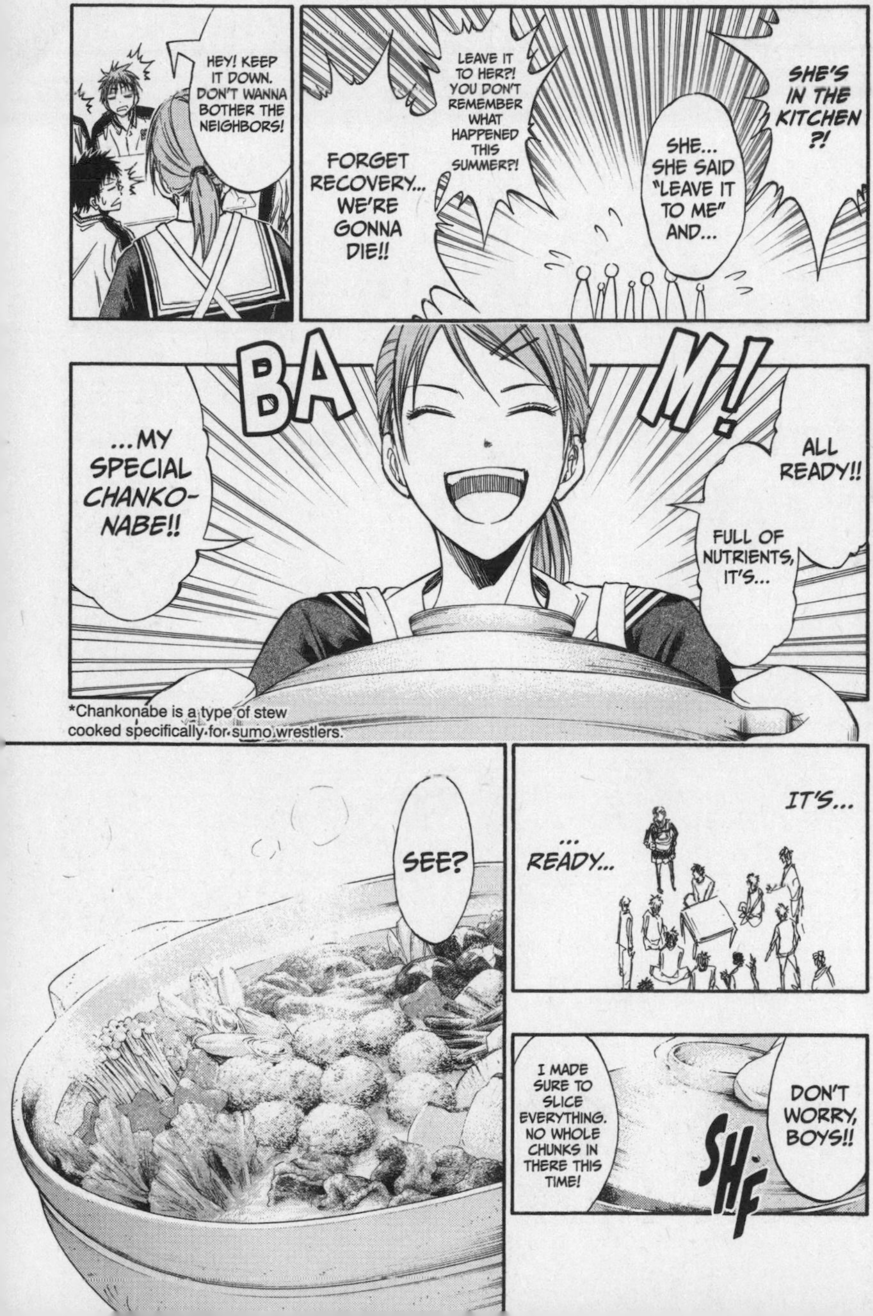
SHE'S IN THE KITCHEN?!
SHE... SHE SAID "LEAVE IT TO ME" AND...
LEAVE IT TO HER?! YOU DON'T REMEMBER WHAT HAPPENED THIS SUMMER?!
FORGET RECOVERY... WE'RE GONNA DIE!!
HEY! KEEP IT DOWN. DON'T WANNA BOTHER THE NEIGHBORS!
BAM!
ALL READY!!
FULL OF NUTRIENTS, IT'S...
...MY SPECIAL CHANKO-NABE!!
IT'S...
... READY...
DON'T WORRY, BOYS!!
SHF
I MADE SURE TO SLICE EVERYTHING. NO WHOLE CHUNKS IN THERE THIS TIME!
SEE?
*Chankonabe is a type of stew cooked specifically for sumo wrestlers.

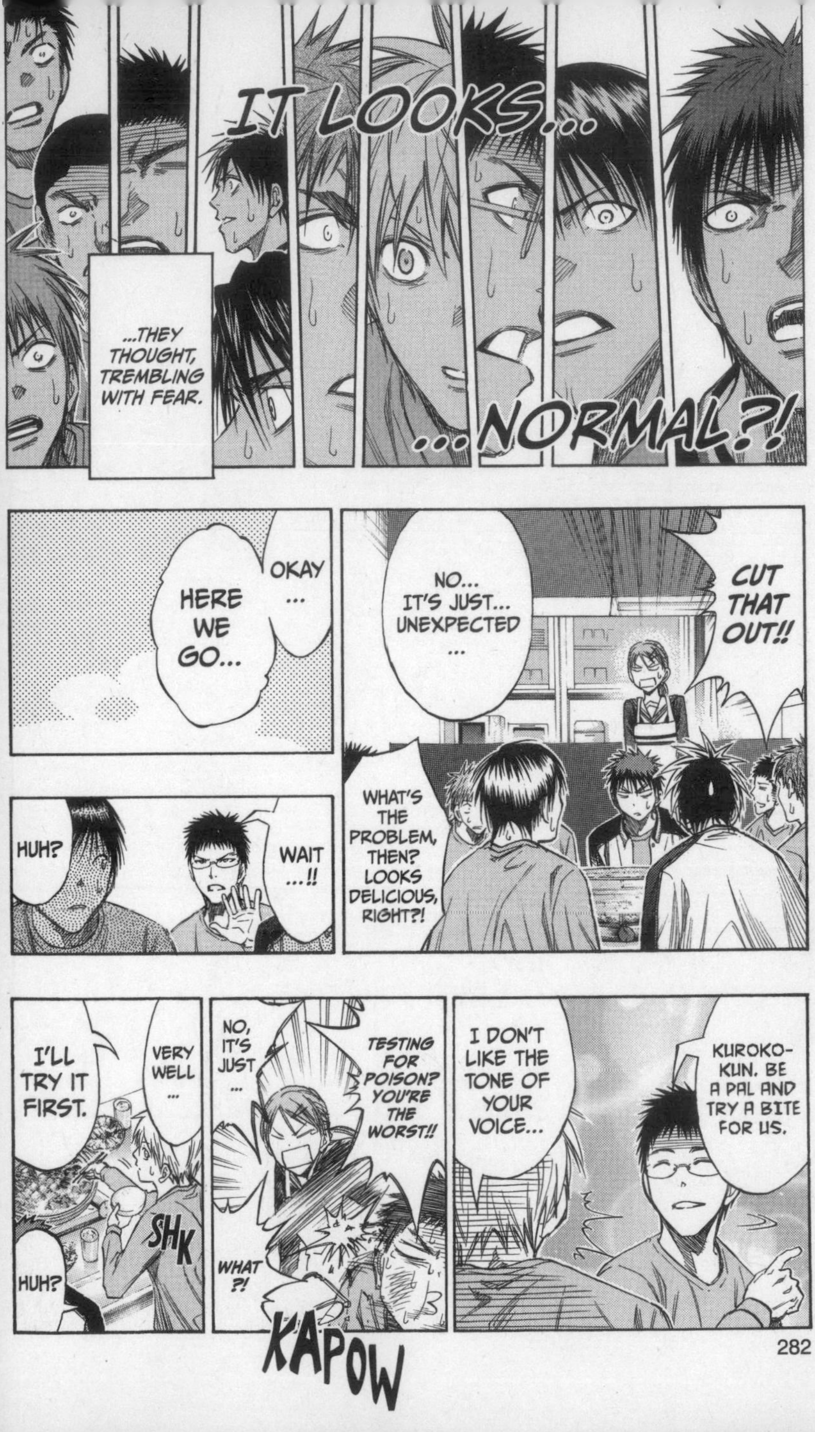
IT LOOKS...
...NORMAL?!
...THEY THOUGHT, TREMBLING WITH FEAR.
CUT THAT OUT!!
NO... IT'S JUST... UNEXPECTED...
WHAT'S THE PROBLEM, THEN? LOOKS DELICIOUS, RIGHT?!
OKAY...
HERE WE GO...
WAIT...!!
HUH?
KUROKO-KUN. BE A PAL AND TRY A BITE FOR US.
I DON'T LIKE THE TONE OF YOUR VOICE...
TESTING FOR POISON? YOU'RE THE WORST!!
NO, IT'S JUST...
WHAT?!
KAPOW
VERY WELL...
I'LL TRY IT FIRST.
SHK
HUH?

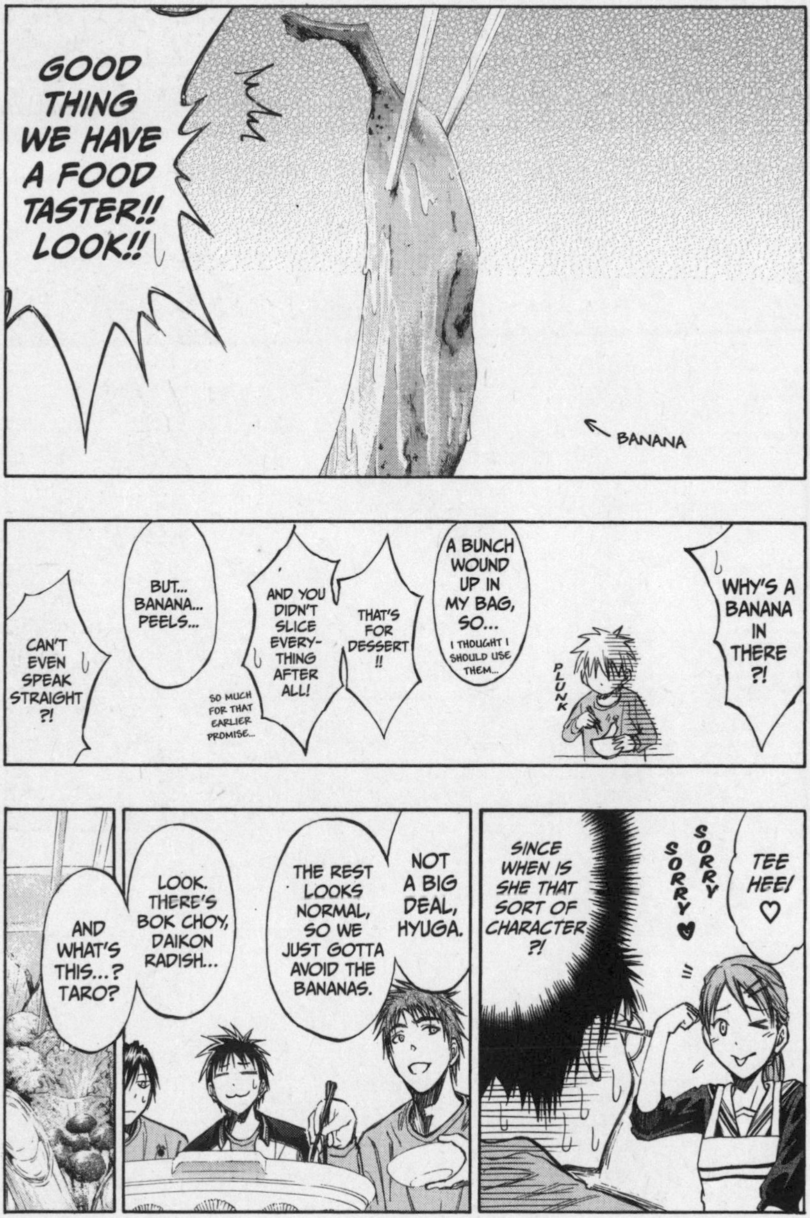
GOOD THING WE HAVE A FOOD TASTER!! LOOK!!
BANANA
WHY'S A BANANA IN THERE ?!
A BUNCH WOUND UP IN MY BAG, SO...
I THOUGHT I SHOULD USE THEM...
PLUNK
THAT'S FOR DESSERT!!
AND YOU DIDN'T SLICE EVERY-THING AFTER ALL!
SO MUCH FOR THAT EARLIER PROMISE...
BUT... BANANA... PEELS...
CAN'T EVEN SPEAK STRAIGHT ?!
TEE HEE! ♡
SORRY SORRY ♥
SINCE WHEN IS SHE THAT SORT OF CHARACTER ?!
NOT A BIG DEAL, HYUGA.
THE REST LOOKS NORMAL, SO WE JUST GOTTA AVOID THE BANANAS.
LOOK. THERE'S BOK CHOY, DAIKON RADISH...
AND WHAT'S THIS...? TARO?

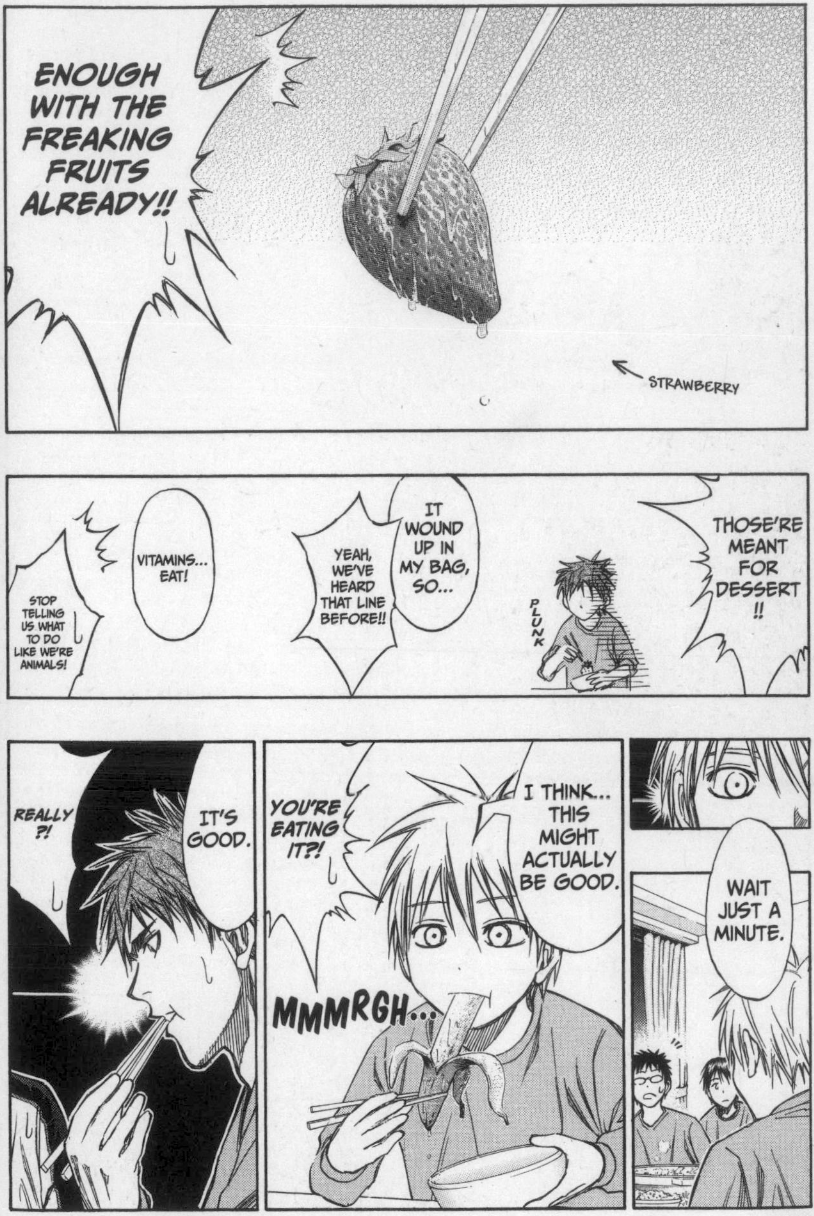
ENOUGH WITH THE FREAKING FRUITS ALREADY!!
STRAWBERRY
THOSE'RE MEANT FOR DESSERT!!
PLUNK
IT WOUND UP IN MY BAG, SO...
YEAH, WE'VE HEARD THAT LINE BEFORE!!
VITAMINS... EAT!
STOP TELLING US WHAT TO DO LIKE WE'RE ANIMALS!
WAIT JUST A MINUTE.
I THINK... THIS MIGHT ACTUALLY BE GOOD.
YOU'RE EATING IT?!
MMMRGH...
IT'S GOOD.
REALLY?!

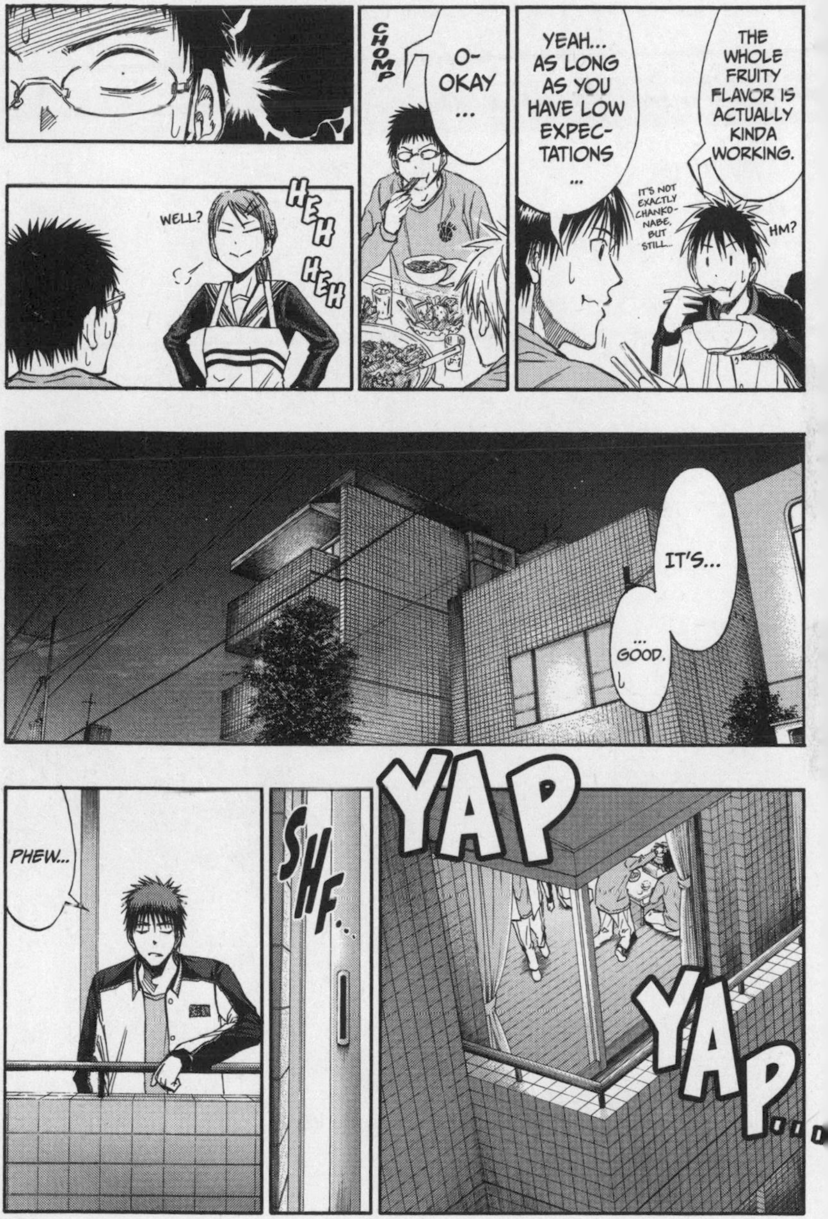
THE WHOLE FRUITY FLAVOR IS ACTUALLY KINDA WORKING.
HM?
IT'S NOT EXACTLY CHANKO-NABE, BUT STILL...
YEAH... AS LONG AS YOU HAVE LOW EXPEC-TATIONS...
O-OKAY...
CHOMP
HEH HEH
WELL?
IT'S...
...GOOD.
YAP
YAP...
SHF...
PHEW...

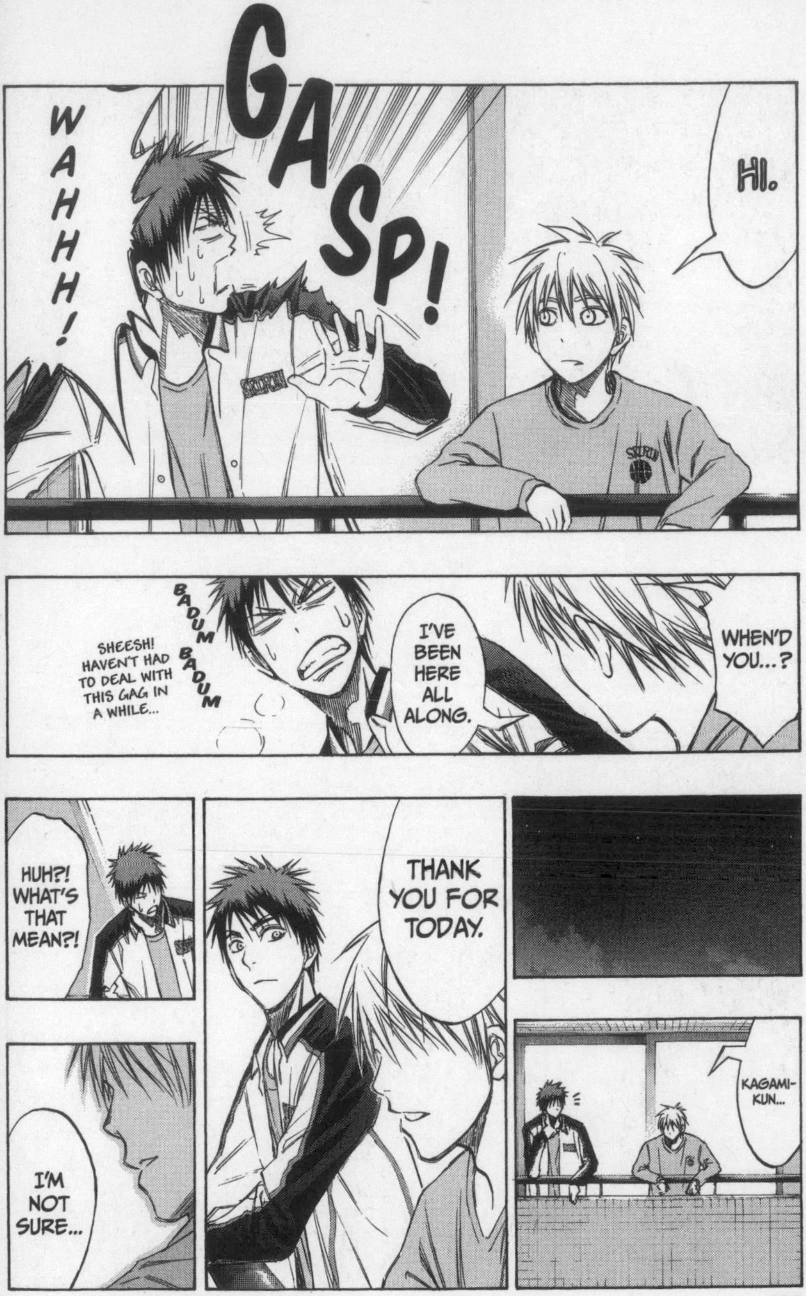
HI.
GASP!
WAHHHH!
WHEN'D YOU...?
I'VE BEEN HERE ALL ALONG.
BADUM BADUM
SHEESH! HAVEN'T HAD TO DEAL WITH THIS GAG IN A WHILE...
KAGAMI-KUN...
THANK YOU FOR TODAY.
HUH?! WHAT'S THAT MEAN?!
I'M NOT SURE...

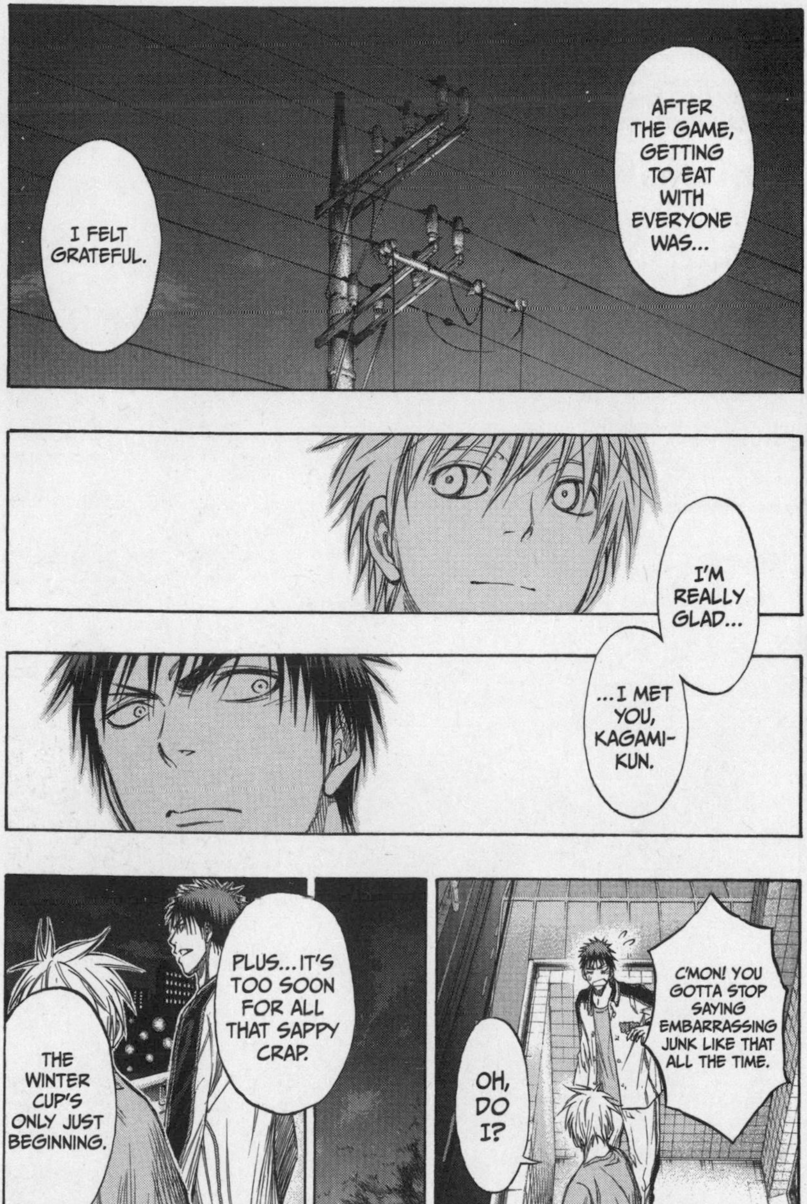
AFTER THE GAME, GETTING TO EAT WITH EVERYONE WAS...
I FELT GRATEFUL.
I'M REALLY GLAD...
...I MET YOU, KAGAMI-KUN.
C'MON! YOU GOTTA STOP SAYING EMBARRASSING JUNK LIKE THAT ALL THE TIME.
OH, DO I?
PLUS...IT'S TOO SOON FOR ALL THAT SAPPY CRAP.
THE WINTER CUP'S ONLY JUST BEGINNING.

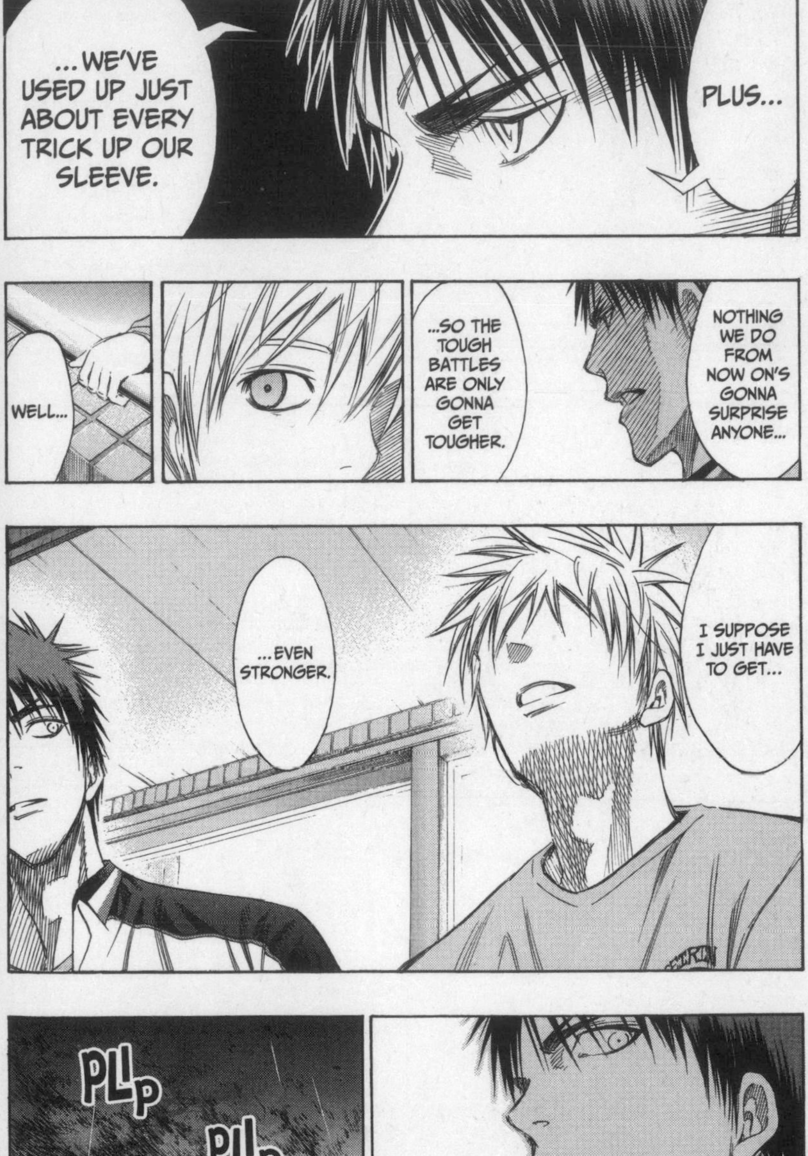
...WE'VE USED UP JUST ABOUT EVERY TRICK UP OUR SLEEVE.
PLUS...
NOTHING WE DO FROM NOW ON'S GONNA SURPRISE ANYONE...
...SO THE TOUGH BATTLES ARE ONLY GONNA GET TOUGHER.
WELL...
I SUPPOSE I JUST HAVE TO GET...
...EVEN STRONGER.
PLIP
PLIP

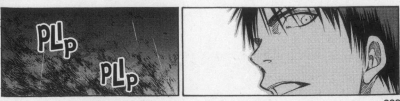

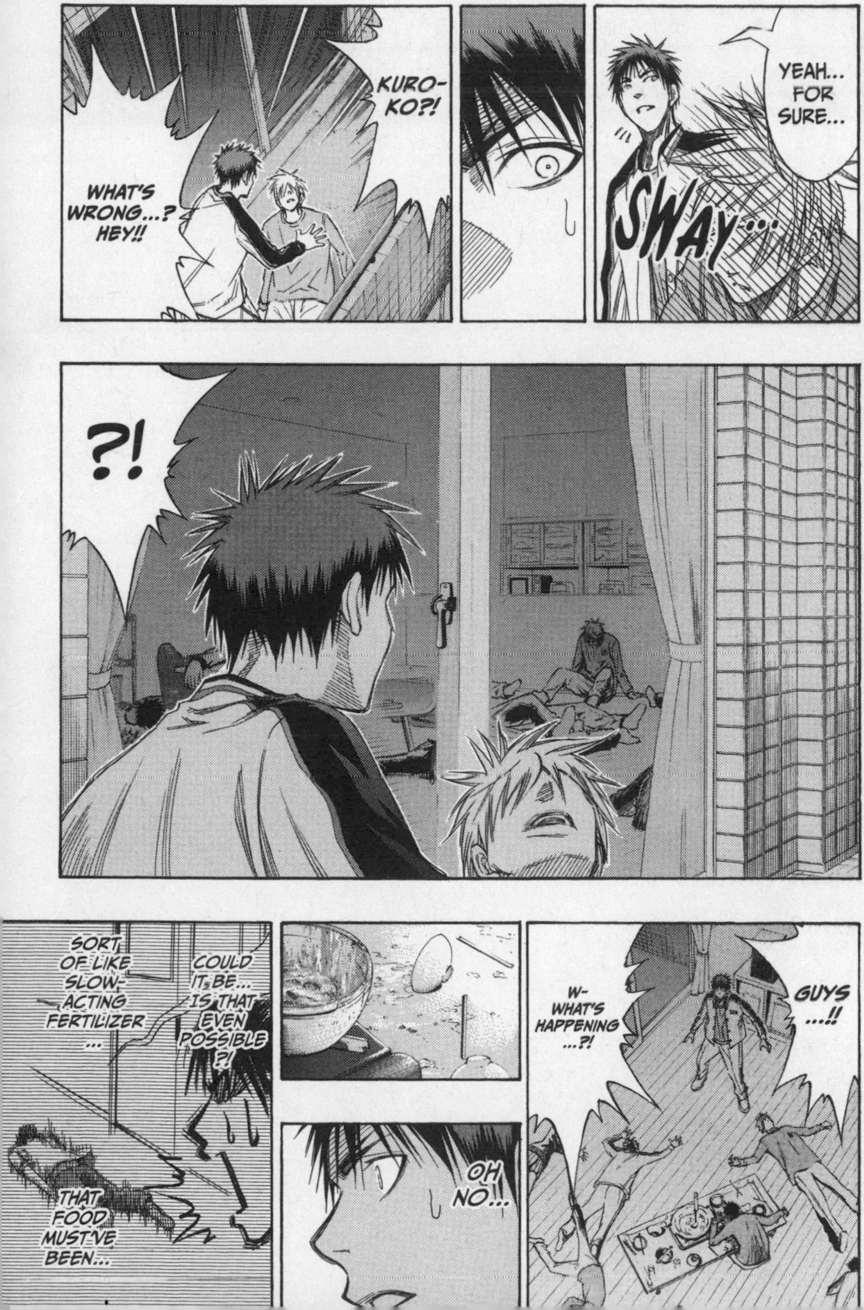
YEAH... FOR SURE...
SWAY...
KURO-KO?!
WHAT'S WRONG...? HEY!!
?!
GUYS ...!!
W-WHAT'S HAPPENING ...?!
OH NO...
COULD IT BE... IS THAT EVEN POSSIBLE ?!
SORT OF LIKE SLOW-ACTING FERTILIZER ...
THAT FOOD MUST'VE BEEN...

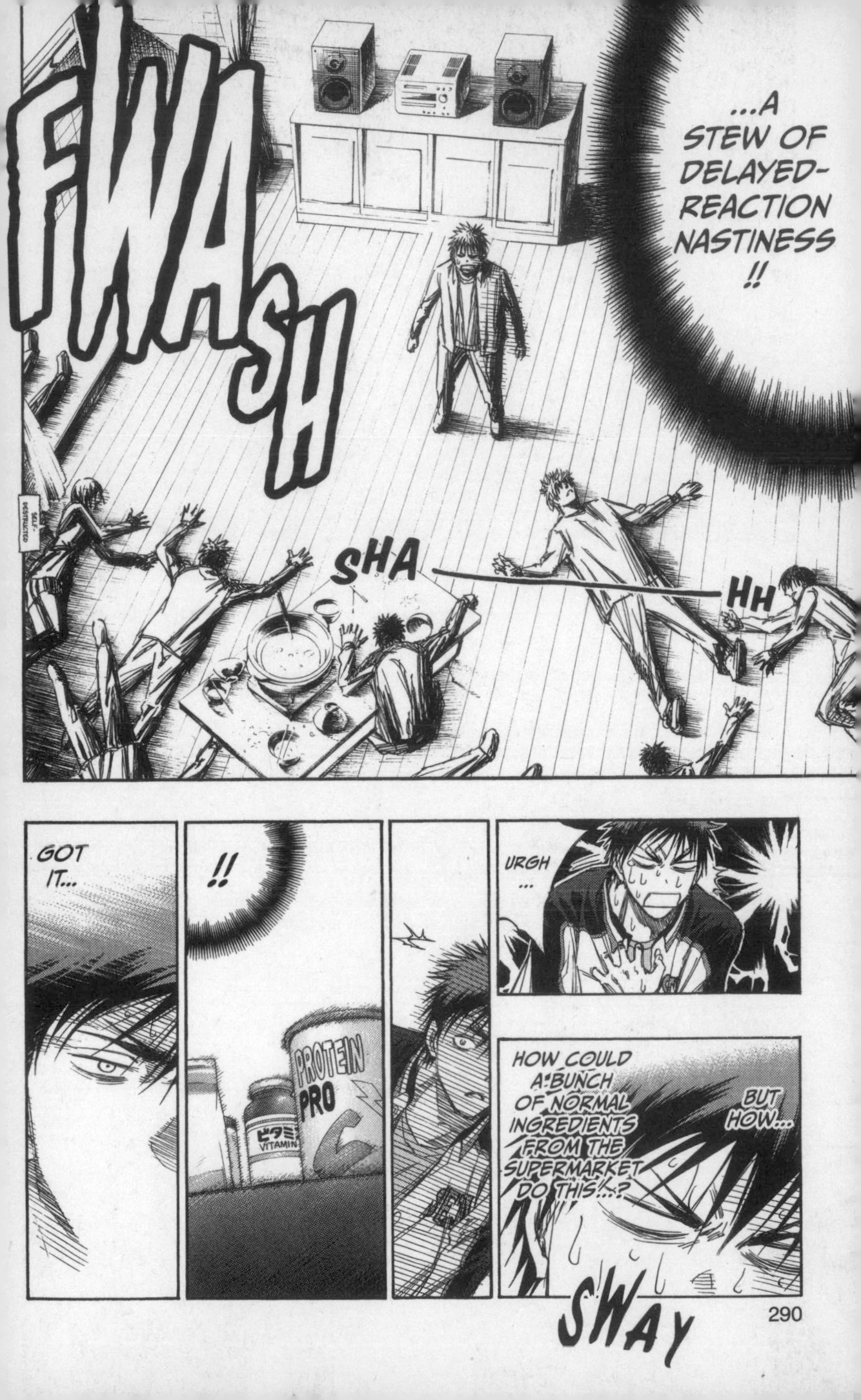
...A STEW OF DELAYED-REACTION NASTINESS !!
FWASH
SELF-DESTRUCTED
SHA—HH
URGH ...
HOW COULD A BUNCH OF NORMAL INGREDIENTS FROM THE SUPERMARKET DO THIS!..?
BUT HOW...
SWAY
!!
PROTEIN PRO
VITAMIN
GOT IT...

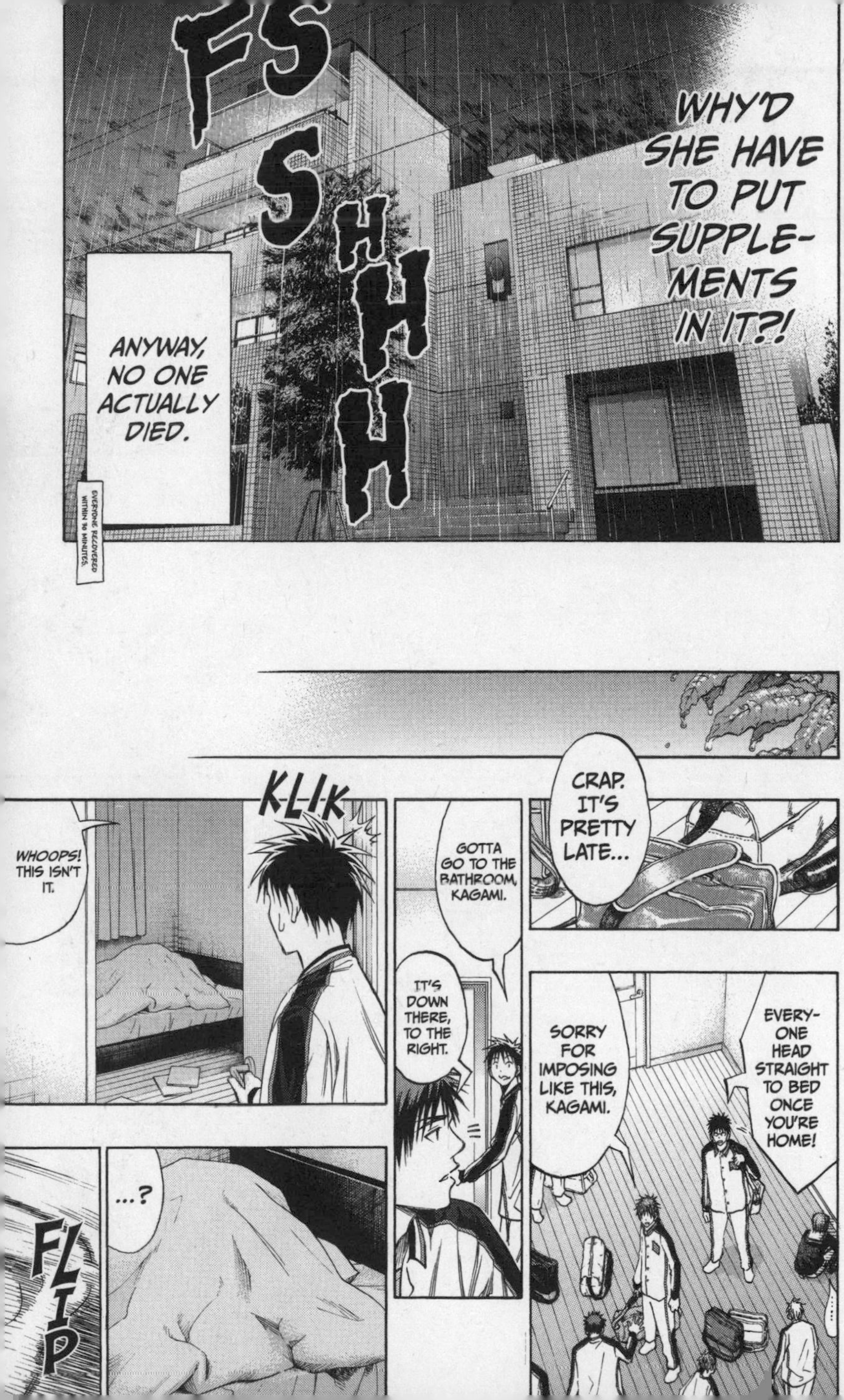
FSSHHHH
WHY'D SHE HAVE TO PUT SUPPLE-MENTS IN IT?!
ANYWAY, NO ONE ACTUALLY DIED.
EVERYONE RECOVERED WITHIN 30 MINUTES.
CRAP. IT'S PRETTY LATE...
EVERY-ONE HEAD STRAIGHT TO BED ONCE YOU'RE HOME!
SORRY FOR IMPOSING LIKE THIS, KAGAMI.
GOTTA GO TO THE BATHROOM, KAGAMI.
IT'S DOWN THERE, TO THE RIGHT.
KLIK
WHOOPS! THIS ISN'T IT.
...?
FLIP

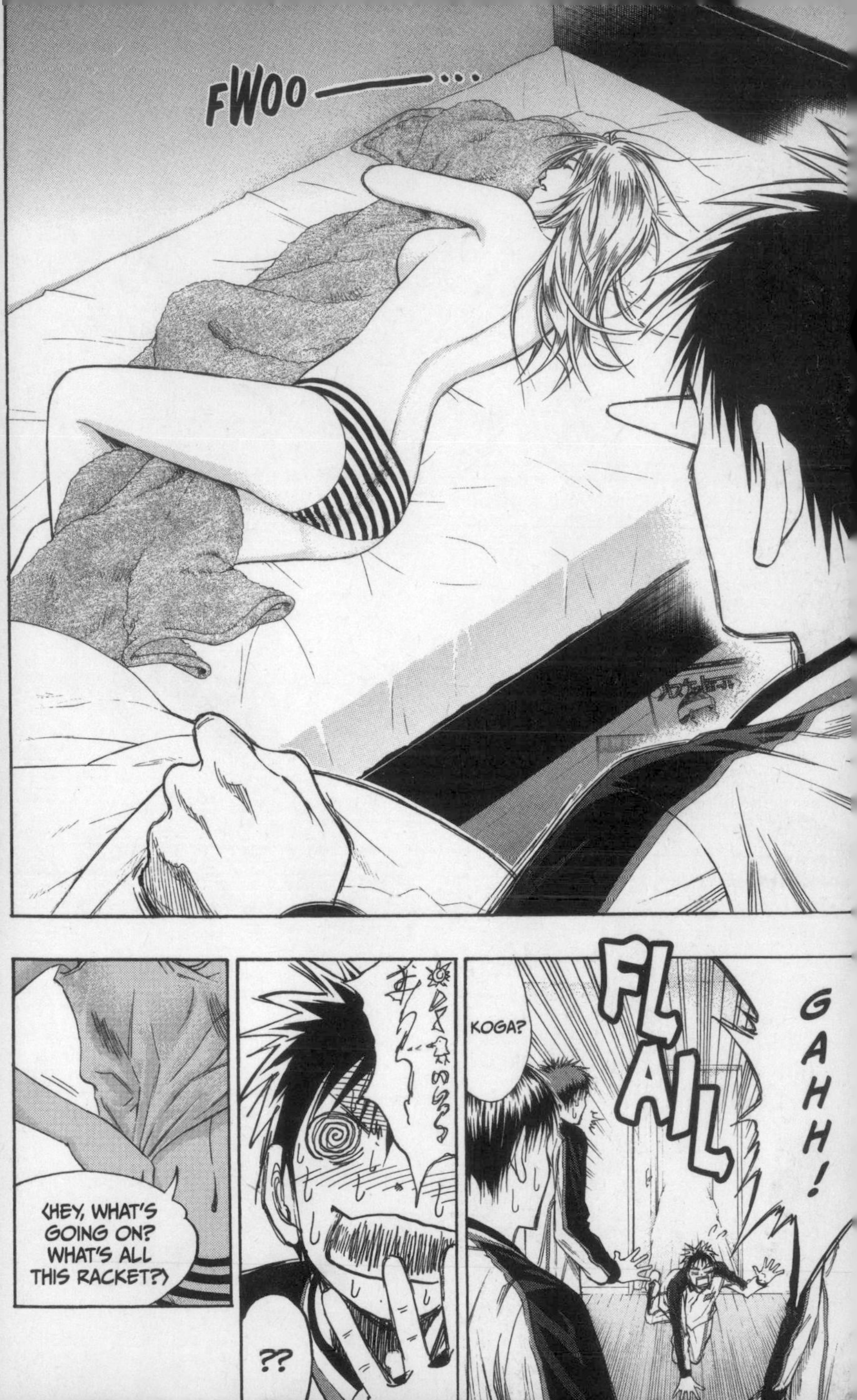
FWOO———...
FLAIL
GAHH!
KOGA?
??
<HEY, WHAT'S GOING ON? WHAT'S ALL THIS RACKET?>

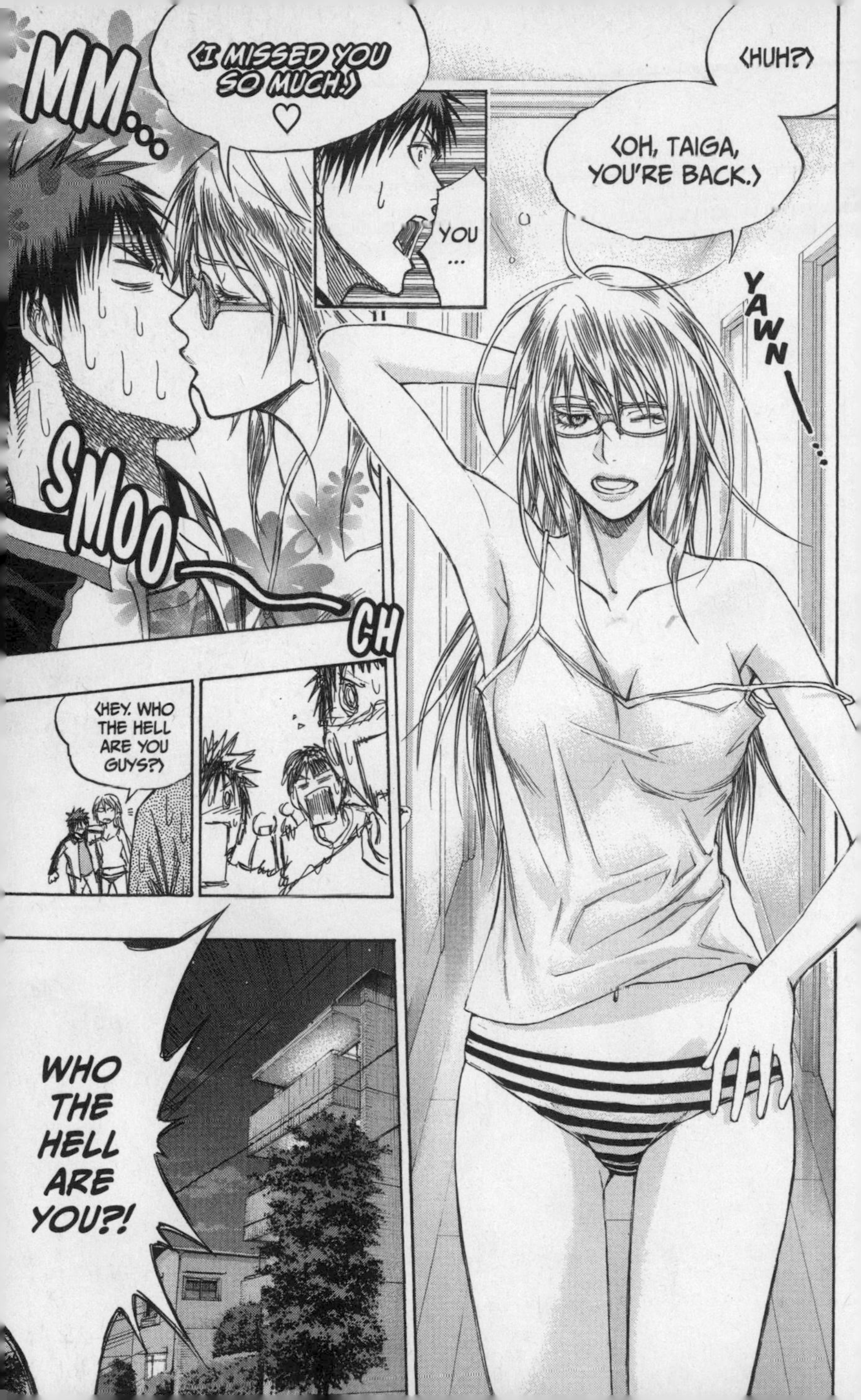

<HUH?>
<OH, TAIGA, YOU'RE BACK.>
YAWN...
YOU ...
<I MISSED YOU SO MUCH.> ♡
MM...
SMOO—CH
<HEY. WHO THE HELL ARE YOU GUYS?>
WHO THE HELL ARE YOU?!

KUROKO'S BASKETBALL BLOOPERS TAKE 3

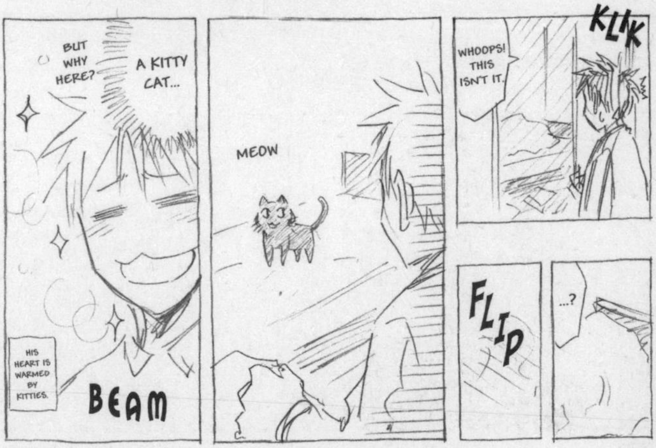
KLIK
WHOOPS! THIS ISN'T IT.
...?
FLIP
MEOW
A KITTY CAT...
BUT WHY HERE?
BEAM
HIS HEART IS WARMED BY KITTIES.

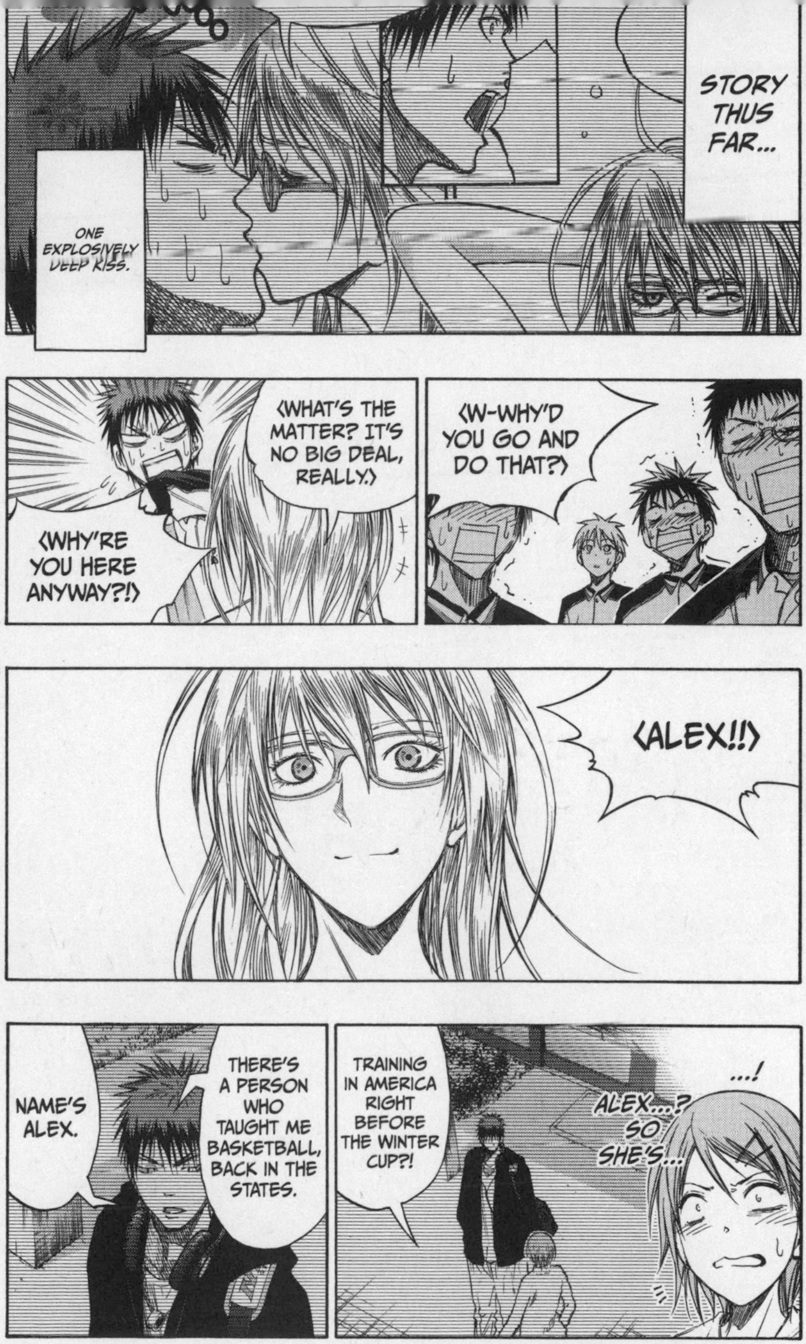
STORY THUS FAR...
ONE EXPLOSIVELY DEEP KISS.
‹W-WHY'D YOU GO AND DO THAT?›
‹WHAT'S THE MATTER? IT'S NO BIG DEAL, REALLY.›
‹WHY'RE YOU HERE ANYWAY?!›
‹ALEX!!›
...!
ALEX...? SO SHE'S...
TRAINING IN AMERICA RIGHT BEFORE THE WINTER CUP?!
THERE'S A PERSON WHO TAUGHT ME BASKETBALL, BACK IN THE STATES.
NAME'S ALEX.

141ST QUARTER: <NICE TO MEET YOU!>

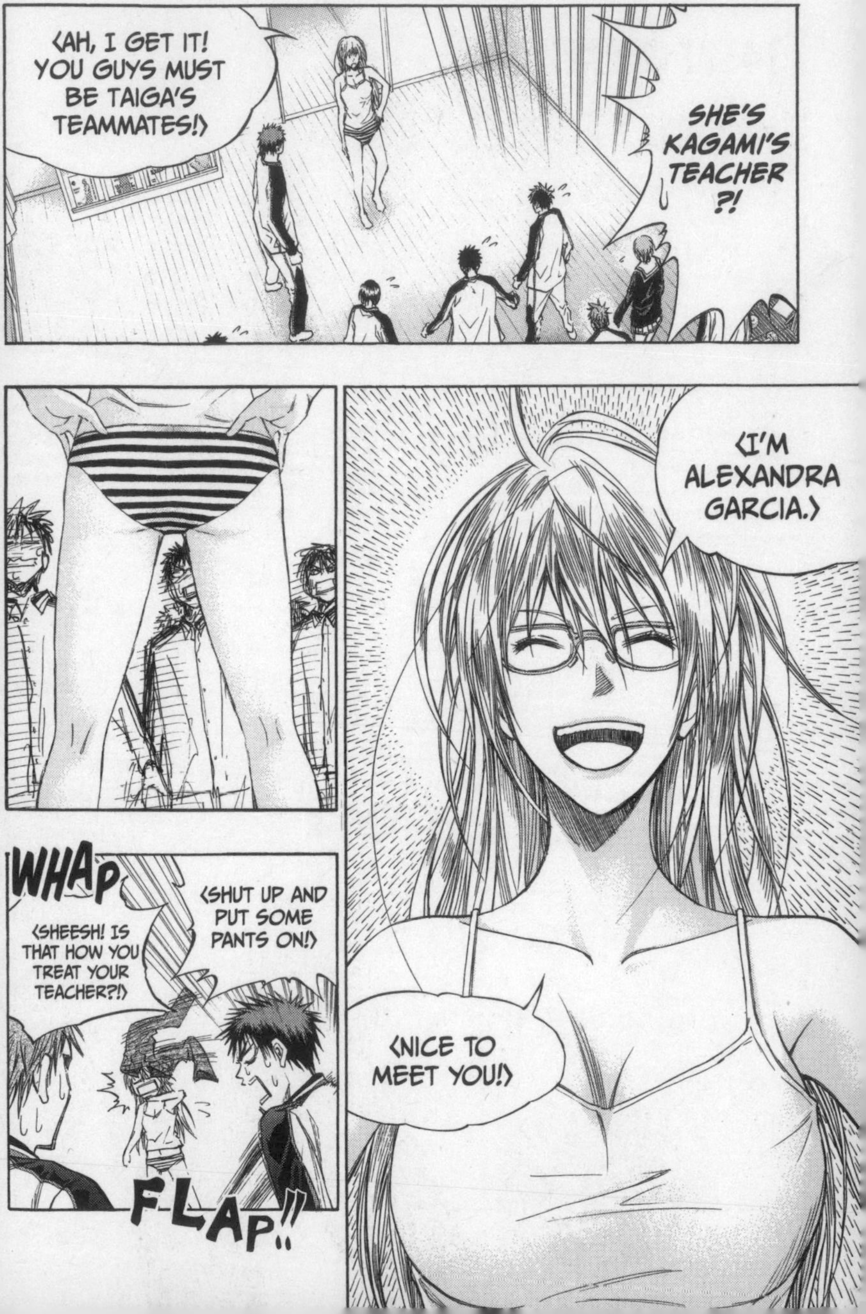
SHE'S KAGAMI'S TEACHER ?!
‹AH, I GET IT! YOU GUYS MUST BE TAIGA'S TEAMMATES!›
‹I'M ALEXANDRA GARCIA.›
‹NICE TO MEET YOU!›
‹SHUT UP AND PUT SOME PANTS ON!›
WHAP
‹SHEESH! IS THAT HOW YOU TREAT YOUR TEACHER?!›
FLAP!!

141ST QUARTER:
<NICE TO MEET YOU!>

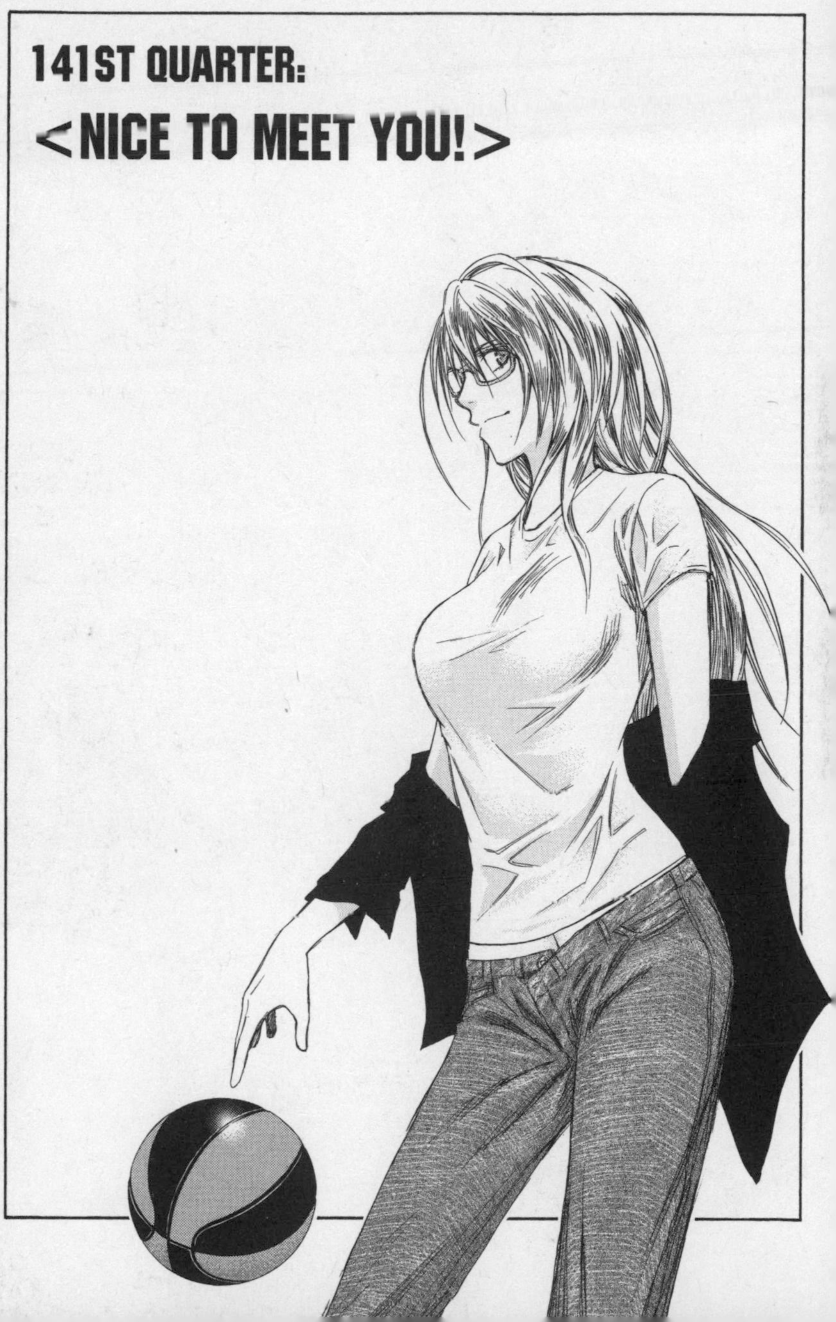

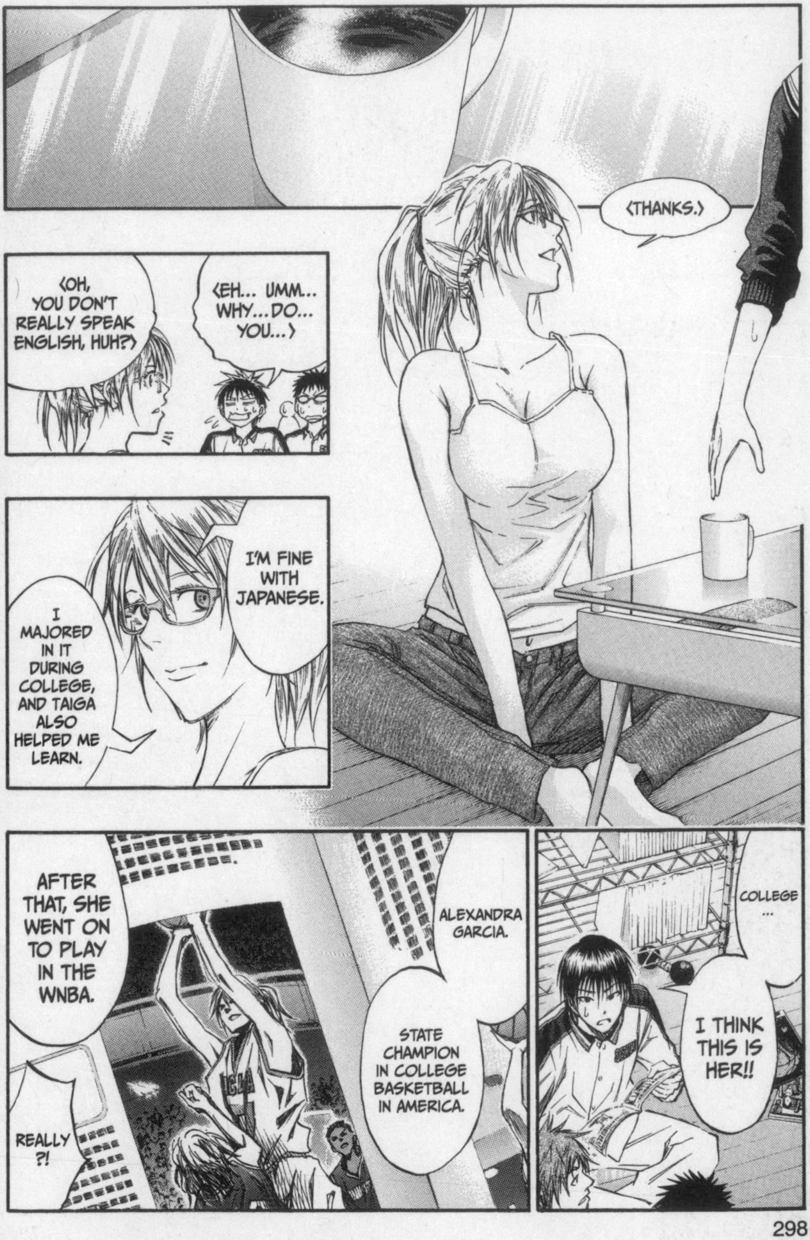

⟨THANKS.⟩
⟨EH... UMM... WHY...DO... YOU...⟩
⟨OH, YOU DON'T REALLY SPEAK ENGLISH, HUH?⟩
I'M FINE WITH JAPANESE.
I MAJORED IN IT DURING COLLEGE, AND TAIGA ALSO HELPED ME LEARN.
COLLEGE ...
I THINK THIS IS HER!!
ALEXANDRA GARCIA.
STATE CHAMPION IN COLLEGE BASKETBALL IN AMERICA.
AFTER THAT, SHE WENT ON TO PLAY IN THE WNBA.
REALLY ?!

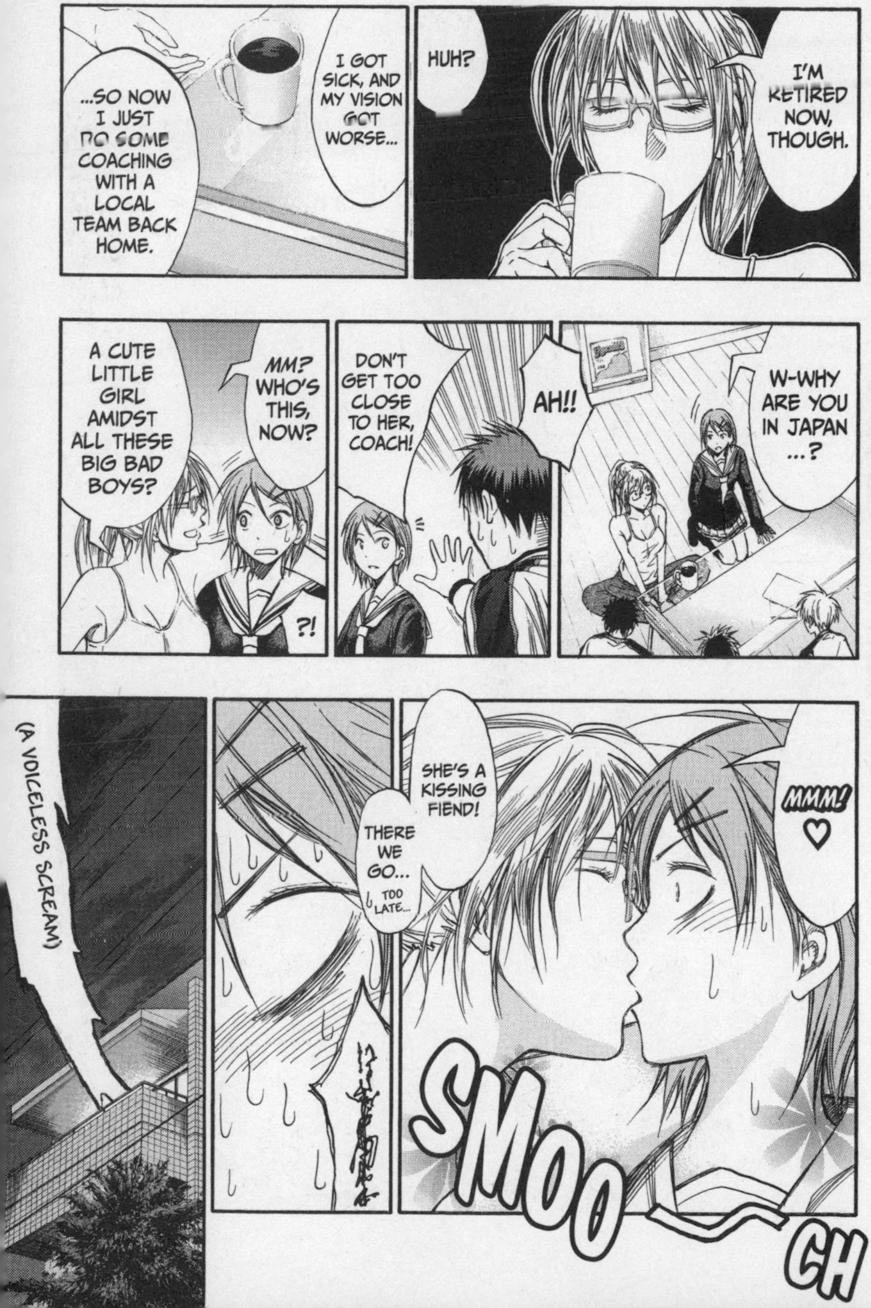
I'M RETIRED NOW, THOUGH.
HUH?
I GOT SICK, AND MY VISION GOT WORSE...
...SO NOW I JUST DO SOME COACHING WITH A LOCAL TEAM BACK HOME.
W-WHY ARE YOU IN JAPAN ...?
AH!!
DON'T GET TOO CLOSE TO HER, COACH!
MM? WHO'S THIS, NOW?
A CUTE LITTLE GIRL AMIDST ALL THESE BIG BAD BOYS?
?!
MMM! ♡
SHE'S A KISSING FIEND!
SMOO~CH
THERE WE GO...
TOO LATE...
(A VOICELESS SCREAM)

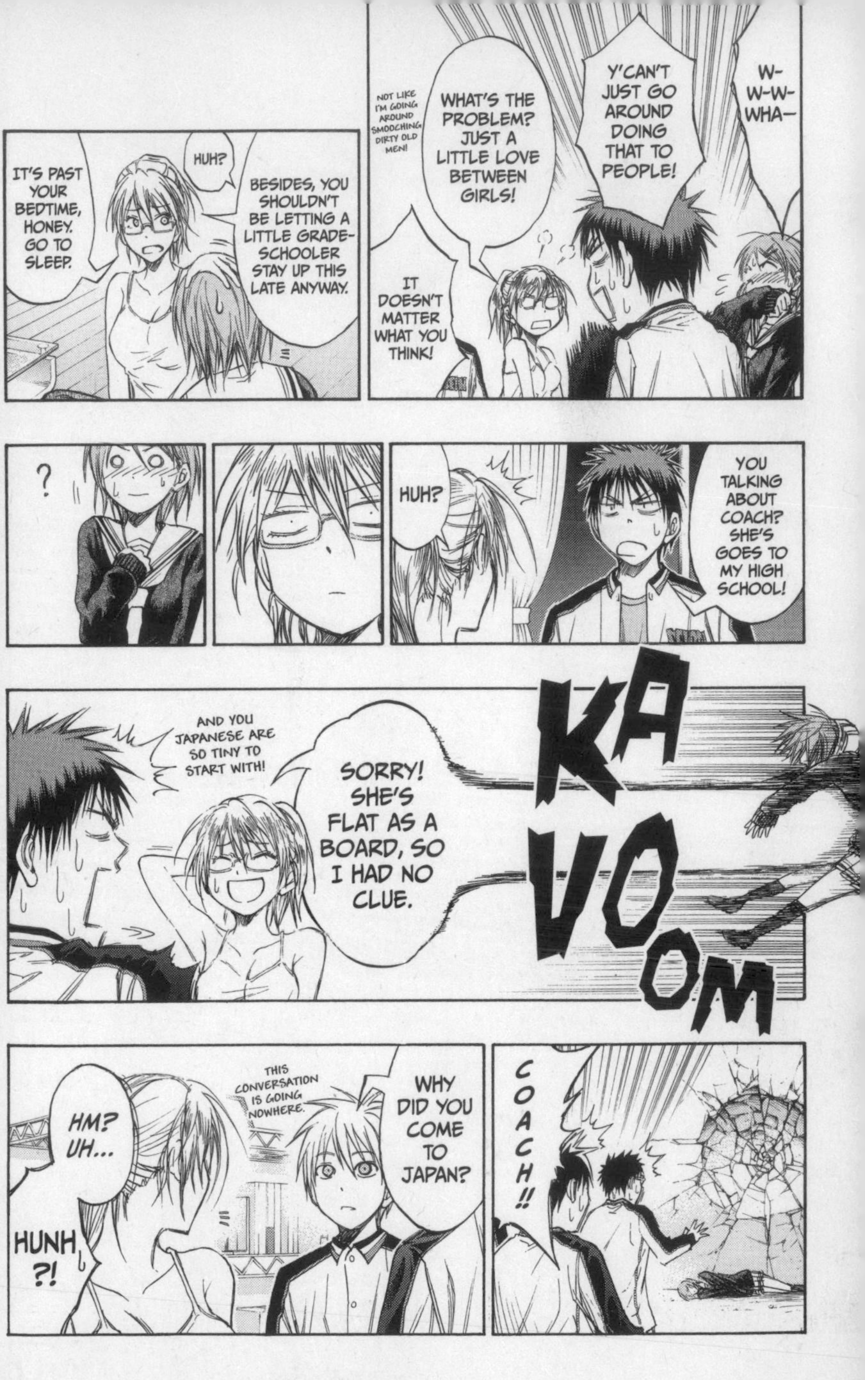
W-W-W-WHA—
Y'CAN'T JUST GO AROUND DOING THAT TO PEOPLE!
WHAT'S THE PROBLEM? JUST A LITTLE LOVE BETWEEN GIRLS!
NOT LIKE I'M GOING AROUND SMOOCHING DIRTY OLD MEN!
IT DOESN'T MATTER WHAT YOU THINK!
HUH?
BESIDES, YOU SHOULDN'T BE LETTING A LITTLE GRADE-SCHOOLER STAY UP THIS LATE ANYWAY.
IT'S PAST YOUR BEDTIME, HONEY. GO TO SLEEP.
YOU TALKING ABOUT COACH? SHE'S GOES TO MY HIGH SCHOOL!
HUH?
?
KA VOOM
SORRY! SHE'S FLAT AS A BOARD, SO I HAD NO CLUE.
AND YOU JAPANESE ARE SO TINY TO START WITH!
COACH!!
WHY DID YOU COME TO JAPAN?
THIS CONVERSATION IS GOING NOWHERE.
HM? UH...
HUNH?!

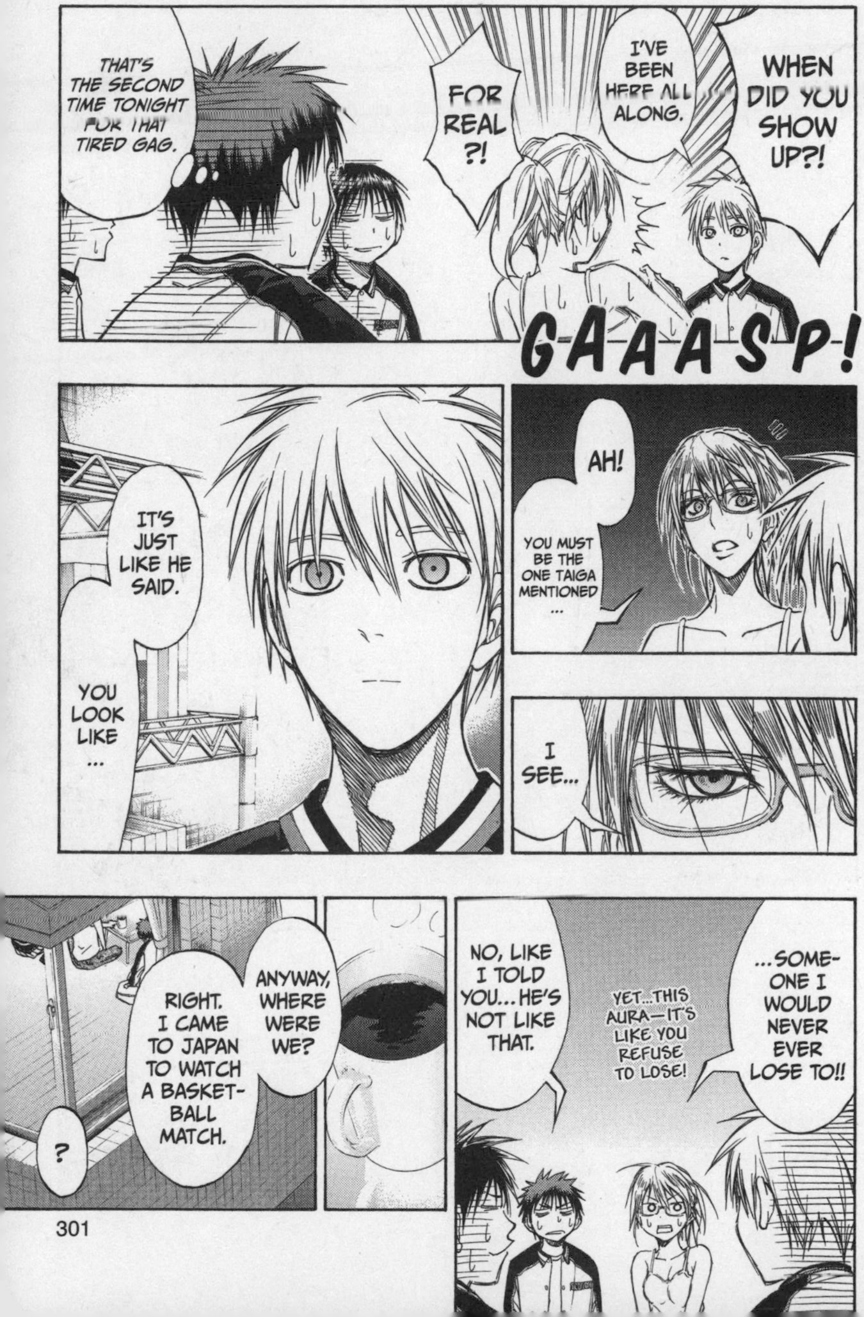
WHEN DID YOU SHOW UP?!
I'VE BEEN HERE ALL ALONG.
GAAASP!
FOR REAL?!
THAT'S THE SECOND TIME TONIGHT FOR THAT TIRED GAG.
AH!
YOU MUST BE THE ONE TAIGA MENTIONED...
I SEE...
IT'S JUST LIKE HE SAID.
YOU LOOK LIKE...
...SOMEONE I WOULD NEVER EVER LOSE TO!!
YET...THIS AURA—IT'S LIKE YOU REFUSE TO LOSE!
NO, LIKE I TOLD YOU... HE'S NOT LIKE THAT.
ANYWAY, WHERE WERE WE?
RIGHT. I CAME TO JAPAN TO WATCH A BASKETBALL MATCH.
?

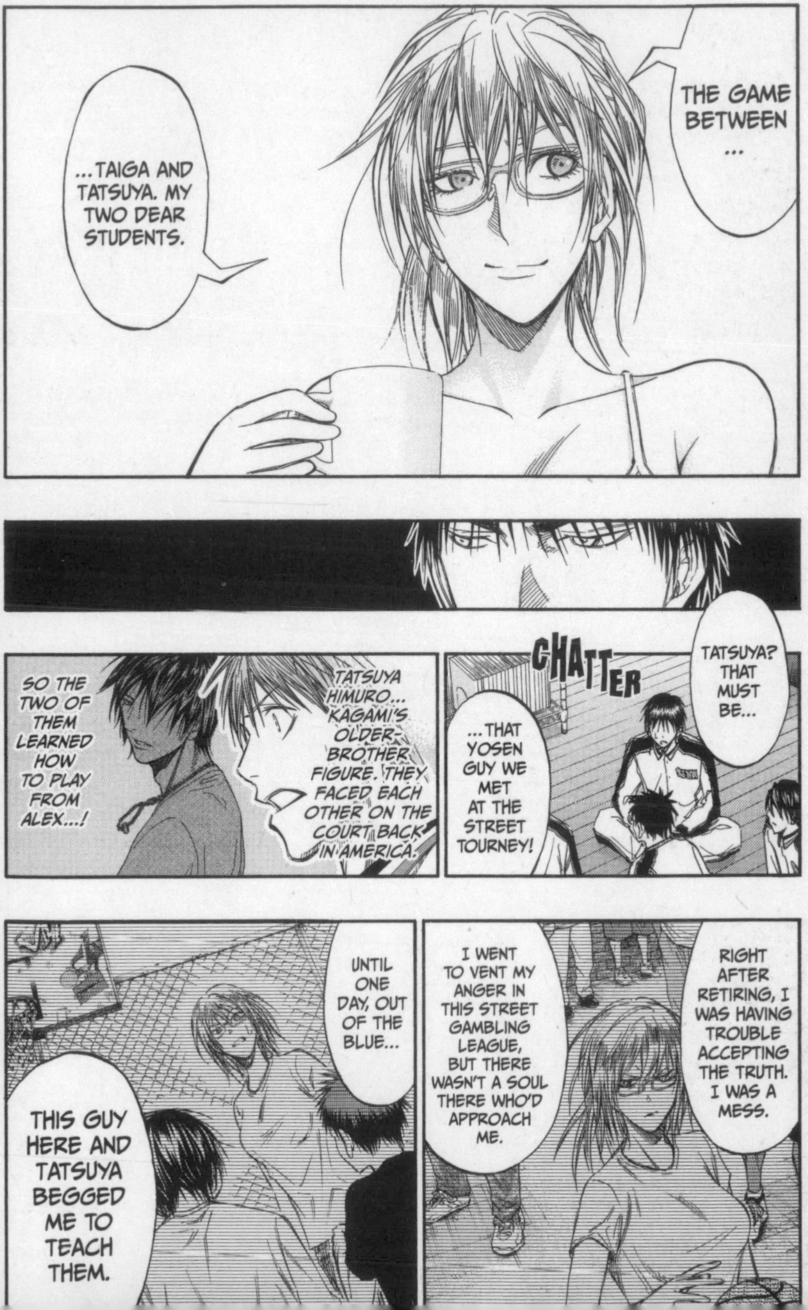
THE GAME BETWEEN ...
...TAIGA AND TATSUYA. MY TWO DEAR STUDENTS.
TATSUYA? THAT MUST BE...
CHATTER
...THAT YOSEN GUY WE MET AT THE STREET TOURNEY!
TATSUYA HIMURO... KAGAMI'S OLDER-BROTHER FIGURE. THEY FACED EACH OTHER ON THE COURT BACK IN AMERICA.
SO THE TWO OF THEM LEARNED HOW TO PLAY FROM ALEX...!
RIGHT AFTER RETIRING, I WAS HAVING TROUBLE ACCEPTING THE TRUTH. I WAS A MESS.
I WENT TO VENT MY ANGER IN THIS STREET GAMBLING LEAGUE, BUT THERE WASN'T A SOUL THERE WHO'D APPROACH ME.
UNTIL ONE DAY, OUT OF THE BLUE...
THIS GUY HERE AND TATSUYA BEGGED ME TO TEACH THEM.

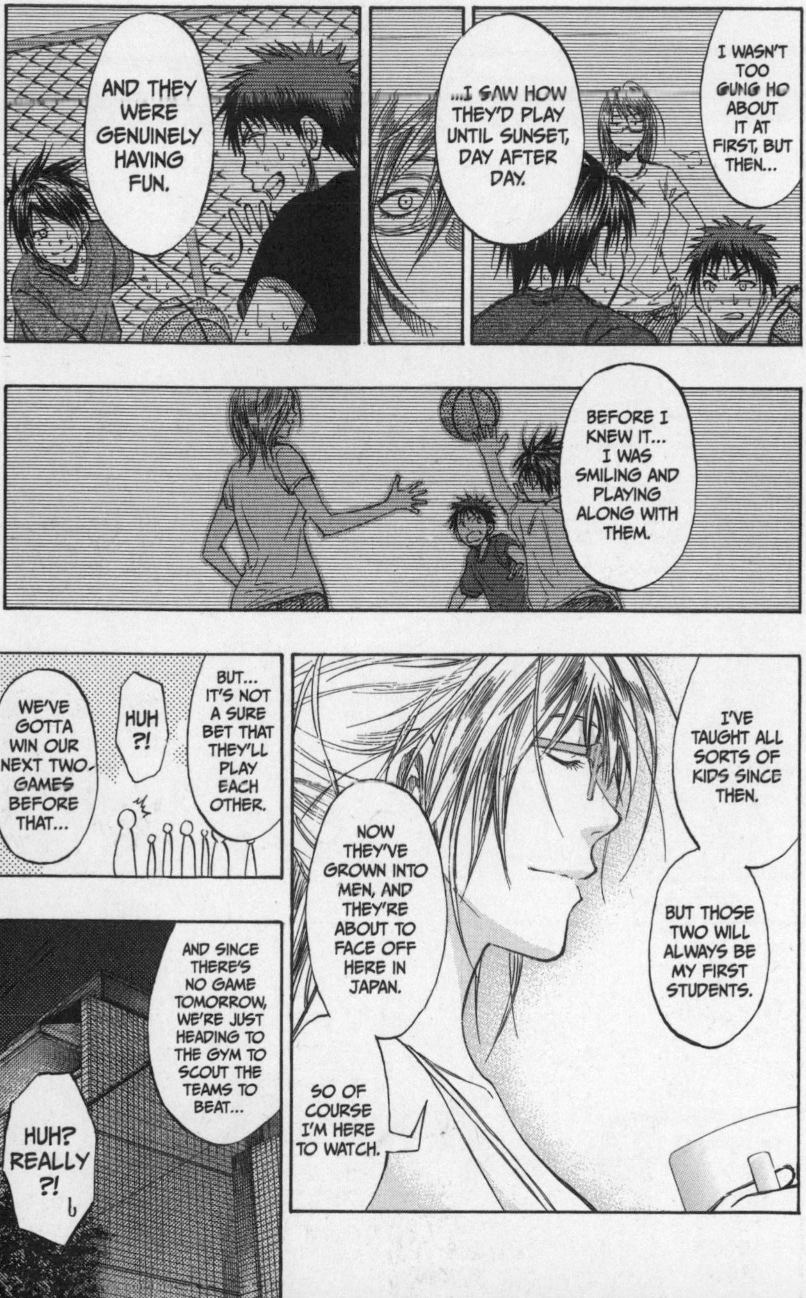
I WASN'T TOO GUNG HO ABOUT IT AT FIRST, BUT THEN...
...I SAW HOW THEY'D PLAY UNTIL SUNSET, DAY AFTER DAY.
AND THEY WERE GENUINELY HAVING FUN.
BEFORE I KNEW IT... I WAS SMILING AND PLAYING ALONG WITH THEM.
I'VE TAUGHT ALL SORTS OF KIDS SINCE THEN.
BUT THOSE TWO WILL ALWAYS BE MY FIRST STUDENTS.
NOW THEY'VE GROWN INTO MEN, AND THEY'RE ABOUT TO FACE OFF HERE IN JAPAN.
SO OF COURSE I'M HERE TO WATCH.
BUT... IT'S NOT A SURE BET THAT THEY'LL PLAY EACH OTHER.
HUH ?!
WE'VE GOTTA WIN OUR NEXT TWO GAMES BEFORE THAT...
AND SINCE THERE'S NO GAME TOMORROW, WE'RE JUST HEADING TO THE GYM TO SCOUT THE TEAMS TO BEAT...
HUH? REALLY ?!

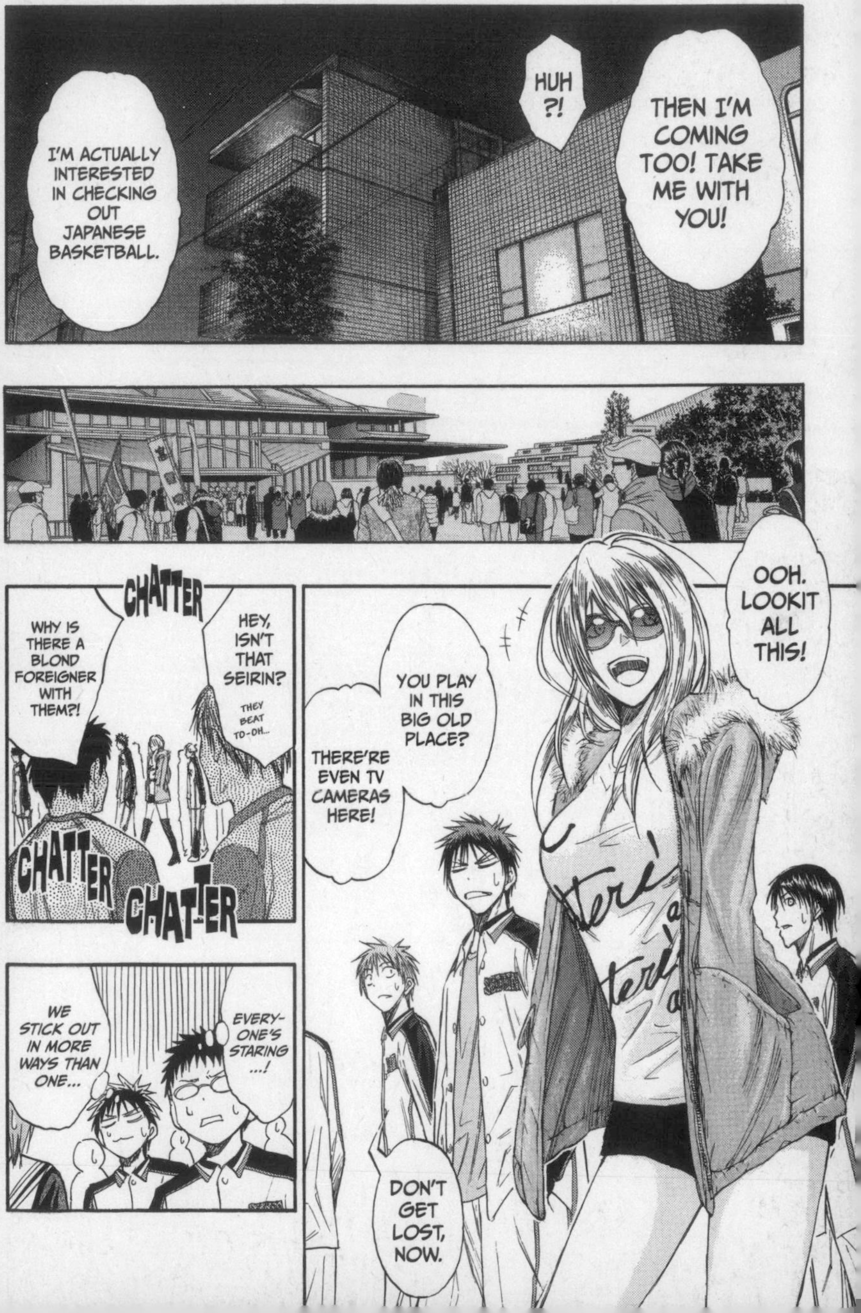
THEN I'M COMING TOO! TAKE ME WITH YOU!
HUH ?!
I'M ACTUALLY INTERESTED IN CHECKING OUT JAPANESE BASKETBALL.
OOH. LOOKIT ALL THIS!
YOU PLAY IN THIS BIG OLD PLACE?
THERE'RE EVEN TV CAMERAS HERE!
DON'T GET LOST, NOW.
CHATTER
HEY, ISN'T THAT SEIRIN?
THEY BEAT TO-OH...
WHY IS THERE A BLOND FOREIGNER WITH THEM?!
CHATTER
CHATTER
EVERY-ONE'S STARING ...!
WE STICK OUT IN MORE WAYS THAN ONE...

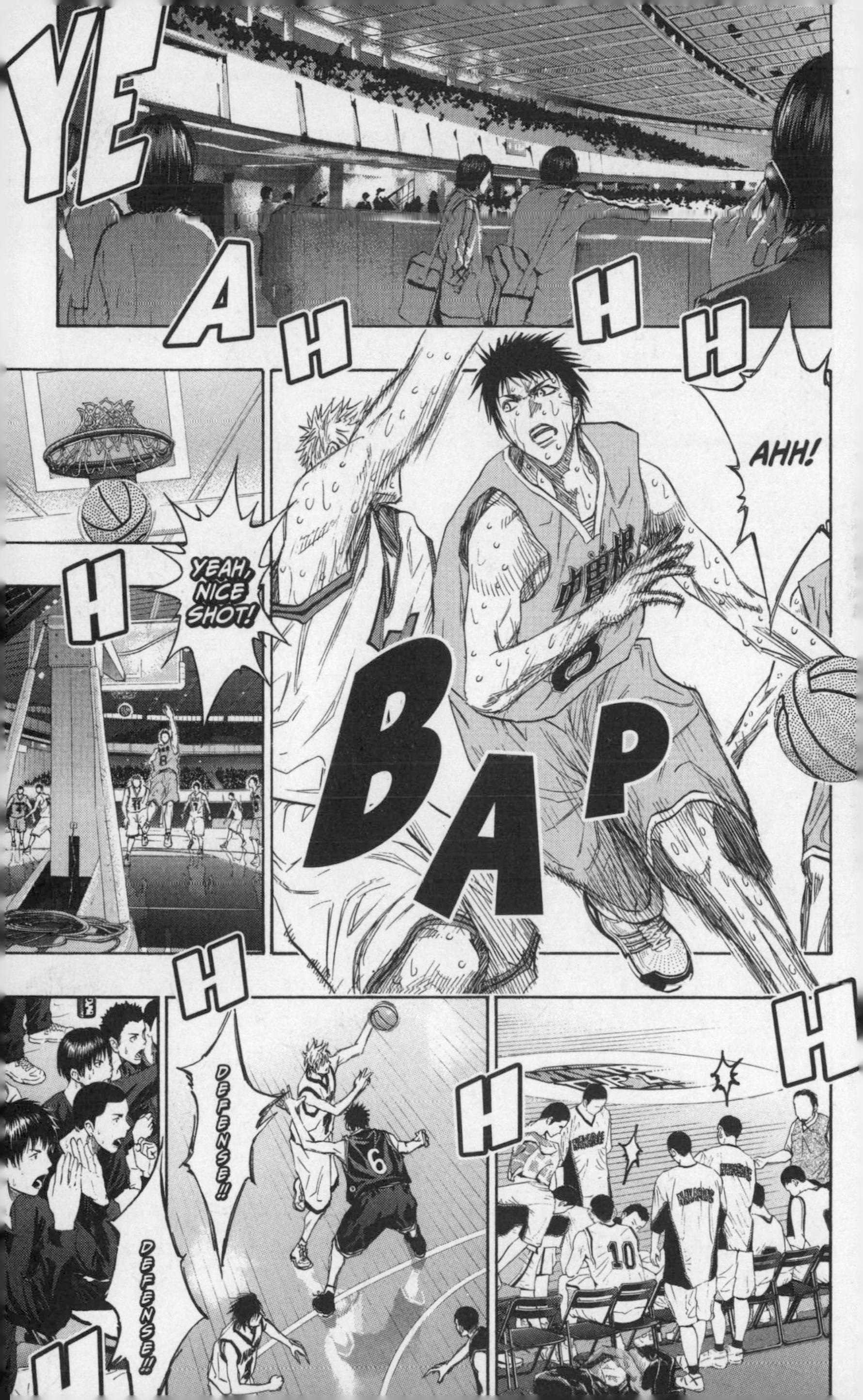
YEAHHHHHHHH
AHH!
BAP
YEAH, NICE SHOT!
DEFENSE!!
DEFENSE!!

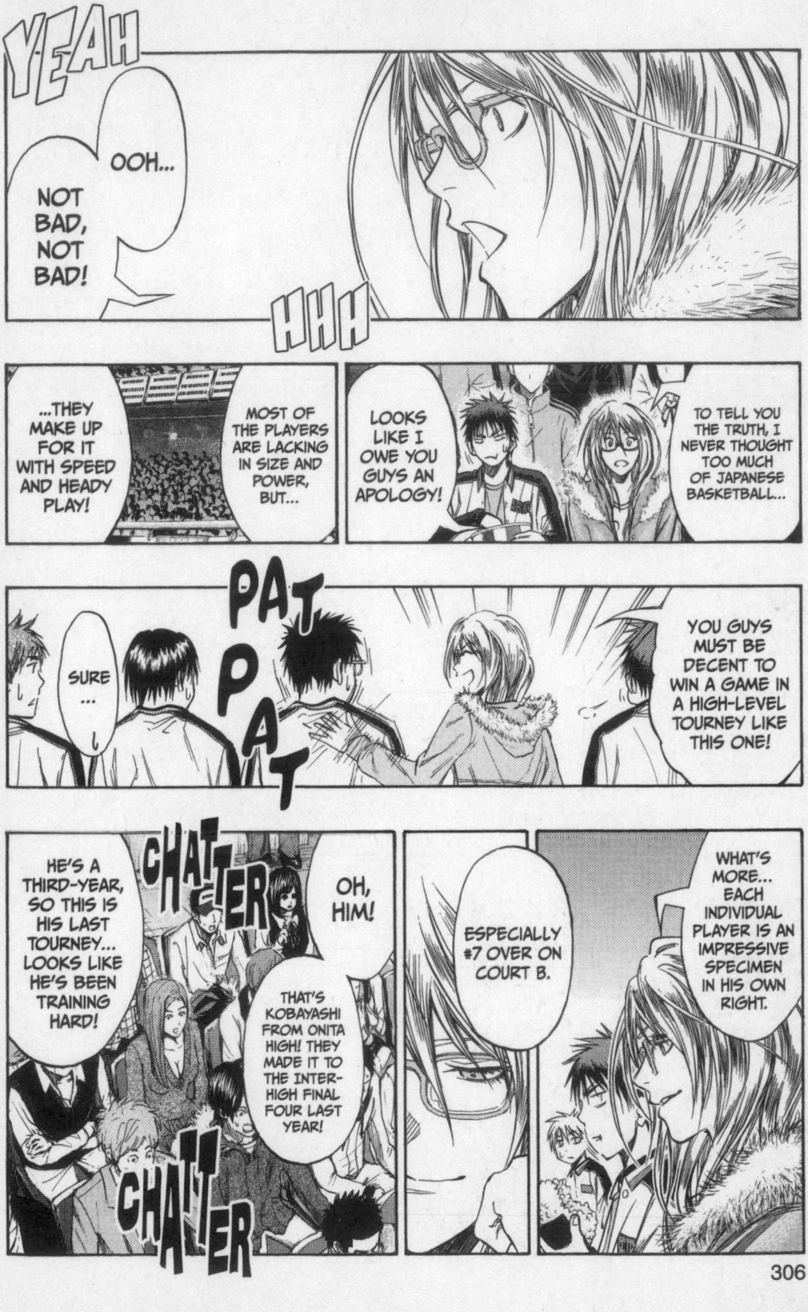
YEAH
OOH...
NOT BAD, NOT BAD!
HHH
TO TELL YOU THE TRUTH, I NEVER THOUGHT TOO MUCH OF JAPANESE BASKETBALL...
LOOKS LIKE I OWE YOU GUYS AN APOLOGY!
MOST OF THE PLAYERS ARE LACKING IN SIZE AND POWER, BUT...
...THEY MAKE UP FOR IT WITH SPEED AND HEADY PLAY!
YOU GUYS MUST BE DECENT TO WIN A GAME IN A HIGH-LEVEL TOURNEY LIKE THIS ONE!
PAT
PAT
PAT
SURE...
WHAT'S MORE... EACH INDIVIDUAL PLAYER IS AN IMPRESSIVE SPECIMEN IN HIS OWN RIGHT.
ESPECIALLY #7 OVER ON COURT B.
OH, HIM!
THAT'S KOBAYASHI FROM ONITA HIGH! THEY MADE IT TO THE INTER-HIGH FINAL FOUR LAST YEAR!
CHATTER
HE'S A THIRD-YEAR, SO THIS IS HIS LAST TOURNEY... LOOKS LIKE HE'S BEEN TRAINING HARD!
CHATTER

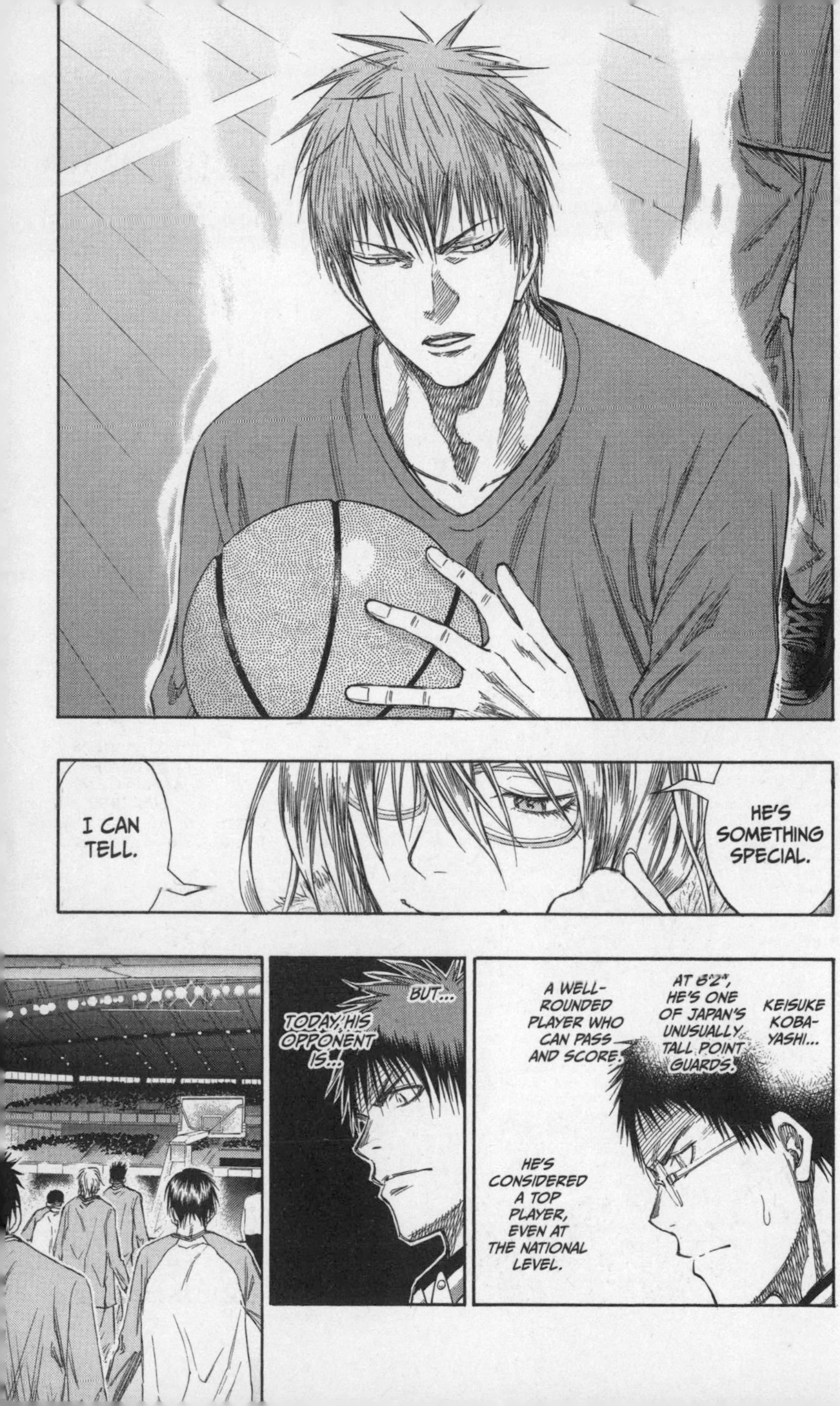
HE'S SOMETHING SPECIAL.
I CAN TELL.
KEISUKE KOBAYASHI...
AT 6'2", HE'S ONE OF JAPAN'S UNUSUALLY TALL POINT GUARDS.
A WELL-ROUNDED PLAYER WHO CAN PASS AND SCORE.
HE'S CONSIDERED A TOP PLAYER, EVEN AT THE NATIONAL LEVEL.
BUT...
TODAY, HIS OPPONENT IS...

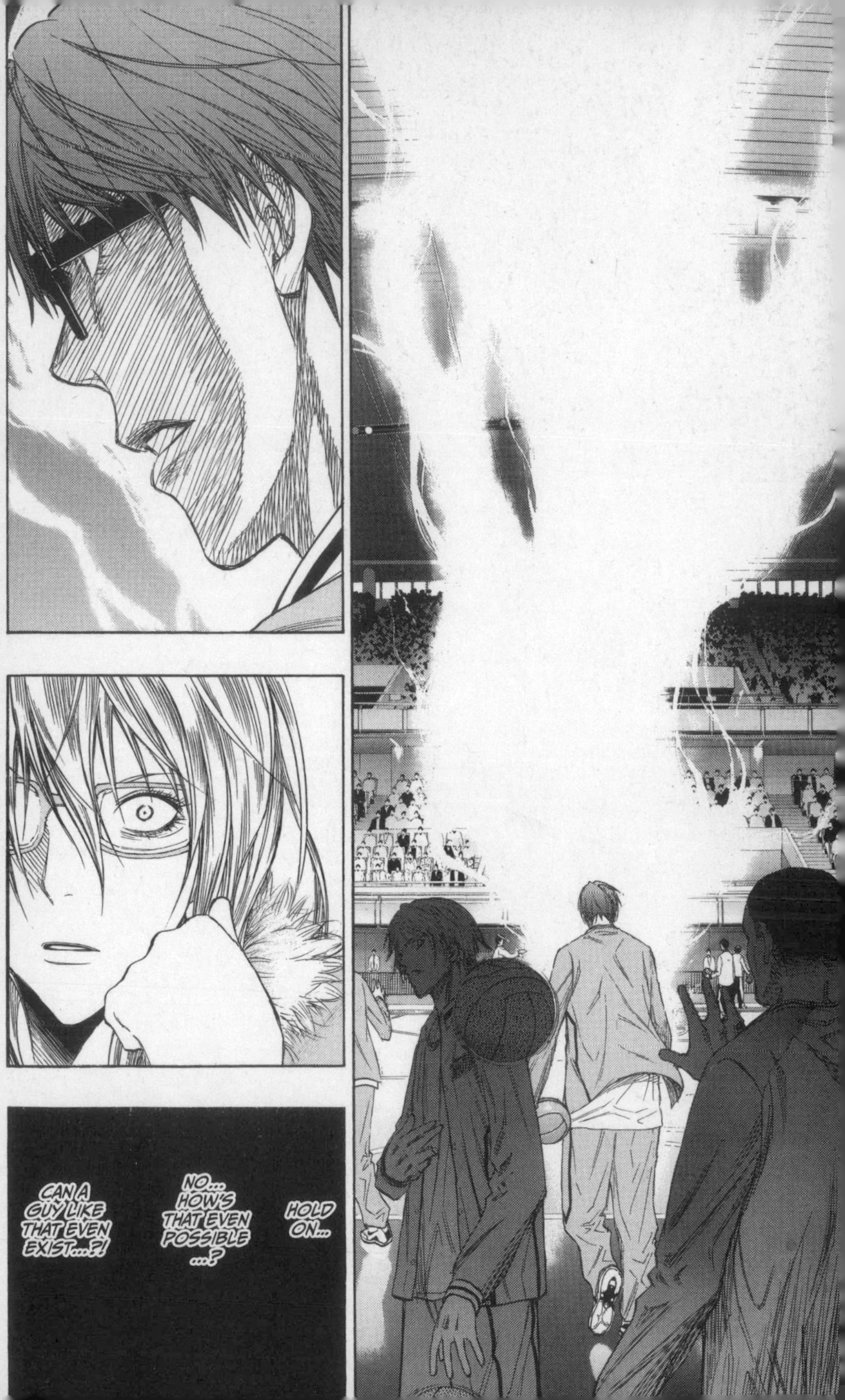
HOLD ON...
NO... HOW'S THAT EVEN POSSIBLE ...?
CAN A GUY LIKE THAT EVEN EXIST...?!

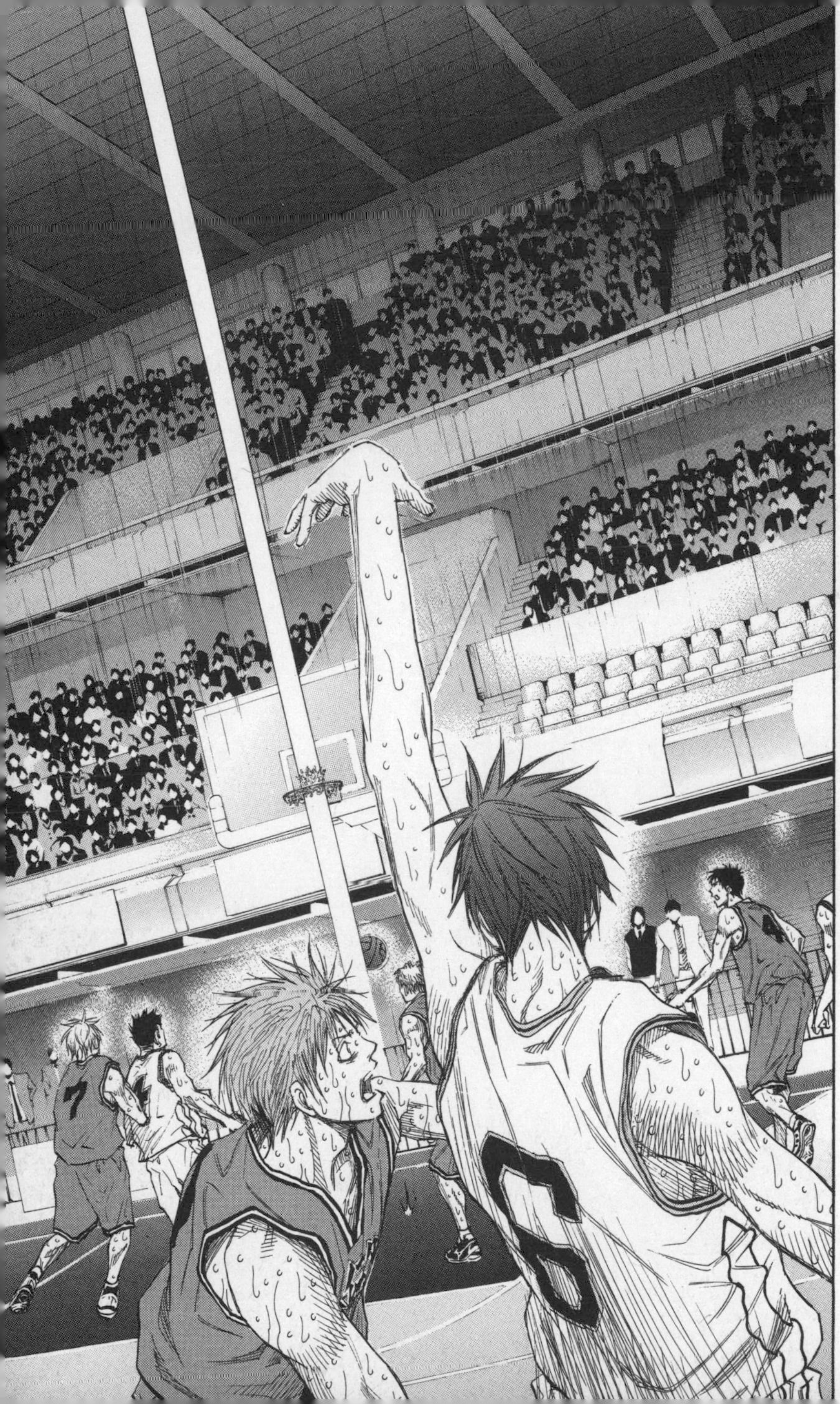

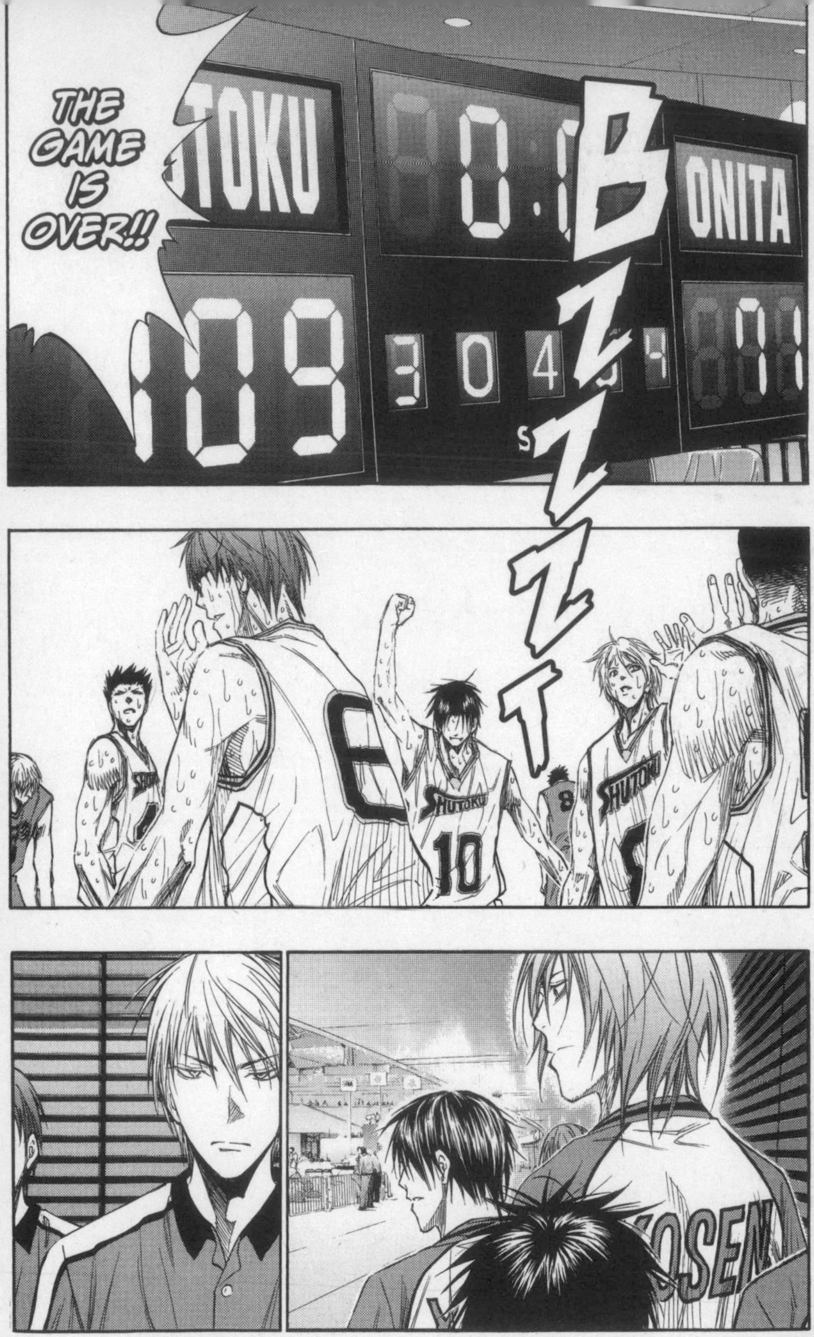
THE GAME IS OVER!!
BZZZZT
TOKU
ONITA
109
SHUTOKU
10
SHUTOKU
OSEN

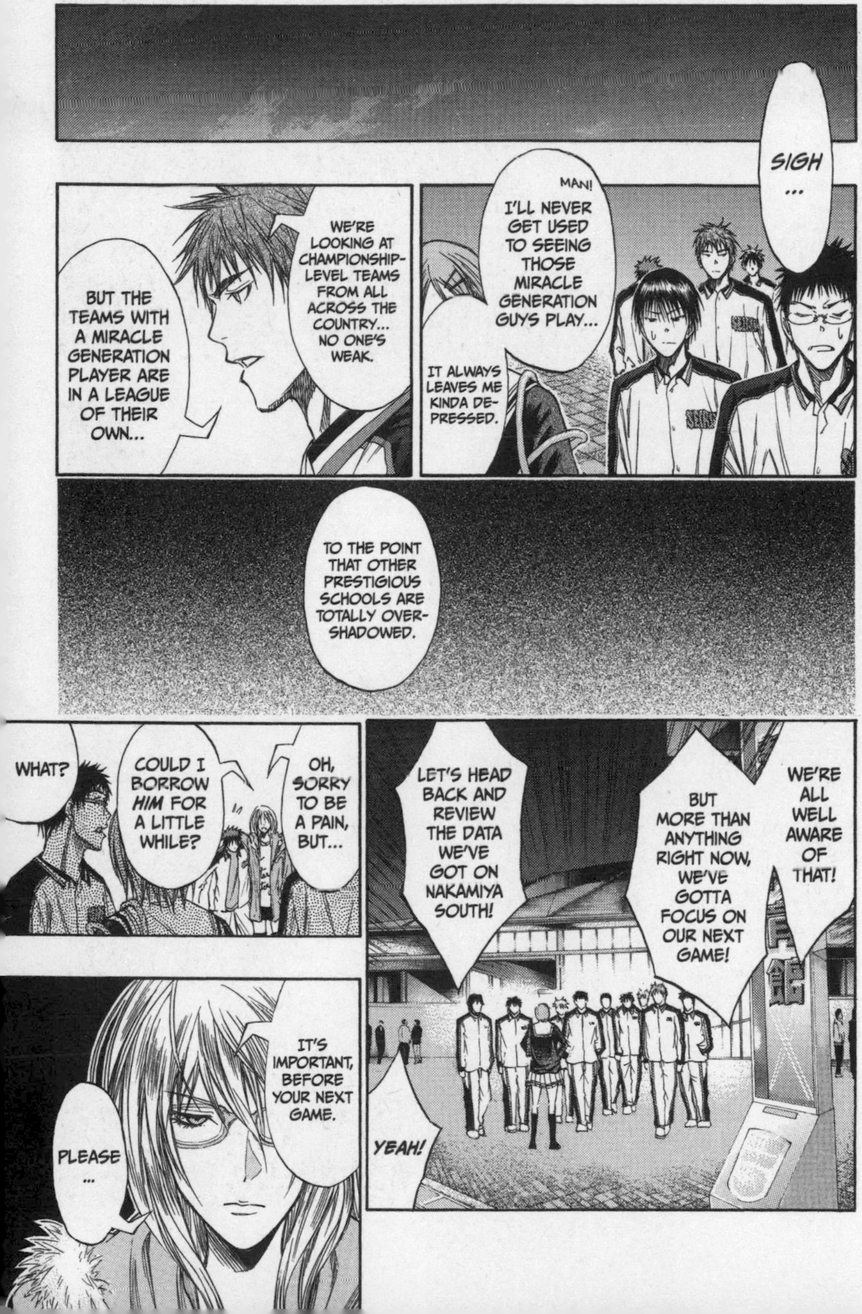
SIGH...
MAN! I'LL NEVER GET USED TO SEEING THOSE MIRACLE GENERATION GUYS PLAY...
IT ALWAYS LEAVES ME KINDA DE-PRESSED.
WE'RE LOOKING AT CHAMPIONSHIP-LEVEL TEAMS FROM ALL ACROSS THE COUNTRY... NO ONE'S WEAK.
BUT THE TEAMS WITH A MIRACLE GENERATION PLAYER ARE IN A LEAGUE OF THEIR OWN...
TO THE POINT THAT OTHER PRESTIGIOUS SCHOOLS ARE TOTALLY OVER-SHADOWED.
WE'RE ALL WELL AWARE OF THAT!
BUT MORE THAN ANYTHING RIGHT NOW, WE'VE GOTTA FOCUS ON OUR NEXT GAME!
LET'S HEAD BACK AND REVIEW THE DATA WE'VE GOT ON NAKAMIYA SOUTH!
YEAH!
OH, SORRY TO BE A PAIN, BUT...
COULD I BORROW *HIM* FOR A LITTLE WHILE?
WHAT?
IT'S IMPORTANT, BEFORE YOUR NEXT GAME.
PLEASE...

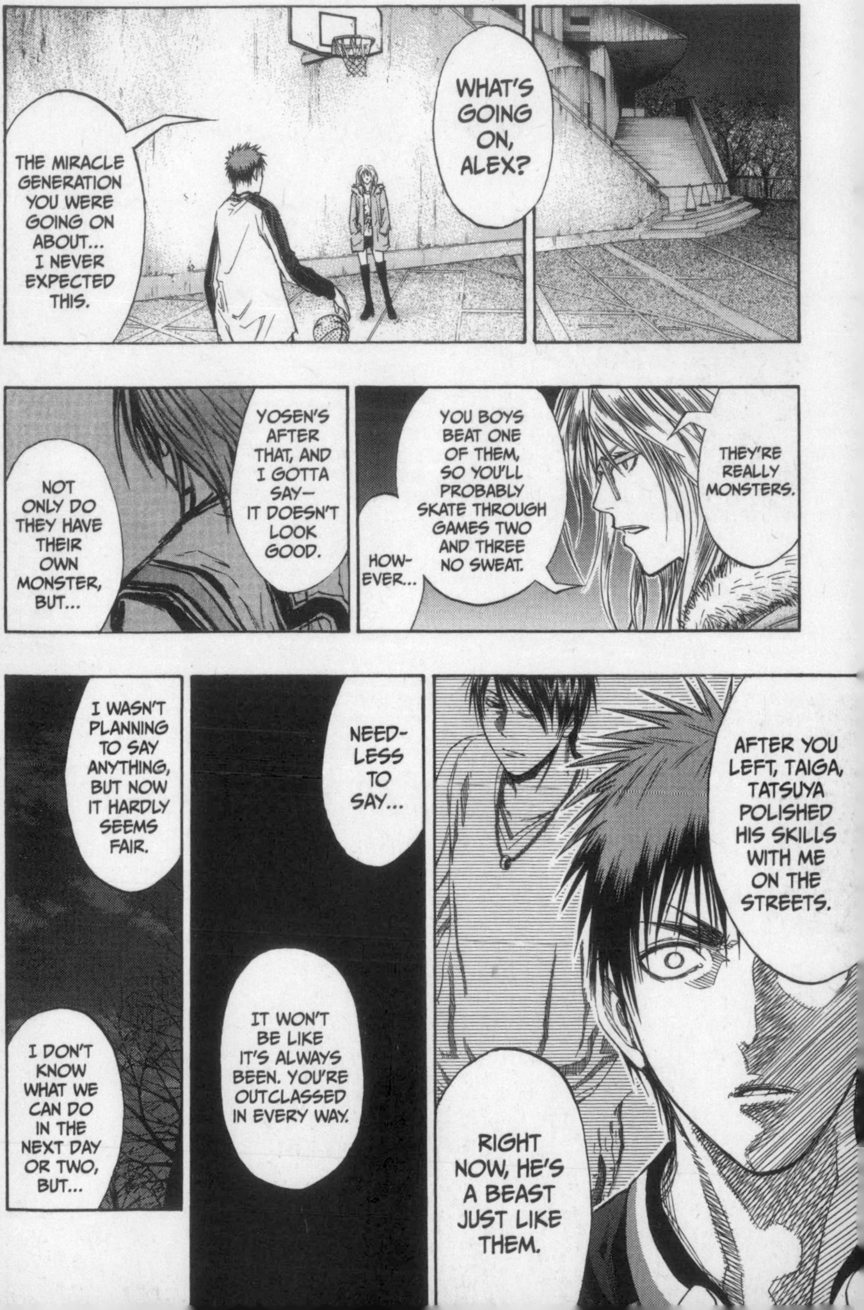
WHAT'S GOING ON, ALEX?
THE MIRACLE GENERATION YOU WERE GOING ON ABOUT... I NEVER EXPECTED THIS.
THEY'RE REALLY MONSTERS.
YOU BOYS BEAT ONE OF THEM, SO YOU'LL PROBABLY SKATE THROUGH GAMES TWO AND THREE NO SWEAT.
HOW-EVER...
YOSEN'S AFTER THAT, AND I GOTTA SAY— IT DOESN'T LOOK GOOD.
NOT ONLY DO THEY HAVE THEIR OWN MONSTER, BUT...
AFTER YOU LEFT, TAIGA, TATSUYA POLISHED HIS SKILLS WITH ME ON THE STREETS.
RIGHT NOW, HE'S A BEAST JUST LIKE THEM.
NEED-LESS TO SAY...
IT WON'T BE LIKE IT'S ALWAYS BEEN. YOU'RE OUTCLASSED IN EVERY WAY.
I WASN'T PLANNING TO SAY ANYTHING, BUT NOW IT HARDLY SEEMS FAIR.
I DON'T KNOW WHAT WE CAN DO IN THE NEXT DAY OR TWO, BUT...

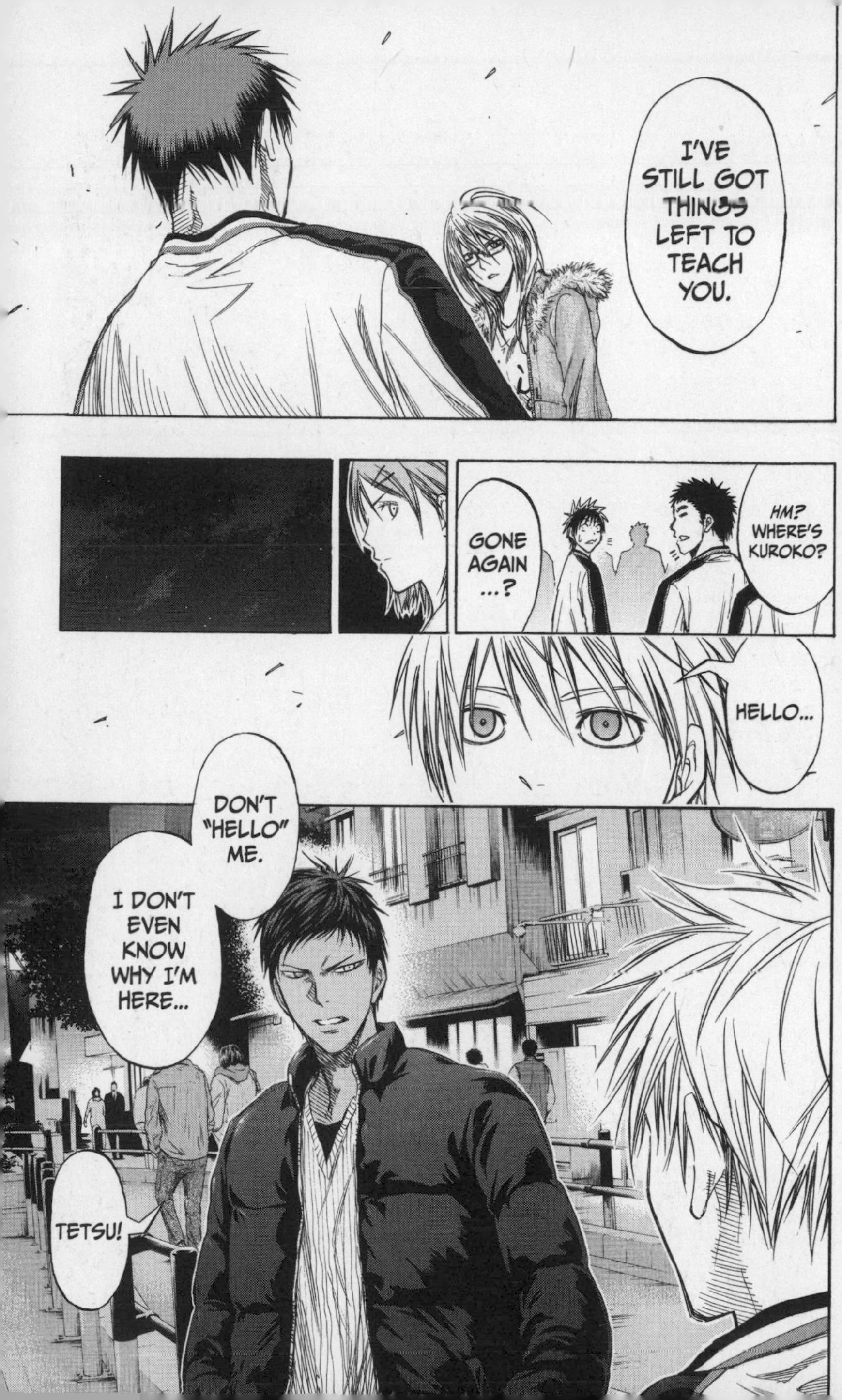
I'VE STILL GOT THINGS LEFT TO TEACH YOU.
HM? WHERE'S KUROKO?
GONE AGAIN ...?
HELLO...
DON'T "HELLO" ME.
I DON'T EVEN KNOW WHY I'M HERE...
TETSU!

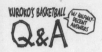

KUROKO'S BASKETBALL Q&A (W/ HALFWAY-DECENT ANSWERS)

Q. DOES RIKO HAVE ANY FRIENDS WHO ARE GIRLS?
(CONGRATS ON THE ANIME!! from CHIBA PREFECTURE)

A. I DON'T PORTRAY THEM THAT OFTEN, BUT YES, OF COURSE SHE DOES. NOT TOO MANY, THOUGH.

KUROKO'S BASKETBALL BLOOPERS TAKE 7

HOLD ON...
NO... HOW'S THAT EVEN POSSI-BLE...?
THAT STEAM IS CRAZY...
HUH ?!
THAT'S STEAM ?!
WRONG!!

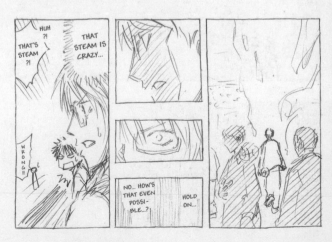

142ND QUARTER: PLEASE TEACH ME

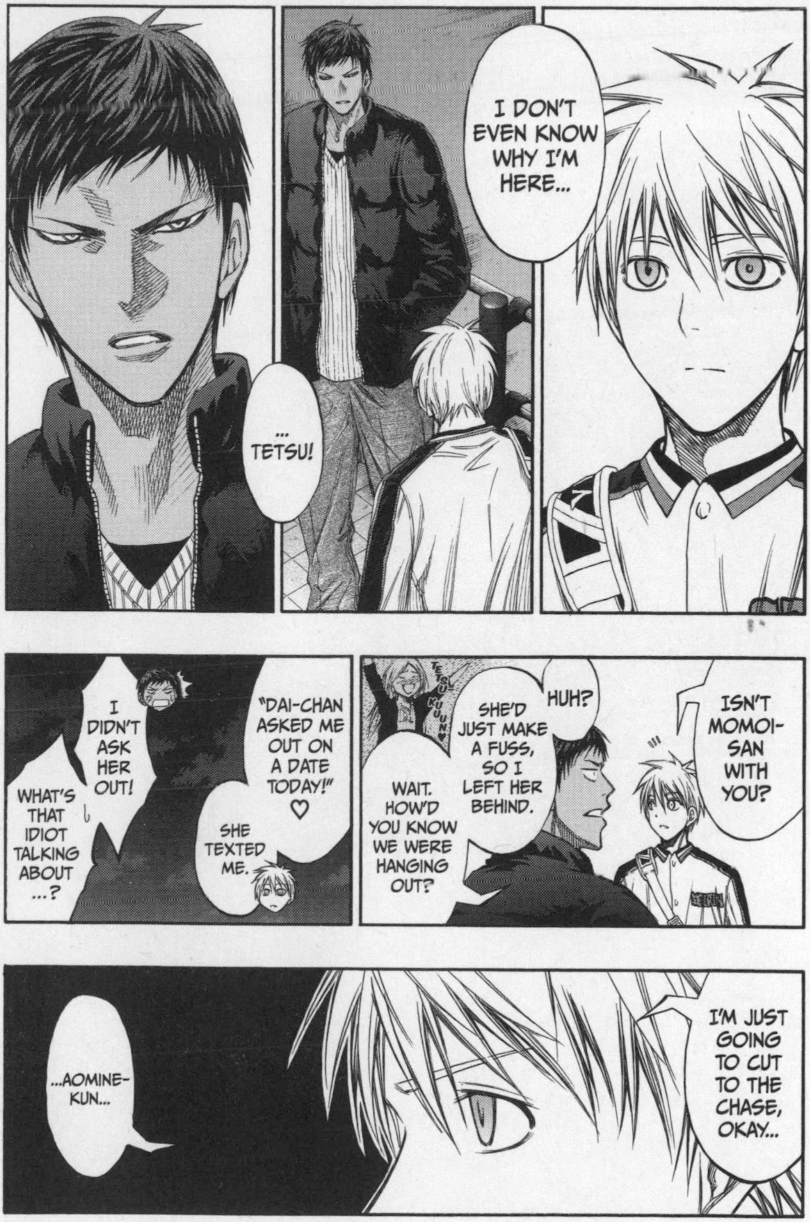
I DON'T EVEN KNOW WHY I'M HERE...
... TETSU!
ISN'T MOMOI-SAN WITH YOU?
HUH?
SHE'D JUST MAKE A FUSS, SO I LEFT HER BEHIND.
WAIT. HOW'D YOU KNOW WE WERE HANGING OUT?
TETSU KUUUN♥
"DAI-CHAN ASKED ME OUT ON A DATE TODAY!" ♡
SHE TEXTED ME.
I DIDN'T ASK HER OUT!
WHAT'S THAT IDIOT TALKING ABOUT ...?
I'M JUST GOING TO CUT TO THE CHASE, OKAY...
...AOMINE-KUN...

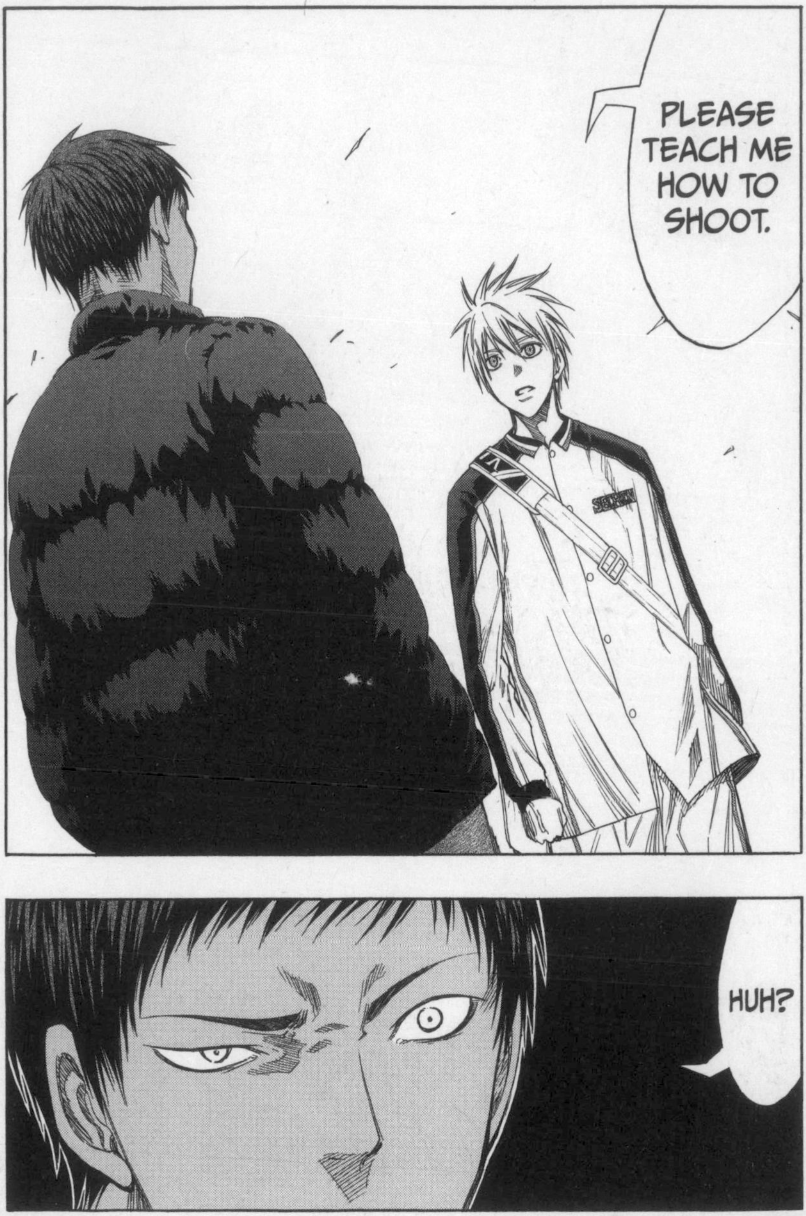
PLEASE TEACH ME HOW TO SHOOT.
HUH?

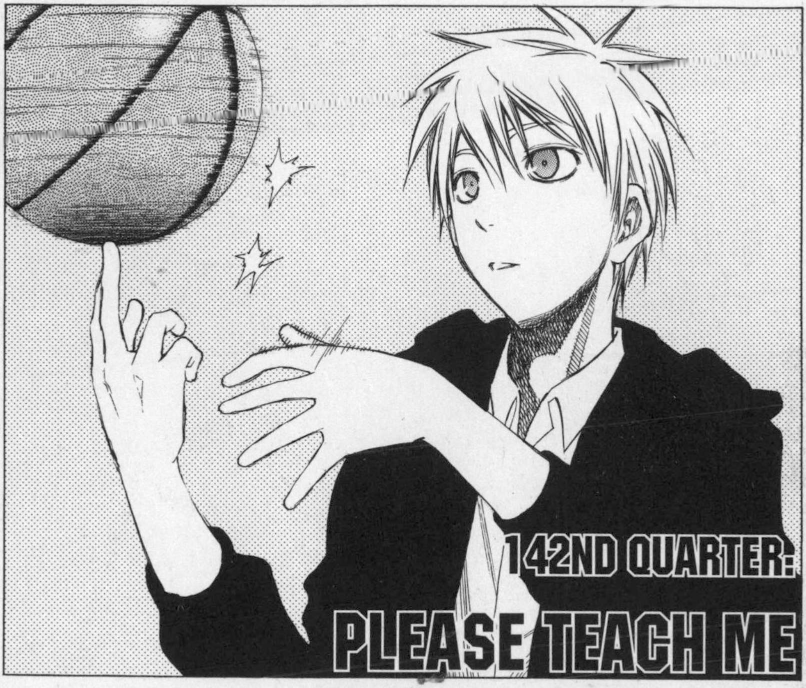
142ND QUARTER:
PLEASE TEACH ME

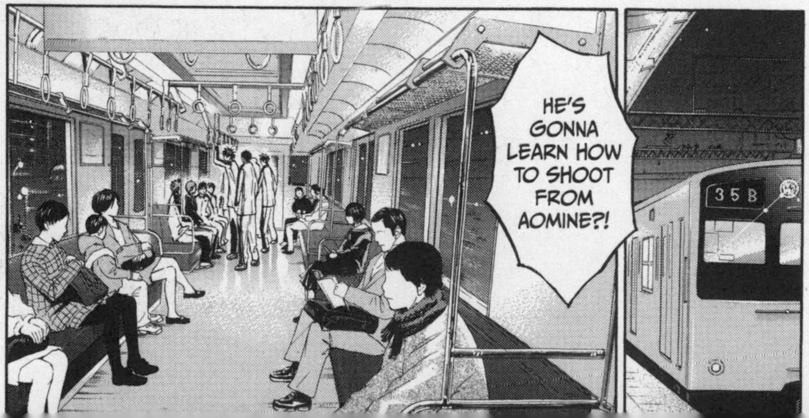
35 B
HE'S GONNA LEARN HOW TO SHOOT FROM AOMINE?!

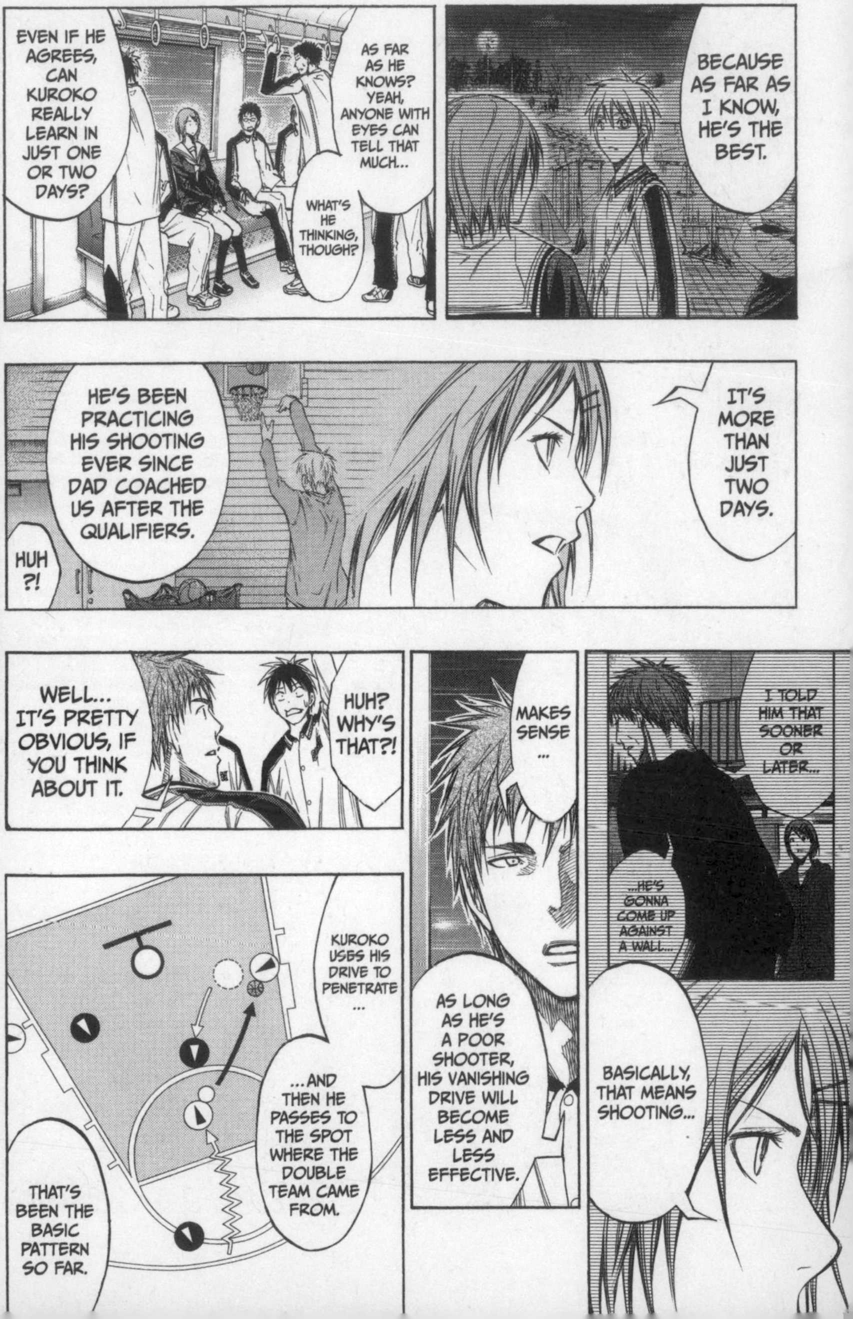
BECAUSE AS FAR AS I KNOW, HE'S THE BEST.
AS FAR AS HE KNOWS? YEAH, ANYONE WITH EYES CAN TELL THAT MUCH...
WHAT'S HE THINKING, THOUGH?
EVEN IF HE AGREES, CAN KUROKO REALLY LEARN IN JUST ONE OR TWO DAYS?
IT'S MORE THAN JUST TWO DAYS.
HE'S BEEN PRACTICING HIS SHOOTING EVER SINCE DAD COACHED US AFTER THE QUALIFIERS.
HUH ?!
I TOLD HIM THAT SOONER OR LATER...
...HE'S GONNA COME UP AGAINST A WALL...
BASICALLY, THAT MEANS SHOOTING...
MAKES SENSE ...
AS LONG AS HE'S A POOR SHOOTER, HIS VANISHING DRIVE WILL BECOME LESS AND LESS EFFECTIVE.
HUH? WHY'S THAT?!
WELL... IT'S PRETTY OBVIOUS, IF YOU THINK ABOUT IT.
KUROKO USES HIS DRIVE TO PENETRATE ...
...AND THEN HE PASSES TO THE SPOT WHERE THE DOUBLE TEAM CAME FROM.
THAT'S BEEN THE BASIC PATTERN SO FAR.

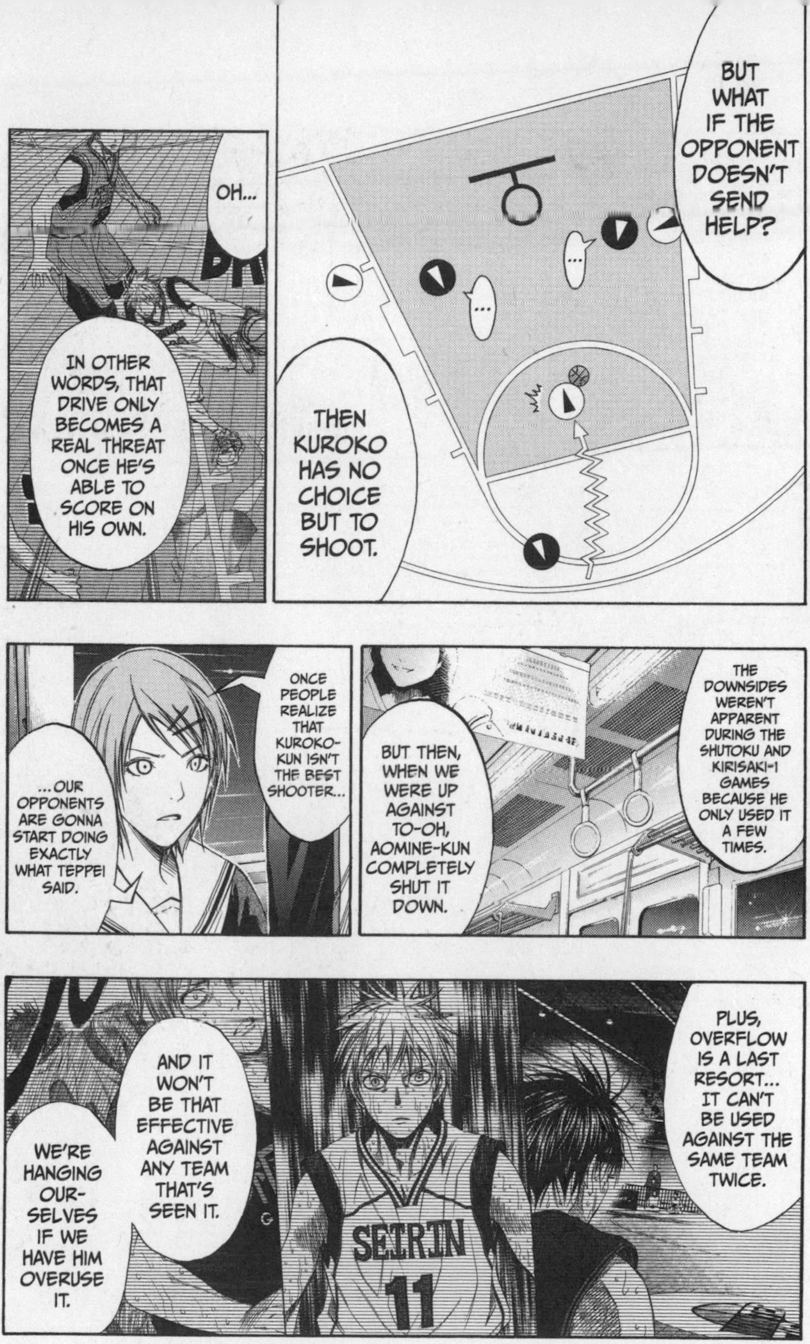
BUT WHAT IF THE OPPONENT DOESN'T SEND HELP?
...
...
THEN KUROKO HAS NO CHOICE BUT TO SHOOT.
OH...
IN OTHER WORDS, THAT DRIVE ONLY BECOMES A REAL THREAT ONCE HE'S ABLE TO SCORE ON HIS OWN.
THE DOWNSIDES WEREN'T APPARENT DURING THE SHUTOKU AND KIRISAKI-1 GAMES BECAUSE HE ONLY USED IT A FEW TIMES.
BUT THEN, WHEN WE WERE UP AGAINST TO-OH, AOMINE-KUN COMPLETELY SHUT IT DOWN.
ONCE PEOPLE REALIZE THAT KUROKO-KUN ISN'T THE BEST SHOOTER...
...OUR OPPONENTS ARE GONNA START DOING EXACTLY WHAT TEPPEI SAID.
PLUS, OVERFLOW IS A LAST RESORT... IT CAN'T BE USED AGAINST THE SAME TEAM TWICE.
AND IT WON'T BE THAT EFFECTIVE AGAINST ANY TEAM THAT'S SEEN IT.
WE'RE HANGING OUR-SELVES IF WE HAVE HIM OVERUSE IT.
SEIRIN
11

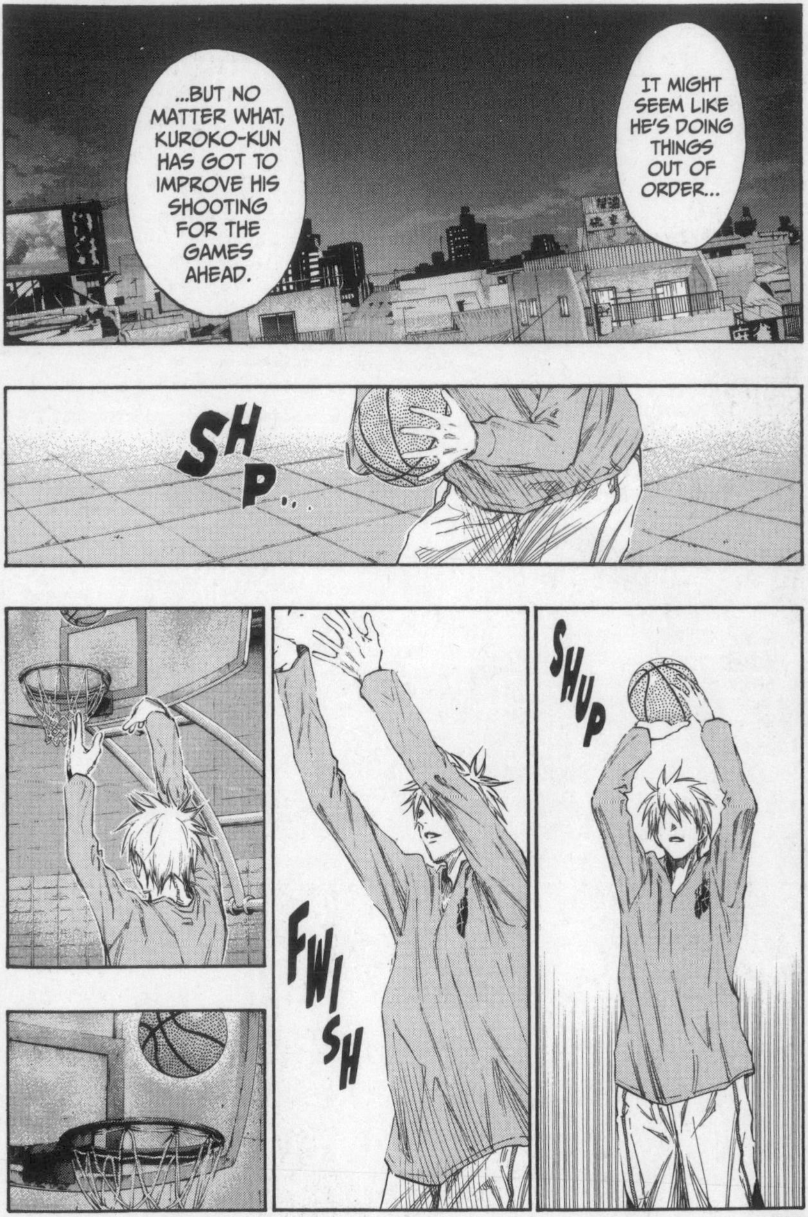
IT MIGHT SEEM LIKE HE'S DOING THINGS OUT OF ORDER...
...BUT NO MATTER WHAT, KUROKO-KUN HAS GOT TO IMPROVE HIS SHOOTING FOR THE GAMES AHEAD.
SHP...
SHUP
FWISH

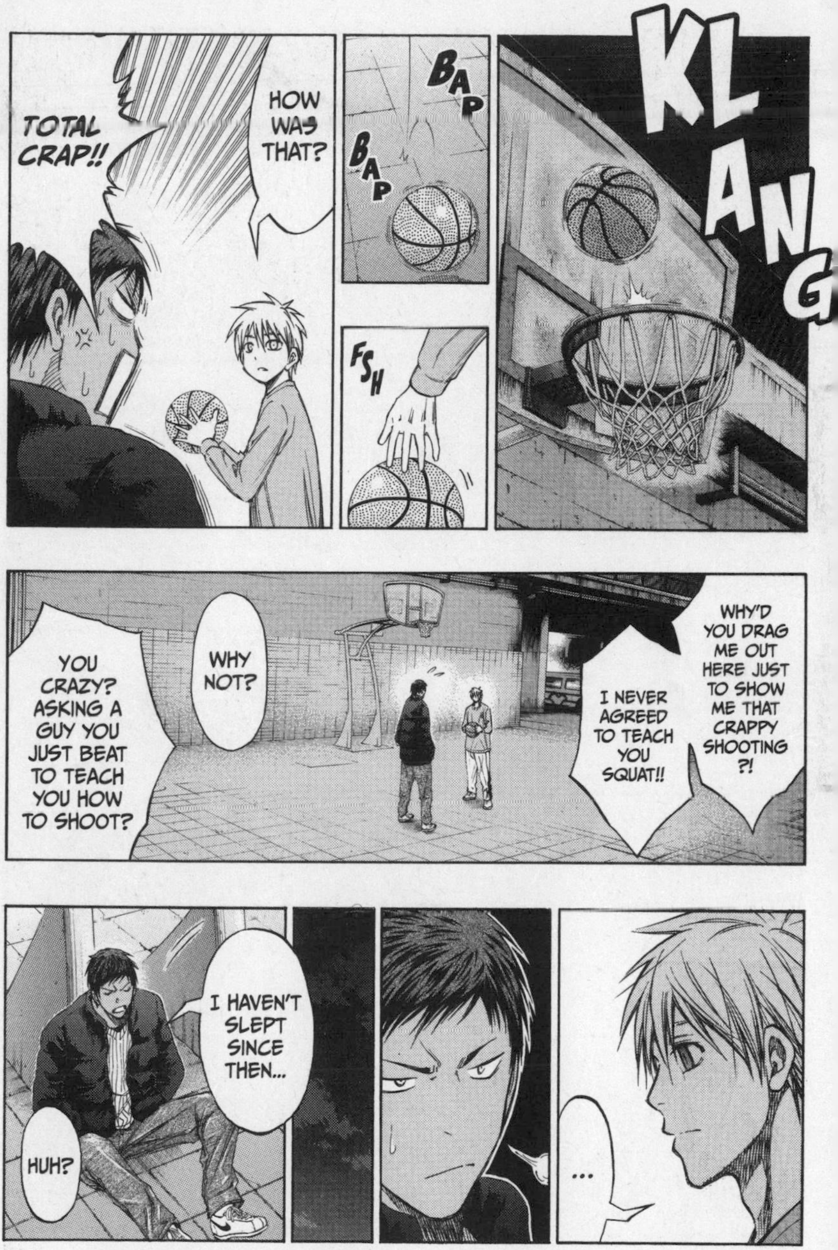
KLANG
BAP
BAP
FSH
HOW WAS THAT?
TOTAL CRAP!!
WHY'D YOU DRAG ME OUT HERE JUST TO SHOW ME THAT CRAPPY SHOOTING?!
I NEVER AGREED TO TEACH YOU SQUAT!!
WHY NOT?
YOU CRAZY? ASKING A GUY YOU JUST BEAT TO TEACH YOU HOW TO SHOOT?
...
I HAVEN'T SLEPT SINCE THEN...
HUH?

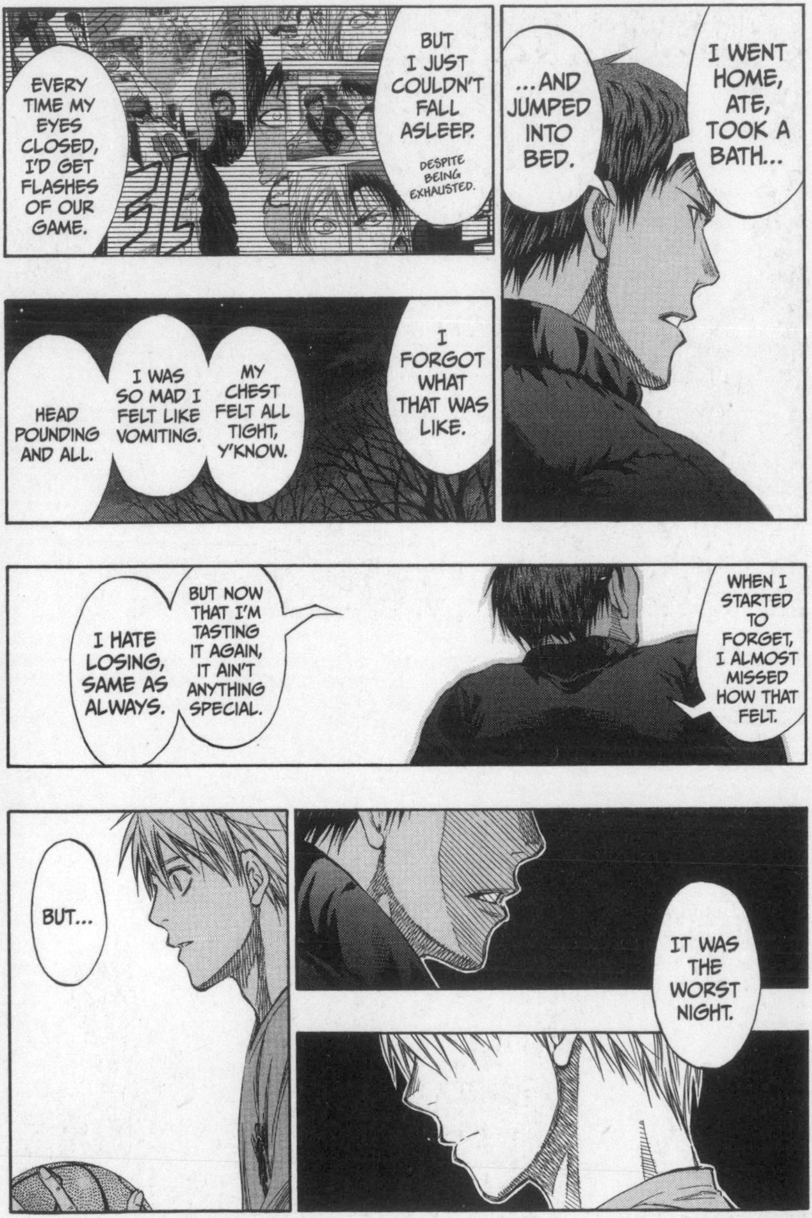
I WENT HOME, ATE, TOOK A BATH...
...AND JUMPED INTO BED.
BUT I JUST COULDN'T FALL ASLEEP.
DESPITE BEING EXHAUSTED.
EVERY TIME MY EYES CLOSED, I'D GET FLASHES OF OUR GAME.
I FORGOT WHAT THAT WAS LIKE.
MY CHEST FELT ALL TIGHT, Y'KNOW.
I WAS SO MAD I FELT LIKE VOMITING.
HEAD POUNDING AND ALL.
WHEN I STARTED TO FORGET, I ALMOST MISSED HOW THAT FELT.
BUT NOW THAT I'M TASTING IT AGAIN, IT AIN'T ANYTHING SPECIAL.
I HATE LOSING, SAME AS ALWAYS.
IT WAS THE WORST NIGHT.
BUT...

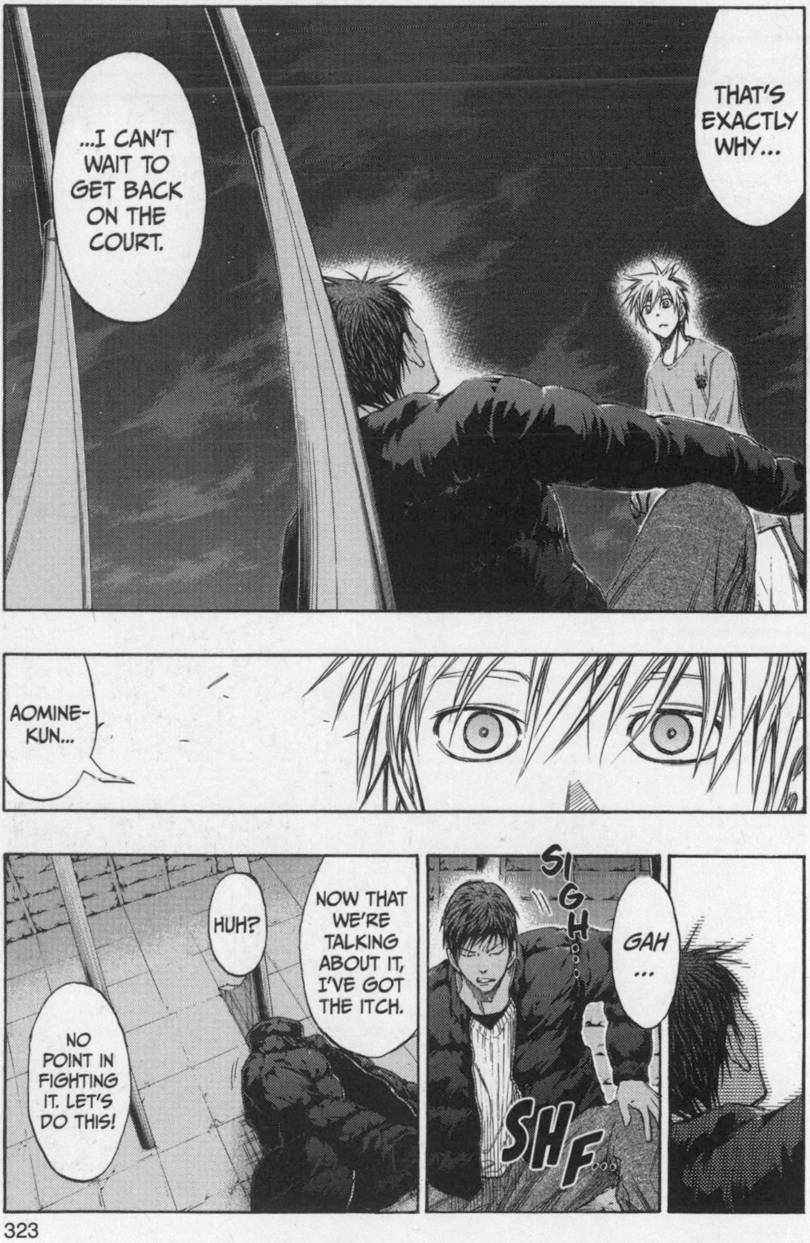
THAT'S EXACTLY WHY...
...I CAN'T WAIT TO GET BACK ON THE COURT.
AOMINE-KUN...
GAH...
SIGH...
SHF...
NOW THAT WE'RE TALKING ABOUT IT, I'VE GOT THE ITCH.
HUH?
NO POINT IN FIGHTING IT. LET'S DO THIS!

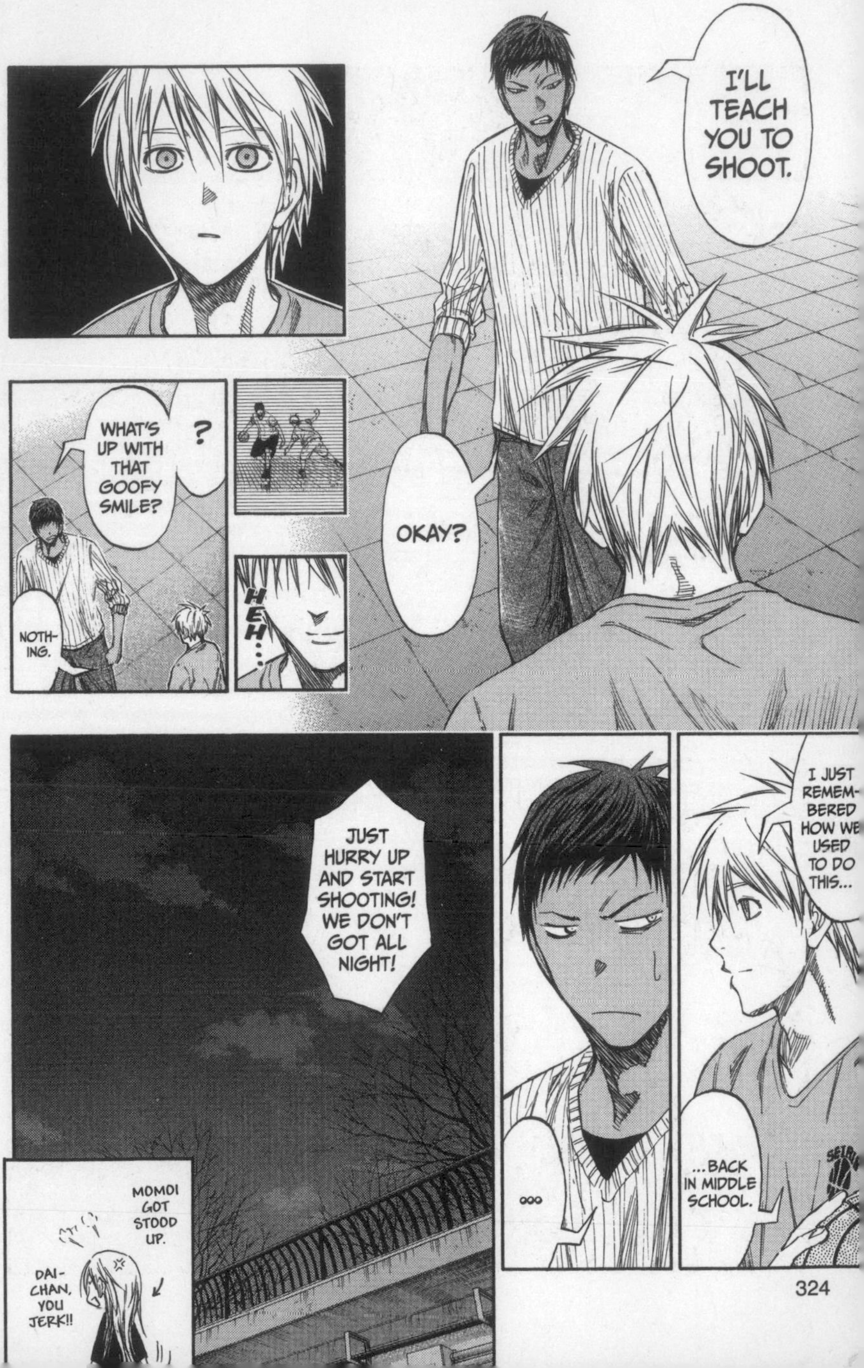
I'LL TEACH YOU TO SHOOT.
OKAY?
HEH...
?
WHAT'S UP WITH THAT GOOFY SMILE?
NOTHING.
I JUST REMEMBERED HOW WE USED TO DO THIS...
...BACK IN MIDDLE SCHOOL.
...
JUST HURRY UP AND START SHOOTING! WE DON'T GOT ALL NIGHT!
MOMOI GOT STOOD UP.
DAI-CHAN, YOU JERK!!

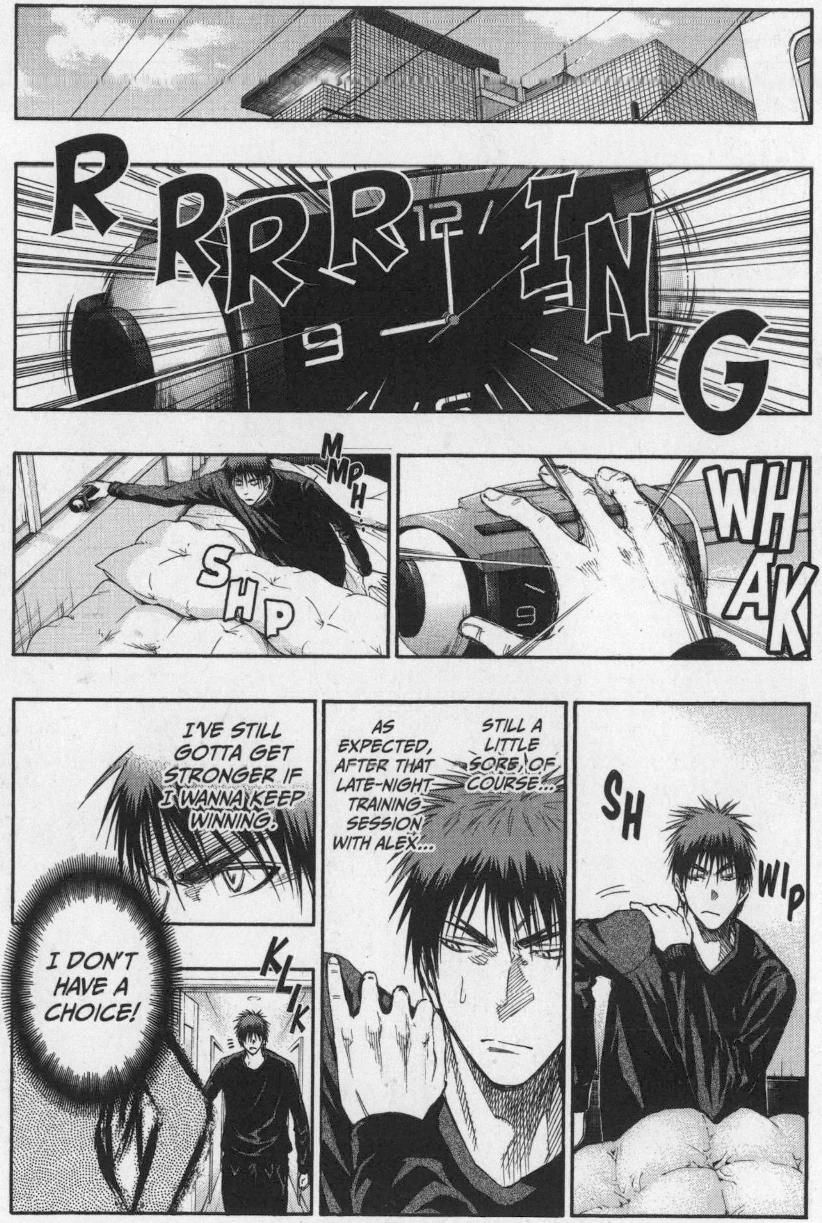
RRRRRING
WHAK
MMPH
SHP
SH WIP
STILL A LITTLE SORE, OF COURSE...
AS EXPECTED, AFTER THAT LATE-NIGHT TRAINING SESSION WITH ALEX...
I'VE STILL GOTTA GET STRONGER IF I WANNA KEEP WINNING.
KLIK
I DON'T HAVE A CHOICE!

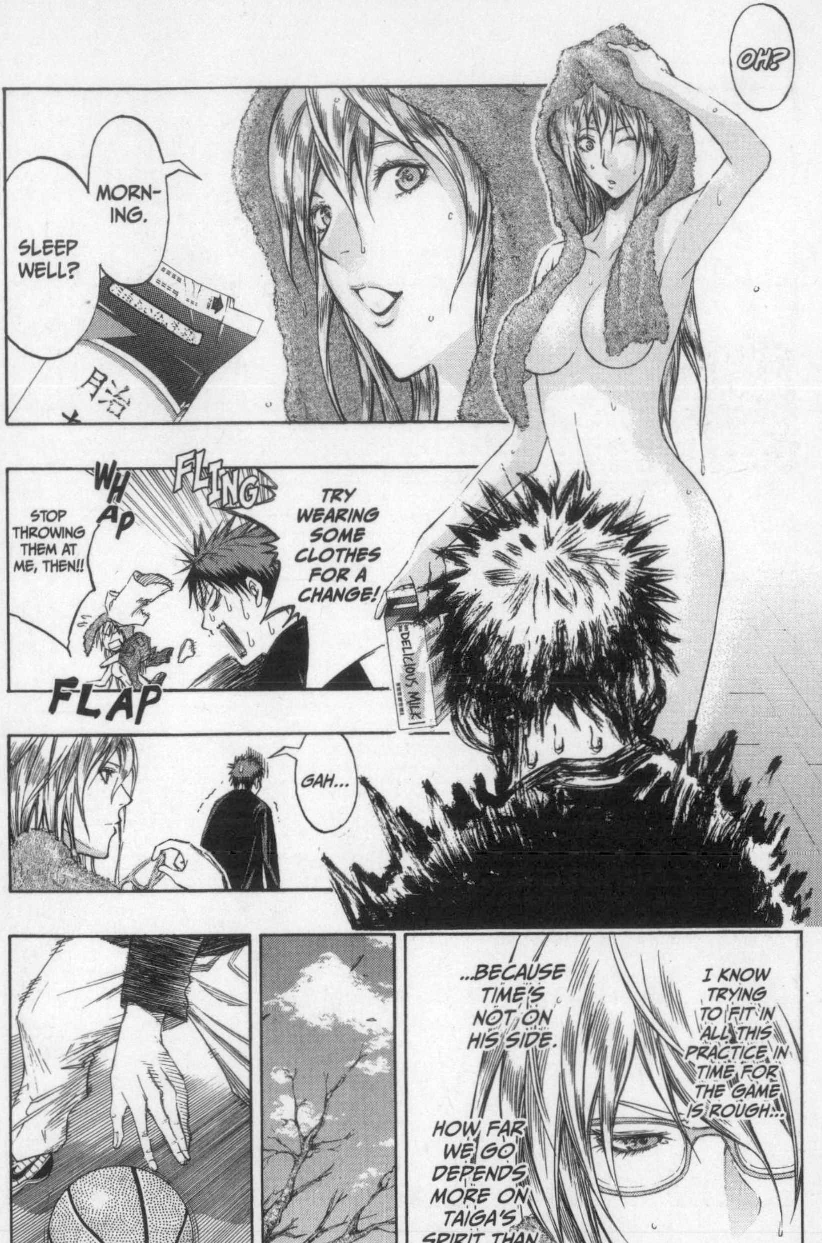
OH?
MORNING. SLEEP WELL?
FLING
TRY WEARING SOME CLOTHES FOR A CHANGE!
WHAP
STOP THROWING THEM AT ME, THEN!!
FLAP
DELICIOUS MILK
GAH...
I KNOW TRYING TO FIT IN ALL THIS PRACTICE IN TIME FOR THE GAME IS ROUGH...
...BECAUSE TIME'S NOT ON HIS SIDE.
HOW FAR WE GO DEPENDS MORE ON TAIGA'S SPIRIT THAN HIS STAMINA.

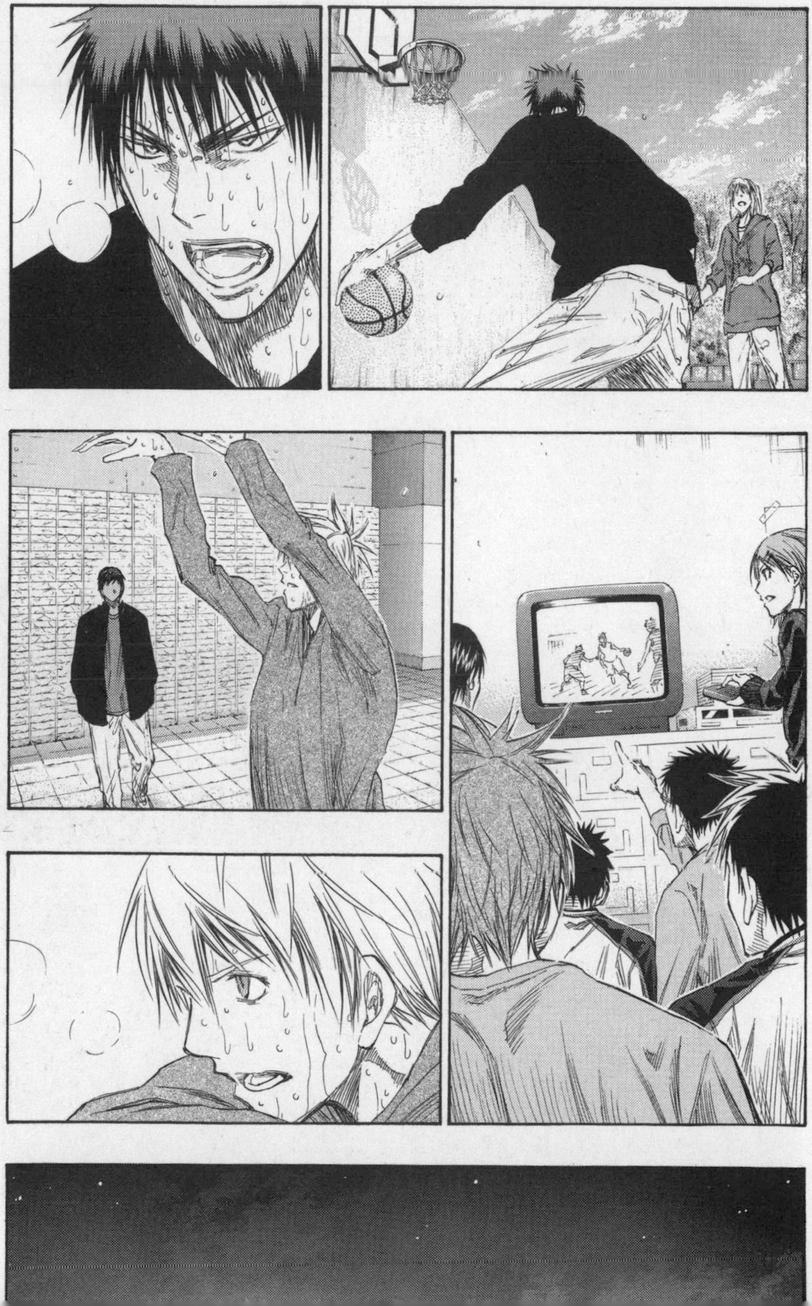

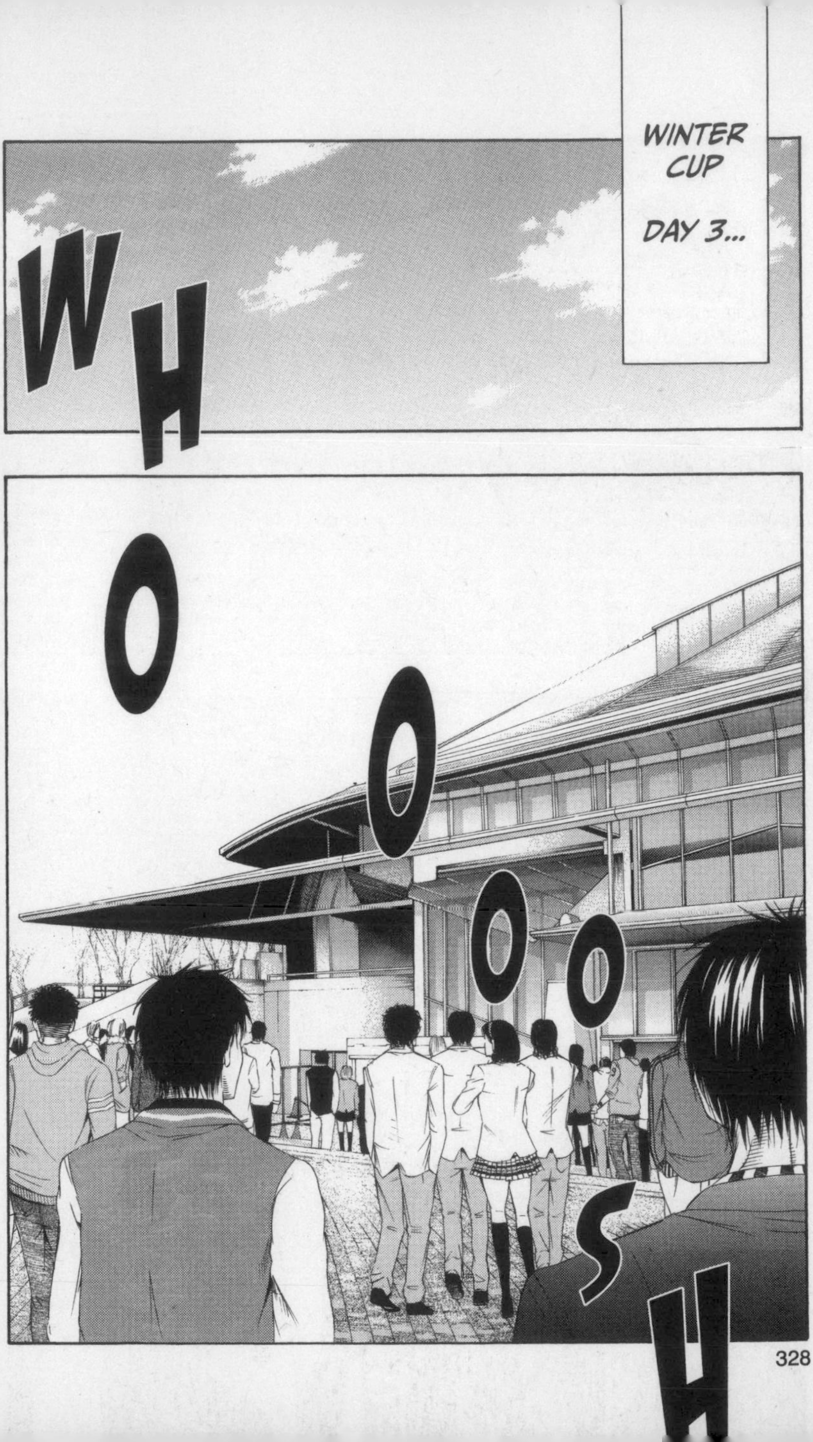
WINTER CUP

DAY 3...
WHOOOOSH

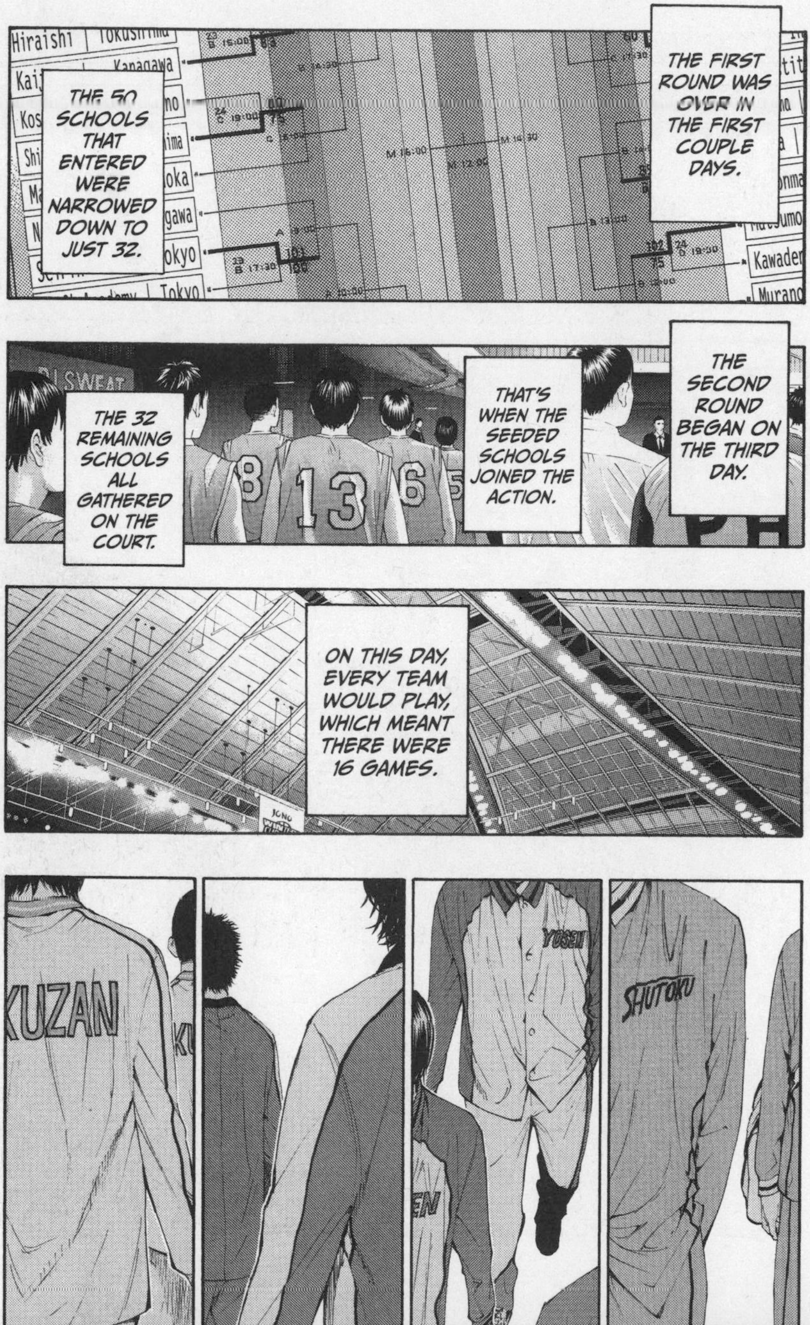

THE FIRST ROUND WAS OVER IN THE FIRST COUPLE DAYS.
THE 50 SCHOOLS THAT ENTERED WERE NARROWED DOWN TO JUST 32.
THE SECOND ROUND BEGAN ON THE THIRD DAY.
THAT'S WHEN THE SEEDED SCHOOLS JOINED THE ACTION.
THE 32 REMAINING SCHOOLS ALL GATHERED ON THE COURT.
ON THIS DAY, EVERY TEAM WOULD PLAY, WHICH MEANT THERE WERE 16 GAMES.
SHUTOKU
YOSEN

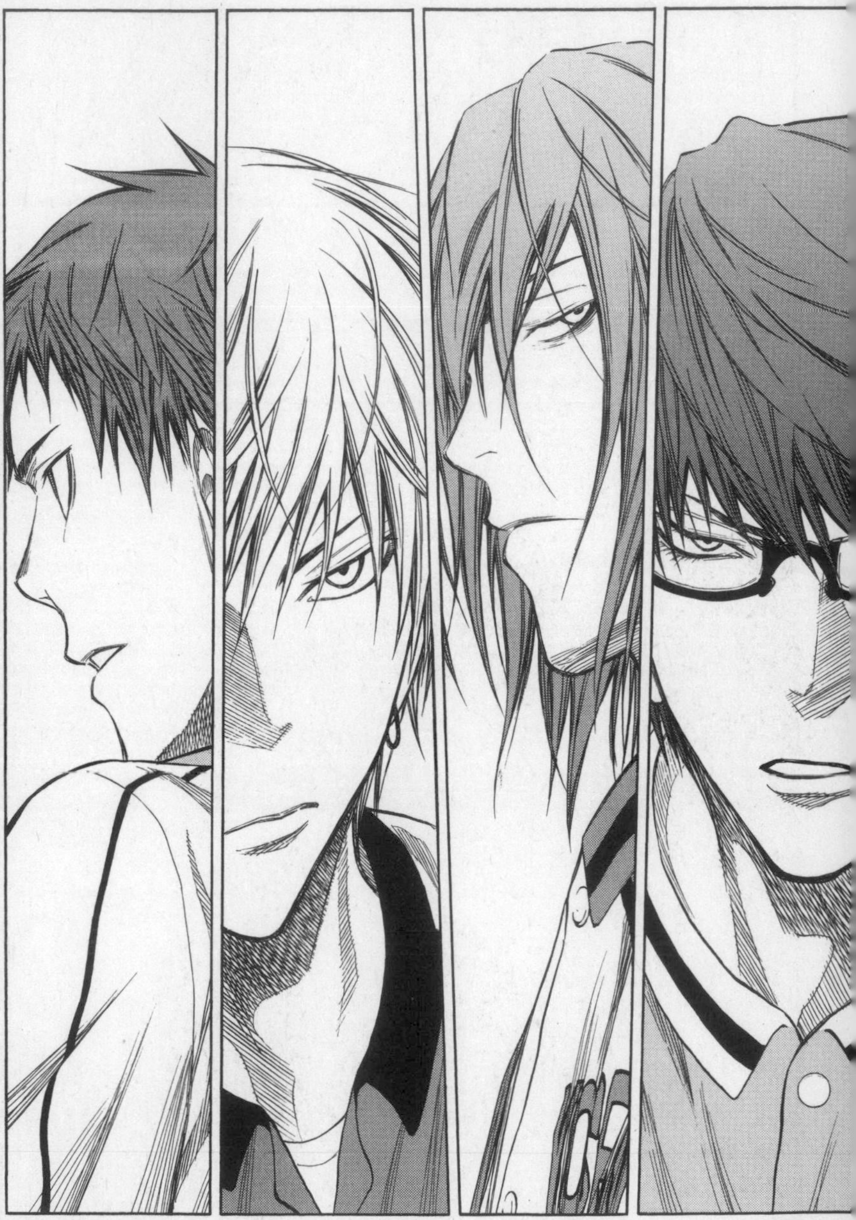

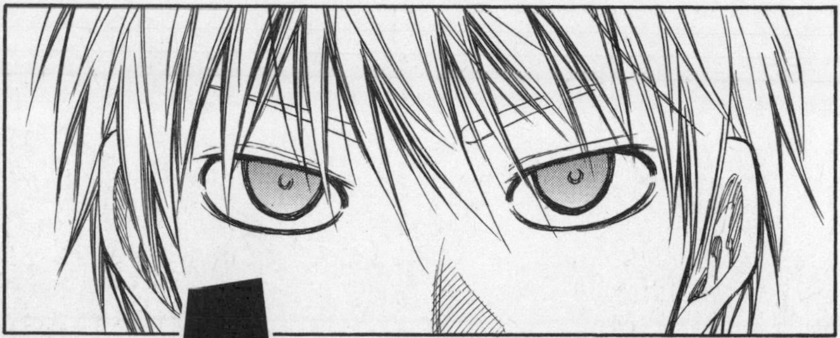

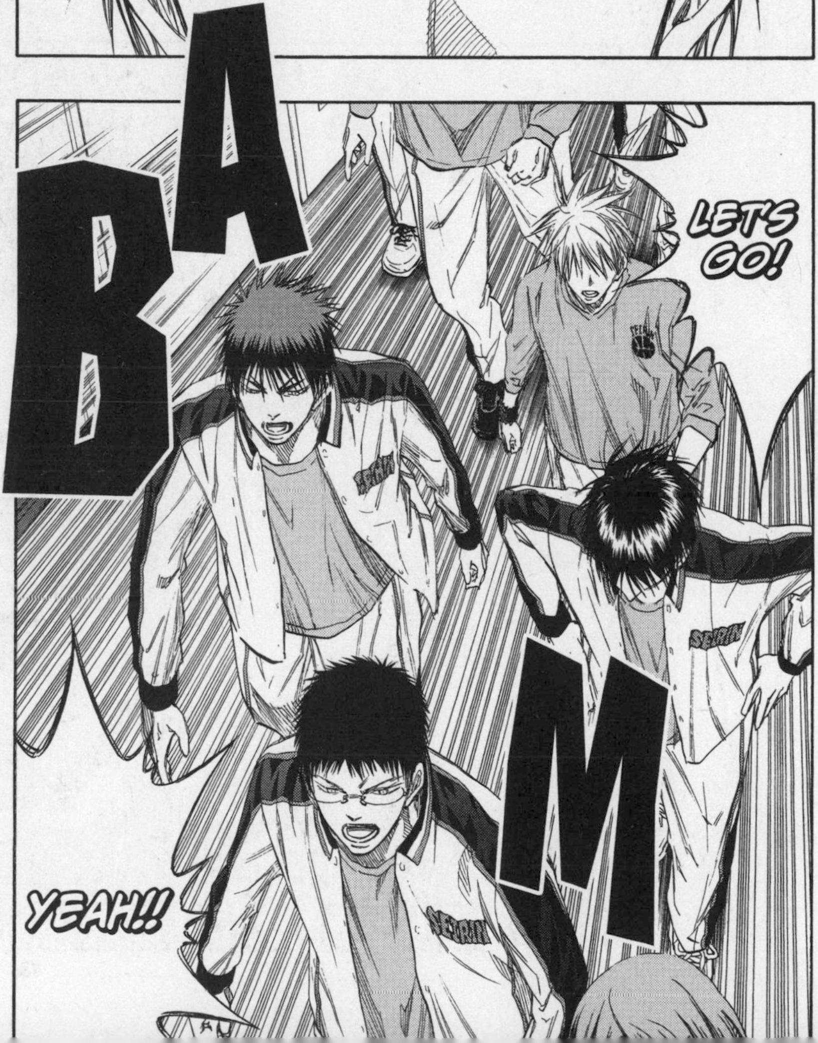
LET'S GO!
BAM
YEAH!!

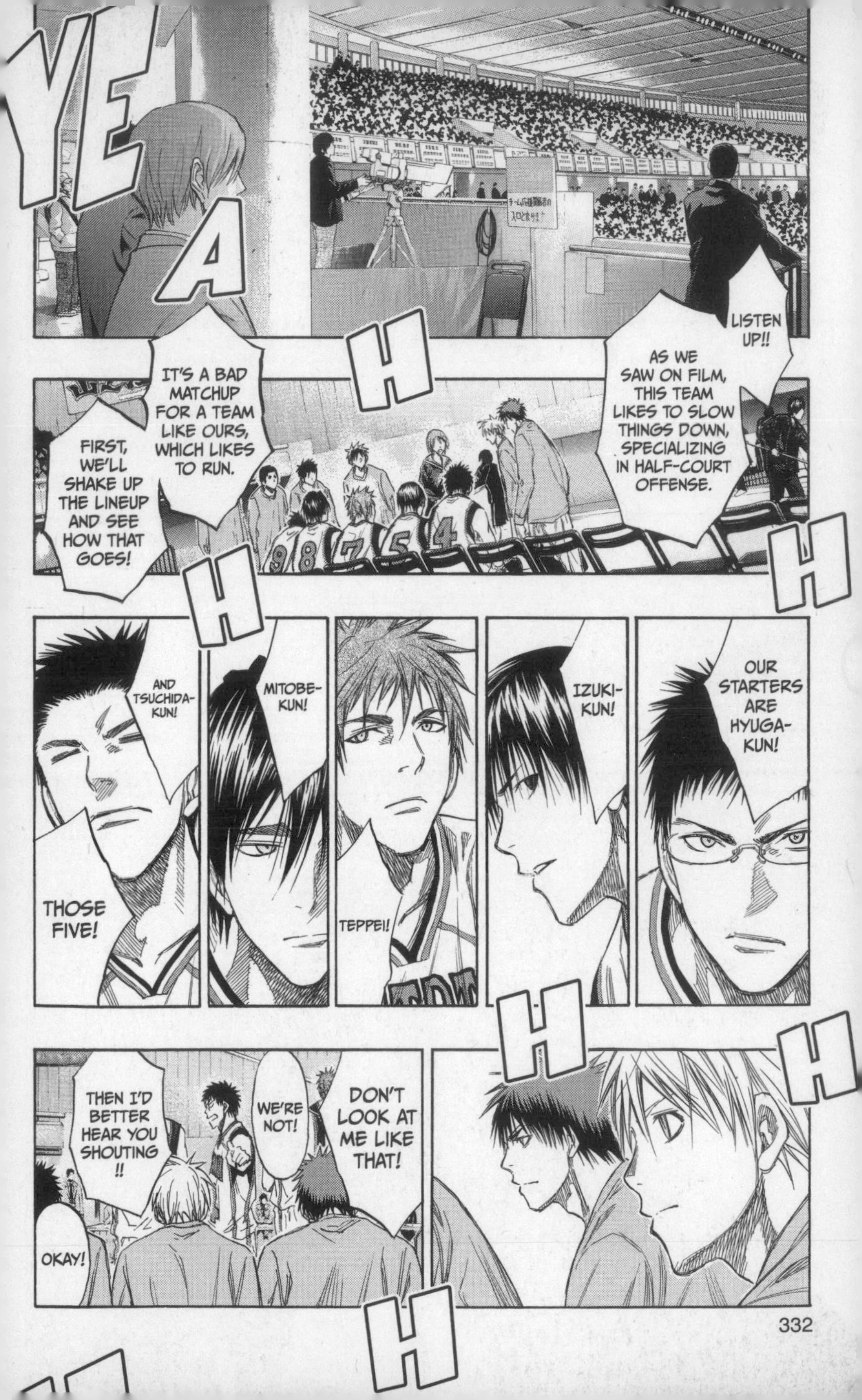
LISTEN UP!!
YEAHHHHHHH
AS WE SAW ON FILM, THIS TEAM LIKES TO SLOW THINGS DOWN, SPECIALIZING IN HALF-COURT OFFENSE.
IT'S A BAD MATCHUP FOR A TEAM LIKE OURS, WHICH LIKES TO RUN.
FIRST, WE'LL SHAKE UP THE LINEUP AND SEE HOW THAT GOES!
OUR STARTERS ARE HYUGA-KUN!
IZUKI-KUN!
TEPPEI!
MITOBE-KUN!
AND TSUCHIDA-KUN!
THOSE FIVE!
DON'T LOOK AT ME LIKE THAT!
WE'RE NOT!
THEN I'D BETTER HEAR YOU SHOUTING!!
OKAY!

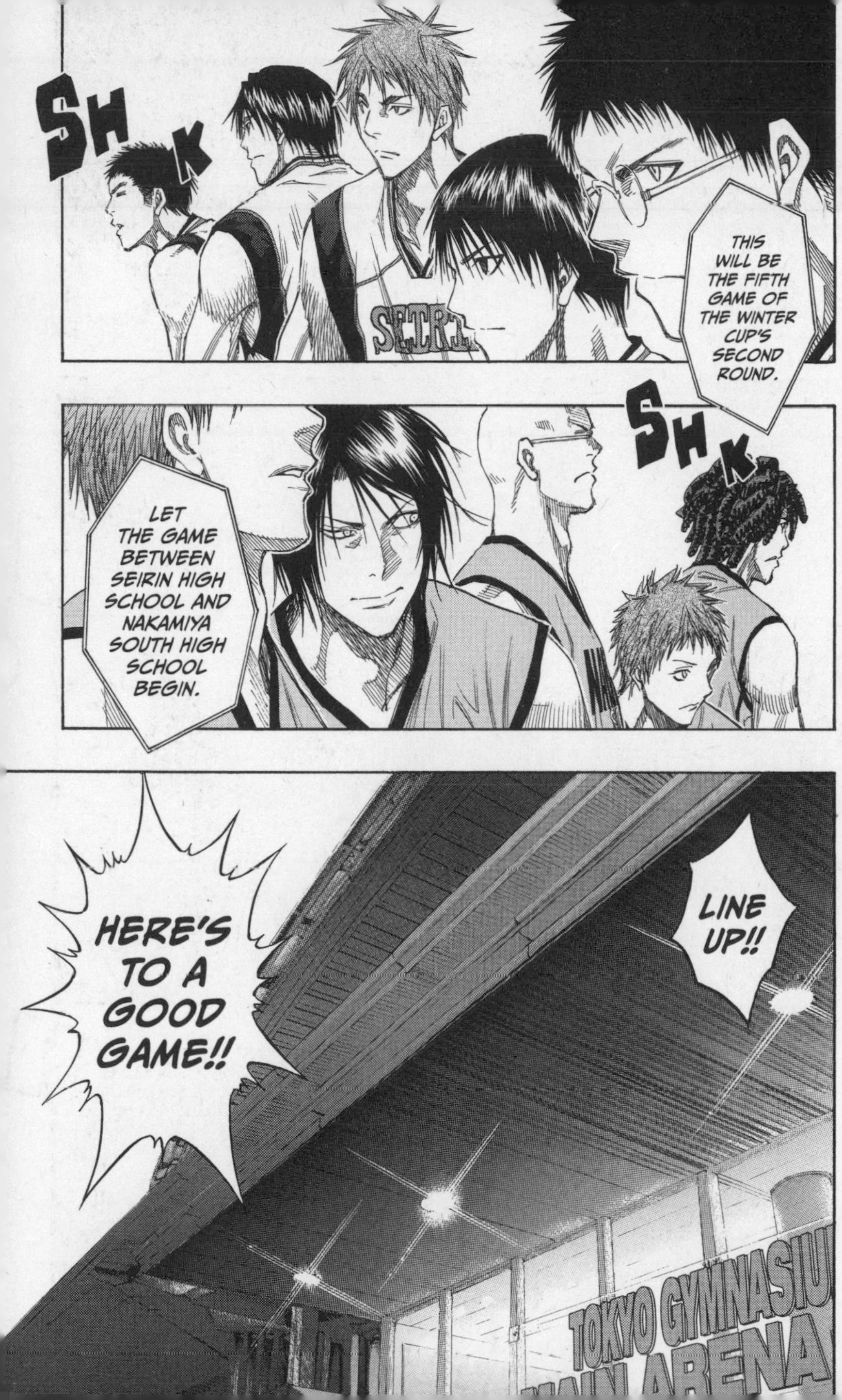
SHK
THIS WILL BE THE FIFTH GAME OF THE WINTER CUP'S SECOND ROUND.
SEIRIN
SHK
LET THE GAME BETWEEN SEIRIN HIGH SCHOOL AND NAKAMIYA SOUTH HIGH SCHOOL BEGIN.
LINE UP!!
HERE'S TO A GOOD GAME!!
TOKYO GYMNASIU
ARENA

KUROKO'S BASKETBALL BLOOPERS
TAKE 1

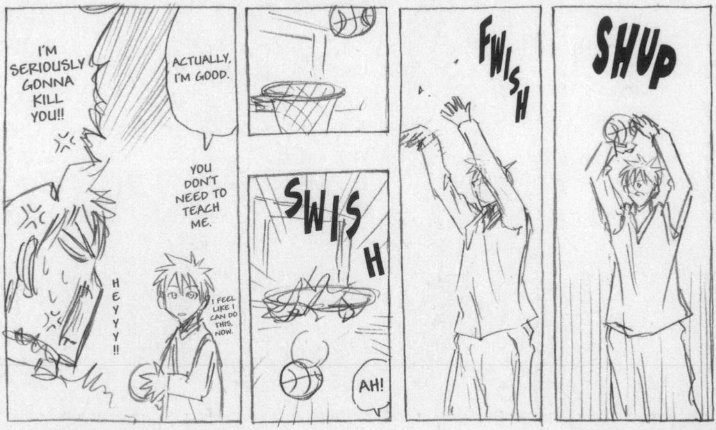
SHUP
FWISH
SWISH
AH!
ACTUALLY, I'M GOOD.
I'M SERIOUSLY GONNA KILL YOU!!
YOU DON'T NEED TO TEACH ME.
I FEEL LIKE I CAN DO THIS, NOW.
HEYYY!!

143RD QUARTER:
NO SMALL FEAT

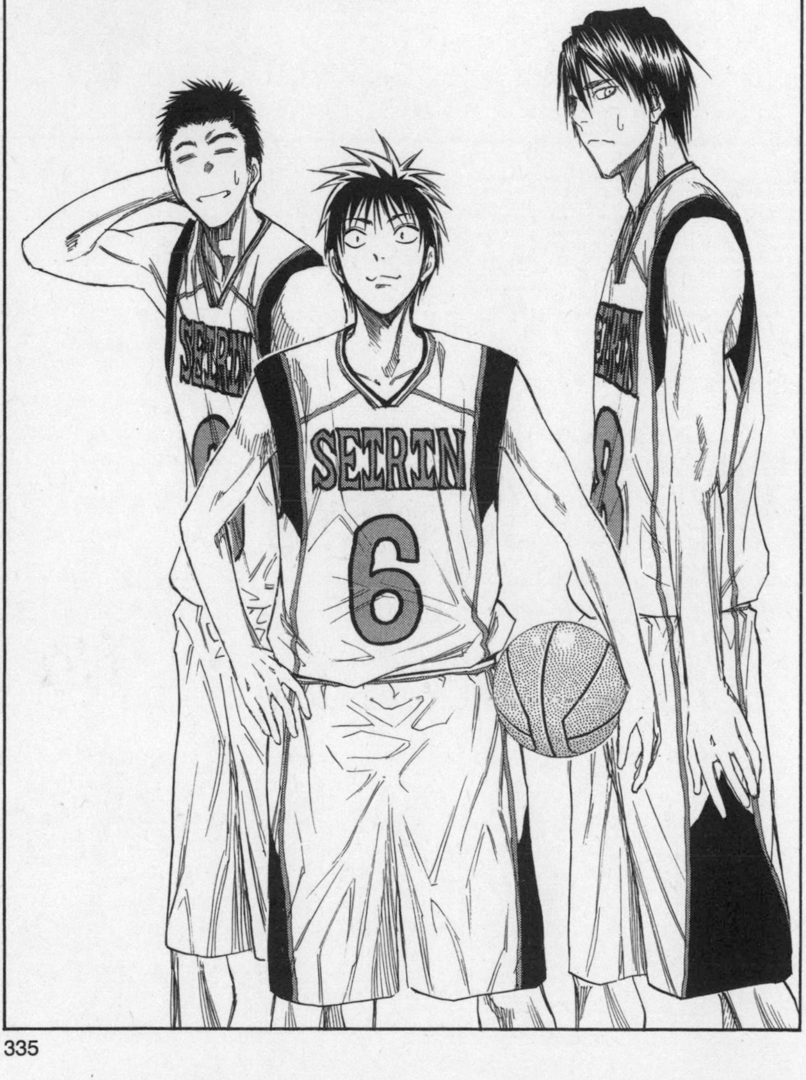
SEIRIN
6

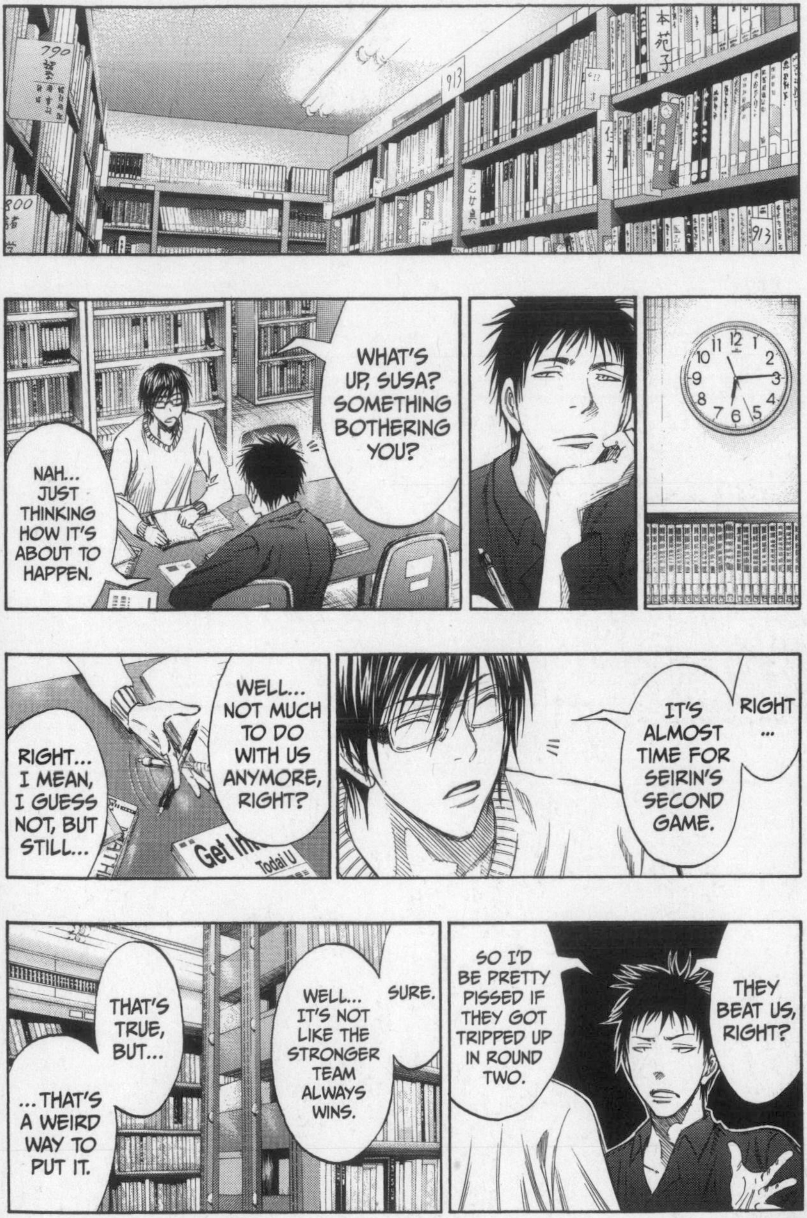
WHAT'S UP, SUSA? SOMETHING BOTHERING YOU?
NAH... JUST THINKING HOW IT'S ABOUT TO HAPPEN.
RIGHT ...
IT'S ALMOST TIME FOR SEIRIN'S SECOND GAME.
WELL... NOT MUCH TO DO WITH US ANYMORE, RIGHT?
RIGHT... I MEAN, I GUESS NOT, BUT STILL...
Todai U
THEY BEAT US, RIGHT?
SO I'D BE PRETTY PISSED IF THEY GOT TRIPPED UP IN ROUND TWO.
SURE.
WELL... IT'S NOT LIKE THE STRONGER TEAM ALWAYS WINS.
THAT'S TRUE, BUT...
...THAT'S A WEIRD WAY TO PUT IT.

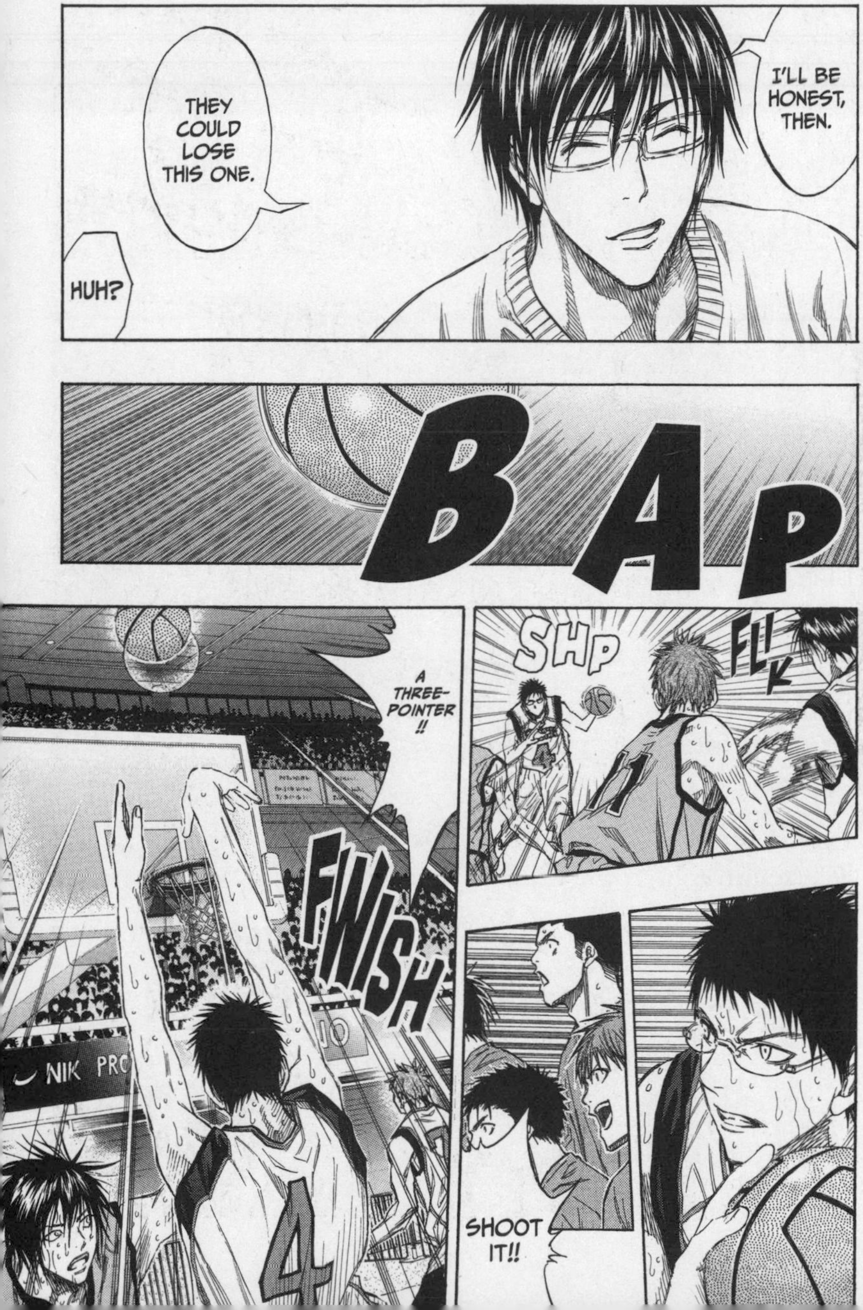
I'LL BE HONEST, THEN.
THEY COULD LOSE THIS ONE.
HUH?
BAP
SHP
FLIK
SHOOT IT!!
A THREE-POINTER!!
FWISH
NIK PRO

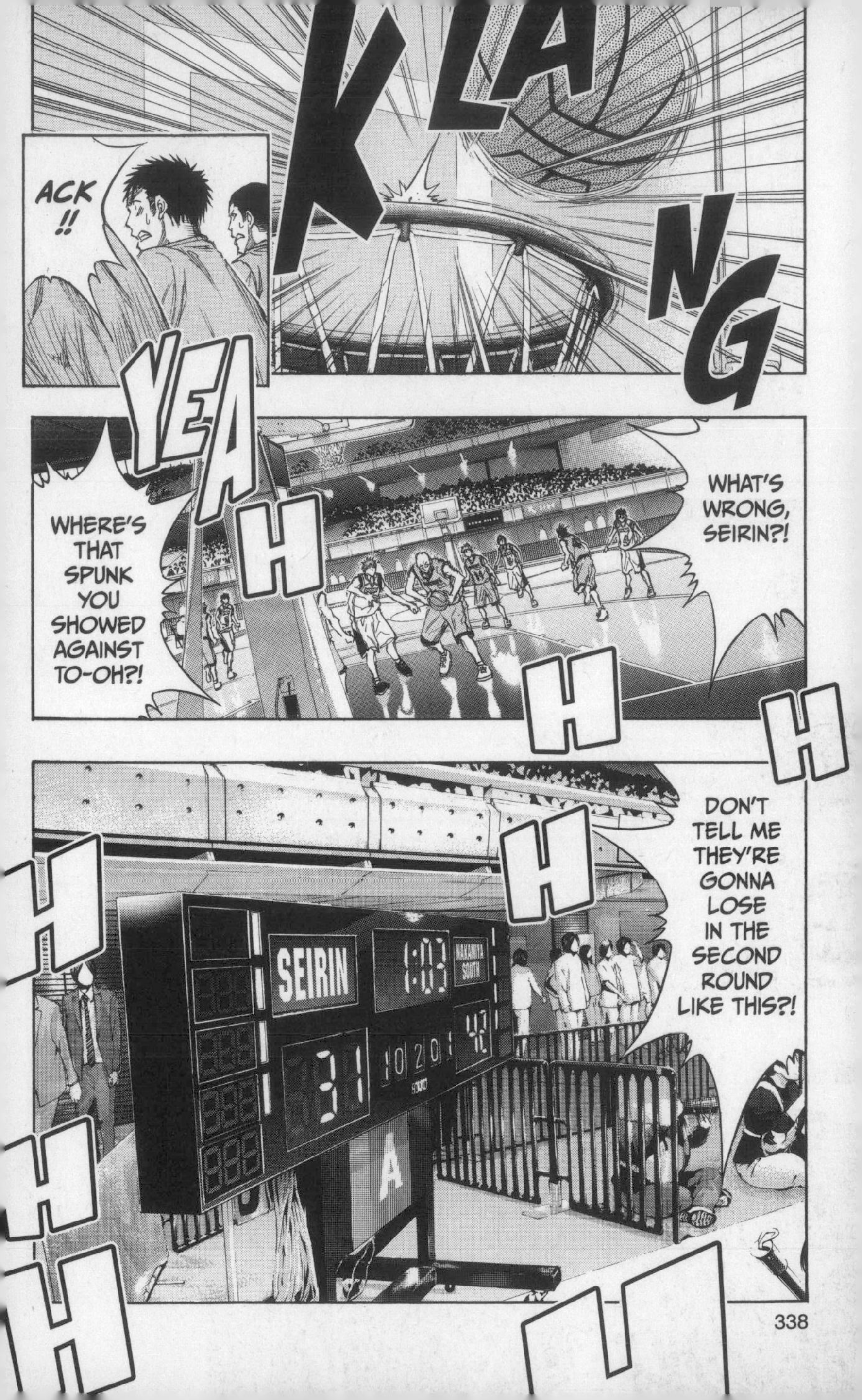
KLANG
ACK!!
YEAHHHHHHHH
WHAT'S WRONG, SEIRIN?!
WHERE'S THAT SPUNK YOU SHOWED AGAINST TO-OH?!
DON'T TELL ME THEY'RE GONNA LOSE IN THE SECOND ROUND LIKE THIS?!
SEIRIN
1:03
NAKAMIYA SOUTH
31
42

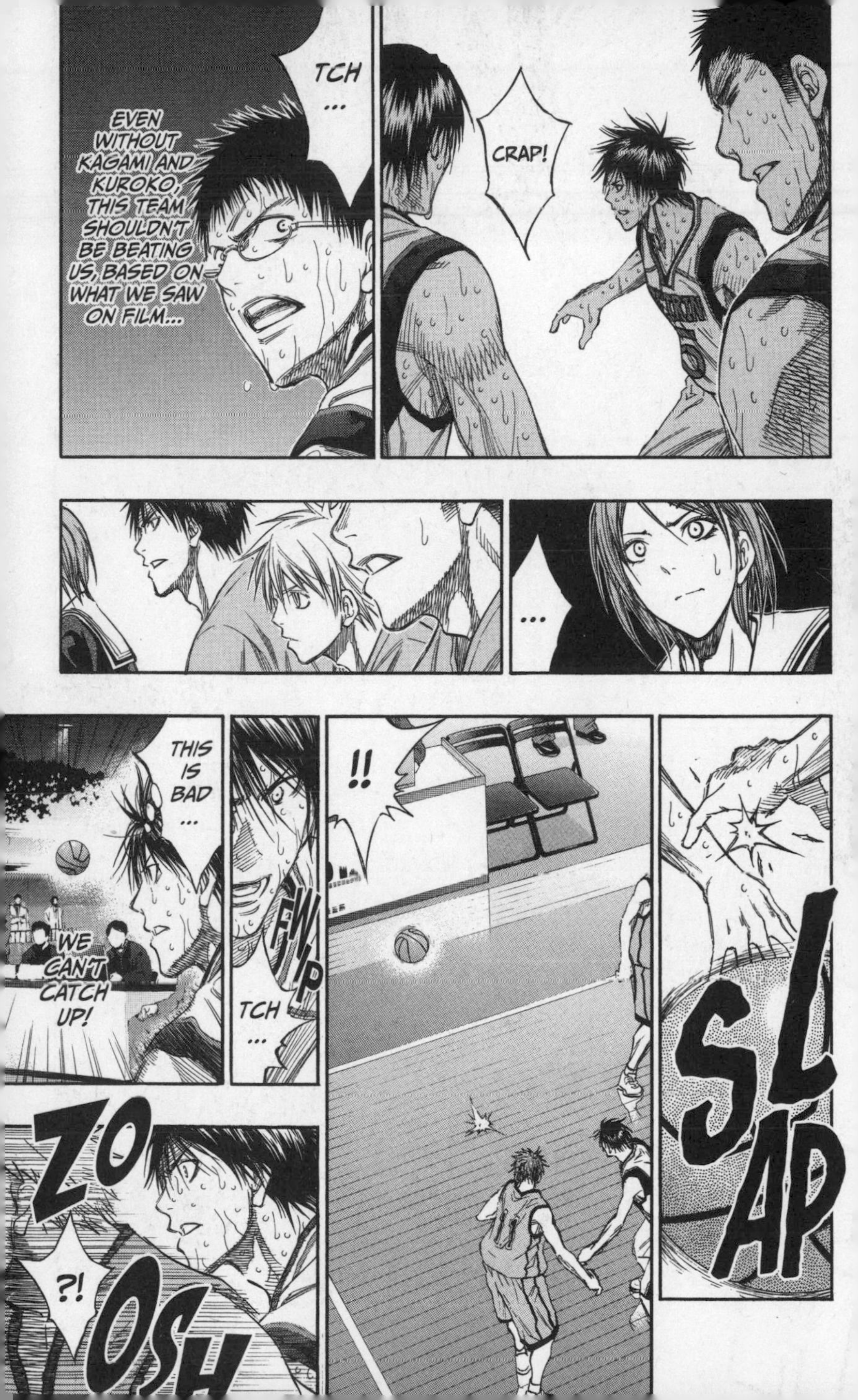
CRAP!
TCH ...
EVEN WITHOUT KAGAMI AND KUROKO, THIS TEAM SHOULDN'T BE BEATING US, BASED ON WHAT WE SAW ON FILM...
...
SLAP
!!
FWIP
TCH ...
THIS IS BAD ...
WE CAN'T CATCH UP!
ZOOSH
?!

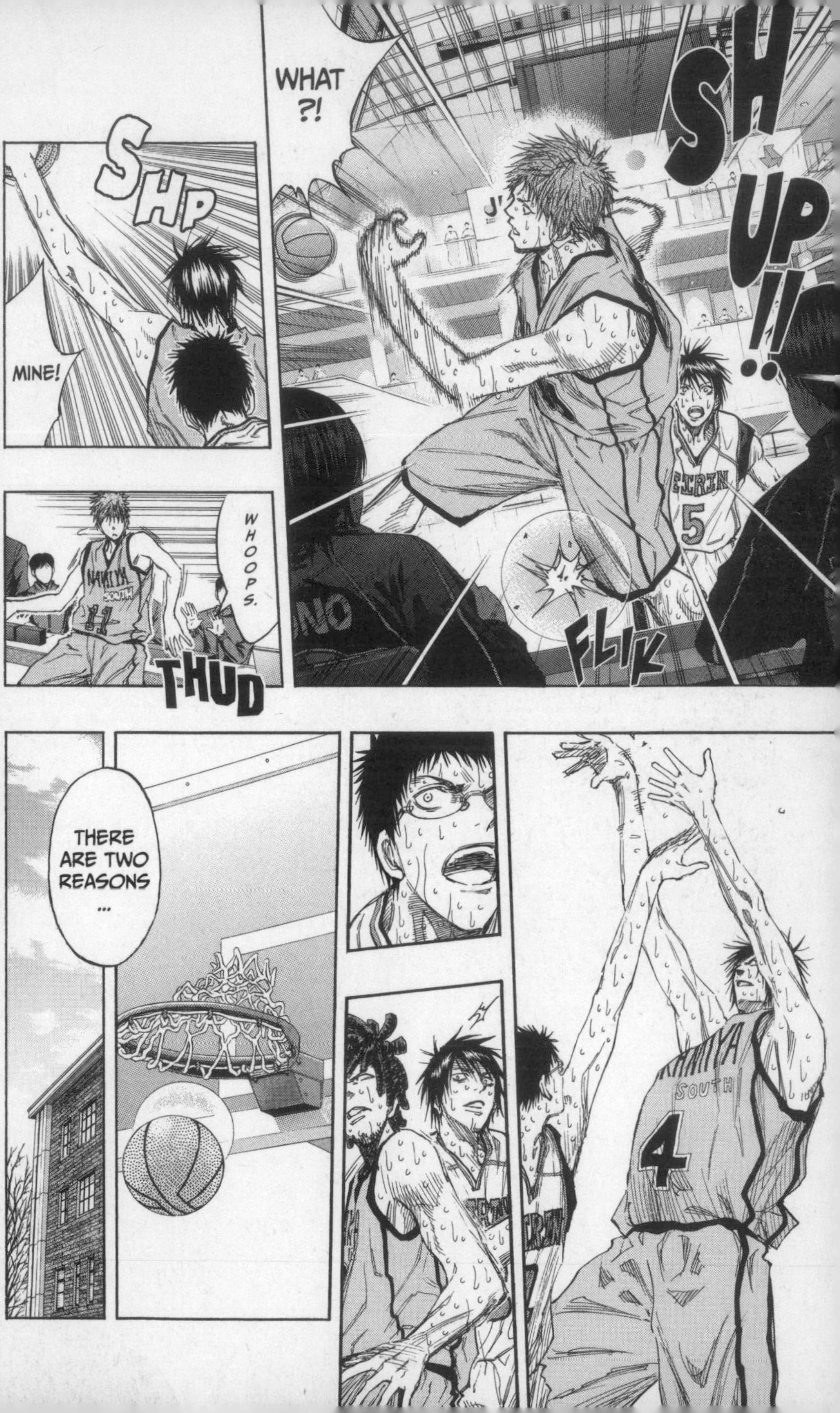
SHUP!!
WHAT ?!
FLIK
SHP
MINE!
WHOOPS.
THUD
THERE ARE TWO REASONS ...

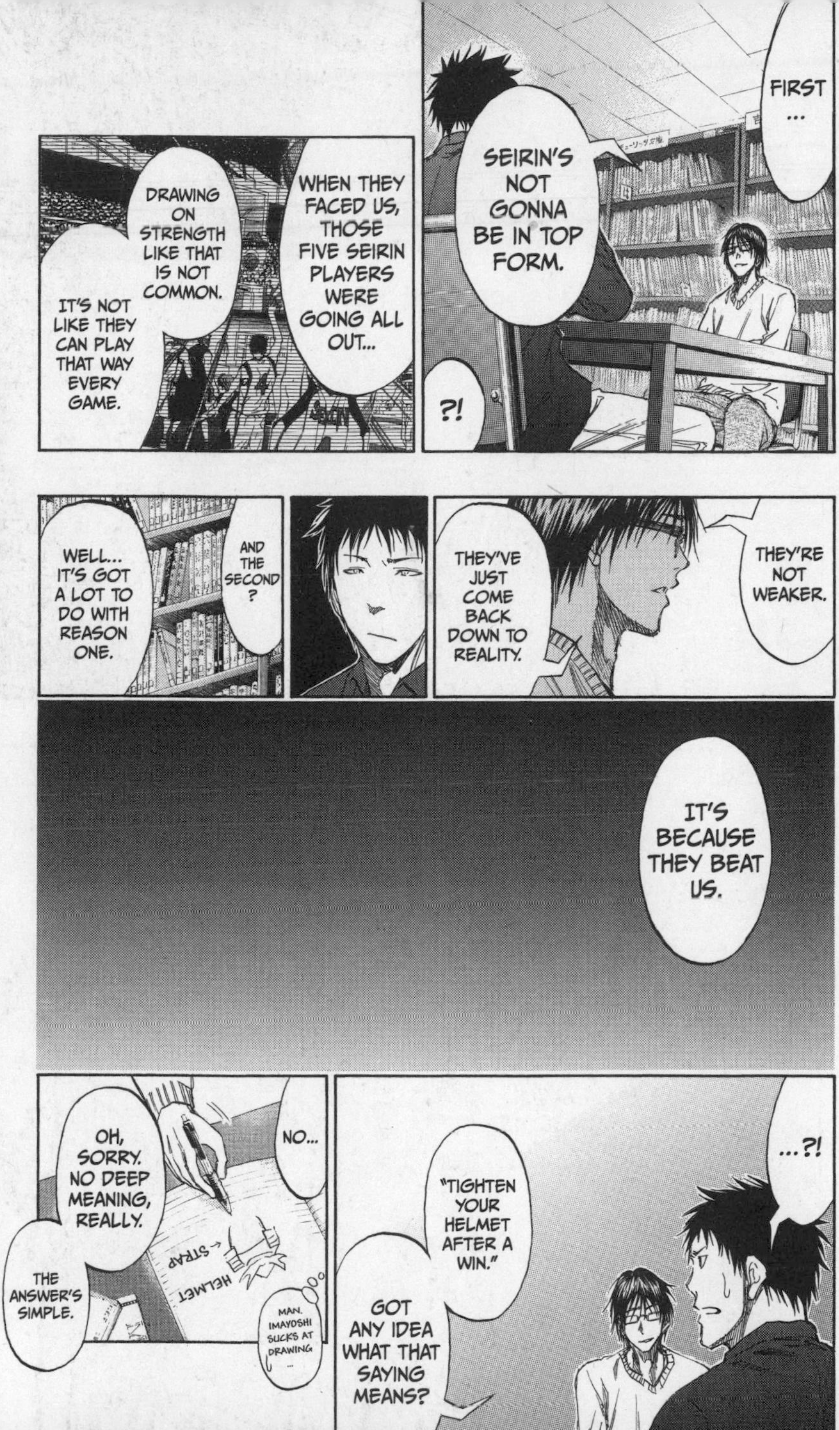

FIRST ...
SEIRIN'S NOT GONNA BE IN TOP FORM.
?!
WHEN THEY FACED US, THOSE FIVE SEIRIN PLAYERS WERE GOING ALL OUT...
DRAWING ON STRENGTH LIKE THAT IS NOT COMMON.
IT'S NOT LIKE THEY CAN PLAY THAT WAY EVERY GAME.
THEY'RE NOT WEAKER.
THEY'VE JUST COME BACK DOWN TO REALITY.
AND THE SECOND ?
WELL... IT'S GOT A LOT TO DO WITH REASON ONE.
IT'S BECAUSE THEY BEAT US.
...?!
"TIGHTEN YOUR HELMET AFTER A WIN."
GOT ANY IDEA WHAT THAT SAYING MEANS?
NO...
OH, SORRY. NO DEEP MEANING, REALLY.
STRAP
HELMET
MAN. IMAYOSHI SUCKS AT DRAWING ...
THE ANSWER'S SIMPLE.

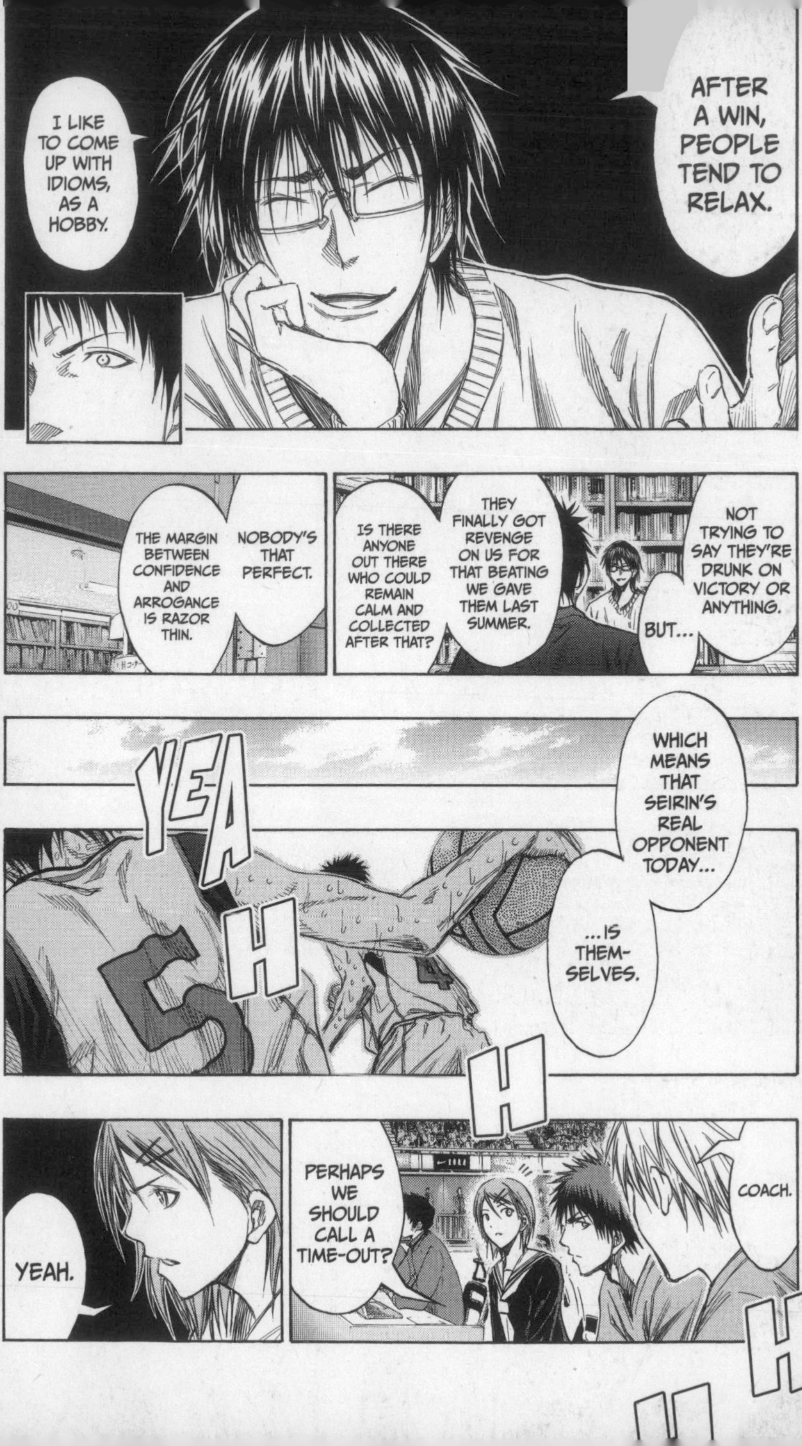

AFTER A WIN, PEOPLE TEND TO RELAX.
I LIKE TO COME UP WITH IDIOMS, AS A HOBBY.
NOT TRYING TO SAY THEY'RE DRUNK ON VICTORY OR ANYTHING.
BUT...
THEY FINALLY GOT REVENGE ON US FOR THAT BEATING WE GAVE THEM LAST SUMMER.
IS THERE ANYONE OUT THERE WHO COULD REMAIN CALM AND COLLECTED AFTER THAT?
NOBODY'S THAT PERFECT.
THE MARGIN BETWEEN CONFIDENCE AND ARROGANCE IS RAZOR THIN.
WHICH MEANS THAT SEIRIN'S REAL OPPONENT TODAY...
YEA
H
...IS THEM-SELVES.
H
COACH.
PERHAPS WE SHOULD CALL A TIME-OUT?
YEAH.
H

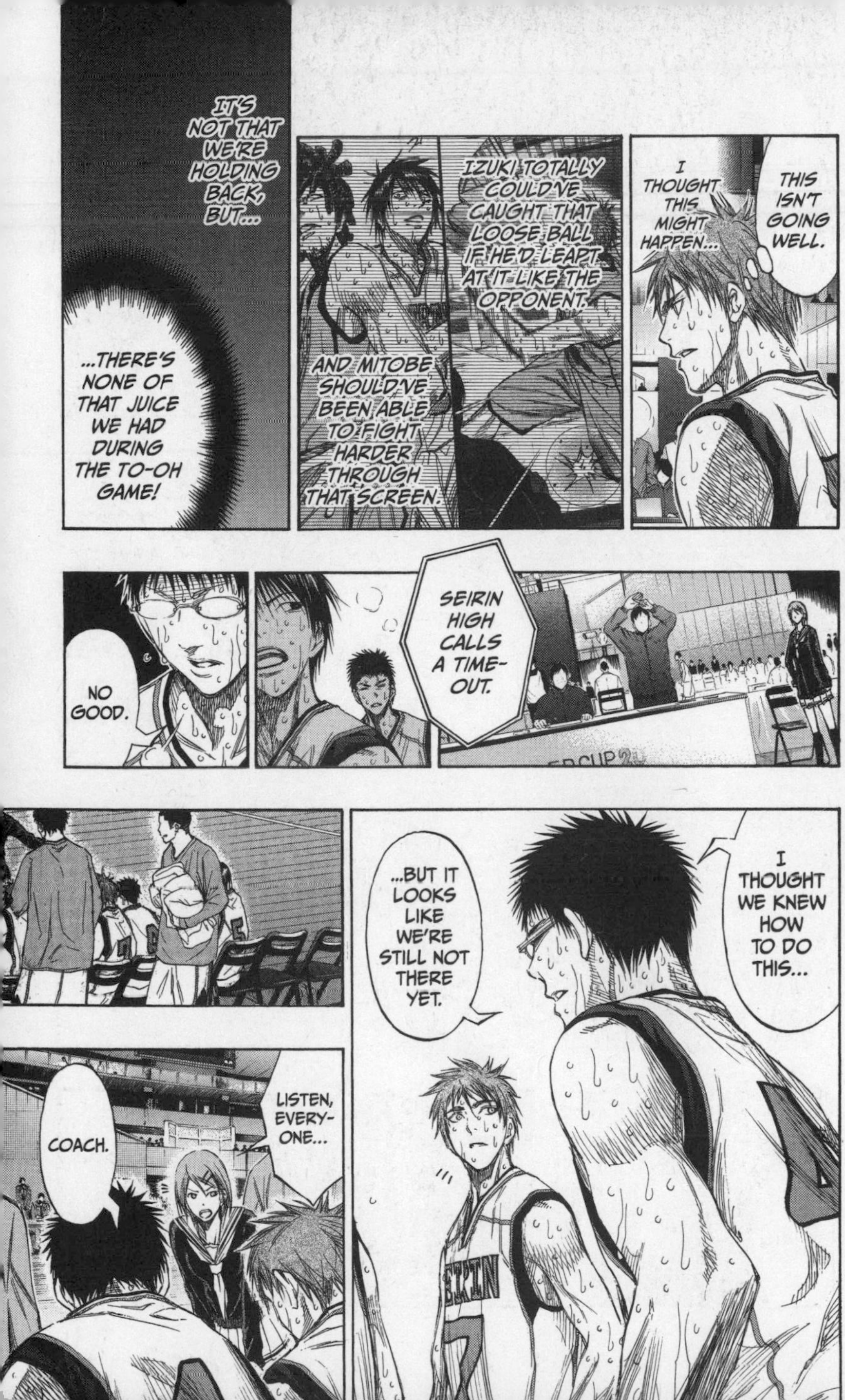
THIS ISN'T GOING WELL.
I THOUGHT THIS MIGHT HAPPEN...
IZUKI TOTALLY COULD'VE CAUGHT THAT LOOSE BALL IF HE'D LEAPT AT IT LIKE THE OPPONENT.
AND MITOBE SHOULD'VE BEEN ABLE TO FIGHT HARDER THROUGH THAT SCREEN.
IT'S NOT THAT WE'RE HOLDING BACK, BUT...
...THERE'S NONE OF THAT JUICE WE HAD DURING THE TO-OH GAME!
SEIRIN HIGH CALLS A TIME-OUT.
NO GOOD.
I THOUGHT WE KNEW HOW TO DO THIS...
...BUT IT LOOKS LIKE WE'RE STILL NOT THERE YET.
LISTEN, EVERYONE...
COACH.

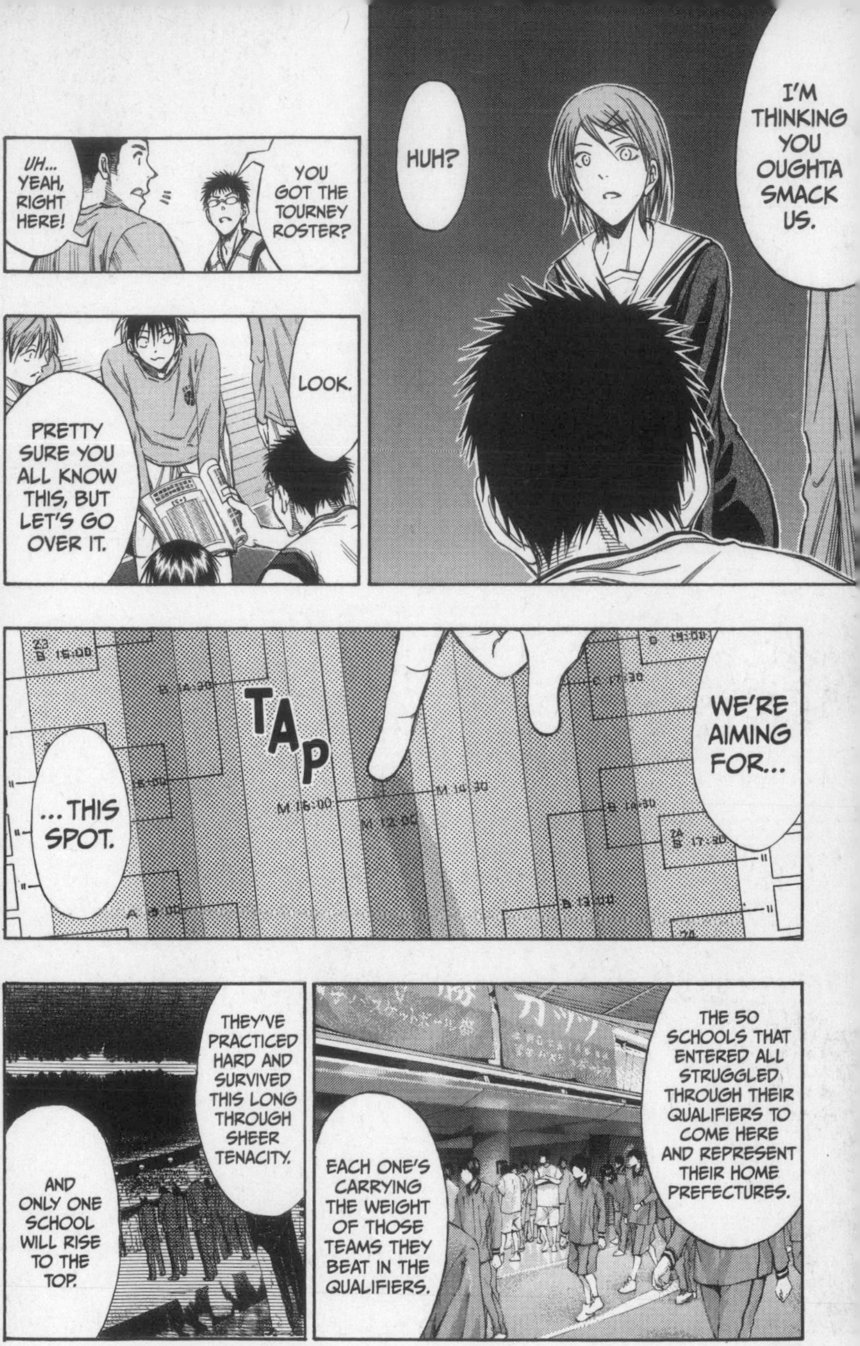
I'M THINKING YOU OUGHTA SMACK US.
HUH?
YOU GOT THE TOURNEY ROSTER?
UH... YEAH, RIGHT HERE!
LOOK.
PRETTY SURE YOU ALL KNOW THIS, BUT LET'S GO OVER IT.
WE'RE AIMING FOR...
TAP
...THIS SPOT.
THE 50 SCHOOLS THAT ENTERED ALL STRUGGLED THROUGH THEIR QUALIFIERS TO COME HERE AND REPRESENT THEIR HOME PREFECTURES.
EACH ONE'S CARRYING THE WEIGHT OF THOSE TEAMS THEY BEAT IN THE QUALIFIERS.
THEY'VE PRACTICED HARD AND SURVIVED THIS LONG THROUGH SHEER TENACITY.
AND ONLY ONE SCHOOL WILL RISE TO THE TOP.

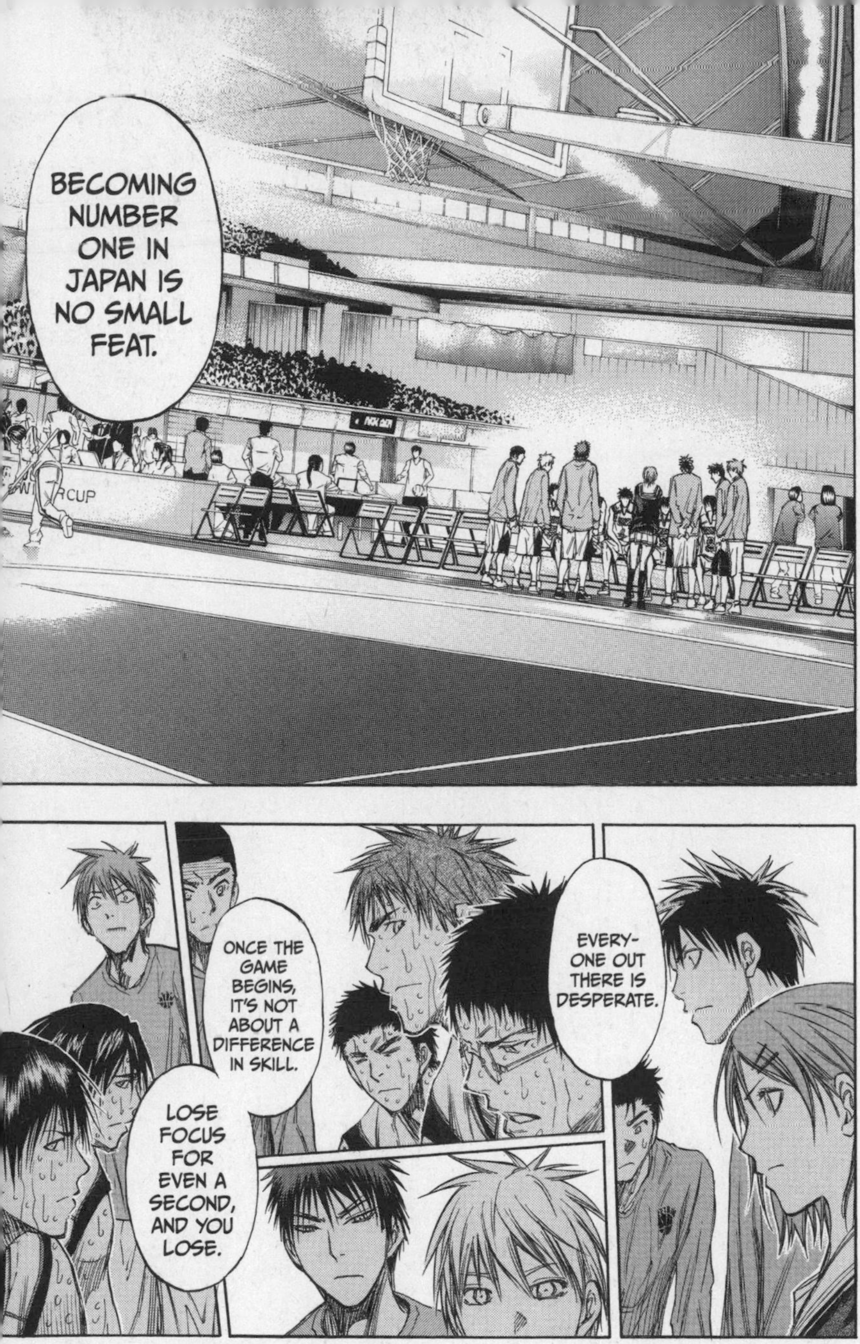
BECOMING NUMBER ONE IN JAPAN IS NO SMALL FEAT.
EVERY-ONE OUT THERE IS DESPERATE.
ONCE THE GAME BEGINS, IT'S NOT ABOUT A DIFFERENCE IN SKILL.
LOSE FOCUS FOR EVEN A SECOND, AND YOU LOSE.

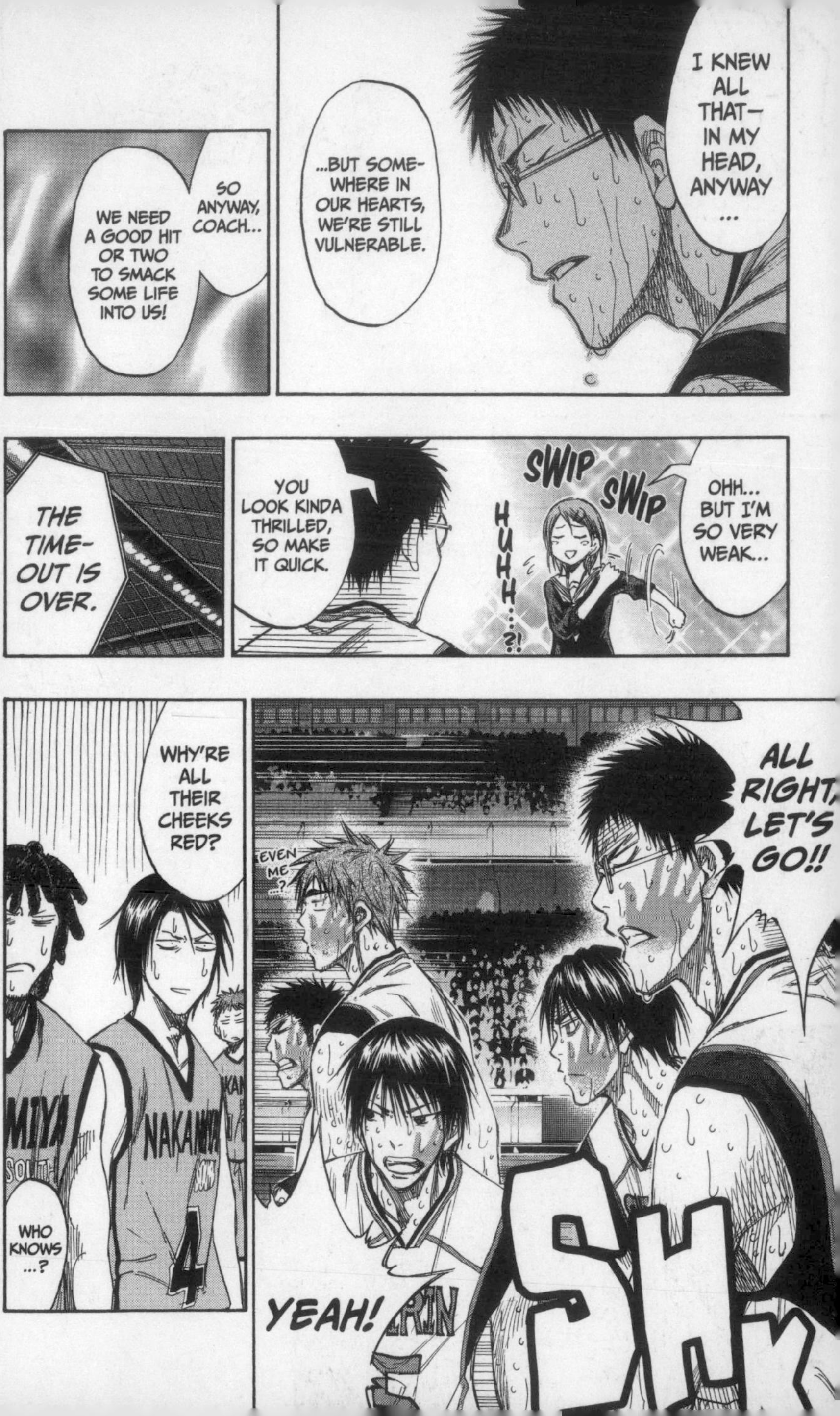
I KNEW ALL THAT— IN MY HEAD, ANYWAY...
...BUT SOMEWHERE IN OUR HEARTS, WE'RE STILL VULNERABLE.
SO ANYWAY, COACH...
WE NEED A GOOD HIT OR TWO TO SMACK SOME LIFE INTO US!
OHH... BUT I'M SO VERY WEAK...
SWIP SWIP
HUHH...?!
YOU LOOK KINDA THRILLED, SO MAKE IT QUICK.
THE TIME-OUT IS OVER.
ALL RIGHT, LET'S GO!!
EVEN ME...?
YEAH!
SHK
WHY'RE ALL THEIR CHEEKS RED?
WHO KNOWS...?

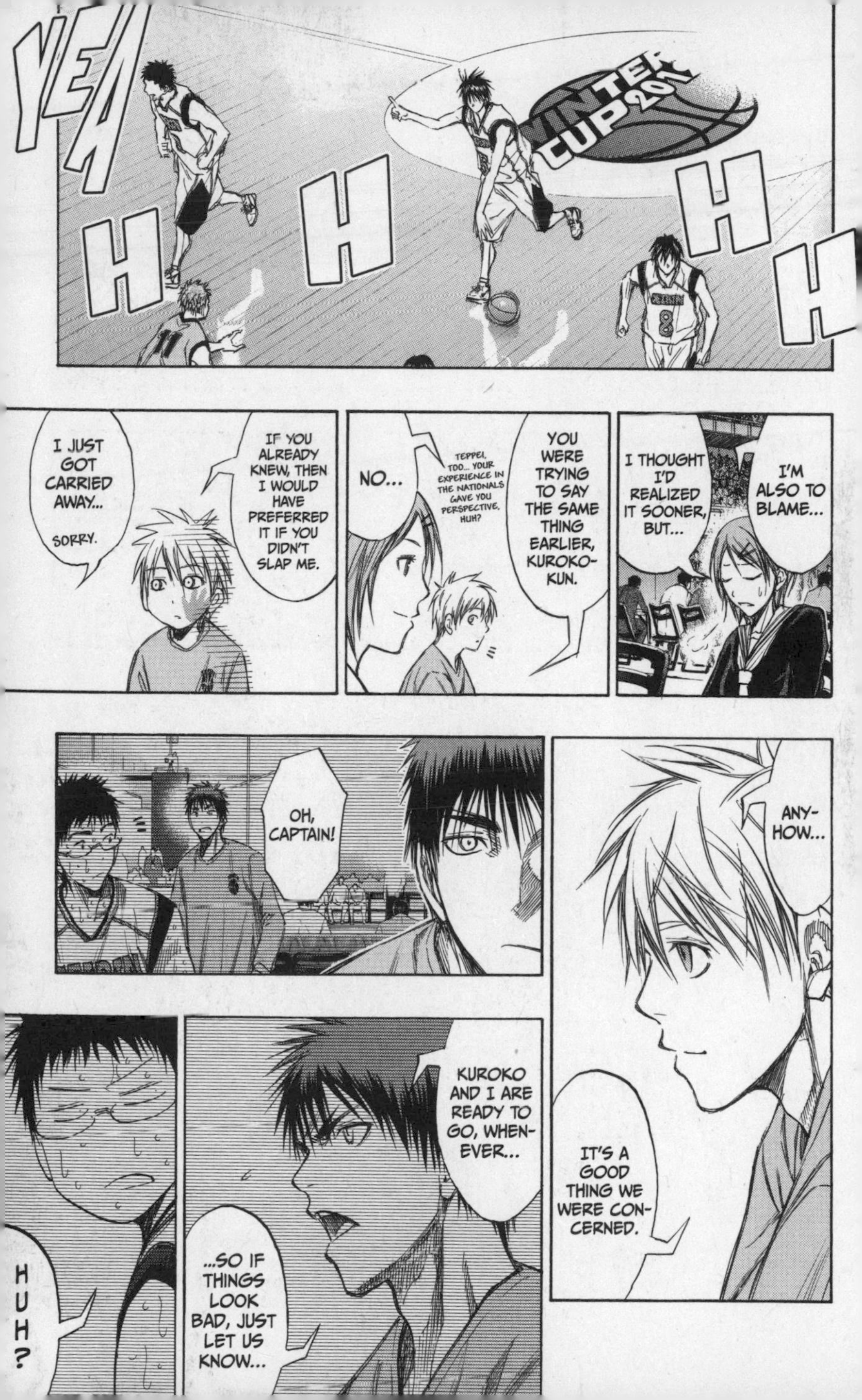
YEA
H
H
H
H
I'M ALSO TO BLAME...
I THOUGHT I'D REALIZED IT SOONER, BUT...
YOU WERE TRYING TO SAY THE SAME THING EARLIER, KUROKO-KUN.
TEPPEI, TOO... YOUR EXPERIENCE IN THE NATIONALS GAVE YOU PERSPECTIVE, HUH?
NO...
IF YOU ALREADY KNEW, THEN I WOULD HAVE PREFERRED IT IF YOU DIDN'T SLAP ME.
I JUST GOT CARRIED AWAY...
SORRY.
ANY-HOW...
IT'S A GOOD THING WE WERE CON-CERNED.
OH, CAPTAIN!
KUROKO AND I ARE READY TO GO, WHEN-EVER...
...SO IF THINGS LOOK BAD, JUST LET US KNOW...
HUH?

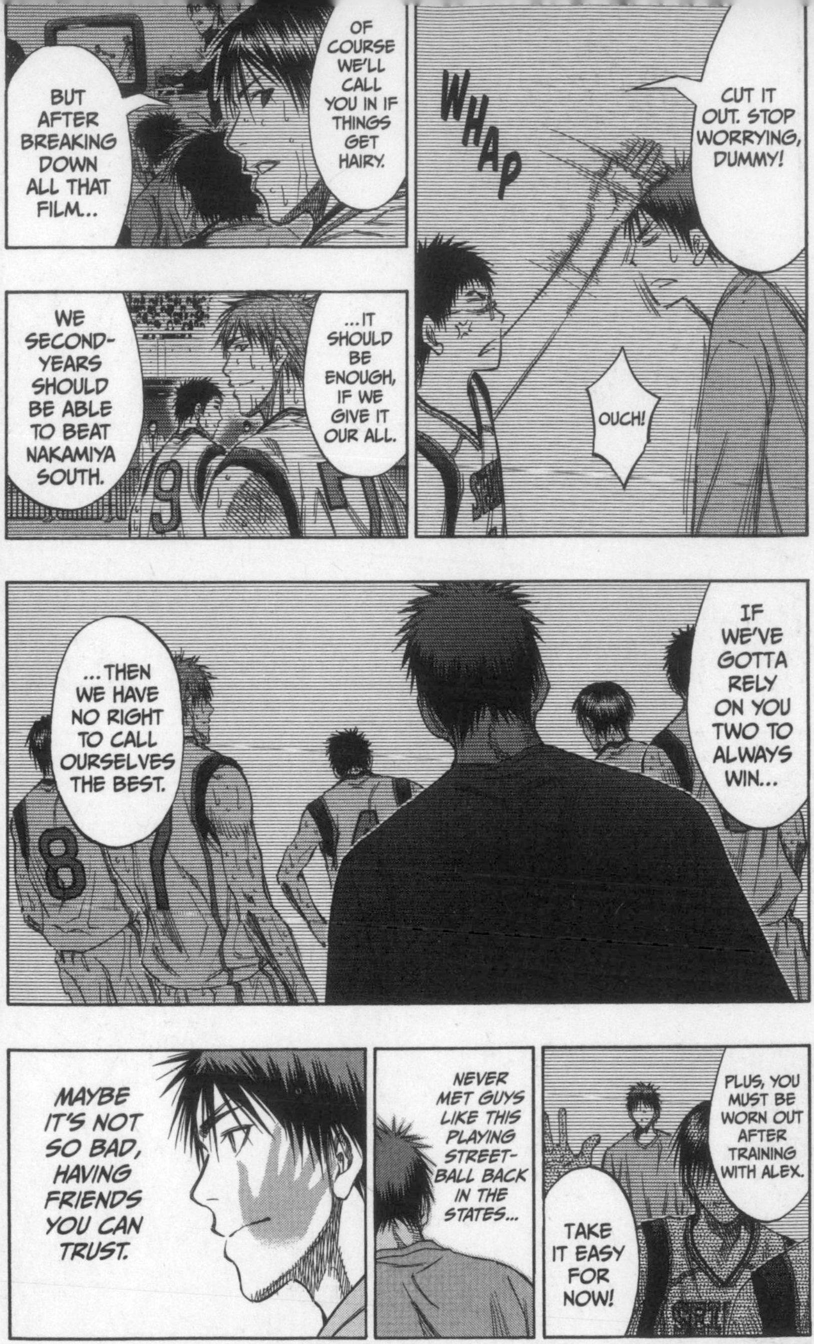
CUT IT OUT. STOP WORRYING, DUMMY!
WHAP
OUCH!
OF COURSE WE'LL CALL YOU IN IF THINGS GET HAIRY.
BUT AFTER BREAKING DOWN ALL THAT FILM...
...IT SHOULD BE ENOUGH, IF WE GIVE IT OUR ALL.
WE SECOND-YEARS SHOULD BE ABLE TO BEAT NAKAMIYA SOUTH.
IF WE'VE GOTTA RELY ON YOU TWO TO ALWAYS WIN...
...THEN WE HAVE NO RIGHT TO CALL OURSELVES THE BEST.
PLUS, YOU MUST BE WORN OUT AFTER TRAINING WITH ALEX.
TAKE IT EASY FOR NOW!
NEVER MET GUYS LIKE THIS PLAYING STREET-BALL BACK IN THE STATES...
MAYBE IT'S NOT SO BAD, HAVING FRIENDS YOU CAN TRUST.

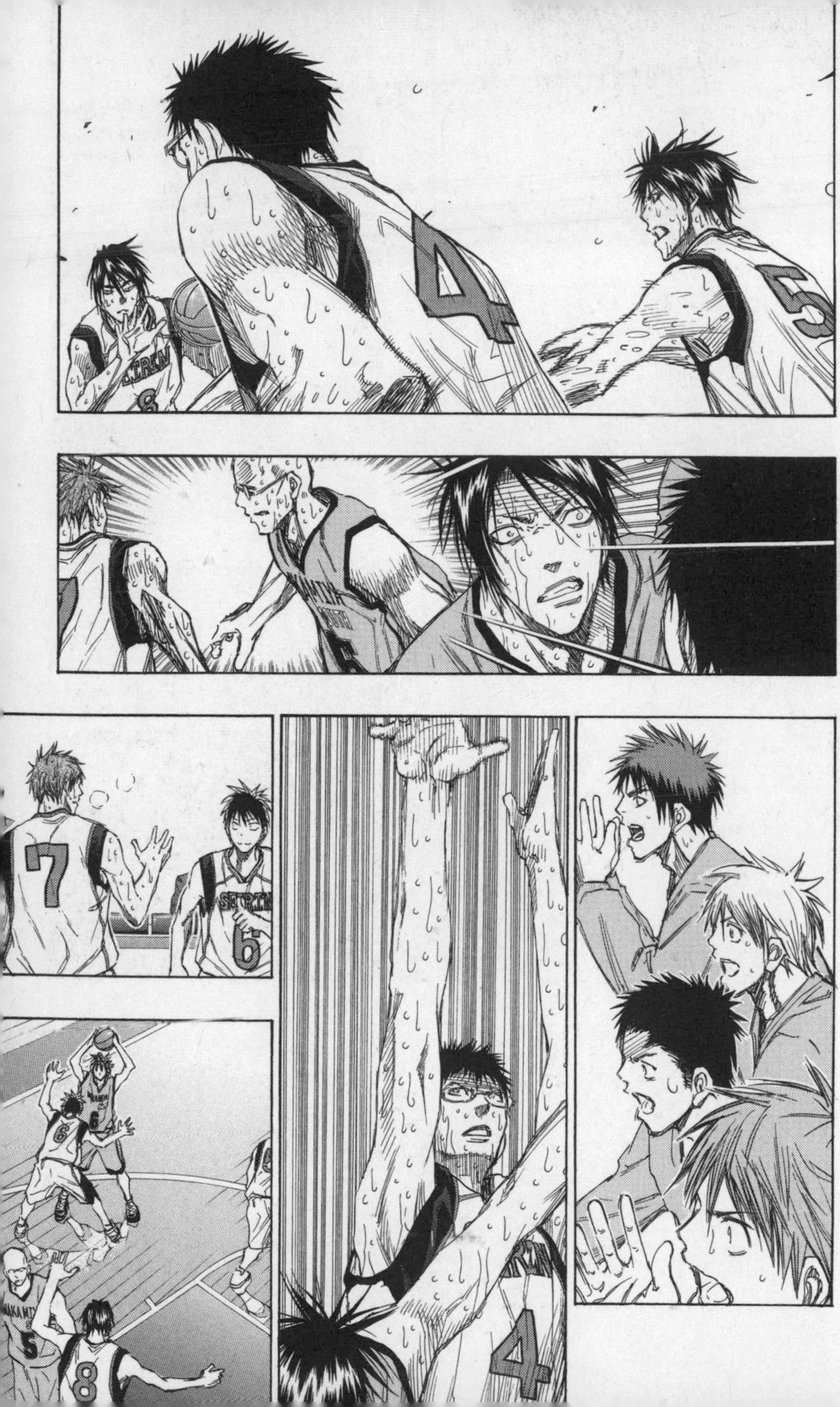

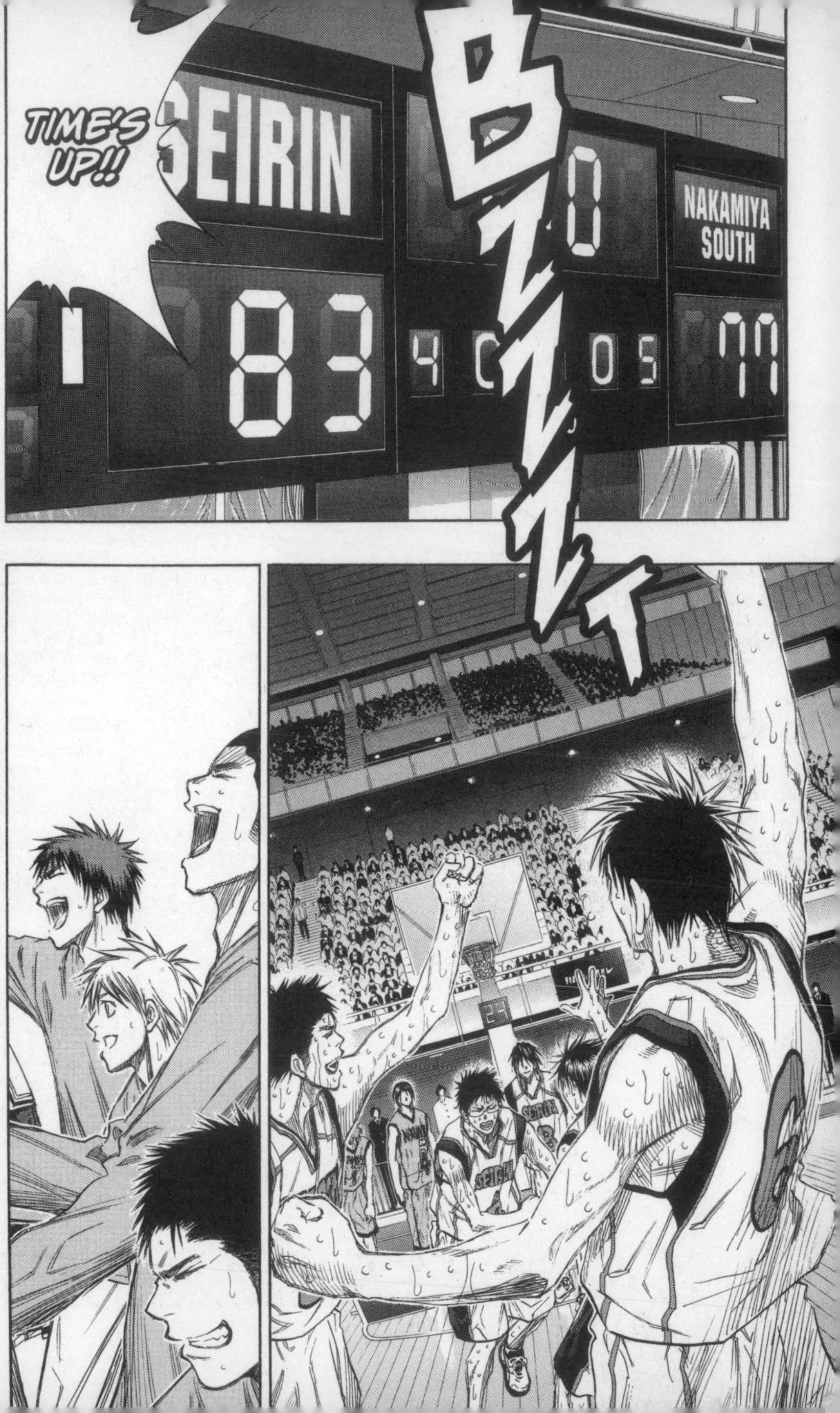
TIME'S UP!!
SEIRIN
83
NAKAMIYA SOUTH
77

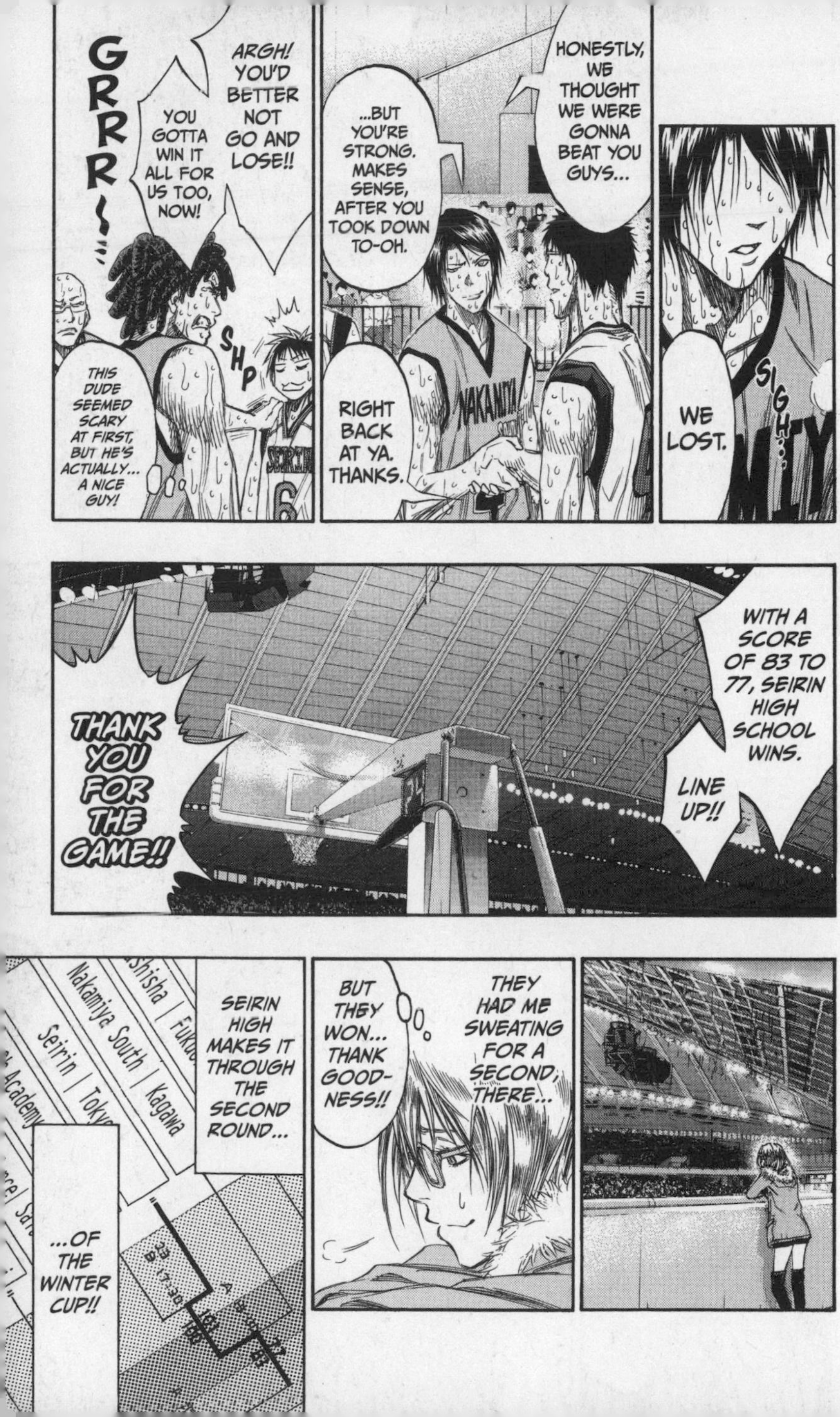
SIGH...
WE LOST.
HONESTLY, WE THOUGHT WE WERE GONNA BEAT YOU GUYS...
...BUT YOU'RE STRONG. MAKES SENSE, AFTER YOU TOOK DOWN TO-OH.
RIGHT BACK AT YA. THANKS.
ARGH! YOU'D BETTER NOT GO AND LOSE!!
YOU GOTTA WIN IT ALL FOR US TOO, NOW!
GRRR~
SHP
THIS DUDE SEEMED SCARY AT FIRST, BUT HE'S ACTUALLY... A NICE GUY!
WITH A SCORE OF 83 TO 77, SEIRIN HIGH SCHOOL WINS.
LINE UP!!
THANK YOU FOR THE GAME!!
THEY HAD ME SWEATING FOR A SECOND, THERE...
BUT THEY WON... THANK GOODNESS!!
SEIRIN HIGH MAKES IT THROUGH THE SECOND ROUND...
Nakamiya South | Kagawa
Seirin
...OF THE WINTER CUP!!

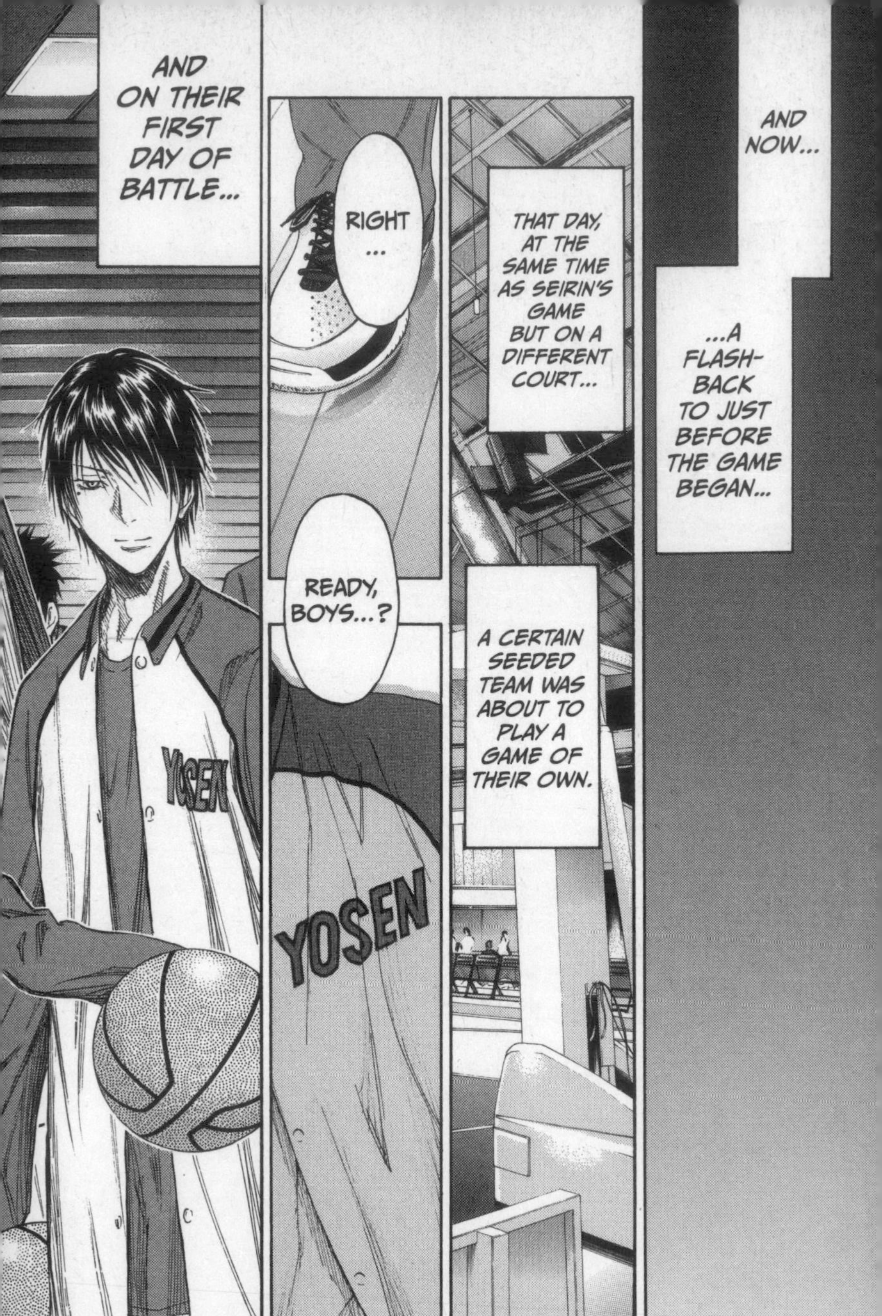
AND NOW...
...A FLASH-BACK TO JUST BEFORE THE GAME BEGAN...
THAT DAY, AT THE SAME TIME AS SEIRIN'S GAME BUT ON A DIFFERENT COURT...
A CERTAIN SEEDED TEAM WAS ABOUT TO PLAY A GAME OF THEIR OWN.
RIGHT...
READY, BOYS...?
YOSEN
YOSEN
AND ON THEIR FIRST DAY OF BATTLE...

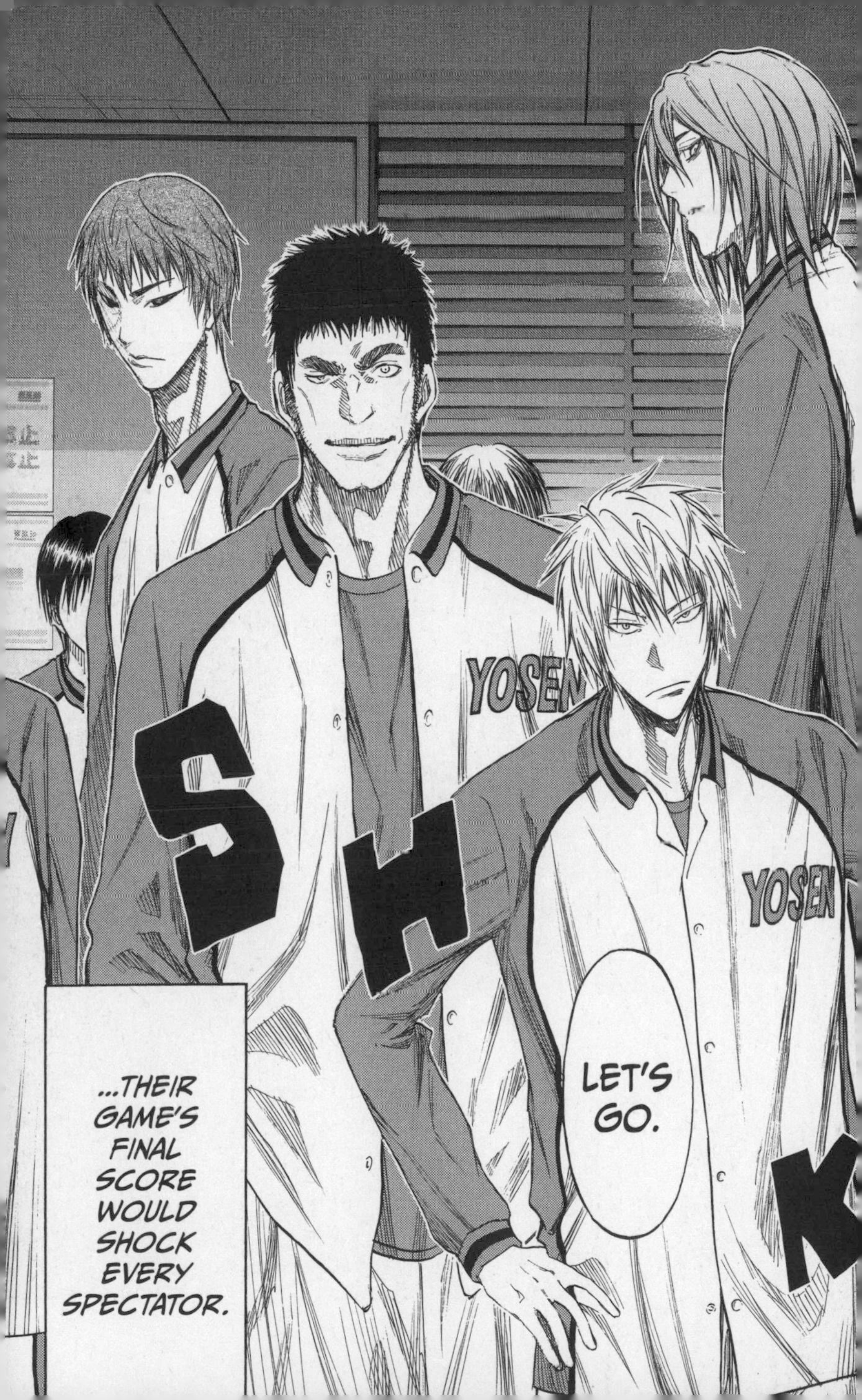
LET'S GO.
...THEIR GAME'S FINAL SCORE WOULD SHOCK EVERY SPECTATOR.
YOSEN
YOSEN

KUROKO'S BASKETBALL Q&A (W/ HALFWAY-DECENT ANSWERS)

Q. **QUESTION FOR MIDORIMA-KUN! HOW DO YOU MANAGE TO DRINK UP ALL THE CHUNKS IN YOUR CANNED OSHIRUKO DRINK?**
(WHEN SETO JUST CAN'T THINK UNLESS HIS FOREHEAD'S SHOWING, I TOTALLY UNDERSTAND HOW HE FEELS from SHIZUOKA PREFECTURE)

A. WHEN THERE'S JUST A LITTLE BIT LEFT, HE BLOWS INTO THE CAN AND THEN IMMEDIATELY GULPS IT ALL DOWN.

KUROKO'S BASKETBALL BLOOPERS TAKE 4

...?!
"TIGHTEN YOUR HELMET AFTER A WIN."
GOT ANY IDEA WHAT THAT SAYING MEANS?
NO ...
OH, SORRY. NO DEEP MEANING, REALLY.
THE ANSWER'S SIMPLE.
SKRTCH
SKRTCH
WHOA!
WHAT'S HE EVEN DRAWING?!
DOES HE KEEP SOME KIND OF ILLUSTRATED DIARY?
HELMET/ KABUTO (BEETLE)

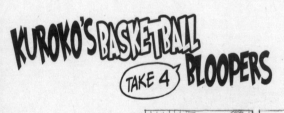

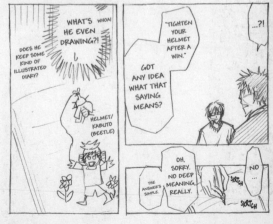

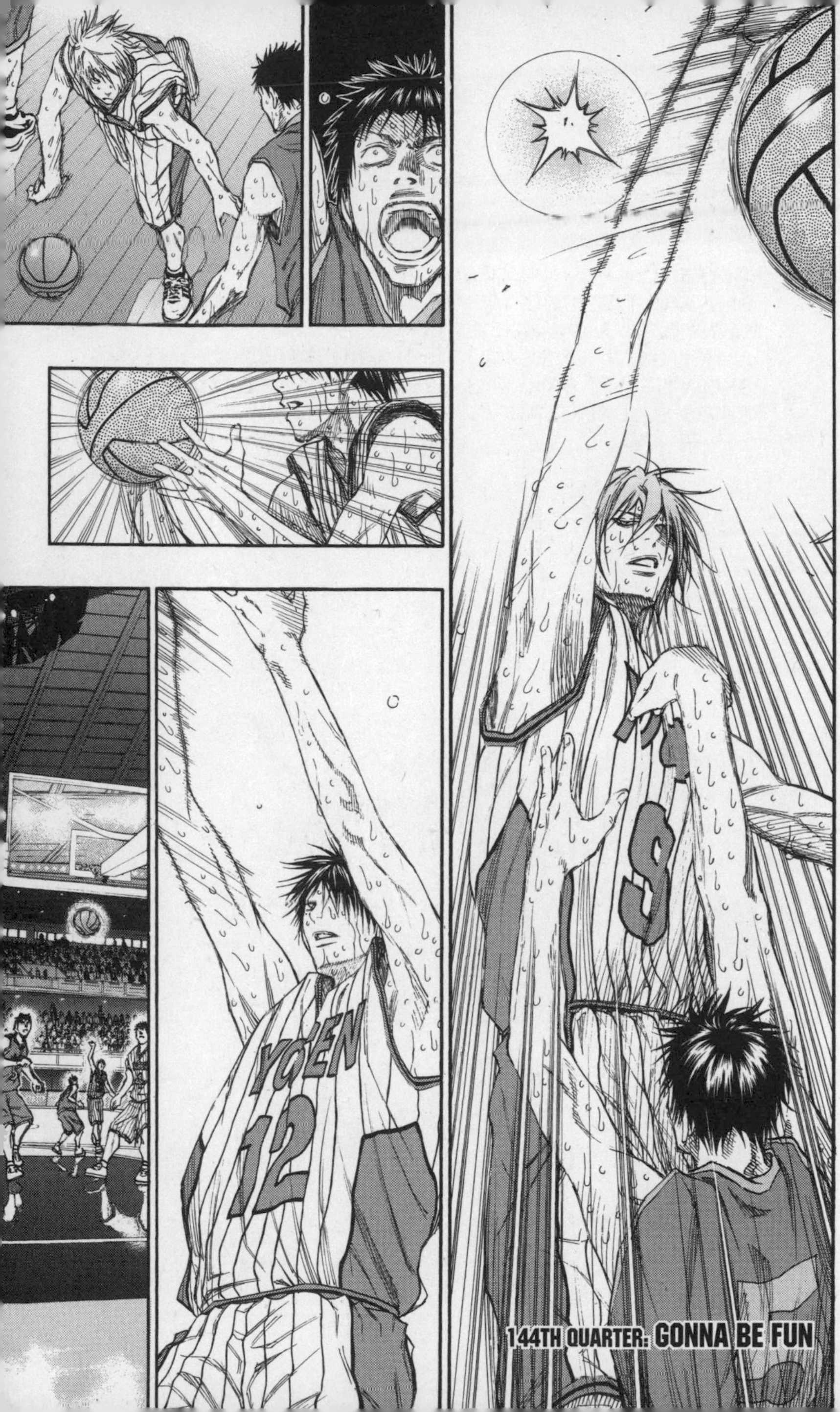
YOSEN
12
144TH QUARTER: GONNA BE FUN

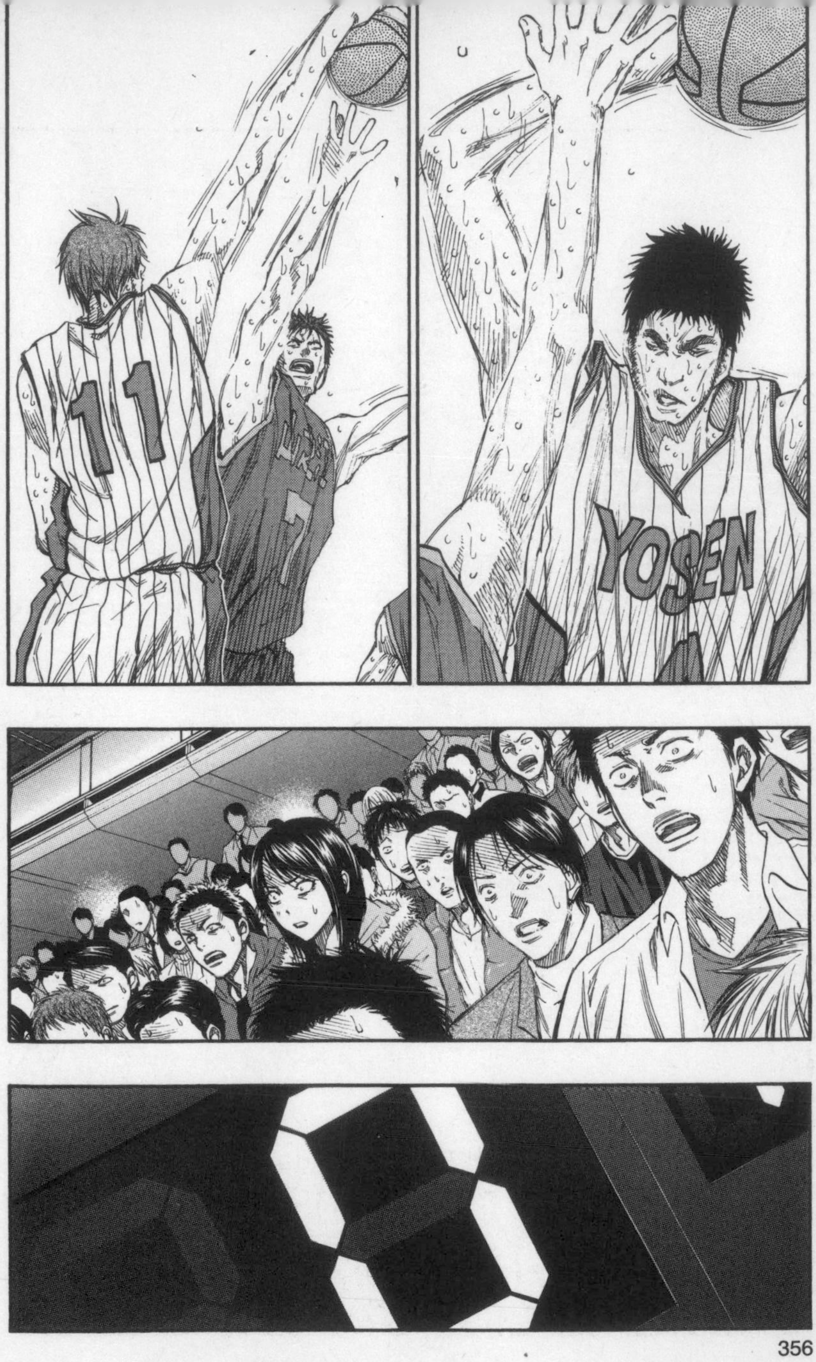
YOSEN

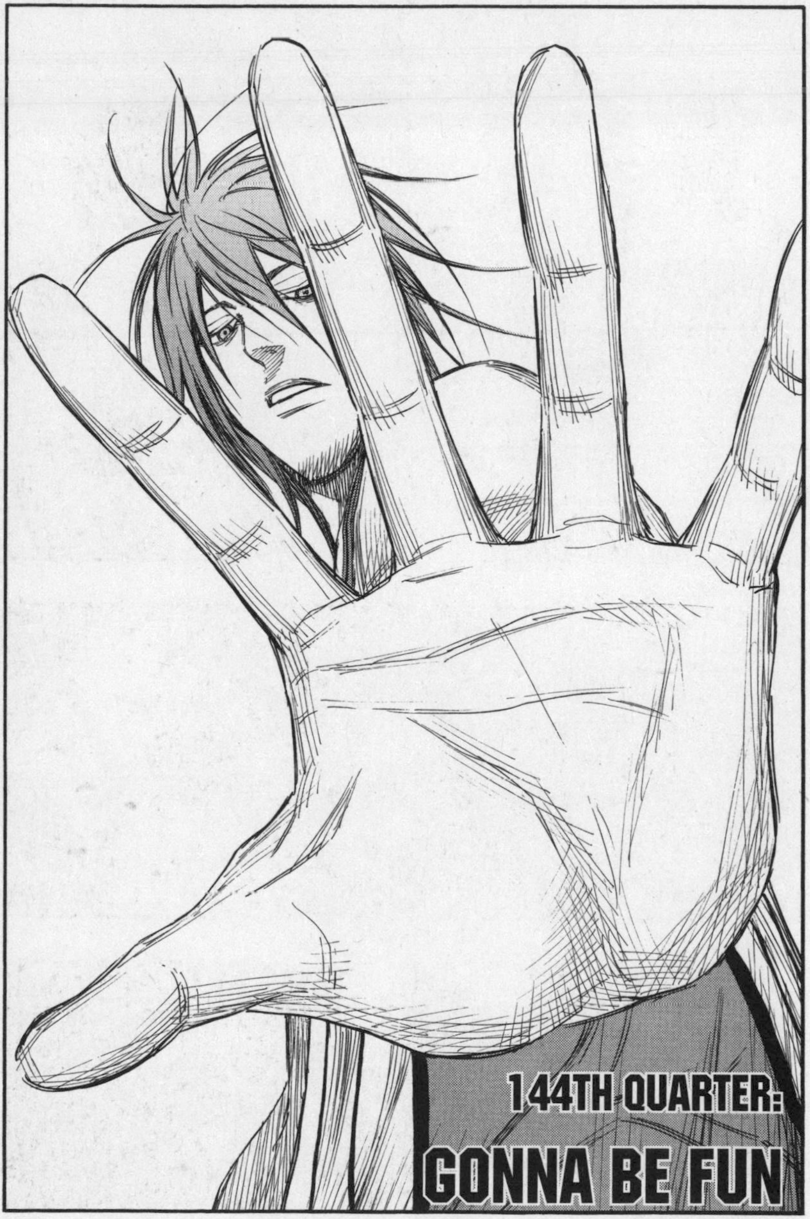
144TH QUARTER:
GONNA BE FUN

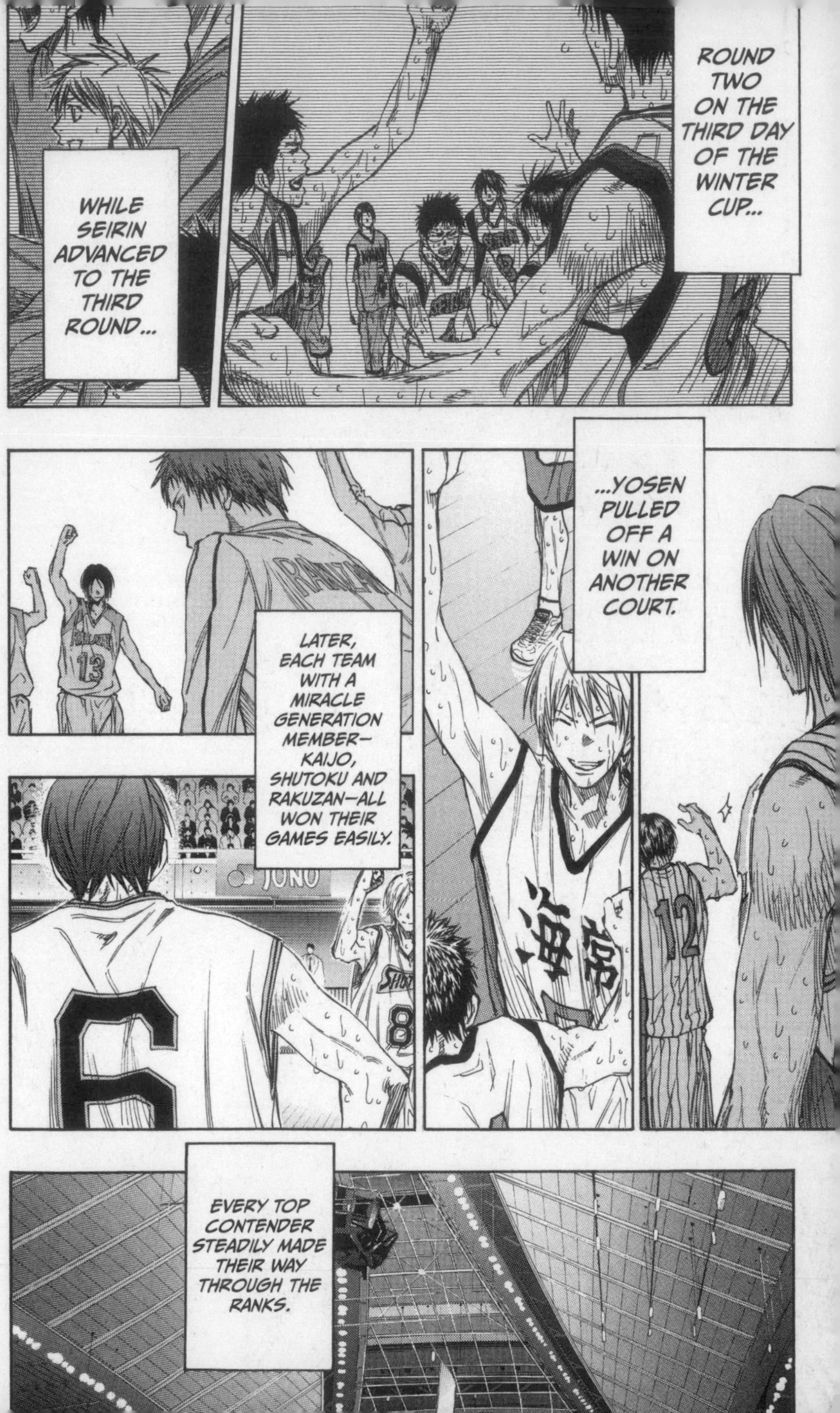
ROUND TWO ON THE THIRD DAY OF THE WINTER CUP...
WHILE SEIRIN ADVANCED TO THE THIRD ROUND...
...YOSEN PULLED OFF A WIN ON ANOTHER COURT.
LATER, EACH TEAM WITH A MIRACLE GENERATION MEMBER—KAIJO, SHUTOKU AND RAKUZAN—ALL WON THEIR GAMES EASILY.
EVERY TOP CONTENDER STEADILY MADE THEIR WAY THROUGH THE RANKS.

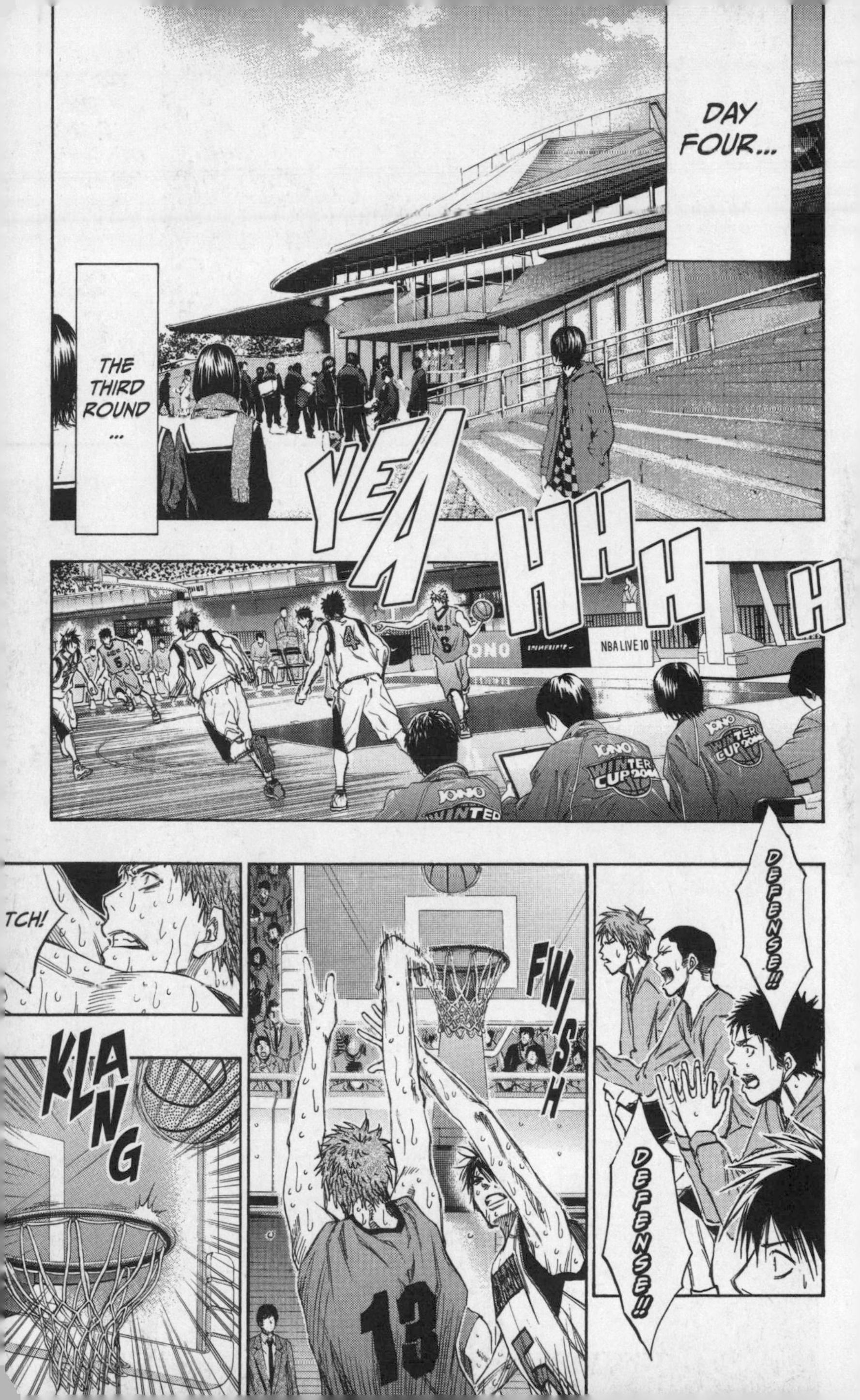
DAY FOUR...
THE THIRD ROUND ...
YEAHHHH
NBA LIVE 10
DEFENSE!!
DEFENSE!!
FWISH
TCH!
KLANG

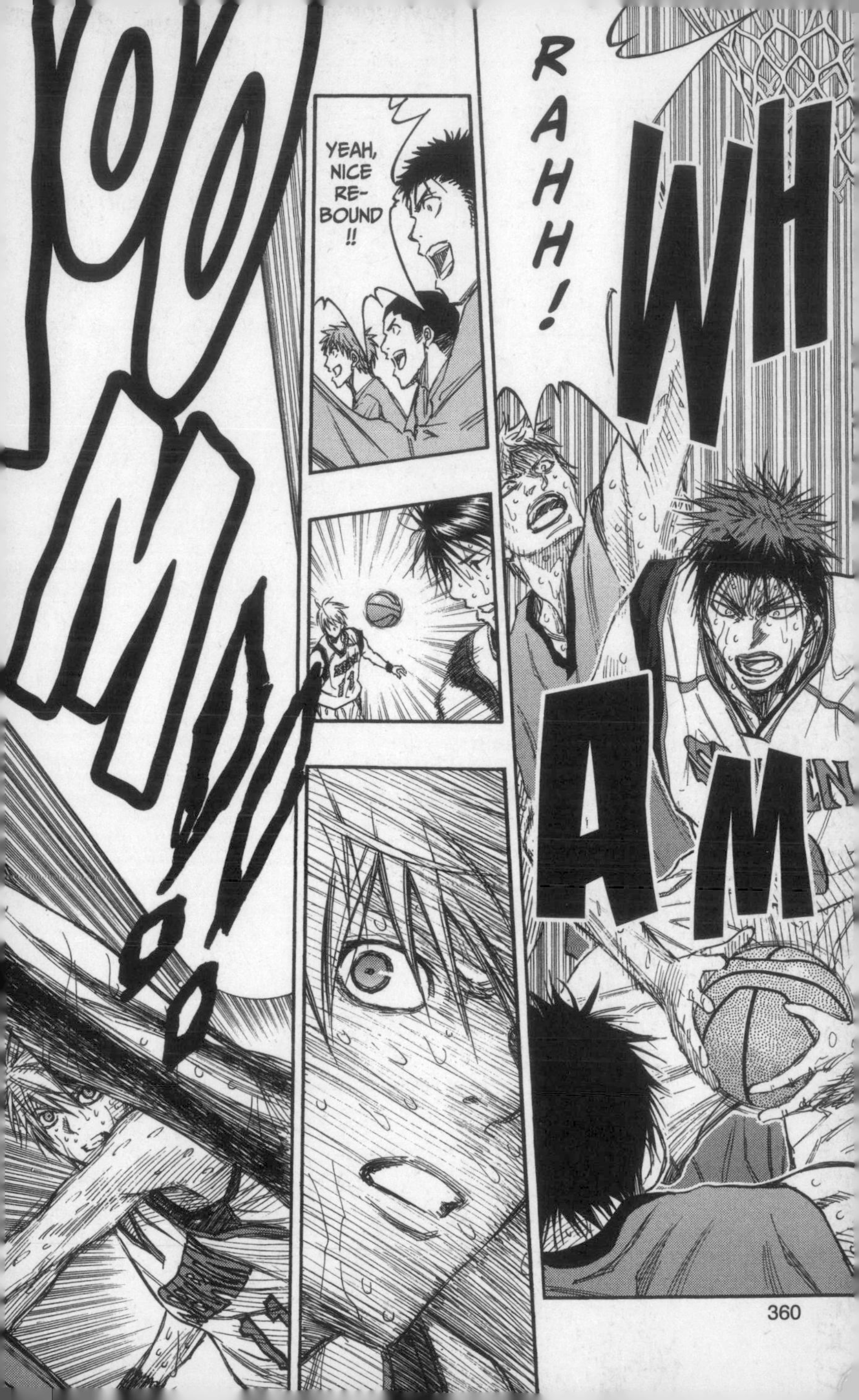
RAHH!
WHAM
YEAH, NICE RE-BOUND!!

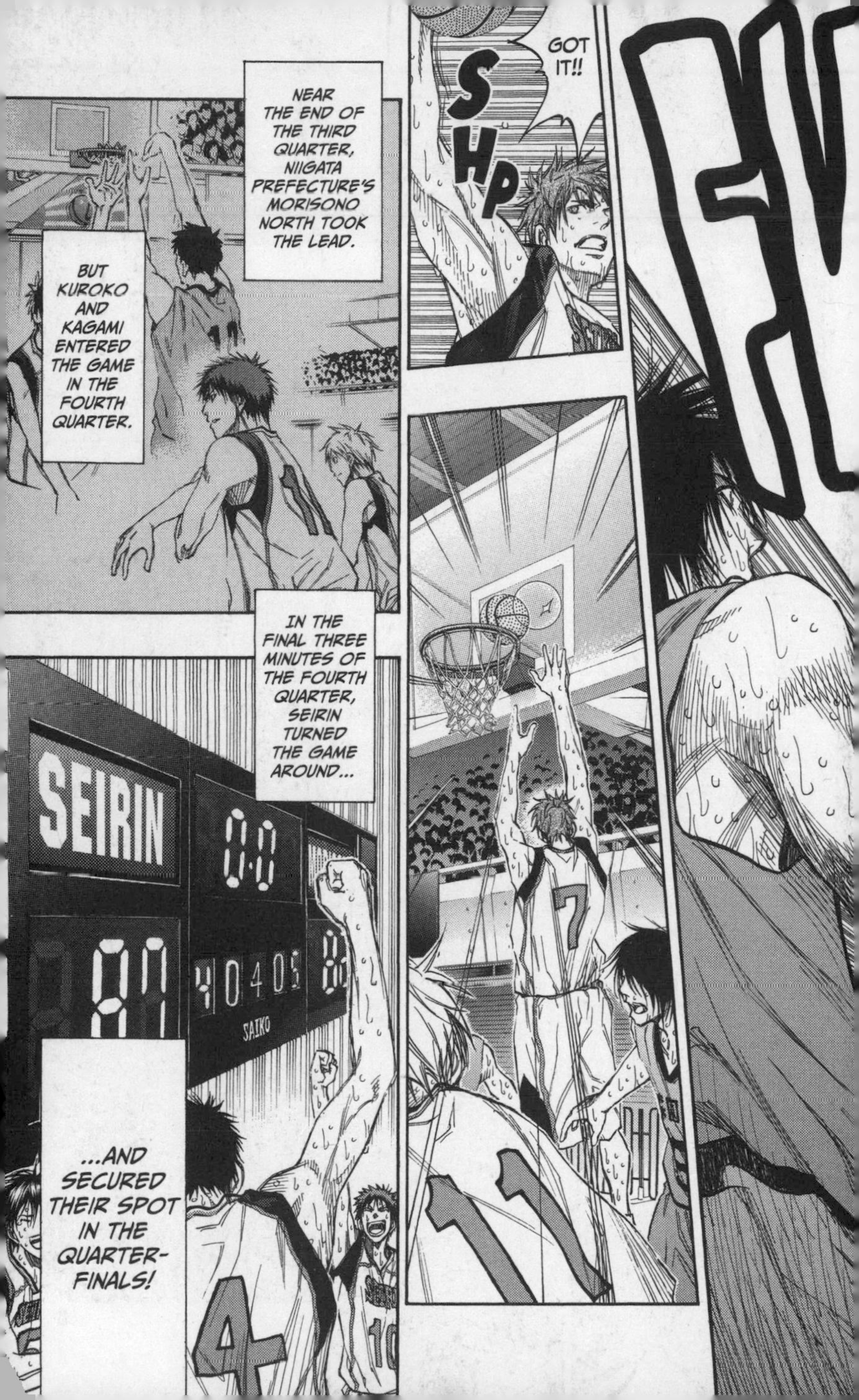
GOT IT!!
SHP
NEAR THE END OF THE THIRD QUARTER, NIIGATA PREFECTURE'S MORISONO NORTH TOOK THE LEAD.
BUT KUROKO AND KAGAMI ENTERED THE GAME IN THE FOURTH QUARTER.
IN THE FINAL THREE MINUTES OF THE FOURTH QUARTER, SEIRIN TURNED THE GAME AROUND...
SEIRIN
...AND SECURED THEIR SPOT IN THE QUARTER-FINALS!

MEAN-
WHILE...

THE
GAME IS
OVER!!

BZZZNNT

YOSEN
HIGH
SCHOOL
MOVES
ON TO
THE
QUARTER-
FINALS!!

YOSEN

12

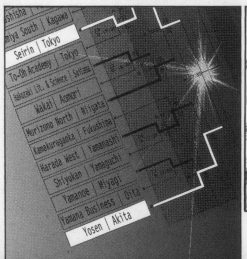

Shisha

miya South | Kagawa

Seirin | Tokyo

To-Oh Academy | Tokyo

Hanzaki Lit. & Science | Saitama

Nakai | Aomori

Morizono North | Niigata

Kamakuragaoka | Fukushima

Harada West | Yamanashi

Shiyukan | Yamaguchi

Yamanoe | Miyagi

Yamana Business | Oita

Yosen | Akita

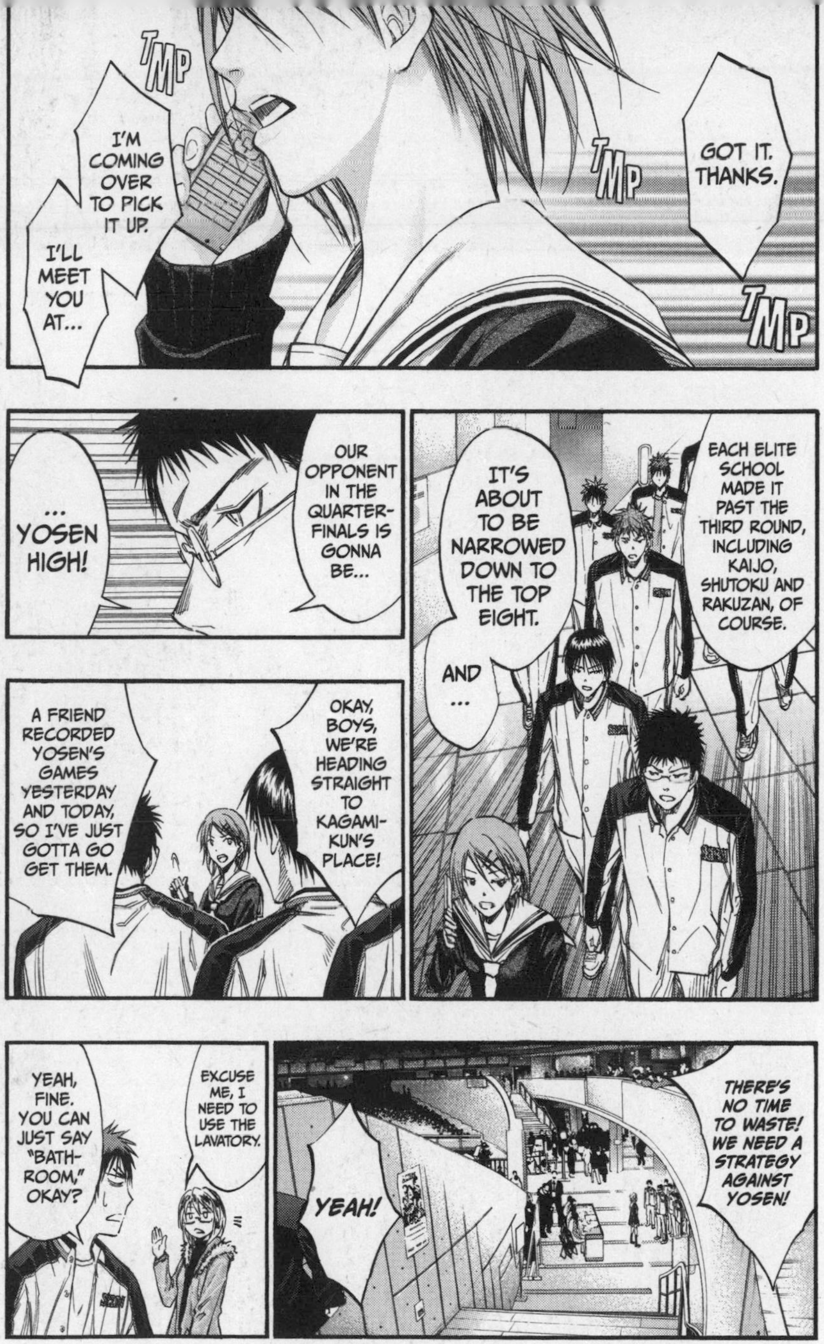
GOT IT. THANKS.
TMP
TMP
TMP
I'M COMING OVER TO PICK IT UP.
I'LL MEET YOU AT...
EACH ELITE SCHOOL MADE IT PAST THE THIRD ROUND, INCLUDING KAIJO, SHUTOKU AND RAKUZAN, OF COURSE.
IT'S ABOUT TO BE NARROWED DOWN TO THE TOP EIGHT.
AND ...
OUR OPPONENT IN THE QUARTER-FINALS IS GONNA BE...
... YOSEN HIGH!
OKAY, BOYS, WE'RE HEADING STRAIGHT TO KAGAMI-KUN'S PLACE!
A FRIEND RECORDED YOSEN'S GAMES YESTERDAY AND TODAY, SO I'VE JUST GOTTA GO GET THEM.
THERE'S NO TIME TO WASTE! WE NEED A STRATEGY AGAINST YOSEN!
YEAH!
EXCUSE ME, I NEED TO USE THE LAVATORY.
YEAH, FINE. YOU CAN JUST SAY "BATH-ROOM," OKAY?

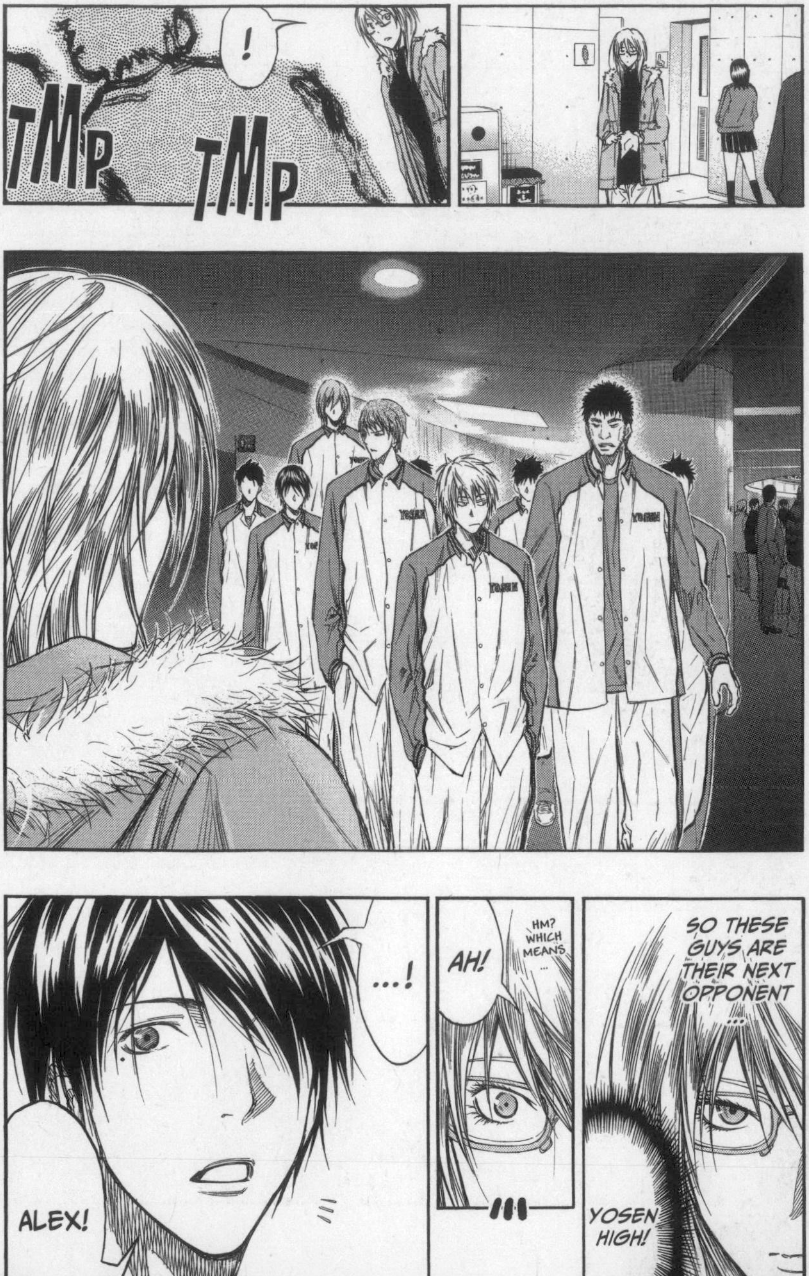
!
TMP
TMP
SO THESE GUYS ARE THEIR NEXT OPPONENT...
YOSEN HIGH!
HM? WHICH MEANS...
AH!
...!
ALEX!

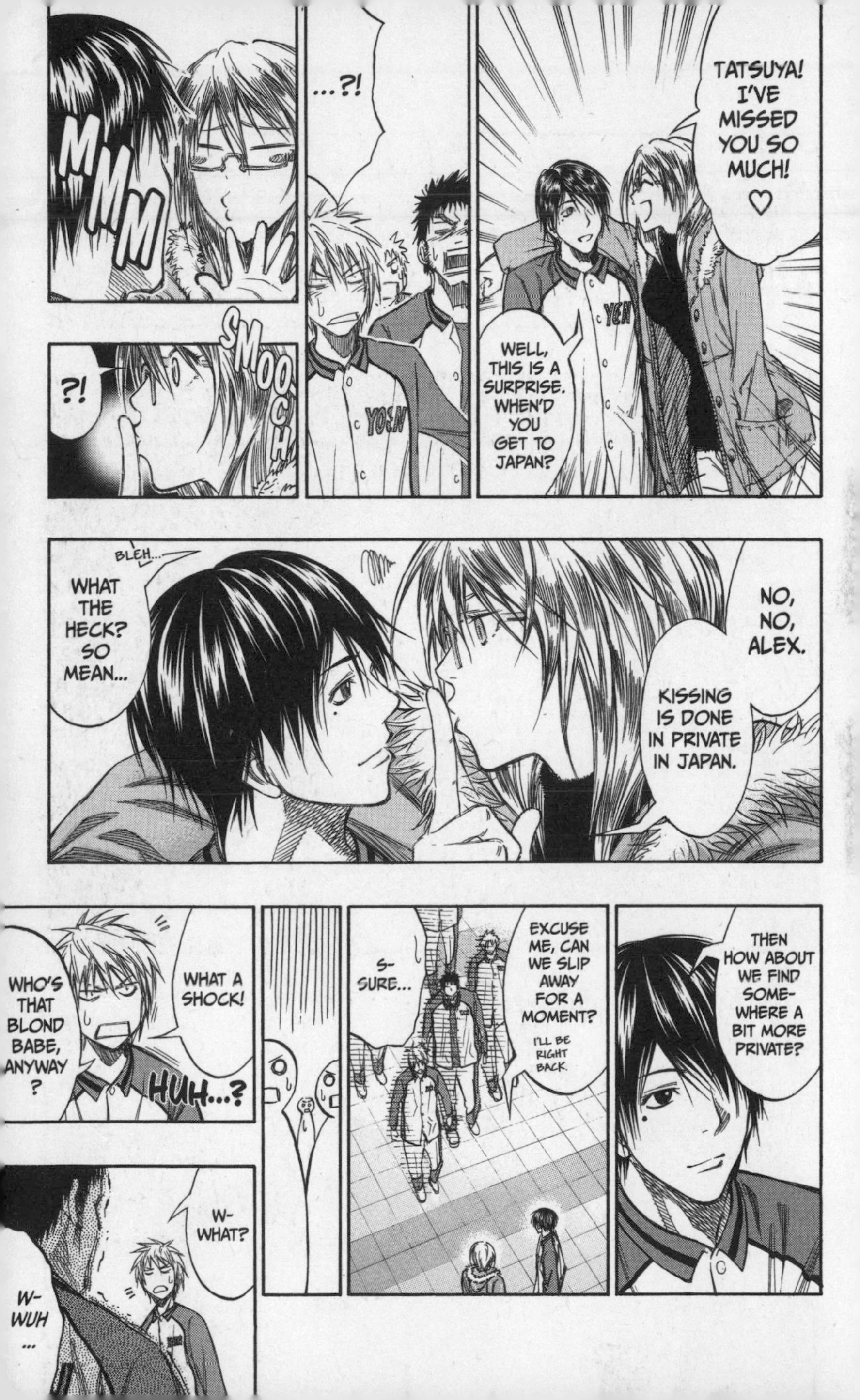
TATSUYA! I'VE MISSED YOU SO MUCH! ♡
WELL, THIS IS A SURPRISE. WHEN'D YOU GET TO JAPAN?
...?!
MMMM
SMOOCH
?!
NO, NO, ALEX.
KISSING IS DONE IN PRIVATE IN JAPAN.
BLEH...
WHAT THE HECK? SO MEAN...
THEN HOW ABOUT WE FIND SOME-WHERE A BIT MORE PRIVATE?
EXCUSE ME, CAN WE SLIP AWAY FOR A MOMENT?
I'LL BE RIGHT BACK.
S-SURE...
WHAT A SHOCK!
HUH...?
WHO'S THAT BLOND BABE, ANYWAY?
W-WHAT?
W-WUH...

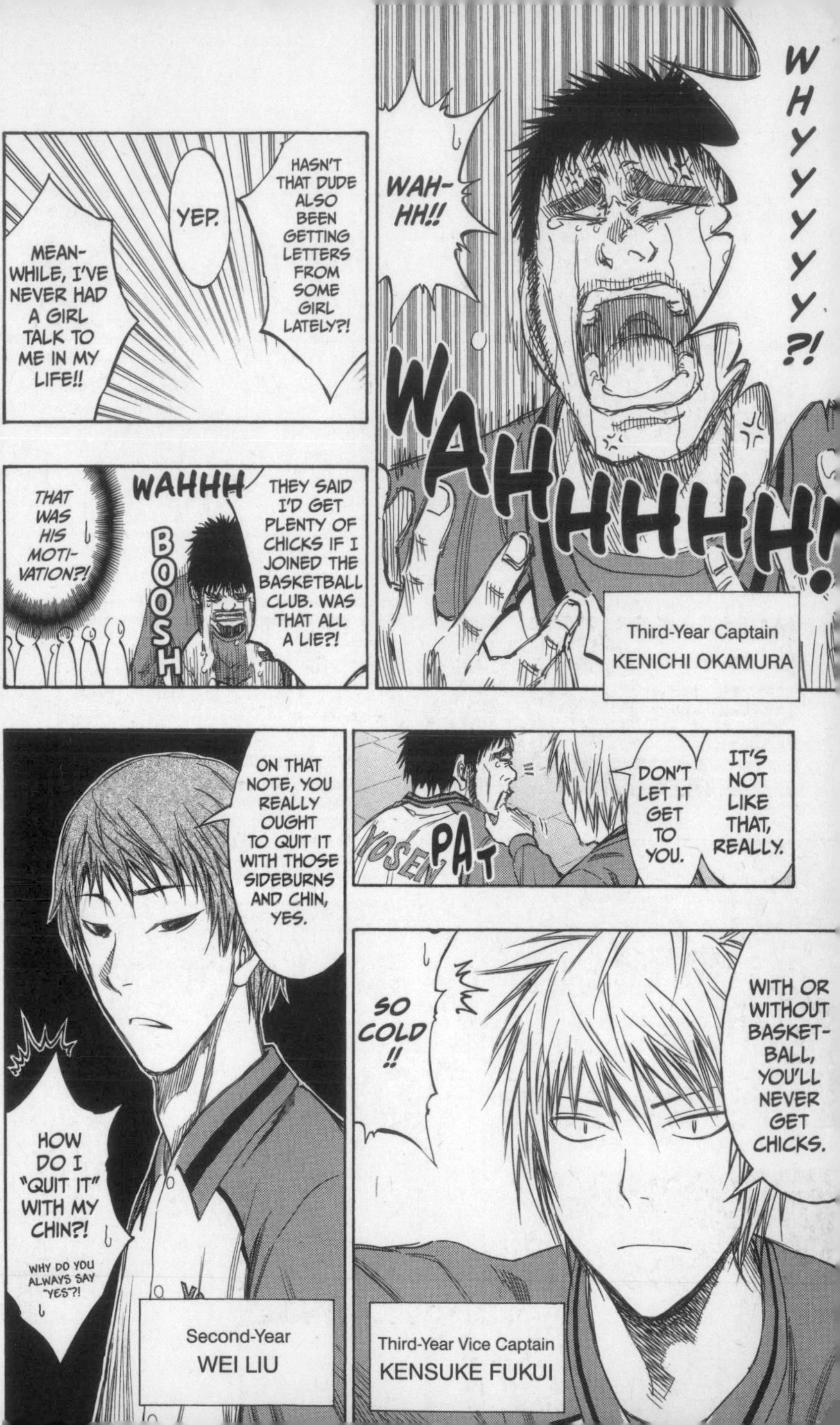
WHYYYYYYY?!
WAH-HH!!
WAHHHHHH!
Third-Year Captain
KENICHI OKAMURA
HASN'T THAT DUDE ALSO BEEN GETTING LETTERS FROM SOME GIRL LATELY?!
YEP.
MEAN-WHILE, I'VE NEVER HAD A GIRL TALK TO ME IN MY LIFE!!
THEY SAID I'D GET PLENTY OF CHICKS IF I JOINED THE BASKETBALL CLUB. WAS THAT ALL A LIE?!
WAHHH
BOOSH
THAT WAS HIS MOTI-VATION?!
IT'S NOT LIKE THAT, REALLY.
DON'T LET IT GET TO YOU.
PAT
WITH OR WITHOUT BASKET-BALL, YOU'LL NEVER GET CHICKS.
SO COLD!!
Third-Year Vice Captain
KENSUKE FUKUI
ON THAT NOTE, YOU REALLY OUGHT TO QUIT IT WITH THOSE SIDEBURNS AND CHIN, YES.
HOW DO I "QUIT IT" WITH MY CHIN?!
WHY DO YOU ALWAYS SAY "YES"?!
Second-Year
WEI LIU

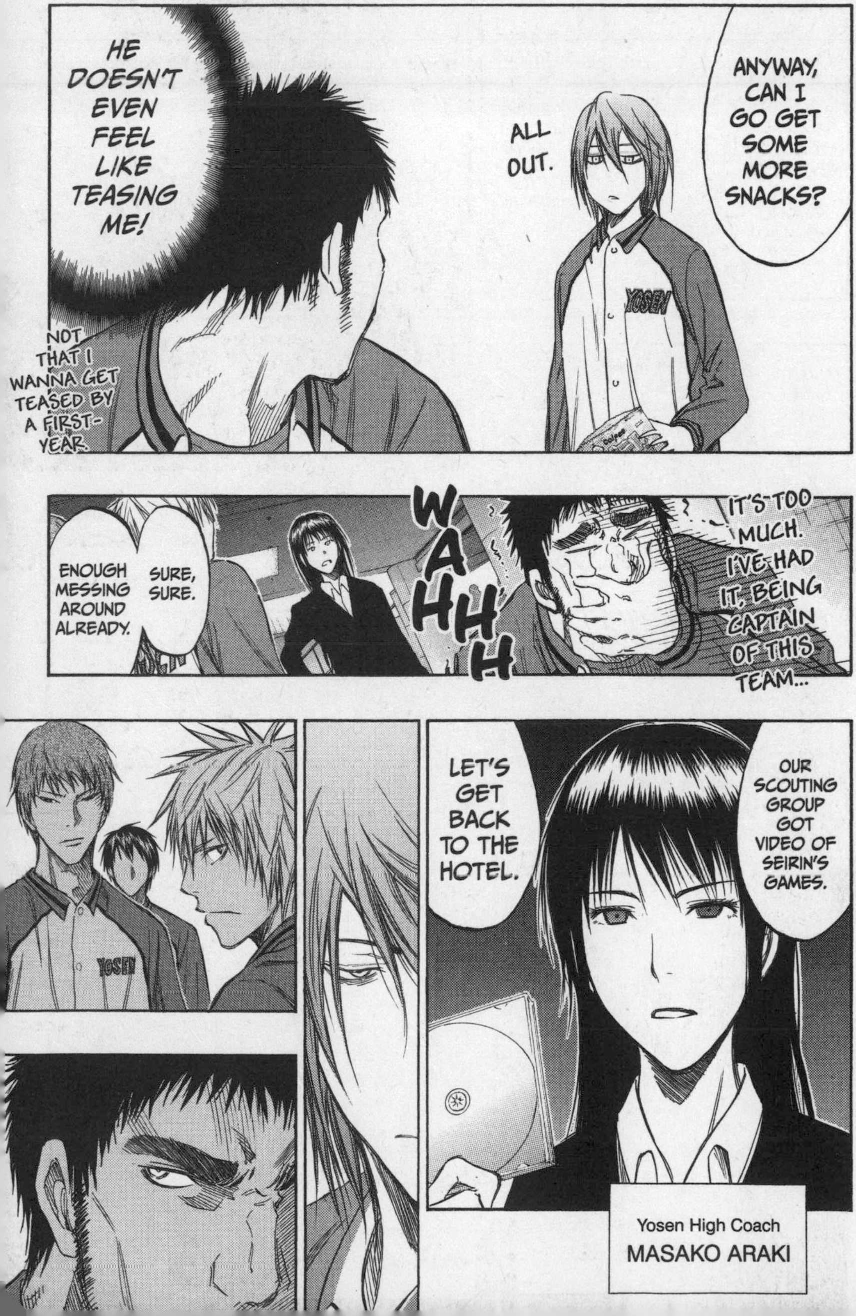
ANYWAY, CAN I GO GET SOME MORE SNACKS?
ALL OUT.
HE DOESN'T EVEN FEEL LIKE TEASING ME!
NOT THAT I WANNA GET TEASED BY A FIRST-YEAR.
IT'S TOO MUCH. I'VE HAD IT, BEING CAPTAIN OF THIS TEAM...
WAHHH
SURE, SURE.
ENOUGH MESSING AROUND ALREADY.
OUR SCOUTING GROUP GOT VIDEO OF SEIRIN'S GAMES.
LET'S GET BACK TO THE HOTEL.
Yosen High Coach
MASAKO ARAKI

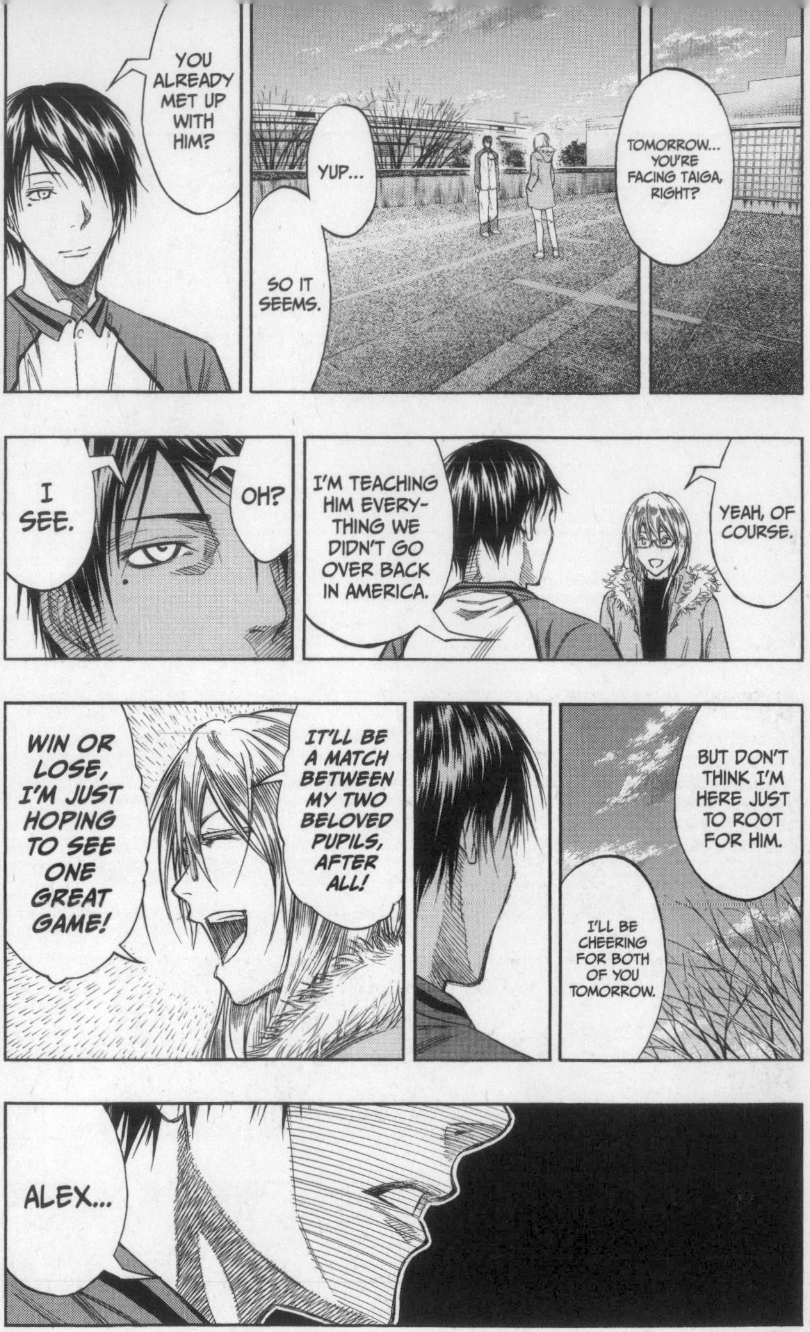
TOMORROW... YOU'RE FACING TAIGA, RIGHT?
YUP...
SO IT SEEMS.
YOU ALREADY MET UP WITH HIM?
YEAH, OF COURSE.
I'M TEACHING HIM EVERY-THING WE DIDN'T GO OVER BACK IN AMERICA.
OH?
I SEE.
BUT DON'T THINK I'M HERE JUST TO ROOT FOR HIM.
I'LL BE CHEERING FOR BOTH OF YOU TOMORROW.
IT'LL BE A MATCH BETWEEN MY TWO BELOVED PUPILS, AFTER ALL!
WIN OR LOSE, I'M JUST HOPING TO SEE ONE GREAT GAME!
ALEX...

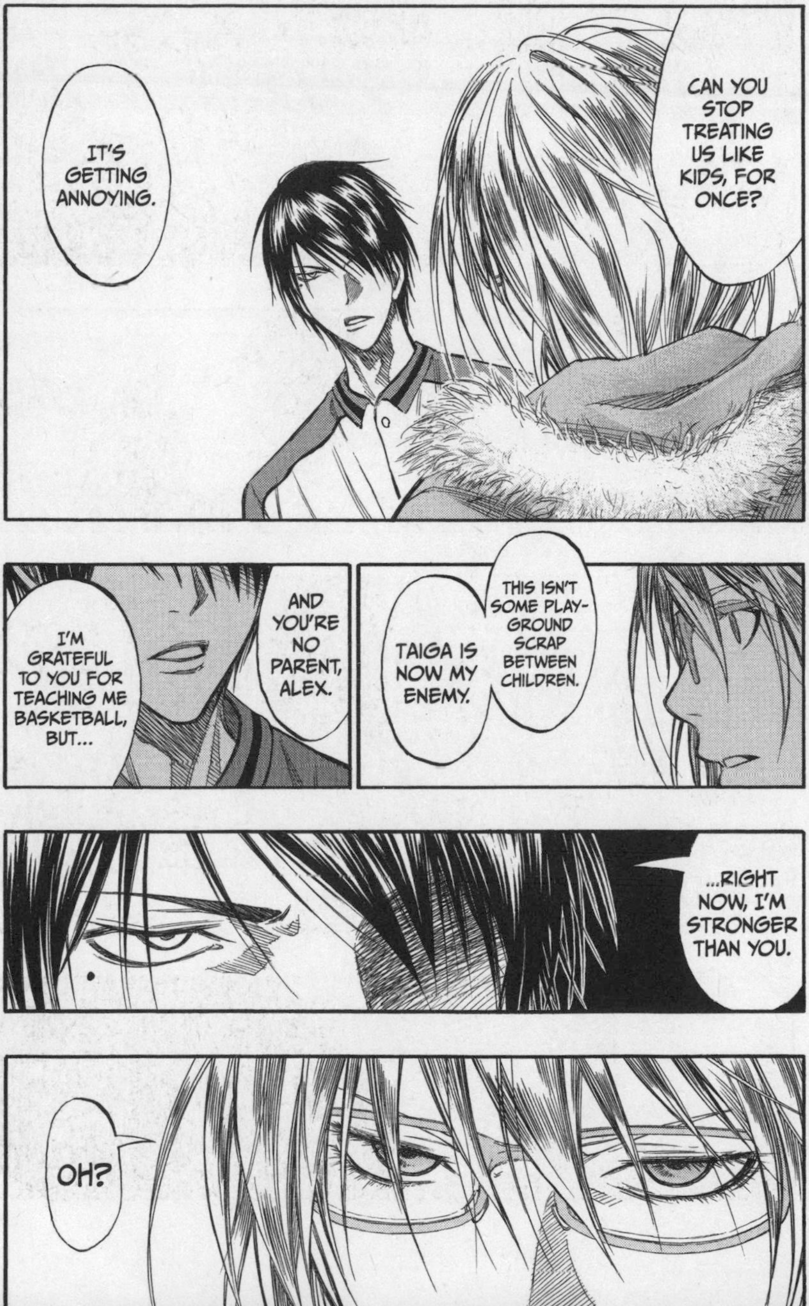
CAN YOU STOP TREATING US LIKE KIDS, FOR ONCE?
IT'S GETTING ANNOYING.
THIS ISN'T SOME PLAY-GROUND SCRAP BETWEEN CHILDREN.
TAIGA IS NOW MY ENEMY.
AND YOU'RE NO PARENT, ALEX.
I'M GRATEFUL TO YOU FOR TEACHING ME BASKETBALL, BUT...
...RIGHT NOW, I'M STRONGER THAN YOU.
OH?

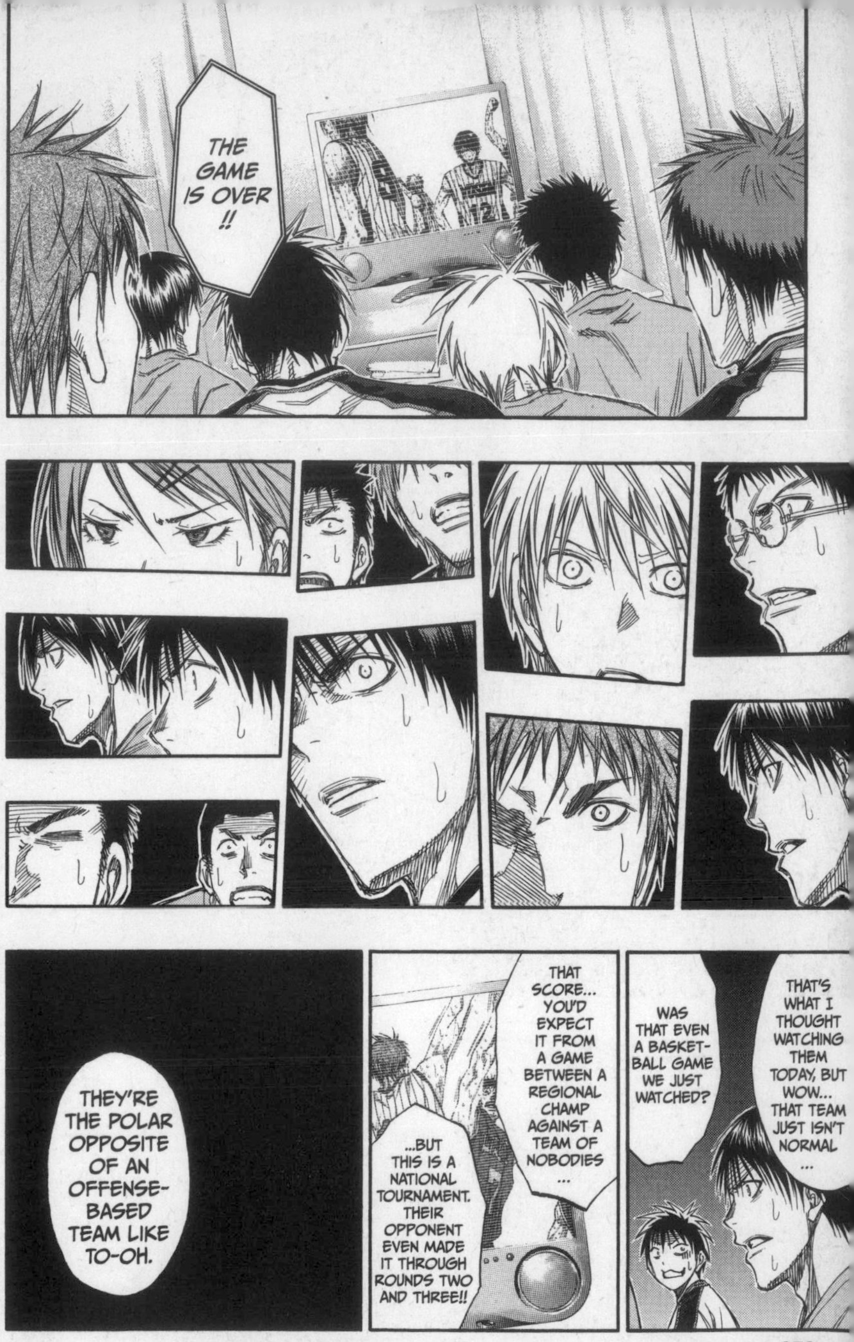
THE GAME IS OVER !!
THAT'S WHAT I THOUGHT WATCHING THEM TODAY, BUT WOW... THAT TEAM JUST ISN'T NORMAL ...
WAS THAT EVEN A BASKETBALL GAME WE JUST WATCHED?
THAT SCORE... YOU'D EXPECT IT FROM A GAME BETWEEN A REGIONAL CHAMP AGAINST A TEAM OF NOBODIES ...
...BUT THIS IS A NATIONAL TOURNAMENT. THEIR OPPONENT EVEN MADE IT THROUGH ROUNDS TWO AND THREE!!
THEY'RE THE POLAR OPPOSITE OF AN OFFENSE-BASED TEAM LIKE TO-OH.

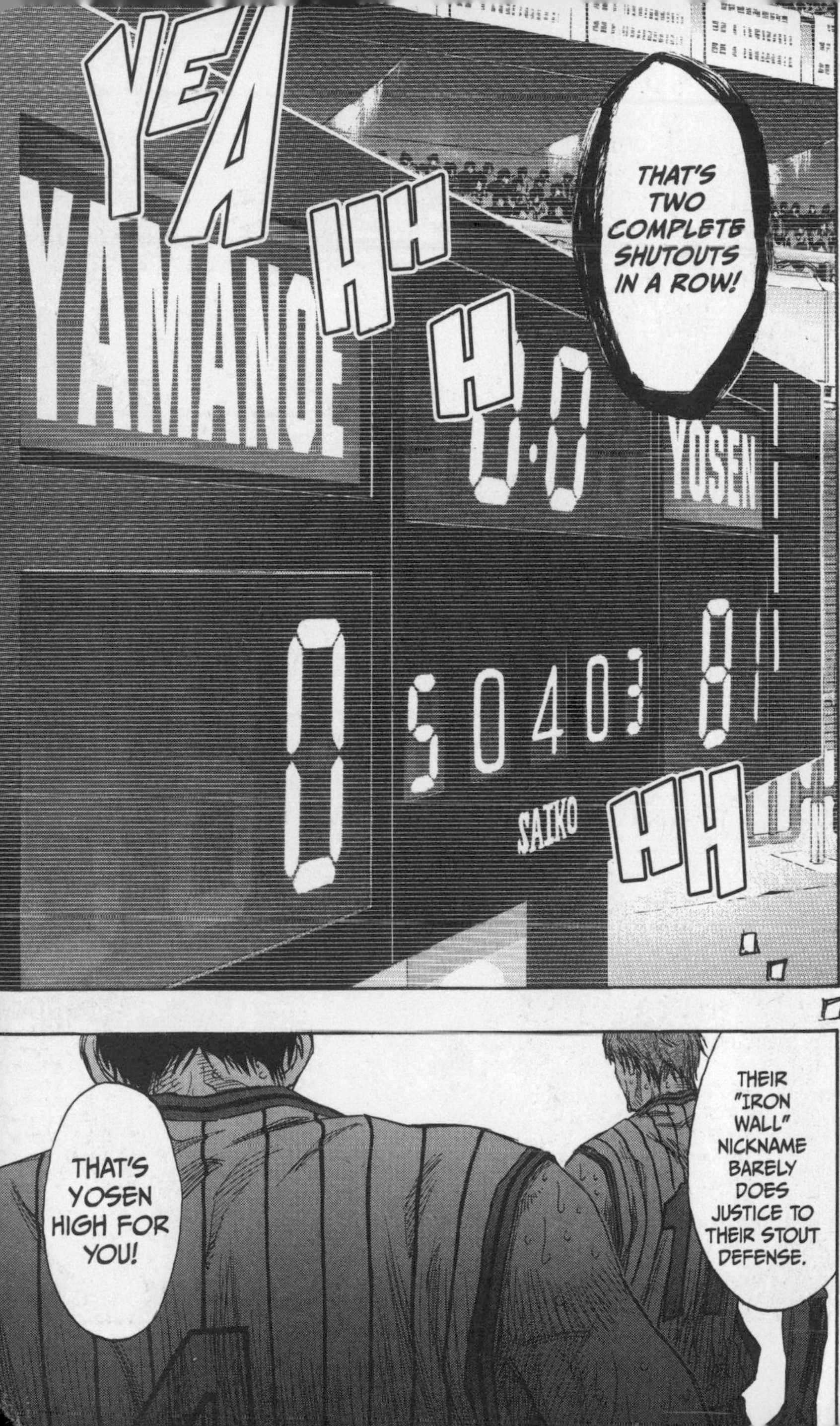

YEAHHHHH
YAMANOE
YOSEN
SAIKO
THAT'S TWO COMPLETE SHUTOUTS IN A ROW!
THEIR "IRON WALL" NICKNAME BARELY DOES JUSTICE TO THEIR STOUT DEFENSE.
THAT'S YOSEN HIGH FOR YOU!

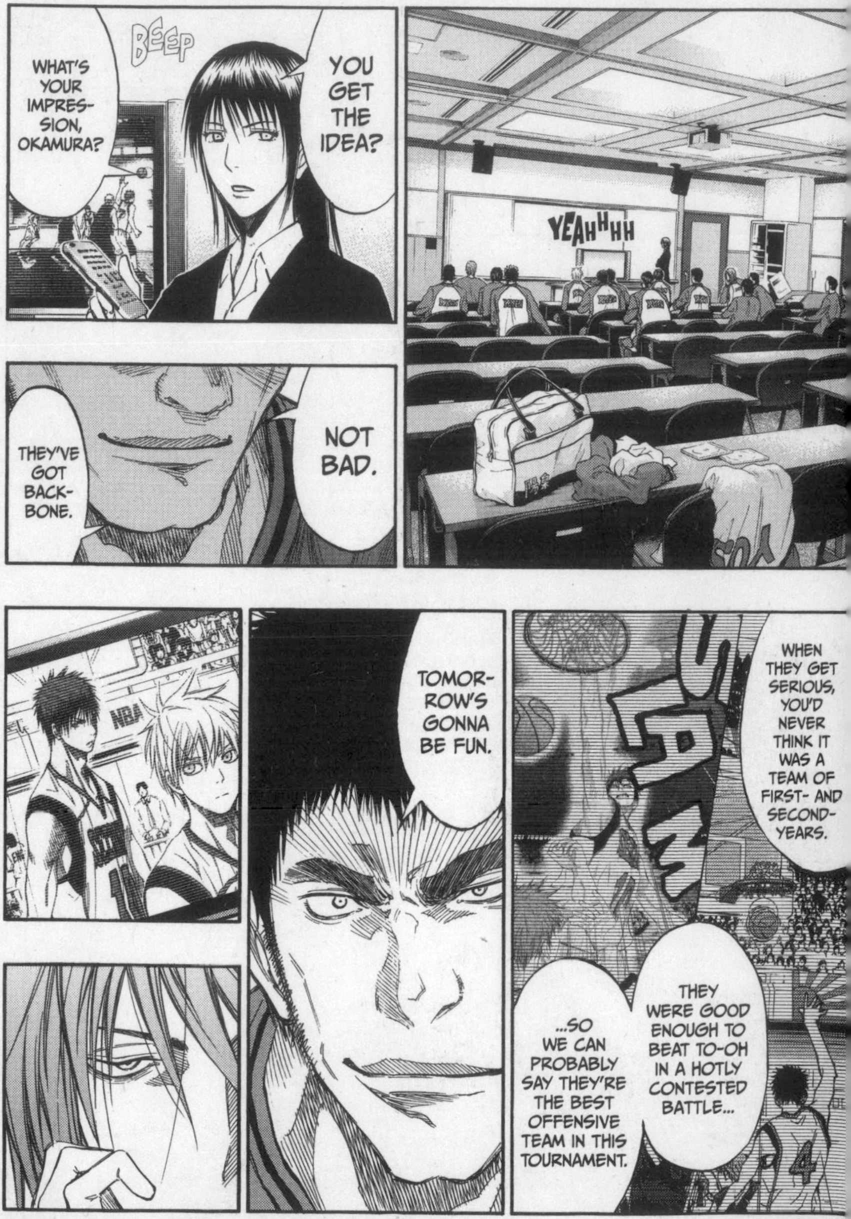
YEAHHHH
YOU GET THE IDEA?
BEEP
WHAT'S YOUR IMPRESSION, OKAMURA?
NOT BAD.
THEY'VE GOT BACKBONE.
WHEN THEY GET SERIOUS, YOU'D NEVER THINK IT WAS A TEAM OF FIRST- AND SECOND-YEARS.
SLAM
THEY WERE GOOD ENOUGH TO BEAT TO-OH IN A HOTLY CONTESTED BATTLE...
...SO WE CAN PROBABLY SAY THEY'RE THE BEST OFFENSIVE TEAM IN THIS TOURNAMENT.
TOMORROW'S GONNA BE FUN.
NBA

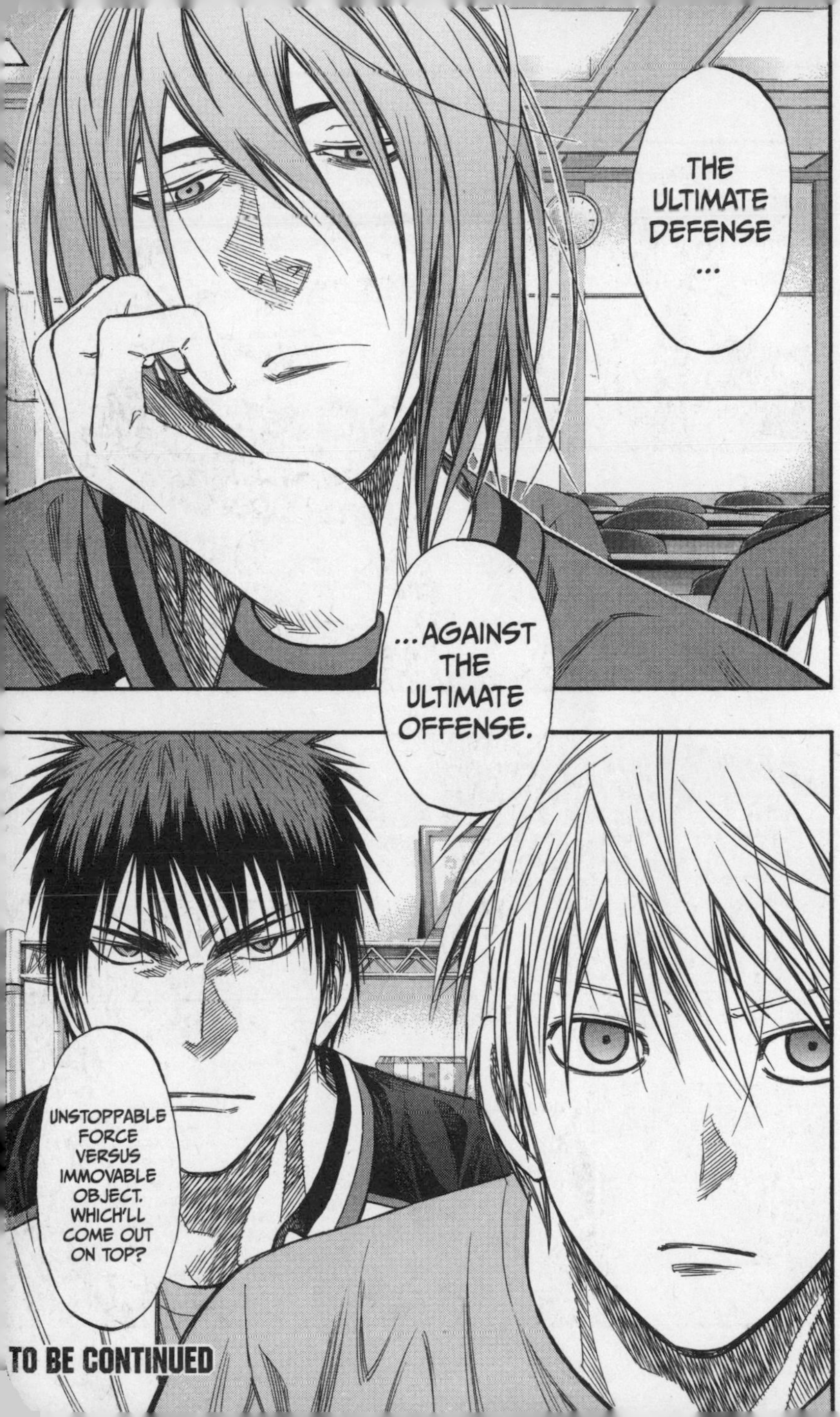
THE ULTIMATE DEFENSE ...
...AGAINST THE ULTIMATE OFFENSE.
UNSTOPPABLE FORCE VERSUS IMMOVABLE OBJECT. WHICH'LL COME OUT ON TOP?
TO BE CONTINUED

KUROKO'S BASKETBALL BLOOPERS

TAKE 2

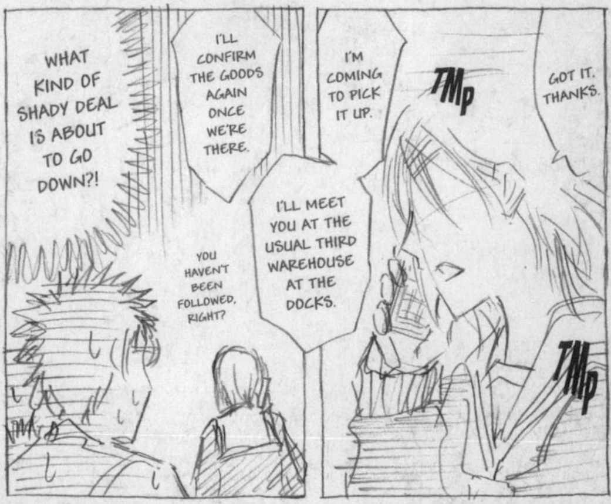
GOT IT. THANKS.
TMP
I'M COMING TO PICK IT UP.
I'LL MEET YOU AT THE USUAL THIRD WAREHOUSE AT THE DOCKS.
TMP
I'LL CONFIRM THE GOODS AGAIN ONCE WE'RE THERE.
WHAT KIND OF SHADY DEAL IS ABOUT TO GO DOWN?!
YOU HAVEN'T BEEN FOLLOWED, RIGHT?